GEOFFREY CHAU(

Geoffrey Chaucer is widely acknowledged as the greatest English poet of the Middle Ages. His texts are studied extensively but, in order to be fully appreciated, they demand a nuanced understanding of the medieval period. This volume provides freshly illuminated access to Chaucer's writing through an unrivalled repertoire of contextual information and perspectives designed to enhance the independence and critical capacities of his modern readers. The featured chapters are written not only by distinguished literary scholars but also by leading international historians. *Geoffrey Chaucer in Context* is an essential reference tool for anyone studying Chaucer and will help readers to identify his different voices and engage with the complexity and colour of his times with new awareness.

IAN JOHNSON is Reader in English at the University of St Andrews. He is, with Alastair Minnis, co-editor of *The Cambridge History of Literary Criticism*, Vol. II: *The Middle Ages* (Cambridge, 2005); and author of *The Middle English Life of Christ: Academic Discourse, Translation, and Vernacular Theology* (2013).

GEOFFREY CHAUCER IN CONTEXT

EDITED BY

IAN JOHNSON

University of St Andrews

CAMBRIDGE
UNIVERSITY PRESS

University Printing House, Cambridge CB2 8BS, United Kingdom

One Liberty Plaza, 20th Floor, New York, NY 10006, USA

477 Williamstown Road, Port Melbourne, VIC 3207, Australia

314-321, 3rd Floor, Plot 3, Splendor Forum, Jasola District Centre, New Delhi - 110025, India

79 Anson Road, #06-04/06, Singapore 079906

Cambridge University Press is part of the University of Cambridge.

It furthers the University's mission by disseminating knowledge in the pursuit of education, learning and research at the highest international levels of excellence.

www.cambridge.org
Information on this title: www.cambridge.org/9781009010603
DOI: 10.1017/9781139565141

First published 2019
First paperback edition 2021

A catalogue record for this publication is available from the British Library

Library of Congress Cataloging in Publication data
Names: Johnson, Ian R. (Ian Richard), editor.
Title: Geoffrey Chaucer in context / edited by Ian Johnson.
Description: Cambridge: Cambridge University Press, 2019. |
Includes bibliographical references and index.
Identifiers: LCCN 2019002335 | ISBN 9781107035645 (hardback)
Subjects: LCSH: Chaucer, Geoffrey, –1400 – Criticism and interpretation. |
English literature – Middle English, 1100–1500 – History and criticism.
Classification: LCC PR1905.G464 2019 | DDC 821/.1–dc23
LC record available at https://lccn.loc.gov/2019002335

ISBN 978-1-107-03564-5 Hardback
ISBN 978-1-009-01060-3 Paperback

Contents

List of Illustrations *page* ix
List of Contributors xi
List of Abbreviations xv

Introduction: Contextualising Contexts of Chaucer 1
Ian Johnson

PART I CHAUCER AS CONTEXT

1 What Was Chaucer Like? 7
†J. A. Burrow

2 Chaucer's Life and Literary 'Profession' 14
Andrew Galloway

PART II BOOKS, DISCOURSE AND TRADITIONS

3 Chaucer's Linguistic Invention 27
Jeremy J. Smith

4 Chaucer and London English 35
Jeremy J. Smith

5 Manuscripts and Manuscript Culture 43
Rhiannon Purdie

6 Chaucer's Books 50
Wendy Scase

7 Authority 58
Mishtooni Bose

8 Literary Theory and Literary Roles 65
Ian Johnson

9 Metre and Versification 72
Ad Putter

10 Dialogue 83
Sarah James

11 Romance 89
Stephen H. A. Shepherd

12 Love 97
Corinne Saunders

13 Chaucer and the Classics 106
Vincent Gillespie

14 The French Context 117
Stephanie A. Viereck Gibbs Kamath

15 The Italian Tradition 126
K. P. Clarke

16 The English Context 132
Marion Turner

17 Chaucer's Competitors 140
Wendy Scase

18 Boethius 147
Tim William Machan

PART III HUMANS, THE WORLD AND BEYOND

19 Chaucer's God 157
Ryan Perry

20 Holiness 167
Marlene Villalobos Hennessy

21 Secularity 178
Alastair Minnis

22 The Self 187
Valerie Allen

23 Women 194
Rosalynn Voaden

24 Sex and Lust 201
Bruce Holsinger

25 Animals in Chaucer 209
Gillian Rudd

PART IV CULTURE, LEARNING AND DISCIPLINES

26 Childhood and Education 219
Nicholas Orme

27 Philosophy 230
Stephen Penn

28 The Medieval Universe 239
Seb Falk

29 Medicine and the Mortal Body 252
Samantha Katz Seal

30 The Law 259
Richard W. Ireland

31 Art 266
Julian Luxford

32 Architecture 273
Richard Fawcett

33 Heraldry, Heralds and Chaucer 286
Katie Stevenson

PART V POLITICAL AND SOCIAL CONTEXTS

34 Dissent and Orthodoxy 295
John H. Arnold

35 The Church, Religion and Culture 301
Rob Lutton

36 England at Home and Abroad 308
Anne Curry

37 Chaucer's Borders 315
Anthony Bale

38 Rank and Social Orders 324
Chris Given-Wilson

39 Chivalry 331
Craig Taylor

40 Chaucer and the Polity 337
Gwilym Dodd

41 The Economy 346
Christopher Dyer

42 Towns, Villages and the Land 355
Mark Bailey

43 London's Chaucer: A Psychogeography 363
John J. Thompson

44 Everyday Life 371
Wendy Childs

45 Household and Home 378
Peter Fleming

46 Marriage 385
Sally Dixon-Smith

47 Dress 393
Laura F. Hodges

PART VI CHAUCER TRADITIONS

48 The First Chaucerians: Reception in the 1400s 403
Robert J. Meyer-Lee

49 The Reception of Chaucer in the Renaissance 410
Alex Davis

50 The Reception of Chaucer from Dryden to Wordsworth 419
Bruce E. Graver

51 The Reception of Chaucer from the Victorians to the Twenty-First Century 429
David Matthews

52. Cyber-Chaucer 436
Stephen Kelly

Further Reading 445
Index 467

Illustrations

1.1 Miniature in colours of Chaucer clutching a rosary and pointing at the text from the *Regiment of Princes* by Thomas Hoccleve. © The British Library Board *page* 9

20.1 *Ampulla* from the shrine of St Thomas Becket at Canterbury, Museum of London. By permission of the Museum of London 169

20.2 Reliquary casket with scenes from the martyrdom of Thomas Becket, Metropolitan Museum of Art. By permission of the Metropolitan Museum of Art 170

20.3 Devotional 'postcard' and parchment painting of the Holy Rood of Bromholm, pasted into the Lewkenor Hours, London, Lambeth Palace Library MS 545, fols. 184v–185r 175

28.1 The nine spheres, in John of Sacrobosco, *De sphera*, Cambridge University Library, MS Ii.3.3, fol. 25v. Reproduced by kind permission of the Syndics of Cambridge University Library 241

28.2 The daily and annual rotations of the heavens 243

28.3 The heavens, in John of Sacrobosco, *De sphera*, London, British Library, MS Harley 3647, fol. 29r. © The British Library Board 244

28.4 Horoscope diagram, adapted from one by Māshā'allāh ibn Atharī, Cambridge, Peterhouse, MS 75.I, fol. 64v. © The Master and Fellows of Peterhouse, Cambridge 245

28.5 '[A] suffisant Astrolabie as for oure orizonte, compowned after the latitude of Oxenforde' (*Astr*, Pro.8–10), London, British Museum, 1909,0617.1. © Trustees of the British Museum 246

28.6 'Zodiac man' showing the parts of the body governed by each sign, in a copy of the Calendar of John Somer, Cambridge, St John's College, MS K.26, fol. 41v. By permission of the Master and Fellows of St John's College, Cambridge 249
32.1 Snettisham Church, the west window 274
32.2 Ely Cathedral, Lady Chapel, interior 275
32.3 Gloucester Cathedral, choir elevation, from Francis Bond, *Gothic Architecture in England* (London: Batsford, 1905), p. 59 277
32.4 Winchester Cathedral, nave interior, from Robert Willis, *Proceedings at the Annual Meeting of the Archaeological Institute* (London: Longman, Brown, Green and Longmans, 1846), p. 71 279
32.5 Canterbury Cathedral, nave interior 280
32.6 Warkworth Castle, the great tower 281
32.7 Bodiam Castle 283
49.1 *The true portraiture of GEFFREY CHAUCER the famous English poet*, from *The Workes of Our Antient and Learned English Poet, Geffrey Chaucer*, ed. Thomas Speght (London: Adam Islip, 1602), facing sig. b1r. Used by permission of the Folger Shakespeare Library 411

Contributors

VALERIE ALLEN is Professor of English at John Jay College of Criminal Justice, City University of New York.

JOHN H. ARNOLD is Professor of Medieval History at the University of Cambridge.

MARK BAILEY is the High Master of St Paul's School, London and Professor of Later Medieval History at the University of East Anglia.

ANTHONY BALE is Executive Dean of Arts and Professor of Medieval Studies at Birkbeck College, London.

MISHTOONI BOSE is Christopher Tower Official Student in Medieval Poetry in English and Associate Professor of English, University of Oxford.

The late J. A. BURROW was Emeritus Professor of English at the University of Bristol.

WENDY CHILDS is Emeritus Professor of Later Medieval History at the University of Leeds.

K. P. CLARKE is Senior Lecturer in Medieval Literature at the University of York.

ANNE CURRY is Professor of Medieval History at the University of Southampton.

ALEX DAVIS is Senior Lecturer in English at the University of St Andrews.

SALLY DIXON-SMITH is Curator (Collections), HM Tower of London, Historic Royal Palaces.

GWILYM DODD is Associate Professor of History at Nottingham University.

CHRISTOPHER DYER is Emeritus Professor of History at the University of Leicester.

SEB FALK is Rosamund Chambers Research Fellow at Girton College, Cambridge.

RICHARD FAWCETT is Emeritus Professor of Art History at the University of St Andrews.

PETER FLEMING is Emeritus Professor of History at the University of the West of England.

ANDREW GALLOWAY is Professor of English at Cornell University.

VINCENT GILLESPIE is J. R. R. Tolkien Professor of English Literature and Language at the University of Oxford.

CHRIS GIVEN-WILSON is Emeritus Professor of History at the University of St Andrews.

BRUCE E. GRAVER is Professor of English at Providence College, Rhode Island.

MARLENE VILLALOBOS HENNESSY is Associate Professor, Hunter College, City University of New York.

LAURA F. HODGES holds a doctorate in literature from Rice University.

BRUCE HOLSINGER is Linden Kent Memorial Professor of English at the University of Virginia.

RICHARD W. IRELAND was until retirement Senior Lecturer in Law at Aberystwyth University.

SARAH JAMES is Senior Lecturer in Medieval Literature, School of English, University of Kent.

IAN JOHNSON is Reader in English at the University of St Andrews.

STEPHANIE A. VIERECK GIBBS KAMATH is an independent researcher, based in northern Virginia.

STEPHEN KELLY is Lecturer in English (Later Medieval Literature) at Queen's University Belfast.

ROB LUTTON is Lecturer in History at the University of Nottingham.

JULIAN LUXFORD is Professor of Art History at the University of St Andrews.

TIM WILLIAM MACHAN is Professor of English at the University of Notre Dame.

DAVID MATTHEWS is Professor of Medieval and Medievalism Studies at the University of Manchester.

ROBERT J. MEYER-LEE is Associate Professor of English at Agnes Scott College.

ALASTAIR MINNIS is Douglas Tracy Smith Professor Emeritus of English at Yale University and Emeritus Professor of Medieval Literature at the University of York.

NICHOLAS ORME is Emeritus Professor of History at the University of Exeter.

STEPHEN PENN is Lecturer in English Studies at the University of Stirling.

RYAN PERRY is Senior Lecturer in Medieval Literature, School of English, University of Kent.

RHIANNON PURDIE is Reader in Medieval English at the University of St Andrews.

AD PUTTER is Professor of Medieval English Literature at the University of Bristol.

GILLIAN RUDD is Professor of English at the University of Liverpool.

CORINNE SAUNDERS is Professor of Medieval Literature in the Department of English Studies and Co-Director of the Institute for Medical Humanities at the University of Durham.

WENDY SCASE is the Geoffrey Shepherd Professor of Medieval English Literature at the University of Birmingham.

SAMANTHA KATZ SEAL is Assistant Professor of English at the University of New Hampshire.

STEPHEN H. A. SHEPHERD is Professor of English Literature at Loyola Marymount University.

JEREMY J. SMITH is Professor of English Philology at the University of Glasgow.

KATIE STEVENSON is Assistant Vice-Principal (Collections and Digital Content) at the University of St Andrews.

CRAIG TAYLOR is Reader in Medieval History at the University of York.

JOHN J. THOMPSON is Emeritus Professor of English at Queen's University Belfast.

MARION TURNER is Tutorial Fellow in English Literature at Jesus College and Associate Professor of English at the University of Oxford.

ROSALYNN VOADEN is Professor Emeritus of English at Arizona State University.

Abbreviations

CHAUCER'S WORKS

Abbreviations referring to the works of Chaucer are identical to those used in *The Riverside Chaucer*, gen. ed. Larry D. Benson, 3rd edn (Oxford: Oxford University Press, 1988). All Chaucer quotations are from the *Riverside* edition unless otherwise stated.

Adam	*Chaucers Wordes unto Adam, His Owne Scriveyn*
Anel	*Anelida and Arcite*
Astr	*A Treatise on the Astrolabe*
BD	*Book of the Duchess*
Bo	*Boece*
CT	*Canterbury Tales*
CYT	*Canon's Yeoman's Tale*
FranT	*Franklin's Tale*
FrT	*Friar's Tale*
GP	*General Prologue*
HF	*House of Fame*
KnT	*Knight's Tale*
LGW	*Legend of Good Women*
Mel	*Tale of Melibee*
MerT	*Merchant's Tale*
MilT	*Miller's Tale*
MkT	*Monk's Tale*
MLT	*Man of Law's Tale*
NPT	*Nun's Priest's Tale*
PF	*Parliament of Fowls*
PhyT	*Physician's Tale*
Pity	*Complaint unto Pity*
Pro	*Prologue*

Retr	*Retractions*
Riverside Chaucer	*The Riverside Chaucer*, gen. ed. Larry D. Benson, 3rd edn (Oxford: Oxford University Press, 1988)
ShipT	*Shipman's Tale*
SqT	*Squire's Tale*
Tr	*Troilus and Criseyde*
Ven	*Complaint of Venus*
WBPro	*Wife of Bath's Prologue*
WBT	*Wife of Bath's Tale*

OTHER ABBREVIATIONS

DH	digital humanities
EETS es	Early English Text Society extra series (1867–1920)
EETS os	Early English Text Society original series (1864–)
L-R	Martin M. Crow and Clair C. Olson, eds., *Chaucer Life-Records* (Oxford: Clarendon Press, 1966)
MED	*Middle English Dictionary*, ed. Hans Kurath and S. M. Kuhn (Ann Arbor: University of Michigan Press; London: Oxford University Press, 1952), http://quod.lib.umich.edu/m/med/
ODNB	*Oxford Dictionary of National Biography*, ed. H. C. G. Matthew and Brian Harrison, 60 vols. (Oxford: Oxford University Press, 2004), www.oxforddnb.com
OED	*Oxford English Dictionary* (Oxford: Oxford University Press, 2009), www.oed.com
PL	*Patrologia cursus completus series latina*, ed. Jacques-Paul Migne *et al.*, 221 vols. (Paris: Migne, 1844–65)
PMLA	*Publications of the Modern Language Association*
PROME	Chris Given-Wilson *et al.*, *The Parliament Rolls of Medieval England 1275–1504*, 16 vols. (Woodbridge: Boydell Press, 2005); also available on CD-ROM (Leicester: Scholarly Digital Editions and the National Archives, 2005)
Spurgeon 1	Caroline F. E. Spurgeon, *Five Hundred Years of Chaucer Criticism and Allusion (1357–1900)*, 3 vols. (London: Chaucer Society, 1914–25), Vol. 1
TEI	Text Encoding Initiative

Introduction
Contextualising Contexts of Chaucer

Ian Johnson

This is not a collection of essays on Chaucer in the normal sense. Neither is it a 'Companion' or 'Guide' or 'Handbook' to Chaucer. It does not have the primary intention of providing readings of the texts of Chaucer (even though it contains much illuminating treatment of his works). Its key aim is to enhance the independence and critical capacities of modern readers of Chaucer by giving them a rich repertoire of contexts – historical and conceptual information and perspectives – through which to read, interpret and enjoy his works with greater confidence and assurance.

Different chapters set about this intention in different ways. Some offer and elaborate an invaluable conspectus of relevant information that categorises itself pretty self-evidently as 'history'. The best scholars to do this are, as a rule, 'real' historians rather than Chaucer specialists: hence the unusual number of chapters (unusual, that is, for a book contributing to Chaucer Studies) written by historians rather than colleagues in Middle English literature. Our historians write variously about the material and socio-political circumstances of Chaucer's England (like the economy, the polity, social orders, everyday life, home, marriage, religious life, heresy) or aspects of culture (such as chivalry, heraldry, art, architecture). Sometimes, chapters do not need to contain much in the way of reference to Chaucer to achieve their contextual aim. Often, however, our historians combine their historical expertise with insights and evidence from Chaucer's works. So often, Geoffrey Chaucer provides a rich and satisfying (and sometimes challenging) context for Geoffrey Chaucer.

A number of chapters shed light on vitally important aspects of the literary culture of Chaucer's time, be it, for example, the French, Italian, classical or English contexts; form and textual culture (e.g. romance, metre, authority, literary roles, love); distinctive conditions of textual production (London, manuscript culture and the likely books available to Chaucer); or, less tangibly but unignorably, considerations such as holiness, secularity, God, sex and the self – not forgetting, of course, the life of Geoffrey

Chaucer himself. The closing five chapters of the book discuss the reception of Chaucer and his works, from the agenda-driven invention of his status as 'Father of English Poetry' in the fifteenth century through to the intellectual problems and opportunities posed by his twenty-first-century digital afterlife.

This book addresses a whole host of questions likely to be in the minds of those studying Chaucer. What was Chaucer like himself? What was heraldry about? What were the pathways of children's education? How did a medievalised classical tradition impinge on Chaucer? What kind of understanding did someone like Chaucer have of the heavens and cosmology? What was chivalry? How did medieval marriages work – or go wrong? What did the commercial and social life of town and country involve? How did verse scan? What was a normal day in the life of someone of Chaucer's time like? What were medieval romance and love about? Who and what were heretics/Lollards? And what about Boethius? Answers to questions like this, and the perspectives and food for thought provided across the sweep of essays in this volume, should go some way to help readers to prepare and develop their readings of Chaucer's works and their critical responses to a whole world of further issues raised (and characteristically exacerbated) by his texts.

Geoffrey Chaucer in Context has not exactly been the most straightforward editorial task. While the coverage is reasonably comprehensive, there are inevitably gaps, which owe themselves to limitations of space, time, configurability and other circumstances. The user of this book would do well to make habitual use of the index and (in the best tradition of medieval *compilatio*) to read across and amongst chapters at will, according to their own needs and interests. Like any compiler, I gratefully acknowledge the authority and the value of the work of the contributors to this volume. I am particularly grateful to Vincent Gillespie, Chris Given-Wilson and Alastair Minnis for their invaluable advice during the process of recruiting contributors. I'd also like to thank colleagues at Cambridge University Press – Anna Bond, Linda Bree and Alison McMenemy, and in particular Emily Hockley, Sarah Lambert, Tim Mason, Carrie Parkinson, Dawn Preston and Robert Whitelock for their support and expertise before and during production.

It is the hope of *Geoffrey Chaucer in Context* that it will assist readers in listening to the voice(s) of Chaucer and in taking on board the complexity and colour of his times with heightened appreciation, but not to do so passively. To contextualise is not passively to accept the past on its own terms, but to put that past – and by extension oneself and the constructedness of one's own culture and situation – in a more self-aware, historically contingent, context. No writer was more inventive and tempting than Geoffrey Chaucer in making his readers perform the work of interpreting his own writings and take responsibility for it. The same belief in the independence and answerability of the Chaucerian reader lies at the heart of this book.

PART I

Chaucer as Context

CHAPTER 1

What Was Chaucer Like?

†J. A. Burrow

Readers of Chaucer's poetry hear in it a distinctive and individual voice. This is most often audible where Chaucer is speaking in the first-person singular as the narrator in his longer poems – as dreamer in the dream poems, as historian of love in *Troilus and Criseyde*, and as pilgrim in the *Canterbury Tales*. These speakers share certain characteristics that between them contribute to a sense that we are here encountering someone of a marked personality. So, more than any other medieval English poet, Chaucer seems to invite the question raised in this chapter. What was he like?

Geoffrey Chaucer's life is much better documented than that of any English poetic contemporary or predecessor: the volume of his 'life records' compiled by modern scholars runs to all of 549 pages, based on no fewer than 493 documentary sources.[1] Yet, as the author of the best recent biography ruefully remarks, these are 'none of them intimate and many of them extremely uninformative'.[2] This is not surprising, for the documents are all official – administrative, financial and legal – and they have no occasion to report how Chaucer may have struck those who knew him: what he was like.

There are however two sources of a different kind, dating from a time shortly after the poet's death, which do have some bearing on this question. One of the witnesses is Thomas Hoccleve (1367?–1426). In the prologue to his *Regiment of Princes*, composed in 1410–11, Hoccleve encounters an old man who, as soon as he learns his name, says:

> Sone, I have herd or this men speke of thee;
> Thow were aqweyntid with Chaucer, pardee.[3]

There follow later in the poem three passages in which Hoccleve laments Chaucer's death (lines 1958–74, 2077–107, 4978–98). These plangent laments – 'O maistir, maistir, God thy soule reste' (line 2107) – are chiefly concerned to praise Chaucer as 'the honour of Englissh tonge' (line 1959); but they also recall occasions when he tried to help the young Hoccleve write better poems:

My deere maistir, God his soule qwyte,
And fadir, Chaucer, fayn wolde han me taght,
But I was dul and lerned lyte or naght.
(lines 2077–9)

It was such affectionate memories that prompted the younger poet to arrange that a portrait of his dear master should appear in copies of the *Regiment* (see Figure 1.1).[4] In the accompanying verses, Hoccleve says that the picture will enable others to recall what Chaucer looked like:

Althogh his lyf be qweynt, the resemblance
Of him hath in me so fressh lyflynesse
That to putte othir men in remembrance
Of his persone, I have heere his liknesse
Do make.
(lines 4992–6)

Unusually for a medieval portrait, this one really does seem to be a 'liknesse', showing an elderly and rather chubby Chaucer, with a pen-holder around his neck and a rosary in his left hand. This extraordinary act of piety towards Chaucer on the part of a disciple allows us a rare opportunity to visualise an English poet of the time. Such, evidently, must be what Chaucer was like – what he looked like, that is.

The second and much the most revealing of these two sources is to be found in John Lydgate's *Troy Book*, composed between 1412 and 1420. This passage also concerns Chaucer's dealings with young would-be poets. Unlike Hoccleve, Lydgate claims no more than second-hand knowledge of his predecessor – '(I have herde telle)' – but he had ready access to an authoritative source, his acquaintance Thomas Chaucer, the poet's son, and it was probably from Thomas that he received his information:[5]

For he þat was gronde of wel-seying
In al hys lyf hyndred no makyng,
My maistir Chaucer, þat founde ful many spot –
Hym liste nat pinche nor gruche at every blot,
Nor meve hym silf to parturbe his reste
(I have herde telle) but seide alweie þe best,
Suffring goodly of his gentilnes
Ful many þing enbracid with rudnes.[6]

Although there is less personal warmth here than in the Hoccleve, Lydgate also speaks highly of '[m]y maistir Chaucer'. He praises in particular the poet's 'gentilnes' as it appeared in his treatment of young literary aspirants. Not wishing to discourage their efforts or hinder the progress of poetry ('makyng'), he 'seide alweie the best', commending their efforts

Figure 1.1 Miniature in colours of Chaucer clutching a rosary and pointing at the text from the *Regiment of Princes* by Thomas Hoccleve.

without drawing attention to the many faults that he no doubt saw in them. Yet Lydgate also notices another, more singular reason for such 'wel seying': Chaucer on such occasions chose not to 'meve hym silf to parturbe his reste'. He reserved his true opinions, that is, in part because he did not wish to exert himself in the discussion of particulars. So, one may imagine that young poets like Hoccleve would have gone away still wondering what the master really thought of their efforts.

Lydgate's little anecdote brings us much closer than any other document of the time, I think, to the Chaucer that we encounter in his poetry. For there too Chaucer 'says always the best', generally representing his subjects in the most favourable light possible, and there too the well-saying will often leave readers to wonder what the poet really thought – about Criseyde, it may be, or about the Merchant. In the *General Prologue* to the *Canterbury Tales*, as is well known, Chaucer gives enthusiastically positive accounts of all his fellow pilgrims, representing each of them as an outstanding example of his or her particular calling. In some of these portraits the praise seems to leave nothing more to be said: there is no call to suspect reservations, let alone criticism, in the lines about the Parson – 'A bettre preest I trowe that nowher noon is' (*CT*, I.524) – nor, despite some recent opinion to the contrary, is the Knight to be understood as anything other than what Chaucer calls him, 'a verray, parfit gentil knyght' (I.72). Yet we are clearly not expected to accept praise of the Pardoner as 'a noble ecclesiaste' (I.708), or to go along with the judgement passed on the Monk's very worldly take on his monastic vocation, 'And I seyde that his opinion was good' (I.183). Other cases are less clear-cut. The Prioress is praised for qualities most of which may be thought, at best, irrelevant to her religious vocation – elegant French, good table manners and the like – yet such misdirected praise does not suggest any outright condemnation. Indeed, her portrait creates an effect so elusive that critics and readers who look for an authorial judgement have quite failed to agree on one.

Passages of this questionable kind have raised the large question of Chaucer's irony. The word derives from *eiron*, a Greek term that denotes someone who deliberately undersells himself, the classic example being the philosopher Socrates in Plato's *Dialogues*, where he defers to others while himself playing the part of a puzzled beginner. Praise of others and dispraise of self are, for the *eiron*, two sides of the same coin. And so it is with Chaucer. Not only does he persistently credit others with the best that can be said of them, he also discredits himself.

The first-person narrators in the longer poems – addressed as 'Geoffrey' in the *House of Fame* – all cut sorry figures. They are not even any good at the one thing where they might be expected to excel – that is, in reporting what they see and read. Although their favourite subject is love, they have no first-hand experience of it. When, in the *Legend of Good Women*, the God of Love himself condemns the poet for his blundering treatments of the matter, Alceste comes to his defence with a most unflattering argument: poor man, he is just a bookworm who does nothing but translate books at random, paying no attention to what may be in them (*LGW*, G Pro 342–3). Nor can he even claim that his own verses are well written. The Man of Law in the *Canterbury Tales* complains that Chaucer has used up so many good stories with his incompetent versions that

> I kan right now no thrifty tale seyn
> That Chaucer, thogh he kan but lewedly
> On metres and on rymyng craftily,
> Hath seyd hem in swich Englissh as he kan.
> (II.46–9)

So, when Chaucer himself is later called on for a contribution, he can offer nothing better than his *Tale of Sir Thopas*, a poem that amply justifies the Man of Law's strictures on his metres, his rhyming and his English.

Eirons do not speak their mind, reserving to themselves what they really think. So it is appropriate that the ironic Chaucer should represent himself as a reserved and private sort of person. In the *House of Fame*, Jove's eagle explains that the god has taken pity on the bookish Geoffrey, deciding to grant him at least some tidings of those love-affairs about which he writes so sedulously; for his present way of life is such that he never knows what is going on:

> But of thy verray neyghebores,
> That duellen almoost at thy dores,
> Thou herist neyther that ne this;
> For when thy labour doon al ys,
> And hast mad alle thy rekenynges,
> In stede of reste and newe thynges
> Thou goost hom to thy hous anoon,
> And, also domb as any stoon,
> Thou sittest at another book
> Tyl fully daswed ys thy look.
> (*HF*, 649–58)

Here for once Chaucer allows us a glimpse of his everyday life, working during the day on his 'rekenynges' in the Port of London and spending his evenings buried in yet more books. This is the same unsociable Chaucer who figures in the *Canterbury Tales* at the moment when, a long way into the poem, the Host notices him for the first time: 'What man artow?' (VII.695). This pilgrim has evidently been playing no part in the life of the company, as the Host complains: 'He semeth elvyssh by his contenaunce, / For unto no wight dooth he daliaunce' (VII.703–4). Elves are not friendly little creatures in Chaucer, and the epithet 'elvyssh' here conveys a certain aloofness in the pilgrim, a reserved and distant demeanour that the professionally sociable landlord of the Tabard finds provoking.

This elvishness appears again in a passage in the *House of Fame*. Having arrived at Fame's house and observed the goddess's dealings with those who sue for her favours, Geoffrey is asked by a bystander whether he has himself come there in the hope of being promised fame. He answers with an emphatic negative:

> Sufficeth me, as I were ded,
> That no wight have my name in honde.

I wot myself best how y stonde;
For what I drye, or what I thynke,
I wil myselven al hyt drynke,
Certeyn, for the more part,
As fer forth as I kan myn art.
(*HF*, 1876–82)

In these lines Geoffrey addresses the one activity of his that might give him a claim on the favours of the goddess: his practice of 'myn art', surely the art of poetry.[7] But he does not, he declares, look to his writings for any kind of personal fame, being content that 'no wight have my name in honde'. Nor does he wish to display his inner life to the opinion of others: 'I wot myself best how y stonde'. So far as he can, accordingly, he will drink up all his private thoughts and experiences – rather than pour them out, that is to say. It is a remarkable statement of intent, and one that is borne out by Chaucer's writings. For in these we do indeed find very little of 'what I drye, or what I thynke'.

To the question put in the title of this chapter, 'What was Chaucer like?', there can never be any direct answer, certainly not on the evidence of the *Life-Records*. The anecdotes of Hoccleve and Lydgate afford some revealing glimpses of Chaucer's behaviour in real life, but all the other evidence cited here comes from his poems, and these may be supposed to display no more than the literary persona that he chose to assume in them. Yet the self-representations in his poetry are so consistent with each other, and in some respects so singular, that it is hard to believe that they bear no relation to the ways in which Chaucer also presented himself in his real-life dealings – as a reserved and ironical sort of person. Certainly, an elvish Chaucer such as that – the Chaucer of Lydgate's anecdote – would have been well equipped to cope with the many vicissitudes of his time, as the poet evidently did.

NOTES

1 *L-R.*
2 Derek Pearsall, *The Life of Geoffrey Chaucer: A Critical Biography* (Oxford: Blackwell, 1992), p. 2. See also Andrew Galloway's chapter in the present volume.
3 Thomas Hoccleve, *The Regiment of Princes*, ed. Charles R. Blyth (Kalamazoo: Medieval Institute, 1999), lines 1866–7. Blyth discusses the references to Chaucer on pp. 12–14 of his introduction. Line numbers of this work will henceforth be indicated in this chapter after each quotation.

4 The picture is reproduced from fol. 88 of London, British Library, MS Harley 4866. For a full discussion of this and other portraits of Chaucer, see Appendix 1 in Pearsall's *Life*.

5 On Lydgate's acquaintance with Thomas Chaucer, himself a man of some eminence in his time, see Derek Pearsall, *John Lydgate* (London: Routledge and Kegan Paul, 1970), pp. 161–2.

6 John Lydgate, *Troy Book*, ed. H. Bergen, EETS es 97, 103, 106, 126 (1906–20), Book v, lines 3519–26.

7 The word 'art' can have a quite general sense (something like 'the trick of it') elsewhere, as in *HF*, 355, where it refers to the devices by which women might evade the wiles of men. But 'my art' sounds more specific than that.

CHAPTER 2

Chaucer's Life and Literary 'Profession'

Andrew Galloway

In a deposition of 1386 for a long dispute in the Court of Chivalry between two powerful knights who claimed the same heraldic bearings, Chaucer stated that he was 'forty years and more' and had borne arms for twenty-seven years, thus indicating that he was born in the 1340s, though the precise date is unknown.[1] From the deed enrolling Chaucer's sale of a tenement he had inherited, on Thames Street in the Vintry, we know he was the son of John Chaucer, a London vintner (wine wholesaler) who was well connected to the civic elite and some gentry, and Agnes de Copton, who was young enough at John's death in 1366 to marry another vintner.[2] Fragmentary household accounts and other records show that Geoffrey spent the 1350s and 1360s as a lowly but rising servant of high nobility: first the King's sister-in-law, Elizabeth, Countess of Ulster; subsequently her husband, Prince Lionel; then in King Edward III's own household, where he served as esquire, a rank just high enough to explain his participation later in the Court of Chivalry dispute between Sir Richard Scrope and Sir Robert Grosvenor (Chaucer gave testimony 'pur la partie de Monsieur Richard Lescrop', the ultimate victor in the dispute, who was in turn supported by Edward III's brother, John of Gaunt, with whom Chaucer was by then closely affiliated). In the 1386 deposition, Chaucer says he had seen Scrope bearing the disputed armorial bearings 'outside the town of Réthel' near Rheims, 'and throughout the entire journey so long as he [Chaucer] was on it': although Chaucer's stray reminiscences supporting Gaunt's man may not have been as innocently spontaneous as they sound, their incidental details confirm Chaucer's travel with Lionel or the Black Prince during Edward III's campaign against Rheims from late 1359 until 11 January 1360. At this point Edward abandoned the siege and led his army southward to Paris through devastated French villages and fields, where guerilla forces killed or captured for ransom any members of the English forces who strayed seeking provisions. Chaucer was himself captured on this campaign sometime before March 1360, when his £16 ransom is listed among other ransoms, ranging from 52 s. for two 'boys';

to £10 for a valet of the Countess of Ulster (the sort of position Chaucer had recently held); up to £50 for a King's esquire, Sir Richard Stury, whose Francophile literary interests and (mildly heretical) English-centred religious interests show other sides of Chaucer's courtly setting besides the war with France that waxed and waned throughout his life.[3]

Chaucer's marriage and early professional life followed courtly service, not civic mercantilism, in spite of his roots in and continued contact with the latter. We know nothing of his life between 1360 and 1366, when he married Philippa (probably *née* Roet), herself a *demoiselle* for the Countess of Ulster, then *domicella* of the chamber for Edward's wife Queen Philippa. After the Queen's death in August 1369 – less than a year after Gaunt's first wife Blanche of Lancaster had also died, in childbirth – Philippa Chaucer continued in Gaunt's domestic household; then from 1371 she served Gaunt's second wife Constance of Castile, heiress to Pedro 'the Cruel' of Castile ('worthy Petro, glorie of Spayne' in the *Monk's Tale* (*CT*, VII.2375)). By 1371, Philippa Chaucer's sister Katherine Swynford, who had been the governess of Gaunt's three legitimate children from his marriage with Blanche, was openly acknowledged as Gaunt's mistress and bore him four more children over the following decade, coyly surnamed 'Beaufort' (in 1396, to everyone's surprise, Gaunt married her). By 1369 Chaucer was an esquire in Edward III's chamber, although after 1372 he was called simply King's esquire. Sometime between Blanche of Lancaster's death on 12 August 1368 and mid-1372, he wrote the *Book of the Duchess* commemorating Blanche's death, a poem unmistakably (if cryptically) offered to Gaunt, Duke of Lancaster and (until July 1372) Earl of Richmond, whose name and titles are conveyed in riddles near the end of the poem: 'A long castel with walles white, / Be Seynt Johan, on a ryche hil' (*BD*, 1319–20). For all datable purposes (and this is the only poem by Chaucer that can be dated even this precisely), this elegant poem, in which the narrator emphasises beyond any plausible verisimilitude his naive misunderstanding of courtly conceits but shows his usefulness in helping his betters mourn, represents the start of Chaucer's poetic and more professionally distinguished career.

Chaucer's fluency in 'reading' armorial bearings, crucial to his testimony in the Scrope–Grosvenor trial, was just one of the kinds of elite literacies he acquired. He certainly had enough early education to read and memorise selectively not just the basic Latin school-texts such as 'Cato' and Claudian's *De raptu Proserpinae*, but also Statius's *Thebaid*, Alan of Lille's *Plaint of Nature*, Boethius's *Consolation of Philosophy*, and quantities of Ovid and Virgil, all works used in St Paul's Almonry School, which he might have attended as a child in London.[4] But his poetry tends to draw on French translations of Latin literature where available, and its uses of French poetry, chronicles and commentaries – by writers from Jean de Meun to Nicholas Trevet, Guillaume de Machaut, Jean Froissart, Oton de Grandson, Eustace Deschamps and others – are much wider and deeper than any other kinds of sources. His (usually minor) roles in many legal actions show adept but not unusual knowledge of the law, some knowledge of which many kinds of professional and personal management and conflict demanded in this litigious period, in settings from Great Houses down to villages. Apart from serfs, whose legal status denied them access to the royal courts of the Common Law (and whose numbers in that status were in any case rapidly dwindling), nearly everyone in the period seems to have been in one court or another at some point.[5] Thus there is more than one reason to be sceptical of the uncorroborated story from 1598 mentioning the memory of a record of a fine Chaucer had paid for beating a friar while Chaucer was studying law at the Inner Temple.[6] Chaucer's reading in theology was thin (Boethius, which he knew well and translated – with assistance from a French translation – was almost as fully appropriated by 'courtly' culture as Ovid), but he cultivated remarkable expertise in astronomy, many sophisticated uses of which appear in his poetry, and the use of the astrolabe, an English guide which he composed for a ten-year-old boy, whom he addresses as 'lyte Lowys my sone' (*Astr*, 1), probably the Louis Chaucer listed as man-at-arms in 1403 alongside Thomas Chaucer, Chaucer's other son, who went on to a much more stellar career than either his brother or father (as chief butler of England and elected speaker of the House of Commons five times). Chaucer's more professionally modest claims that 'on bokes for to rede I me delyte' around all other demands and distractions (*LGW*, 30; *HF*, 652–60; *PF*, 695–9) are supported by the continually widening sources of the poetry he wrote, evidence of lifelong intellectual as well as literary enquiry. An increased preoccupation with rhetorical theory, for example, appears in works written towards the end of his career, such as the *Nun's Priest's Tale*; perhaps not coincidentally, around the same time a new interest in rhetorical guides is notable at Oxford.[7]

Chaucer's work for the King's civil service expanded to both diplomacy, where rhetoric was a highly practical skill, and regulatory supervision, where precise accounting and investigation were essential. In 1372–3, Chaucer was sent by the aged King or his advisers on a mission to Genoa to negotiate a dedicated English port for the Genoese traders – a goal that the English crown and Genoese merchants desired, but most London merchants detested. Submitting his expenses, Chaucer also noted a journey to Florence, where Dante was lauded and near where Boccaccio was living, not far from Padua where a very old Petrarch was living as well. Any official reason for the Florentine leg is lost, but thereafter Chaucer increasingly used Italian as well as French literature as his sources and models. Upon his return he was engaged for a long stretch, 1374–86, as a controller of the London subsidy and wool custom. Though again serving as royal agent in the civic world, as customs controller Chaucer was surrounded by the operations of late medieval London mercantilism. His job was to check the accounting of the higher merchants who served as the 'collectors'; to supervise the 'searchers' (who could confiscate uncustomed goods), packers and porters; and to deal regularly with the troner, the official who used the tronage beam for weighing taxable wool in a barnlike wharfside office, near the current Custom House, with a 'solarium', or sunroom, for accounting.[8] In July 1376 Chaucer gained the bounty of £71. 4s. 6d. for discovering a shipment of uncustomed wool. This suggests he quickly learnt how to benefit from the attentiveness and 'practical' literacy that a customs controllership required.

In this period he lived rent-free above Aldgate, continuing to make occasional official journeys, suspending his duties as customs controller (he appointed a succession of deputies, and during his entire last year as controller was allowed the unique privilege of appointing a permanent deputy).[9] When Chaucer travelled again in 1378 to Italy, this time to Lombardy, he gave Richard Forester and the other major London courtly poet, John Gower, who exchanged poetic sources and tales with Chaucer as Chaucer did with him, power of attorney.[10] This journey's purpose was to request military support for the King from the Italian-based English mercenary Sir John Hawkwood, who may be alluded to in the portrait of the Knight in the *General Prologue* (I.43–78). Other literary traces of this journey are visible throughout Chaucer's writing: he mentions 'tirauntz of Lombardye' in the *Legend of Good Women* (F 374), and describes Bernabò Visconti in the *Monk's Tale* (VII.2399–406), both works from the late 1380s or later. Chaucer also travelled in this period to Brittany and France to assist knights like Sir Richard Stury in diplomacy and perhaps royal marriage negotiations for the young King Richard II, such as those that took place in 1380 when Richard, Charles of France and Friedrich of Meissen were all bidding for marriage with Anne of Bohemia, which has been suggested as the occasion for the *Parliament of Fowls*. That poem and the contemporaneous *House of Fame* display close knowledge both of Italian literature and of raucously 'urban' mob voices to a degree that does not appear earlier in Chaucer's poetry. The sense of a wider civic world seeping into his writing in this period includes his depiction of himself as a less-than-courtly literary drudge, although his two longest and most 'courtly' single works derive from this busy period: the translation of Boethius's *Consolation of Philosophy*, and *Troilus and Criseyde*.

Although there is no evidence of Chaucer's direct dealing with either Edward III or Richard II, his well-situated friends were no doubt responsible for his avoiding the many political and social crises of these decades, in which a young Richard was in constant and often bloody conflict with his uncles, and in which England saw its largest coordinated popular rebellion (in June 1381) followed by its largest popular heresy, Lollardy, whose adherents involved some of the King's chamber knights, including Stury.[11] Not surprisingly, Chaucer's personal life is barely visible in such records, apart from his giving Gower power of attorney and regularly collecting his wife's annuities on her behalf. Philippa Chaucer, while serving the Queen and a succession of other noble ladies, rotated among castles in Staffordshire, Hertfordshire and especially Lincolnshire, where Katherine Swynford lived and where, apparently, Philippa Chaucer died in 1387. In 1380, Chaucer was 'released' from all charges of *raptus* 'and anything else' by one Cecily Chaumpaigne, an event in which Chaumpaigne also released two others from charges, one of whom signed a recognisance of debt to her of £10.[12] It seems clear that *raptus* here is sexual rape, rather than (as sometimes) abduction; but whether this was a single event or a situation coming to a head, and whether it involved Chaucer centrally or peripherally, remain unanswered. The most skilful legal machinations involved here are probably those deflecting focus from Chaucer's exact role, capped by the usual method of gathering influential supporters.[13] Chaucer's release carries as witnesses five of the most powerful lords and London figures of the period, suggesting networks of power and mutual favours like those Pandarus mentions to Criseyde when he is seeking to overcome her reluctance to begin a love affair with Prince Troilus: 'swych love of frendes regneth al this town' (*Tr*, II.379).

By the mid 1380s Chaucer may have moved to Kent, or at any rate had left his Aldgate residence; in 1386 he was Justice of the Peace for Kent (on a kind of grand jury in which he joined a quorum of eighteen magnates, lawyers and gentry in considering cases for indictment, though at that time JPs did not pass judgements), and was elected to Parliament, usually considered an expensive obligation rather than an honour.[14] This seems the likeliest period for his first version of the *Legend of Good Women* – where the poet-narrator has to answer to a king and queen who look remarkably like Richard II and Anne of Bohemia; the sections referring to Anne were omitted from a revised version of the prologue, thus usually dated after her death in 1394. The later 1380s also marked the start of the *Canterbury Tales*, where in the introduction to the *Man of Law's Tale* the narrator looks back on 'Chaucer's' prolific and renowned literary career. But he was not yet retired. In 1389–91 he took up his most arduous job in royal service: Clerk of the Works, where he had to oversee construction and remodelling at Westminster; the Tower of London; St George's Chapel, Windsor; and other manors and lodges; to which were added other projects when in 1390 Chaucer was appointed along with Stury as Commissioner of Walls and Ditches in Kent. The same year he supervised construction of scaffolds at Smithfield for jousts, which have been connected to Theseus's construction of an ampitheatre in the *Knight's Tale* (1.1881–2088).[15] After 1391 he retired fully, living on annuities given by Edward III; John of Gaunt; Richard II; and finally, in Chaucer's last year, Henry IV, conferred without detailed explanation for 'good service'. In 1399 he returned to London, taking out a fifty-three-year lease on a house in the garden of the Lady Chapel of Westminster Abbey, where he died in 1400: 25 October is the date on the mid-sixteenth-century monument. It is usually thought that Chaucer wrote many of the *Canterbury Tales* in the decade after retirement from his position as Clerk of the Works, including his brief final year in the grounds of Westminster Abbey – for which his fifty-three-year lease, like the 116 tales that the *General Prologue* promises, provides a remarkable if not surreal optimism for longevity.

Thus, in brief, Chaucer's life. That so much evidence survives for it is itself noteworthy – as is the contribution that biographical information made to later ideas about this secular author's literary stature and vice versa (medieval 'biography' being closely intertwined with hagiography). Thomas Hoccleve, the unstable poet-clerk at the Privy Seal Office, can be credited with establishing the post-mortem 'presence' of Chaucer in terms more vivid than anyone earlier managed. Most notably this appears in Hoccleve's distinctive portrait of him (see Figure 1.1) in the *Regiment of Princes*, written in 1412 for Henry, Prince of Wales. Chaucer stands penitent with rosary, but with pen-case rather than cross dangling from his neck, his finger pointing to Hoccleve's passage recalling Chaucer as the 'firste fyndere of our faire langage'.[16] Hoccleve's portrait seems the model for the etching on Chaucer's mid-sixteenth-century monument in Westminster Abbey, where he gazes out on what by John Dryden's time was called 'Poets' Corner'. By then, Chaucer had become the Father of English Poetry, his biography inflated accordingly. 'I hold him in the same degree of veneration as the Grecians held Homer, or the Romans Virgil', Dryden declared in 1700; 'I need say little of his parentage, life, and fortunes; they are to be found at large in all the editions of his works. He was employed abroad, and favoured, by Edward the Third, Richard the Second, and Henry the Fourth, and was poet, as I suppose, to all three of them.'[17]

Having a biography of any kind distinguishes Chaucer from most medieval poets. But in spite of Dryden's comment on 'all the editions', only one before Dryden described Chaucer's life: Thomas Speght's edition of the *Canterbury Tales* (1598, reprinted 1602), which recounted his origins, parentage, education, marriage, service, income, friends, literary works and death.[18] Speght consulted records in the Exchequer and the Tower, but also drew, with unfortunately long-lasting consequences, on two non-Chaucerian works, *The Court of Love* and Thomas Usk's *Testament of Love*, both included without attribution among Chaucer's works by the earlier editor William Thynne. Taken as Chaucer's words, Usk's pleas for release from prison led to a long-lasting view that Chaucer himself had fallen from political grace in 1388, and had been not imprisoned but exiled in France, eventually regaining his sovereign's favour. This confusion was dispelled only by W. W. Skeat's 1894 edition of the *Testament*.[19] Speght's more reliable information concerns Chaucer's marriage and genealogy, gathered from heralds. That source is understandable, and not only because Chaucer became brother-in-law to John of Gaunt. Chaucer's son Thomas married a wealthy heiress of Sir John Burghersh; their daughter Alice's third marriage to William de la Pole, Duke of Suffolk, produced John, Earl of Lincoln, whom Richard III, his uncle, designated heir to the throne. After Richard III's fall, John and his younger brother Edmund de la Pole persisted unsuccessfully in claims to the throne; Edmund – Chaucer's last direct male descendant – died in the Tower.

But just as Chaucer's poetic achievements had nothing to do with his original burial in another part of Westminster Abbey (the result of his abbey tenancy and probably of his professional labours for the King), so those poetic achievements had little to do with the documentation that allows us to chart his life better than that of any other English writer before Shakespeare. None of the surviving 493 life-records from his period mention his role as poet, much less a 'firste fyndere' of fair English. Like Speght's genealogical tree (see Figure 49.1), in which Chaucer stands only tenuously connected to the illustrious lineages that burgeon around him, we possess a biographical trove for a major but far from uniquely important medieval English poet, not because Chaucer's literary genius magnetically drew such historical evidence, but because a well-connected and historically fortunate royal and civil servant, living in a time and place of proliferating bureaucracy, happened to express his literary genius by writing English poetry.

This linguistic choice was not inevitable. It was not, to be sure, uncommon in Chaucer's courtly world to produce 'amateur' poetry – that is, in a gentlemanly vein like Jean Froissart and Oton de Grandson, or even simply like Chaucer's Squire, who 'koude songes make and wel endite, / Juste and eek daunce, and weel purtreye and write' (*CT*, I.95–6). Such refined amateurism was far from professional minstrelsy: thus the joke of *Sir Thopas* is exquisitely elitist. But apart from some conventional French lyrics by 'Ch' that may or may not be early works of Chaucer (preserved in a single copy along with lyrics by other French poets whom Chaucer certainly read or knew – Guillaume de Machaut, Grandson and others), Chaucer made an early, unusual and apparently exclusive commitment to English verse, even when addressing the royal court.[20] When Chaucer began his literary career, major works in English were beginning to be copied more widely than ever before: *Piers Plowman*, which mixes Latin (and some French) abundantly into its English verse, was copied widely from the 1360s; and romances in English were well represented, as shown by the collection of them in the early fourteenth-century London 'Auchinleck' manuscript.[21] The period's most popular English poem – though this too uses Latin verses regularly to structure its English – is the didactic mid-fourteenth-century *Prick of Conscience*, surviving in 119 copies: a product of and for the expanding English readership of priests entrusted with the laity's annual confessions. The occasional inclusion of Middle English romances and other works, including Chaucer's *Parliament of Fowls*, in volumes containing the *Prick of Conscience* shows how readily even didactic tastes for English could broaden into wider literary ones.[22] But in noble spheres, works in French were more routinely copied or at least preserved; and spoken French – in a distinctively 'English' style (which in the *General Prologue* Chaucer points to in his portrait of the Prioress (*CT*, 1.123–6)) – was the norm in all the worlds that Chaucer occupied. Latin remained the language of more learned poetry, certain administrative records and nearly all academic religious writing (making Wycliffite efforts to disseminate sermon cycles and the Bible in English in the 1390s at first shocking in their medium, although the Wycliffite Bible became spectacularly widespread). John Gower, Chaucer's associate, friend and competitor for literary patronage, wrote in all three languages in roughly equal measure: approximately 30,000 lines each in Latin, French and English. From all the literary productions we can identify as his, it remains apparent that Chaucer chose English alone.

Peeling away the Renaissance and later claims about his 'fatherhood of English poetry', then, we are still left with a central biographical mystery. Did Chaucer's 'English bias' derive from his persistent sense of social difference from the exclusively 'courtly poetry' in the vein of Grandson and Froissart? Was Chaucer's unusual commitment to English for his own literary writing (not, to be sure, for his official memoranda or diplomacy) displaying his cosmopolitanism, distinguishing himself from continental French and Italian poets of whom he was unusually aware? Was it inspired by the vernacular commitments of the Lollards?[23] Did it express a personal as well as wider antipathy to the French after his capture in 1360 (a possibility canvassed by John Bowers) – although, if so, why do Chaucer's works so often follow and elaborate the structures of French poetry, including such consummately skilful adaptation of French 'fixed forms' as the 'complaint' in *Anelida and Arcite* (as James Wimsatt shows)?[24] Or was English so little inflected with national prestige in this period that it possessed no distinctive, representative authority – beyond, perhaps, a special sense of *dependence* on other languages (as argued by Ardis Butterfield)?[25]

Perhaps Chaucer's signature literary monolinguism was based not on a commitment to 'realism' or quasi-democratic invitation to wider audiences – famous as he has been for both – but instead on a calculated linguistic constraint, sharply contrasting his world's constant mixing of languages, to contain and counter his unusually wide interests in forms, genres and perspectives. Chaucer's poetry famously juxtaposes fundamentally different outlooks, social castes, 'styles'. Restricting his artistic medium to English alone to accomplish this would virtually force him to invent or develop new literary properties, in metre, genre, 'free indirect discourse' and much else: an aesthetic commitment, like using a mirrored 'double chant royal' form for Anelida's 'complaint' in *Anelida and Arcite*. Such a restriction to monolinguism marks off Chaucer's literary production from everything else that he wrote or said, or that surrounded him in his courtly and professional worlds: a focusing of literary skill into a language purer and rarer than any of the official 'rekenynges' over which he pored all day (*HF*, 653–8). In the 1394 revision of the *Legend of Good Women*, he frames his linguistic commitment via Alceste's command to him: 'the naked text in English to declare' (*LGW*, G 86). However we try to explain it away, it is hard not to see in this a settled plan.

NOTES

1 *L-R*, pp. 370–4.
2 *Ibid.*, pp. 1–12.
3 *Ibid.*, p. 24; see Jonathan Sumption, *The Hundred Years War II: Trial by Fire* (Philadelphia: University of Pennsylvania Press, 1999), pp. 426–35. Stury owned a copy of the *Roman de la Rose* that survives as London, British Library, MS Royal 19 B XIII. For Stury's association with Lollardy, see below.
4 Edith Rickert, 'Chaucer at School', *Modern Philology*, 29 (1932), 257–74.
5 See J. G. Bellamy, *Bastard Feudalism and the Law* (Portland, OR: Areopagitica Press, 1989); Robert C. Palmer, *English Law in the Age of the Black Death, 1348–1381: A Transformation of Government and Law* (Chapel Hill: University of North Carolina Press, 1993).
6 *L-R*, pp. 12, 21.
7 Marijane Osborn, *Time and the Astrolabe in the 'Canterbury Tales'* (Norman: University of Oklahoma Press, 2002); Martin Camargo, 'Chaucer and the

Oxford Renaissance of Anglo-Latin Rhetoric', *Studies in the Age of Chaucer*, 34 (2012), 173–207.

8 *L-R*, p. 233.

9 *Ibid.*, pp. 168–70.

10 *Ibid.*, p. 54. For Gower see Andrew Galloway, 'Gower's Quarrel with Chaucer, and the Origins of Bourgeois Didacticism in Fourteenth-Century London Poetry', in Annette Harder, Geritt Reinink and Alasdair MacDonald, eds., *Calliope's Classroom: Didactic Poetry from Antiquity to the Renaissance* (Leuven: Peeters, 2007), pp. 245–68.

11 E.g. Thomas Walsingham, *The St Albans Chronicle*, Vol. II: *1394–1422*, ed. John Taylor, Wendy Childs and Leslie Watkiss (Oxford: Clarendon Press, 2011), pp. 26–7.

12 *L-R*, pp. 343–7; a further record is presented and discussed by Christopher Cannon, '*Raptus* in the Chaumpaigne Release and a Newly Discovered Document Concerning the Life of Geoffrey Chaucer', *Speculum*, 68 (1993), 74–94.

13 A useful collection of the relevant primary documents of this case, with images of the original documents, is available at http://chaumpaigne.org/ (last accessed 1 December 2018).

14 *L-R*, pp. 348–69. Although most scholars accept the long-established view that Chaucer lived at least periodically in Kent during this period (Paul Strohm describes the anti-Ricardian political atmosphere with special animus against royally appointed controllers of customs like Chaucer that made his departure from London a 'constrained choice' (*Chaucer's Tale: 1386 and the Road to Canterbury* (New York: Viking, 2014), p. 183), there is no definitive proof he resettled in Kent. Tracing records linking Gower and Gower's Southwark neighbours and supporters to Chaucer, Sebastian Sobecki argues in contrast that Chaucer spent much of his time in the 1380s and 1390s in Southwark: 'A Southwark Tale: Gower, the 1381 Poll Tax, and Chaucer's *The Canterbury Tales*', *Speculum*, 92 (2017), 630–60.

15 *L-R*, pp. 490–3, 472–3.

16 Thomas Hoccleve, *The Regiment of Princes*, ed. Charles R. Blyth (Kalamazoo: Medieval Institute, 1999), lines 4978–5005, with illustration of the image on p. 187.

17 In J. A. Burrow, *Geoffrey Chaucer: A Critical Anthology* (Harmondsworth: Penguin, 1969), pp. 63–4.

18 *The Workes of our Ancient and Learned English Poet, Geoffrey Chaucer, newly printed*, ed. Thomas Speght (London: Adam Islip, 1602), fols. b.ii–c.ii.

19 W. W. Skeat, ed., *Chaucerian and Other Pieces* (Oxford: Clarendon Press, 1894), pp. xviii–xxxi, 1–147.

20 See James I. Wimsatt, ed., *Chaucer and the Poems of 'Ch'*, rev. edn (Kalamazoo: Medieval Institute, 2009).

21 See http://auchinleck.nls.uk/index.html (last accessed 1 December 2018).

22 Oxford, St John's College, MS 57; London, British Library, MS Cotton Galba E. IX; see those and others in Robert E. Lewis and Angus McIntosh,

A Descriptive Guide to the Manuscripts of the 'Prick of Conscience' (Oxford: Society for the Study of Mediaeval Languages and Literature, 1982).

23 See Andrew Cole, *Literature and Heresy in the Age of Chaucer* (Cambridge: Cambridge University Press, 2008), pp. 75–100.

24 John Bowers, 'Chaucer after Retters: The Wartime Origins of English Literature', in D. N. Baker, ed., *Inscribing the Hundred Years' War in French and English Cultures* (Albany: State University of New York Press, 2000), pp. 91–125; James I. Wimsatt, *Chaucer and His French Contemporaries: Natural Music in the Fourteenth Century* (Toronto: University of Toronto Press, 1991), pp. 116–26.

25 Ardis Butterfield, *The Familiar Enemy: Chaucer, Language, and Nation in the Hundred Years War* (Oxford: Oxford University Press, 2009).

PART II

Books, Discourse and Traditions

CHAPTER 3

Chaucer's Linguistic Invention

Jeremy J. Smith

'INVENTIO'

Famously, the early fifteenth-century English poet Thomas Hoccleve referred to Chaucer, in his *Regiment of Princes*, as the 'firste fyndere of oure faire langage', and the expression *fyndere* can puzzle modern readers.[1] Hoccleve was well qualified to give an opinion. Not only was he a poet in his own right – literary criticism in the medieval period seems often to be expressed through a creative response – but also his association with Chaucer was personally as well as professionally close, as demonstrated by the presence of his handwriting in the Hengwrt manuscript of the *Canterbury Tales*, a text copied, it is has been argued, by Chaucer's 'own scribe', Adam Pinkhurst.[2] It seems likely therefore that the word *fyndere* is carefully chosen, as a modified translation of the first 'canon' of classical and medieval rhetoric: Latin *inventio* (noun, cf. *invenire*, verb), the ancestor of present-day English *invention*.

Invention refers to novelty, but according to the classical and medieval rhetoricians *inventio* had a distinct meaning, i.e. discovering something. Reflecting widespread views on the subject, the nineteen-year-old Cicero composed *De inventione*, defining the notion as 'the discovery of valid or seemingly valid arguments that render one's thoughts plausible';[3] and this discovery of arguments can be extended to the broader notion of 'materials', i.e. the words available to the author. If Chaucer, according to Hoccleve, was *the firste* to undertake this process in *oure … langage*, that *langage* was the London English whose character will be outlined in the next chapter.

However, any assessment of Chaucer's 'poetic art' requires us not just to identify the linguistic choices available to him; it also requires us to ask how those choices relate to his broader poetics. These questions will be addressed throughout the remainder of this chapter.

AN EXAMPLE OF 'FINDING': THE PRONOUNS OF POWER

A commonly praised feature of Chaucer's writing is his use of conversational interaction, as in the links between the pilgrim-narrators. Such interaction is also well illustrated by the *Parliament of Fowls*:

> 'Wel bourded', quod the doke, 'by myn hat!
> That men shulde loven alwey causeles!
> Who can a resoun fynde or wit in that?
> Daunseth he murye that is myrtheles?
> Who shulde recche of that is recheles?'
> 'Ye queke', seyde the goos, 'ful wel and fayre!
> There been mo sterres, God wot, than a payre!'
>
> 'Now fy, cherl!' quod the gentil tercelet,
> 'Out of the donghill cam that word ful right!
> Thow canst nat seen which thyng is wel beset!
> Thow farst by love as oules don by lyght:
> The day hem blent, ful wel they se by nyght.
> Thy kynde is of so low a wrechednesse
> That what love is, thow canst nouther seen ne gesse.'
> (*PF*, 589–602)

We might compare:

> She neyther answerde wel, ne seyde amys.
> So sore abasht was she, tyl that Nature
> Seyde, 'Doughter, drede yow nought, I yow assure.'
> (*PF*, 446–8)

The use of second-person pronouns in such passages is of particular interest. Present-day standard English has only one form of the pronoun: *you* and its inflected forms (*your*, *yours*). However, other languages such as German or French make a distinction between singular and plural – *du*/*ihr*, *tu*/*vous* – and many non-standard varieties of English usage include analogous formations such as *youse*, *y'all*. Earlier forms of English similarly made a distinction between a singular form *thou* and a plural form *ye*, a usage now regarded as archaic and restricted to very special forms of discourse, e.g. in prayer. Further, present-day German and French deploy *du*/*ihr*/*Sie* and *tu*/*vous* respectively, not simply to flag plurality but also as so-called 'pronouns of power', with *tu*, *du* and *ihr* used with intimates or to address children or perceived social inferiors, while *vous* and *Sie* are 'polite' forms, even when addressing individuals. A similar usage with *thou*/*ye* seems to have existed in earlier forms of English, disappearing gradually, for complex reasons, during the course of the eighteenth and nineteenth centuries.[4]

Given the history of these pronouns, the usage in such passages as that just cited from the *Parliament of Fowls* becomes much more explicable. The goose addresses the duck with the plural form, but the tercelet rebukes the waterfowl with the singular *thou/thee/thy*, a choice flagging not only disapproval but an assertion of social superiority.

CHAUCERIAN STYLE

Chaucer's use of pronouns to characterise his birds is a particular choice from the linguistic resources available to him, and thus a matter of *style*, a notion for which classical and medieval literary theoreticians had their own terminology. They distinguished *high*, *middle* and *low* styles, widely recognised as having distinct functions.

However, the distinction between the three styles was, as David Burnley emphasised, 'complicated by shifting moral, social, and artistic values';[5] high style is variously described by medieval authorities as ornate, as the language appropriate for addressing kings and thus of social display, and as the language of elevated moral fervour, while low style is the undecorated language of villainous churls. Thus William Caxton, England's first printer, in the prologue to his translation of the *Aeneid*, distinguished between *curious* (high/ornate), *plain* (middle) and *rude* (low/'vplondyssh') styles, recommending the use of 'a meane bytwene bothe, appropriate for a clerke & a noble gentylman that feleth and vnderstondeth in faytes of armes in loue & noble chyualrye'.[6] Similarly Chaucer's Host in the *Clerk's Prologue* speaks of 'Heigh style, as whan that men to kinges write' (*CT*, IV.18). It is perhaps better (using modern stylistic terminology) to refer to *norm* and *foregrounding*; speakers and writers can vary against a stylistically neutral norm by using 'lower' or 'higher' styles, as appropriate. Each can be seen not as a separate category, but as a pole on a stylistic cline.

This notion of a cline is helpful for many aspects of Chaucerian style. With regard to mode of delivery, for instance, it is interesting that – as Derek Brewer demonstrated – Chaucer is, in linguistic terms, 'poised between oral and literate cultures'.[7] Brewer points out that this poise has implications for certain stylistic choices, notably in Chaucer's deployment of familiar, formulaic – even, in terms of literal meaning, 'redundant' – expressions. Such usage typically happens at the beginning of poems, in order to meet readers or audiences on, as it were, familiar territory, as in the following example from Chaucer's early poem the *Book of the Duchess*. The italicised phrases represent formulaic expressions:

I have gret wonder, *be this lyght,*
How that I lyve, *for day ne nyght*
I may nat slepe *wel nygh noght*;
I have so many an ydel thoght
Purely for defaute of slep
That, by my trouthe, *I take no kep*
Of nothing, *how hyt cometh or gooth,*
Ne me nys nothyng *leef ne looth.*
(*BD*, 1–8)

Such usages were drawn from a domain familiar to the poet's audience, namely the tail-rhyme romances that come down to us from the great vernacular repositories such as the mid-fourteenth-century Auchinleck manuscript: '[t]heir familiarity establishes a link between poet and audience, makes attention easier, characters and actions clearer and more memorable'.[8]

Deployment of usage familiar from the tail-rhyme romance tradition can also be seen in individual words, e.g. 'heroic epithets' *hende*, *joly* etc. in the *Miller's Tale* to refer to the anti-heroes Nicholas and Absolon respectively.[9] But this tale also illustrates well Chaucer's ability to move up and down the stylistic cline, modulating his usage, as when the Miller attempts 'high style' with the heavily subordinated syntax appropriate to formal tenor, and a specialised vocabulary associated with the domain of astrology – but then runs first out of control and then steam altogether:

With hym ther was dwellynge a poure scoler,
Hadde lerned art, but al his fantasye
Was turned for to lerne astrologye,
And koude a certeyn of conclusiouns,
To demen by interrogaciouns,
If that men asked hym in certain houres
Whan that men sholde have droghte or elles shoures,
Or if men asked hym what sholde bifalle
Of every thyng; I may nat rekene hem alle.
(*CT*, I.3190–8)

There are several features of interest in this passage, in addition to the obvious parallelism between the subordinating conjunctions ('If that … Whan that … Or if …'), accelerating towards the end of the period with 'what sholde … Of every …', and finally shifting to a separate, simple coordinated clause, 'I may nat rekene hem alle'. It is also interesting that, according to both *MED* and *OED*, this quotation contains the first recorded use of *interrogacioun*, and one of the earliest of *conclusioun*; the Miller is clearly ambitious to *lykne* himself *to gentill men*, but simply cannot sustain the effort.

This passage also demonstrates a further aspect of Chaucer's style – his handling of metre: it is as a metrist that Chaucer's skill as a 'finder' is perhaps most subtly demonstrated. Here again, the distinction between norm and foregrounding is basic. As Derek Attridge has noted, 'Organized rhythm [i.e. metre] sets up expectations, and any departure from the expected norm is potentially a matter of emphasis.'[10]

In the natural rhythm of speech, it is an observed fact that stress is assigned according to the grammatical category of the word in question. Closed-class (sometimes *grammatical*) words are prototypically less stressed than open-class (*lexical*) words, since the information-content of the former is largely predictable from context. Thus, in a phrase such as *the book*, *the* will be unstressed and *book* will be stressed, yielding an *iamb*, x /. With open-class words of two or more syllables, one syllable will prototypically be more prominent, and thus receives stress: *booking* is therefore a *trochee*, / x. Verse-metre draws on these rhythms but, in the hands of skilled poets, natural rhythm and metre do not invariably coincide: modulation is essential. If poetry is 'invention', a species of 'finding', then poets exploit the linguistic resources available to them, allowing for a tension between rhythm (performance) and metre (expectation) to exist, with 'potential … for emphasis', i.e. foregrounding.

The passage just quoted from the *Miller's Tale* is written in the metre known as iambic pentameter, a verse-form consisting of five iambs (x /) in sequence, but of course it will be observed that many lines, if stressed according to expected patterns of prominence, do not accord with the simple pattern of x/ x/ x/ x/ x/, e.g.:

> x x / / x / x / x / x
> If that men asked hym in certain houres

This stress-pattern is in line with the rhythms of contemporary Middle English, but it deviates from the 'expected' metrical norm, and is thus foregrounded. Of course, alternative scansions are possible, perhaps with unexpected emphasis placed on the conjunction *If* given the parallelism that is being set up between the conjunctions *And … If … Whan … Or*. It is important to realise that an audience's apprehension of stress in verse is a matter of artistic (not scientific) interpretation, and a reader's – or a critic's – scansion of verse is rather like that undertaken on a piece of music.

Nevertheless, a plausible interpretation of a piece of verse should be informed by an understanding of linguistic structure, and in this case our knowledge of Middle English is relevant. The effect of the deviation from the metrical norm is to emphasise the complexity of utterance; by placing two stresses side-by-side (*men asked*) in a spondee, Chaucer slows down the utterance immediately after the speedier pyrrhic (*If that*). The effect is plausibly mimetic, capturing the stumbling character of the Miller's expression. Such special prosodic effects can be achieved because English speech naturally alternates stressed and unstressed syllables; and in Chaucer's time, when final syllables such as *-e*, *-ed*, *-es* were pronounced, the alternation must (as has just been suggested) have been more insistent. The rhythm of the line – the natural stressing of the language – is in tension with the metre, the expected pattern, and thus stylistic foregrounding is achieved.[11]

Chaucer did not always use the iambic pentameter; in his earliest verse he used a shorter measure shared with earlier Middle English romances such as *Sir Orfeo*: the iambic tetrameter. Here, for instance, is the opening of another early poem, the *House of Fame*:

God turne us every drem to goode!
For hyt is wonder, be the roode,
To my wyt, what causeth swevenes
Eyther on morwes or on evenes;
And why th'effect folweth of somme,
And of somme hit shal never come …
(*HF*, 1–6)

Two characteristics of this opening are especially striking. First, Chaucer is already a skilled manipulator of the tension between metre and rhythm; but second, it is fairly clear that he struggled here to sustain enjambment, the run-on of sense-units such as phrases and clauses across lines. Derek Attridge has argued, controversially, that the 'four-beat measure', to be found in such disparate verse-forms represented by the Sanskrit *Rig-Veda* and the Old English poem *Beowulf*, relates to the prototypical shape of syntactic units in Indo-European languages, which would imply that line-ends tend to coincide with ends of sense-units, thus making enjambment more difficult.[12]

Chaucer's eventual response to the difficulty – seemingly simple – was to develop the iambic pentameter, since the addition of an extra beat made enjambment much easier.[13] The advantages this change offered him become very clear from the much less strained opening of *Troilus and Criseyde*:

The double sorwe of Troilus to tellen,
That was the kyng Priamus sone of Troye,
In lovynge, how his aventures fellen
Fro wo to wele, and after out of joie,
My purpos is, er that I parte fro ye.
Thesiphone, thow help me for t'endite
Thise woful vers, that wepen as I write.
(*Tr*, 1.1–7)

In this opening stanza of the poem Chaucer is able to abandon tag-expressions ('be the roode' etc.) needed to flesh out lines, and as a result produces a much more grammatically coherent piece of verse, appropriate for the solemn matter with which he is to engage. Chaucer based *Troilus* on Boccaccio's *Il filostrato*, and it seems almost certain that, in an act of cross-linguistic invention, he adopted the five-beat measure from the Italian poet's *endecasillibi*: an action entirely appropriate for 'le grant translateur' identified by his contemporary Eustache Deschamps.[14]

In so doing Chaucer changed the history of English poetry, but it seems unlikely he was thinking about that. Rather he did what any skilled poet does: he was assisted in his stylistic choices by what antiquity would have called his own peculiar 'genius', the particular linguistic resources of his time and place: the Middle English of London. Had he lived at another time and place, he would have expressed himself differently, and adopted a different poetic strategy. He would have 'invented' different things.

NOTES

1 See D. S. Brewer, ed., *Chaucer: The Critical Heritage*, Vol. 1: *1385–1837* (London: Routledge and Kegan Paul, 1978), p. 63.

2 See Linne R. Mooney, 'Chaucer's Scribe', *Speculum*, 81 (2006), 97–138; for another recent view, see importantly Jane Roberts, 'On Giving Scribe B a Name, and a Clutch of London Manuscripts from *c.* 1400', *Medium Ævum*, 80 (2011), 247–70. For the identification of Hoccleve's hand in the Hengwrt manuscript, i.e. Aberystwyth, National Library of Wales, MS Peniarth 392 D, see the *Late Medieval English Scribes* website, www.medievalscribes.com (last accessed 26 November 2017). The copyist of the Hengwrt manuscript has been generally accepted as the same hand as in the manuscript that is the basis for almost all editions of the *Canterbury Tales*, the Ellesmere manuscript: San Marino, Huntington Library, MS EL 26 C 9. See the seminal article by A. I. Doyle and M. B. Parkes, 'The Production of Copies of the *Canterbury Tales* and the *Confessio Amantis* in the Early Fifteenth Century', in M. B. Parkes and A. G. Watson, eds., *Medieval Scribes, Manuscripts and Libraries: Essays Presented to N. R. Ker* (London: Scolar Press, 1978), pp. 163–210.

3 Summarised in James J. Murphy, *Rhetoric in the Middle Ages* (Berkeley: University of California Press, 1974), p. 11.

4 For a discussion of 'pronouns of power', see famously R. Brown and A. Gilman, 'The Pronouns of Power and Solidarity', in T. A. Sebeok, ed., *Style in Language* (Boston, MA: MIT Press, 1960), pp. 253–76; for Chaucer, see Simon Horobin, *Chaucer's Language* (Basingstoke: Palgrave Macmillan, 2007), pp. 100–3. For dialectal forms, see Joseph Wright, *The English Dialect Grammar* (Oxford: Frowde, 1905), p. 237; and Clive Upton, David Parry and

J. D. A. Widdowson, *Survey of English Dialects: The Dictionary and Grammar* (London: Routledge, 1994), p. 486.

5 J. D. Burnley, *A Guide to Chaucer's Language* (Basingstoke: Macmillan, 1983), p. 199. Further discussion of the three styles is offered in Christopher Cannon, 'Chaucer's Style', in Piero Boitani and Jill Mann, eds., *The Cambridge Chaucer Companion*, 2nd edn (Cambridge: Cambridge University Press, 2004), pp. 233–50; Cannon refers to an 'undistinguished' level of style against which other levels may be positioned, but the more usual norm/foregrounding distinction is adopted here.

6 Cited in W. F. Bolton, ed., *The English Language: Essays by English and American Men of Letters I: 1490–1839* (Cambridge: Cambridge University Press, 1966), p. 3.

7 D. S. Brewer, 'Chaucer's Poetic Style', in Piero Boitani and Jill Mann, eds., *The Cambridge Chaucer Companion*, 1st edn (Cambridge: Cambridge University Press, 1986), pp. 227–42 (p. 227). Brewer's important discussion is supplemented rather than replaced by Cannon, 'Chaucer's Style'.

8 Brewer, 'Chaucer's Poetic Style', p. 229. Auchinleck (Edinburgh, National Library of Scotland, Advocates' MS 19.2.1) includes such well-known Middle English works as *Sir Orfeo, Amis and Amiloun, Guy of Warwick, Bevis of Hampton* and *King Alisaunder*. There is no direct indication of his engagement with this book, but it seems plausible that Chaucer knew it or something very like it.

9 For analysis of these forms, see most famously E. Talbot Donaldson, 'Idiom of Popular Poetry in *The Miller's Tale*', in *Speaking of Chaucer* (London: Athlone, 1970), pp. 13–29.

10 Derek Attridge, *Poetic Rhythm* (Cambridge: Cambridge University Press, 1995), p. 15.

11 For further discussion, see Derek Attridge, *The Rhythms of English Poetry* (Harlow: Longman, 1983). For cases where emphasis can be (arguably) placed on 'grammar-words' such as determiners, see J. J. Smith, 'Chaucer's Use of the Demonstrative', *English Studies*, 93 (2012), 593–603.

12 See Attridge, *Rhythms of English Poetry*, pp. 81–3.

13 See Martin J. Duffell, '"The craft so long to lerne": Chaucer's Invention of the Iambic Pentameter', *Chaucer Review*, 34 (2000), 269–88, and references there cited.

14 See Brewer, *Chaucer: Critical Heritage*, Vol. 1, pp. 40–1.

CHAPTER 4

Chaucer and London English

Jeremy J. Smith

ON LONDON

Geoffrey Chaucer's London was a very different place from the modern global city, not least in that almost all of its inhabitants were largely unaware of communities much beyond Europe and the Mediterranean littoral. The London conurbation in Chaucer's day was restricted to the modern City on the north bank and an enclave around Southwark on the south bank, linked to the City by the old London Bridge. To the west, and still a distinct settlement separated from the City by intervening fields, was Westminster, with its abbey and royal seat of government. The whole conurbation's population, estimated by historical demographers at around 50,000 in 1400, was roughly equivalent to that of comparatively small present-day centres such as Llanelli or Penzance.[1]

However, there are similarities between the modern and medieval city as well as differences. Ever since Eilert Ekwall's pioneering study, there has been an awareness that immigration to London from elsewhere within England had been growing apace during the fourteenth century, in part at least because of the massive social disruption caused by the Black Death.[2] Toponymic surname-evidence for post-1300 London shows that immigration to the capital came from the Home Counties; the Midlands; and, increasingly in the fifteenth century, Yorkshire. As with the cities of the so-called 'Third World' today, London may have been disease-ridden, but it also was a social magnet for those *arrivistes* willing to take a gamble for an improved life: something, notoriously, more attractive to those with nothing to lose than for those with an established stake in the community.[3] And some incomers were successful gamblers, for the story of Richard (Dick) Whittington, a real figure who famously travelled to London to make his fortune, dates from this period: he was not alone.[4]

In addition, living in a port city, Londoners would regularly come across traders not only from the further reaches of England – until the railway age it was always easier to transport bulky goods by water than by land – but also from beyond, both from the other polities within the British Isles and from further afield. These communities rapidly set up their own social structures: Scots, Welsh, Irish, Flemings, Florentines, Hanseatics and so on.[5] The outcome for London society of these processes of immigration, from inside and beyond the medieval English polity, was that it became a city of multiple identities, both in terms of class and of ethnicity. These multiple identities necessarily implied polyvocality.

LONDON'S LANGUAGES

French, Dutch, Italian and German were therefore to be heard in London streets – as were other usages, such as the macaronic 'trading language', a Latin/English/French pidgin found in the financial records associated with the management and maintenance of London Bridge, e.g.: 'fremasons operantur in operibus pontis hoc anno in hewyng & apparellyng lapides vocatur Bridge assheler ac in posicione le Groyne orientale ex parte boriali illius archus sub ponte vocatur seynt mary loke'.[6] But foreign languages and pidgins were only one element in the London sound-world. English-speakers, whether from London or beyond, also contributed linguistic variation.

Such variation is manifested in the range of variants found in London texts and indeed the development of London English during the late medieval period. It may be illustrated by a simple example: the evolution of the third-person plural pronominal system. Chaucer's system, as revealed in the 'best' Chaucerian witnesses such as the Ellesmere and Hengwrt manuscripts of the *Canterbury Tales*,[7] combined northern- (and Norse-) derived nominative *thei* with the oblique forms *hem* and *here*, the latter two being inherited from the Old English paradigm (cf. Old English *him*, *hiera* etc.). *Þ-/th*-type forms in the nominative, e.g. *þai/þei*, are recorded in London from the middle of the fourteenth century, even if still alongside *h*-type forms derived from Old English *hie*. The selection of this innovative usage was probably functionally driven: a more distinctive pronominal system was required as the old inflexional methods of sustaining grammatical cohesion continued to decay, and this situation would have been particularly acute in the nominative case, where the usual positioning of the subject at the beginning of the clause was key for the meaning of the whole utterance.[8] However, at roughly the same time as Ellesmere and Hengwrt were being copied, a new northern-derived oblique form *thair*, the ancestor of present-day English 'their', is recorded in certain London documents, prefiguring future developments.[9] This emerging usage reflects an analogical extension of the *þ*-forms, eventually resulting in the present-day English standard paradigm; but it also reflects the ongoing impact of more northerly varieties on London's polyvocality.

That Chaucer and his circle were aware of – and in Chaucer's case well informed about – northern speech is illustrated by his depiction of that variety in the *Reeve's Tale*. Here is a diplomatic transcription from the Hengwrt manuscript of the *Tale*, demonstrating several features characteristic of northern usage at the end of the fourteenth century:

By god / right by the hop*er* / wol I stande
Quod Iohn / and se how the corn gas In
Yet saw I neuere / by my fader kyn
How þ*at* the hop*er* / wagges til and fra
¶ Aleyn answerde / Ioh*a*n wiltow swa
Thanne wol I be byneth / by my crown
And se / how þ*at* the mele falles down
In to the trogh / that sal be my desport
ffor Iohn in faith / I may been of youre sort
I is as ille a Millere / as ar ye[10]

The two young students, John and Alan, are distinguished by a range of northernisms, such as: the *-s* inflexion in third-person singular verbs ('gas', 'wagges', 'falles') (cf. southern forms in *-eth*); the form *sal* (cf. southern *s(c)hal*); the use of <a> as the reflex of Old English *ā* in *swa*, 'so'; and vocabulary items such as *til and fra*, 'to and fro'. Such an appreciation of linguistic difference suggests not only that Chaucer was well acquainted with speakers of northern English usage, but also that the courtly individuals who made up his first audiences would have been similarly acquainted, since the representation of the students' speech would have been otherwise baffling rather than amusing.

A more delicate example of polyvocality is illustrated by the rhyming-practice in the following rhyme-royal stanza from Chaucer's *Troilus and Criseyde*:

This Troilus, withouten reed or loore
As man that hath his joies ek forlore,
Was waytyng on his lady ever more
As she that was the sothfast crop and more
Of al his lust or joies heretofore.
But Troilus, now far-wel al this joie,
For shaltow nevere sen hire eft in Troie!
(*Tr*, v.22–8)

In rhyme royal *a-* and *b-*rhymes should be kept distinct, and despite appearances Chaucer seems to have done so. The *a-*rhymes in the stanza consist of words that, in Chaucer's day, contained the reflexes of Old English *ā*, i.e. *loore* (Old English *lār*, 'teaching, learning'), *more* (Old English *māra*, 'more'); however, the vowels in the *b-*rhyme words, i.e. *forlore* (Old English *forloren*, 'abandoned', past participle), *more* (Old English *moru*, 'root'), *heretofore* (Old English *-foran*) reflect a different historical development. Although rhyming practice in Middle English verse localisable to the Midlands demonstrates a merger of reflexes of Old English *ā* and Old English lengthened *o*, it seems that prestigious London accents maintained the difference,[11] and Chaucer exploits this distinction for his own poetic purposes: a demonstration of his 'good ear', celebrated many years ago by Dorothy Everett.[12]

CHAUCER AND THE LANGUAGE OF SOCIAL CLASS

Chaucer was sensitive, then, to geographical distinctions in language; he was also sensitive to emerging social differences. The evidence of Chaucer's verse is of a writer exceptionally aware of such matters, contrasting the Knight with the Miller, who *quites* him. And although Chaucer was – as well as a diplomat, an MP and a senior civil servant – John of Gaunt's brother-in-law, and thus moved in the circle of Ricardian magnates, he was also quite capable of playing with his own persona's position in relation to contemporary social elites.

Chaucer famously shows awareness of social distinction in the *Parliament of Fowls*, contrasting the speeches of the 'gentil foules' with those of the 'sed-' and 'water-foul'. Here, for instance, is a speech by the 'royal tersel', the 'hyest' of the birds:

And if that I be founde to hyre untrewe,
Disobeysaunt, or wilful necligent,
Avauntour, or in proces love a newe,
I preye to yow this be my iugement:
That with these foules I be al torent,
That ilke day that evere she me fynde
To hir intrewe, or in my gilt unkynde.
(*PF*, 428–34)

Here, however, are contrasting speeches by the duck and the goose, 'water-foul' that 'sat lowest in the dale' (*PF*, 327):

'Wel bourded', quod the doke, 'by myn hat!
That men shulde loven alwey causeles!

Who can a resoun fynde or wit in that?
Daunseth he murye that is myrtheles?
Who shulde recche of that is recheles?'
'Ye queke', seyde the goos, 'ful wel and fayre!
There been mo sterres, God wot, than a payre!'
(*PF*, 589–95)

Analysis of these two passages shows some interesting differences. Some are obvious: the waterfowl use what are clearly idiomatic expressions ('by myn hat', 'God wot') and the goose deploys a proverb – 'There been mo sterres … than a payre' – as a point of authority. Such usage is clearly presented as humorous: the cracker-barrel wisdom to be expected of such a figure identified later by the 'gentil tercelet' as a 'cherl'. The royal tercel is clearly a very different creature, striking the heightened social attitudes to be expected of the stereotypical courtly lover.

The most obvious difference between the two speeches is in terms of vocabulary. The duck and the goose use well-established words in recorded circulation since at least the beginning of the fourteenth century. Forms such as *loven*, *fynde*, *murye* are all reflexes of attested Old English forms (*lufian*, *findan*, *myrig*). The form *resoun* is first recorded in *OED* in 1225, while *queke(n)*, 'quack' (verb), described by *OED* as 'imitative', is found, according to *MED*, in glosses dating from the 1320s. The verb 'bourded' relates to the noun *bourd(e)* 'jest', cited first in *OED* and *MED* from romances of the 1330s, and the lexeme *dance* (cf. *daunseth*), although earliest recorded in *MED* from the third quarter of the fourteenth century, is first recorded in *OED* from around 1300. The word *causeles* is an exception to this pattern in the waterfowls' speech, being recorded in *OED* only from Chaucer's time, but the item *cause* (to which the reflex of Old English *-lēas* has been suffixed) first occurs, according to *OED*, around 1315.

By contrast, the royal tercel's vocabulary is not only heightened; it seems to be novel. Words such as *disobeysaunt*, *necligent*, *avauntour*, *process* are all, it seems, innovations in the history of the English lexicon, indicated by the fact that, in both *OED* and *MED*, Chaucer is not only cited frequently for these words but also is often the earliest source given. Even allowing for the well-known over-citation from major poets to be found in both *MED* and *OED*, it seems fairly clear (if not absolutely conclusive) that the tercel's vocabulary is innovative.[13] It would seem therefore that the tercel is flagging his status as an aristocratic bird by studding his language with French-derived vocabulary.

Such an interpretation would of course be in line with what we know about the role of French in English – and indeed wider British – society in the late fourteenth century. The relationship between English and French during the medieval period was not simple, and indeed shifted through time. To simplify massively: Norman French – which later developed into Anglo-Norman – was the language of the new elite after the Conquest of 1066, and sustained that position until the middle of the thirteenth century. After that date, Anglo-Norman continued to be used, but seems to have been increasingly perceived as old-fashioned, and indeed many words appear to have been regarded as native and not perceived as having any connection with French. Chaucer himself seems to have regarded the word *fruyt*, 'fruit', as English, using it in the *Parson's Tale* to translate Latin *fructus*, even though *fruyt* was derived from Anglo-Norman, replacing the Old English form *wæstm*.

Central French took over as the language of politeness. Although the ability to speak English was increasingly a marker of national identity as the medieval period progressed, the ability to speak French retained a considerable social cachet for Chaucer and his contemporaries.[14] Richard II habitually spoke French as well as English; he wrote in French too (e.g. to the Abbess of Barking in about 1395), as did most of his magnates.[15] The extension to English discourse of novel, French-derived words seems to be a linguistic marker of social difference that was becoming increasingly salient in the late medieval period, and indeed underlies the present-day register distinctions between forms inherited from Old English, such as *begin*, and French-derived *commence*. Such usages available in the language gave Chaucer numerous opportunities for invention; how he exploited these opportunities is the subject of Chapter 3.

NOTES

1 See www.visionofbritain.org.uk/atlas/theme/T_POP (last accessed 22 November 2017).

2 Eilert Ekwall, *Studies on the Population of Medieval London* (Stockholm: Almquist and Wiksell, 1956).

3 Caroline Barron, 'London 1300–1540', in D. M. Palliser, ed., *The Cambridge Urban History of Britain I: 600–1540* (Cambridge: Cambridge University Press, 2000), pp. 395–440; see p. 399 and references there cited.

4 Whittington (*c.* 1350–1423) came from Gloucestershire. Although the third son of a minor nobleman, he began his life in the capital as a mercer's apprentice, rising to become Lord Mayor in 1397. Other figures from the period include Simon Eyre (d. 1458, Mayor 1445) from Suffolk, who began as an apprentice 'upholder' (dealer in second-hand clothes); Adam Fraunceys (d. 1375, Mayor 1352) from Yorkshire, a man of uncertain origins but it seems primarily a dealer

in wool; and John Pyel (d. 1382, Mayor 1372) from Northamptonshire, who had been 'sent to London to be apprenticed to trade'. *ODNB* offers short biographies of these men; see also Barron, 'London 1300–1540', p. 399.

5 *Ibid.*, pp. 401–2.

6 With modifications, after Laura Wright, ed., *Sources of London English: Medieval Thames Vocabulary* (Oxford: Clarendon Press, 1996), p. 23. For further discussion of such macaronic language, see Laura Wright, 'Macaronic Writing in a London Archive, 1380–1480', in M. Rissanen, O. Ihalainen, T. Nevalainen and I. Taavitsainen, eds., *History of Englishes* (Berlin: Mouton de Gruyter, 1992), pp. 762–70.

7 Aberystwyth, National Library of Wales, MS Peniarth 392 D ('Hengwrt') and San Marino, Huntington Library, MS EL 26 C 9 ('Ellesmere').

8 See J. J. Smith, 'Pronominal Systems in the Auchinleck Manuscript', in C. J. Kay and L. M. Sylvester, eds., *Lexis and Texts in Early English: Studies Presented to Jane Roberts* (Amsterdam: Rodopi, 2001), pp. 225–35.

9 Examples appear in R. W. Chambers and M. Daunt, eds., *A Book of London English, 1384–1425* (Oxford: Clarendon Press, 1931), such as 'The Appeal of Thomas Usk against John Northampton', dated to 1384, which has 'thair' alongside 'they' and 'hem' (pp. 22–31).

10 Hengwrt MS; cf. *CT*, I.4036–45. See also, famously, J. R. R. Tolkien, 'Chaucer as a Philologist: *The Reeve's Tale*', *Transactions of the Philological Society*, 33 (1934), 1–70.

11 See R. Jordan, trans. E. J. Crook, *A Handbook of Middle English Grammar: Phonology* (Berlin: Mouton, 1974), pp. 47–8; also J. J. Smith, *Sound Change and the History of English* (Oxford: Oxford University Press, 2007), Chapter 5 and Appendix 2, and references there cited. I have argued elsewhere that the distinction between these reflexes contributed to the emergence of the Great Vowel Shift in the southern half of England; see Jeremy Smith, *An Historical Study of English: Function, Form and Change* (London: Routledge, 1996), chapter 5, and Smith, *Sound Change*, chapter 6.

12 Dorothy Everett, 'Chaucer's "Good Ear"', *Review of English Studies* os 91 (1947), 201–8.

13 Interestingly, the late fourteenth and early fifteenth centuries see a good deal of experimentation with different forms for particular semantic slots: information now possible to retrieve through C. Kay, J. Roberts, M. L. Samuels and I. Wotherspoon, eds., *Historical Thesaurus of the Oxford English Dictionary* (Oxford: Oxford University Press, 2009). Thus, *disobeysaunt* sits in late Middle English alongside not only such forms as *inobedient* (last recorded 1805), *unobeisant* (last recorded 1400) and the current form *disobedient*, but also forms recorded only once in the *OED*: *inobeisant* (1382), *unobeishing* (1382), *disobeyant* (1422). It would seem plausible to explain such experimentation as relating to the period of extensive lexical transfer ('borrowing'), just described, from higher-status languages to English.

14 See Thorlac Turville-Petre, *England the Nation: Language, Literature and National Identity, 1290–1340* (Oxford: Clarendon Press, 1996).

15 See William Rothwell, 'Stratford-atte-Bowe revisited', *Chaucer Review*, 36 (2001), 184–207. On 'trilingual England', see William Rothwell, 'The Trilingual England of Geoffrey Chaucer', *Studies in the Age of Chaucer*, 16 (1994), 45–67. For Chaucer's relationship with the French language and wider francophone culture, see Ardis Butterfield, *The Familiar Enemy: Chaucer, Language and Nation in the Hundred Years War* (Oxford: Oxford University Press, 2009). See also Jocelyn Wogan-Browne *et al.*, eds., *Language and Culture in Medieval Britain: The French of England, c. 1100–c. 1500* (Woodbridge: Boydell and Brewer, 2009).

CHAPTER 5

Manuscripts and Manuscript Culture

Rhiannon Purdie

This chapter looks at how Chaucer's works reached medieval readers, and how medieval readers accessed Chaucer in the age of manuscript circulation. It also considers what insights are to be gained for the modern reader from a heightened awareness of the manuscript context through which his works come down to us. Not all of Chaucer's audience encountered his work in manuscript, of course. The famous frontispiece (see front cover of this book) to the early *Troilus* manuscript Cambridge, Corpus Christi College, MS 61, which appears to show Chaucer (or at very least the Chaucerian narrator) declaiming to an elegant assembly, reminds us that many members of Chaucer's medieval audience would have heard, rather than read, his texts. But a manuscript is still required for such social readings even if Chaucer does not appear to have one in the frontispiece, so this chapter focuses firmly on the circulation of Chaucer's texts in late medieval manuscript culture.

A medieval reader in search of Chaucer's texts needed money, connections and above all patience. On the evidence of the manuscripts (which for the most part are relatively modest) and their ownership inscriptions, the core readership for Chaucer's works was drawn from the ranks of the gentry and the well-to-do merchant and professional classes from which he himself had emerged. The majority of the manuscripts are copied on parchment, evidently considered more appropriate for Chaucer's works even though it was roughly eight times the price of paper and the latter was certainly available in late-fourteenth-century England. Materials were never the primary expense in producing a medieval book, however: roughly three-quarters of the outlay went on scribal labour. Medieval copying speeds have been estimated at about 2–3 folios (i.e. 4–6 sides) a day, which gives some sense of how long a text such as *Troilus* – copies of which are almost all over 100 folios long – would take to produce even were a scribe to work on it full-time.[1]

Some would-be book-owners avoided this expense by turning scribe themselves. In the later fifteenth century, one John Brode Jr copied for his own use a 195-folio volume of the *Canterbury Tales* (Manchester, John Rylands Library, MS Eng. 113, in which he writes firmly 'Iste liber constat [this book belongs to] Iohanni Brode Iuniori'), as well as another compilation including the *Parliament of Fowls* and *Anelida and Arcite* (Oxford, Bodleian Library, MS Digby 181 part 1).[2] In a legal suit of 1405, a Southwark scrivener called Thomas Spencer claimed that he had settled part of the disputed debt in 1394 with 'quendam librum vocatum Troylous' (a certain book called *Troilus*) worth 20 s., possibly copied by himself.[3] This apparent use of a *Troilus* manuscript as currency in the 1390s is notable in the light of suggestions that the relative cost of manuscripts spiked in the later fourteenth century, perhaps as a consequence of successive waves of plague beginning with the Black Death of 1348–9: these seem to have hit particularly hard the urban communities where scribes worked.[4] Is an unusual shortage of professional scribes in this period partly why no early manuscripts of Chaucer's first works, such as the *Book of the Duchess* and the *House of Fame*, survive, and why copies of them remain rare in the fifteenth century?

Stationers (i.e. booksellers) and professional scribes seem to have worked on commission, often subcontracting out copying and decoration to other scribes and artists. If no exemplar (i.e. a manuscript from which to copy) was to hand, one would have to be borrowed. An inventory of the books of the fifteenth-century Norfolk gentleman John Paston II scrupulously records borrowed items such as 'A boke had off myn ostesse at þe George', as well as loaned ones: 'a boke off Troylus whyche William Bra[...] hathe hadde neer x yer and lent it to Da[...] Wyngfelde'.[5] (That a copy of Chaucer's *Troilus* loaned out almost a decade earlier should be so carefully tracked indicates the value placed upon it.) Borrowing and lending on a much greater scale were practised by John Shirley (d. 1456), a key figure in the circulation of Middle English literature, including Chaucer, in the opening decades of the fifteenth century. Based in London but in the service of Richard Beauchamp, Earl of Warwick, Shirley appears to have operated a kind of informal lending library for acquaintances who, without his own literary or social connections, might have found it difficult to access literary works. In one of the anthologies he copied he wrote proudly:

Þis litell booke with myn hande
Wryten I haue ye shul vnderstande
And sought þe copie in many a place
To haue þe more thank of youre grace
And doon hit bynde In þis volume
þat boþe þe gret and þe comune
May þer on looke and eke hit reede.[6]

Once acquired, an exemplar could yet prove to be incomplete or otherwise unsatisfactory, be recalled early by its owner, or be borrowed by an impatient fellow scribe hurrying through another commission. An 'exemplar' will often have consisted of an unbound booklet containing a single text, a group of shorter texts or part of a longer text (dividing a long text allowed several scribes to copy it at once). The individual booklets that make up surviving manuscripts sometimes have visibly worn outer leaves, a legacy of independent circulation while still unbound. Such piecemeal circulation increased the danger of loss (of leaves or whole quires of text), but it also allowed fifteenth-century readers great freedom in creating their own anthologies. The ordering and presentation of texts within surviving manuscript volumes can offer a valuable window onto the attitudes of their compilers towards their contents.

One obvious but important consequence of circulation exclusively by manuscript is that no two copies of a text will ever be the same. A modern editor has likened the experience of reading the sixteen manuscript copies of *Troilus* to 'taking up – to look at the same object – a number of sets of binoculars each adjusted to somebody else's eyesight'.[7] There was no standardised spelling system in Middle English and thus little pressure to reproduce that of an exemplar: the scribe who copied the two earliest and most authoritative manuscripts of the *Canterbury Tales* opened with 'Whan that Aprill with hise shoures soote …' in Ellesmere but 'Whan that Aueryll w[t] his shoures soote' in the earlier Hengwrt. This scribe's dialect of English was close to Chaucer's own, but other copyists spoke very different regional dialects, and without any kind of written standard to follow, they tended to create dialectal 'translations' of varying degrees of thoroughness. When this is combined with accidental misreadings and deliberate rewritings of the exemplar, it can result in substantial differences between manuscript copies. Based on the majority of the manuscript readings, the *Riverside Chaucer*'s *Parliament of Fowls* prints: '… the nyghtyngale, / That clepeth forth the grene leves newe' (lines 351–2), but the Scottish copyist of the Selden MS wrote '… the nyghtingale / That callis on thir fresche loueris newe', substituting the Old Norse-derived 'call' for 'clepe', replacing the southerly present third-person singular ending *-th* with Scots *-is*, and apparently deciding that the nightingale must be calling upon 'thir loueris' – 'these lovers', with the Scots plural demonstrative article – as nightingales are wont to do in lyric poetry.

The bespoke nature of the medieval manuscript also allowed for deliberate customisation of a text. In the copy of the *Canterbury Tales* in British Library, MS Harley 7333, part of a compilation made for a house of

Augustinian canons in Leicestershire in the second half of the fifteenth century, there are several omissions and alterations at points where the integrity of the clergy had been impugned: in the *Reeve's Tale*, the miller's wife is no longer a parson's daughter fostered in a nunnery, but the daughter of a 'swanneherde' (*CT*. I.3943) fostered in a 'dayrye' (I.3977), and the Pardoner's disgraceful attempt to sell relics and pardons to the pilgrims is omitted (I.919–68), as is the whole of the *Shipman's Tale* with its misbehaving monk. Elsewhere, several manuscripts of *Troilus* – although not the earliest – omit Troilus's soliloquy on predestination (IV.953–1079). His despairing arguments against free will are drawn directly from Boethius's *Consolation of Philosophy*, but the pagan Troilus does not include Lady Philosophy's firm rebuttal of them, which perhaps persuaded an anxious scribe or disapproving client to cut this section: of the surviving manuscripts, the earliest to do so is the great Chaucer anthology Cambridge University Library, MS Gg.4.27 of *c*. 1420. It is less easy to imagine how Bodleian Library, MS Rawlinson Poet.163 came to omit the proems of Books II, III and IV, with no gaps to indicate that the scribe was aware of missing text.

Where some alterations to a text were deliberate, others were forced upon a scribe for lack of a complete or satisfactory exemplar. The scribe of the copy of *Troilus* in San Marino, Huntington Library, MS HM 114 evidently worked from an exemplar missing the 'predestination' soliloquy, but he inserted it on extra leaves, presumably having tracked down a more complete exemplar after completing his original copying stint. A more extreme response to an incomplete exemplar (if it is not a deliberate rejection of Chaucer's ending) can be seen in the *Parliament of Fowls* as it appears in the Scottish MS Arch Selden B.24: its text departs abruptly from Chaucer's at line 601, losing the end of the birds' debate and the formel eagle's bashful request to be allowed a year's respite before choosing a mate. Instead, a suspiciously Chauntecleer-like cockerel complains about the fickleness of his 'seuen loues'; a peacock persuades Nature to ensure that all birds are paired off as planned, including the eagles; and the birds all then fly off apart from one self-pitying owl. Both peacock and discontented owl are clear allusions to a mid-fifteenth-century Scottish poem, *The Buke of the Howlat* (*The Book of the Owl*), which also features 'Dame Natur', a peacock-pope and a raucous parliament of birds. Such freedom to rewrite a text was rarely exercised so brazenly with works by authors of Chaucer's status, but it illustrates how far it was possible, within a culture of manuscript circulation, for a text to move from an author's original without any indication of what has taken place.

This gives context to the anxiety that Chaucer so famously expresses about the fate of his poetry at the end of *Troilus* (v.1793–8). Even the author's name could be lost in transmission (see the 'Poems Not Ascribed to Chaucer in the Manuscripts' in the *Riverside Chaucer*) or the wrong name could be attached: one wonders how pleased Chaucer would be to have Lydgate's *Complaint of the Black Knight* attributed to him as it is in the Selden MS and related Scottish productions. It may be in response to such loss of control over his oeuvre that Chaucer lists his other compositions within some texts (e.g. at *MLT*, II.57–76; *Retr*, X.1085–7; *LGW*, F 417–28, G 405–18), or embeds a recognisable version of himself as author, such as his poet-pilgrim in the *Canterbury Tales* or the narrator 'Geffrey' in the *House of Fame* (named at line 729).

An understanding of the variations between surviving medieval copies of Chaucer's works will sooner or later prompt the question 'but what did Chaucer write?'. Fifteenth-century manuscripts can reveal all sorts of interesting things about copyists', compilers' and later readers' responses to Chaucer, but as long as Chaucer is held up as the acme of medieval English poetic achievement, there is no dispensing with this fundamental question. Since nothing survives in his hand as far as we know, the extant manuscripts – with their multiplicity of variants – are the sole witnesses available. Questions of scribal authority in representing Chaucer came to a dramatic head in 2004 when Linne Mooney identified the single scribe responsible for the Hengwrt and Ellesmere manuscripts of the *Canterbury Tales* as one Adam Pinkhurst, who recorded his oath in the Common Paper of the Scriveners' Company of London in *c.* 1395.[8] Mooney subsequently traced his career through the records of later-fourteenth-century London, including possible intersections with that of Chaucer. Malcolm Parkes and Ian Doyle had labelled the Hengwrt–Ellesmere copyist 'Scribe B' from his work in a manuscript of Gower's *Confessio Amantis* on which their study focused; they also noted that, although the Gower manuscript seems to have been copied after 1408, Scribe B's hand looks fourteenth-century.[9] Mooney argued for the identity of Pinkhurst's and Scribe B's hands and proposed that he must therefore be the 'Adam Scriveyn' to whom Chaucer addressed his wry complaint. (This poem and its ascription to Chaucer survive in a unique copy by John Shirley, but most scholars are willing to accept his testimony to Chaucer's authorship.) Pinkhurst's autograph Latin oath and the Hengwrt–Ellesmere scribe's hand are not identical, as Mooney acknowledges, but professional scribes could write in a variety of different hands, and identifying differing hands as the products of a single scribe is a judgement-call that very few scholars have the expertise to make: the present author certainly does not. Mooney's identification of Pinkhurst has been widely accepted, but it is perhaps inevitable that it has not been universally so.[10]

If Hengwrt and Ellesmere *were* copied by Adam Pinkhurst, who worked as a professional scrivener in London during Chaucer's lifetime, and if Pinkhurst *is* the 'Adam Scriveyn' who supposedly irritated Chaucer with his faulty copies of *Boece* and *Troilus* (the criticism is usually assumed to be joking), then the Hengwrt and Ellesmere *Canterbury Tales* are the work of a scribe who did not merely have access to some early drafts, as previously assumed, but had worked *directly* under Chaucer over an extended period of time, since both *Boece* and *Troilus* are compositions from the 1380s. 'The readings in Hengwrt and Ellesmere, then, are likely the closest we can come in the surviving materials to Chaucer's own authorial version of the *Tales*', Mooney concludes.[11] And if this is the case, the Hengwrt–Ellesmere texts should also serve as a guide to the extraction of genuine Chaucerian text from the manuscript matrix, as should any other Chaucerian texts copied by Scribe B/Pinkhurst, such as the Hatfield fragment of *Troilus*.[12]

But Hengwrt and Ellesmere may yet raise more questions than they answer about what Chaucer wrote. Despite their common scribe, early date and authoritative status, there are significant differences between their ordering of the tales, and their texts themselves are not identical. Manuscript variants are normally treated as the product of cumulative scribal activity, with the astute modern editor having to identify which, if any, is the 'correct' reading, but this assumes that there was a single authorial reading in the first place. Virginia Woolf famously altered the proofs of many of her novels between the British and American printings, giving two distinct but equally 'authorial' readings: how much easier would it have been for Chaucer to correct the occasional passing copy of one of his poems, or even to commission a revised copy? Unlike with Woolf's corrections, Chaucer's hand in the process would become invisible once such copies (re-)entered the haphazard world of manuscript circulation. Such a scenario may account for the myriad textual differences between the extant copies of *Troilus*, although the case has yet to be proven.[13] Either way, a modern reader's understanding of Chaucer is significantly impaired if the manuscript context from which all modern editions of Chaucer have been reconstructed is ignored.

NOTES

1 Daniel Wakelin, 'Writing the Words', in Alexandra Gillespie and Daniel Wakelin, eds., *The Production of Books in England 1350–1500*

(Cambridge: Cambridge University Press, 2011), pp. 34–58 (p. 35). See also Joanne Filippone Overty, 'The Cost of Doing Scribal Business: Prices of Manuscript Books in England, 1300–1483', *Book History*, 11 (2008), 1–32 (p. 7).

2 M. C. Seymour, *A Catalogue of Chaucer Manuscripts*, 2 vols. (Aldershot: Scolar Press, 1995–7), Vol. I, pp. 30–1, and Vol. II, pp. 154–8.

3 Martha Carlin, 'Thomas Spencer, Southwark Scrivener (d. 1428): Owner of a Copy of Chaucer's *Troilus* in 1394?', *Chaucer Review*, 49, no. 4 (2015), 387–401.

4 Overty, 'Cost of Doing Scribal Business', p. 7.

5 Norman Davis, ed., *Paston Letters and Papers of the Fifteenth Century*, 2 vols. (Oxford: Clarendon Press, 1971–6), Vol. I, pp. 516–18.

6 London, British Library, Add. MS 16165, fol. iir, lines 13–19, quoted from Margaret Connolly, *John Shirley: Book Production and the Noble Household in Fifteenth-Century England* (Aldershot: Ashgate, 1998), p. 206.

7 Geoffrey Chaucer, *'Troilus and Criseyde': A New Edition of 'The Book of Troilus'*, ed. Barry Windeatt (London and New York: Longman, 1984), p. 32.

8 Announced in July 2004 and published in full as 'Chaucer's Scribe', *Speculum*, 81 (2006), 97–138. Richard Firth Green adjusted her initial 1392 dating of the Scriveners' Common Paper to *c.* 1395 in 'The Early History of the Scriveners' Common Paper and Its So-Called Oaths', in Simon Horobin and Linne Mooney, eds., *Middle English Texts in Transition* (Woodbridge: York Medieval Press, 2014), pp. 1–20.

9 A. I. Doyle and M. B. Parkes, 'The Production of Copies of the *Canterbury Tales* and the *Confessio Amantis* in the Early Fifteenth Century', in M. B. Parkes and A. G. Watson, eds., *Medieval Scribes, Manuscripts and Libraries: Essays Presented to N. R. Ker* (London: Scolar Press, 1978), pp. 163–210 (p. 208). 'Hand' is the term normally encountered in palaeographical discussions. On the distinction between this and 'script', Parkes observes: 'A *script* is the model which the scribe has in his mind's eye when he writes, whereas a *hand* is what he actually puts down on the page.' M. B. Parkes, *English Cursive Book Hands, 1250–1500* (Oxford: Clarendon Press, 1969), p. xxvi.

10 For the most coherent case against, see Jane Roberts, 'On Giving Scribe B a Name and a Clutch of London Manuscripts from *c.* 1400', *Medium Ævum*, 80 (2011), 247–70; and Lawrence Warner, 'Scribes, Misattributed: Hoccleve and Pinkhurst', *Studies in the Age of Chaucer*, 37 (2015), 55–100.

11 Mooney, 'Chaucer's Scribe', p. 105.

12 Doyle and Parkes, 'Production of Copies', p. 208.

13 Chaucer, *Troilus and Criseyde*, ed. Windeatt, pp. 36–54.

CHAPTER 6

Chaucer's Books

Wendy Scase

Chaucer's writings show that the poet engaged in an extensive and rich variety of reading, ranging from fashionable continental vernacular literature to classical authors, from philosophical and religious treatises to works of science, and from proverbs and maxims to penitential works. This chapter will briefly survey Chaucer's sources and then explore how this astonishing range of reference might map on to what we know about the books and access to reading material a person of Chaucer's background, education, social status and life history might have experienced. We shall see that knowledge of the book-history context for Chaucer may modify the inferences modern readers are likely to make on the basis of the evidence of his works, and offer a deeper understanding and appreciation of the meanings and literary functions of Chaucer's implicit and explicit references to his encounters with books.

Much of Chaucer's work evidences sustained engagement with identifiable sources and models. The texts to which Chaucer is extensively indebted include the French allegorical dream vision the *Roman de la Rose* (translated in Chaucer's *Romaunt* and used extensively in, for example, the prologues of the Wife of Bath and the Pardoner); Boethius's *De consolatione philosophiae* (translated in *Boece* and used in, for example, the *House of Fame* and *Troilus*); Ovid's *Metamorphoses* (the source, for example, for the legends of *Thisbe*, *Lucrece*, and *Philomela*); Boccaccio's *Il Teseida* (the main source for the *Knight's Tale*) and *Il filostrato* (the main source for *Troilus*); Dante's *Comedìa* (used for example in the *House of Fame* and *Parliament of Fowls*); and Petrarch's Latin version of the story of Griselda (an important source for the *Clerk's Tale*). Throughout there are borrowings from the *Disticha Catonis* (a Latin school-text) and the Bible.

Chaucer's range of reference goes well beyond such main sources. He enthusiastically embraces the medieval habit of citing authorities and refers to a large number of other authors and texts by name. A survey of some of those under the letter 'A' in Chaucer's 'reading list' will give a flavour of the range and variety of material cited in his work. 'Aleyn' and his 'Pleynt of Kynd' (*PF*, 316) are Alan of Lille, *De planctu Naturae*; the same author's *Anticlaudianus* is cited in the *House of Fame* (line 986). Ptolemy's *Almagest* is mentioned by the Wife of Bath (*CT*, III.182–3), in *Boece* (II, pr. 7.33) and in the *Astrolabe* (I.17.9). St Ambrose's preface to the Mass is cited in the *Second Nun's Tale* (*CT*, VIII.271–2). The first-century *Argonautica* is recommended as follow-up reading in the legend of *Hypsipyle and Medea* (*LGW*, 1457). Aristotle is mentioned as an authority several times, and his *Physics* is cited in *Boece* (V, pr. 1.63). Augustine is a frequent authority; he is quoted in *Melibee* (*CT*, VII.1617) and in the *Parson's Tale* (*CT*, X.97), for example, while Averroes, commentator on Aristotle, is cited alongside Avicenna as one of the medical authors known to the 'Doctour of Phisik' (*CT*, I.432–3). But even when Chaucer is not acknowledging his literary debts by name, his work is steeped in them. It is perhaps not an exaggeration to describe Chaucer's oeuvre as a journal of his reading. How and in what form could he have accessed this material?

We have no external evidence for Chaucer's books. No manuscripts known to have been used by him survive (even the earliest manuscripts of his own works may postdate his death). We have no will or post-mortem inventory of Chaucer's goods. No accounts survive recording book purchases made by him; no wills survive recording bequests to him. To answer the question of how Chaucer accessed his reading matter we have two recourses – to references to reading in his works, and to the context: book production, ownership and circulation in later-fourteenth-century England.

Chaucer refers frequently to the encounters with books of his fictional alter egos. Especially in his earlier work, he often locates the origins of particular poems in experiences of reading. The poet in the *Parliament of Fowls* describes himself as a frequent reader of books about love. He describes a particular instance. He 'happede' upon an old book (written with 'lettres olde' (lines 18–19)) containing Cicero's story of the *Dream of Scipio*. He reads all day until night falls, robbing him of light by which to read, and he goes to bed thinking about his reading. At the end of the poem the poet continues his reading, turning to other books.

The *Book of the Duchess* opens with a description of an insomniac poet. He describes an occasion when he cannot sleep and so he sits up in bed and asks for a book to be brought. He reads the story of Ceyx and Alcione and learns about Morpheus, the god of sleep. Reading this story sends the poet to sleep – on top of his book. At the end of the poem when the poet awakes he finds himself in bed with the book still in his hand.

The prologue to the *Legend of Good Women* begins with an appreciation of old books, and the narrator describes himself as someone who delights in old books and can be rarely torn away from them by other pursuits. In his dream, when the Dreamer cannot identify Alceste, the God of Love asks him if he does not have a book about her lying in his 'chest' (*LGW*, F 510). Later (F 556) the God of Love instructs the poet that he will find the other ladies about whom he is to write in his books. The poet takes up his books and begins to compose his legendary.

The *Parliament* and *Legend* offer us a picture of a poet with access to many old books at home. The poet in *Book of the Duchess* uses a book kept close to hand in his house; in the *Legend*, the Dreamer is said to keep his many books in a chest. These Chaucer figures read alone and in private places. The *Legend* portrays a poet so addicted to private reading that he can rarely be enticed away to social events. The poet in *Book of the Duchess* reads in bed. Joyce Coleman's '"ethnography of reading" in Chaucer' offers a detailed analysis of passages of this kind, showing that the portrait Chaucer draws of himself as a reader marks him as belonging to a particular category of reader – that of the literary professional – and that the experience of this group was not at all the norm among lay readers.[1] Coleman is interested in reading practices rather than access to books, but if we analyse the implications of these passages for Chaucer's access to books a similar picture emerges: for all that the conditions described chime so readily with modern experience, they were not at all the norm in Chaucer's day. These descriptions of the poet as a bookish figure, always reading and with a large collection of books to hand for his personal and private use, chime so readily with the impression of access to books given by Chaucer's manner of composition that it is easy to overlook the fact that they are quite at odds with the norms for a person of Chaucer's background and circumstances in the later fourteenth century. The contextual, historical evidence provides us with a lens through which to interpret his responses to his sources and the internal descriptions of Chaucer and his books.

Dying some fifty years before Gutenberg's invention of printing with movable type (1450s) and some three-quarters of a century before the first book was printed in England (1476), Chaucer had to access texts exclusively in manuscript. The earliest printed books imitated the appearance of manuscripts, but manuscript differed from print in fundamental ways. Manuscript books varied a great deal in their appearance and the expense involved in their production. At one end of the spectrum were de luxe books, lavishly decorated and copied in an ornate script that was slow (and expensive) to write and could be difficult to read. At the other end of the spectrum were books that seem to have been produced as economically as possible (for example, in cases where books were copied by the owner for his own use). Books at all points on this spectrum, however, were expensive, requiring prepared material to write on (usually, in fourteenth-century England, parchment rather than paper), binding of some kind, and above all the labour of scribes and decorators (if used). Quite apart from involving considerable expense, purchasing a new book in Chaucer's England was not the straightforward matter it is in our age of online and high-street retailers. Almost all new books were made to order and the production process, at least for the kind of material Chaucer was reading, may have been engineered afresh for each new commission. There is evidence that the 'stationer' served as coordinator of the various artisans involved in production. Stationers appear to have held stocks of, or known how to access, exemplars for copying. Nonetheless, obtaining particular texts could be difficult, especially if they were recent works. The expense and difficulties of manuscript production mean that it is unlikely that Chaucer would have commissioned the making of a great many new books.

As a consequence of this method of production, every manuscript book was a unique, and potentially unstable, artefact. Each scribe introduced changes to the text, either inadvertently or on purpose for a particular audience, patron or purchaser. In two famous passages Chaucer fears that his own work will be corrupted in future as a consequence of being transmitted in manuscript (*Tr*, v.1793–6; *Adam*). Decoration, binding and contents were all special to each volume, depending upon the taste of the patron, the style of the decorators and the funds available. Furthermore, manuscript books were not stable objects. Many were not the result of a single production campaign but were accumulations of content gathered over time. Many contain texts squeezed into spare space by later readers. In Chaucer's time the term *book* could refer to little unbound quires of no more than a few pages. Some volumes comprise such 'books' – originally separate booklets bound up together much later: these have been described as miniature libraries.[2] Jankyn's 'book of wikked wyves' sounds like just such a book (*CT*, III.685). Even individual works could have a compilatory and accretive character. Medieval readers encountered classical and authoritative authors via compilations, anthologies and commentaries. For example, Chaucer most likely accessed the *Dream of Scipio* from its inclusion in the *Romance of the Rose*, while some of his references to medieval dream lore could have come from the *Disticha Catonis*. It is easy to be misled by Chaucer's many references to authors and his use of passages from their work into inferring that he had access to the original texts. Chaucer's books may well have been compilations of sources and little quires, rather than the original texts and weighty codices the modern reader may imagine.

If Chaucer is likely to have had fewer codices than his source referencing might suggest, how many books is he likely to have had to hand in his personal collection? It is very difficult to estimate the numbers of books a prosperous family of London merchants such as Chaucer's might have been expected to own.[3] The main sources of information are wills and inventories and, in some cases, surviving books. If a family owned any book it was most likely a Book of Hours, a prayer book that could be used for devotional purposes and to display taste and status.[4] We know about some exceptionally large book collections that were amassed by individuals. John Erghome owned over 220 books, including scientific, astrological, historical and medical material.[5] An Augustinian friar of York who became prior of the house in 1385, Erghome is hardly a parallel with Chaucer, however. Thomas of Woodstock (d. 1397) was evidently a bibliophile; the post-mortem inventory of his collection records that he had 126 books in his Essex residence and more in his London house. His collections ranged across law, history and romance material in Latin, French and English.[6] Manuscripts surviving from his collection show that he lavished considerable expense on de luxe copies (for example his Wycliffite Bible: London, British Library, MSS Egerton 617–18). A wealthy nobleman, however, Thomas is not comparable with Chaucer.

If he is unlikely to have had a personal library on such a scale, Chaucer could have borrowed books or elicited gifts by virtue of his connections and status. Informal lending must have been common and is attested by ownership inscriptions and anathemas against those who did not return books to their owners.[7] Chaucer clearly moved in bookish circles and in the orbit of persons of sufficient wealth and social standing to own books. London lawyer and author Ralph Strode (d. 1387), one of the dedicatees of *Troilus*, was a former fellow of Merton College, Oxford and clearly had access to works of logic, philosophy and theology.[8] Chaucer's administrative activities brought him into contact with noblemen such as William Beauchamp, patron of at least one cleric with an interest in copies of the latest literature.[9] Acquaintance with soldier and courtier Lewis Clifford (d. 1404) appears to have provided Chaucer with access to French courtly poetry by Eustache Deschamps, if we are to believe the scenario painted in Deschamps's *ballade* in praise of Chaucer, where Deschamps begs Chaucer to look kindly upon his 'schoolboy' verses, sent to back to the poet in England via Clifford (presumably as a gift rather than a loan).[10]

Some institutional libraries and book collections could have furnished Chaucer with access to some of his classical and religious sources. At this date, of course, there were no public libraries, and organised schemes for lending to laypeople not rich enough to own books were still to develop.[11] Religious houses had libraries, though they were normally exclusively for the use of members of the order. Parish churches would have collections of basic service books and sometimes held other material. Books held in such institutions are likely to have been chained; Chaucer may have been able to access such material, though clearly he could not have read it in bed. Schools and colleges too had libraries and collections. Chaucer is not known to have attended university but it is possible that he attended grammar school. St Paul's almonry school in London had copies of the classical Latin authors cited by Chaucer.[12] 'Cato', quoted in the *Nun's Priest's Tale* (VII.2971, 3940) and elsewhere, would have been encountered at grammar school.

Some staples may have been readily available (for example service books, school books and law books), but obtaining more recent, fashionable, literary material must have often depended on personal connections along the lines suggested by Deschamps's poem. Chaucer's access to the Italian poets is perhaps the most difficult to explain. He would have encountered talk of Dante, Boccaccio and Petrarch during his trips to Italy in the 1370s. However, it seems unlikely that he could have arranged for the copying of a book in the few months available to him abroad. Another possibility is that he used Italian merchants trading out of London as go-betweens or sources of material.[13] A further possibility is that he could have bought second-hand copies while he was abroad. Acquisition of second-hand volumes was one of the key ways in which book-owners could add to their collections.[14]

Conditions of book production, availability and use in later-fourteenth-century England shaped authors' outputs and the means of dissemination they could imagine for their work. There was no equivalent of the modern publishing industry, where the production and marketing of books are financed speculatively on the expectation of profits from sales. Books were made at the expense of an author or patron and investments in book production were part of economies of gift-exchange, both secular and religious, rather than economies driven primarily by monetary profit. For example, a presentation copy of a work might be gifted by an author to a nobleman in the hope of gaining patronage or favour (e.g. the manuscript of *Contra Lollardorum*, by Roger Dymmok, presented to Richard II), or to a church or religious house by a patron in the expectation that the donor would be remembered in the recipients' prayers (e.g. in 1384, several missals in

St George's Chapel, Windsor were the gifts of noblemen).[15] When the God of Love instructs Chaucer to present a copy of the *Legend of Good Women* to the Queen 'at Eltham or at Sheene' (F 496–7), Chaucer imagines that he is working within the secular model of presentation and patronage. His request to readers and audience members in the *Retractions* 'that ye preye for me' (*CT*, x.1084) inscribes his investment in book-making in the economy of salvation.

NOTES

1 Joyce Coleman, *Public Reading and the Reading Public in Late Medieval England and France* (Cambridge: Cambridge University Press, 1996), pp. 148–78.

2 Phillipa Hardman, 'A Medieval "Library in Parvo"', *Medium Ævum*, 47 (1978), 262–73.

3 Sylvia L. Thrupp, *The Merchant Class of Medieval London* (Chicago: University of Chicago Press, 1948).

4 Eamon Duffy, *Marking the Hours: English People and Their Prayers 1240–1570* (New Haven, CT: Yale University Press, 2006).

5 M. R. James, ed., 'The Catalogue of the Library of the Augustinian Friars at York', in *Fasciculus Joanni Willis Clark dicatus* (Cambridge: Cambridge University Press, 1909), pp. 2–96; Michael J. Curley, 'John of Bridlington (*c.* 1320–1379)', *ODNB*, www.oxforddnb.com/view/article/14856 (last accessed 20 September 2013).

6 Viscount Dillon and W. H. St John Hope, 'Inventory of the Goods and Chattels Belonging to Thomas, Duke of Gloucester', *Archaeological Journal*, 54 (1897), 275–308.

7 For example, in British Library, Add. MS 37787, fol. 183, which says that the manuscript belongs to the Cistercian monk John Northwood.

8 J. D. North, 'Strode, Ralph (*d.* 1387)', *ODNB*, www.oxforddnb.com/view/article/26673 (last accessed 24 September 2013).

9 Wendy Scase, ed., *The Making of the Vernon Manuscript: The Production and Contexts of Oxford, Bodleian Library, MS Eng. poet. a. 1* (Turnhout: Brepols, 2013), pp. 269–93.

10 T. Atkinson Jenkins, 'Deschamps' Ballade to Chaucer', *Modern Language Notes*, 33 (1918), 268–78 (p. 270); for Clifford's visit to France see Peter Fleming, 'Clifford, Sir Lewis (*c.* 1330–1404)', *ODNB*, www.oxforddnb.com/view/article/50259 (last accessed 24 September 2013).

11 Wendy Scase, 'Reginald Pecock, John Carpenter, and John Colop's "Common-Profit" Books: Aspects of Book Ownership and Circulation in Fifteenth-Century London', *Medium Ævum*, 61 (1992), 261–74.

12 Pointed out by Douglas Gray, 'Chaucer, Geoffrey (*c.* 1340–1400)', *ODNB*, www.oxforddnb.com/view/article/5191 (last accessed 23 September 2013).

13 Nick Havely, 'The Italian Background', in Steve Ellis, ed., *Chaucer: An Oxford Guide* (Oxford: Oxford University Press, 2005), pp. 313–31.

14 David Rundle, 'English Books and the Continent', in Alexandra Gillespie and Daniel Wakelin, eds., *The Production of Books in England 1350–1500* (Cambridge: Cambridge University Press, 2011), pp. 276–91 (pp. 287–9).

15 Cambridge, Trinity Hall, MS 17, fol. 1 bears a dedication to the King; see Christopher de Hamel, 'Books and Society', in Nigel J. Morgan and Rodney M. Thomson, eds., *The Cambridge History of the Book in Britain*, Vol. II: *1100–1400* (Cambridge: Cambridge University Press, 2008), pp. 3–21 (p. 16).

CHAPTER 7

Authority

Mishtooni Bose

'Myn auctour shal I folwen if I konne' (*Tr*, II.49): thus the narrator of *Troilus and Criseyde* encapsulates Chaucer's profound, fruitful ambivalence towards literary authority. This may appear a straightforward statement of narratorial intent, but there are creative tensions between the line's main and subordinate clauses. Most obviously, *Troilus and Criseyde* has no single 'auctour': 'Lollius', the alleged authority to whom the narrator ostensibly defers, is fictional; Giovanni Boccaccio, whose *Il filostrato* is followed most substantially throughout and sometimes translated line for line, is unnamed; and the narrator's professed obligation to 'follow' an authoritative source is considerably complicated by the fact that in this poem Chaucer interpolates substantial portions of Boethius via his own translation of the *Consolation of Philosophy*, for which he consulted not only the Latin original and Latin commentary tradition but a French intermediary. Innovation to this extent suggests that the narrator's apparently self-deprecatory 'if I konne' may be intended to keep open some textual and imaginative space for the many experiments in omission, compression, amplification and interpolation whereby *Troilus and Criseyde* repeatedly distinguishes itself from its immediate parent-text, *Il filostrato*, as well as from the literary territory of the other *auctores* – Boethius, as well as 'Virgile, Ovide, Omer, Lucan, and Stace' (V.1792) – who had, in various direct and indirect ways, made the poem possible. '[I]f I konne' thus points the reader away from narratorial deference and towards an exercise of authorial will just as surely as 'yif I kan' had done in the *House of Fame* (line 143), where, as a notorious addition to the rendering of the *Aeneid*'s opening line, it signalled the thick layer of mediation between English readers and Latin source. As these examples suggest, Chaucer was resolutely uninhibited by the anxieties surrounding fidelity and authorial accountability that he habitually foisted onto his surrogate narrators. Rather, at such moments he stages the wresting of initiative from a concept of literary authority dependent on 'following' – with all the cultural deference and faithful replication that this implies – in the service of far more complex kinds of mimesis.

Medieval authority was not, of course, granted and exercised exclusively in the literary sphere. In Chaucer's lifetime, the exercise of authority was radically challenged in both ecclesiastical and socio-political spheres.[1] For example, the Wycliffite controversies were shot through with the rhetoric of confrontation between legitimacy and illegitimacy in authority and doctrine, a preoccupation encapsulated in the recycling of biblical imagery drawn from the Parable of the Sower (Matthew 13:24–30), with the eventual separation of wheat and tares at the final harvest functioning as a metaphor concerning the drawing of distinctions between true and false doctrine. In Latin, the tares, or illegitimate doctrine in this polemical context, had been signified by the word *lolium*. Chaucer's writings are hardly impervious to the implications of such events: it has been speculated that he may have intended to activate the connotation of illegitimacy when burdening the narrator of *Troilus and Criseyde* with the fruitless task of following a single, fictional source named 'Lollius' (I.394; V.1653).[2] But as even this example suggests, his interrogations of the contingency of institutional authority are characteristically articulated through, or even displaced by, more obvious concerns with the paradoxes generated by specifically *literary* authority, which is accordingly the main focus here.

While retaining juridical and political senses from its classical past, as well as an habitual collocation with *potestas* (denoting civic power), the Latin lexeme *auctoritas* later acquired further valence in the literary sphere, where it denoted quotations or longer pieces of discourse, as well as the credibility or deference traditionally accorded to them.[3] *Auctoritas* thus came to signal the preservation and transmission of institutionally or culturally forged connections between utterances and their reception. An *auctor* (author), who generated such discourse, was 'someone … to be respected and believed'.[4] The medieval canon of *auctores* gradually swelled to encompass a host of Christian and classical writers in every discipline from grammar, rhetoric and dialectic to Canon Law, theology and poetry; and academic paratexts, such as prologues (*accessūs*) and commentaries, were substantially devoted to explaining how *auctoritas* manifested itself, for example in the intentions behind the literary work and in its rhetorical modes of procedure.[5]

Auctoritas was typically the outcome of long periods of scholarly rumination and eventual consensus. Antiquity was thus a fundamental criterion for the conferring of authority, leading Walter Map in the twelfth century to joke that 'old copper' was habitually preferred to 'new gold', and permitting Chaucer not to name his principal source in *Troilus and Criseyde*, the recently deceased Boccaccio.[6] *Auctoritas* thus set in motion complex negotiations between the voices of the dead and the living. In scholastic disputations, for example, the voices of *auctoritates* temporarily halt the flow of magisterial rumination, obliging theologians and philosophers to negotiate between *auctoritates* such as Aristotle and Augustine en route to formulating their own solutions to the questions they have posed. The creativity of such disputations is thus forged through the setting up of dialectical relationships not only between philosophy and theology, but also between the old authorities and the new, living contenders. The resulting atmosphere of vigorous but usually constructive contention between old and new voices is reflected in *Piers Plowman*, in which abbreviated Latin quotations are habitually sampled, carrying some of their authoritative energy into the poem even as the vernacular lines in which they have been recontextualised subject them to new kinds of scrutiny and commentary.

Far from serving as repositories of truth transcending the moral and political priorities and ideologies of particular interpretative communities, *auctoritates* both reflected and sustained such ideologies: 'an *auctor* had to say the right things'.[7] Medieval constructions of *auctoritas* habitually prioritised the needs of contemporary literate communities over respect for the milieux in which the *auctores* themselves, whether Christian or pagan, had originally written. The preservation and transmission of *auctoritas* often involved excerption and deracination, the uprooting of quotations from their original settings so that they could be 'replanted' in *florilegia* (collections of literary 'flowers'), used for the composition of sermons; or in the *quaestiones* (questions) that functioned for centuries as the principal unit of scholastic discourse. Tradition paradoxically entailed distortion, as the words of the original *auctor* were recontextualised in order to serve different readerly and writerly imperatives. The conferring of cultural authority thus had a variety of textual outcomes, such as false attributions (for example the long association of Alcher of Clairvaux's *Liber de spiritu et anima* with St Augustine). Much more than being purely linguistic acts, translations involved a variety of interventions between the words of the original *auctor* and different target audiences, resulting in texts such as the *Ovide moralisé*, an early fourteenth-century translation of the pagan *auctor* Ovid into French octosyllabic verse accompanied by a commentary that enacted the conscription of his poetry to Christian ends. Medieval authors were well aware, moreover, that it was not always easy to impose boundaries between *auctoritas* and other, less formally acknowledged, forms of influence. The Clerk's narrative energies may be fuelled by the knowledge that his acknowledged source, Petrarch, is 'deed and nayled in his cheste' (*CT*, IV.29), but Chaucer knew that physical death was only the beginning as far as literary negotiations between the living and the dead were concerned. Likewise, in *Le livre de la cité des dames* (1405), Christine de Pizan attests to the malevolent psychological power exerted by a thirteenth-century misogynist text, the *Lamentations* of Matheolus, 'which I considered to be of no authority'.[8]

Given that the role of *auctoritas* was essentially pragmatic, it is not surprising that the foundations for Chaucer's ambivalence towards the literary system that simultaneously overshadowed and fuelled his own vernacular experiments had been laid centuries before he began to write. The literary traditions that nourished Chaucer's poetry also transmitted creative scepticism towards both the content of authoritative pronouncements and the agency of the *auctores* themselves. This critical mentality is nowhere better expressed than in Alan of Lille's famous pronouncement that authority, in the form of a citation from a trusted source, has a metaphorical 'wax nose', in that it is capable of being twisted in opposite directions, and thus requires strengthening with arguments ('Sed quia auctoritas cereum habet nasum, id est, in diversum potest flecti sensum, rationibus roborandum est').[9] Although Alan is writing specifically about theological *auctoritas* here, his image perfectly captures the potential vulnerability of literary authority and its distance from unassailable truth. This vulnerability extended to the person of the *auctor* himself. The lust-filled lives of Solomon and David, both eminent scriptural *auctores*, proved particularly problematic to medieval readers.[10] Thus, when, in the *Merchant's Tale*, Proserpyne attacks Solomon's reputation – 'He was a lecchour and an ydolastre' (IV.2298) – Chaucer is vocalising the ambivalence of his intellectual forebears. The acknowledged vulnerability of the *auctores* could even serve as the basis on which a modern, vernacular author could stake his claim to credibility: 'Sithen Seint Jerom had manye detractouris and inpugners of hise writingis, as he himself witnessith, what merveyle is if Y so have?', wrote Reginald Pecock, a fifteenth-century orthodox participant in the Wycliffite controversies, in a rhetorical flourish from the prologue to *The Donet* that boldly and instantaneously narrows the gap between the ancients and himself.[11]

The efflorescence of European vernacular literature in the Middle Ages has been described in terms of a *translatio auctoritatis*, a 'transferring of authority', as later medieval writers acknowledged different degrees of authorial subjectivity.[12] Among English authors, Julian of Norwich firmly disclaims a conventionally authoritative stance in order to create a fresh discursive space: 'God forbade that ye schulde saye or take it so that I am a techere.'[13] In *Le Morte Darthur*, however, Sir Thomas Malory's slippery evocations of his alleged source, the 'French book', constitute a spectrum of gestures of pseudo-deference whereby authorial subjectivity is rhetorically disavowed even though, as in Chaucer's works, it is not actually suppressed.[14] In the *Book of Margery Kempe*, the reader's access to Margery throughout is heavily mediated and controlled by the voices and the narrative framing of her clerical scribes. Claiming the role of the *compilator* (compiler) was another way to disclaim outright originality, but Chaucer himself was to expose, through the Wife of Bath, the fact that compilations of voices from the *auctores* had always been creative and even opportunistic acts.[15] Replication of the textual norms signalling the scholastic validation of *auctoritas* was another, more obvious method of achieving authority of one's own. Thus, in the case of Dante's *Convivio*, a commentary on his own lyrics, 'the point is being made loudly and clearly that Dante's vernacular works merit the full scholarly apparatus of commentary which for generations had been lavished on Latin *auctores*'.[16] But Chaucer was temperamentally and critically very distant from Dantesque self-canonisation. In the *House of Fame*, he parodies and deconstructs authorial privilege, exposing the mechanisms whereby Fame is achieved as fragile, arbitrary and circumstantial. The concept of authority, and the textual strategies that serve to construct and validate it, are subjected to a variety of textual depredations throughout his works, the lexemes *auctor* and *auctorite* frequently acting as signals of their seminal and revisionary energies. The fragility of the *auctor*'s name alone is acknowledged in the mangling of 'Marcus Tullius Scithero' by the earnest Franklin (V.722). The ceaseless tension between what was permanent and what perishable about the written word is, in the *Nun's Priest's Tale*, mercilessly exposed in Chauntecleer's insouciant mistranslation of *mulier est hominis confusio* (VIII.3164). The deadpan recommendation, in the *House of Fame*, that the reader consult both Ovid and Virgil on the subject of Dido, when in fact she is presented quite differently in the *Aeneid* and the *Heroides*, can be read as Chaucer's frank acknowledgement that a critical approach to 'matter' as a whole may be a more worthwhile endeavour than putting one's trust in any particular *auctor*.[17] And the pilgrim Chaucer's apparently innocuous pronouncement about the authors of the four Gospels – 'doutelees hir sentence is al oon' (VII.952) – tellingly contrasts with the earnest protestation of the anonymous Carthusian author of the *Speculum devotorum* that all four Evangelists 'wryten wel and trewly, and that one levyth anothyr supplyeth'.[18] All of these gestures shift the locus of authority away from the cultural and ideological norms according to which *auctoritas*, and vernacular would-be *auctores*, conventionally operated. The narrator of *Troilus and Criseyde* could be left to worry about those.

Bonnie Wheeler characterises *Le Morte Darthur* as 'a thicket of experience', and this phrase could be extended to describe much late medieval vernacular secular literature in which *auctoritas* has been dismantled and authority transferred to the critical reader, whose sceptical stance is nurtured by the kind of text offering nothing of the hermeneutic containment and direction once supplied by academic prologues.[19] Sir Philip Sidney would later prove himself a particularly adept reader of Chaucer in valorising him in the context of commending 'the poet' on the grounds that 'he nothing affirms, and therefore never lieth'.[20] Chaucer is thus identified with a literary arena far from the polarities of truth and lies, and beyond the control of any one institution.[21] In this form of vernacular humanism, authority is distributed amongst writers, readers and the unprecedented text itself, where experience, irreducible to paraphrase, is given priority. The *translatio auctoritatis* enacted in the *House of Fame* has recently been described as 'the dynamic creative explosion of [Chaucer's] own mental world, constantly remaking itself in new forms'.[22] This adeptly captures the poem's inward gaze, the sense it gives of a mind scrutinising both its own machinery and the various, selective impressions made upon it by the literary systems on which it has nourished itself. In this and other works, Chaucer chose repeatedly to dismantle and expose the inner contradictions of *auctoritas*, and the price – in terms of the elisions, distortions and arbitrary privileging of some interpretations over others – at which it was achieved and preserved. That he was granted a measure of posthumous *auctoritas* may be regarded as one of the paradoxes of English literary history.

NOTES

1 Andrew Galloway, 'Authority', in Peter Brown, ed., *A Companion to Chaucer* (Oxford: Blackwell, 2000), pp. 23–39 (pp. 24–6).

2 Richard J. Utz, '"As writ myn auctor called Lollius": Divine and Authorial Omnipotence in Chaucer's *Troilus and Criseyde*', in H. Keper, C. Bode and R. J. Utz, eds., *Nominalism and Literary Discourse: New Perspectives* (Amsterdam and Atlanta: Rodopi, 1997), pp. 123–44 (p. 141).

3 For a nuanced account, see Jan Ziolkowski, 'Cultures of Authority in the Long Twelfth Century', *Journal of English and Germanic Philology*, 108 (2009), 421–48 (pp. 425–7 are particularly relevant here).

4 A. J. Minnis, *Medieval Theory of Authorship: Scholastic Literary Attitudes in the Later Middle Ages* (London: Scolar Press, 1984; 2nd edn with a new preface by the author, Philadelphia: University of Pennsylvania Press, 2010), p. 10.

5 *Ibid.*, pp. 15–33.

6 *Ibid.*, p. 12.

7 *Ibid.*, p. 10.

8 Christine de Pizan, *The Book of the City of Ladies*, trans. Rosalind Brown-Grant (Harmondsworth: Penguin, 1999), p. 5.

9 *De fide catholica contra haereticos*, *PL*, 201, 305C–422A (333C).

10 A. J. Minnis, 'The Author's Two Bodies? Authority and Fallibility in Late-Medieval Textual Theory', in P. R. Robinson and R. Zim, eds., *Of the Making of Books: Medieval Manuscripts, Their Scribes and Readers. Essays Presented to M. B. Parkes* (Aldershot: Scolar Press, 1997), pp. 259–79 (pp. 261–2).

11 Wogan-Browne *et al.*, eds., *The Idea of the Vernacular*, p. 101.

12 Minnis, *Medieval Theory of Authorship*, p. xiii.

13 Wogan-Browne *et al.*, *The Idea of the Vernacular*, p. 81.

14 Bonnie Wheeler, '"As the French book seyeth": Malory's *Morte Darthur* and Acts of Reading', *Cahiers de recherches médiévales et humanistes*, 14 (2007), 115–25 (p. 117).

15 Ralph Hanna III, '*Compilatio* and the Wife of Bath: Latin Backgrounds, Ricardian Texts', in *Pursuing History: Middle English Manuscripts and Their Texts* (Stanford: Stanford University Press, 1996), pp. 247–57.

16 Minnis, 'The Author's Two Bodies?', p. 261.

17 Katherine Terrell, 'Reallocation of Hermeneutic Authority in Chaucer's *House of Fame*', *Chaucer Review*, 31 (1997), 279–90 (p. 286).

18 Wogan-Browne *et al.*, *The Idea of the Vernacular*, p. 75.

19 Wheeler, 'As the French book seyeth', p. 124.

20 Sir Philip Sidney, *An Apology for Poetry; or, The Defence of Poesy*, ed. G. Shepherd, 2nd edn (Manchester: Manchester University Press, 1973), p. 123.

21 Galloway, 'Authority', pp. 29–30.

22 Ashby Kinch, '"Mind like wickerwork": The Neuroplastic Aesthetics of Chaucer's House of Tidings', *postmedieval*, 3 (2012), 302–14 (p. 312).

CHAPTER 8

Literary Theory and Literary Roles

Ian Johnson

Medieval literary theory was generated in the educational system and, most importantly, in commentaries on the authoritative works at the commanding heights of medieval culture. It consisted of systems and conceptual tools for interpreting and communicating the teachings and significance of canonical works, the most important and challenging being the Bible, but also including para-biblical, exegetical, patristic and classical texts – which often served as sources and inspirations for further literary creativity in both Latin and the vernacular.[1]

Neither Latin nor vernacular writers put themselves on a par with canonical authors. Nevertheless, in accessing, adapting and re-voicing their sources they were able to tap and repurpose their authority, sometimes with genuine originality. We have to remember that this time writers did not make up their works solely from inside their own heads: they always used sources, written or passed down through oral tradition. The recycling of pre-existing textual matter was in a perpetual dialectic with rhetorical and interpretative invention. Fortunately, medieval literary thought offered an ideologically propitious range of roles that a writer might adopt or cite for the purposes of reworking authors (*auctores*) and authority (*auctoritas*), as well as materials of lesser prestige. In the thirteenth century, a fascinating hierarchy of literary roles, as variously practised by writers, was delineated by St Bonaventure. This hierarchy ascended from the humble scribe (a mere copyist), via the compiler (a rearranger adding nothing of his own) and then the commentator (who ostensibly only explicates the words of the others), to the author, an autonomous asserter who only resorts to the words of others to confirm his own self-styled materials:

> The method of making a book is fourfold. For someone writes the materials of others, adding or changing nothing, and this person is said to be merely the scribe. Someone else writes the materials of others, adding, but nothing of his own, and this person is said to be the compiler. Someone else writes both the materials of other men, and of his own, but the materials of others

> as the principal materials, and his own annexed for the purposes of clarifying them, and this person is said to be the commentator, not the author. Someone else writes both his own materials and those of others, but his own as the principal materials, and the materials of others annexed for the purposes of confirming his own, and such must be called the author.[2]

Scribes occupy the least important role, though they were important enough to Chaucer, who in his *Troilus* (v.1795–6) begged subsequent copyists not to miswrite or mis-metre his work, and even penned a witty stanza to his scribe, 'Adam scriveyn', complaining that his negligence and haste result in errors that Chaucer has to rub out himself (see Chapter 5).

Turning now to the other end of the spectrum, although medieval writers did not as a rule dare to call themselves authors, they frequently showed real independence in handling materials. The role of commentator in particular was one of enormous power and range, and was exploited by writers throughout the Middle Ages with good reason. In the educational system and in commentary tradition, those who formulated and interpreted the syllabus of set works decided what authoritative texts (including the Bible), in all their complexity, actually meant – even to the point of bending the 'waxen nose of authority' with meanings suiting themselves (see Chapter 7). This formidable hermeneutic role was available to vernacular writers, not least because, in an age when most literature (including the bulk of Chaucer's own writings) was translation of one kind or another, translation itself was authoritatively defined as a species of interpretative commentary. The most important dictionary of the age, the *Catholicon* (1286) of Joannes Januensis, declared that 'translation is the exposition of meaning/teaching through/by another language' ('translatio est expositio sententie per aliam linguam').[3] To translate was to expound the *sententia* (in Middle English *sentence* – a word energetically deployed by Chaucer himself) – the significance, teaching, deeper meaning. This required an effort of interpretative intelligence. Makers of literary texts like Chaucer's, then, were accordingly interpreters re-performing sources in new linguistic and cultural circumstances and with new opportunities. Just as a commentator might elaborate selectively, inventively and at length on the moral or spiritual themes of a text, so might a vernacular writer find and adapt various significances and angles in his sources, sometimes changing them in remaking them. Chaucer's repertoire of *expositio sententie* runs a vernacular gamut from his highly academic prose translation of Boethius's *De consolatione philosophiae* – which incorporates Englished glosses from learned Latin commentary tradition – via his free yet closely attentive adaptation in the *Knight's Tale* of Boccaccio's *Teseida*, to his retranslation of the same plot into *fabliau* format in the *Miller's Tale*.

Unlike Geoffrey Chaucer, most of the writers of texts made in England in the later Middle Ages were a specially sanctioned breed of commentators: priests. Supported by the institutional authority of the Church and their ordained status, they had enhanced access (so it was believed) to divine grace, shedding light upon what their minds were attempting to judge. As a layman, Chaucer was not in this position, but he still had access to terms and forms used by clerics in interpreting divine textuality. Like any reasonably educated individual, he would have known that Scripture was routinely appraised in terms of its four levels of meaning. The historical sense is the sense in which the human author narrates historical events. The allegorical sense is the spiritual meaning extracted from the literal and historical levels (where, for example, the three days spent by Jonah in the whale before re-emerging symbolise the three days spent by Christ between Good Friday and Easter Sunday before His Resurrection). The tropological sense refers to moral teachings that may be taken from Scripture. Finally, the anagogical sense refers to heaven and the afterlife, as, for example, when the earthly city of Jerusalem is taken to denote the celestial city.

In addition to fourfold exegesis, Chaucer would have been routinely aware of another conventional system of distinctions used by commentators for discriminating between textual levels, such as that of Hugh of St Victor in his *Didascalicon* (1130s), a standard medieval text-book on reading and exposition:

> The letter (*littera*) is the proper arrangement of words which we also call construction. The sense (*sensus*) is a straightforward and open interpretation which the letter offers at first sight. The sentence (*sententia*) is a deeper understanding which is discovered in no other way except by exposition or interpretation.[4]

In the fourteenth century, the separation of literal sense and *sententia* (often allegorised by commentators against the intention of the original author and the grain of the text) was challenged. Around 1331, Nicholas of Lyra argued forcefully, in his highly influential *Postilla* on the literal sense of the whole of the Bible, that only the *sensus literalis* – and not the allegorical senses – could form a valid basis for theological argument. This valorisation of the level at which the intention of the human authors of Scripture operated raised the status of authors in general.[5]

Other theoretical options openly available to Chaucer were the terms commonly deployed to teach set texts. These were primarily to be found in the prologues (*accessūs*) to commentaries, where the procedures for interpreting the canonical work were disclosed. They influenced vernacular translators' descriptions and justifications (in their own prologues and self-comment) of how they were setting about their business. They also look recognisable enough today as tools for interpreting a text. Typically, they cover the use/value of a work (*utilitas*); its intentionality (*intentio*); its name/title (*nomen libri*); its procedure/style (*modus agendi*); its structure, order of materials and physical layout (*ordinatio/forma tractatus*); the name and/or life of its author (*nomen auctoris ... vita auctoris*); its sources/subject matter (*materia*); and the question of which part of the educational syllabus the work belongs to (*pars philosophiae*).[6]

So much for the commentator: what about the rather less elevated compiler, who, in the scheme of Bonaventure 'writes the materials of others, adding, but nothing of his own'? This is a role with which Chaucer repeatedly plays, especially in the *Canterbury Tales*. Although compilers may typically make out that they are doing no more than repeating immediately the words of the sources, their choices in selecting, ordering, combining and formatting materials determined what and how readers read. Many authoritative works were consumed as extracts in compilations, with the authority for the contents referred to the original authors but with the responsibility for their arrangement being the compiler's. As Vincent of Beauvais announced in the *Libellus apologeticus* prefacing his colossal encyclopedia, the mid-thirteenth-century *Speculum maius*:

> This work is not in the true sense of the word mine, but it is the work of those authors from whose writings I have put together almost the whole book. For I have added little or nothing that is my own (*ex mea pauca et quasi nulla addidi*). So the authority (*auctoritas*) is theirs, while the ordering of the various parts (*partium ordinatio*) is ours.[7]

Chaucer followed this tradition in his prologue to the *Astrolabe*, claiming to have originated nothing but obediently compiled the work of 'olde astrologiens': 'But considre wel that I ne usurpe not to have founden this werk of my labour or of myn engyn. I n'am but a lewd compilator of the labour of olde astrologiens, and have it translatid in myn Englissh oonly for thy doctrine' (*Astr*, Pro.59–64). Chaucer was immensely inventive in exploiting the genre of compilation. The *Canterbury Tales* are a ludic *compilatio*, with a miscellaneous diversity of materials and a fictional pilgrim-narrator claiming to report faithfully the tales of fictional tellers. The Miller parodies the learned crediting/blaming of sources by citing not a text, but the ale of Southwark for any deficiencies in his output

(*CT*, I.3136–40). Chaucer then breaks dramatic illusion in mock-compilatory fashion when the Miller invites readers to exercise their freedom by turning the page and looking elsewhere in the collection if they do not like his tale. It has to be stressed that compilation was predicated on *lectoris arbitrium*, literally the 'free will/judgement of the reader', answerable through their inalienably God-given free will for negotiating and responding to the contents of any compilation, just as a writer should take responsibility for how s/he reads and re-performs sources. Such a responsibility ostensibly motivates Chaucer, in his *Retractions* at the end of the *Canterbury Tales*, to retract those tales that tend/conduce towards sin ('sownen into synne' (*CT*, X.1086)). But which tales are these? Conducing to sin will vary from reader to reader, and so the retractability of any given tale must vary too. Here Chaucer perhaps provides at least a wittily thin and enjoyable excuse for otherwise morally questionable tales surviving in the collection. It has been said more seriously, however, that by genuinely taking a degree of moral responsibility before God for his output, despite the playful compilatory rhetoric, Chaucer is acknowledging himself as an author rather than compiler.[8] This, however, is complicated further when at the same time he 'defends' his good intentions by deploying a dictum conventionally used to justify the reading and writing of anything one wishes to read or write, the much-cited words from St Paul in Romans 15:4: 'Al that is writen is writen for oure doctrine' (X.1083). This universal licence could conceivably excuse anything written by Chaucer or read by his readers, consequently bringing into question the need to retract anything.[9] For all this, nevertheless, ethical reading and writing are not abandoned. Clearly, the way that Chaucer plays with the genre and role of compiling reveals a playful literary-theoretical sensibility mixing earnest with game – a sensibility assuming and inviting the moral and hermeneutic discretion of the reader.

Chaucer's *Retractions* are constituted by theoretical attitudes rhetoricised creatively. Any account of medieval literary theory and notions of literary roles connected with it therefore has to acknowledge, however briefly, the place of rhetorical tradition not only for its own conceptions of the relationship between interpretation and invention, but also as a source and resource for the provision of literary models and roles.

Medieval grammatical education was about teaching Latin reading and correct usage. From the twelfth century onwards, however, grammatical education became notably more interested not only in the 'grammatical exposition of the canonical authors (*enarratio poetarum* or *auctorum*)' but in the teaching of prescriptive poetics centring on good style, narrative effectiveness, appropriate use of figures, and the general exercise of discretion in observing and applying poetic decorum.[10] Much attention was given to textual examples, thereby coalescing practices of interpretation and imitation. Such prescriptive poetics gave budding poets exemplary roles to grasp and to replay. Works like Matthew of Vendôme's *Ars versificatoria* (*c.* 1175), Geoffrey of Vinsauf's *Poetria nova* (*c.* 1210), Gervase of Melkley's *Ars versificaria* (*c.* 1215) and John of Garland's *Parisiana poetria* (*c.* 1230) gave 'prescriptive advice about how to generate a new text by imitating canonical models'.[11] Inasmuch as such imitation was linked to interpretation, it had affinities with the activities of the commentator. Medieval rhetorical arts were, then, about far more than listing and exemplifying rhetorical figures: Geoffrey of Vinsauf's *Poetria nova*, for example,

> covers all five of the canons of rhetoric, from the teaching of invention as conceptual planning (the archetype), to disposition or arrangement through the natural and artificial orders of narration, and then to style, as both a material function (amplification and abbreviation of the matter devised) and a verbal (elocutionary) function (stylistic ornaments), and finally to advice about memory and delivery.[12]

Here, as with the continuum of literary roles outlined by St Bonaventure, was a resource for the purposeful and creative remaking of the materials of others. No late medieval English writer used the repertoire of such theoretically derived roles more brilliantly or tellingly than Geoffrey Chaucer.

NOTES

1 A. J. Minnis, *Medieval Theory of Authorship: Scholastic Literary Attitudes in the Later Middle Ages* (London: Scolar Press, 1984; 2nd edn with a new preface by the author, Philadelphia: University of Pennsylvania Press, 2010), pp. 10–12.

2 *Ibid.*, p. 94, for this translation. For further discussion, see pp. 94–5.

3 Joannes Januensis, *Catholicon* (Westmead: Gregg, 1971 [1460]), s.v. *glossa* (unfol.).

4 Cited and translated in M. B. Parkes, 'Punctuation; or, Pause and Effect', in James J. Murphy, ed., *Medieval Eloquence: Studies in the Theory and Practice of Medieval Rhetoric* (Berkeley: University of California Press, 1978), pp. 127–42 (p. 131).

5 See *ibid.*, p. 132. For a wide-ranging study of changing exegetical approaches, see Beryl Smalley, *The Study of the Bible in the Middle Ages*, 3rd edn (Oxford: Blackwell, 1983).

6 For academic literary prologues and literary roles, see Minnis, *Medieval Theory of Authorship*, pp. 9–39, 73–117, 160–5.

7 Alastair Minnis, '*Nolens auctor sed compilator reputari*: The Late-Medieval Discourse of Compilation', in Mireille Chazan and Gilbert Dahan, eds.,

La méthode critique au Moyen Age (Turnhout: Brepols, 2006), p. 48, translating *Speculum maius, Apologia totius operis*, ed. A.-D. von den Brincken, in 'Geschichtsberachtung bei Vincenz von Beauvais', *Deutsches Archiv für Erforschung des Mittelalters*, 34 (1978), 409–99 (pp. 469–70).

8 Minnis, *Medieval Theory of Authorship*, pp. 208–10.

9 For the use of this dictum, see Vincent Gillespie, 'From the Twelfth Century to *c.* 1450', in Alastair Minnis and Ian Johnson, eds., *The Cambridge History of Literary Criticism*, Vol. II: *The Middle Ages* (Cambridge: Cambridge University Press, 2005), pp. 145–235 (p. 200).

10 Rita Copeland and Ineke Sluiter, eds., *Medieval Grammar and Rhetoric: Language Arts and Literary Theory, AD 300–1475* (Oxford: Oxford University Press, 2009), p. 546.

11 *Ibid.*, p. 547.

12 *Ibid.*, p. 595.

CHAPTER 9

Metre and Versification

Ad Putter

Throughout his writings Chaucer expressed concerns about the formal properties of his verse. Thus, at the end of *Troilus*, where Chaucer addresses his book, he worried about the damage that scribes could (and did) inflict on his metre:

> And for ther is so gret diversite
> In Englissh and in writing of oure tonge,
> So prey I god that non myswrite the
> Ne the mysmetre for defaute of tonge.
> (v.1793–6)

Chaucer had to coin the word 'mysmetre', because no one had said this kind of thing in English before. In the *House of Fame*, he asks Apollo, the god of wisdom, to make his poetry 'agreable / Though som vers fayle in a sillable' (lines 1097–8). Chaucer was especially concerned with the syllable count, and conscious both of the liberties he himself took and of those taken by scribes. He knew that scribes might write in different dialects and could damage the metre by misrepresenting its articulation. Uncertainty about which final *-es* should be pronounced with 'tonge' was a particular problem for Chaucer's earliest readers, and has remained so ever since. Rhyme, too, preoccupied Chaucer. Again in *Troilus*, for instance, he promises to relay Troilus's words, 'As I may my rymes holde' (III.91). He could have made life easier by allowing self-rhyme, but Chaucer's way was never that of least resistance. The rhyming of 'tonge' with 'tonge' in the lines above may look like a slip, but the 'tongues' in 'oure tonge' (the vernacular language) and 'defaute of tonge' (mispronunciation) do not mean the same thing; rhyming on different senses of the same word or on homonyms, known as *rime riche* or *rime équivoque*, was not merely permitted but admired, and Chaucer, too, showed his skill here (e.g. *CT*, I.17–18, 3275–6).

In his youth Chaucer had been a page at the French-speaking court of Countess Elizabeth of Ulster, and so had grown up hearing poetry not only in English but also in French. His poetry is deeply indebted to courtly French verse, which was strict in terms of both the number of syllables allowed per line and the exactness of rhymes required. Imperfect rhymes, common enough in many Middle English poems,[1] were not tolerated by the French poets who influenced Chaucer, and he allowed them only in *Sir Thopas*, his parody of medieval English romance. This blithely rhymes, for instance, 'Thopas' with 'grace' (elsewhere disyllabic in Chaucer, as in refined medieval French pronunciation) and flaunts various other vices that Chaucer had noticed in English verse, such as the thudding monotony of its end-stopped lines, and its arbitrary departures from self-imposed rhyme-schemes and stanza-forms.

Chaucer's ear for French also helped him in other respects. In Chaucer's England, French had not long ceased to be a mother tongue, and French-derived words had not been fully assimilated to English stress patterns. Chaucer could therefore say words like 'comfort' or 'colour' with stress on either syllable. The exploitation of this flexibility is an important aspect of his art. In the *Summoner's Tale*, for instance, the accent on the name 'Thomas' shifts within a single line: 'O Thómas, *je vous dy*, Thomás, Thomás' (*CT*, III.1832; my stress marks). The code-switch into French is characteristic of the speaker, a Friar who likes to show off his learning and refinement; but it also entitled Chaucer to shift from the English pronunciation of 'Thomas' to the French one, and in so doing to meet the demands of metre (iambic pentameter) and rhyme (here on *-as*).

The most exacting of Chaucer's literary models were French lyrics in the *formes fixes*, with stanzas that followed a fixed rhyme-scheme with a very restricted set of rhyme-sounds. In the prologue to the *Legend of Good Women*, Chaucer's oeuvre is said to have included 'balades, roundels, virelayes' (F 423). Possibly some of these were in French,[2] but he certainly wrote 'balades' and 'roundels' in English. The *ballade* is especially taxing, for in the strict form of this genre, which Chaucer followed, all stanzas (apart from the *envoi*) must follow the same rhyme scheme *and* rhyme on the rhyme-sounds as fixed by the first stanza. All stanzas must also end with the same refrain line. An illustration is provided by the first *ballade* in the *Complaint of Venus* (a sequence of three *ballades* inspired by Chaucer's French contemporary Oton de Grandson), with the rhyme words (Table 9.1).

This meets the required standards, but only by imitating the 'French' style of rhyming on suffixes. To medieval ears, this sounded graceful and dignified, and it is Chaucer's verse in this vein that begot the 'aureate' poetry of the fifteenth century.[3] However, Chaucer also managed to find

Table 9.1 *Ballade* rhyme scheme in the *Complaint of Venus*

Stanza 1	**Stanza 2**	**Stanza 3**
pleasaunce	governaunce	suffisaunce
hevynesse	gesse	humblesse
remembraunce	avaunce	countenaunce
worthynesse	richesse	besynesse
stidfastnesse	noblesse	sikernesse
dure	Nature	aventure
creature	assure	honoure [read 'honure'?]
gentilesse	gentilesse	gentilesse

some very 'un-French' rhymes, including one in the *envoi* to the *Complaint of Venus*. Here he complains about the difficulty of rhyming in English ('rym in Englissh hath such skarsete' (line 80)), while simultaneously showing how easily he himself could handle a ten-line *envoi* with only two rhyme-sounds. He begins:

> Princes, receyveth this compleynt in gre
> Unto your excellent benignite,
> Direct after [*Composed according to*] my litel suffisaunce.
> For elde, that in my spirit dulleth me,
> Hath of endityng al the subtilte
> Wel nygh bereft out of my remembraunce[.]
>
> (lines 73–8)

The elevated address to 'princes' shows Chaucer's awareness of French lyric conventions;[4] but, here as elsewhere, he introduces some self-deprecating humour, representing himself as 'dul' (slow-witted) (cf. *PF*, 162). Paradoxically, it is Chaucer's endearingly plain 'me' that helps to solve the problems of a rhyme-scheme that is purportedly beyond him.

The *rondeau* is another *forme fixe* with which Chaucer experimented. In this genre, only two rhyme sounds were normally permitted, with the opening lines being repeated as refrain lines. The rhyme-scheme of Chaucer's roundels is *ABB abAB abbABB* (capitals denote refrain lines). An example is the roundel 'Now welcome, somer, with thy softe sonne', sung by the birds at the end of the *Parliament of Fowls* (lines 686–92). In *Merciles Beaute*, Chaucer attempted a triple roundel, and the poem works brilliantly as a sequence. The key to its success is the comic contrast between the earnest despair of the first two roundels and the breeziness of the third, which begins:

> Sin I fro love escaped am so fat,
> I never thenk to ben in his prison lene;
> Sin I am free, I counte him not a bene.
> (lines 27–9)

Our poet has escaped from love's tyranny, and we sense the relief in the unpretentiousness of the rhymes as compared with those of the preceding roundel, which uses exclusively French-derived rhyme-words.

Chaucer was unusually sensitive to the effects of combining (or not combining) Romance words with Germanic words in rhyme. A fine example is the Miller's address to the Reeve:

> An housebonde shal nat been inquisityf
> Of Goddes pryvetee, nor of his wyf.
> So [*As long as*] he may fynde Goddes foyson [*plenty*] there,
> Of the remenant nedeth nat enquere.
> (*CT*, I.3163–6)

God has mysterious secrets ('pryvetee'), and so have wives, but as long as a man finds God's plenty 'there' – that is, in his wife's 'pryvetee' (now in the sense of private parts) – no further questions need to be asked. The wordplay is obviously funny, but Chaucer's comedy also depends on aspects of versification: on the rhyming of the quasi-scholastic 'inquisityf' and 'enquere' with plain-English 'wyf' and 'there', and finally on the enjambment in 'inquisityf / Of Goddes pryvetee', which ensures that the rhetorical pause falls not at the end of line 3163, but halfway down the next line, where it draws attention to the incongruity of what Chaucer has coordinated on either side of the caesura.

There are precedents for Chaucer's remarkable use of enjambment both in earlier English narrative verse in short couplets (e.g. *Cursor mundi*) and in French courtly poetry and English versifiers influenced by that poetry, such as John Gower.[5] In Old and Middle English alliterative poetry (characterised not by end-rhyme but by the repetition of the same sound at the beginning of stressed syllables), however, the line was end-stopped, and the verse line was in turn divided into two half-lines. Chaucer alludes to this tradition when the Parson (in the prologue to his tale) says: 'I am a Southren man. / I kan nat geeste "rum, ram, ruf" by lettre' (X.42–3). That Chaucer, despite being himself a 'Southren man', was nevertheless familiar with alliterative verse is indicated by his deliberate use of alliteration in epic-style battle scenes (*CT*, I.2605–16; *LGW*, 635–42).[6] However, the native verse-form to which Chaucer owes much more is the rhymed couplet, which he adopted for his earliest narrative poems, the *Book of the Duchess* and the *House of Fame*. The four-beat couplet had become the mainstream medium for story-telling in fourteenth-century England, but if Chaucer's adoption of the form is not remarkable, his treatment of it assuredly is, for he handled it with unusual fluidity, as a passage from the *Book of the Duchess* will illustrate. Alcyone has learned that her husband is lost at sea:

> And she, forweped and forwaked,
> Was wery; and thus the dedë slep
> Fil on hir or she tooke kep,
> Thorgh Juno, that had herd hir bonë,
> That ma[ked] hir to slepë sonë.
> For as she prayed, right so was don
> In dedë; for Juno ryght anon
> Called thus hir messager
> To doo hir erande, and he com ner.
> (lines 126–34)

My diereses indicate which final *-es* should probably be pronounced. A useful rule of thumb for the non-specialist is that at line-ending final *-e* should always be pronounced, but at mid-line only where doing so avoids clashing stress; before a vowel or weak *h-* it is normally elided. A fuller explanation involves historical grammar. For instance, in the lines above, the adjective 'dedë' has pronounced final *-e*, because it is a weak adjective (i.e. an adjective preceded by a definite article or demonstrative/possessive pronoun), while 'tooke' does not, because it is a strong verb, which had no ending in first- and third-person singular past tense; 'sonë' is disyllabic because it has an organic final vowel etymologically (from Old English *sōna*). Similar explanations account for 'slepë' (with infinitive inflection), 'bonë' (which acquired final *-e* by analogy), and so on. However, the scansion of Chaucer's verse still presents some imponderables. Our biggest problem is that the manuscripts that transmit it (none of them autographs) are unreliable, particularly in the case of the *Book of the Duchess*.[7] For instance, line 130, as it stands in the manuscripts (and in *The Riverside Chaucer*), actually reads 'made' for 'maked'; but the metre requires a disyllable, and 'maked' is clearly the variant that Chaucer used elsewhere when he needed the disyllabic form in eliding contexts (cf. *CT*, 1.526, 1046, 1730, 1907 etc.).

The French ancestor of the short line, the octosyllabic couplet, allowed very little scope for variation: the line had eight syllables (or nine, in the case of feminine rhymes). The English equivalent, with alternating rhythm, is the iambic tetrameter, the template of which is *wswswsws*(*w*) (where *w* stands for an offbeat, *s* for a beat, and (*w*) for the optional unstressed final syllable). In Chaucer, however, this template is at best a norm, as the passage above shows. One variation, common in Chaucer but entirely absent from John Gower's English verse, is the so-called headless line, in which the weak syllable at the start is missing, as in lines 128 ('*Fil* on hir …') and 133 ('*Called* thus …'). That Chaucer used headless lines deliberately is evident from his apology in the *House of Fame* ('Though som vers fayle in a sillable' (line 1098)). The apology was quite unnecessary, since Chaucer's headless lines are usually very effective. For instance, he often begins a line with a beat when the preceding line enjambs. Lines 128 and 134 in the passage above show us why: the lack of the initial anacrusis helps to bolt the verb onto the preceding line, which needs it to make grammatical sense. Elsewhere, headless lines give a sense of urgency – which is why Chaucer frequently uses them for line-initial imperatives (cf. *BD*, 41, 110, 139, 144, 153; *HF*, 58, 78, 853, 893).

Another Chaucerian departure from strict iambics is the reinforcement of a mid-line caesura by the addition of an unstressed syllable (or, more rarely, by its omission, resulting in clashing stress: e.g. *CT*, VII.214; *Tr*, II.1721; *Pity*, 41). Not every scholar is convinced that Chaucer really wrote lines with such 'epic caesuras', and some examples may be more apparent than real.[8] In the above-cited passage, lines that offer possible examples are 127, 131, 132 and 134, but none of these is straightforward. Thus 'prayed' should probably be read as 'prayde', Chaucer having at his disposal both syncopated and unsyncopated preterites of verbs with vocalic stems. At line 127, the *-y* possibly merges in pronunciation with the following schwa: known as *synklisis*, this merger is not uncommon in Chaucer's verse (e.g. *CT*, I.130: 'Wel koude she car*ie a* morsel and wel kepe'). Finally, it could be argued that in line 132 the final *-e* in 'dede' should not be pronounced, and that in line 134 Chaucer intended the syncopated form ('ernde'). However, he does not use *errand* and *deed* as monosyllables elsewhere, and many other examples of epic caesuras in Chaucer's tetrameter and pentameter lines cannot easily be explained away (e.g. *BD*, 517, 609, 750, 981; *CT*, I.2458; *PF*, 337). While the possibility of scribal corruption cannot be ruled out, it seems significant that the hypermetrical unstressed syllable consistently occurs after the caesura, where its use is apt. Like the anacrusis at line opening, the unstressed syllable after the caesura indicates a new beginning mid-line. Line units and sense units are not the same thing, and in Chaucer they are sometimes heard in counterpoint.

From this perspective, the epic caesura is linked to another metrical resource that gives the Chaucerian line its fluidity: enjambment. In earlier English alliterative poetry, enjambment is vanishingly rare; in earlier couplet verse it occurs infrequently, but Chaucer really embraced it. Once or twice he uses it feebly, to force a word into rhyme position (e.g. *BD*, 78), but he generally employs it very effectively to increase the tempo. In the passage from the *Book of the Duchess*, for example, the enjambment actualises the haste implied by the adverbs ('sone', 'ryght so', 'ryght anon'). Another adverb that frequently gives rise to enjambment in Chaucer is 'suddenly'. It occurs twice in the *Book of the Duchess* and on both occasions triggers enjambment (lines 272–6, 838–40; cf. *CT*, I.1118–19, 1574–5).

Chaucer's greatest contribution to English verse, however, was to abandon the short line in favour of the longer, five-beat, iambic pentameter. His models for this were French and Italian: French had the *vers de dix*, as exemplified by, for example, Oton de Grandson's *ballades*, and Italian had the *endecasillabo* (eleven-syllable verse), which Chaucer encountered in his sources for the *Knight's Tale* and *Troilus*: Boccaccio's *Teseida* and *Filostrato*. The influence of the *endecasillabo* is especially important;[9] it accounts for Chaucer's flexible placement of the caesura,[10] also variable in Italian, but in French usually fixed after the fourth syllable, and it also explains Chaucer's partiality to feminine rhyme. The *endecasillabo* ended in an unstressed syllable, and the sound pattern evidently grew on Chaucer. Thus, in Book I of *Troilus* (156 stanzas), 16 stanzas end in masculine couplets; in Book II (251 stanzas) that number goes down to 12; and finally, in Book V (267 stanzas) there is only one.[11] Boccaccio also taught Chaucer to write narrative verse in stanzas, which in both poets are just as fluid as their lines, showing frequent enjambment. Boccaccio's *Filostrato* and *Teseida* are in eight-line stanzas rhyming *abababcc*. Chaucer abridged the *ottava rima* to the seven-line rhyme-royal stanza (*ababbcc*). Chaucer would have been familiar with the rhyme-royal stanza from lyrics.[12] Gower, for example, used it in his French *ballades*, and in English for 'In Praise of Peace' and the 'Supplication to Venus' at the end of *Confessio Amantis*, while it is significant that Chaucer's earliest experiment with the rhyme-royal stanza, the *Complaint unto Pity*, was also a lyric. Chaucer, however, pioneered its use for narrative verse, first in the *Parliament of Fowls*, then in *Troilus*, and finally in the *Canterbury Tales*, where it became the vehicle for stories of high pathos and gravity.

The deep structure of Chaucer's pentameter is iambic, that is, *wswswswsws*(*w*), and the fact that he wrote with this structure in mind emerges clearly from the strategic choices he made on the basis of an impressive repertoire of metrical variants. Thus, as metre required, Chaucer alternated between proper names in Latin/Greek form (e.g. 'Almachius' (*CT*, VIII.435); 'Pandarus' (*Tr*, I.761)) and their vernacular counterparts ('Almache' (*CT*, VIII.413); 'Pandare' (*Tr*, I.1070)); longer and shorter forms of the same verb (e.g. 'lyest' at *CT*, VIII.486, but 'lixt' at *CT*, III.1618; 'rideth' at *Tr*, II.688, but 'rit' at *CT*, I.123); contracted and uncontracted verb-forms (e.g. 'nolde' at *CT*, I.550, but 'ne wolde' at *Tr*, II.1473); words with and without prefix (e.g. 'doun' at *CT*, I.1541, but 'adoun' at *CT*, I.1758; 'rise' at *CT*, I.1041, but 'arise' at *CT*, I.1047), and so on.[13]

But while Chaucer was good at 'rigging' the metre, he also knew that metrical regularity is partly an effect produced by our expectations, and that, to compose iambic pentameter, it is neither necessary nor desirable for a poet to write verses in which strongly stressed syllables invariably alternate with weakly stressed ones. The point is illustrated by my last example from the *Pardoner's Tale*, a passage in which the Old Man's solemn warnings go unheeded by the three revellers, who are in reckless pursuit of personified Death and find it, unpersonified, by a heap of gold, over which they soon kill each other:

/ x x / x / x / x / x
'Se ye that ook? Right there ye shal hym fynde.

x /x / x / x / x / x
God save yow, that boghte agayn mankynde,

x x x/ x x / x /x /
And yow amende!' Thus seyde this oldë man,

x / x x x /xx x /
And everich of thise riotoures ran

x x x x x / x / x / x
Til he cam to that tree, and ther they founde

x / x / x / x / x / x
Of floryns fine of gold ycoyned rounde

x / x / x / x x x / x
Wel ny an eighte bushels, as hem thoughte.

x / x / x /x / x / x
No lenger thanne after Deeth they soughte ...
(*CT*, VI.764–71)

In a *metrical* analysis of beats and offbeats, all lines except the first scan as regular iambics, but I have here given a *linguistic* scansion (/ representing a strongly stressed syllable and x a weak one) in order to reveal the tension that exists, in all good poetry, between the underlying metrical design and the manifestation of that design in actual lines. The first line has an inverted foot, which is common enough in Chaucer and here gives logical emphasis to the interrogative 'Se'.[14] Especially noticeable in the lines that follow is Chaucer's ability to create iambic pentameter, not by mechanically alternating weak linguistic stresses with strong ones, but by producing rhythmical contours – in this case runs of three weakly stressed syllables – that can readily be assimilated to iambic metre, either because the weakly stressed syllable that takes the beat is more prominent relative to its neighbours, or simply because a metre, once established, will predispose us to hear the rhythm we expect to hear. This metrical conditioning explains why Chaucer can also put strongly stressed syllables in offbeat position, as in the following line from the *Knight's Tale*:

x / / / / / x / x /
As ook, firre, birche, aspe, alder, holm, popler
(*CT*, I.2921)

Sequences of stressed and unstressed syllables are perfectly reconcilable with the prevailing metre: *ceteris paribus* we will hear their rhythm as iambic. Metre has 'assimilative powers',[15] and one of Chaucer's achievements as a poet is to let the metre do the work for him (but note in the above-cited line Chaucer's skilful distribution of Germanic 'alder', with first-syllable stress, and French-derived 'popler', with natural stress on the suffix).

The key difference between sequences of stressed syllables and sequences of unstressed ones, however, is that the latter move much more quickly. This returns us to the passage from the *Pardoner's Tale*, in which tempo and meaning are admirably integrated. The Old Man's words are *measured* in a way that has everything to do with verse-form. As well as being end-stopped, his lines are checked mid-line by a pronounced caesura that falls in every case in its classic place, after the second beat. In lines 764 and in 765 this means after the fourth syllable, but in 766 an extra unstressed may be at play. Assuming the final *-e* after the subjunctive ('amende') is pronounced, as it certainly is in the preceding subjunctive ('save'), the conclusion of the Old Man's direct speech is marked with an epic caesura. The revellers, however, do not stop to listen: they are off – and Chaucer dashes after them in a couple of lines in which there is no end-stopping and in which the iambic pulse quickens because the beat is made to fall repeatedly on the second of a series of three weakly stressed syllables.

Tempo is relative, however, and the breathless speed of 767–70 is all the more noticeable because the next line slams the brakes on: 'No lenger thannë after Deeth they soughte.' The adverb *then* is generally monosyllabic in Chaucer (except at line-ending), but it is precisely this general rule that allowed him to deploy 'thanne' as an emphatic variant, as in the *Nun's Priest Tale*, when Chauntecleer is surprised by the fox: 'Nothyng ne liste hym thannë for to crowe' (*CT*, VII.3276).[16] Disyllabic 'thanne' in line 771 of the *Pardoner's Tale* is similarly pointed, but even more remarkable, since final *-e* normally elides before a vowel. The only exceptions occur when the final *-e* is separated from the following vowel by a caesura[17] – so here, too, a pause after 'thanne' must be assumed. Through metre, then, Chaucer controls speed, and variations in speed in turn enrich meaning. For the grim irony is that the revellers find death precisely when they no longer seek it, and the deliberateness of 'thanne' brings that irony home.

In conclusion, Chaucer's poetic practice and his pronouncements on rhyme and metre make it very clear that he cared about verse form. To see how his poetry benefited as a result of this care, all we need to do is to read it with Chaucer's concerns in mind.

NOTES

1 See E. G. Stanley, 'Rhymes in Medieval English Verse: From Old English to Middle English', in Edward Donald Kennedy, Ronald Waldron and Joseph Wittig, eds., *Medieval English Studies Presented to George Kane* (Cambridge: D. S. Brewer, 1988), pp. 19–54; and Judith A. Jefferson, Donka Minkova and Ad Putter, 'Perfect and Imperfect Rhyme: Romances in the *abab* Tradition', *Studies in Philology*, 111 (2014), 631–51.

2 See James I. Wimsatt, ed., *Chaucer and the Poems of 'Ch'*, 2nd edn (Kalamazoo: Medieval Institute, 2009).

3 The point was made by C. S. Lewis, *The Allegory of Love*, 2nd edn (New York: Oxford University Press, 1958), p. 164.

4 Eustache Deschamps named various kinds of *ballades* with envoys that should begin with 'Princes' in his *Art de dictier*, ed. and trans. Deborah M. Sinnreich-Levi (East Lansing: Colleagues Press, 1994), pp. 78–9.

5 On enjambment in the French court poetry see Adolf Tobler, *Vom französischen Versbau alter und neuer Zeit*, 4th edn (Leipzig: Hirzel, 1903), pp. 26–9; and on enjambment in the native couplet tradition see Ad Putter, 'In Appreciation of Metrical Abnormality: Headless Lines and Initial Inversion in Chaucer', *Critical Survey*, 29 (2017), 65–85.

6 See N. F. Blake, 'Chaucer and the Alliterative Romances', *Chaucer Review*, 3 (1969), 163–9 (pp. 164–5).

7 See N. F. Blake, 'The Textual Tradition of *The Book of the Duchess*', *English Studies*, 62 (1981), 237–48.
8 See O. Bischoff, 'Über zweisilbige Senkung und epische Caesur bei Chaucer', *Englische Studien*, 24 (1898), 353–92; 25 (1899), 339–98.
9 See Martin J. Duffell, '"The craft so long to lerne": Chaucer's Invention of the Iambic Pentameter', *Chaucer Review*, 34 (2000), 269–88.
10 Examples in Elizabeth Solopova, 'The Survival of Chaucer's Punctuation in the Early Manuscripts of the *Canterbury Tales*, in A. J. Minnis, ed., *Middle English Poetry: Texts and Traditions. Essays in Honour of Derek Pearsall* (Cambridge: D. S. Brewer, 2001), pp. 27–40.
11 See Howard Buck, 'Chaucer's Use of Feminine Rhyme', *Modern Philology*, 26 (1928), 13–14.
12 See Martin Stevens, 'The Royal Stanza in Early English Literature', *PMLA*, 94 (1979), 62–76.
13 More examples in Joseph Bihl, *Die Wirkungen des Rhythmus in der Sprache von Chaucer und Gower* (Heidelberg: Winter, 1916).
14 Compare my earlier comments (p. 77 above) on headless lines and imperatives.
15 W. K. Wimsatt, 'The Rule and the Norm: Halle and Keyser on Chaucer's Meter', *College English*, 31 (1970), 774–88 (p. 785).
16 See Ad Putter, Judith Jefferson and Myra Stokes, *Studies in the Metre of Alliterative Verse* (Oxford: Society for the Study of Medieval Languages and Literature, 2007), pp. 237–8.
17 See Derek Pearsall, 'Chaucer's Meter', in A. T. Gaylord, ed., *Essays on the Art of Chaucer's Verse* (London: Routledge, 2001), pp. 131–44 (p. 135).

CHAPTER 10

Dialogue

Sarah James

The topic of dialogue as a context for Chaucer's work may seem a strange choice, given that it is a word he does not use at any point in his oeuvre.[1] The word is first attested in Middle English in the early thirteenth century, when it appears to have been restricted to literary works in the form of an exchange between two or more persons; it seems to have acquired its more modern sense of 'conversation' only from the beginning of the fifteenth century, at the very moment when Chaucer's output was complete.[2] This chapter therefore focuses on the earlier attested sense and considers Chaucer's poetry in relation to the literary dialogue, demonstrating that while he is not generally regarded as a producer of such texts, an examination of his works quickly reveals the extent to which he has absorbed both the form and its characteristic concerns into his own writings.

The literary dialogue has a long and distinguished history, its most famous early incarnation being in the Socratic *elenchus* as reported in Plato's dialogues. In pursuit of dialectic, dialogue has the advantage of permitting the juxtaposition of opposing points of view, in support of which can be adduced a range of evidence and opinions; but arguably it also functions rhetorically, serving to persuade the reader through its artistry.[3] These two elements in combination form a powerful philosophical method, grounded not in authoritative pronouncements but in the Socratic *elenchus*, and thus dialogue becomes a type of heuristic practice. But while the ostensible aim of such a method may be to resolve the question at issue, the Socratic dialogues quite explicitly allow for a failure of resolution (*aporia*); a final answer need not be found. For Socrates, the emphasis is upon the dialogic process itself; the sequential questioning is designed not so much to expose transcendent truth as it is the prejudices and preconceptions of the dialogue's participants. In this sense the concluding *aporia* carries a powerful message both intellectual and moral: what we think we know is far less significant than recognising the limits of our knowledge.

The Socratic tradition is not, however, the only one available to later writers; far more influential for medieval poetic invention is that deriving from the *Consolation of Philosophy* by Boethius, which Chaucer translated into prose in its entirety.[4] The famous dialogue between the Prisoner and Lady Philosophy was translated and adapted throughout the Middle Ages, making its ethical and spiritual content accessible to ever larger audiences; but its importance to the history of poetry is derived from much more creative reworkings, and the influence not just of its form but of its broader spiritual and ethical concerns.[5] Indeed, arguably the most significant element of the literary dialogue, whether Socratic or Boethian, is its intimate connection with questions of politics, ethics and religion. Whatever its ostensible subject, it poses searching questions about how we should live, both as individuals and within our communities, and about our ontological status, questions with which the reader is invited to engage in an active process of coming to self-knowledge.[6] For medieval universities, themselves seeking an effective methodology for answering questions of pressing political and ethical importance, the dialectic and techniques of disputation borrowed, at least in part, from these classical and late antique precursors were an obvious choice.[7]

Medieval works as disparate as the *Summa theologiae* of Thomas Aquinas and the anonymous *Owl and the Nightingale* exploit the advantages of the literary dialogue, demanding that the reader or listener engage first with one side of an argument and then with another. The final outcome of such dialogues varies, of course. Aquinas intends to produce a comprehensive work of reference providing definitive answers to a range of theological questions; thus, having aired the points *pro* and *contra* his point of dispute, he offers an explicit resolution to the problem with a level of certainty entirely appropriate to a work of theological enquiry. By contrast, in *The Owl and the Nightingale* something rather closer to the Socratic example of concluding *aporia* is adopted; the poem ends uncertainly with the protagonists embarking on a journey to seek a certain 'Maistre Nichole' who will arbitrate between the contending parties.[8] Similar examples of *aporia* proliferate in medieval poetry; it seems that regardless of which, if either, tradition they were explicitly drawing upon, medieval poets were particularly alive to the possibilities for both education and entertainment offered by an inconclusive ending.

Although Chaucer's is a name we might not automatically associate with the production of literary dialogues – a form that, despite contemporary claims to the contrary, can sometimes feel stale and contrived – several of his poems do take this form; and even when they do not, the influences are still much in evidence. The significance of the Boethian tradition in particular to an understanding of Chaucer's poetry has been restated by Winthrop Wetherbee, who remarks that 'reminiscences of the *Consolation* are perceptible in virtually any reflective passage of [Chaucer's] poetry'.[9] For example, both the *Knight's Tale* and *Troilus and Criseyde* are profoundly Boethian in their concerns, which are articulated at least in part through conversational exchanges between their protagonists, although neither text could properly be described as a literary dialogue. There are, however, examples of Chaucer's poetry that conform more closely to dialogic conventions. Despite its initial foregrounding of the anxieties of its naïve narrator, the *Book of the Duchess* quickly settles into an extended dialogue between the narrator and the Black Knight, providing the latter with an opportunity to remind himself of the qualities of his lost lady. The narrator's very obtuseness also serves to compel his interlocutor to articulate his plight more emphatically than might otherwise be the case; in asserting 'She ys ded!' (*BD*, 1309) it may be argued that the Black Knight finally accepts the truth he has previously resisted, the whole dialogue becoming an act of remembrance that combines regret with the possibility of resignation. In this example an element of resolution or certainty has at last been attained; the dialogue has fulfilled its function. By contrast, the squabbling birds in the *Parliament of Fowls* for the most part engage in something much closer to the medieval concept of debate: that is, arguing and contention.[10] Yet beyond the altercations among individuals there is a larger question at stake: which of the three tercel eagles should the formel choose as her mate? This question itself leads to one of much wider ethical significance: how are we to evaluate different aspects of character and calculate the force and value of love? Nature, unable to disentangle the claims of the tercels, leaves it to the formel to choose among the qualities of her three suitors:

> For sith it may not here discussed be
> Who loveth hire best, as seyde the tercelet,
> Thanne wol I don hire this favour, that she
> Shal han right hym on whom hire herte is set,
> And he hire that his herte hath on hire knet:
> Thus juge I, Nature, for I may not lye …
> (*PF*, 624–9)

The formel is unable to make a decision and Nature permits her to delay her choice for a year, an inconclusive ending that reflects the Socratic *aporia*. By offering no resolution the dialogue becomes, in some sense, one between the poem and the reader; like the formel, the reader is asked to engage actively with the discussions and must judge for herself which outcome is most desirable.

The *Tale of Melibee* is in some respects perhaps the most conventional of Chaucer's literary dialogues. Its exploration of the characteristics of good counsel, the perils of vengeance and the cultivation of prudence is highly moralistic and clearly indebted to the Boethian tradition. Melibee, like Boethius's Prisoner, is all too human, consumed with his own worldly concerns and incapable, at least initially, of grasping the broader ethical context within which he must act. His dialogue with his wife, Dame Prudence, combines the dialectical and rhetorical qualities characterising the best examples of the genre, and at last he accepts her counsel. However, the text is more compelling than its conventional qualities might suggest. Chaucer's careful delineation of the character of Dame Prudence raises her above the level of an uncomplicated supernatural adviser;[11] she is revealed as a strategic thinker, fully aware of Melibee's weaknesses and prepared to exploit them in order to ensure that her views prevail. Furthermore, *Melibee* contains within itself a pronouncement that seems to gesture towards Chaucer's broader expectations of his readers: at Melibee's first assembly of counsellors, a wise advocate reminds his audience that 'men seyn that ilke juge is wys that soone understondeth a matiere and juggeth by leyser' (*CT*, VII.1031). As author of a literary dialogue, Chaucer hopes for a reader who, like the wise judge, will quickly grasp the issues at stake but nevertheless ponder the case carefully before arriving at a judicious conclusion. His poetry continually reveals his desire to involve his readers in this way, although often the question we are invited to consider is posed implicitly rather than explicitly, as when we reach the end of the *Parliament of Fowls*, discussed above. It is in the *Canterbury Tales*, however, where the possibilities of the literary dialogue are brought most consistently into play. Throughout the different layers of the text Chaucer encourages, cajoles and provokes the readerly responses that are a crucial element of the form. Within individual tales questions are hinted at but not answered; for example, is the punishment of the knight in the *Wife of Bath's Tale* sufficient for his crime? Between the tales the pilgrims are asked to adjudicate, as when, at the end of his tale, the Franklin addresses his interlocutors directly: 'Lordynges, this question, thanne, wol I aske now, / Which was the mooste fre, as thynketh yow?' (V.1621–2). Finally, as readers we find ourselves faced with questions about the structure, purposes and even sincerity of the *Canterbury Tales* as a whole. This text demands that its readers enter into conversation with it; it becomes one side of an exchange in which the reader is compelled to participate, required to stand up and be counted, to make a determination – or at least to assess the different sides of the argument before concluding that there is no satisfactory answer. This most ambitious and capacious of

Chaucer's literary dialogues exposes both the intra-textual characters and his extra-textual readers to the ethical demands of engagement with society.

Paul Strohm emphasises this aspect of Chaucer's works when he writes of their 'provisional and unfinished qualities, their willingness to entertain alternatives without pressing for premature resolution, their frankly exploratory approach'.[12] Strohm's particular concern is to explore the relationship of Chaucer's poetry to medieval social relations, but these same qualities seem to me to extend to a much wider range of issues in which Chaucer is interested, and with which he invites his readers to engage. Those readers are totally implicated in this procedure; rather than remaining at a distance and watching Chaucer and his characters unfold before them, they are forced to participate in the quest for wisdom, to engage with the debates that are initiated and never truly concluded in the poetry. The very act of reading becomes, in this sense, an extended heuristic Chaucerian dialogue. Chaucer is, of course, familiar at quite an intimate level with at least part of his initial audience and therefore writes with them in mind. Thus he is not simply inviting his audience to enter into dialogue with the ethical concerns of the text, but is in fact building into the work itself some acknowledgement of the existence of that audience, and their preferences, prejudices and weaknesses. As Strohm comments, 'the utterance is formed and received within the larger social milieu that embraces both speaker and listener and the more particular social relationship that exists between them'; the audience shapes the work by the mere fact of its existence.[13]

Chaucer, like many of his contemporaries, is alive to the creative possibilities afforded by the literary dialogue. Beyond the ideas explored here, it also surely forms the foundation upon which he builds his use of direct speech as a means of revealing and developing character in his poetry. However, he is also clearly drawn to its use for the serious examination of social, political, religious and ethical questions, and in his most deeply reflective work the influence of Boethius is unmistakable. These questions are not merely the subjects of his poetry, however; he insists that they become pressing concerns for his audience too as he returns again and again to the Socratic example of inconclusivity, that productive *aporia* that demands the reader's ethical engagement with his works.

NOTES

1 Akio Oizumi, ed., *A Complete Concordance to the Works of Geoffrey Chaucer*, 15 vols. (Hildesheim: Olms-Weidmann, 1991).

2 See the citations in the *MED* and *OED* for details.

3 This was a feature of Plato's writing much admired by Cicero; see Robert A. Watson, 'Dialogue and Invention in the "Book of the Duchess"', *Modern Philology*, 98 (2001), 543–76. Among medieval writers, Henry Suso (writing *c.* 1320) claims that he employs the dialogue form to convey matters 'ad ferventiorem modum' (in a more vivid manner); see Henry Suso, *Wisdom's Watch upon the Hours*, trans. Edmund Colledge, O.S.A. (Washington, DC: Catholic University of America Press, 1994), p. 55. Reginald Pecock, writing over 100 years after Suso, suggests that 'bokis in foorme of a dialog' are particularly favoured by readers; see Reginald Pecock, *The Book of Faith*, ed. J. L. Morison (Glasgow: Maclehose and Sons, 1909), p. 122.

4 *Consolation of Philosophy*, in Boethius, *The Theological Tractates and the 'Consolation of Philosophy'*, ed. H. F. Stewart, E. K. Rand and S. J. Tester (Cambridge, MA: Harvard University Press, 1973).

5 Winthrop Wetherbee, 'The *Consolation* and Medieval Literature', in John Marenbon, ed., *The Cambridge Companion to Boethius* (Cambridge: Cambridge University Press, 2009), pp. 279–302.

6 Janet Coleman, 'The Science of Politics and Late Medieval Academic Debate', in Rita Copeland, ed., *Criticism and Dissent in the Middle Ages* (Cambridge: Cambridge University Press, 1996), pp. 181–214.

7 See Martin Grabmann, *Die Geschichte der scholastischen Methode*, 2 vols. (Freiburg: Herdersche Verlagshandlung, 1909, 1911), esp. pp. 98, 193–4, 222–4, 264, 317–22.

8 *The Owl and the Nightingale*, ed. Neil Cartlidge (Exeter: University of Exeter Press, 2001), line 1778.

9 Wetherbee, 'The *Consolation*', p. 291.

10 *MED*, definition 1.

11 For example, his constant emphasis on the care with which she chooses her time to speak (*CT*, VII.1051, 1728, 1832).

12 Paul Strohm, *Social Chaucer* (Cambridge, MA: Harvard University Press, 1989), p. xii.

13 *Ibid.*, p. 49.

CHAPTER 11

Romance

Stephen H. A. Shepherd

Chauser ... was evir (God wait [knows]), all wommanis frend.[1]

So the Scots poet Gavin Douglas, writing just over a century after Chaucer's death. His immediate concern is with Chaucer's counter-Virgilian defence of Dido in the *Legend of Good Women*. But in another sense Douglas is also praising Chaucer as chivalrous, as aspiring to the service of worthy women – 'ladeis lilly quhyte (lily-white, fair)', he adds – in a fashion essential to any good knight in a courtly romance. Yet, at first glance, some of Chaucer's adaptations of the romance mode – the *Knight's Tale*, *Franklin's Tale*, *Man of Law's Tale*, *Clerk's Tale*, *Wife of Bath's Tale* and *Squire's Tale* – reveal no shortage of women put through extraordinary and often seemingly gratuitous ordeal. Douglas's chivalrous analogy may then be more modish than it is nuanced; but it also suggests an analytical perspective on Chaucer's apprehension of the romance mode that goes beyond an engagement with individual texts, their conventions or their sources. It can be useful, in other words, to think of authorial practice as itself an extension of romance.

In the English context, a universal definition of medieval romance is difficult to apply. The customary paradigm, derived from the late-twelfth-century French romances of Chrétien de Troyes, is that of the lone knight riding out to destined adventure, engaging in chivalric combat (often in marvellous, preternatural or supernatural circumstances), and undergoing a spiritual and moral improvement in the process. The hand of a powerful noblewoman, or access to something as exalted as the Grail, are familiar prizes. By Chaucer's time, we know of the composition of just over sixty romances in English, almost none of which, save a translation of Chrétien such as *Ywain and Gawain*, adheres fully to the French paradigm.[2] An early (*c.* 1280) and excellent English poem such as *Havelok*, for instance, while employing copious amounts of combat and supernatural prophecy, presents a boy hero who grows into his predestined kingship rather than undergoing a process of self-correction. *Sir Orfeo*, a couple of decades later, features a recovery narrative, going so far as to reorientate the classical tale of Orpheus and Eurydice, both by placing it in an England invested with the magic of *faerie*, and by seeing that the legendary harpist gets to bring his wife back alive and for good. In lieu of combat, there is the transcendent music of Orfeo's Breton harp. *Sir Gawain and the Green Knight*, written in the northwest Midlands around the time Chaucer was writing the *Canterbury Tales* in London, acknowledges the customary paradigm by unravelling it. As Gawain's long journey to satisfy the Green Knight's challenge comes to its end, he becomes a better knight only in the sense that he now knows his traditionally vaunted 'literary' courage has an emblematic, material and earthly limit. So concerned is the poet to envelop Gawain in the relentless menace of the Green Knight's natural (indeed 'green' and somewhat pre-Christian) domain, that the many combative adventures of the rest of Gawain's journey – the substance of a paradigmatic romance – are effectively compressed into twenty-three lines (lines 713–35), a fraction of just one of the poem's 101 stanzas.[3]

Chaucer seems to have much in common with the *Gawain*-poet, sharing a wariness about emblems, pronouncements, tradition and the expectations invited by literary genre. It is suspected that, like Chaucer, the *Gawain*-poet served a noble court; and that is a context more likely to be survived through empiricism than idealism. The *Knight's Tale*, given the occupation of its teller, a 'verray, parfit gentil knyght' who 'loved chivalrie' (*CT*, I.72), portends a perfect, noble testament to the virtues of chivalry – surely something along the lines of Chrétien. What emerges, however, is an unrelenting tale of devastation brought on by two knights in full knowledge of, and yet defiant against, the inevitability of misfortune. Like *Gawain*, Chaucer's poem tends to eschew the conventional progress of knightly adventures, and concentrates combat into a few rather ignoble moments, the most notable being the tournament between Palamon and Arcite for the hand of Emily. On the face of it, certain romance paradigms seem to be fulfilled, but the winner, Arcite, crushed under his horse during the victory lap, dies thereafter by slow putrefaction – and Emily, for all the fuss over her, had already declared love for neither knight, and, if forced to marry, asked only that the one who loved her most be victor.

As with Gawain, each knight fails to adhere to authoritative narratives to which they initially claim they are bound. For Gawain there was his traditional romance identity, as well as the dominant livery he sported, a gold pentagram on a red background, signifying the 'five fives' of his chivalric and spiritual perfections. These are soon obviated when, in fear for his life, he acquires two new emblems: a nick on his neck commemorating his flinching beneath the Green Knight's axe, and a green sash he had been led to believe, by his host's impressive lady, would ward off just such injuries. In identifying his new livery to Arthur's court, Gawain declares his irredeemability to tradition:

> ... I mot nedez hit were wyle I may last;
> For mon may hyden his harme, bot vnhap ne may hit,
> For þer hit onez is tachched, twynne wil hit neuer.
> (lines 2510–12)

> [... I must wear it as long as I live;
> For a man may conceal his harm, but may not do away with it,
> For there where it once is fastened, it will never separate.]

As if to try to return to tradition, Arthur's court responds by substituting self-remonstration with a fashion statement, where all don a green sash for Gawain's sake (lines 2513–18).

A comparable moment occurs toward the end of the *Knight's Tale*. Chaucer has complicated the chivalric deportment of his two lover-knights by having their pagan world subscribe to a philosophy arguably at odds with the self-formative ambitions of romance, that of the inexorable workings of Fortune. Chaucer's source for the philosophy is Boethius's *Consolation of Philosophy*, which he adds to his narrative source, the *Teseida* of Boccaccio. In his first speech, the imprisoned Arcite speaks Boethian wisdom to Palamon:

> ... taak al in pacience
> Oure prisoun, for it may noon oother be.
> Fortune hath yeven us this adversitee
> ...
> We moste endure it; this is the short and pleyn.
> (*CT*, 1.1084–91)

When Arcite dies horribly, after years of defeating his own advice, the only one who seems to provide comfort to the grieving is Egeus, father of Duke Theseus. His utterance is as stolid as had been Arcite's, and, in the fashion of Fortune's Wheel itself – after all the trials and ordeals – as unproductive as it is *circular*:

> 'Right as ther deyed nevere man', quod he,
> 'That he ne livede in erthe in some degree,
> Right so ther livede never man', he seyde,
> 'In al this world, that som tyme he ne deyde.
> This world nis but a thurghfare ful of wo,

And we ben pilgrimes, passinge to and fro.
Deeth is an ende of every worldly sore.'
(I.2843–9)

Boethian pronouncements such as this constitute a trivialising rhetorical green sash for the tale. Such an analogy takes us some way towards that extra-literary level of Chaucer's engagement with his material suggested by Gavin Douglas.

In a larger sense for Chaucer, as with the *Gawain*-poet, the task at hand is not only to adapt romance convention, but to invite us to assess it, and to experience in the new work a certain degree of experimentation. A feature often identified with medieval romance is the marvellous – magic, *faerie*, the preternatural, the superhuman, and people empowered by such things – suggesting a longstanding appreciation of romance as a medium for revelling in what is conventionally held as *im*possibility. Chaucer, moreover, is often careful to distinguish the impossible from the *unthinkable*, and he plays on our expectations of the marvellous in romance to test the difference. For Chaucer, this has a scholastic dimension. At universities of his time, a statement of the impossible might be presented to a student with the challenge rhetorically to make it 'possible' – for instance, to resolve a proposition such as that expressed by the late-thirteenth-century scholar Siger of Brabant: 'it is possible for something both to be and not be, and for contradictories to be true of each other or of the same thing'.[4] Chaucer alludes or refers to scholastic *impossibilia* in three of the *Canterbury Tales*, most obviously in the *Summoner's Tale*, where a manservant answers the implicit question of how the Holy Spirit – that which surely cannot be divided – could be divided evenly amongst the apostles. He solves this 'inpossible' (III.2231) by demonstrating with a wagon wheel how a 'fart sholde evene deled be' among twelve friars (III.2249). The unthinkable is indeed not impossible.

The other two *impossibilia* are associated with romances. Like the *Summoner's Tale*, the *Franklin's Tale* presents an ingenious empirical solution to a seemingly insurmountable challenge, in this case making the black rocks of the Brittany coast disappear. The challenge is apparently Chaucer's invention, certainly not present in his main source, Boccaccio's *Filocolo*. 'This were an impossible!', cries Aurelius, the squire-suitor to Dorigen, a lonely but loyal married woman who thinks she has just given the man a task he can never complete (V.1009). As in *Orfeo*, the marvellous (or at least the appearance of it) plays a much greater role than the marital in breaking up impasses. Aurelius contracts the help of a magician of Orleans, who, notwithstanding a *show* of magic, knows his astrological authorities well enough to predict the arrival of a rare high tide: all the rocks get covered. A harrowing *new* formula for impossibility results: the loyal wife must now keep her word to husband and suitor alike, and the poor suitor must now pay an unmanageable debt to the magician. This in turn is resolved by high 'magic' of a very human order: an indivisible nexus of pity, honour and generosity, through which, and without violence, each figure releases the other. A significant aspect of romance – we see it in *Orfeo*, *Havelok*, *Gawain*, the *Franklin's Tale* and the *Knight's Tale*, indeed in most English romances – is the testing of agreements contracted through principles of chivalric honour. In the *Franklin's Tale* Chaucer has rather turned the test on its head: chivalric values are preserved only by unbinding contracts once held together on chivalric principle.

The *Wife of Bath's Prologue and Tale* could be Chaucer's most interrogative engagement with romance. *Sir Thopas* is a rival, but lacks a lengthy 'confessional' teller's prologue, which complicates our reception of the ensuing tale. The Wife tells a version of the popular 'Loathly Lady' romances, in which a woman breaks a spell put upon her that condemns her to exist as a dissolute hag until she can marry and win sovereignty over a great knight. It is hard not to read the Wife's take on the traditional tale as an expression of the yearnings she discloses in her prologue, among them a desire to be free of the constraints placed on women by the dictates of learned male authorities:

> For trusteth wel, it is an impossible
> That any clerk wol speke good of wyves,
> Ne of noon oother womman never the mo.
> . . .
> By God, if wommen hadde writen stories,
> As clerkes han withinne hire oratories,
> They wolde han writen of men moore wikidnesse
> Than al the mark of Adam may redresse.
> (III.688–96)

If only women had written stories – but that seems as much an *impossibilium* as a wife's good reputation among clerks (including her last husband, Oxford-trained, who may inadvertently have provided her with her scholastic rhetoric). And yet, the Wife *does* modify a traditional story enough to warrant the unthinkable status of a female author; and her tale, so modified, does tend to throw women into a better light than men. Throughout, what once was Loathly becomes Wife-of-Bathly, and female sovereignty becomes authorial where it once was only matrimonial. Chaucer has seen to it that that marvellous transformation characteristic of the traditional romance now emanates from the plangent 'reality' and non-rhetorical *possibility* of its female teller.

Whether unfinished or cut short, two of the romances in the *Canterbury Tales*, the *Squire's Tale* and *Sir Thopas*, prove 'impossible'. Siger might say that both tales 'are, and are not'. The arc of a traditional romance is one of happy closure, of which, even in the *Knight's Tale* (as in *Gawain*), there is at least a semblance. And it may be no coincidence that, against Chaucer's usual practice, neither short poem has a dominant source, standing largely as its own invention. Yet, in terms of marvellous adventure, both (allowing also for *authorial* adventure) do have it, of an evanescent nature perhaps, but transfixed nonetheless by each tale's prompt dis-invention and liberation from the expectation of denouement.

What remains in the *Squire's Tale* is a fantastic *premonition* of romance made more sublime. As if suggesting a new ambition for the form, the Squire speaks of classical romance matter as 'olde' (v.211), and of 'Gawayn, with his olde curteisye' as now confined to 'Fairye' (v.95). And Lancelot? – 'he is deed' (v.287). Thus, in the Squire's romance, a mechanical horse brings gifts of invincibility that remain uncompromised – 'nevere yet was herd so grete mervailles' (v.660). There is no prospect in the Squire's telling of a *Gawain*-like rescinding of gifted supernatural powers, nor the kind of ironic promises made by a Mars to an Arcite, or a Loathly Lady to a knight made to experience the answer he seeks before he hears it (v.661–70). And Canacee, Cambyskan's daughter, enabled by a magic ring to converse with a wounded female falcon, encounters an avatar of the abused heroines found in the *Man of Law's Tale*, the *Clerk's Tale* and the wide tradition of Constance-Griselda legends from which those tales borrow. The Squire proposes to dwell on the healing of the heroine instead of chronicling her compounded abuse, the tale itself projecting a kind of hypergeneric sanctuary not unlike the cage Canacee herself makes for the falcon (v.641–57). Such absolute triumphs as are guaranteed by the gifts of the mechanical horse and the ring could be put down to the Squire's youthful naïveté, but Chaucer dignifies the Squire's revisive (yet chivalric) ambition by suspending the tale between its soaring projections and uncritiqued closure.

Thopas is really neither incomplete nor a pejorative send-up of the many English romances to which it alludes by way of its metrical form, its tags, its lists of heroes or its description of the workings of the marvellous. It is perhaps better understood as bad writing done so very well, a mock-insipid sublimation of its (real) author's preposterous talent. Much of the poem is simply impossible, as in VII.807–13, where a dangerous, seemingly

Saracenic giant (or perhaps just a big man), named Sir Elephant (or is it Sir War-Horn?), will kill the hero's *horse* (Thopas is safe), bludgeoning it extra-metrically 'with mace'. How could such thorough incoherence, beyond anything to be found in later burlesque/travesty romances such as *The Weddyng of Syr Gawen and Dame Ragnell*, *The Tournament of Tottenham* or *Ralph Coilyear*, be resolved by an ending? However self-effacing, on Chaucer's part, the poem's heated dismissal by the Host may seem (VII.919–35), the dismissal cauterises and sustains one of his great and unprecedented adventures in high-functioning vernacular nonsense (one might argue that it even supersedes his unfinished epistemological quest in the *House of Fame*). Here we see the perilous (but also marvellous) boundary between authority and nonsense, a higher literary venture into matters of epistemic impossibility, investigating how, how better, or whether what is authorised can be known, or known anew.

As *Thopas* is about to begin, Chaucer describes himself (through the Host) as 'elvyssh', having the properties of an otherworldly creature, of a kind known to inhabit the marvellous side of romance sought by Thopas himself (VII.703). The Wife of Bath, that living 'impossible', yearns for it:

> … ther as wont to walken was an elf
> There walketh now the lymytour hymself
> In undermeles and in morwenynges,
> And seyth his matyns and his hooly thynges
> As he gooth in his lymytacioun.
> Wommen may go saufly up and doun.
> In every bussh or under every tree
> Ther is noon oother incubus but he,
> And he ne wol doon hem but dishonour.
> (III.873–81)

'Lymytour' refers to a mendicant friar, but also plays on the broader notion of someone who imposes limits; and 'in his lymytacioun' in turn suggests someone with limited views, certainly not an innovator. To the Wife the elfin world does not limit, and we have seen the Wife herself (as befriended by her author, to recall Gavin Douglas) become something new and previously unthinkable in her imaginings of that world. Whenever one encounters Chaucer's engagement with romance (including such texts as *Troilus and Criseyde*, the *Miller's Tale*, the *Merchant's Tale*, the *Parliament of Fowls*, the *Book of the Duchess* and the prologue to the *Legend of Good Women*), the Wife's case models an important distinction to keep in focus: it is a difference between romance as *read* and romance as *acted out, or upon*, by character and author alike. What might be read traditionally in an escapist manner becomes in Chaucer's hands a revision of impossibility into possibility, at once scholastic in foresight and empirical in application.

NOTES

1 Quoted in Derek Brewer, ed., *Chaucer: The Critical Heritage*, Vol. 1: *1385–1837* (London: Routledge, 1978), p. 86.

2 Still the most useful summary resource on Middle English romances is J. Burke Severs, ed., *A Manual of the Writings in Middle English*, Fascicle 1: *Romances 1050–1500* (New Haven: Connecticut Academy of Arts and Sciences, 1967).

3 All citations are from *Sir Gawain and the Green Knight*, ed. J. R. R. Tolkien and E. V. Gordon, 2nd rev. edn, ed. Norman Davis (Oxford: Clarendon Press, 1967).

4 Antoine Côté provides a good summary of Siger's types and examples in 'Siger and the Skeptic', *Proceedings of the Society for Medieval Logic and Metaphysics*, 6 (2006), 3–18 (p. 5):

> Siger's *Impossibilia* deal with several kinds of impossibility: metaphysical impossibility … (God does not exist); physical impossibility … (The Trojan war is happening in this instant) and … (Some unimpeded, upward lying heavy object would not fall); ethical impossibility … (In human affairs there is no evil action in virtue of whose evil that action should be prohibited or someone punished for committing it); logical impossibility … (It is possible for something to both be and not to be, and for contradictories to be true of each other or of the same thing); and finally, epistemic impossibility … (everything that appears to us are illusions [simulacra] and similar to dreams, so that we are not certain of the existence of anything).

CHAPTER 12

Love

Corinne Saunders

Love is Chaucer's great subject. He addresses it in many forms and across all genres, from comic to high tragic. He is not alone in his focus on love but his variety and flexibility are unique. They reflect and are inspired by a rich and complex set of traditions – classical, continental and English; and a range of genres – epic, lyric, romance, devotional. The conventions of classical poetry, the courtly and chivalric ideals and practices that underpin romance, and the great tropes of Christianity all shape Chaucer's treatment of love.

Like his medieval predecessors, Chaucer found particular inspiration in Virgil and Ovid, though he draws on a range of classical writings. Virgil provided the great example of consuming passion and the conflict between love and duty in the love of Dido and Aeneas, set against the dynastic model of Aeneas's marriage to Lavinia. Ovid's *Metamorphoses* offered a series of instances of unruly, transformative desire, while his *Heroïdes* articulated the loves and losses of a sequence of celebrated women. Ovid's *Amores* and *Ars amatoria* provided a set of powerful conventions, in particular, of the concept of love as a powerful and invasive external force affecting mind and body, a sickness caused by the arrows of the God of Love. These secular classical examples were complemented by the profound love at the heart of the Christian story: the sacrifice of Christ's life for mankind, emulated by the saints. Dante, whose work was a profound influence on Chaucer, merges secular and sacred patterns in the *Divina commedia*: Beatrice is both the earthly beloved and the celestial rose.

Chaucer draws on all these models, both directly and as refracted through medieval writers – though he is careful to present himself as following in the footsteps of the great classical authors, Homer and Virgil. While Latin, French and Italian texts provide frequent sources and analogues for his work, English is a less conspicuous source of inspiration – most directly signalled in the tale of *Sir Thopas*, with its parody of metrical romance. English romances, however, often more naturalistic than their continental counterparts, may well have played a shaping role in Chaucer's distinctive mode of realism.

Late medieval writers also inherited the conventions of *fin'amor*, the term used by twelfth-century French poets to convey a refined, rarefied emotion that elevated the sufferer to new heights of feeling and action, ritualised in courtly practices. For C. S. Lewis, such 'courtly love' (a term translating the French scholar Gaston Paris's phrase *amour courtois*, which he used to characterise a distinctively medieval mode of love) equated to a religion, and in its ideal form, as in the *Comedìa*, was not consummated.[1] The other face of such love, he argued, was found in the great medieval narratives of adulterous love – Lancelot and Guinevere, Tristan and Isolde, Troilus and Criseyde. For Lewis, married love represented a debased version of courtly love. His *The Allegory of Love* draws in particular on the thirteenth-century treatise of Andreas Capellanus, *De arte honeste amandi*, powerfully to convey the conventions of medieval depictions of love. Yet his concept of a code of love is too fixed, ignoring the fact that many medieval romances treat married love, while narratives of adultery are comparatively few.[2] Nor are the courtly conventions associated with love as clearly defined or emotion as consistently idealised as Lewis's argument suggests.

Fluidity and variety of treatment are already evident in twelfth-century romance. Marie de France and Chrétien de Troyes employ many of the conventions of idealised love-sickness used in the lyrics of the *troubadours* and *trouvères*, as well as in Ovid; they also draw on Ovid's self-conscious, sometimes artificial, sometimes satirical treatment of emotion. In Chrétien's *Le chevalier de la charrete* (*Lancelot*), love and reason are at war, but it is precisely the irrationality of great love that can inspire great deeds of prowess; in *Le chevalier au lion* (*Yvain*), prowess and love come into conflict, leading to a journey through madness to self-realisation and integration; *Erec et Enide* treats similar themes, but *Cligès* adopts a more satirical perspective. *Le chevalier de la charrete* offers the first account of the adulterous love of Lancelot and Guinevere, but *Erec et Enide* and *Le chevalier au lion* celebrate married love, while Chrétien's last romance, *Le conte du graal* (*Perceval*), takes spiritual love as its central theme, contrasting this with secular, temporal concerns. All these works were read in England, while Chrétien's quest pattern and Arthurian themes established a genre and subject matter that became popular across Europe, elaborated and adapted across the subsequent centuries. Perhaps most influential for Chaucer, however, was the thirteenth-century *Roman de la Rose*, which developed the conventions of *fin'amor* and love-sickness in its archetypal narrative of the Lover's wounding by the God of Love and pursuit of the beautiful Rose. Guillaume de Lorris's allegorical dream vision is balanced by Jean de Meun's much more cynical completion of the narrative, with its sophisticated debate between Nature and Reason. For Chaucer, this work, parts of which he translated, offered a crucial model in its combination of nature and artifice; its multiple, conflicting perspectives on love; and its polyvocality.

In Chaucer's earliest narrative poem, the *Book of the Duchess*, that ambiguity of tone and shifting perspective are already evident, and his treatment of love combines rhetorical and literary sophistication with a probing, naturalistic quality. The literary and cultural contexts of the poem are complex: Chaucer weaves together and adapts an English subject, a tale from Ovid's *Metamorphoses*, and parts of a series of French courtly poems (the *Roman de la Rose*; Machaut's *Dit de la fonteinne amoureuse*, *Jugement dou roy de Behaingne* and *Jugement dou roy de Navarre*; Froissart's *Paradys d'amours*). He creates a narrative interweaving three stories of love and loss: the narrator's mysterious sickness and insomnia, we presume because of unrequited love; the tragic tale of Ceyx and Alcyone, who dies of grief on hearing of her husband's drowning; and the narrator's dream encounter with the Man in Black, who is grieving for his lost beloved. The poem commemorates the death of John of Gaunt's wife Blanche, Duchess of Lancaster (*c.* 1368), using cryptic wordplay to evoke their names and titles. The dialogue between Dreamer and Man in Black moves through various stages, which draw closely on stylised courtly traditions of love and lament, but also depict a process of grief through the gradual exposition of the Man in Black's feeling, his memory of the past, and finally the actuality of his loss. Like Sisyphus – 'alway deynge and be not ded' – he is the essence of sorrow: 'y am sorwe, and sorwe ys y' (*BD*, 588, 597). Chaucer develops the physiology of love found in his sources, drawing on medical theory of the period to emphasise the physical effect on the knight; 'Hys sorwful hert gan faste faynte / And his spirites wexen dede' (*BD*, 488–9): his blood retreats into his heart, causing deathly pallor and lassitude. The narrator's questions lead the Man in Black far into the recollection of the past, as he reconstructs his service to the 'craft' of love (*BD*, 791); their courtship is related as an inset courtly romance. Like the physiology of love, the workings of memory are conveyed with realism, drawing on medieval understandings of the mind: Chaucer recounts the inner dialogue of the knight and the recreation of his lady through the images stored in the memory, an act of 'sorwful ymagynacioun' (*BD*, 14). The final interchange between Man in Black and Dreamer is discordant, comic yet painful in the Dreamer's lack of comprehension: '"Sir … where is she now?" / … "She ys ded!" "Nay!" "Yis, be my trouthe!" / "Is that youre los? Be God, hyt ys routhe!"' (*BD*, 1298–1310). The blunt statement contrasts strikingly with the Man in Black's first lament, a 'lay, a maner song, / Withoute noote, withoute song' (*BD*, 471–2), which is highly formalised, its conventional antitheses typical of courtly lyrics such as those of Machaut or Froissart. Through the process of question and answer, the Dreamer comes to realise that the images of loss are literal rather than figurative, while the knight comes to a new, direct expression of death. The *Book of the Duchess* is a poem about writing love – about the process of inspiration, and the search for new forms of writing that marry convention with originality, literary authority with individual experience.

The *Book of the Duchess* sets the tone for Chaucer's writing of love in its combination of natural and conventional, serious and comic, and its shifts and ambiguities. Chaucer's narrators repeatedly draw back from love, and if Chaucer celebrates the joys of love he also depicts it as an irresistible and potentially destructive force. Only because he is not a lover can the narrator-dreamer in the *Parliament of Fowls* safely enter the gates that, in a rewriting of Dante's message 'Lasciate ogni speranza, voi ch'entrate' (Abandon every hope, you who enter) (*Inferno*, 3.9), promise both delight and dread. Dread is more evident than delight: the stories depicted on the walls of the temple of Venus in the *Parliament of Fowls* are all tragic, and in the narrative of the parliament itself no decision concerning the most deserving lover is reached: perhaps the three rivals for the formel eagle's hand will re-enact the negative paradigm. Chaucer narrates a sequence of such tragic love stories in his late dream-vision poem the *Legend of Good Women*, drawing from and adapting parts of Virgil's *Aeneid*, Ovid's *Heroïdes* and *Metamorphoses*, Vincent of Beauvais's *Speculum historiale*, the *Ovide moralisé*, and other works, and weaving the whole into a tapestry of passion, betrayal and death. Chaucer complicates classical legend by portraying his protagonists as Christian saints, creating a series of ambiguities and tensions. These women are all victims of love, whose sorrows end in death, often through suicide. Yet they are also given agency, both through Chaucer's careful depiction of their processes of thought and feeling, and through his vivid realisations of their lamenting voices.

In a more extended way, ambiguity and multi-vocality distinguish the *Canterbury Tales*. The *Knight's Tale*, Chaucer's grandest and most literary tales rewrites classical epic and continental romance, setting the actions of the classical gods against Boethian Christian philosophy. Chaucer exploits the sophisticated rhetoric of love inherited from his sources to point up the painful physiology of love. Elaborating and going beyond the familiar neo-Platonic convention of love striking through the eyes to wound the heart, he demonstrates a detailed awareness of contemporary physiological theory in his depiction of the ensuing bodily and mental illness: Arcite not only wastes away physically, but also suffers from a malady 'lyk manye, / Engendred of humour malencolik / Biforen, in his celle fantastik' (*CT*, I.1374–6).[3] Chaucer is specific about the part of the brain affected, the front ventricle controlling the imagination (the 'celle fantastik'), and about the humoral nature of the illness.[4] The destructive effects of passion are vividly evoked, as Palamon and Arcite, cousins and blood-brothers, are reduced to wild animals fighting in a forest glade, up to their ankles in blood (I.1655–60). The pains of love are emphasised in the images painted in Venus's temple, and concluded only by Saturn's action of sending a 'furie infernal' (I.2684) to throw Arcite to his death. Troubling too is Emily's lack of choice: it is difficult to reconcile her supposed happiness with the earlier extremes of passion and death. The destinies played out by callous gods do not readily coincide with Theseus's image of divine providence, 'the faire cheyne of love' (I.2991), that binds the elements and moves the spheres. Yet it is crucial too that the tale offers this positive view of divine love – looking beyond temporal passion to the eternal. Chaucer interweaves classical and Christian, conventionality and realism, to present an uneasy and compelling account of love in its existential contexts.

The *Canterbury Tales* depict many other faces of love, none perhaps as heightened as this epic version, yet often playing on the tensions between secular and sacred, positive and negative, comic and serious, and on the underlying creative tension between inherited literary conventions and naturalism. As in the *Legend of Good Women*, Chaucer repeatedly returns to the subject of force in love, problematising the conventions of *fin'amor*. The *Knight's Tale* finds a brilliantly parodic response, including at a structural level, in the *Miller's Tale*, with its narrative of willing, adulterous love and trickery, in which both cuckolded husband and cunning clerk get their comeuppances. The tale is a *tour de force* in its parody of courtly language and conventions, and life-enhancing in its comedy, though it also hints at a moral concerning the dangers of jealousy: the young wife Alison is kept 'narwe in cage' (I.3224) by her older husband. The darker aspects of *fabliau* become more evident in the *Reeve's Tale*, with its structuring motifs of rape, revenge and cruelty, and in the January–May tale offered by the Merchant, which sets adulterous love against a chilling portrayal of the wedding night, with the bride brought to bed 'as stille as stoon' (IV.1818).

Romance repeatedly offers a means to probe the subject of female agency in love. In the *Franklin's Tale*, Chaucer turns to the form of the Breton *lai* to challenge romance assumptions through an exploration of love, force and free will – also the subject of the *Wife of Bath's Tale*, with its examination of female desire and sovereignty, and interweaving of Arthurian romance with legal realism.[5] The subject of rape central to the *Wife of Bath's Tale* recurs in the *Physician's Tale*, where desire is presented as a demonic, invasive force leading to death: the tale of Virginia, killed by her father to prevent her ravishment, combines the genres of classical *exemplum* and moral tale. Secular love is balanced by sacred in the *Second Nun's Tale*, which recounts the life of Saint Cecilia: here, the earthly becomes a mere shadow of the celestial, and, by contrast to the *Physician's Tale*, martyrdom is willing, as Cecilia re-enacts Christ's teaching and his sacrifice, inspiring the same act in others. In their different ways, all these narratives realise the power but also the dangers of love, its inexorable hold over body and mind, its potential destructiveness. They also, however, suggest love's transformative quality – its ability to effect joy, inspire forgiveness and generosity, and open onto divine vision. Its message is that of the gates in the *Parliament of Fowls*, both delight and dread.

It is in *Troilus and Criseyde* that Chaucer paints his most extensive canvas of love, rewriting a celebrated tale of betrayal that found its roots in Homer's *Iliad* and the chronicles of the Trojan war of Dares and Dictys, was first recounted by the French *romancier* Benoît de Sainte-Maure and was elaborated by the Italians Guido delle Colonne and Giovanni Boccaccio, whose poem *Il filostrato* was Chaucer's direct source. Chaucer's creative translation and adaptation is most notable in his treatment of Criseyde, whose enigmatic character is at the heart of the poem. But it is through Troilus that the subject of love is most elaborated. In Troilus's experience, the bodiliness of desire is especially striking, as Chaucer again develops the physiology of love rooted in the neo-Platonic convention of the connection between the eyes and the heart. When he sees Criseyde, Troilus's heart is caused to 'sprede and rise', wounding and quickening his affections (*Tr*, I.278); he manifests the typical symptoms of the malady of love: weeping, sighing, swooning, melancholy and physical decline.[6] Love and death are interwoven throughout: Troilus becomes a pale figure of death reminiscent of the Man in Black in the *Book of the Duchess*, his speeches infused with images of death. While Chaucer uses a familiar set of conventions derived from *Il canzoniere* of Petrarch (*c.* 1327–74), the physicality of his descriptions is remarkable and the imagery medically alert. In Books IV and V, Troilus is literally unmade by love, his suffering characterised by swoons, frenetic madness, nightmares and silence, until, finally, he wastes away to a shadowy figure of his former self:

He ne et ne drank, for his malencolye,
And ek from every compaignye he fledde:
This was the lif that al the tyme he ledde.

He so defet was, that no manere man
Unneth hym myghte knowen ther he wente;
So was he lene, and therto pale and wan,
And feble, that he walketh by potente [*crutch*].
(v.1216–22)

His complaint is of grievous pain around his heart (v.1231–2). Chaucer uses ancient notions of the heart as seat of both thought and feeling, and plays on the cognitive aspects of emotion, the ways that it affects the mind, producing *phantasmata* or thought-images of Criseyde: Troilus makes 'a mirour of his mynde' in which he sees 'al holly hire figure' (I.365–6).[7]

Yet if love unmakes Troilus, it also shapes his identity: his sufferings open onto love's sublimity.[8] Interwoven with the classical context is a profound Christian emphasis. The narrative is interspersed with Troilus's lyrics, which include the first translation into English of a sonnet of Petrarch, 'If no love is, O God, what fele I so?' (*Tr* I.400–20), and, preceding the consummation scene, a Boethian song, 'Benigne Love, thow holy bond of thynges' (III.1261–74), which echoes Theseus's vision of the fair chain of love at the end of the *Knight's Tale*. The fulfilment of desire opens onto a vision of divine love; the song praises God's harmony and the ordering of the world through love: secular and sacred, earthly and spiritual love intersect. For Troilus, Criseyde opens the way to the celestial: in her eyes, Paradise stands 'formed' (v.817). The end of Book III offers a further celebration of love as a force in the universe in Troilus's song 'Love, that of erthe and se hath governaunce' (III.1744–71). The elements 'discordable' are held in harmony; peoples and individuals in virtuous accord. The effect of love is to elevate the individual in virtue, so that Troilus demonstrates surpassing moral excellence: he is without pride ('Benigne he was to ech in general' (III.1802)), and eschews vice ('Pride, Envye, Ire, and Avarice / He gan to fle' (III.1805–6)).

The sublimity of love articulated through Troilus, however, is balanced – and troubled – by other perspectives. Pandarus offers a pragmatic and wryly comic view of Troilus's sufferings, laments and swoons: while he lies in bed, Pandarus promotes the affair, carrying letters, negotiating meetings and physically placing Troilus in bed with Criseyde while he looks on as if reading 'an old romaunce' (III.980). He plays the role of Fortune, turning Troilus's desire into reality – and in Book IV, of opportunist, urging Troilus to take a new lover. In Pandarus's manipulation of Criseyde, pragmatism becomes more sinister, and this work too gestures towards the potential connection between desire and force. Criseyde, for all her apparent independence, is also portrayed as a victim – of social constraints, of her uncle, of politics and of her own fearfulness. It is not coincidental that the poem evokes the tale of Philomela, celebrated victim of rape, or that in the consummation scene Boccaccio's sexually precocious Criseida is rewritten as the innocent lark held in the sparrowhawk's claws.

Chaucer also reworks Boccaccio's poem by incorporating elements of Boethius's *Consolation of Philosophy*, which he was translating at the same time, into Pandarus's optimistic speeches concerning Fortune, Criseyde's rationalism and Troilus's laments, most famously his monologue concerning his lack of free will in Book IV. The three main characters enact different philosophical perspectives in relation to love – and, at the end of the poem, Chaucer draws on Boccaccio's *Il Teseida* to present another perspective again, as Troilus looks down from the seventh sphere and laughs at 'this wrecched world' (V.1817). Through the double sorrow of Troilus, his sufferings in love and then his betrayal by Criseyde, the poem raises unanswerable questions concerning the value and meaning of love, with its capacity to open onto the sublime, to transform the individual, but also to destroy, and, ultimately, with all things, to pass away.

Chaucer finds in the subject of love both matter and mode. The works of classical, French and Italian authors provided the narratives in which many of his works are rooted; they also provided the conventions of *fin'amor* so crucial to the language of love. To them, Chaucer brought new interests in physiology and philosophy, and new modes of realism and comedy. His writing is inspired by, but also exploits, adapts and goes beyond, the complex literary and cultural traditions that shape medieval portrayals of love. In probing the tensions between classical and Christian perspectives, and in depicting the darker side of love, Chaucer's writings ask uneasy existential questions, and call into doubt any simple celebration of love.

NOTES

1 C. S. Lewis, *The Allegory of Love: A Study in Medieval Tradition* (Oxford: Oxford University Press, 1936). See also C. S. Lewis, *The Discarded Image: An Introduction to Medieval and Renaissance Literature* (Cambridge: Cambridge University Press, 1964).

2 An intelligent critique of Lewis's view is offered by E. Talbot Donaldson, 'The Myth of Courtly Love', in *Speaking of Chaucer* (London: Athlone Press, 1970), pp. 154–63. Peter L. Allen emphasises the clerical, scholarly context of Andreas

Capellanus's *De arte honeste amandi*: 'Andreas's inscribed reader, "Gualterius", is a young man, and the history of the text's reception suggests that its public, for centuries, was essentially male'; see *The Art of Love: Amatory Fiction from Ovid to the 'Romance of the Rose'* (Philadelphia: University of Pennsylvania Press, 1992), p. 59. On the reception of *De arte honeste amandi*, see Alfred Karnein, *'De amore' in volkssprachlicher Literatur: Untersuchungen zur Andreas-Capellanus-Rezeption im Mittelalter und Renaissance*, Germanisch-Romanische Monatsschrift, Beheift 4 (Heidelberg: Carl Winter, 1985). For a sensitive treatment of 'the social and emotional dimensions' of medieval marriage, which argues against the predominant association of love with adultery in the literature of the period, see Neil Cartlidge, *Medieval Marriage: Literary Approaches, 1100–1300* (Cambridge: D. S. Brewer, 1997), esp. pp. 1–32 (p. 1).

3 On medieval medical notions of mind and body see Simon Kemp, *Medieval Psychology* (New York: Greenwood Press, 1990). On medieval medicine, see M. L. Cameron, *Anglo-Saxon Medicine* (Cambridge: Cambridge University Press, 1993); Faye Getz, *Medicine in the English Middle Ages* (Princeton: Princeton University Press, 1998); Nancy G. Siraisi, *Medieval and Early Renaissance Medicine: An Introduction to Knowledge and Practice* (Chicago: University of Chicago Press, 1990); and C. H. Talbot, *Medicine in Medieval England* (London: Oldbourne, 1967). For a comprehensive discussion of the malady of love, see Mary Frances Wack, *Lovesickness in the Middle Ages: The 'Viaticum' and Its Commentaries* (Philadelphia: University of Pennsylvania Press, 1990).

4 Chaucer draws on precise medical ideas about the influence of affect on the brain, available to him, for instance, through Bartholomaeus Anglicus's *De proprietatibus rerum* (see 5.3), and the translation of this by John of Trevisa (see 1:173). See further Jacqueline Tasioulas, 'Dying of Imagination in the First Fragment of the *Canterbury Tales*', *Medium Ævum*, 82 (2013), 213–35.

5 On rape and ravishment in Chaucer's writings, and in their classical and medieval contexts, see my *Rape and Ravishment in the Literature of Medieval England* (Cambridge: D. S. Brewer, 2001).

6 On Troilus's love-sickness, see also my discussion in '"The thoghtful maladie": Madness and Vision in Medieval Writing', in Corinne Saunders and Jane Macnaughton, eds., *Madness and Creativity in Literature and Culture* (Houndmills: Palgrave Macmillan, 2005), pp. 67–87 (pp. 74–5).

7 On thought-images, see Mary Carruthers, *The Book of Memory: A Study of Memory in Medieval Culture* (Cambridge: Cambridge University Press, 1990), pp. 17, 47–60.

8 See further my chapter, 'Love and the Making of the Self: *Troilus and Criseyde*', in Corinne Saunders, ed., *A Concise Companion to Chaucer* (Oxford: Blackwell, 2006), pp. 135–56.

CHAPTER 13

Chaucer and the Classics

Vincent Gillespie

I wol now synge, yif I kan,
The armes, and also the man.
(*HF*, 143–4)

In the *House of Fame*, Chaucer begins his retelling of the Troy story with a characteristically hesitant citation of the *Aeneid*. Virgil's decisive 'Arma virumque cano', a bold present-tense statement of his epic's subject, becomes in Chaucer's version a statement of uncompleted intent ('I wol now synge'), and an uneasy acknowledgement of uncertainty that he has the knowledge and skills to emulate his epic poetic *exemplum* ('yif I kan'). Except, of course, these acts of verbal hesitancy and provisionality are not Chaucer's. They are the voice of a brass tablet fixed to the wall of the glass Temple of Venus into which the narrator's dream has deposited him, the first of a series of ekphrastic accounts of the Troy story that will seamlessly segue from Virgil's account of the fall of the city and the exploits of Aeneas into an account of the doomed affair of Dido and Aeneas, drawn largely from Ovid. So, the hesitancy comes not from Chaucer's modesty in the face of classical tradition, but rather from an apparent uncertainty at the heart of that very tradition as it was received by medieval readers and writers.

On the face of it, the richly decorated and ornamented glass temple stands as a glorious monument to the inherited classical traditions of epic and love poetry. The narrator (uniquely in Chaucer's work named, and named as 'Geffrey') calls it a 'chirche' (*HF*, 473), and it enshrines an extensive array of epic love stories from the classical past, calling particularly on the indistinguishably blended authority of 'Virgile in Eneydos' and 'the Epistle of Ovyde' (378–9) (i.e. the *Heroides*), as well as referring the audience eager to know more about Virgil's exploits to 'rede many a rowe / On Virgile or on Claudian, / Or Daunte' (448–50). But when Geffrey comes to interrogate it more carefully, he finds it a strangely deracinated, lifeless and anonymous edifice. The Temple of Glass represents a literary tradition that has no named author or maker, and lacks geographical, national or linguistic identity:

> A, Lord,' thoughte I, 'that madest us,
> Yet sawgh I never such noblesse
> Of ymages, ne such richesse,
> As I saugh graven in this chirche;
> But not wot I whoo did hem wirche,
> Ne where I am, ne in what contree.
> (lines 470–5)

The 'ymages' embody the inherited deposit of classical literature, but in the course of the poem Chaucer shows us how complex his relationship with that tradition actually was. In the later Temple of Fame, where texts are whimsically judged by the goddess and assigned their fate of renown or oblivion, the landscape and architecture gradually deteriorate from a place of order and degree, where named authors stand on metal pillars, to a place of animalistic chaos and nightmarishly clashing voices, the labyrinthine House of Rumour:

> The halle was al ful, ywys,
> Of hem that writen olde gestes
> As ben on treës rokes nestes;
> But hit a ful confus matere
> Were alle the gestes for to here.
> (lines 1514–18)

The *House of Fame*, a pivotal poem for Chaucer's thinking about the name and nature of poetry, traces a fearful journey into the heart of darkness of literary transmission, away from the seeming certainty of the literary canon as represented in the classical order of the palace of Fame, into the promiscuous echo chamber of the House of Rumour, a market place of narrative, where stories are denuded of their generic markers of status and value (epic, romance, tragedy, satire, lay) and are reduced to their lowest common denominator status of 'tydynges', pure discourse, where gossip and slander are indistinguishable from truth and wisdom. Here, stories change hands cheaply in the market place, growing and distorting in the telling to a shape and form unrecognisable to their first tellers (or authors). This is profoundly unsettling for the narrator, Geffrey, himself a love poet, who constantly seeks to interpret the events of his journey by reference to older classical texts, such as the *Metamorphoses* of Ovid (which his eagle guide refers to as 'thyn oune bok' (712)). Not only is the instability of the literary tradition a source of anxiety to Geffrey but, as the eagle points out, his reliance on an exegetical toolkit constructed from the written authority of antecedent texts actually gets in the way of his experience of the wonders he is being shown. Throughout the *House of Fame*, Chaucer is imaginatively exploring his own understanding of and relationship to antecedent literature, and particularly to the literature of Latin antiquity as it had survived into his lifetime.

That very contingency of literary survival was itself part of the problem. How reliable is a literary tradition that appears to deconstruct itself over the course of the poem? The palace of Fame is built on foundations of ice, and Geffrey notes that the names of many authors carved into the ice have melted away in the sun, whereas those carved on more sheltered parts of the foundation are still legible. This models the high attrition of classical texts, known perhaps to have once existed but no longer available, and more worryingly raises the possibility that those named authors that survive and are still legible may represent texts that never enjoyed the heat of fame and survived through neglect or accident. In Geffrey's journey through the temple of glass, he is exposed to a multi-sensory array of classical literature, which he variously sees, hears and reads at different points, suggesting how omnipresent classical materials were in the world of the visual and verbal arts. Yet even in the retelling, Geffrey hints that the survival of classical inheritance is partial and incomplete: recounting the destruction of Troy, he tells us of the flight of Aeneas, carrying his father Anchises:

> The whiche Anchises in hys hond
> Bar the goddes of the lond,
> Thilke that unbrende were.
> (lines 171–3)

In rescuing only those household gods that have remained unburnt in the sack of the city, Anchises models the patchy and incomplete survival of classical literature. In Chaucer's own lifetime, the diligent manuscript scholarship of humanist book historians such as Petrarch, Boccaccio and Salutati was remapping the knowledge of classical antiquity, discovering long-lost texts, discrediting medieval forgeries attributed to classical authors (especially to Ovid) and reinforcing the contingency of the body of literature available to Chaucer's generation of readers.

Chaucer emerges from his own rewritings of classical texts as a very bookish reader. This bookishness is on display from the opening lines of the *Legend of Good Women*, a passionate defence of the importance of books and reading:

> Than mote we to bokes that we fynde,
> Thurgh which that olde thinges ben in mynde.

And to the doctrine of these olde wyse,
Yeve credence, in every skylful wise,
That tellen of these olde appreved stories …
That tellen of. G: And trowen on
And yf that olde bokes were aweye,
Yloren were of remembraunce the keye.
Wel oughte us thanne honouren and beleve
These bokes, there we han noon other preve.
(*LGW*, F 17–28)

Rebuked by Cupid for his sins against the law of love, he is criticised for the authorial choices he has made to 'translate' the *Roman de la Rose* and *Troilus and Criseyde*:

Was there no good matere in thy mynde,
Ne in alle thy bokes ne coudest thow nat fynde
Som story of wemen that were goode and trewe?
Yis, God wot, sixty bokes olde and newe
Hast thow thyself, alle ful of storyes grete,
That bothe Romayns and ek Grekes trete[.]
(*LGW*, G 270–5)

The irascible god of love returns several times to Chaucer's literary sources and resources, urging him to draw on them to make his commissioned legendary of Cupid's saints and martyrs:

And in thy bokes alle thou shalt hem fynde;
Have hem now in thy legende al in mynde.
(*LGW*, F 556–7)

Hast thow nat in a bok, lyth in thy cheste,
The grete goodnesse of the queene Alceste …?
(*LGW*, G 498–9)

It is natural to assume that these books are classical works in Latin. But we would be wrong to make this assumption. Cupid emphatically does not say that Chaucer's 'sixty bokes' are all in Latin. Even in his account of the glass temple of the *House of Fame*, Geffrey has urged his readers to 'rede many a rowe / On Virgile or on Claudian, / Or Daunte' (*HF*, 449–50). While the citation of Dante reminds us of the *Comedìa*'s use of Virgil as a spirit guide through the lower stages of Dante's journey, it also reminds us not to assume that writers like Chaucer either had the linguistic skills or the literary resources only to have direct access to works of classical literature. Chaucer's classical knowledge was a *bricolage* made up of direct knowledge of some Latin works (especially those of Ovid and Virgil); some knowledge of Latin works supported by translations or commentaries in the European vernaculars in which he was comfortable, especially French (he used a French translation of Boethius in his own translation) and Italian (such as his use of the commentaries of Filippo Ceffi to help him with Ovid); and some knowledge of vernacular reworkings of earlier Latin materials that he was able to finesse and nuance by referring back to the Latin originals (such as his tendency to move Boccaccio's *Teseida* back towards the *Thebaid* of Statius by the judicious reinsertion of narrative details). Even Geffrey's awestruck journeying through the literary canon presented in the *House of Fame* has him drawing on medieval aids to assist him. His reading of the Dido legend, in its blended Virgilian-Ovidian form, displays a moralistic mode of reading that reduces this most sublime and tragic narrative to a convenient peg on which to hang rather banal proverbs (All that glitters is not gold; only he who fully knows the herb can safely put it in his eye). 'Al this seye I *be* Eneas / And Dido' (*HF*, 286–7), he concludes, the 'be' ('about' or 'concerning', or 'by means of') revealing that he is using them as *exempla* in the great tradition of moralised Ovid readings, especially those in the contemporary French *Ovide moralisé*.

Chaucer's literary imagination is fuelled by a highly mediated and contextualised access to his classical sources, almost always supported by, filtered through or read against the vernacular works of European contemporaries. Petrarch described Dante as the 'dux vulgaris' (the duke of the vernacular), and the same phrase might be applied to Chaucer in England. Like Dante, he is a cultural synapse between Latin literature and the vernaculars of medieval Europe. We get a glimpse of this pervasive mediation in the dream chamber, in which the Dreamer awakes in his early exploration of grief and consolation in the *Book of the Duchess*. Having been unable to sleep, the narrator 'bad oon reche me a book / A romaunce' (*BD*, 47–8):

> And in this bok were written fables
> That clerkes had in olde tyme,
> And other poetes, put in rime
> ...
> This bok ne spak but of such thinges,
> Of quenes lives, and of kinges.
> (lines 52–8)

The tale of Ceyx and Alcyone which follows is retold originally from Ovid's *Metamorphoses*, but in fact in this case filtered through a French intermediary performance in Machaut's *Dit de la fonteinne amoreuse*. The story of kings and queens (making it fit treatment for epic and Chaucer's Boethian definition of tragedy) comes from the 'olde tyme' and is the work of 'clerkes' and 'other poetes', but the Dreamer calls it a 'romaunce', a distinctively medieval, if decidedly baggy, generic label for writing in the vernacular. As with Chaucer's other reworkings and creative borrowings from the French tradition in this poem, there is only that slight verbal hint that the material is being creatively filtered through an effectively bilingual synthesis. That doubleness of cultural focus persists throughout the poem, as the Man in Black goes through his paces as an aspirant francophone love poet who also knows the main lineaments of Boethian lament, and despairs of the abilities of the *remedia amoris* of Ovid and the songs of Orpheus to heal his grief. In seeking to describe his lost beloved's face he comments 'Me lakketh both Englyssh and wit / For to undo hyt at the fulle' (*BD*, 898–9), and the implication is that it would be easier to do it in French or Latin. That doubleness is already on display in the decoration of the narrator's dream chamber, suggesting that, whatever else divides the protagonists in the unfolding dialogue, they share similar literary reference points:

And sooth to seyn, my chambre was
Ful wel depeynted, and with glas
Were al the windowes wel yglased
Ful clere, and nat an hoole ycrased,
That to beholde hyt was gret joye.
For hooly al the story of Troye
Was in the glasynge ywroght thus
...
And alle the walles with colours fyne
Were peynted, bothe text and glose,
Of al the Romaunce of the Rose.
My wyndowes were shette echon,
And throgh the glas the sonne shon.
(lines 321–36)

This ekphrastic portrait effectively represents the inside of the Dreamer's head, the cultural terms of reference with which he will navigate the profoundly literary landscape he will encounter when he takes his horse and, apparently stark naked, leaves the bedchamber on his quest. On the one hand the windows are decorated with the great classical epic of the fall of Troy, and the sun shining through windows closed against the outside world is coloured as it passes through these images, filtering reality and gilding it with an epic sheen. On the other, the walls are 'peynted' (a word often used to describe the words of poetry) with the great French vernacular masterpiece the *Roman de la Rose*, the dominant francophone text of the previous century and a half, of which every vernacular poet was aware, and with which every literary imagination of medieval Europe was decorated, not only with the text but also, as here, 'bothe text and glose' (*BD*, 333), that is both the original work and its various reworkings and imaginative engagements.

The cohabitation of Latin and vernacular models is part and parcel of the furnishing of every medieval mind. Chaucer's literary landscape, like the Dreamer's, is always coloured by interpenetrating traditions of Latin texts and their vernacular reworkings. Even when he claims to be using a Latin source, as in *Anelida and Arcite*, the truth is invariably more complex:

> For hit ful depe is sonken in my mynde,
> With pitous hert in Englyssh to endyte
> This olde storie, in Latyn which I fynde,
> Of quene Anelida and fals Arcite,
> That elde, which that al can frete and bite,
> As hit hath freten mony a noble storie,
> Hath nygh devoured out of oure memorie.
> . . .
> First folowe I Stace, and after him Corynne.
> (*Anel*, 8–21)

Although he claims to follow the *Thebaid*, his source is in fact Boccaccio's *Teseida* (his first sustained engagement with that seminal work), and Corynne, never convincingly identified, appears to be as much a textual shibboleth as the Latin *auctor* Lollius whom Chaucer invokes as a proximate source for his book of Troilus, also largely reworked from Boccaccio's *Il filostrato*. While the survival of Boccaccio's own annotated copy of the *Thebaid* allows us to see something of his creative alchemy in reworking Statius into the *Teseida*, nothing comparably concrete survives for Chaucer to allow us insight into his imaginative processes. His classical knowledge is often available to us inferentially and allusively. Marginal citations from classical sources in some manuscripts of his works suggest that he or his early scribes and readers assumed that his readers would recognise and appreciate the intertexts he was creating and the aphorisms and *auctoritates* he was invoking. But we can be more certain of his knowledge of sententious extracts and proverbial utterances than we can in most cases of his knowledge of whole works.

Or perhaps, more accurately, we should say that we can really only deduce from this Chaucer's confidence that his intended audience would recognise and respond to such sententiousness. It may be that many of these citations came through *florilegia* of excerpts from classical texts.

Chaucer certainly uses one such *florilegium*, the *Communiloquium* of the thirteenth-century Franciscan John of Wales. But a feature of florilegial compilation was that extracts from a wide variety of available classical texts were collected under topical headings or alphabetical citations, deprived of their original context and repurposed to serve as proof texts or examples in preaching environments. The great encyclopedias of Vincent of Beauvais (whose work is mentioned by Chaucer) or Bartholomaeus Anglicus, *On the Nature of Things*, ensured that many classical aphorisms were in wide circulation, utterly denuded of their strategic role in their original texts and reapplied in locally tactical ways. Citations of Cato, Seneca, Juvenal and many other classical authorities probably reflect a shared cultural awareness of such materials among grammar-school-educated readers. So does his proven use of the *Elegies* of Maximian and Claudian's *De raptu Proserpinae*, and some of the shorter epistles of Ovid. These fleeting engagements with classical authorities throughout his writings suggest that, like many of his contemporaries, Chaucer was recalling materials he would have encountered in his own education. The Chaucerian tendency to *bricolage*, and to rapid syntheses of materials, and the willingness to tolerate or even celebrate unusual juxtapositions of genre and source may reflect the diverse and protean syllabus of Latin reading texts that were encountered at school.[1] It is hard to think of examples of sustained, patient engagement with classical materials in Chaucer that are not heavily mediated by and filtered through earlier vernacular engagements with those materials. Chaucer's work emerges out of an echo chamber of literary voices, glossing, paraphrasing, tweaking and repackaging earlier classical materials. David Lawton has recently argued that '[l]iterary texts are all dialogues: their voice arises from and speaks to other texts, and it may stage its own movement as an interchange of voices on that and other, more crafted, levels … In that sense the craft of the writer is an *ars combinatoria* to do with voice.'[2] The classical texts engaged with by Chaucer are only one strand in this colourful tapestry of multi-vocal and multi-lingual narrative threads.

The possible exception to this is Chaucer's pervasive and recursive use of Ovid, or at least of Ovidian techniques of narrativity and playful creation of conflicting narrative *personae* in different works. But even here, an evanescent play of voice is fundamental to his appreciation of what he could learn from Ovid. Ovid allowed Chaucer to find lots of other voices, none of them his own. Ovid haunts contemporary assessments of Chaucer, perhaps even his own: the *Man of Law's Prologue* has him comically patronising Chaucer with a checklist of his literary output that he says almost outdoes Ovid's:

> … But nathelees, certeyn,
> I kan right now no thrifty tale seyn
> That Chaucer, thogh he kan but lewedly
> On metres and on rymyng craftily,
> Hath seyd hem in swich Englissh as he kan
> Of olde tyme, as knoweth many a man;
> And if he have noght seyd hem, leve brother,
> In o book, he hath seyd hem in another.
> For he hath toold of loveris up and doun
> Mo than Ovide made of mencioun
> In his Episteles, that been ful olde.
> What sholde I tellen hem, syn they been tolde?
> (*CT*, I.45–56)

The complexity of Chaucer's cultural engagement with Ovid is made clear in this passage. The fact that he has made tales of lovers 'Mo than Ovide made of mencioun' draws our attention to the augmentative as well as the imitative dimension of medieval narrative on these themes. Ovid provides a way of talking about such topics, but the work of literary expansion and elaboration goes on.

Chaucer's 'large volume' (the *Legend of Good Women*) encourages good love, just as many medieval commentators and moralists saw Ovid's epistles as doing. But, in a clear reference back to the criticisms of the God of Love in the prologue to that poem, the Man of Law remarks that Chaucer avoids stories that give a 'wikke ensample' (*CT*, II.78) of immoral love and sexual violence.

The Chaucerian popularity of the complaint or lament as the genre of disempowerment for both male and female speakers may derive some of its impetus from medieval readings of the *Heroides* and *Metamorphoses* that saw them creating a feminine space for male readers to think through and in. The representation of thoughtful and aspiringly autonomous women in such Ovidian imitations as *Pamphilus* and in the carefully gendered voices of Chaucerian narration may be linked. Ovid, or perhaps the medieval commentaries on him, taught Chaucer how to 'do the police in different voices'. 'Antiquity's proximity and yet also difference gave medieval poets a way of thinking otherwise, imagining something outside their ideological envelope.'[3] Chaucer embraces this wholeheartedly in his disciplined and richly imagined creation of self-contained pagan worlds in the *Knight's Tale* and *Troilus and Criseyde*. But that imaginative alterity is shot through by Chaucer's deep imbrication in the textures and techniques of contemporary medieval vernacular story-telling, which has almost always already begun that process in their own narratives.

Chaucer's elaborately mannered gestures of submission at the end of *Troilus and Criseyde* when he orders 'litel myn tragedye' (*Tr*, v.1786) to kiss the steps where 'Virgile, Ovide, Omer, Lucan, and Stace' (1792) have passed, is rather conventional, reminiscent of Dante's praise of the 'bella scuola'. Yet the phrase 'litel myn tragedye' deliberately echoes Dante's Virgil, who describes the *Aeneid* as 'alta mia tragedia' (my high tragedy).[4] Chaucer is typically engaged in a multi-lingual act of homage and respect. The canonised authors on the pillars in the *House of Fame* are not ranked chronologically or historically; they exist in an eternal and timeless narrative now, sorted more by narrative mode than by mortality and temporality. That Chaucer problematises and challenges that stasis in his model of the production of discourse in the House of Rumour does not detract from the restless and iterative 'nowness' in which narrative is endlessly generated there and is received in the palace of Fame.

When Chaucer's contemporary Deschamps calls him 'Ovide grans en ta poetrie' ('a great Ovid in your poetry') he is acknowledging his place in an endlessly self-refining cavalcade of literary emulation and admiration that transcends linguistic and national boundaries.[5] (He also calls him a Socrates full of philosophy and a Seneca of morals, and praises him for translating the *Roman* into English, and establishing a literary orchard planted with grafts from other countries.) Chaucer's imaginative poetics restlessly demonstrate a tirelessly recursive intertextuality between vernacular and Latin authors, between Latin philosophy and vernacular rumination, in a chain that stretches backwards to the limits of literary memory and imagination. Relatively little of Chaucer's translation of classical texts is direct and unmediated: rather it might be said that his art is infused with an all-pervasive classicism and an instinctive Ovidianism. That much is clear in Deschamps's denouement, where he calls Chaucer a 'grand translateur' ('great translator'). To describe Chaucer thus is not to historicise him or even categorise him. Rather it is to recognise Chaucer as an avatar of a timelessly playful and imaginative narrative art that replicates, reduplicates and remonstrates with the literary performances of other poets.

NOTES

1 See now Christopher Cannon, *From Literacy to Literature: England 1300–1425* (Oxford: Oxford University Press, 2016).

2 David Lawton, *Voice in Later Medieval English Literature: Public Interiorities* (Oxford: Oxford University Press, 2017), p. 136.
3 Rita Copeland, 'Introduction: England and the Classics from the Early Middle Ages to Early Humanism', in Rita Copeland, ed., *The Oxford History of Classical Reception in English Literature*, Vol. 1: *800–1558* (Oxford: Oxford University Press, 2016), p. 12.
4 Dante Alighieri, *Inferno*, 20.113.
5 Eustace Deschamps, *Autre balade*, in Derek Brewer, ed., *Chaucer: The Critical Heritage*, 2 vols. (London: Routledge and Kegan Paul, 1978), Vol. 1, p. 40.

CHAPTER 14

The French Context

Stephanie A. Viereck Gibbs Kamath

The medieval French poet Eustache Deschamps (*c.* 1346–1406), or Eustache de Morel, wrote more than 1,000 *ballades* with a remarkable range of subjects; even the overuse of mustard as a condiment makes an appearance. One holds signal importance for Chaucerian scholars: a *ballade* Deschamps addresses to the 'grant translator noble geffroy chaucier' notes his English contemporary's transplantation of the French allegorical *Roman de la Rose* to England and requests further poetic exchange.[1] As Ardis Butterfield has ably demonstrated, this unique record of French praise for Chaucer's writing that can be dated to Chaucer's own lifetime raises many unresolved questions: we do not know the extent of Chaucer's translation of the *Roman de la Rose* – only one or two of the surviving fragments of the Middle English *Romaunt* may be attributable to Chaucer[2] – and we also do not know what knowledge Deschamps might have had of it; moreover, the date, tone and even the meaning of particular words of the *ballade* are subject to debate.[3] Nonetheless, this act of translation not only reflects the importance of the *Rose* to Chaucer and his contemporaries but also indicates the poet's interest in multiple dialects, peoples and places that can be termed French.[4] The connection Deschamps establishes between Chaucer and the *Rose* thus offers a lens through which to view his extensive engagement with French literary culture. Chaucer read, emulated and adapted French works produced by a variety of major literary figures, not only Deschamps but also Guillaume de Machaut, Jean Froissart, Christine de Pizan, Oton de Grandson, John Gower and Guillaume de Deguileville (or Digulleville): all, like Chaucer, demonstrably wrote in response to the *Rose*, sharing strategies of claiming vernacular authority with this influential poem even when diverging from its model.

The *Rose* conjoins verses composed by Guillaume de Lorris in *c.* 1230 with a lengthy continuation crafted by Jean de Meun some four decades later. The nearly 300 medieval manuscripts that survive today indicate the poem's popularity; by way of contrast, there are fewer than 100 manuscripts of Chaucer's *Canterbury Tales*. The *Rose* recounts a quest for a beloved rosebud, framed as a dream vision, told from a first-person perspective and peopled by a host of personifications; its innovative form combines elements found in a range of French literary traditions: the love lyrics of the troubadours and their northern successors, the *trouvères*; the quest narratives of romance; the prosopopoeic philosophy of Alain de Lille's twelfth-century neo-Platonic Latin allegory; and also, especially in Jean de Meun's continuation, the satiric comedy typical of *fabliaux* and beast fables.[5] Chaucer's richly varied corpus drew from these same traditions, not only through the witness of the *Rose*.[6] Yet the *Rose* claims an authority that exceeds that of the French literary tradition, and its manner of staking this claim appealed to many later writers in the French and English vernaculars, including Chaucer.

The *Rose* is the earliest major vernacular allegory to feature a first-person narrator who is identified as both protagonist and author of the narrative.[7] This duality extends the interpretative energies typically centred on an allegory's protagonist to the author as well; the verses of Guillaume de Lorris insist on hermeneutic attention like that devoted to works of antiquity, featuring a Macrobian meditation on the nature of dreams at the outset and claiming to enclose the entire art of love in the manner of Ovid. Moreover, Jean de Meun's method of recording the conjoined nature of the *Rose*'s authorship both aligns the poem with Latin literary tradition and reopens the question of how the roles of lover, dreamer and writer relate. Jean envisions the God of Love weeping for the deaths of the greatest authors of amatory verse, as Love does in Ovid's *Amores*. After mourning Ovid, Gallus, Catullus and Tibullus, Love announces the impending death of Guillaume de Lorris and predicts the birth of Jean de Meun and his completion of the *Rose*, citing lines that have already occurred in the poem as the passage of transition. Love's declaration thus sets vernacular authors within an authoritative literary canon even as it complicates the identity of the poem's first-person voice. There are numerous complex voices within the *Rose*, notably that of the *Vielle* (Old Woman), who instructs the rosebud with purportedly experiential knowledge cribbed from Ovid's *Remedia*, and the duplicitous friar *Faux Semblant*, whose very name openly announces that he is not what he seems: Chaucer drew upon both as sources for his Wife of Bath and Pardoner respectively.[8] But the *Rose*'s strategy of calling interpretative attention to the authority and identity of the vernacular author shaped the later French literature read by Chaucer, who translates from these sources as well as the *Rose* in crafting his own self-presentation.

Guillaume de Machaut (*c.* 1300–77), the major French poet and composer of the fourteenth century, created an allegorical prologue to his extensive corpus. In the prologue, Love exhorts Machaut to write, but the poet has already pledged to use Nature's gifts to this end before Love speaks. Although Machaut's depiction of his artistic development emulates the *Rose*, Machaut displays greater interest in poetic skill than erotic engagement, not only in this prologue but throughout his works. The sleepless first-person narrator of Machaut's *Dit de la fonteinne amoureuse* finds surcease not in the expression of his own love but in recording the overheard love lament of another, who likens his sufferings to those described by the Ovidian myth of Alcyone; the lover is his patron, and the marvellous element of this narrative is not love itself, but rather the narrator's ability to furnish a perfect record of the patron's love when requested. The same strategic presentation of the poet as witness to lovers' laments and the centrality of a patron figure recur in Machaut's *Jugement dou Roy de Behaingne*. His *Remede de fortune* is another notable example of how the poet queries and displaces ownership of emotion and text. Chaucer borrowed much from Machaut, perhaps most markedly in his *Book of the Duchess*; beyond particular elements, such as the retelling of Alcyone's story and the overheard complaint of the Black Knight, Chaucer adopts a poetic voice laying claim to a literary inheritance from classical myth as well as the *Rose* but doing so as obliquely as his predecessor.

Chaucer's corpus, including his *Book of the Duchess*, also reflects the influence of another emulator of the *Rose* and of Machaut: Jean Froissart (*c.* 1337–1404). Although best known today for his prose chronicles, Froissart also crafted a sizable poetic corpus, including lyrics, narrative *dits* and a chivalric romance featuring inset lyrics attributed to a patron (*Meliador*). Marion Turner's contribution to this volume notes the political closeness of Froissart and Chaucer as well as the direct debt of Chaucer's *Book of the Duchess* to Froissart's *Paradys d'amours*; the similar opening lines of both poems represent innovative, emphatic use of the first-person voice in their respective vernaculars and they also share the addition of a newly named character to Ovid's myth of Morpheus.[9] Froissart, in truth, goes beyond Machaut in his invention of pseudo-Ovidian materials as well as in his poetic worship of the *marguerite* (daisy or pearl flower); as in the *Rose* and Machaut's flower-centred poems, the thematic motif of this flower in Froissart's poetry symbolises the poetic expression of love as often as any particular beloved. Chaucer's first-person narrators are similarly more skilled in textual than erotic service, and Alceste of Chaucer's prologue to the *Legend of Good Women*, a patron figure for English literature, is memorably crafted through both mythic invention and the rhetoric of flower worship.

Eustache Deschamps, with whom we began our examination, contributed to the tradition of *marguerite* poetry as well; although differing from Machaut and Froissart in the sheer profusion and variety of his short lyrics, Deschamps also sought to identify vernacular composition as worthy of serious attention, notably in his treatise *L'art de dictier* (*c.* 1392). Chaucer's borrowings from Deschamps are less easily particularised, but he may have known the long narrative poem Deschamps left unfinished, the allegorical *Miroir de mariage*. The *Miroir* responds to the satiric elements of Jean de Meun's *Rose*, relating how the personified Free Will debates the question of whether he should marry; characters such as Desire and Folly wax enthusiastic, whereas Collected Wisdom condemns the idea. There are evident parallels in Chaucer's writings, not only in the local structure of the *Merchant's Tale* but in the English poet's recurrent interest in meditations on marriage and love.

Deschamps's *ballade* to Chaucer itself merits a closer look in relation to Chaucer's own compositions. The *ballade* suggests that the English poet's efforts to translate the *Rose* assert a claim of literary authority; Chaucer is addressed not only as a great translator but as an *Ovides grans*, for example. And the authority ascribed to the English poet depends on his identification with the personification represented in the *Rose* as controlling the poem's authors: Ardis Butterfield notes how Deschamps declares 'Chaucer is the earthly God of love in Albion, and the God of the Rose which he translates into "bon anglès" (good English).'[10] Chaucer's own depiction of his literary production in the *Legend of Good Women* prologue envisages the God of Love as a literary patron and judge, as in the *Rose*. Yet Chaucer's Love also represents the poet's English context, for the work he judges is Chaucer's own love poetry, particularly his *Rose* translation and *Troilus and Criseyde*, a pseudo-classical narrative based upon Giovanni Boccaccio's *Filostrato*, which also draws extensively from the *Rose* and the poetry of Machaut and Froissart. The defence of Chaucer's poetry against Love's harsh condemnation in the *Legend of Good Women* prologue represents further creative engagement with the *Rose* tradition. The French literary context of Chaucer's defender Alceste has been noted above, and Alceste's reference to Chaucer's *Boece* as a composition likely to ameliorate Love's judgement would have entertained an audience able to recall that the vernacular translation of Boethius is precisely what the personification Reason urges within the *Rose* as a defence against Love's folly. Reason's praise for anyone who undertakes such translation refers indirectly to her author, Jean de Meun, who adapted the allegory of Boethius into Reason's speeches in the *Rose* and also created a full translation of *De consolatione* for King Philip IV of France. Chaucer's *Boece* drew from Jean's French translation as well as from the Latin Boethius,[11] a salient reminder that French served Chaucer as an intermediary to a wider literary tradition not only in the manner of the *Rose*'s claim to Ovidian authority, but also more practically, as in the *Physician's Tale* or the *Tale of Melibee*. Chaucer both translated from French compositions and used French translations to approach sources in other languages; he also, like the writers of the *Rose* and their successors, recombined the elements of first-person voice, myth and dream allegory to direct attention to the value and authority of his poetry in relation to his predecessors.

Unlike Love in Chaucer's *Legend of Good Women* prologue, we are not in a position to judge Chaucer's *Rose* translation, if indeed he ever completed this work. But when we examine the two best attested survivals of Chaucer's direct translations from French poetry, we find that the influence of the *Rose* tradition persists. Chaucer's *Complaint of Venus* both translates and lauds the French love poetry of the Savoyard Oton de Grandson. The *envoi* suggests that translated expression of passion meant less to the English poet than establishing his connection to Oton and the princely patrons addressed in conclusion. The alteration of the beloved object's gender from female to male similarly suggests the openness of poetic voice to reanimation by successive writers.[12] Chaucer's *Complaint* selectively engages with Grandson's collection of five *ballades* to craft a tripartite complaint. The skill Chaucer demonstrates in recasting French into English forms in his *Complaint* is equally apparent in the *ABC to the Virgin*, his only surviving complete translation from a single French source, a Marian prayer found within the *Pèlerinage de la vie humaine* of the Cistercian monastic Guillaume de Deguileville. Chaucer's translation alters the metre and rhyme of his source and ends at *Z*, omitting the scribal abbreviation stanzas, yet maintains Deguileville's stanzaic acrostic of the alphabet, a feat not undertaken in Dutch, German or Castilian translations of this lyric.

Even Deguileville's Marian prayer represents a French source inseparable from the lineage of the erotic *Rose*; Deguileville's *Pèlerinage* is the first lengthy allegory to acknowledge a debt to the *Rose* explicitly. In the *c.* 1331 version, Deguileville's first-person narrator-author declares that reading the *Rose* inspires his pilgrimage dream, recalling the meditation on dreams and interpretation composed by Guillaume de Lorris. In Deguileville's *c.* 1355 *Pèlerinage* revision, a malevolent Venus claims the *Rose* as her own work and critiques 'borrowed' elements within it, diverging from her purposes.

Deguileville's use of pilgrimage as an organising principle for this dream-framed allegory and two others (*Pèlerinage de l'âme*, *Pèlerinage de Jésus-Christ*) reconverts to salvific purposes the erotic pilgrimage narrative in Jean de Meun's conclusion of the *Rose*. Although notably different from the *Canterbury Tales*, Deguileville's allegory may have inspired Chaucer's own interest in the pilgrimage framework, as well as his interest in the interpretative connections of books and dreams that surfaces in the *House of Fame* and *Parliament of Fowls*.[13] The connection between Deguileville and Chaucer certainly seems to reach beyond the *ABC*; both write first-person accounts witnessing the ruling characters of the *Rose* (Love, Venus) laying claim to literary proprietorship, yet offering condemnatory judgements on the text or its adaptation.

The manner in which both Chaucer and Deguileville thus recognise yet diverge from the *Rose* resembles Christine de Pizan's strategy in her *Epistre au dieu d'Amours* (*c.* 1399), which purports to be a letter in which Love condemns the *Rose* for its defamation of women. The Italian-born Christine (*c.* 1364–1430), hailed today as the first professional woman writer in French, encouraged scrutiny of the *Rose* with a collection of letters and texts known as the *Querelle de la rose*, the first recorded literary debate concerning a French composition. Christine's narrative allegories also employ a first-person voice identified with the name of the writer, yet claim a new literary lineage for the vernacular writer of allegory and a new mythography for women. Despite the lack of definite evidence of interaction, '[t]he texts and careers of Geoffrey Chaucer and Christine de Pizan crisscross each other with dizzying complexity'.[14]

The discrete borrowings from, direct translations of and looser parallels with French literature observed in our brief overview extend across Chaucer's canon, challenging any rigid adherence to the notion of an early period of predominantly French influence that gave way to one of emulating Italian models and finally to one of crafting more thoroughly 'English' compositions. This 'three-period' model has been often criticised, but scholars have yet to generate a chronology for Chaucer's oeuvre that does not depend on the probable time periods of visits to Italy to date his works.[15] Nonetheless, French literary culture is increasingly acknowledged as a pervasive rather than juvenile influence on Chaucer's poetry. After all, the *Rose* was influential in Italy and may also have been influenced by Italian works.[16] The distinction between what is culturally English and French is similarly far from clear, particularly in light of the extensive Anglo-Norman and Anglo-French traditions, as Marion Turner observes.[17] Although the lines of influence are thus permeable, there are inescapable reminders of more sharply drawn battle lines in the Italo-French works of Christine de Pizan, who castigates English fickleness and praises Joan of Arc, as well as in the lyrics of poets at the French royal court, such as Deschamps, who laments the destruction of his home and village by the English. The Hundred Years War ranged poets sharing a literary culture on opposing sides. In the records of the Scrope–Grosvenor trial, Chaucer alludes to his imprisonment and release during the English siege of Rheims, at which Deschamps fought in defence, although time spent in captivity may have fostered rather than hindered literary exchange, if the later examples of Charles d'Orléans and the Duke of Suffolk are indicative.[18]

The trial records recount Chaucer's speech in French, and although 'Chaucer's' French here could represent the choice of the scribe rather than of the speaker, it raises the intriguing question of whether Chaucer composed in French. One surviving manuscript collection of fourteenth-century French lyrics includes poems temptingly signed 'Ch', giving rise to speculation about Chaucer's authorship, although the chance appears slim.[19] Still, it is not impossible that Chaucer may have been a multi-lingual poet; certainly, his compatriot John Gower wrote in French as well as Latin and English. Gower refers explicitly to Chaucer only in one version of his major English work, yet he does so in a way that reflects the *Rose* tradition: in the earliest recension of his *Confessio Amantis*, the first-person narrator-author-lover beholds Venus, both commending Chaucer for his compositions in her service and bidding him to make conclusion of his work. English and continental responses to Chaucer in his lifetime thus share their association of Chaucer with the *Rose* and its technique of authorising literary production through a first-person narrator-author depicted diegetically as in thrall to the imagined characters populating the narrative. In the eyes of his contemporaries, as much as in his own presentation of his corpus, Geoffrey Chaucer was a *grant translator* of the *Rose*-tinted tradition of late medieval French literary production.

NOTES

1 No. 285, in Deschamps, *Œuvres complètes de Eustache Deschamps*, ed. le Marquis de Queux de Saint-Hilare (Paris: Firmin-Didot, 1880), Vol. 11, pp. 138–40.

2 On attribution, see Charles Dahlberg, 'Authorship', in Geoffrey Chaucer, *The Romaunt of the Rose*, ed. Charles Dahlberg (Norman: University of Oklahoma Press, 1999), pp. 3–24; Simon Horobin describes an additional manuscript witness in 'A New Fragment of the *Romaunt of the Rose*', *Studies in the Age of Chaucer*, 28 (2006), 205–15.

3 Ardis Butterfield, *The Familiar Enemy: Chaucer, Language and Nation in the Hundred Years War* (Oxford: Oxford University Press, 2009), pp. 143–51; cf. Laura Kendrick, 'Deschamps' Ballade Praising Chaucer and Its Impact', *Cahiers de recherches médiévales et humanistes*, 29 (2015), 215–33.

4 Florence Bourgne's 'Chaucer: Poète multilingue, mais jusqu'où?', *Cahiers de recherches médiévales et humanistes*, 29 (2015), 199–214 nicely outlines both Chaucer's linguistic interests and the forms of French he knew.

5 Armand Strubel sets the *Rose* in context with other allegorical and literary forms in *'Grant senefiance a': Allégorie et littérature au Moyen Age* (Paris: Champion, 2002).

6 For more broadly focused study of medieval French and English literary interaction, see William Calin, *The French Tradition and the Literature of Medieval England* (Toronto: University of Toronto Press, 1994); for a seminal *Rose*-focused study, see Charles Muscatine, *Chaucer and the French Tradition: A Study in Style and Meaning* (Berkeley: University of California Press, 1957).

7 On the distinctive manner in which medieval manuscripts of the *Rose* mark this innovation with rubrication, see S. Huot, '"Ci parle l'aucteur": The Rubrication of Voice and Authorship in *Roman de la Rose* Manuscripts', *SubStance*, 17:2 (1988), 42–8.

8 On Chaucer's *Canterbury Tales* characters and their *Rose* counterparts with regard to Guillaume de Machaut's intervening influence, see Calin, *French Tradition*, pp. 328–30, 337–46.

9 On innovations in voice, see Butterfield, *Familiar Enemy*, pp. 271–5. For a more extensive study of Chaucer's relation to Machaut and Froissart, as well as Deschamps and Grandson, see James I. Wimsatt, *Chaucer and His French Contemporaries: Natural Music in the Fourteenth Century* (Toronto: University of Toronto Press, 1992).

10 Butterfield, *Familiar Enemy*, p. 146.

11 See A. J. Minnis and T. W. Machan, 'The *Boece* as Late-Medieval Translation', in A. J. Minnis, ed., *Chaucer's 'Boece' and the Medieval Tradition of Boethius* (Cambridge: D. S. Brewer, 1993), pp. 167–88.

12 On this alteration's significance in light of John Gower's *ballades* and the relations of French and English lyric more broadly, see Butterfield, *Familiar Enemy*, pp. 252–4.

13 See my *First-person Allegory and Authorship in Late Medieval France and England* (Cambridge: Boydell and Brewer, 2012), pp. 65–71.

14 Theresa Coletti, '"Paths of Long Study": Reading Chaucer and Christine de Pizan in Tandem', *Studies in the Age of Chaucer*, 28 (2006), 1–40 (p. 2).

15 On the debate, see my 'The *Roman de la Rose* and Middle English poetry', *Literature Compass*, 6 (2009), 1109–26 (pp. 1112–13).

16 Luciano Rossi suggests that Bolognese records of a Johannes de Mauduno refer to Jean de Meun, speculating that the poet's Italian experience may have influenced his *Rose* continuation; see 'Du nouveau sur Jean de Meun', *Romania*, 121 (2003), 430–60.

17 One worthwhile collection on insular French is Jocelyn Wogan-Browne *et al.*, eds., *Language and Culture in Medieval Britain: The French of England c. 1100–c. 1500* (Woodbridge: York Medieval Press, 2009).

18 Charles wrote extensively in French – and possibly in English – during his twenty-five years of captivity in England, at times under the watch of Suffolk. According to John Shirley, Suffolk wrote and copied French lyrics during his time as a prisoner in the castle of Charles's half-brother Dunois in France (1430–2). See John Fox and Mary-Jo Arn, eds., with Stephanie A. V. G. Kamath, *The Poetry of Charles d'Orléans and His Circle: A Critical Edition of BnF MS. fr. 25458, Charles d'Orléans's Personal Manuscript*, trans. R. Barton Palmer (Tucson: Center for Medieval and Renaissance Studies, Arizona State University Press, 2010), pp. xlix–l.

19 See James I. Wimsatt, *Chaucer and the Poems of 'Ch'* (Kalamazoo: Medieval Institute Publications, 2009); Elizaveta Strakhov, 'The Poems of "Ch": Taxonomizing Literary Tradition', in E. Steiner and L. Ransom, eds., *Taxonomies of Knowledge* (Philadelphia: University of Pennsylvania Press, 2015).

CHAPTER 15

The Italian Tradition

K. P. Clarke

The Italian influences on the work of Geoffrey Chaucer are very pronounced and have been studied extensively. Documents survive for two visits Chaucer made to Italy. Over a six-month period between 1372 and 1373, he went to Genoa, accompanying two Genoese merchants, Giovanni del Mare (known to the English as John de Mari) and Jacopo Provano (known as Sir James de Provan), both men of high rank in the service of Edward III. On this trip Chaucer went to Florence, and while the records give no indication of the purpose of the visit, we do know that he was there on the King's secret business ('secrees busoignes'). The second visit to Italy took place in 1378, where he went with a delegation, including Sir Edward de Berkeley, to Milan, negotiating with Bernabò Visconti and a man well known there as Giovanni Acuto, but more easily recognisable to Chaucer as his fellow Englishman John Hawkwood. These were two relatively important trips, with both economic and political dimensions, but it is also true that Chaucer was not a senior member of these delegations. Indeed, not a single trace of Chaucer's presence survives in any Italian archive, and Chaucer himself leaves no account of what he did there, whom he met, or what he read.

It is after these visits that Chaucer's work begins to show discernible traces of contact with the works of the century's greatest writers, Dante Alighieri (1265–1321), Giovanni Boccaccio (1313–75) and Francesco Petrarca (1304–74). *Anelida and Arcite* (generally dated to the mid-to-late 1370s) is an early engagement with Boccaccio's vernacular epic poem, *Teseida*, which undergoes a much more sustained reworking in the *Knight's Tale*. The *Parliament of Fowls* (late 1370s or early 1380s) and the *House of Fame* (1379–80) owe much to Dante's poem *Comedìa*. But it is a romance by Boccaccio, the *Filostrato*, that is most closely worked on by Chaucer to produce his own great poem, *Troilus and Criseyde* (early-to-mid 1380s). Into this poem he places his translation of a sonnet (number 132 in the collection known as the *Rerum vulgarium fragmenta*, or later more commonly referred to as the

Canzoniere) by Petrarch, and it is Petrarch's translation of the final tale in Boccaccio's great collection of stories, *Decameron*, that Chaucer translates and assigns to the Clerk to tell on the way to Canterbury. Chaucer also had contact with Latin work by Boccaccio, such as the *De casibus virorum illustrium* and the *De claris mulieribus*.

The decade of Chaucer's two visits to Italy was a crucial time for the development of vernacular literature in Florence. In 1373 city officials commissioned a series of public lectures on Dante's *Comedìa*, and Giovanni Boccaccio, the century's greatest Dante scholar (and himself a master of Tuscan prose), was chosen for the task. It was a highly charged civic attempt at a cultural repatriation of a Dante who had never returned from exile. Boccaccio began his *lecturae* in the Church of Santo Stefano in Badia, and continued until January of the following year, when ill health prevented him from continuing. The middle of the decade, in a sense, saw a close of the great age of the *Tre Corone* (Three Crowns) with the death of both Boccaccio and Petrarch, in 1374 and 1375 respectively. Benedetto Croce famously defined the century that followed as the 'secolo senza poesia' (century without poetry), and while the characterisation does not take sufficient account of the lively context of 'minor' poetry, it was not until the circle around Lorenzo de' Medici that we get what Croce would have called poetry. Indeed, 'minor' literary figures such as Antonio Pucci and Franco Sacchetti were well known in the city, and exchanged poems with Boccaccio, while Sacchetti wrote poems commemorating the deaths of Petrarch and Boccaccio.

It was with the appointment of Coluccio Salutati as Chancellor of Florence that the decade saw the inauguration of a new era, one of crucial importance for the city's incipient humanism. Salutati can be thought of as a pivotal figure in Florence's negotiation of its politics and its literature, both within the city and in its relations with the rest of Italy (and indeed the rest of Europe). He has been described as a key link between Petrarch and humanism as it developed and matured in the fifteenth century, but his attention was also directed at the vernacular, and he owned manuscripts of the *Comedìa* and the *Rerum vulgarium fragmenta*. He translated two of Petrarch's vernacular poems into Latin, perhaps even during Petrarch's lifetime. Chaucer's second Italian visit, to the Visconti in Lombardy in 1378, saw him enter an often-fraught context of diplomacy between Lombardy and Florence, one in which the literary vernacular was deeply imbricated.

Dante was born in Florence in 1265 to a family of minor nobility. His early life was marked by precocious literary activity in the vernacular. He wrote numerous lyric poems, and in these early years exchanged sonnets with contemporaries, such as Dante da Maiano, Chiaro Davanzati and Forese Donati. In the early 1290s, Dante put together poems with explicatory prose in an extraordinary work known as the *Vita nova*. It appears to have been prompted by the death, in 1290, of a woman named Beatrice, a female figure of great power for the poet and who would come to dominate the later epic poem *Comedìa*. In the late 1290s he became more actively involved in Florentine politics, whose ferocious factionalism left few participants unscathed. In 1302, during a visit to Rome as part of a Florentine delegation negotiating with the Pope, an abrupt change in government resulted in Dante being accused of corruption and subjected to an order of exile. He never returned to his native city, and the experience left an indelible mark on his work.

Dante spent his post-exile years in the north of Italy, moving between cities and courts: for example Forlì, the Casentino, Verona and latterly Ravenna, where he died in 1321. The first years of exile produced an unfinished Latin treatise – the first of its kind – on the use of the vernacular (*De vulgari eloquentia* (*c.* 1304–5)), and an ambitious, unfinished vernacular work of philosophy combining his poems with prose commentary, *Convivio* (1304–7). A Latin treatise on secular and papal power, *Monarchia*, probably dates from sometime between 1314 and 1318. But most of Dante's years in exile were occupied by the writing of his great vernacular poem *Comedìa* (begun not earlier than 1307, and finished not long before the poet's death in 1321). Told in the first person, the poem is divided into three parts (*cantiche*), and narrates a journey to the afterlife, beginning with a descent to hell, proceeding to purgatory and culminating with the poet experiencing heaven. It is written in *terza rima*, an interlocking rhyme-scheme *ababcbcdc*, apparently first devised by Dante, with the line in hendecasyllables (in *De vulgari eloquentia*, II.v.3, Dante had called this metre 'superbius' – 'most excellent' – both for its measured movement and for the scope it offers for subject matter, constructions and vocabulary). The poem enjoyed a very remarkable success and a wide circulation. Writers in the vernacular, certainly in the Trecento, had to engage head-on with this monumental poem. This was also the case for the century's other two great writers, Giovanni Boccaccio and Francesco Petrarca. While Boccaccio was much more open about his admiration for Dante, Petrarch was famously cool. But even in Petrarch's work the (sometimes powerful) traces of engagement with Dante are to be discerned. Giovanni Boccaccio was born in Florence in 1313. He was raised in a mercantile environment, his father, Boccaccio (or Boccaccino) di Chelino, working for Florence's powerful Bardi bank. Sent to Naples at the age of fourteen to learn his trade, Boccaccio soon developed literary leanings, which were greatly resisted by his father, who pushed him towards Canon Law at the city's Studio. The Neapolitan period was one of intellectual richness for the young poet: he went to law lectures delivered by the poet Cino da Pistoia and was surrounded by some of the most important cultural figures of the time, drawn to the court of Robert of Anjou with its splendid royal library. It is to this period that Boccaccio's earliest work is dated, such as the *Caccia di Diana* (*c.* 1334) and the *Filostrato* (1335). The *Filostrato* is a narrative poem in *ottave* (eight-line stanzas in hendecasyllables, with the rhyme-scheme *abababcc*), a metre thought to have been devised by Boccaccio himself for this poem. It is divided into nine parts (*canti*), and based on the *Roman de Troie* by Benoît de Sainte-Maure and the *Historia destructionis Troiae* of Guido delle Colonne. The *Teseida* is traditionally dated 1339–41, and thus was begun in Naples and finished after Boccaccio's return to Florence between 1340 and 1341. Written in *ottave*, it is an imposing poem of just over 9,900 lines in twelve books, telling the story of the rivalrous love of two Theban knights, Palemone and Arcita, for Emilia, sister-in-law to the Athenian ruler Theseus. Ostensibly, it responds to Dante's observation in *De vulgari eloquentia*, II.ii.10 that no Italian had treated of the theme of arms in vernacular poetry. Indeed, the autograph manuscript of the *Teseida* (Florence, Biblioteca Medicea Laurenziana, MS Acquisti e Doni 325) is also equipped with a detailed classicising commentary by Boccaccio himself, rendering the poem a serious enterprise, for both author and reader.

The work for which Boccaccio is most famous, the *Decameron*, was (probably) written between 1349 and 1351 in Florence. It comes, then, in the wake of the destruction of the Black Death, and is set squarely in the middle of that destruction: ten youths (seven women and three men) gather in the Church of Santa Maria Novella, and decide to flee the city and take refuge in the surrounding hills, where they tell stories on selected themes to each other to pass the time. After the *Decameron*, Boccaccio's work takes a decidedly Latinate turn, perhaps triggered by contact with Petrarch, the century's greatest Latinist. Over the following two decades Boccaccio would begin and continue to rework and revise a series of ambitious Latin works, such as the *Genealogia deorum gentilium*, a genealogy of the pagan gods; the *De montibus*, a geographical dictionary; the *De casibus virorum illustrium*, a catalogue of famous men; and the *De mulieribus claris*, a catalogue of famous women. During these later years Boccaccio acted on behalf of the city, especially on ambassadorial missions to Naples, Rome and Avignon, for example. In 1373 he delivered a series of lectures on Dante's *Comedìa*, and from the bitter tone of self-recrimination in several late poems at opening the poem's secrets to the vulgar masses, one can only conclude they were a roaring success.

Boccaccio's literary activity was not limited to the composition of his own work but also extended to its copying. Numerous autographs survive, such as the famous copy of the *Decameron* (Berlin, Staatsbibliothek Preussicher Kulturbesitz, MS Hamilton 90), as well as that of the *Teseida* (mentioned above). He is also a fundamentally important figure in the early copying and transmission of works by Dante and Petrarch. Three copies in his own hand survive of the *Comedìa* (Toledo, Biblioteca Capitular, MS 104.6; Florence, Biblioteca Riccardiana, MS 1035; Vatican City, Biblioteca Apostolica Vaticana, MS L VI 213), while Dante's *Vita nova* and Petrarch's *Rerum vulgarium fragmenta* are copied in Vatican City, Biblioteca Apostolica Vaticana, MS L V 176. This editorial and 'bookish' side of Boccaccio was a crucial aspect of the fourteenth-century circulation of his work and the work of Petrarch and Dante.

Francesco Petrarca was born in Arezzo in 1304, his father having been exiled from Florence two years previously (in the same exile order expelling Dante). In the hope of obtaining work at the papal court, his father, ser Pietro, moved with his family to Avignon in 1312, and Francesco grew up in its learned, international, cosmopolitan environment. After initial training as a notary, Petrarch studied law at Montpellier and Bologna. With the death of his father in 1326, Petrarch turned his attention fully to literary pursuits, the study of the Latin classics and the collecting of books. During this period, he worked on his much-anticipated nine-book Latin epic *Africa*, and his stature as a Latinist and humanist grew immensely. Petrarch struggled greatly with the *Africa*, which would remain unfinished, a fact the great humanist Coluccio Salutati despaired of when he eventually managed to get hold of it after Petrarch's death. In 1341, he was examined by King Robert of Naples, and chose to be crowned with laurel on Easter Sunday, 8 April 1341 (his *Collatio laureationis* marks the honour). His reputation was sealed with a wide range of Latin works, perhaps most famously his collections of letters addressed to contemporaries and to classical figures, *Rerum familiarum libri*, started in the early 1350s, revised again in 1359–60, and again in 1363–4; the *Rerum senilium libri* was worked continuously from 1361 until his death in 1374. During this time of intense Latin scholarship, Petrarch was also composing vernacular poems, and began ordering them into a collection of 366 poems entitled *Rerum vulgarium fragmenta*, for which two important manuscripts survive that were supervised and in part written by Petrarch himself (Vatican City, Biblioteca Apostolica Vaticana, MS Vat. lat. 3195, containing the final 'edition', and MS Vat. lat. 3196, containing the drafts). A remarkable collection of verse, they are a relentless, if not to say obsessive, labour of deconstructing and reconstructing the self, especially his love for Laura, whom he saw for the first time in Avignon, at the Church of Santa Chiara on 7 April 1327.

In 1352, returning to Italy from Avignon, Petrarch went to Milan and remained there under the patronage of the ruling Archbishop Giovanni Visconti, much to the dismay of his friends, including Boccaccio. This dismay was rendered even more acute because in 1350, while on his way to Rome for the Jubilee, Boccaccio had met Petrarch outside Florence, and the following year the Signoria sent him to Padua to invite Petrarch to take up a position in the city's Studio, an offer he politely declined. It is thus that Petrarch's absence from Florence was felt to be, in a sense, a pointed one. Chaucer's Clerk locates Petrarch outside both Florence and Milan, specifying that he learnt the story of his tale from the master himself in Padua ('at Padowe' (*CT*, IV.27), where Petrarch spent his final years and died. It was from here that he wrote his last letters, including a set of four letters that together would make up the penultimate book of the *Seniles*, one of which (*Seniles*, 17.3) was a translation of the final tale of Boccaccio's *Decameron*, the story of Griselda. It was a translation that would launch the story on a vast and highly fecund European circulation, starting with Chaucer's own Clerk on the way to Canterbury.

CHAPTER 16

The English Context

Marion Turner

Chaucer's *Book of the Duchess* ends with a series of multi-lingual puns (lines 1318–19). The Black Knight, who represents John of Gaunt, son of Edward III, rides to a 'long castel' (he was Duke of Lancaster), with 'walles white' (representing Blanche of Lancaster, his dead wife) on a 'ryche hil' (Gaunt was also Earl of Richmond). Lancaster and Richmond are English locations, but their names bear traces of England's colonial and colonised past. Lancaster was originally a Roman fort; the word *castel* came to Middle English from Latin, via Old North French and then Old English. Chaucer's suggestion that *lan* has its origin in *long* is mistaken – the word comes from Lune, a river in Cumbria and Lancashire with a Celtic name. The name reaches back to the years before the Anglo-Saxon invasions, reminding us of the Celtic peoples and language so comprehensively displaced by the Germanic invasions of the Migration Age. Chaucer's lack of familiarity with the River Lune is hardly surprising; indeed, he had less acquaintance with regions of England distant from London than he had with continental Europe. London is far closer to Calais, or even to Ghent, or Bruges, or Valenciennes, than it is to Lancaster. And Chaucer would certainly have found more words to puzzle him in the work of contemporary north-western poets than in the work of his French contemporaries.

French, of course, had been an important language in England since the Norman Conquest, and Richmond, in Yorkshire, was a legacy of that conquest. Built in the later eleventh century, it took its name from Richemont in Normandy and was usually attached to the dukedom of Brittany. A few years after Chaucer wrote the *Book of the Duchess*, Gaunt gave up the earldom of Richmond, which was returned to the Duke of Brittany, an ally of Edward III's against the French. These titles, Chaucer's punning references to them, their roots in conquests and wars, and the witness they bear to the embeddedness of the English language in other languages, show something of the complexity of the 'English context' of Chaucer's writings. An 'English' person at this time could lay claim to various ethnic and linguistic identities – indeed, in 1417, the English representatives at the Council of Constance claimed Gascon as one of the five English languages.[1] And back in 1354, Gaunt's father-in-law, Henry of Grosmont, the first Duke of Lancaster, had chosen to announce his Englishness in French: 'jeo sui engleis'.[2]

The hybridity and diversity of the literary traditions in England in Chaucer's era make it hard to define the 'English context'. Should Henry of Grosmont's book, written in Anglo-Norman, be considered part of this context? Should it include the three major poems written by Chaucer's English contemporary John Gower – or only the one written in the English language, excluding the Latin and Anglo-Norman poems? Should it include poems written at the English court, for the King and Queen of England, even though these poems were written in French, by Hainault poets?

It is hard to see how poems by the Hainault poets Jean Froissart and Jean de la Mote, written under the patronage of the English crown, could be primarily part of the 'French context', even though their poems are written in the French language. Both these writers were attached to Queen Philippa's entourage. De la Mote came to England with Philippa of Hainault in 1328; during the next fifteen years, he was awarded a generous annuity by Edward III, wrote an elegiac poem for Philippa on the death of her father, and entertained the King as a minstrel at Eltham.[3] He was involved in a sharp exchange of poems with the French poet Philippe de la Vitry, who criticised him for serving the English King. De la Mote's response was to assert the value of serving in England, and to declare (in French) that he had nothing to do with France: 'Ne je ne sui point de la nacion / De terre en Grec Gaulle' ('And I in no way belong to the nation / Of the Land in Greek called Gaul') (*La response*, lines 9–10).[4] Froissart, also from Hainault, spent several years in England in the 1360s and composed many of his works while in royal service. For Chaucer, poems by de la Mote and Froissart might have had the same kind of status as, for instance, Gower's *Mirour de l'homme*: these were poems written in an English context but in the French language. French and its dialects were not the exclusive possessions of the inhabitants of France; to write in French was a normal thing for people in England, including English people, to do.

The relative statuses of French and English, however, were going through a time of change. The court poets of Edward III wrote in French, but by the early fifteenth century, Henry V and his family were commissioning poems in English by poets such as Lydgate and Hoccleve. While the

Hundred Years War in some ways encouraged a more militant desire to use English as opposed to enemy French, French was not consistently seen as the possession of the enemy. Just as Gascon was claimed as an English language, so the English crown was asserting that it had natural dominion over French-speaking territories. But as the fourteenth century wore on, English was being used in more and more areas of government and law; religious, historical, scientific and philosophical texts were increasingly being translated into English; vernacular theology, mysticism and Bible translation flourished (controversially); and English established itself as the pre-eminent literary language for English writers who might previously have chosen to write in Latin or French.

Much literature in English was translated from other languages and bore the linguistic traces of those source texts in word-borrowings and coinages, and sometimes in syntactical structures too. The author of the General Prologue to the English Wycliffite Bible, for instance, writes in Latinate cadences, with Latinate word order and diction.[5] Both Chaucer and his contemporaries and predecessors borrowed words extensively from Romance languages. And some poets wrote macaronic verse incorporating more than one language; we might think of lyrics such as 'Of one that is so fair and bright', which is in Latin and English, with two separate rhyme-schemes for the two languages.

The English context, then, is utterly dependent on other contexts, in particular on the Latin and French texts that formed its foundations. Many of the 'native' English romances mocked so relentlessly by Chaucer in *Sir Thopas*, for instance, came from Anglo-Norman sources. Equally, the hugely popular *Mandeville's Travels* was first written in Anglo-Norman and then translated into English. Just as the English language was a hybrid and derivative entity, so literature in English did not come from a native tradition untouched by the literature of other languages and countries; on the contrary, it is impossible to separate the English context from its broader European heritage.

The range of literature in English produced both before and during Chaucer's lifetime is showcased in fourteenth-century manuscripts such as the Vernon or Auchinleck manuscripts, both of which contain a dazzling range of texts written in English. Chaucer may even have had access to the Auchinleck manuscript; it certainly contains many texts with which he was familiar.[6] It includes hagiography, didactic poems, chronicle, humorous poems, bird debate, satire and complaint, but it is known primarily for its collection of eighteen romances. Many of them focus on English heroes;

others draw on antiquity or the French tradition; some have an Arthurian theme; some are partly set in otherworlds of *faerie*.

The traditional way to talk about Chaucer's English context is to point out that while his poems are dense with sophisticated allusions to continental poets such as Dante, Boccaccio and Machaut, he chooses to lampoon his English heritage as 'drasty rymyng' that makes Harry Bailly's ears ache and is 'nat worth a toord' (*CT*, VII.930, 923).[7] Indeed, Harry coins the word 'dogerel' (VII.925) to characterise Chaucer-the-pilgrim's hilariously bad tale, set firmly in the tradition of English tail-rhyme romances. Chaucer here ostentatiously departs from his usual range of styles, using a metre that appears nowhere else in his oeuvre. The short lines, the tail-rhyme scheme, the use of formulae and the choice of diction all mark the tale's indebtedness to popular romances such as *Guy of Warwick* and *Bevis of Hampton.* Some comic aspects of the tale – such as Thopas's running away from combat, or the bathetic praise of his nose (VII.729, 827–30) – – directly draw on serious elements of *Guy* and exploit potentially silly aspects of popular romance.[8] Most of all, the jarringly awkward rhythm, set against the flowing pentameters that Chaucer commonly employs and his masterly deployment of schemes such as rhyme royal, characterises popular English romances as banal, their poets as incompetent.

Chaucer is merciless in his forensic dissection of aspects of the genre of popular romance, exposing its bare bones for ridicule. But it would be absurd to take this as his only or final word on literature in English (or on romance as a whole). His indebtedness to major authors writing in English is clear: in particular, he and John Gower, author of a dense and learned tale collection, *Confessio Amantis*, refer to each other by name in their texts. English romance was itself a diverse genre, including poems such as the hauntingly brilliant *Sir Orfeo*. The Auchinleck manuscript also bears witness to a number of other texts and genres in English that were important to Chaucer. For instance, the last poem in the manuscript is *The Simonie*. Written around 1321 (twenty years before Chaucer was born) this is a traditional estates satire, attacking the vices and follies of different levels of society, starting with the clergy, including monks, parsons and friars, and continuing through knights, squires, justices, bailiffs, sheriffs, beadles and merchants. Chaucer may well have known this particular poem; the important point, though, is that estates satire already had a solid tradition in English before Chaucer penned his masterful *General Prologue*. William Langland and Gower also wrote estates satire – Langland in English and Gower in French.

If we examine *The Simonie*, it articulates many of the same specific concerns that Chaucer (along with many others) highlights. For instance, the Monk's hunting practice is singled out:

> And þise abbotes and priours don aȝein here rihtes:
> Hii riden wid hauk and hound and contrefeten knihtes.
> Hii sholde leue swich pride and ben religious.
> (lines 121–3)[9]

Similarly, Chaucer emphasises the Monk's love of hunting, repeatedly calling him a 'lord', telling us about his greyhounds and his disdain for the idea that hunters are not holy men (*CT*, I.165–207). It is a theme also explicitly taken up by Langland in *Piers Plowman* and by Robert Mannyng in his mid-century *Handlyng Synne*. There was a varied English context for some of the things that Chaucer was doing; he had a wealth of vernacular precedents to draw on for at least some of his writings.

The Simonie is one of the few Auchinleck texts that utilises alliteration – in a flexible and broken-down form – as a metrical technique. While alliterative poetry remained primarily a northern genre, it was undoubtedly an important part of Chaucer's English context. Indeed, some alliterative poems were clearly related to the south, such as *St Erkenwald*, and Chaucer himself uses alliterative techniques occasionally in his work (*CT*, I.2605–16; *LGW*, F 635–49). Some of the most interesting and enduring poems of the later fourteenth century are alliterative. *Wynnere and Wastoure*, for instance, dramatises the tension between a stereotypically mercantile attitude to wealth, focused on accumulating and hoarding, and a stereotypically aristocratic attitude, focused on reckless spending and magnificent display. It addresses some of the greatest social and political concerns of the 1350s: Edward III's reliance on merchants to finance the war in France, the behaviour of aggressive lordly retinues, the provision of charity, the financial power of the Church. While it seems to draw a contrast between merchant and noble, the social reality was much more complicated than this. Nonetheless, there were certainly some differences and perceived differences in lifestyle and in world-views between these groups. And these were two sectors of society with which Chaucer was profoundly concerned as the son of a merchant who, as a teenager, entered the service of the daughter-in-law and the son of the King, living in a great household and fighting in the Hundred Years War as part of Prince Lionel's retinue. Chaucer went on in later life to work closely with London merchants while also maintaining important connections with the King's household.

Other alliterative poems such as those by the *Gawain*-poet bear witness to the sophistication of the alliterative tradition both in form and content. *Pearl*, an astonishingly emotive and powerful dream vision, is structurally exceptionally complex and intricate, bound together by concatenation words that unify each stanza-group and bind the end to the beginning, and containing an apocalyptically significant overall number of lines (1,212). And, while rhymed poetry comes from the French tradition and alliterative poetry from Old English poetic forms, it would be wrong to assume that alliterative verse is therefore a native form untouched by continental influence. Indeed, *Pearl* uses rhyme as well as alliteration (although Chaucer's Parson assumes that the two techniques are mutually exclusive (*CT*, x. 43–4)). *Pearl* also draws on the *Roman de la Rose*, the most important French poem of the later Middle Ages. *Gawain*, like most later medieval English Arthurian literature, is indebted to traditions emerging from Chrétien de Troyes's Arthurian romances.[10] As we see over and over again, English literary traditions, like the English language, are inextricably intertwined with other traditions.

This is also evident in another of Chaucer's poems: the *ABC to the Virgin*. Based on Guillaume de Deguileville's French *Pèlerinaige de la vie humaine*, Chaucer also makes use of specifically English terminology, such as 'bench' for 'court' (line 159). The very idea of writing an English Marian lyric is also an entirely normal thing for an English poet to do at this time. In the later Middle Ages, in the wake of the 'twelfth-century Renaissance', vernacular genres such as the romance and the lyric developed quickly in Europe and appealed to lay audiences, including women, often dramatising the experiences of people for whom family life was of central importance.[11] English lyrics such as *Stond wel moder under rode* allowed the audience to empathise with Mary as a parent, to see Christ as son or lover, not as untouchable divinity. This lyric even explicitly discusses the pain of childbirth, focusing on an extremely important but little-written-about aspect of female experience.

While Chaucer's lyrics often draw on French sources, they are also part of a huge body of English lyrics that can be found scattered over diverse manuscripts, and that bear witness to the popularity of these kinds of poems within wide-ranging sectors of society. Women (who were less likely than men to read Latin) were increasingly involved in reading and in patronising the work of vernacular poets, and the growth of vernacular literature was partly driven by women's desire to participate in literary culture.[12] Indeed, longer poems such as the F-version of the prologue to the *Legend of Good Women* may have found their immediate audience amongst women: Nicola McDonald has argued that this text emerged from a female-dominated courtly circle, where vernacular game-playing, riddling, and risqué discussion were the norm in the 1380s.[13] Chaucer mentions the Queen – Anne of Bohemia – in line 496. She, of course, was not herself English-born, but may nonetheless have been instrumental in sponsoring English writings.

Englishness is a topic particularly susceptible to skewed nationalistic commentary, but there can be no doubt that Chaucer was not 'the Father of his nation rather in the style of George Washington' without whom we would all be writing in French today (G. K. Chesterton). Nor did he single-handedly abandon declensions, linguistic gender and the inflections of the definite article (John A. Weisse). Nor was he 'the Bard who first adorn'd our Native Tongue' (John Dryden).[14] Chaucer's English context, along with his French and Italian contexts and his classical heritage, was vital and varied. These contexts gave him all kinds of building blocks. His achievement was to construct a dazzlingly complex edifice out of this rich and diverse set of materials. He was an exceptional poet, not because he wrote in English but because of his unerring capacity to knit together multiple, interlinked, multi-lingual sources and traditions to create new things of wonder.

NOTES

1 David Wallace, 'Constance', in *Europe: A Literary History, 1348–1418*, 2 vols. (Oxford: Oxford University Press, 2016), Vol. II, pp. 655–82 (p. 673).

2 *Le livre de seyntz medicines: The Unpublished Devotional Treatise of Henry of Lancaster*, ed. E. J. Arnould (Oxford: Blackwell, 1940), p. 239, available at www.anglo-norman.net/sources/ (last accessed 6 December 2018).

3 Ardis Butterfield, *The Familiar Enemy: Chaucer, Language, and Nation in the Hundred Years War* (Oxford: Oxford University Press, 2009), pp. 120–30.

4 James I. Wimsatt, ed., *Chaucer and MS French 15 (Penn)* (Kalamazoo: Medieval Institute Publications, 2009), available at www.lib.rochester.edu/camelot/teams/wjchms.htm (last accessed 6 December 2018).

5 James M. Dean, ed., 'Anticlerical Poems and Documents: Introduction', in *Medieval English Political Writings* (Kalamazoo: Medieval Institute Publications, 1996), available at http://d.lib.rochester.edu/teams/publication/dean-medieval-english-political-writings (last accessed 6 December 2018).

6 Edinburgh, National Library of Scotland, Advocates' MS 19.2.1, available in transcription and facsimile at http://auchinleck.nls.uk/ (last accessed 6 December 2018).

7 Thomas Tyrwhitt, *The Poetical Works of Geoffrey Chaucer* (London: Edward Moxon, 1843), p. lxvi; Robert M. Correale and Mary Hamel, eds., *Sources and*

Analogues of the 'Canterbury Tales', 2 vols. (Cambridge: D. S. Brewer, 2005), Vol. II, pp. 650–1.
8 Correale and Hamel, *Sources*, pp. 664, 685.
9 Dean, *Medieval English Political Writings*.
10 Ad Putter, *'Sir Gawain and the Green Knight' and the French Arthurian Romance* (Oxford: Clarendon Press, 1995).
11 R. W. Southern, *The Making of the Middle Ages* (New Haven, CT: Yale University Press, 1953), chapter 5.
12 *Riverside Chaucer*, p. 1076.
13 Nicola McDonald, 'Games Medieval Women Play', in Carolyn P. Collette, ed., *'The Legend of Good Women': Context and Reception* (Cambridge: D. S. Brewer, 2006), pp. 176–97.
14 Christopher Cannon, *The Making of Chaucer's English: A Study of Words* (Cambridge: Cambridge University Press, 1998), pp. 4, 53, 14, 12–13.

CHAPTER 17

Chaucer's Competitors

Wendy Scase

Thomas Hoccleve, one of the first generation of poets inspired by Chaucer's example, praised the poet as 'the honour of Englyssh tong'.[1] Others followed suit, and Dryden's sobriquet 'Father of English Poetry' continues to modern times.[2] To be sure, there is a great deal of justification for claiming Chaucer as the founding father of English literary tradition on the basis of his embellishment of the language. Chaucer was the first English poet to write in iambic pentameter. He was the first to use the sonnet form in English. Troilus's letter to Criseyde (*Tr*, v.1317–34) is the first letter in English to apply dictaminal conventions.[3] Chaucer's works provide the earliest example of 1,960 words and 5,421 first uses of words in a particular sense, and Chaucer is the third most cited author in the *OED*, outranked only by Scott and Shakespeare.[4] There is no question that Chaucer won, early, decisively and enduringly, recognition as the founder of English literary language. However, this narrative of exceptionalism can become questionable if the context for his achievement is overlooked. Chaucer was one among many late medieval writers engaged in making English a language for literature. This chapter looks at the 'competition' Chaucer faced and finishes by considering how far the narrative of Chaucer as literary founder is modified when his work is considered as part of this wider context.

Chaucer's experiments with metre and stanza-form were ambitious and extensive. He set himself to the discipline of writing in English in some of the most challenging metres of continental poetry. These included the *formes fixes* of French lyric love poetry. At the end of the *Parliament of Fowls* some of the birds conclude the proceedings by singing a 'roundel' (*PF*, 675). This form required two rhyming sounds, which are introduced in the opening stanza and then interwoven in the following stanzas and the refrain (a repeat of the opening stanza). Chaucer's rhymes are 'softe', 'on-lofte' and 'ofte', and 'overshake', 'blake', 'sake', 'make' and 'wake' (lines 680–92). Many of his free-standing shorter poems are in the form of the *ballade*. This form was particularly exacting. Chaucer's *ballades* have three eight-line *ballade* stanzas that use three rhymes only, the third rhyme being repeated in refrain (the last line of each stanza), followed in some cases by a shorter *envoi* that concludes with a couplet on the third rhyme-sound. *Truth*, for example, rhymes on the sounds *-esse*, *-al* and *-ede*. Chaucer sometimes set himself the even more exacting task of sequencing *ballades*, for example in *Fortune*, where the plaintiff's case and Fortune's response and their counter-responses are sequenced in three *ballades* and an *envoi*. Chaucer evidently also attempted to write virelays in English (*LGW*, F 423), though no examples by him survive.

Chaucer invites us to compare his achievement with those of continental models. One example must suffice. In his *Complaint of Venus*, another *ballade* sequence, he apologises for his 'litel suffisaunce' (*Ven*, 75) in composing, blaming his shortcomings partly on the infirmities of age and partly on 'the skarsite' of rhyme in English, which, he says, make it very burdensome to follow the 'curiosite' (*Ven*, 80–1) of his model, the illustrious French poet Oto de Grandson. Although Chaucer led the way in bringing such fixed continental forms into English, he was not alone in trying to write in English in complex and exacting metres and stanza forms. The anonymous dream vision *Pearl* arguably set the bar even higher. An example is this stanza, where the Dreamer calls into question the Pearl-Maiden's claim to be a queen in heaven:

> 'Blysful', quoþ I, 'may þi be trwe? –
> Dysplesez not if I speke errour –
> Art þou þe quene of heuenez blwe,
> Þat al þys worlde schal do honour?
> We leuen on Marye þat grace of grewe,
> Þat ber a barne of vyrgyn flour.
> Þe croune fro hyr quo moȝt remwe
> Bot ho hir passed in sum fauour?
> Now, for synglerty o hyr dousour,
> We calle hyr Fenyx of Arraby,
> Þat fereles fleȝe of hyr Fasor –
> Lyk to þe quen of cortayse.'[5]

As this example shows, *Pearl* uses a twelve-line stanza with the rhyme-scheme *ababababbcbc*, also called the *ballade* stanza, a demanding form requiring four rhymes on the first rhyme-sound and six on the second. Six rhymes are also required on the third rhyme-sound, and in this case there is an added complexity. *Pearl* sequences stanzas in groups of five, each of which ends with a variant of the same line and concludes on the same key word, meaning that the *c* rhyme-sound appears ten times and requires six different rhyme-words. In the sequence from which the example is drawn, 'cortayse' rhymes with 'Arraby', 'bayly', 'hyȝe', 'byȝe' (ring) and 'byye' (buy). An exception is the fifteenth stanza-group, which includes six stanzas. *Pearl* has twenty stanza-groups in all, thus 1,212 lines in the twelve-line stanza, reflecting the numerical properties of the heavenly Jerusalem as described towards the end. The line in *Pearl* is less exacting than that in Chaucer's *ballades* in that it is accentual, being based on four stressed syllables with a flexible number of unstressed syllables, whereas Chaucer's line is syllabic – the iambic pentameter – but the *Pearl*-poet increases the difficulty by using frequent ornamental alliteration to accent key words, for example in lines 10–11 above. We do not know the precise date of the composition of *Pearl*, but it has been convincingly argued that it could have been 1375–85 – precisely contemporary with Chaucer's imitations of the French *ballade* form, dated 1380–1400.[6] *Pearl* is by no means the only example of the use of complex stanza-forms in this period. At about the same time, poems in complex stanza-forms were being collected and sequenced in the Vernon and Simeon manuscripts: two huge, related, compilations of vernacular material.[7] There is no evidence that the authors of *Pearl* or the Vernon lyrics were aware of Chaucer's ambitious experiments or vice versa, but it is clear that Chaucer was not alone in attempting to demonstrate the potential of Middle English poetry to rival the virtuosity achieved in the continental vernaculars.

If we cannot demonstrate that Chaucer knew other examples of the Middle English *ballade*, it is clear that he was aware of other Middle English stanzaic and lyric poetry. His parody of the tail-rhyme romance in *Sir Thopas* suggests that he viewed such material as simply no competition – famously, the Host describes it as 'drasty rymying' (*CT*, VII.930) – while his association of the vocabulary and cadences of the Middle English secular love lyric with uncourtly and morally disreputable characters, for example the Pardoner and the Summoner (I.672–3), and even the pretentious chickens Chauntecleer and Pertelote (VII.2879), serves much the same purpose. Chaucer does, however, acknowledge the tradition of the alliterative long line with respect. His persona in the *Canterbury Tales* rejects the Host's suggestion that he recite a tale 'in geeste' (VII.933), while the Parson explicitly declares his inability to compose in the form: 'I kan nat geeste "rum", "ram", "ruf", by lettre' (X.43). Like the Middle English *ballade* stanza, the alliterative long line was a medium for ambitious poetic experiment in the period Chaucer was working. Particularly accomplished examples dating from the later fourteenth century include *Piers Plowman*, *Sir Gawain and the Green Knight* and the *Morte Arthure*.

A passage from the *Morte Arthure* in which Arthur and the members of the Round Table celebrate Christmas offers a good example of the challenges of the form and the virtuosity it enabled:

Then after at Carlisle a Christenmass he holdes,
This ilk kidd conquerour and held him for lord
With dukes and douspeeres of diverse rewmes,
Erles and erchevesques and other ynow,
Bishoppes and bachelers and bannerettes noble
That bowes to his banner, busk when him likes.
But on the Christenmass-day when they were all sembled,
That comlich conquerour commaundes himselven
That ilk a lord sholde lenge and no leve take
To the tende day fully were taken to the end.
Thus on real array he held his Round Table
With semblaunt and solace and selcouthe metes;
Was never such noblay in no mannes time
Made in mid-winter in tho West Marches![8]

The basic unit of alliterative verse is a line of flexible length but always divided by a caesura. Normally, each line has a minimum of four stressed syllables, two before and two after the caesura. Alliteration falls on the first three stressed syllables, serving to link the two halves of the line, while the fourth stressed syllable does not normally alliterate. The number of unstressed syllables is flexible. The line 'With dukes and douspeeres of diverse rewmes' illustrates the pattern. Although not demanding in terms of requiring adherence to syllabic metres and rhyme-schemes, the alliterative long line required a wealth of synonyms so that alliteration could be sustained on different sounds. Here the poet uses several synonyms that suggest magnificence: 'real array', 'noblay', 'semblaunt'. The form also encouraged use of specialised vocabularies, offering opportunities for the poet to display his lexical resources and his virtuosity in deploying them in the alliterative line, and to flatter the audience by implying that they would share his knowledge of courtly language. In this example the poet demonstrates knowledge of the specialised vocabulary of the various ranks of those assembled at court, such as the terms for degrees of knight – 'bannerettes' and 'bachelers' – and those for the higher nobility: 'dukes' and 'douspeeres'.

Chaucer may have chosen not to participate in the alliterative project but he made significant contributions to another important late medieval literary enterprise: the composition of Middle English prose of learning and devotion. Chaucer's *Boece* was the first of a number of Middle English translations of the *Consolation*, becoming sufficiently well known to influence later Boethian works.[9] His *Treatise on the Astrolabe* offers instruction on the use of a scientific instrument devised for calculations involving planets and stars. As a practical scientific treatise in Middle English prose it was unusual but not unique. Comparable and from around the same later-fourteenth-century date is a treatise on an instrument called the *Navicula de Venitiis* (little ship of Venice), thought to be so called on account of its shape.[10] Another instrument treatise from this period is the *Equatorie of the Planetis*, sometimes argued to be by Chaucer though this attribution remains in doubt.[11] If we widen the context to include all prose of practical use, the corpus expands considerably.[12] Chaucer's *Parson's Tale* belongs with a large corpus of Middle English prose associated with religious teaching and the sacrament of penance.[13] Much of the material in both corpora and indeed the corpus of Middle English prose more generally is undatable, but there is no question that Chaucer is working here in a vigorous and innovatory enterprise marked by several ground-breaking achievements, such as the Wycliffite Bible translations and related commentary and sermon materials,[14] John Trevisa's translations of the *Polychronicon* (a compendious historical work) and the encyclopedic *De proprietatibus rerum*,[15] and the anonymous prose *Brut*.[16]

The literary projects described above were carried out alongside the development of English as a language of administrative process.[17] It is possible that Chaucer employed a scribe who copied one of the earliest surviving petitions in English.[18] These documents display English equivalents for the conventional phrasing of petitions and letters, such as the opening salutation. Chaucer's translation into English of dictaminal conventions in *Troilus* is comparable with, and may be related to, this larger bureaucratic enterprise.[19]

This chapter has shown that Chaucer's radical experiments with fashioning a literary language in English were part of a larger enterprise. Chaucer made his own unique and enduring contributions to what was a larger movement. His contributions survived, and influenced and shaped English literature irrevocably. Much of his context is largely forgotten and little of it had an enduring legacy. Nonetheless, viewing his work in this context offers us fresh and unusual perspectives on it.

NOTES

1 Thomas Hoccleve, *Regiment of Princes*, in *Selections from Hoccleve*, ed. M. C. Seymour (Oxford: Clarendon Press, 1981), line 1959.

2 E.g. Helen Cooper, '600 Years Dead: Chaucer's Deserved Reputation as "the Father of English Poetry"', *Times Literary Supplement*, 27 October 2000.

3 Norman Davis, 'The *Litera Troili* and English Letters', *Review of English Studies* ns 16 (1965), 233–44.

4 'Top 1,000 Sources in the *OED*', *OED Online*, www.oed.com (last accessed 13 November 2017). Chaucer is sixth in the ranking of all sources, including multi-author sources.

5 *Pearl*, lines 421–32, in Malcolm Andrew and Ronald Waldron, eds., *The Poems of the 'Pearl' Manuscript*, rev. edn (Exeter: University of Exeter Press, 1987):

> 'Blissful [one]', I said, 'may this be true? Do not be displeased if I speak error. Are you the queen of heaven, that all this world should honour? We believe that of Mary from whom grace grew, who bore a child, flower of the virgin. Who might remove the crown from her unless she surpassed her in favour? Now on account of the uniqueness of her sweetness we call her the phoenix of Arabia, which flew without peer from her creator, just like the queen of courtesy.'

6 Susanna Fein, 'Twelve-Line Stanza Forms and the Date of *Pearl*', *Speculum*, 72 (1997), 367–98.

7 Wendy Scase, ed., *The Vernon Manuscript: A Facsimile Edition of Oxford, Bodleian Library, MS Eng. poet. a. 1*, Bodleian Digital Texts, 3 (Oxford: Bodleian Library, 2011), fols. 407–12; John Thompson, 'The Textual Background and Reputation of the Vernon Lyrics', in D. Pearsall, ed., *Studies in the Vernon Manuscript* (Cambridge: D. S. Brewer, 1988), pp. 210–24.

8 Larry D. Benson, ed., *King Arthur's Death: The Middle English Stanzaic 'Morte Arthur' and 'Alliterative Morte Arthure'*, rev. edn, ed. Edward E. Foster, TEAMS Middle English Texts (Kalamazoo: Medieval Institute, 1996), lines 64–77:

> Then afterwards at Carlisle he holds Christmas, this same renowned conqueror, comporting himself as a lord, with dukes and peers of various realms, earls and archbishops and plenty of others, bishops and bachelors and noble bannerets that approach his banner, make ready when it pleases him. But on Christmas Day, when they were all assembled, the handsome conqueror himself commands that each lord should stay and not take their leave until ten days have passed. So he held his Round Table in a royal manner with courteousness and comfort and wonderful food. Such magnificence had never been displayed in midwinter in the western marchlands.

9 Ian Johnson, 'Making the *Consolatio* in Middle English', in Noel Harold Kaylor and Philip Edward Phillips, eds., *A Companion to Boethius in the Middle Ages* (Leiden: Brill, 2012), pp. 413–46.

10 D. J. Price, 'The Little Ship of Venice – A Middle English Instrument Tract', *Journal of the History of Medicine and Allied Sciences*, 15 (1960), 399–407.

11 *The Equatorie of the Planetis*, ed. D. J. Price (Cambridge: Cambridge University Press, 1955); Kari Anne Rand, *The Authorship of the 'Equatorie of the Planetis'* (Cambridge: Cambridge: D. S. Brewer, 1993).

12 Laurel Braswell, 'Utilitarian and Scientific Prose', in A. S. G. Edwards, ed., *Middle English Prose: A Critical Guide to Major Authors and Genres* (New Brunswick, NJ: Rutgers University Press, 1984), pp. 337–87.

13 Alexandra Barrett, 'Works of Religious Instruction', in Edwards, *Middle English Prose*, pp. 412–31.

14 Anne Hudson, ed., *Selections from English Wycliffite Writings* (Cambridge: Cambridge University Press, 1978).

15 John Trevisa, *On the Properties of Things: John Trevisa's Translation of Bartholomaeus Anglicus's De proprietatibus rerum: A Critical Text*, ed. M. C. Seymour *et al.*, 3 vols. (Oxford: Clarendon Press, 1975–88); Churchill Babington, ed., *'Polychronicon Ranulphi Higden monachi Cestrensis' Together with the English Translations of John Trevisa and of an Unknown Writer of the Fifteenth Century*, 9 vols. (London: Longman, Green, Longman, Roberts and Green, 1865–86).

16 Friedrich Brie, ed., *The Brut; or, The Chronicles of England*, EETS os 131, 136 (London: Kegan Paul, Trench, Trübner, 1906–8).

17 R. W. Chambers and Marjorie Daunt, eds., *A Book of London English* (Oxford: Clarendon Press, 1931); John H. Fisher, Malcolm Richardson and Jane L. Fisher, eds., *An Anthology of Chancery English* (Knoxville: University of Tennessee, 1984).

18 For the identification of the scribe, see Linne Mooney, 'Chaucer's Scribe', *Speculum*, 81 (2006), 97–138.

19 Wendy Scase, *Literature and Complaint in England 1272–1553* (Oxford: Oxford University Press, 2007), pp. 65–77, 177–9.

CHAPTER 18

Boethius

Tim William Machan

According to the fifteenth-century Italian humanist Lorenzo Valla, Anicius Manlius Severinus Boethius (*c*. 475–*c*. 525) was the 'last of the Romans, first of the Scholastics'. Whatever the truth of Valla's claim, Boethius did indeed lead a life marked all at once by political intrigue, public duty and intellectual accomplishment, ending with imprisonment (during which he wrote his greatest work, *De consolatione philosophiae*) and execution. Early *vitae* and legends offer many details of this life, though their reliability is always in doubt (e.g. the claim that the young Boethius studied in Alexandria), and for all of Boethius's prominence in the Middle Ages, few facts seem completely reliable. Even the reason for his seizure by Theodoric, the Ostrogothic King of Italy, is not certain. Some sources cite questions about Boethius's religious beliefs (unlike Boethius, Theodoric adhered to the Arian denial of Christ's divinity); others have doubts about his political allegiances, whether to Theodoric or to the Emperor Justin I, who at the time were contending over influence and authority. The formal charges raise other accusations: that Boethius practised magic, or that he aspired to become emperor. One thing that is clear is that upon his father's early death, Boethius had moved to the household of the influential aristocrat Quintus Aurelius Memmius Symmachus, who introduced the boy to literature and philosophy as well as to the power politics of late antique Rome. And it was Symmachus's daughter Rusticiana whom Boethius later married and with whom he had two accomplished sons – for all of whom he expresses admiration and devotion in the *Consolatio*. In and around ninth-century Pavia Boethius was already venerated as a martyr, and in 1883 he was beatified as St Severinus Boethius, with his feast day set for 23 October.

It was the benefit of his learning at Symmachus's house that enabled Boethius to pursue an intellectual undertaking whose ambition and explanatory rigour very probably would have impressed the scholastics of whom Valla speaks. For in his commentary on Aristotle's *De interpretatione*,

Boethius claims that his goal is to translate into Latin as many of Aristotle's works as he could find, along with Plato's *Dialogues*; to provide these translations with detailed commentaries; and in the process to demonstrate that on the most crucial philosophical issues Aristotle and Plato were in agreement with each other. That he failed to realise this ambition perhaps goes without saying. He was in fact able to translate only Aristotle's *De interpretatione*, *De topiciis differentiis*, *Praedicamenta* (*Categories*), and the sections on the prior and posterior analytics and the thirteen fallacies (*De sophisticis elenchis*) from the *Organon*, though it is clear that he knew other works as well, including the *Metaphysics* and *Poetics*. He also wrote commentaries on these Aristotelian works (only some of which survive), on Cicero's *Topics* and on Porphyry's *Isagaoge* (an introduction to logic), which he also translated.

To say that Boethius failed to realise his lofty goal, then, is to risk underestimating just how much he did accomplish. Limited in number though his Latin translations from Greek may be, it was substantially through these translations that the Middle Ages came to know Greek philosophy, for it was not until the time of humanists like Valla that Western Europeans had either their own access to Greek manuscripts or Hellenic skills to rival those of Boethius. Moreover, Boethius translated other Greek works and composed original academic treatises, though not all of these have survived. He claims to have compiled works on each of the four parts of the quadrivium (the word and concept are his creations). Cassiodorus echoes this claim, though only *De arithmetica* and *De musica* survive in something like their entirety; the work on geometry is fragmentary, and that on astronomy, which probably was in part a translation of Ptolemy's *Almagest*, is lost. Boethius also composed several original treatises on logic, and *Opuscula sacra*, also known as the five theological tractates, which deal with matters of faith, such as the Trinity and Christ's nature as both divinity and human being. And he did all this, at least in the *Consolatio*, with metrical virtuosity and a prose style that, while not exactly Ciceronian, has a grace, clarity and precision that transcend a great deal of medieval Latin.

It is *De consolatione philosophiae* on which Boethius's considerable fame in the Middle Ages rested. Purporting to be written while Boethius was in prison awaiting execution, the book offers, as its title suggests, the consolation that philosophy can provide in a tumultuous world of uncertainty, specifically to a man such as Boethius: learned, accomplished, successful, loyal, wealthy, civically responsible and above all (the work insists) innocent. Beginning with Boethius's verse lament about the injustice of his situation, the *Consolatio* consists of five books, each of which has alternating sections of instructive or descriptive prose (*prosae*) and emotive poetry (*metra*), the latter of which amplifies or extends the preceding arguments. The work is built around the fiction that while in his prison cell Boethius is visited by Philosophia, an imposing and imperious figure, whose garments are marked by a ladder illustrating the mind's ascent from practical matters to theoretical ones. In a dialogue the two review Boethius's success, his sudden downfall and his complaints about the world's unreliability. Philosophia assures the desolate and almost inconsolable Boethius that the same love that governs the heavens governs life on earth. And she voices the sentiments of yet another allegorical figure, Fortuna, whose only constancy is inconstancy and according to whom those (like Boethius) who agree to ride on her wheel to fame and success must also recognise that, inevitably, the wheel will bring them down. During the course of the first three books of the *Consolatio*, Philosophia systematically undercuts the value of all the worldly goods Boethius has lost; nobility, for example, is shown to be the achievement of the parents who acquire it, not the children who inherit it.

Having illustrated the weaknesses and indulgence of Boethius's self-pity, Philosophia uses an elegant poem about Orpheus's ascent from Hades, illustrating the need for Boethius (and his readers) to ascend from intellectual darkness to unity with God, as a transition to her own arguments about life, its triumphs and its disappointments. In an explicitly neo-Platonist framework, she stresses the hierarchical structure of the universe, the innate desire for all to do good and the need to transcend the vicissitudes of life. One all-encompassing order embraces everything, she says, and the closer individuals are to the centre of that order and the better they perform within their allotted cosmic status, the happier they will be. Turning to fate and free will, Philosophia, who by Book v has come to dominate the dialogue, explains that the former exists only to the extent that our limited capacities prevent us from viewing the universe as God does, in an eternal present. God's omniscience does not cause us to do things, she says, but only reflects his awareness of our choice to do them. Understanding all this, Boethius and his readers are urged to rise above petty concerns, live virtuously, and accept the love that unites the whole of experience with God.

Summarised in this way, the *Consolatio* might not seem particularly compelling. Its explanation of God's foreknowledge in particular has proved unsatisfying to some modern readers. Yet in the *Summa theologiae* Thomas Aquinas cites this explanation with approval, and in general it is difficult to overestimate the impact of the *Consolatio* on the Middle

Ages. Indeed, after the Bible and St Augustine's *City of God*, Boethius's work may be the most cited and influential in the period. As a set university text, it inspired lengthy commentaries by learned authorities such as Remigius of Auxerre, William of Aragon, William of Conches, Nicholas Trevet and others. Typically accompanying the *Consolatio*, whether marginally framing the text or intercalated with it, these commentaries explain everything from grammatical nuances to historical and literary allusions to planetary motion. Anyone who read the *Consolatio* in the Middle Ages probably read it along with one of these commentaries, and learned readers had ample opportunity to do so, for hundreds of manuscripts of the *Consolatio* and of the various commentaries survive.

Beyond this enthusiastic reception of the Latin text, thriving vernacular traditions also demonstrated the popularity of the *Consolatio*. From the court of King Alfred the Great emerged an Old English translation. Notker Labeo rendered it in Old High German, and diverse hands (among them those of Jean de Meun, author of the *Roman de la Rose*) in Old French. Also extant are medieval translations in Dutch, Middle High German, Italian, Catalan, Spanish, Greek and Hebrew. Chaucer translated the work into Middle English as the *Boece* (on which more below), as did the fifteenth-century poet John Walton and the sixteenth-century monarch Queen Elizabeth I. Judged by the number of surviving manuscripts – over twenty, and so more than twice that of the *Boece* – Walton's translation was especially popular in the fifteenth century. The indirect influence of Boethius's work was just as great. Gower's *Confessio Amantis* owes its dialogue format to the *Consolatio*, Lydgate's *Fall of Princes* and Hoccleve's *Regiment of Princes* use it for many of their sentiments, and Langland draws on its ideas and expressions in *Piers Plowman*. The image of Fortune's wheel alone appears in the *Fall of Princes*, Malory's *Works*, *The Awntyrs off Arthure*, the *Stanzaic Morte Arthure*, Henryson's *Testament of Cresseid* and elsewhere.

And what was never doubted in the Middle Ages (though it has been since then) was that Boethius was a sincere and devout Christian, worthy of veneration and deserving (eventually) of sainthood. If he nowhere mentions Christian doctrine or Christ in the *Consolatio*, everything he does say harmonises not only with neo-Platonism but with the thought of St Augustine. It is the consolation of philosophy, rather than theology, that Boethius provides; for the latter, readers might look to his *Opuscula sacra*, which in many ways are counterparts to the *Consolatio*, using the same principles of logical argument to affirm the dictates of belief. It is not surprising, then, that in *Paradiso*, 10.121–9 Dante not only places Boethius in heaven but describes him as a martyr and fellow exile.

Nor is it surprising that Chaucer, a particularly philosophical and learned writer, should have taken deep interest in Boethius's ideas, which are scattered throughout Chaucer's works. It is Boethius's views on true gentility that the old hag quotes to the young knight in their marriage bed in the *Wife of Bath's Tale* (*CT*, III.1109–1206), and his views on misplaced happiness, providence and fortune that the imprisoned Arcite expresses to his cousin Palamon in the *Knight's Tale* (I.1081–6). As in the latter case, or again at the end of the tale when, in his 'Prime Mover speech', Theseus voices Boethius's comments on the chain of divine love (I.2987–3074), Chaucer did far more than parrot the *Consolatio*. He rather used it selectively both to historicise his pagan characters and to show the limits of their thinking; the conclusion Boethius draws from what Theseus says is not that we should make the best of things in this world but that we must look past this world to a transcendent divinity. Boethian influence also appears in the *Book of the Duchess*, the *Parliament of Fowls*, the *House of Fame* and the *Legend of Good Women*, although in some cases it may come indirectly, through Jean de Meun or Dante.

Chaucer's most sustained literary use of the *Consolatio* occurs in *Troilus and Criseyde*, where he rewrites his Italian source (Boccaccio's *Il filostrato*) into a meditation on fate, free will, chance and human destiny by introducing arguments from the Latin text. Like Boethius, the poem's main characters are imprisoned (in Troy), and like him they seek philosophical explanations for the events that yoke them together and then pull them apart. When Troilus rides past Criseyde's window for the first time in Book II, causing her to exclaim 'Who yaf me drynke' (II.651), his appearance seems to identify their love as destined, just as much as the second time he rides past (II.1245–67), under the guidance of Pandarus's machinations, illustrates fate to be an illusion that human beings only partly understand or control. Troilus's questions in Book IV about necessity come straight from the *Consolatio* but with a literary twist reminiscent of the *Knight's Tale*, since it is again left to the reader to supply the answers that Boethius provides (IV.953–1085). Similarly, as carefully and thoughtfully as Chaucer expresses the views of the *Consolatio*, to the reader who knows these views Pandarus functions as a kind of anti-Philosophia, failing to offer any real consolation to Troilus (or the reader) and perhaps in the process raising doubts about the consolation that even Boethius can provide.

Chaucer engaged in more direct representations of the *Consolatio* as well. The five so-called Boethian 'Balades' (*The Former Age*, *Fortune*, *Truth*, *Gentilesse* and *Lak of Stedfastness*) are earnest, close and artful presentations of some of Boethius's central ideas, with *The Former Age* being a close rendering of parts of the fifth *metrum* from Book II. 'A blissful lyf, a paisable and a swete', it begins, 'Ledden the peples in the former age' (lines 1–2). But Chaucer's most painstaking engagement with Boethius's text is the *Boece*, a close prose translation of the whole of the *Consolatio*. In the best medieval academic tradition, Chaucer employed a range of sources in order to explicate fully Boethius's thought. He used a Latin text, though in a distinctly late medieval version known as the Vulgate. He also drew on both the tradition of interlinear glosses associated with Remigius of Auxerre and the commentary of the fourteenth-century Dominican Nicholas Trevet. And he had a copy of Jean de Meun's Old French translation, which provided a model for turning the entire *Consolatio* into prose.

For the variety of its sources, their length and the complexity of their ideas, the *Boece* is thus among Chaucer's most ambitious undertakings. In the Eagle's language from the *House of Fame*, the translation must have required many a night of Chaucer sitting 'also domb as any stoon' (*HF*, 656) with his Boethian materials when he returned home from a day of 'rekenynges' (line 656). For beyond being ambitious, the *Boece* is also accomplished, with its artistry measured less by modern standards of dictionary accuracy and more by late medieval ones of exposition and linguistic invention. Throughout the work Chaucer moves between his sources, using Latin-derived lexis within French-derived syntax (say), or following a close translation of the Latin with a looser translation from the French, or glossing classical allusions with commentary material. While lacking the verve and charm that have attracted many readers to Chaucer's poetry, the *Boece* bespeaks the engagement of a powerful mind with a powerful text, and it would seem to bespeak the translator's own sense of pride that on the few occasions when he mentions the canon of his works (in the *House of Fame* (line 972) and the *Retractions* to the *Canterbury Tales* (x.1087)), the *Boece* is cited by name.

Just as along with the Bible and Augustine's *City of God* the *Consolatio* was among the most foundational works of the Middle Ages, so was it crucial to Chaucer's own intellectual formation. Already in the *Book of the Duchess*, generally regarded as Chaucer's earliest extant long poem (composed around 1370), there are allusions to the falseness of Fortune that can be traced, ultimately, to the *Consolatio*; and even the late, short comic *Lenvoy* to Bukton, probably written in 1396, echoes Boethius's ideas on the importance of 'trouthe' and 'sothfastnesse'. Whether Chaucer wrote the *Troilus* and the *Knight's Tale* as he did because he already had translated the *Consolatio* and doing so encouraged his interest in fate and free will (as is often argued), or translated the *Consolatio* after he composed the poems because working with its ideas in his poetry made him want to understand the work better (as I tend to believe), may never be known. It is clear that as much as Chaucer was intrigued by poetic expression and the natural world, like many of his contemporaries he took significant interest in the scholasticism that Valla saw. That he sometimes expresses this interest in a characteristically Chaucerian way only affirms the importance of Boethius in his own thought. Indeed, the Nun's Priest may dismiss the ideas of 'Boece' on necessity, but in doing so he links them with two of the most respected thinkers in the late fourteenth century: 'the hooly doctour Augustyn' and 'the Bishop Bradwardyn' (*CT*, VII.3241–2). For Chaucer, finding a place for Boethius in the whimsy and intellectual *tour de force* of the *Nun's Priest's Tale* may be the highest compliment of all.

PART III

Humans, the World and Beyond

CHAPTER 19

Chaucer's God

Ryan Perry

> We know the good, for it is written. But God is not only in what is written … His commandments are the smallest part of Him. We may keep the commandments to the letter, and yet be very far from God.[1]

God, appropriately enough for the omnipresent creator, is everywhere in the works of Geoffrey Chaucer. Although Chaucer was not a writer of conventionally pious literature, a cursory glance at a concordance to his works will illustrate how ubiquitous are his mentions of the Christian Trinitarian God, whether as the one God, or according to his separable entities: the Father, 'hye God'; the Son, 'Jhesu Crist'; or the considerably less frequently individuated 'Hooly Goost'. Chaucer's use of the word 'God' to signify the Christian deity most often reveals less about the author's spiritual or theological engagement with the supreme being, and more about the texture of everyday speech in late-fourteenth-century England: 'God you spede'; 'For Goddes love', 'God foryeue yow', 'By God and the hooly sacrament', 'By Goddes bones', 'A Goddes name', 'For Goddes love', 'So God me save', 'God have yow in his grace', 'I prey to God that it may plesen.'[2] God is invoked in conventions of polite greeting and farewell; in gratuitous curses; in blessings, promises, prayerful incantations; and in all manner of hackneyed aphorisms, blurted at appropriate or artfully inappropriate moments by the people who populate Chaucer's fiction.

Despite the relative religiosity of the times, the sheer volume of invocations in the name of God suggest that such phrases contained relatively little force as conscious addresses to the Christian deity, but were instead units in the fabric of language as spoken by Chaucer's contemporaries. In his literary reconstructions of the linguistic tics of fourteenth-century English society, Chaucer's characters inevitably deploy such phrases in manners that relate to the speaker, or to the tenor of the tale being told. Harry Bailey's earthy, tavern-learned irreverence, for example, may be imputed from the stream of oaths that pour from his mouth, swearing frequently by God and by the materials, events and wounds pertaining to Christ's Passion in an inventive variety of ways. His blasphemous invocations of God are echoed in the language of other scurrilous and drunken figures from the *Canterbury Tales*, including Robyn the Miller, who 'swoor' to respond to the tale told by the Knight 'By armes, and by blode and bones' (of the Crucified Christ), and insists on telling his tale 'By Goddes soule' (*CT*, I.3125–8). This 'ydel sweryng' (VI.638), something for which the Host is upbraided by the Parson in the epilogue to the *Man of Law's Tale* (II.1171), is also practised by the three sinful 'riotoures' in the *Pardoner's Tale*, with such speech becoming a focus within the Pardoner's digressive sermon on tavern sins. The language of the Pardoner's doomed revellers unambiguously parallels the Host's own demented swearing immediately preceding the *Pardoner's Tale*, when 'Oure Hooste gan to swere as he were wood' (VI.287).

GOD WOOT

Other invocations of God hint at conventional lay understandings of the nature of the Christian deity, and to His relationship with creation. Variations on the phrase 'God woot' (God knows) are regularly repeated within the *Canterbury Tales*. On one level the term is rooted in the most basic theological understanding of the deity, indicating God's omniscience: God *woot*, because God sees all. In pragmatic linguistic terms, it serves for characters to emphasise the truth of a situation being described – God is witness to otherwise unverifiable events described by a speaker – as He is, for instance, to the suffering of the Wife of Bath's husbands: 'God it woot', she assures her fellow pilgrims with an implied grin, 'I chidde hem spitously' (III.223).

It would, in fact, be deeply surprising if the majority of Chaucer's characters in the *Canterbury Tales* did much more than refer to God in such humdrum ways, and were instead to enquire on challenging theological matters pertaining to God and His relationship to humanity. As he interrupts the order of tale-telling in order to *quite* the Knight, Chaucer's drunken Miller provides a comic reminder that speculation about God is not advisable for most people, and certainly not for the unlearned:

> An housbonde shal nat been inquisityf
> Of Goddes pryvetee nor of hys wyf,
> So he may fynde Goddes foyson there,
> Of the remnant nedeth nat enquere.
>
> (I.3163–6)

Attached to the Miller's bawdy homosocial joke about it being best for married men to avoid ruminating upon the unseen activities of their wives, is the understanding that it is unwise to 'been inquisityf' in respect of the divine mysteries of God.[3] There is an echo here of what was a common reflex in the contemporary religious education of laypeople in respect of difficult theological concepts – do not question, merely accept. The idea of 'symple soules' avoiding thinking too much about the nature of divine mysteries is one that is underscored in a meditative treatise penned by the Carthusian prior Nicholas Love, *The Mirror of the Blessed Life of Jesus Christ* (written in the decade after Chaucer's death).[4] Whilst much of Love's work is aimed at encouraging its audience to meditate on events from the earthly lives of incarnate deities (the lives of Jesus Christ and his mother Mary), the author is much more careful when dealing with heavenly beings, and with matters of difficult doctrine, such as the nature of the Trinity:

> Bot now beware here þat þou erre not in imaginacion of god & of þe holi Trinite ... study not to fer in þat matere[,] occupy not þi wit ... And þerfore when þou herest any sich þing in byleue þat passeþ þi kyndly reson, trowe soþfastly þat it is soþ as holy chirch techeþ & go no ferþer.[5]

If spiritual phenomena go beyond one's common-sense understanding of the material world – that is, if it 'passeþ þi kyndly reson' – then one must avoid dangerous speculation and trust in the teachings of the ordained officers of the Church. This is a dynamic Chaucer deploys in the *Second Nun's Tale*, where St Cecilia explains the Trinity to the heathen Tiburce in easily digestible lay terms when he queries how there can be one God and yet three (VIII.335–6): 'There nys but o God ... / ... of three how maystow bere witnesse?' This theme of lay simplicity in respect of the nature of the supreme deity is raised again within the *Miller's Tale* itself, as John the Carpenter frets over what he believes to have been the dire spiritual consequences of Nicholas, his scholarly boarder, attempting to discern divine secrets through the quasi-science of astronomy:

> This man is falle, with his astromye,
> In some woodnesse, or in som agonye.
> I thoghte ay wel how that it sholde be!
> Men sholde nat knowe of Goddes pryvetee.
> (I.3451–4)

Instead of considering the mysteries of an ineffable God – a being that from John's perspective is unknowable and dangerous to attempt to know – the Carpenter attempts to direct Nicholas to God incarnate, Jesus Christ, and specifically to the Passion, the biblical event around which most late medieval religious ritual and devotional practice revolved. 'Awak, and thenk on Cristes passioun' (I.3478), he immediately exhorts Nicholas. When, a few lines later, he advises 'Thynk on God, as we doon, men that swynke' (line 3491), he again appears to be directing the scholar away from God's ineffability to the comprehensible life of Christ; this is the version of God open for contemplation by 'men that swynke', those members of the social orders whose job it is to work for the benefit of society (as opposed to the orders of professional religious who were tasked with praying for the greater good and might engage in more sophisticated varieties of devotional contemplation).[6] The Carpenter's words thus suggest that ways of thinking about God might differ depending on one's social station and access to learning. Certainly, for the unlearned lay members of Chaucer's imaginary worlds, engagement with the idea of the heavenly God is often limited to characters' uttering basic formulae, whether ostensibly profane or devout.

GOD FORWOOT

Considerably rarer than the expression 'God woot' in the writings of Chaucer, and opening up a set of much more theologically sophisticated issues, is the expression 'God forwoot' (God foreknows). The complex philosophical implications of God's 'forwityng' (or 'purveiaunce') for the human world are something that clearly absorbed Chaucer, and it is a theme raised in a number of his writings.[7] Most vexed is the intrinsically related issue of the individual's capacity for free will if God has already foreseen future events. Are the actions of people necessarily constrained, predestined to a particular course, if God has already witnessed them? The issue receives sustained expression in the *Nun's Priest's Tale* when the tale's teller reflects upon Chauntecleer's decision to ignore his ominous prophetic dream:

> O Chauntecleer, acursed be that morwe
> That thou into that yerd flaugh fro the bemes!
> Thou were ful wel ywarned by thy dremes
> That thilke day was perilous to thee.
>
> (VII.3230–3)

The narrator immediately shifts perspective, moving from suggesting that Chauntecleer had the chance to avert calamity, to weighing up the possibility that he was impelled to take a certain course. The cockerel is perhaps destined, the Nun's Priest muses, to ignore his prophetic dream in order to fulfil God's foreknowledge of his seizure by the fox: 'But what God forwoot moot nedes bee, / After the opinioun of certain clerkis' (VII.3234–5). The Nun's Priest goes on to manifest Chaucer's impressive knowledge of contemporary scholarly contention concerning the issue of divine foreknowledge and free will, as he announces the 'greet altercacioun / In this mateere' (VII.3237–8). The text enumerates three alternative understandings of the implications of God's 'forwyting' (VII.3243) that might be understood as representing the differing views of Bishop Bradwardine, St Augustine and Boethius – authorities on the issue invoked directly by the Nun's Priest in lines 3241–2.[8] The possibilities listed by the Nun's Priest are: that there can be no free will – that God's foreknowledge compels a particular course – 'Goddes worthy forwityng / Streyneth me nedely for to doon a thing' (a position that can be associated with not only Bradwardine but also John Wyclif); that free will happens if God grants someone the opportunity to choose – 'free choys be graunted me / To do that same thyng, or do it noght / Though God forwoot it, er that it was' (an argument equatable with St Augustine's understanding); or that God's foreknowledge has no influence upon free will, 'his wityng streyneth nevere a deel / But by necessitee condicioneel' (VII.3243–50). This final perspective is outlined by Dame Philosophy in Boethius's *Consolation of Philosophy*, where she uses the term 'conditional necessity' in opposition to 'simple necessity'. 'Conditional necessity' describes something that happens (necessarily because God has foreseen it), but nevertheless through the agency of a person – as opposed to something that inevitably happens through its nature ('simple necessity'). The example of someone walking, in contrast with the rising of the sun, is used by Dame Philosophy to exemplify the point (here in Chaucer's translation): 'Ryght so is it here, that the thinges that God hath present, withoute doute thei shollen ben. But some of hem descendith of the nature of thinges (as the sonne arysynge); and some descendith of the power of the doeris (as the man walkynge)' (*Bo*, V, pr. 6.227–32). The past, present and future are to God an eternal present, and thus when He witnesses a human act it does not necessitate that thing happening in the same way as with the universal laws of nature. A person deciding to walk necessarily happens, because God witnesses it happening, but his witnessing of it did not compel the act of walking. Dame Philosophy's description of 'conditional necessity' in the *Consolation of Philosophy* is demanded in response to Boethius's own depressingly fatalistic cogitations on the implications of God's foreknowledge, with which he is unable to reconcile free will and is left only with the grim possibility of individuals being bundled towards inescapable destinies (*Bo*, V, pr. 3).

Strikingly, in the classical, pagan settings of *Troilus and Criseyde* and the *Knight's Tale*, it is this, Boethius's claustrophobic sense of foreordination, that underwrites the operations of the protagonists who appear to struggle against the aimless whims of blind Fortune and, in the *Knight's Tale*, against the machinations of pagan gods. In the scene in the *Knight's Tale* in which the tragic, oppositional courses of Palamon and Arcite are set into irreversible motion, Palamon yelps with the pain of love-longing as he spies the beautiful Emily from the window of the thickly barred prison cell. His cousin Arcite, mistaking their imprisonment as the reason for the groan, articulates his sense of mankind's utter impotency in a life already mapped out from birth:

> For Goddes love, taak al in pacience
> Oure prisoun, for *it may noon oother be.*
> Fortune hath yeven us this adversitee.
> Som wikke aspect or disposicioun
> Of Saturne, by some consellacioun
> Hath yeven us this, although we hadde it sworn;
> So stood the hevene whan that we were born.
> We must endure it; this is the short and playn.
> (*CT*, I.1084–91; my emphasis)

These men, along with their would-be lover, Emily, cannot steer their own courses even if they were thoroughly set upon taking a particular route – 'although we hadde it sworn'. They must meekly accept whatever comes – something repeatedly borne out in the dark plot-twists of this tale. In *Troilus and Criseyde*, in one of the author's late additions to his story, Troilus muses on free will and predestination as he considers his impotency in being able to prevent the impending loss of his lover Criseyde to the Greek camp. His speech borrows very closely, and at times almost verbatim, from Boethius's words in Chaucer's prose translation of the *Consolation of Philosophy*:

> For som men seyn, if God seth al biforn –
> Ne God may nat deceived ben, parde –
> Than moot it fallen, theigh men hadde it sworn,
> That purveiance hath seyn before to be.
> Wherfore I sey, that from eterne if he
> Hath wist byforn oure thought ek as oure dede,
> We han no fre chois, as thise clerkes rede.
> (*Tr*, IV.974–80)

Although they are characters painted within the classical pagan world, Troilus and Arcite are weighing up issues that ultimately pertain to contemporary debates in Christian theology. And whereas Boethius will have his fatalistic view counteracted by Philosophy's 'conditional necessity', there is no sense of mitigation against an inevitable playing out of history in either the *Knight's Tale* or *Troilus*. Indeed, although these stories have rightly been described as drawing upon Boethian influence, they only do so in as far as they represent Boethius's pessimistic determinism, whilst completely disregarding Philosophy's case for individual self-determination. It is not only universal laws that are inescapable necessities bound to God's foreknowledge, but specifically the activities of mankind; as the Knight announces within his tale, whether it be 'werre or pees, or hate or love / Al is this reuled by the sighte [God's foresight] above' (*CT*, I.1671–2).

It is difficult to be sure, as ever with Chaucer, what exactly his treatment of God's foreknowledge and the capacity for free choice (or lack of it) means in terms of the author's own beliefs. Perhaps he saw a menacingly deterministic world as artfully fitting for certain types of fiction, rather than necessarily representing his own understanding of this branch of theology. A strict sense of predestination might have seemed particularly apt in a treatment of the lives of pagans, and Chaucer may have thus utilised one understanding of foreordination to paint the pagan world in a certain light. The air of foreboding in these tales is intrinsically tied to that sense of inescapable destiny. At the conclusion of *Troilus*, the audience is moved from a depiction of the pagan past into the Christian present, with the author advocating the utter rejection of worldly values (values of the Trojan past, but also of his contemporary world). With the air of a sermoniser he recommends that his audience turn from their 'worldly vanyte' and focus their love upon God instead, and especially Christ, who 'starf, and roos, and sit in hevene above' (*Tr*, V.1837, 1844). There is little hint whether a distinct understanding of predestination applies here in the author's own contemporary Christian world or whether, despite an intellectual interest in the issue, he concludes with the Nun's Priest that 'swich mateere' is best left for clerks to debate (*CT*, VII.3251).

GOD IN A CRUEL WORLD

It is a question that ties comments upon the nature of God in fourteenth-century England to those still uttered in this cynical, postmodern, supposedly post-religious age. The question, ubiquitously blurted accusingly at sheepish clergymen in the wake of tragedy, goes thus: 'How could a loving God oversee such a cruel world?' The worlds Chaucer constructs in his fictions are frequently brutal and seemingly unjust; the turn of Fortune's wheel and the inevitable slip from 'welthe to wo' are rarely part of any discernible working out of divine providence, but are blind, cruel and seemingly characteristic of a universe devoid of mercy. This is especially true of the pagan worlds discussed above. However, the complaints in respect of cosmic injustice as articulated by pagan protagonists appear to be specifically apt within a contemporary Christian context. Palamon poignantly bemoans his fate after the release of Arcite from their shared prison, crying to his pagan deities: 'O cruel goddes that governe / This world with byndyng of youre word eterne' (*CT*, I.1303–4). Despite Palamon's appeal to the pagan gods, his subsequent soliloquy, complaining of unjustified suffering in the lives of good people, who potentially face an afterlife of pain (even after attempting to control worldly appetites in obeisance to the will of God), has universal relevance for pagan and Christian alike:

> What governance is in this prescience,
> That gilteless tormenteth innocence?
> And yet encresseth this al my penaunce,
> That man is bounden to his observaunce,
> For Goddes sake, to letten of his wille,
> Ther as a beest may al his lust fulfille.
> And whan a beest is deed he hath no peyne;
> But man after his deeth moot wepe and pleyne,
> Though in the world he have care and wo.
> Withouten doute it may stonden so.
>
> (*CT*, I.1313–22)

The references to divine foreknowledge, 'prescience' and the Christian obligation of 'penaunce' reveal that Palamon's words are intended to resonate beyond the pagan, fictional context of the *Knight's Tale*. Likewise, questions of divine justice are articulated by pagan characters: famously, in the *Franklin's Tale*, Dorigen complains directly to the creator about the fearsome 'rokkes blake' that form a jagged line along the coast of Brittany. This 'werk unresonable' – a ruinous creation defying human reason – has destroyed a 'hundred thousand bodyes of mankynde' to no discernible providential purpose (V.867, 877). The horrific implications of a cruel and unjust world are subsequently rendered ambiguous in a familiar Chaucerian trope when faced with concluding on a matter of difficult theology. The matter is left by the speaker, with a sense of dissatisfaction, to the theologians, the 'clerkes' – as happens in the discussions of foreknowledge in *Troilus and Criseyde* and the *Nun's Priest's Tale*, and in Palamon's musings on cosmic unfairness: 'The answere of this lete I to dyvynys, / But wel I woot that in this world greet pyne ys' (*CT*, I.1323–4). Theologians may argue 'that al is for the beste' (*CT* v.885), and Dorigen states that she will leave them to their arguments – '[t]o clerkes lete I al disputison' (*CT*, v.890) – but it may be that Chaucer's audience is intended to be left sharing in Dorigen's continuing unease in spite of scholarly attempts to reconcile destructive forces with a sense of divine justice.

The *Clerk's Tale* also carries shocking implications in respect of God's relationship to mankind. This tale, in which Griselda is subjected to cruel psychological torment by her husband and lord, Walter, might be read as an audacious theological thought experiment. It has long been recognised by scholars that one might see Walter as a God figure, and most have been just as keen to demonstrate the perversity of the idea that this is Chaucer's intention. Indeed, the Clerk, at the conclusion to the tale (following his Petrarchan exemplar), deliberately distinguishes between the torment inflicted on mankind by God and that by Walter on Griselda. Although humans face 'sharpe scourges of adversitee' that 'preeveth folk' (that is, hardships through which God tests human spiritual fortitude), the Clerk, citing James 1:13, tells his fellow pilgrims that God 'tempteth' not mankind – a term repeatedly used in respect of Walter's cruel testing of his wife (iv.1153–7). And yet, the very necessity of the Clerk's rejection of a potential comparison between Walter and God indicates the plausibility, at least to a non-clerical audience, of that parallel. Indeed, the subtlety of the distinction between how Walter 'tempteth' and God 'preeveth' might not bear too much scrutiny (and certainly, it is subjected to none when the distinction is aired by the Clerk). James Simpson has suggested that an allegorical reading of this tale collapses, because 'if Walter is a God figure, then God is pathological, even more so since he already knows the result of what he is testing'.[9] Perhaps this is so, but only if the author intended it as an allegory accurately reflecting the dynamics of divine relations with mankind. Chaucer's fiction, if anything, appears consistently to reflect a lack of certain knowledge on matters of difficult theology. His texts raise the knottiest of theological problems and then dismiss them without satisfactory answers; theological uncertainties are deliberately allowed to linger, and continue to be troubling for Chaucer's characters (even as remote 'clerks' babble among themselves, engaged in disagreements supposedly beyond the reckoning of layfolk). The *Clerk's Tale* might, as Kathryn Kerby-Fulton suggests in response to Simpson, be read as a 'deliberately incapacitated allegory', a story with a self-abnegating theme, in which the idea of a cruel God is raised and dismissed.[10] Certainly, a sense of deep unease remains after experiencing the tale, and perhaps this is in part due to the momentary plausibility of the suggestion. It is this gnawing sense of anxiety – borne from Chaucer's intellectual instinct to raise the most challenging and ultimately unanswerable questions – that could be said to be most characteristic of Chaucer's engagements with the nature of God.

NOTES

1 Herman Hesse, *Narziss and Goldmund* (Aylesbury: Penguin, 1976), pp. 33–4.
2 See Larry D. Benson, *A Glossarial Concordance to the 'Riverside Chaucer'*, 2 vols. (New York: Garland, 1993) Vol. 1, pp. 351–60.
3 For the term 'pryvetee', see *MED*, s.v. 'privete' for definitions. The term here relates to definition 3, '[a] sacred mystery, divine secret; revelation'.
4 Nicholas Love, *'The Mirror of the Blessed Life of Jesus Christ': A Full Critical Edition*, ed. Michael G. Sargent (Exeter: University of Exeter Press, 2005), p. 10.
5 *Ibid.*, p. 23.
6 For further discussion of this see Ryan Perry, '"Thynk on God, as we doon, men that swynke": The Cultural Locations of *Meditations on the Supper of Our Lord* and the Middle English Pseudo-Bonaventuran Tradition', *Speculum*, 86 (2011), 419–54.
7 For 'purveiaunce', 'purveien', see Benson, *Glossarial Concordance*, Vol. 1, p. 690.
8 For analysis of the three alternative perspectives see the discussion in Bernard L. Jefferson's seminal study, *Chaucer and the 'Consolation of Philosophy' of Boethius* (New York: Gordian Press, 1968), pp. 78–80; also E. W. Dolnikowski, *Thomas Bradwardine: A View of Time and a Vision of Eternity in Fourteenth-Century Thought* (Leiden: Brill, 1995).
9 James Simpson, *English Literary History: 1350–1547. Reform and Cultural Revolution* (Oxford: Oxford University Press, 2002), p. 319.
10 Kathryn Kerby-Fulton, *Books under Suspicion: Censorship and Tolerance of Revelatory Writing in Late Medieval England* (Notre Dame: University of Notre Dame Press, 2006), p. 349.

CHAPTER 20

Holiness

Marlene Villalobos Hennessy

Chaucer's works depict a vast, densely articulated landscape of holiness. Holiness is implanted in the very soil of the opening lines of the *General Prologue* of the *Canterbury Tales* as the eponymous destination of the pilgrims, who journey to the famously curative shrine of St Thomas Becket: 'The hooly blissful martir for to seke / That hem hath holpen whan that they were seeke' (*CT*, I.17–18). One of the few native words used in this invocation ('hooly', from Old English *hālig*), holiness is also embedded in both the indigenous English topography and the literary aesthetic of the *Tales* and becomes a topic that thereafter never disappears from the collection, sometimes permeating it to the point of saturation. Yet holiness is strangely everywhere and nowhere in the *Tales*: at some times overt subject, at others merely part of the everyday furniture of the pilgrims' stories, more often than not it is sorely lacking and painfully absent from the world, its human inhabitants, and presumed natural home, the Church.[1] Like Becket's shrine, holiness chimerically appears and then recedes into the landscape and social drama of the *Tales* as the distant, longed-for, supreme goal of the pilgrims, finally visible as an idealised reflection at the horizon of the *Parson's Tale*, 'Of thilke parfit glorious pilgrimage / That highte Jerusalem celestial' (X.50–1), yet always just out of view. Holiness proves to be as mutable, as many-hued, and 'chameleon', to borrow Keats's appellation, as the poet himself.

Indeed, in Chaucer's view holiness has a changeable hue and can be twisted and moulded at will – hence the Pardoner's sanguine self-description: 'Thus spitte I out my venym under hewe / Of hoolynesse, to semen hooly and trewe' (VI.421–2). Holiness all too readily lends itself to forgery, fraudulence and hypocrisy, and like the Pardoner's notoriously prolific relic, the 'sholder-boon / Which that was of an hooly Jewes sheep' (VI.350–1), Chaucer takes for granted that it could mean different things to different people at different times. Many scholars have shown that his critique of contemporary practices within the Church unmasks an English social context in which holiness was highly contested and politicised, had a transparently economic dimension, and was inextricably tied to discourses of reform.[2] Yet more troublesome is that with a chef's sleight of hand, Chaucer mixes orthodox and heterodox beliefs, genuine expressions of religious faith with humour and irreligiosity. The Pardoner's breezy allusion to eucharistic debates via culinary metaphor as a 'Lollard joke' is perhaps the most succinct example of this literary strategy: 'Thise cookes, how they stampe, and streyne, and grynde / And turnen substaunce into accident / To fulfille al thy likerous talent' (VI. 538–40).[3]

This chapter will propose that beneath these dazzling contrarieties, Chaucer's works implicitly suggest that holiness has an unchanging essence or reality apart from its diverse and often deceptive human appearances, and was instantiated in the Bible, in the Eucharist, in the person of Christ and His mother Mary, and in the saints. Holiness is also a literary category by which he classifies some of his writings and is a central aspect of his authorial self-conception (for example, *CT*, I.3176–80, X.1088; *LGW*, F 417–30). And although much about holiness in Chaucer's works remains disputed, elliptical or even contradictory, many of his images of religious devotion and popular piety are themselves situated in a broader cultural context than is usually recognised. Central to this context was the widespread veneration of 'holy matter': the body and blood of Christ and His saints.[4]

Chief among the saints who people the religious imaginary of the *Canterbury Tales* is Thomas Becket. His violent murder by armed knights in 1170 transformed him into a national and international saint whose embattled appeal cut across classes, continents and centuries. The grisly nature of his martyrdom made his material remains instantaneously accessible, highly privileged relics. When assassins cut off half his crown, the floor of the cathedral was famously stained red and white with his blood and brains.[5] Thereafter a tinted, chiaroscuro pattern emerged in which Becket's own physical matter would stand at the centre of his cult, a similitude of the water and blood that flowed from Christ's wounded side. Within hours of Becket's death eager souls bottled his shed blood and dipped fingers and shreds of clothing into it; later immersed in water, this diluted blood would become known as 'St Thomas's Water' or 'Canterbury Water', and people who ingested it reportedly experienced miraculous healing. Becket's blood began to feature prominently in his posthumous miracles, the numbers, grandeur and theatricality of which expanded his meteoric popularity. A drop placed in the eye gave sight to the blind; poured into the mouth it restored the dead to life. A dose of this surprisingly abundant liquid

Figure 20.1 *Ampulla* from the shrine of St Thomas Becket at Canterbury, Museum of London. This mid-thirteenth-century lead-alloy *ampulla* shows the scene of Becket's murder and has an inscribed frame that reads 'O[P]TIMVS EGRORVM MEDICVS FIT TOMA BOROR[VM]' (Thomas is the best doctor of the worthy sick). This pilgrim souvenir would have contained a mixture of holy water and, allegedly, Becket's blood.

was widely considered potent medicine for the sick, and *ampullae* filled with watered-down doses were sold in great quantities (Figure 20.1). These movable relics were depicted on pilgrims' badges, hung up in churches and hoarded within monasteries.[6] Even Henry II drank St Thomas's Water and received a phial of it when he made his own pilgrimage to the cathedral in expiation for his role in Becket's murder in July 1174.[7]

King and commoner alike sought intensely physical contact with Becket's material remains. Pilgrims smeared his blood on their eyes, and sipped it with their mouths.[8] His blood would remain the very special liquid at the centre of his cult up to the Reformation. Within two decades of Becket's death, Pope Urban III (1185–7) wrote a letter to the faithful proclaiming that the whole city of Canterbury was rubricated, reddened, and made beautiful with the roseate blood of the martyr.[9] Indeed, Becket's

Figure 20.2 Reliquary casket with scenes from the martyrdom of Thomas Becket, *c.* 1173–80, Metropolitan Museum of Art. This gilded silver box was designed to contain drops of Becket's blood, probably as dried flakes, which were gifted across Christendom. Made within a decade of his canonisation in 1173, the front panel shows the saint being attacked by armoured knights, one of whom slices into the top of his head, while on the triangular lid above an angel looks on. The glass jewel at the top is placed over red-tinted foil that is meant to reflect mimetically the precious blood-drops within.

blood flowed in the city's veins and circulated around the nation's pulsing heart. Drops or dried flakes of it were often placed in ornate metal-casket reliquaries, which diffused his *prima materia* across Christendom more widely (Figure 20.2).

The *General Prologue*'s opening lines assert that it was the saint *himself* the pilgrims sought, not merely the cathedral: 'The hooly blissful martir for to seke' (1.17). The saints, those exemplars of death-in-life, were strongly believed to inhabit their shrines physically through their relics: those bones, body parts, effluvia, clothing and other objects that came into contact with them (known as 'contact relics'). Relics at Becket's shrine included not only his corpse, but also his bloody hair-shirt, ecclesiastical garments, pelisse, cowl, shoes, belt and gloves. Perhaps the most potent symbol of Becket's living presence at his shrine was his blood itself, a substance that was active, renewable, not subject to decay. As Caroline Walker Bynum observes: 'The blood of Christ and of the martyrs cries out, forever fresh.'[10] This idea finds a fitting expression in lines from the *Prioress's Tale* about the murdered little clergeon, who is treated as a saint:

> Mordre wol out, certeyn, it wol nat faille,
> And namely ther th'onour of God shal sprede;
> The blood out cryeth on youre cursed dede.
> (VII.576–8)

The lines also reflect a popular medieval belief that blood sometimes possessed special agency: the body of a murdered person would bleed in the presence of the guilty, a variation on Genesis 4:10, which suggests that blood can 'cry out'. Becket's bloodshed, charged with his sacred presence, loudly proclaimed his physical continuity and survival.

The opening lines of the *General Prologue* suggest that 200 years after Becket's death and the height of his popularity, the saint's cult was still fresh, vividly alive – the stuff not only of religious fervour but also of poetic inspiration – the phrase 'Inspired hath in every holt and heeth' (I.6) an apt analogy for the saint's profound diffusion in English landscape and culture in the fourteenth century. For example, as Chaucer's pilgrims made their way on horseback out of the city on the road followed by all travellers since Roman times, they encountered the saint's indelible imprint on the countryside: 'And forth we riden a litel moore than paas / Unto the watering of Seint Thomas' (I.825–6). This named brook was located about 2 miles outside London, once the boundary of the city liberties, where it served as a landmark for travellers; in this instance, the 'watering' is a fitting signpost of the constant movement to which Chaucer's narration is sensitive. Other bodies of water across England were named for Becket, such as a well near his shrine valued for its medicinal properties. Indeed, Becket's holy matter stretched across the vast, unwieldly map of England, with a total of twelve holy well dedications 'from every shires ende' (I.15), but he was by no means the only saint about whom this was true.[11]

In Chaucer's England, the ways in which holiness was located in the natural world varied from region to region and era to era, but it was often found in such sacred wells and waterways, as well as in holy trees, caves and other topographies where saints were thought to have left their marks. For example, when 'sely John' the Carpenter in the *Miller's Tale* calls upon St

Frideswide, the patron saint of Oxford, he is accurately reflecting a locally inflected religious devotion (I.3449). In late medieval England, the great bulk of visitors to Frideswide's shrine, approximately 75 per cent of them, lived within 40 miles of Oxford.[12] Like Becket, Frideswide had a healing well connected with her cult and came to greatest prominence in the twelfth century; the Augustinian canons of her monastery had been inspired by the success of Becket's cult at Canterbury and actively promoted her, recording over a hundred miracles when her relics were translated in 1180.[13] John's invocation reflects her reputation as a healing saint, since he is worried that 'hende' Nicholas is 'falle, with his astromye, / In some woodnesse or in som agonye' (I.3451–2).[14] Another local touch is seen in the religious oaths sworn to Becket by both John (I.3425, 3461) and Alison (I.3291). Becket was especially revered in Oxford, which had a parish church, a hall and a fraternity named for him.

In contrast to the humorous fabliau context in which Frideswide is invoked, in the *Second Nun's Tale*, Chaucer soberly and eloquently celebrates one of the most venerated female saints in all Europe, St Cecilia.[15] The story of this early Christian virgin, her chaste marriage and subsequent martyrdom had been circulating in England since the Anglo-Saxon period. There were at least four English churches dedicated to her before 1700.[16] St Cecilia also plays a prominent role in the sophisticated theology of Chaucer's contemporary, the anchoress Julian of Norwich (*c.* 1342–*c.* 1416), who assimilates the saint's violent martyrdom to her own internalised devotional practice.[17] Cecilia is also invoked in the proem to Nicholas Love's widely circulated translation, *The Mirror of the Blessed Life of Jesus Christ*, where she is depicted as a model of devout reading: 'Amonge oþer vertuese commendynges of þe holy virgine *Cecile* it is written þat she bare alwey þe gospel of criste hidde in her breste … And so with a liking & swete taste gostly chewing in þat manere þe gospel of crist. She set & bare it euer in þe priuyte of her breste. In þe same manere I conseil þat þou do.'[18] Chaucer likewise embraces a hermeneutics of embodiment, but instead exults in the materiality of her martyrdom. He describes how the executioner boils her alive and, despite three blows, fails to remove her head completely, while a crowd collects her blood on sheets:

> But half deed, with hir nekke ycorven there,
> He lefte hir lye, and on his wey he went.
> The Cristen folk, which that aboute hire were,
> With sheetes han the blood ful faire yhent.
> (VIII.533–6)

This unapologetic blood-piety is starkly reminiscent of that which surrounded Becket's death. Moreover, Chaucer's embrace of orthodox Christian materiality here aligns his devotional interests with those found in a broad range of English religious writings by authors with whom he is not typically connected.

For Chaucer, as for most late medieval Christians of his day, holiness was instantiated in matter, present and manifest in shrines, relics, holy objects and the natural world. The material remains of Christ, His mother Mary and the saints were venerated all over England. Pilgrimage sites associated with Christ and Mary were increasingly popular, unbounded by temporal or geographical constraints, and Chaucer invokes several of these in the *Tales*, including the prosperous shrine at Hailes Abbey in Gloucestershire, famous for owning a relic of Christ's blood. In his excursus on the perilous sins of the tavern, especially swearing and gambling, the Pardoner invokes the holy blood by way of example:

> 'By Goddes precious herte', and 'By his nayles',
> And 'By the blood of Crist that is in Hayles,
> Sevene is my chaunce, and thyn is cynk and treye!'
> (VI.651–3).

According to a contemporary chronicler, when this relic was brought to Hailes in 1267 as a gift from Edmund, son of King Henry III, throngs of pilgrims wept and laughed with joy at its sight and crept on their knees in procession. In the opening years of the fifteenth century even Margery Kempe visited Hailes on one of her pious perambulations. Hailes remained a popular pilgrimage site up to the Dissolution and inspired miracle tales, monastic poems and even 'tourist literature' printed by Richard Pynson in the sixteenth century.[19] The very sight of this relic was said to put one in a state of salvation. Yet it was just one of at least twenty-three relics of the Holy Blood, which many considered to be the authentic, actual blood shed at the Crucifixion, scattered across Europe by the end of the Middle Ages. England possessed three other cruets of the precious blood, housed in shrines at Ashridge, Glastonbury and Westminster.[20]

The Pardoner's example illustrates that swearing oaths by the Holy Blood was commonplace, even if it was considered impious by figures such as the Parson (II.1170–1); John in the *Miller's Tale* likewise avows 'Nay, Crist forbede it, for his hooly blood!' (I.3508). The lines from the *Pardoner's Tale* also depict the practice of swearing on Christ's wounded heart and the nails of the Crucifixion, which were ubiquitous objects of popular devotion in their own right. Lyrics on the heart of Christ, the wounds, and the length of the three nails of the Crucifixion circulated widely, and some of these were illustrated and used as charms for spiritual protection.[21] Some English manuscripts include a drawing of a nail 5¾ inches long, sometimes thought to be the actual measure of the nails.[22]

Indeed, relics connected with Christ and His mother Mary were surprisingly abundant in Chaucer's England and often appear in his works in comic contexts. In the *Reeve's Tale*, when the clerk Alan struggles in the dark with 'hoote deynous' Symkyn (I.3941), his nameless wife cries out: '"Help! Hooly croys of Bromeholm", she seyde, / "In manus tuas! Lord to thee I calle!"' (I.4286–7). The Rood of Bromholm was brought to England between 1205 and 1223, part of the upsurge in relics after the fall of Constantinople in 1204, and was believed to contain a relic of the True Cross at its centre. According to a contemporary chronicler, this shrine at the Cluniac Priory of Bromholm in Norfolk experienced traffic as heavy as Becket's.[23] There are at least four surviving depictions of this Rood in late medieval English manuscripts, sometimes as devotional 'postcards' sewn onto vellum folios (Figure 20.3); these souvenirs were presumably distributed to pilgrims, who were also sold *ampullae* filled with prophylactic water.[24] The alleged apotropaic powers of this relic are also manifest in its alliance here with a macaronic tag from Luke 23:46, often used as a charm to ward off sudden death.

The Rood of Bromholm was just one of the ten pieces of the True Cross that were recorded in England at the Dissolution. St Albans owned the Crown of Thorns; Caversham Abbey possessed the bloody, pointed tip of the spear of Longinus; Durham displayed pieces of Mary's clothing; and there were no fewer than seven specimens of the Virgin's breast milk in medieval Britain, the most illustrious housed at the *über*-shrine of Walsingham in Norfolk. Marian shrines active throughout the fourteenth century include Ipswich, Doncaster, Caversham, Knaresborough, Worcester, Penrice, Westminster and Willesden.[25]

Chaucer inhabited a world thick and heady with images and objects of the holy, and he shows himself attentive to such materiality in his images of popular religion. Holiness is a subject that by turns he interrogates, mocks and celebrates, yet he always reveals it to possess more texture and complexity than a single perspective would allow. Like the magic mirror gifted to Canacee in the *Squire's Tale*, his works are fashioned 'by composiciouns / Of anglis and of slye reflexiouns' (V.229–30). One of Chaucer's unique powers as a writer is his ability to stand apart and gaze unblinkingly at each angle, holding these glimmering tensions in balance.

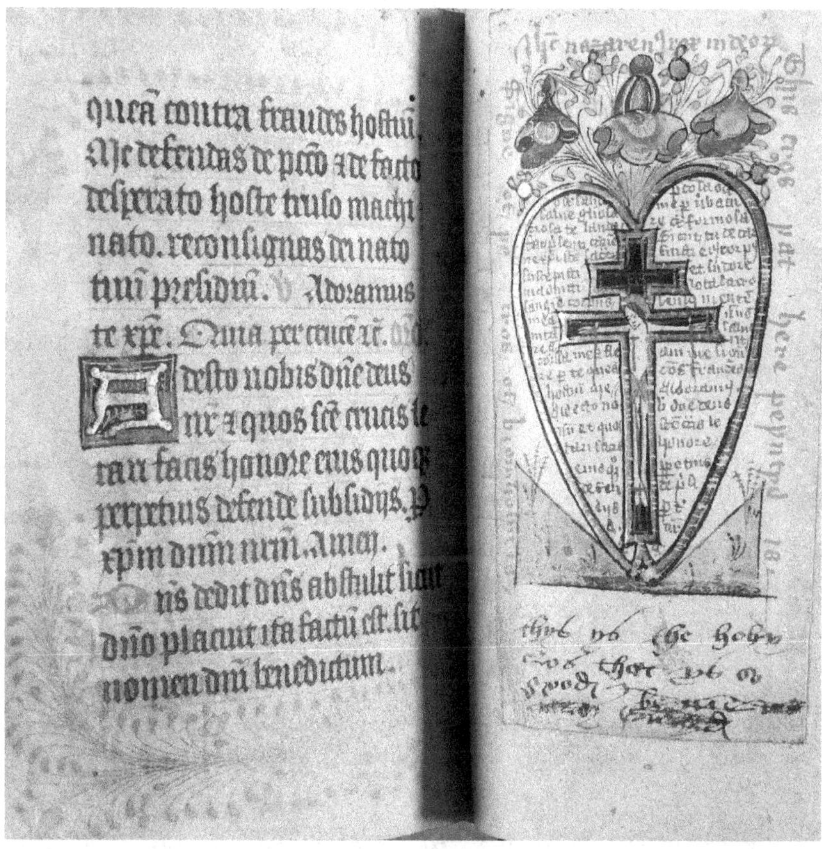

Figure 20.3 Devotional 'postcard' and parchment painting of the Holy Rood of Bromholm, *c.* 1490, pasted into the Lewkenor Hours, London, Lambeth Palace Library, MS 545, fols. 184v–185r.

NOTES

1 A similar point is made in Nicholas Watson, 'Christian Ideologies', in Peter Brown, ed., *A Companion to Chaucer* (Oxford: Blackwell, 2000), pp. 75–89 (p. 86).

2 See, among others, David Aers and Lynn Staley, *The Powers of the Holy: Religion, Politics, and Gender in Late Medieval English Culture* (University Park: Pennsylvania State University Press, 1996); Larry Scanlon, *Narrative, Authority, and Power: The Medieval Exemplum and the Chaucerian Tradition* (Cambridge: Cambridge University Press, 1994); and Andrew Cole, 'Chaucer's English Lesson', *Speculum*, 77 (2002), 1128–67.

3 See Alan J. Fletcher, 'The Topical Hypocrisy of Chaucer's Pardoner', *Chaucer Review*, 25 (1990), 11–26; and Paul Strohm, 'Chaucer's Lollard Joke: History and the Textual Unconscious', *Studies in the Age of Chaucer*, 17 (1995), 23–42.

4 See Caroline Walker Bynum, *Christian Materiality: An Essay on Religion in Late Medieval Europe* (New York: Zone Books, 2011), esp. pp. 15–36.

5 David C. Douglas and G. W. Greenaway, *English Historical Documents 1042–1189*, Vol. II (London: Eyre and Spottiswode, 1968), p. 768. Still useful is Muriel Bowden, *A Commentary on the General Prologue to the 'Canterbury Tales'* (New York: Macmillan, 1960), pp. 19–43.

6 Ronald C. Finucane, *Miracles and Pilgrims: Popular Beliefs in Medieval England* (New York: St Martin's Press, 1977), pp. 157–8, 163. See also Frank Barlow, *Thomas Becket* (Berkeley and Los Angeles: University of California Press, 1986), pp. 265–75.

7 Douglas *et al.*, *English Historical Documents*, Vol. II, p. 776.

8 *Ibid.*, Vol. II, p. 768.

9 'Cantetigitur novum Domino canticum felix Cantuariensis Ecclesia, cuius aram suo purpuravit pretioso sanguine martyr Thomas. Quinimo civitas ipsa tota potest et debet in exsultationis voce non immerito jubilare, quae cruore roseo sui martyris rubricata, pulchra facta est et apparuit speciosa' (*PL*, 190, 979C).

10 Bynum, *Christian Materiality*, p. 257.

11 James Rattue, *The Living Stream: Holy Wells in Historical Context* (Woodbridge: Boydell Press, 1995), pp. 71–2.

12 Finucane, *Miracles and Pilgrims*, p. 16.

13 Simon Yarrow, *Saints and Their Communities: Miracle Stories in Twelfth-Century England* (Oxford: Clarendon Press, 2006), pp. 169–70.

14 Ruth H. Cline, 'Four Chaucer Saints', *Modern Language Notes*, 60 (1945), 480–2.

15 See V. A. Kolve, 'Chaucer's *Second Nun's Tale* and the Iconography of Saint Cecilia', in Donald M. Rose, ed., *New Perspectives in Chaucer Criticism* (Norman, OK: Pilgrim Books, 1981), pp. 137–74.

16 Leslie A. Donovan, *Women Saints' Lives in Old English Prose* (Cambridge: D. S. Brewer, 1999), p. 58.

17 Catherine Sanok, *Her Life Historical: Exemplarity and Female Saints' Lives in Late Medieval England* (Philadelphia: University of Pennsylvania Press, 2007), pp. 3–6.

18 Nicholas Love, *'The Mirror of the Blessed Life of Jesus Christ': A Full Critical Edition*, ed. Michael G. Sargent (Exeter: University of Exeter Press, 2005), p. 11.

19 J. C. T. Oates, 'Richard Pynson and the Holy Blood of Hayles', *The Library*, 5th series, 13 (1958), 276–7.

20 See Nicholas Vincent, *The Holy Blood: King Henry III and the Westminster Blood Relic* (Cambridge: Cambridge University Press, 2001); and Caroline Walker Bynum, *Wonderful Blood: Theology and Practice in Late Medieval Northern Germany and Beyond* (Philadelphia: University of Pennsylvania Press, 2007).

21 Eamon Duffy, *The Stripping of the Altars: Traditional Religion in England c. 1400–c. 1580* (New Haven, CT: Yale University Press, 1992), pp. 234–65, Plates 110, 112.

22 John Shinners, ed., *Medieval Popular Religion, 1000–1500: A Reader* (Peterborough: Broadview Press, 1997), pp. 369–70.

23 Finucane, *Miracles and Pilgrims*, p. 199.

24 Francis Wormald, 'The Rood of Bromholm', *Journal of the Warburg Institute*, 1 (1937), 31–45; R. A. Pratt, 'Chaucer and the Holy Cross of Bromholm', *Modern Language Notes*, 70 (1955), 324–5; and Kathryn M. Rudy, *Postcards on Parchment: The Social Lives of Medieval Books* (New Haven, CT: Yale University Press, 2015), pp. 262–4.

25 Finucane, *Miracles and Pilgrims*, p. 196.

CHAPTER 21

Secularity

Alastair Minnis

The first recorded use of the noun *seculerte* occurs in a Wycliffite text of *c.* 1395, wherein 'prelatis & curatis' are attacked for the worldliness they display in taking Church income for themselves and dispending it as they like. A similar statement occurs in the slightly later *Dives et Pauper* (*c.* 1410), during an explanation of Christ's aversion to anything that belongs to *seculerte* being sold in the temple (cf. Matthew 21:12–13). The related noun *seculer(e)*, like its Latin and French counterparts, designates 'a member of the laity as opposed to a cleric', together with 'a member of the clergy living in the world as opposed to living under a rule, a secular priest'. My interest here is in the first two of these definitions, which implicate (to adopt more phrases from the *MED*) a concern 'with earthly life as opposed to spiritual or eternal life', 'desire' and 'behavior' that are 'worldly' and 'unspiritual', and matters 'belonging to the laity as opposed to the clergy'.[1]

All of these definitions set the 'secular' in simple opposition to the 'religious'. And there is no doubt that, in the age of Chaucer, a 'lay spirit' (so termed in Georges de Lagarde's pioneering work) was developing, on account of a complex confluence of influences at once political, social and ideological.[2] On the ideological front, it is impossible to exaggerate the significance of Aristotle, whose recently recovered treatises (accompanied by a formidable apparatus of commentary by Islamic scholars) quite transformed the learned discourse of European scholasticism. Bodies of specialist 'scientific' knowledge were being created within a wide range of disciplines, including epistemology, psychology, astronomy/astrology, alchemy and medicine, together with the art of war, politics, ethics and economics (i.e. household management, as then understood). The Latin term *scientia* (and, following it, the Middle English *science*) referred to a corpus of secure and reliable doctrine, vouched for by a galaxy of authoritative writers. Such sources of secure and reliable doctrine were burgeoning, and claiming a considerable measure of autonomy from the 'queen of the sciences', theology. But this does not mean that secularity and religiosity were invariably in implacable opposition. Admittedly, they *could* be – and this chapter will end with a clear example of that. But, generally speaking, the reality was more complicated. Competing interests there frequently were, but in many cases the secular and the religious should be seen as complexly interwoven, operating in relationships of complementarity, mutual support or even interdependence.

Aristotle was above all else the philosopher of human experience, responsible for epistemological and psychological theories that held that the acquisition of knowledge begins with data collected through sensory perception of the empirical world, which are then processed by the mental faculties. In Chaucer's day, the terms *experience* (cf. Latin *experientia*) and *experiment* (*experimentum*) were regularly applied in discussion of knowledge acquired through personal observation of natural events, an enquiry that could well reveal that certain marvels of nature had natural causes (however hard they were for mortals to understand), rather than being of supernatural origin. Many instances are offered by a treatise on how atmospheric refraction distorts our sight of the stars, which Nicole Oresme, the most impressive of the scholar-translators sponsored by Charles V, King of France, wrote 'to excite the minds of young men to speculate on noble things'.[3] This passage is typical: 'One experiment [*experientia*] concerns the circumpolar stars. Let one of them be observed on the meridian circle when it is near the zenith.' However, *experientia* is not necessarily in opposition to what one reads in some old book; Oresme can offer a conclusion that 'is clear through experience [*per experientias*] and in every author [*per omnes auctores*]'. What to us is textual authority may have been personal experience to a given author. Talking of a conclusion that can be reached thanks to the gaze (*de oculo*) of the viewer, Oresme remarks that this is no 'discovery newly contrived', for it may be 'proven by authorities and experiments manifested by the ancients'.[4] In this case *auctoritee* and *experience* are mutually supportive, as they are in Chaucer's *Treatise on the Astrolabe*, where the writer appeals to his own experience ('had I of this conclusioun the ful experience …'; 'By experience I wot wel …') in the course of a work that is compiled 'of the labour of olde astrologiens' (*Astr*, II.1.24–5, 3.75, Pro.62). In similar vein, the English mathematician Richard of Wallingford (*c.* 1291/2–1336), who is best known for his creation of scientific instruments (particularly an elaborate astronomical clock) far more sophisticated than an astrolabe, declared that 'the science of the sterries [stars]' involves not just 'the techynge of philosophris but also of thin awn experience'.[5] Here he is citing the great Greco-Roman *auctor* Ptolemy (d. *c.* 168).

A similar confluence of authority and experience may be found in a text of a very different kind, the *Wife of Bath's Prologue*, which begins with Alison's confident assertion that 'Experience, though noon auctoritee / Were in this world' is sufficient for her to speak about marital woe (*CT*, III.1–3), yet proceeds to quote an abundance of *auctoritees* both pagan and Christian. In some cases, of course, one was heavily or totally reliant on textual authority; when the Bible pronounced on a given matter, that was the end of it (though different interpretations could be possible). There were circumstances (relating to the afterlife, for example) in which no one could 'preve' something 'by assay' – determine the truth by personal observation or examination – and God forbid that men should believe only what they 'han seen with ye', that is, have perceived with their own eyes, as Chaucer himself says in the *Legend of Good Women* (F Pro.9–15). Yet, again and again, the poet displays a fascination with the 'auctoryte of experyence', to borrow a phrase from the fifteenth-century writer Osbern Bokenham.[6] One day the Friar's summoner will be able to prove the facts about hell, understanding them all too well – and painfully – by his 'owene experience' (*CT*, III.1514–20). In the *Clerk's Tale*, Walter, Marquis of Saluzzo, puts his wife Griselda through a series of extreme experiments 't'assaye' her true and patient 'wommanheede' (IV.1074–5; cf. 449–62). 'Assay by preve' has its dark side; Chaucer is acutely aware of the anxieties that surround the acquisition of secular *science* through experience, even as (quite evidently) he is attracted by the enterprise.

This is nowhere more evident than in the Canon's *Yeoman's Prologue and Tale*, which include trenchant satire against alchemists who conduct investigations that might well be deemed a genuine scientific quest, yet stage false experiments to deceive the eyes of their victims, from whom they extort money. Thus, the canon and his servant create 'illusioun' (VIII.672) and 'sleightes' (VIII.773). Yet there is more to it than that: alchemists deceive even themselves, when they think they are observing gold and silver actually being produced. No amount of staring can make that happen. 'If that youre eyen kan nat seen aright, / Looke that youre mynde lakke noght his sight' (VIII.1418–19). The testimony of one's own eyes may be unreliable. We should depend rather on the mind's eye and its powers of reason – which the duped priest of the final part of the Canon's *Yeoman's Tale* fails to do, believing the canon's assurance that he will 'seen heer, by experience' quicksilver becoming a precious metal 'right in [his] sighte anon, withouten lye' (VIII.1125–30).

But that does not mean that Chaucer rejected outright the 'slidynge science' of alchemy (VIII.732). He, or at least his character, the Canon's

Yeoman, is quite clear that, at the present time, this 'lore' is fruitless, no 'conclusioun' having been achieved. Here is a 'science' so far ahead of us that it is impossible to 'overtake' (VIII.672, 680–2). But what of 'futur temps' (VIII.875)? Will it continue to elude us then? The Yeoman ends his tale with an anecdote about how Plato refused to name the secret stone; indeed, all the philosophers swore an oath of silence. Even more decisively, Jesus Christ Himself holds the art so dear that He wills it should not be explained, until He decides that the time is right (VIII.1428–71). Here is no categorical prohibition of alchemical enquiry, but rather an expression of the possibility that, one day, Christ may well reveal its secrets to the right people. In short, this is a body of genuine knowledge that awaits full revelation. We are not dealing with impossibilities of nature, pseudo-knowledge that can never be true. 'This craft is wroght be weie of kinde', John Gower remarks, 'So that ther is no fallas [falseness] inne'.[7] Alchemy is not against nature, but works with nature.

In Chaucer's day, attempts were being made to distinguish between natural marvels and the miraculous. Excellent (if rather bizarre) examples may be found in the *Speculum curatorum* of Ralph, or Ranulph, Higden, monk of Chester (*c.* 1285–1364). Higden distinguishes between two basic kinds of magic: deception or black magic (*prestigium vel nigromancia*) and natural magic (*magica naturalis*). The former comes from the devil, who 'offers false knowledge to men' through various creatures, with the intention of leading them into sin.[8] The latter is, in fact, the appearance rather than the reality of magic, since only 'natural operations' are involved, 'and in this there is no work of demons and, even though ignorant men think that such things are evil deeds, learned men are not astonished'. Among his 'many instances of natural magic' Higden includes 'the sudden generation of frogs and lice from a recent mixing of semen with other assistant substances'. Furthermore,

> a candle made of wax and powdered snake skin, burning alone in a place littered with chaff or rushes, makes sticks seem to be snakes leaping about. In this case, the powdering causes the change in form; the movement of the candle flame causes the leaping. Next, an oak leaf at night may seem like a toad or a frog. And a branch variegated by its peeling bark in a shadowy place seems to be a snake. Also, a candle made of wax and the semen of an ass when it burns alone makes men seem to be asses.[9]

Rather a mixed bag of optical illusions and (allegedly) natural phenomena. Nicole Oresme's *De causis mirabilium* (*c.* 1370) is far more rigorous. This was written, Oresme explains, 'to show the causes of some effects which seem to be marvels and to show that the effects occur naturally … There is no reason to take recourse to the heavens, the last refuge of the weak, or demons, or to our glorious God as if He would produce these effects directly, more so than those effects whose causes we believe are well known to us.'[10] That is not to say that some late medieval thinkers were denying the possibility of divine miracles: simply that they were seeking to restrict the sphere of the miraculous. Nature has its own marvels, and people may be 'well satisfied with natural causes', to cite Oresme again.[11]

Chaucer often displays such satisfaction, not least in his treatment of the amazing gifts that, in the *Squire's Tale*, the 'kyng of Arabe and of Inde' bestows upon King Cambyuskan: a bronze flying horse, a large mirror in which the future may be seen, a ring that enables the wearer to understand the language of birds, and a sword that will heal any wound it inflicts. The horse is a sophisticated machine that works through the turning of a system of pegs and manipulation of its reins (v.312–33). A person who 'kan nat [does not know] the craft' is unable to move it, but Cambyuskan receives the requisite instruction from the unnamed knight who has piloted it to his kingdom. In general, says the Squire, 'lewed [ignorant] peple' think the worst about things 'that been maad moore subtilly / Than they kan in hir lewedness comprehende' (v.221–3). The point is that, if a person does not have sufficient knowledge of how something works, he may deem it threatening, judging it 'to the badder ende' (v.224).

Moreover, if no explanation for a given phenomenon is forthcoming, this is not because one does not exist, but simply because one has not yet been discovered. It is well known that glass is made from ashes of fern (according to actual medieval practice). Which may seem strange, admits the Squire, given that glass looks nothing like ashes of fern. But that is the fact of the matter, and therefore there is neither cause for debate nor need for wonder concerning this particular artefact (v.253–7). In contrast, room for debate remains concerning the origins of thunder, of the ebb and flow of the tides, of spiders' webs, and of mist (v.258–9) – and indeed, 'of alle thing, til that the cause is wyst [known/understood]' (v.260). In that category may be included the mysterious mirror, ring and sword. One day, all may be revealed (just as, hopefully, one day the secrets of alchemy will be entrusted to a select few). In the meantime, Cambyuskan's courtiers can only try to make 'skiles after hir fantasies' (v.205), seeking to turn their imaginings into firm explanations. What is perfectly clear is that no devil or evil spirit is being accused of involvement as a means of explaining the strange goings-on in the tale. Here is secularity of a high order.

The same can be said of the *Franklin's Tale*, despite the narrator's over-anxious attempts to distance himself from 'swiche illusiouns and swiche meschaunces [evil practices] / As hethen folk useden in thilke dayes' (v.1291–2). Aurelius does pray to the pagan gods (supposed by Christians to be fallen angels, devils in disguise) for a 'miracle' (v.1056, 1065; cf. 1299) in the form of a high tide of abnormal duration, requiring interference with the moon's natural course for two whole years – a terrifying prospect, indicative of the young man's reckless desires (v.1066–70). But nothing of the kind happens. On the contrary, when Aurelius's brother thinks back to his college days at Orleans he recalls a book of 'magyk natureel' (v.1125), and the two of them set off there to seek a practitioner therof (v.1155). The 'magicien' who takes on the task of making it look as though the terrifying rocks have vanished from the Breton coast uses nothing more disquieting than a set of accurate astrological tables (v.1273–4). Further, a strong emphasis is placed on the subtlety of his calculations, 'hise equacions in every thyng' (v.1279). The implication is that, thanks to the magician's knowledge of planetary motions, he predicts that a high tide is coming, which will cover all the coastal rocks. An unusual event perhaps (at least in terms of its size) but not unnatural; it may last for 'a wyke or tweye' but certainly not for the two years that Aurelius had requested in his 'ravyng' (v.1026).

Chaucer's attribution of astronomical/astrological lore to that magician (or 'philosophre', as he also is called) cannot be taken as *prima facie* evidence that he is of dubious character, any more than we should blame the Physician for his use of 'magik natureel' in diagnosing his patients (I.416). The later distinction between the science of astronomy and the pseudo-science of astrology did not yet exist. However, crucial distinctions were made between acceptable and non-acceptable forms of astrology. To draw on a passage from *Troilus and Criseyde*, the 'influences' of the 'hevenes hye' are, 'under God', 'our hierdes' (shepherds, guides), inasmuch as they do affect our behaviour – but they do not determine it (*Tr*, III.617–20). The freedom of the human will cannot be denied, since one can choose to accept or reject those same 'influences'. Thus, the impulse towards secularity was reconciled with religious imperatives. As Ralph Higden said, while 'celestial bodies can have great power over fundamentally lower natures', 'if stars were responsible for our actions, neither worthiness nor unworthiness could be ascribed to us since we would not be the originators of our actions'. Furthermore, some 'secrets are revealed by astronomy through observations made with an astrolabe or through natural magic', and this process may be quite allowable.[12]

'General predictions', concerning such events as storms, rains, floods, epidemics, famines and wars, were certainly deemed allowable, whereas the practice of casting horoscopes concerning the fates of individuals was frowned upon. Only those 'who are inspired by the deity can predict particulars', declares the Oxford astrologer John Ashenden (a fellow of Merton College), who completed his vast *Summa astrologiae judicialis de accidentibus mundi* in December 1348, here echoing (pseudo-)Ptolemy's *Centiloquium*. Ashenden is defending the right of philosophers like himself to engage in such investigation. However, attempts to make 'particular predictions' were regarded as unacceptable in Christian society, as Chaucer asserts in his *Treatise on the Astrolabe*: 'these ben observaunces of judicial matere and rytes of payens, in whiche my spirit hath no feith, ne knowing of her *horoscopum*' (*Astr*, II.4.57–60). *Troilus and Criseyde*, which ends with a robust attack on 'payens corsed olde rites' (*Tr*, V.1849), features one character who is something of a scientist, namely Calkas. By 'calkulynge' and 'astronomye' (I.72, V.115) he has worked out that the city of Troy will fall (a contingency falling within the category of 'general' prediction). However, Calkas also has recourse to the ambiguous answers of the god he worships, and whose deceitful practices he emulates, namely 'Daun Phebus or Appollo Delphicus' (I.70). Chaucer's distaste is directed against pagan theology rather than pagan science.

Pagan practical philosophy is also treated respectfully, as may be demonstrated by a reading of the *Knight's Tale* in light of doctrine from Aristotle's *Ethics* and *Politics*, which Giles of Rome's popular *De regimine principum* (*c.* 1285) did much to make available to a lay audience. To cite John Trevisa's Middle English translation of Giles, the crowning princely virtue of 'magnificence' involves 'greet spendyng and cost'. It 'hath the name of workes and of *facio*, makynge'; the magnificent man is called 'as it were *magna faciens*, makynge and doynge grete thinges'. Since it is seemly for a king to be magnificent, he should perform magnificent works in respect of God, of the common good of his state, of special persons who are 'worthi worschep', and of himself and his household. The first of these works involves the construction of temples to the glory of God while the last entails the maintenance of a splendid home, paying for splendid weddings for his family-members, and attracting 'wonderfullich cheualrie' to his court.[13] Duke Theseus, lord and governor of Athens, does all of those things to a superlative degree. An exceptional big spender and builder-king, he ensures the construction of new pagan temples and a vast amphitheatre, fit places for top-ranking aristocrats to pray and fight in. Two hundred knights are attracted to Athens to engage in feats of chivalry, in support of Arcite and Palamon. When the battle's lost and won, Palamon weds Emily 'with alle blisse and melodye' (*CT*, I.3097). Admittedly, that event is treated very briefly – but Arcite's appropriately expensive funeral is described at some length.

The *Knight's Tale* and *Troilus and Criseyde* are also poems of passionate love. Chaucer was not writing primarily for celibates and/or those who had withdrawn from regular social exchange to follow the contemplative life, but rather for people of secular estate pursuing careers outside the Church, marrying and raising families. Many writers of his age followed Aristotle in asserting that man is a social animal, and regarded marriage and family life as obvious outcomes of that sociability. According to Giles's *De regimine principum*, 'the Philosopher' taught that great love and friendship should exist between husband and wife.[14] Likewise, Nicole Oresme attributed to Aristotle the belief that nature bestowed sexual pleasure on the human species, 'not only for reproduction of its kind but also to enhance and maintain friendship between man and woman'.[15] Human love can indeed serve the common good; the relationship between a man and a woman is the primal social unit, and happy marriage is conducive to a harmonious society.

Those attitudes permeate Chaucer's love poetry, and do much to account for the ways in which he adapted materials from a masterpiece of early medieval neo-Platonism, Boethius's *De consolatione philosophiae*, to suit that hardly welcoming context. Boethius's denigration of the 'inferior goods' of material wealth, honour, power, fame and bodily pleasure is radically reconfigured. Most radical of all is Chaucer's celebration of 'Love, that of erthe and se hath governaunce' (*Tr*, III.1744) near the end of Book III of *Troilus and Criseyde*. In Book II, metrum 8 of the *Consolatio*, Chaucer found what is reconstructed here as the fullest possible vision of love attainable through secular, philosophical wisdom, without recourse to the love of Him who 'starf' (died) on the cross 'oure soules for to beye' (buy/pay for) (*Tr*, V.1844–5). This served well the poet's project of depicting enlightened pagans who are innocent of Christian love, in itself a striking instance of his valorisation of the secular. Thus, Chaucer emphasised the original's (somewhat minimal) reference to the bond of heterosexual love, rather than its praise of virtuous friendship. But far more striking than any specific alteration is the profound shift of meaning effected by his positioning of this Boethian doctrine. For it comes after the physical consummation of Troilus's love for Criseyde, and its enlightened insights seem to have been prompted by the joy of that experience. Here is a quite extraordinary case of postcoital philosophising.

Little wonder, then, that *Troilus* should head the list of those texts that, in the *Retractions*, the penitent poet revokes as worldly vanities, in contrast with those 'books of legendes of seintes, and omelies, and moralitee, and devocioun' that he is glad to have written (*CT*, x.1087). Throughout his oeuvre Chaucer had negotiated the competing demands of authority and experience – what we see with our own eyes and what the old books tell us to believe; what requires *preve* and what is a matter of faith; what, to adapt the idiom of Mark 12:17, may be rendered unto Caesar and what must be rendered unto God. But now the limits of secularity are frankly, perhaps even fearfully, acknowledged.

NOTES

1 *MED*, s.v. *seculerte* (n.), *seculer(e)* (n.) and *seculer(e)* (adj.).
2 Georges de Lagarde, *La naissance de l'esprit laïque, au déclin du moyen âge*, 5 vols., 3rd edn (Louvain: Nauwelaerrs, 1956–70).
3 Nicole Oresme, *De visione stellarum (On Seeing the Stars)*, ed. D. Burton (Leiden: Brill, 2006), pp. 216–17.
4 *Ibid.*, pp. 122–3, 140–1, 142–3.
5 Richard of Wallingford, *Richard of Wallingford: An Edition of His Writings with Introductions, English Translation and Commentary*, ed. and trans. J. D. North, 3 vols. (Oxford: Clarendon Press, 1976), Vol. 1, p. 241. I quote from an anonymous Middle English translation of Wallingford's Latin *Exafrenon.*
6 *MED*, s.v. *experience*, 2(a).
7 John Gower, *Confessio Amantis*, iv.2508–9, in *The English Works of John Gower*, ed. G. C. Macaulay, 2 vols., EETS os 81–2 (London: Oxford University Press, 1900–1).
8 Ranulph Higden, *Speculum curatorum (A Mirror for Curates)*, Book 1: *The Commandments*, ed. Eugene Crook and Margaret Jennings (Leuven: Peeters, 2012), pp. 103, 109, 111.
9 *Ibid.*, p. 105.
10 Nicole Oresme, *Nicole Oresme and the Marvels of Nature: A Study of His 'De causis mirabilium' with Critical Edition, Translation, and Commentary*, ed. and trans. Bert Hansen (Toronto: Pontifical Institute of Mediaeval Studies, 1985), p. 137.
11 *Ibid.*, p. 361.
12 Higden, *Speculum curatorum*, ed. Crook and Jennings, p. 113.
13 John of Trevisa, *The Governance of Kings and Princes: John Trevisa's Middle English Translation of the 'De regimine principum' of Aegidius Romanus*, ed. D. C. Fowler *et al.* (New York: Garland, 1997), pp. 79–80, 83.
14 *Ibid.*, pp. 182–4, 187. Cf. Aristotle, *Nicomachean Ethics*, viii.12 (1162a).
15 Nicole Oresme, *Le livre de yconomque d'Aristote*, ed. A. D. Menut (Philadelphia: American Philosophical Society, 1957), p. 813.

CHAPTER 22

The Self

Valerie Allen

The only definition offered here of selfhood – a term freely alternated with associated terms – is stipulative, namely, an intuitive sense of 'being me' as opposed to being some other entity, conscious or not. Cultural histories of the western self often begin in the seventeenth century, a departure point in many ways philosophically justifiable but not so helpful in a book on Chaucer. I will engage later with the paradigm shift said to inaugurate this early modern subjectivity, for there is value in taking the long view; as in any complex system of interacting agents, characteristics of that system not apparent at the local level do emerge on the global scale. Most of this chapter, however, deals more nearsightedly with a model we know Chaucer knew, a model that is not a theory but a story: the tale of Narcissus and his mirror, as told by Ovid in the *Metamorphoses* and retold by Guillaume de Lorris in the French *Romance of the Rose*, a poem Chaucer partly translated.[1]

Physically stunning, Narcissus arouses love in all who see him but spurns all suitors. One of his casualties is the nymph Echo, whose fate it has become only to utter the tail-ends of other people's speech. Before she dies of grief, she prays that the youth will become as lovesick as she (this detail by Lorris; Ovid's suppliant is unnamed). Narcissus subsequently catches sight of his reflection in a pool and, like Echo, dies for want of himself, thereby fulfilling the prophecy of the blind seer Tiresias, who had foretold that the youth would live only for as long as he lacked self-knowledge. His last word, 'farewell' (*vale*), is resounded by Echo, now avenged. The tale cautions against preoccupation with surface and illusion, which, in the case of Narcissus, extends beyond the confines of life for, as he enters the underworld, he gazes into the waters of the Styx to catch another glimpse of his image.

Self-awareness comes through looking and is motivated by the epistemological connection between knowing and seeing. Sight and blindness stand in ironic counterpoint: Tiresias is blind but has insight; Narcissus has no insight but has vision, and it destroys him. Chaucer's *Merchant's Tale* satirically enacts this rich theme. Figuratively blind to all sage counsel against marrying a younger (and untrustworthy) woman, January turns literally blind, only to regain his sight and demonstrate yet again his moral blindness. These stories question how much self-knowledge can be endured and suggest that insight and blindness might always entail each other.

Of all sights that arrest the eye, beauty summons the gaze most imperiously because *claritas* (radiance), say classical and medieval philosophers, is an intrinsic property of beauty, beauty here being understood as objective ideal, not personal preference.[2] As light is luminous, so is beauty self-evident (note the Latin root *videre*, to see, in 'evident'). To invoke that just-so sense of loveliness, romance heroines such as Emily in the *Knight's Tale* conform to a regular pattern (*CT*, I.1033–61), for their beauty should be instantly apparent and not a matter for debate any more than one has to be persuaded that 2 + 2 = 4. Like truth, beauty just *is*, and in its deictic presence the only appropriate response is, 'yes, I see'. Blanche's portrait offers Chaucer's most sustained elaboration of true beauty and beautiful truth (*BD*, 817–1033). Beauty gives pleasure, therefore desire is the inevitable response, love making lovers self-aware and limning the boundaries of their self-sufficiency. 'Who yaf me drynke?', Criseyde asks self-reflectively (*Tr*, II.651). While the self-disclosing *studie* into which exiled Arcite falls is admittedly a romance convention of lover's complaint and a narrative stratagem to reconnect him with Palamon (*CT*, I.1528–73), it demonstrates more profoundly how love turns the soul inside out, externalising consciousness into an object of scrutiny.

A lover also, Narcissus already possesses what he lacks, grammatically functioning as his own predicative: 'iste ego sum' (I am that 'he'). *Iste* is logically tricky, for the word is a demonstrative pronoun that means something like 'him over there, near you', and spatially distances addressee from speaker. Narcissus and Echo split and double each other; where he lacks a separable object to his love, she lacks a speaking subject-position, able only to repeat end-words. Her echo 'replies' to his dying 'farewell', as if he had uttered it to her rather than to himself. Her mimicry is recursive, for although she cannot start a sentence, she can continue one indefinitely by echoing her own echo. She may not be able to speak until spoken to, but she will always get the last word.[3] Like mirrors held before each other, creating an infinite series of reflected reflections, self-awareness loops around to feed upon its own feedback, and in the case of Narcissus consumes him as he surrenders fatalistically to Tiresias's prediction. In Ovid's densely textured lines flickers the implosive, dangerous liaison between subject and object. Chaucer closely imitates these recursive structures in moments of falling in love.

Narcissus's watery mirror serves as a primal scene of (often deadly) self-knowledge. Though mirrors were often made of polished metal, it is those of glass that offer the richest associations. Middle English *glas* refers both to the clear substance one looks through (as in a magnifying glass) and to the same substance now metal-backed, opaque and reflective (as in a looking glass). *Mirour* also works double time, denoting both a metal-backed looking glass and a lens or burning glass, as when in the *Squire's Tale* Chaucer speaks 'of queynte mirours and of perspectives' (*CT*, v.234). References to mirrors thus can be equivocal about whether one is supposed to look through or at them. The imprecision is a sign not of confusion between refraction and reflection, but of enigma; like Tiresias's cryptic words but *not* like luminous beauty, mirrors yield images, requiring hermeneutic effort. The outcome of encountering them is forked: deep self-examination or shallow vanity. Their ambages intimate that knowledge of self, acquired by looking *at* the mirror, and knowledge of the other, acquired by looking *through* the mirror, might not be so different. Ovid's supple amphibolies, which play throughout with tensions between seeming and being, enact this duality.

Medieval mirror-makers poured molten metal into the concavity of blown glass to silver its back – a challenging feat because the larger the glass, the higher the likelihood of thermal shock. A shape was then cut from the bubble and framed, by necessity small, circular, convex and distorted in projection, characteristics apparent in the mirror centrally positioned in Jan van Eyck's Arnolfini portrait.[4] The mirror's convexity displays a wide field of vision behind the viewer, perhaps for which reason it shows approaching danger to Canacee (v.132–6). Nature in the *Rose* offers an instructive lecture on the different kinds of images mirrors make. Some magnify, others minify; some show things in their proper size, others invert. Skilled mirror-makers can 'make one image give birth to several'.[5]

Distortion constitutes both the technological weakness and the imaginative strength of the medieval convex mirror, for it offers a conceptual rather than optical perspective. Modelling reality, *mirour* means something like 'paradigm', a sense in which Chaucer regularly uses the word, as when the Man of Law calls Constance 'mirour of alle curteisye' (II.166). A *mirour* magnifies in the old sense of the word, semantically conjoining glorification and amplification. It invites scrutiny, for its smallness requires proximity. Like a miniature medieval book, designed for personal devotion, really only one person at a time can benefit from the mirror, which enframes the viewer's face as if in a painting. Medieval book, portrait and mirror are hermeneutically allied: look into any of them and ruminate.

Rumination, a digestive metaphor for reading and deep, reiterative thought, requires active interpretation. Likewise, the viewer's ruminative gaze back at the mirror should occur at an epistemological level conceptually higher than passive duplication. As the beam of the eye bends back upon itself, to watch itself watching, one sees oneself and *knows* that one does so. Conventionally, this meta-knowledge is an operation of reason, a distinctively human power: because only humans form concepts and only humans are selves. According to Nature in the *Rose*, 'Without doubt, all dumb animals … are by nature incapable of knowing themselves.'[6] So Chaucer's references both to Troilus making 'a mirour of his mynde' when deciding to love Criseyde (*Tr*, I.365), and to January's selection of a bride in the *Merchant's Tale* as analogous to setting up a mirror in a market place (*CT*, IV.1577–87) insinuate that neither lover thinks through the choice as actively and freely as does Walter in the *Clerk's Tale*, whose decision is marked by the vocabulary of measured thoughtfulness: 'in sad wyse', 'ofte avyse', 'considered', 'disposed' (IV.232–45).

Developments in mirror technology, such as a cold process of silvering glass, led through the later Middle Ages and early modern period to the plane mirror, which yields an image more closely approximating optical perspective. In the visual arts, concurrent developments in projective geometry and painterly devices, such as the construction of a vanishing point to convey the illusion of depth, made perspective into a science. The rules of perspective also distort because they do not wholly correspond with what is actually seen (i.e. the viewer uses two eyes to focus, not one); Michel Foucault's analysis of *Las meninas* by Diego Velázquez exposes the epistemological tensions within an interior scene that, like the Arnolfini portrait, uses a central mirror, only this time a flat one.[7] Yet for all its tacit deceptions, the visually plausible scene seems to represent naturalistically what viewers think they really see when they look out on the world.

Where the convex mirror offers visibility from multiple angles, the plane mirror renders a more precise but optically restricted image from the viewer's fixed position in mapped Cartesian space. The viewer controls, perspectivally speaking, what is seen.[8] The more optically verisimilar the vista, the more the viewer in the plane mirror need simply describe the scene; the image presented by the convex mirror in contrast requires explanation. The convex mirror affords an exemplary model for imitation and self-correction; the plane mirror invites critique and self-objectification. It isolates the viewing 'eye' and the viewing 'I', thereby sundering subject from object and one thinking subject from another in a rupture that initiates what philosopher Charles Taylor calls the 'punctual self' – disengaged, autonomous, objectifying, radically reflexive.[9]

Marking this emergent sense of 'being me', 'selfhood' as a word enters English in the seventeenth century, although it carries largely negative associations of egoism and self-absorption.[10] Only in the nineteenth century does it acquire the more neutral sense of personality. Yet the dangers of self-preoccupation are a thoroughly medieval tune, sounding most often in depictions of Pride, chief of the Seven Deadly Sins, who carries a mirror for signature. Idleness in the *Rose* carries one in her hand (*Rom*, 567), and aptly does the narrator call Narcissus's fountain a 'mirrour perilous' (*Rom*, 1601). Beyond signifying *vanitas*, mirrors tap into ancient superstitions about encountering one's own double. The fatal multiplication of reflected reflections brings about what philosopher René Girard calls a 'violent mimesis', in which the principle of differentiation internal to unity is destroyed.[11] Such doubling grotesquely parodies the true complementarity between subject and object; lover and beloved; and, for Alan of Lille in his *Plaint of Nature* (also known to Chaucer), man and woman. The target of Alan's satire is same-sex love, and the narcissine encounter is its paradigmatic negative exemplum. His argument is that self should find itself in difference, not in sameness, as if to say, 'look through the mirror, not at it'. It appeals to the prevalent cosmological model of four elements that mix their differences to create all material things and where each has its designated natural place, or 'kyndely stede' (see *HF*, 729–56): earth lowest, then water, then air, then fire. 'Kyndely enclynyng' makes all matter seek its respective home: stones drop; fire rises. This medieval model of motion both describes physical behaviour and explains its causes in one go. A stone falls because it belongs below among heavy things, because that is how its nature makes it behave. The one statement both describes physical behaviour and prescribes its tendencies in an expository method that is self-justifying and ultimately circular. From this elision of description (the how) and theory (the why), it is only a flea-jump to authorising a world in which kings 'naturally' rule, serfs 'naturally' obey and men 'naturally' love women. Undo that marriage of differences, the inference runs, and things fall apart. Dodging explicit exhortations to know one's place in this 'natural' order, Chaucer explores instead how women in particular might experience how it feels to 'be me', making of his own poetry a mirror that reflects from oblique positions.

Newton's first law of motion – that a moving body with no force acting on it will move indefinitely, at a constant rate and in a straight line – is incompatible with natural motion, which terminates once the moving body has reached its 'propre mansyon' (*HF*, 754). Scientific method rigorously distinguishes between quantitative description, captured best in the mathematical formula, and theoretical rationale, now apportioned to metaphysics. Natural motion, with its home-seeking bodies, is planned motion, meaning that medieval physics is teleological in conception. Such a providential system cannot account for randomness except to accommodate chance or *aventure* by making Fortune a servant of God with jurisdiction over worldly affairs (*Bo*, II). Early probability theory, formulated by Blaise Pascal and Pierre de Fermat when calculating how to anticipate a fair split of the winnings in an interrupted betting game, begins to measure chance, to subject the aleatory to the logic of number, to mathematicise Fortune. The computation of probability has important consequences for modern personality by statistically defining standards and deviances that become psychically internalised. Actuarial calculation infiltrates modern selfhood at every level, creating distinctive challenges (being 'just a number', being only 'average') as well as consolations (being 'normal').[12]

A medieval calculus of human nature also delineates types, but not by numerical aggregation. Where a modern personality type is drawn from a statistical abstraction ever revisable in light of more complete data, a medieval type is a settled abstraction drawn from intuitively self-evident categories, authorised by experience and convention, and not subject to any ordeal of statistical proof. Working within inherited categories such as estate, sex and literary genre, Chaucer also redefines them, and this is most demonstrably so in the instance of female selfhood. Beyond social roles defined by women's sexual relationship to men – maidenhood, motherhood and widowhood – he generalises female nature into a subject position that remains biologically embodied yet performs good theoretical work. Griselda's 'wommanhede' becomes a productive abstraction capable of transcending even gendered divisions to represent 'every wight'.[13] In the story of the western modern subject, as conventionally chronologised, Chaucer's 'pre-natal' selves narrate a story about 'being me' as full of diversely angled perspectives as the rippled surface of Narcissus's mirror.

NOTES

1 I thank Marlene Villalobos Hennessy for valuable feedback. Ovid, *Metamorphoses*, III.341–510, ed. and trans. F. J. Miller, rev. G. P. Goold, 3rd edn (Cambridge, MA: Harvard University Press, 1977), pp. 148–61.

2 St Thomas Aquinas, *Summa theologiae*, ed. and trans. Thomas Gilby (Oxford: Blackfriars, 1964–75), 1.a39.8 corp.

3 See Christine Neufeld's recuperation of Echo as more than a mere reflective surface for Narcissus in *Avid Ears: The Medieval Gossip and the Art of Listening* (London: Routledge, 2019).

4 At the National Gallery, London, www.nationalgallery.org.uk/paintings/jan-van-eyck-the-arnolfini-portrait (last accessed 14 January 2019); Sabine Melchior-Bonnet, *The Mirror: A History*, trans. Katharine H. Jewett (New York: Routledge, 2001), pp. 13–17.

5 Guillaume de Lorris and Jean de Meun, *The Romance of the Rose*, lines 18153–286, trans. Charles Dahlberg, 3rd edn (Princeton: Princeton University Press, 1995), pp. 302–3. For an overview of the historical and metaphoric importance of mirrors in medieval culture, see Nancy M. Frelick, ed., *The Mirror in Medieval and Early Modern Culture: Specular Reflections* (Turnhout: Brepols, 2016); and Miranda Anderson, ed., *The Book of the Mirror: An Interdisciplinary Collection Exploring the Cultural Story of the Mirror* (Newcastle: Cambridge Scholars, 2007), especially two contributions by the editor: 'Chaucer and the Subject of the Mirror', pp. 70–9, and 'Early Modern Mirrors', pp. 105–20.

6 *Romance of the Rose*, trans. Dahlberg, 17793–4 (p. 296).

7 At the Museo Nacional del Prado, www.museodelprado.es/en/the-collection/art-work/las-meninas/9fdc7800-9ade-48b0-ab8b-edee94ea877f (last accessed 14 January 2019); Michel Foucault, *The Order of Things: An Archaeology of the Human Sciences*, trans. from French (London: Routledge, 2002), pp. 3–16.

8 Melchior-Bonnet, *The Mirror*, p. 128.

9 Charles Taylor, *Sources of the Self: The Making of the Modern Identity* (Cambridge: Cambridge University Press, 1989), pp. 159–76; Jerrold E. Seigel, *The Idea of the Self: Thought and Experience in Western Europe since the Seventeenth Century* (Cambridge: Cambridge University Press, 2005), pp. 45–9.

10 *OED*, s.v. *selfhood* (n.). Jonathan Sawday, 'Self and Selfhood in the Seventeenth Century', in Roy Porter, ed., *Rewriting the Self: Histories from the Renaissance to the Present* (London: Routledge, 1997), pp. 29–48 (pp. 29–30).

11 René Girard, *Violence and the Sacred*, trans. Patrick Gregory (Baltimore: Johns Hopkins University Press, 1977), p. 47.

12 Karma Lochrie, *Heterosyncrasies: Female Sexuality when Normal Wasn't* (Minneapolis: University of Minnesota Press, 2005), pp. 1–25.

13 Tara Williams, '"T'assaye in thee thy wommanhede": Griselda Chosen, Translated, and Tried', *Studies in the Age of Chaucer*, 27 (2005), 93–127.

CHAPTER 23

Women

Rosalynn Voaden

Geoffrey Chaucer had a mother. He also had a wife, a daughter, a sister-in-law. He was a page in the household of a noblewoman. He may well have had a lover. Geoffrey Chaucer encountered women of all kinds; all shapes and sizes, ranks and degrees, ages and stages of life; and many versions of these women found their way into his works. This chapter sets out to convey, briefly, a sense of the wide range of women's lives in Chaucer's England. It offers glimpses into the lives of young women, widows, nuns, women of the court, urban women, country women and women of the streets, bolstered by vignettes of historical figures from the period. In all these categories, a woman's social class was, of course, a major factor in the kind of life she led. In the late Middle Ages society was divided into three estates: those who pray – the clergy; those who fight – the aristocracy and landed gentry; and those who work – commoners, encompassing peasants, artisans, merchants and burgesses, among others. Women were usually categorised by virtue of the estate of their father or husband.

Young women of the third estate, that is, commoners, would have been taught domestic skills as well as those skills necessary to help in the family business or on the farm. Urban women may have had basic literacy and numeracy, enough to keep accounts. The fourteenth-century poem *How the Good Wife Taught Her Daughter* gives some indication of the ideal to which young women of this estate were to aspire, which was to become good wives themselves. They should go to church regularly; stay out of taverns; avoid gossip; bake bread; manage their servants; be nice to the neighbours; please their husbands; and, in their turn, prepare their own daughters for marriage. That such guides to conduct existed at all suggests that these behavioural strictures may have been more honoured in the breach than in the observance. This is certainly evident in some of Chaucer's characters. Alison of the *Miller's Tale*, she of the weasel-like body 'gent and smal' (*CT*, 1.3234), is clearly a girl who just wants to have fun, and managing her household or pleasing her husband are low on her list of priorities. In the years after the Black Death, with increasing social mobility, young people of both sexes gravitated to the towns where life seemed more exciting and offered greater opportunities. It has been suggested that this poem and other similar conduct books were not really intended for mothers, whose daughters presumably could learn by seeing and doing, but for the mistresses of domestic servants, who served *in loco parentis*.[1] This is a persuasive argument, as young women frequently spent several years in domestic service. In fact, many children of both sexes at all levels of society were raised to independent adulthood in households other than that of their own family.[2]

This was frequently the case with young gentry and noblewomen. Living with a family other than their own extended social networks for both males and females, and increased opportunities for marriage. Young women of this estate would have been taught courtly etiquette and protocol as well as skills such as needlework, dancing, music, riding, hunting and hawking. They may well have learnt to read for pleasure and for devotional purposes. They would also have acquired, by example or instruction, the ability to manage a household. Chaucer's own wife and sister-in-law, Philippa and Katherine de Roet respectively, were raised in the household of Queen Philippa, wife of Edward III. Their father, Paon de Roet, came to England from Hainault as part of Queen Philippa's household when she married Edward III in 1328.[3] When the girls' mother died they were installed in the Queen's household, and when their father also died, fighting for the Black Prince in Aquitaine, they seem to have been taken under the wing of the Queen, who may have helped to arrange their marriages – Philippa's to the young Geoffrey Chaucer, then a Yeoman of the Chamber of Edward III, and Katherine's to Hugh Swynford, a knight and member of John of Gaunt's retinue.

In most cases, apart perhaps from high-level dynastic marriages, young women had some say in whom they would marry. While social and financial considerations may have played a larger role than they do in our romance-obsessed culture, love and lust certainly featured in medieval marriage. Chaucer's Wife of Bath says that she married her first three husbands for their money, but chose her fifth husband because

> … he hadde a paire
> Of legges and of feet so clene and faire
> That al myn herte I yaf unto his hoold.
> (*CT*, III.597–9)

The Wife's historical contemporary, the visionary Margery Kempe of Lynn (*c.* 1373–after 1438), may have married beneath her station for love – or lust.

Her father, she tells us, was 'meyr fyve tymes of þat worshepful burwgh and aldyrman also many ȝerys', while her husband, John, never elicits any reference to his success or status.[4] Late in her life she admits that 'sche in hir ȝonge age had ful many delectabyl thowtys, fleschly lustys, & inordinat louys to hys persone'.[5]

The Book of Margery Kempe, the first autobiography written in English (*c.* 1438), gives us a fascinating glimpse into the life of a well-off urban woman of the time. Citizens and burgesses of towns and cities could amass considerable wealth and hold civic offices, thereby achieving respectability and standing in the community. Their wives and daughters would enjoy commensurate social standing, and may also have had some degree of independence. Women in many towns could inherit in their own right, run their own businesses and travel without their husbands. Women in the families of wealthy merchants or tradesmen may have had more education, to the extent of owning books and discussing them with like-minded women.

One such woman is the fictional Wife of Bath; another is Margery Kempe. Although ostensibly a spiritual autobiography, *The Book* is replete with details of both daily life and of special events in the time of Chaucer. Margery married when she was about twenty and set up household with her husband, John. Marriage in one's early-to-mid twenties and establishing an independent household was the general practice in England. After the birth of her first child Margery experienced what we would now identify as post-partum depression, considered suicide and feared eternal damnation. The discovery of a subsequent pregnancy filled her with quite understandable dismay. She eventually had fourteen children, at least one of whom led a dissolute life, which worried his mother a great deal. She was an independent businesswoman – though not a very successful one – starting a brewery and a horse mill. She was flirtatious and fashion-conscious, telling us that she wore headdresses with gold pipes and cloaks slashed to show fabric of a different colour underneath. In this she recalls the guildsmen's wives in the *General Prologue* to the *Canterbury Tales*, aping the nobility with long trains to their mantles, and, indeed, the Prioress, with her pleated wimple, elegant cloak and gold brooch (I.378, 151–62). Margery travelled throughout England, sometimes with her husband, sometimes alone, and, like the Wife of Bath, was an inveterate pilgrim, journeying to Jerusalem, Rome and Santiago de Compostela, as well as to shrines in northern Europe. Margery inherited money from her father and used her own money to pay her husband's debts in return for his allowing her to go on pilgrimage to Jerusalem. She complains of illness, of a bad leg, of her dissolute son and of gossiping neighbours; and, as an old woman, she washes the nappies of her incontinent husband. In many ways, she is a fifteenth-century Everywoman.

A woman whose experience is definitely not that of Everywoman is Chaucer's sister-in-law, Katherine Swynford (*c.* 1350–1403), who defied all the odds against mistresses by remaining the lover of John of Gaunt (1340–99), Duke of Lancaster, uncle of Richard II and the most powerful man in England, for more than twenty years until finally becoming his third wife.[6] Yet in the trajectory of Katherine's life she is representative of many women of the court who grew up in fairly sheltered circumstances, made appropriate marriages, bore and raised children, and managed the family estates while their husbands were away at war or involved in government. As stated above, Katherine was from the gentry class and grew up in the royal court, being sufficiently educated to be appointed governess to the two children of John of Gaunt and his first wife, Blanche, Duchess of Lancaster (d. 1368). She married, in her late teens, Sir Hugh Swynford, a man about ten years older than her. Whether this was a love match or simply a suitable marriage is not known. Hugh was not wealthy, but could provide Katherine with his knightly rank and social standing. After their marriage, Katherine spent much of her time at Hugh's rather run-down estates at Kettlethorpe and Coleby in Lincolnshire, managing their affairs while Hugh was away fighting. They had two daughters, Blanche and Margaret (John of Gaunt was godfather to Blanche), and one son, Thomas. Katherine continued to serve in the ducal household, and her children probably spent considerable time there with her, growing up in the courtly environment and acquiring the skills appropriate to their rank.

When Hugh died in Aquitaine in 1371 in the service of John of Gaunt, Katherine was left a widow with three young children and unproductive estates. John of Gaunt gave her some financial support, and appointed her, along with her sister, Philippa Chaucer, to the household of his second wife, Constance of Castile. At some point after 1372 the two became lovers, and thenceforth much of Katherine's life was spent outside the court on her estate at Kettlethorpe. She and John of Gaunt had four children who, after their parents' marriage in 1396, were legitimised by the Pope and took the name Beaufort. From this liaison between Katherine Swynford and John of Gaunt are descended the Tudors, Stuarts and every British monarch since.

Despite the notoriety that attached to her as John of Gaunt's mistress, Katherine Swynford was a pious woman, and established a relationship with the Chapter of Lincoln Cathedral that culminated in her renting a house in the Cathedral Close for many years. In her piety as well as in other aspects of her life she can be seen as representative of women of the second estate, many of whom led devout lives and inculcated spiritual precepts in members of their household through daily prayers and devotional readings. Women with sufficient means could join a religious guild, or a confraternity – organisations of layfolk, both men and women, created to perform special works of Christian charity and promote devotion. Both Katherine Swynford and her sister Philippa Chaucer were members of the fraternity of Lincoln Cathedral. Margery Kempe became a member of the Guild of the Holy Trinity in Lynn in 1438.

Some women chose to become vowesses when their husbands died; that is, they took vows to remain chaste and live simply and devoutly, while continuing to live in the world and manage their affairs and household. An episcopal ceremony was performed in which the widow was blessed by the Bishop and invested with a ring signifying her commitment. She was then dressed in a simple robe, mantle and wimple, often indistinguishable from that of other widows. Being a vowess had both secular and spiritual advantages: the woman was free from pressure to remarry, she retained control of her temporal resources, and as a chaste widow she could hope to achieve a more elevated spiritual state than that of wives.

A monastic life was a possibility for women who wished to retreat from the world, though not all women in convents were there because they had a vocation. Some convents became dumping grounds for unwanted women – widows, unmarried or unmarriageable daughters of minor royalty or aristocracy, noble bastards and the like – where spirituality took a decided second place to material comfort. Chaucer's Prioress, with her genteel manners and pampered lapdogs, was probably the product of such a house. On the other hand, some women's houses were both spiritual bastions and centres for female education and accomplishment. Dartford Priory, a Dominican convent founded in 1346, was a prime example. It attracted some noblewomen, but the majority of the sisters were from gentry or wealthy merchant families. Dartford was a wealthy house and had an impressive library, much of it acquired through gifts and legacies. A similar foundation was Syon Abbey, established in 1415 by Henry V to house a community of Brigittine nuns. Like Dartford, Syon was a centre of women's learning and spiritual erudition. It also had a notable library, shared with the Carthusian monastery of Sheen just across the river, and the convent commissioned devotional books such as the *Myroure of Oure Ladye*. Margaret Swynford, daughter of Hugh and Katherine, and Elizabeth Chaucer, daughter of Geoffrey and Philippa, were both nuns at Barking

Abbey, another prominent women's house. Convents were sometimes open to women visitors for spiritual retreats and conversation; Margery Kempe visited Syon and also Denny Abbey near Ely on her devotional perambulations. Common women without dowries could enter convents as lay sisters. They performed the domestic tasks, or worked in the convent gardens or on the farms, while their wealthier sisters prayed and sang in the choir. One hopes that for the women of both estates the heavenly reward was the same.

Women who wanted a less restrictive spiritual experience could go on pilgrimage. Pilgrimage was the package tour of the Middle Ages, a liminal experience when people of all sorts mingled, as in the *Canterbury Tales*. While Canterbury was the favourite destination in Britain, pilgrims also travelled to Jerusalem, Rome and shrines in northern Europe. Santiago de Compostela was a popular route, with frequent sailings from Bristol to the Spanish port. Women could go on pilgrimage alone, though most women travelling alone went to shrines in England; pilgrims always travelled in groups for safety. Margery Kempe went on pilgrimage both in England and abroad without her husband, and her account speaks of other single women journeying to various sites. A conduct poem, *The Goodwife Would a Pilgrimage*, takes as its premise a mother setting off on pilgrimage and instructing her daughter how to manage the household in her absence.

At the opposite end of the spiritual spectrum from nuns and (most) pilgrims were the women of the streets. Although there were bawdy houses, or stews, in English towns they were not widespread, and prostitution was less institutionalised in England than on the Continent, where prostitutes were more strictly segregated from the rest of society. It seems that in England, common women who lacked family support or opportunities to enter the labour market proper might become hucksters – street-sellers of food and trinkets – or brewsters, and fall into casual prostitution, along with petty thievery and the illicit sale of ale. The *Cook's Tale* briefly introduces a woman of this sort – the wife of Perkyn Revelour's friend, who 'heeld for contenance / A shoppe, and swyved for sustenance' (I.4421–2). Punishment for prostitution could be imprisonment, a fine, banishment from the area or a period of time on the ducking stool.

Woman of the court or woman of the streets – death came to all alike, though not all were commemorated. Queen Philippa lies in Westminster Abbey. There is no record of the death or known tomb of Philippa, Chaucer's own wife, or of Margery Kempe. Katherine Swynford's tomb is in Lincoln Cathedral, alongside that of her daughter Joan. John of Gaunt lies in St Paul's Cathedral, as he directed in his will, beside his 'very dear late consort, Blanche'. The *Book of the Duchess* is Geoffrey Chaucer's moving epitaph to a woman of his time.

NOTES

1 Felicity Riddy, 'Mother Knows Best: Reading Social Change in a Courtesy Text', *Speculum*, 71(1996), 66–86.

2 In his early teens, Chaucer was a member of the household of the Countess of Ulster, daughter-in-law of Edward III, probably serving as a page. See *Riverside Chaucer*, p. vxii.

3 Paon de Roet was a bit-player in the well-known drama at Calais, when Queen Philippa interceded with Edward III to save the burghers of that city. See Jeannette Lucraft, *Katherine Swynford: The History of a Medieval Mistress* (Stroud: The History Press, 2010), pp. 1–2.

4 Sanford Brown Meech and Hope Emily Allen, eds., *The Book of Margery Kempe*, EETS os 212 (London: Oxford University Press, 1940), p. 111.

5 *Ibid.*, p. 181.

6 Information on Katherine Swynford has been drawn from Lucraft, *Katherine Swynford*; and Alison Weir, *Mistress of the Monarchy: The Life of Katherine Swynford, Duchess of Lancaster* (New York: Ballantine, 2009).

CHAPTER 24

Sex and Lust

Bruce Holsinger

Horny friars, adulterous wives, cuckolded old men: the sexual universe depicted in Chaucer's writings can seem a lively and colourful one, full of erotic double entendres and ribald jokes that have given the poet a modern reputation for a bawdy humour targeting every rank and order of medieval society. Yet critics have long recognised the darker, more violent sides of Chaucerian sexualities. His corpus both represents and colludes in the sexual traffic in women, while the *Wife of Bath's Tale* begins with a blithely narrated act of rape that scholars have linked to the strong suggestion in the life records that Chaucer was himself a likely perpetrator of sexual violence. Much of the light humour characterising the poet's treatments of sexuality in fabliau and romance masks quite violent and misogynist attitudes towards its many objects and victims. The subject of Chaucerian sexualities is a difficult and complex one, then, fraught with political and moral implications that extend far beyond the boundaries of his eccentric corpus of writings on the subject.

Sexuality is a modern term, of course, generally used to refer to a particular aspect of our inner lives: a personal disposition; an inherent quality or instinct; that distinct and distinguishing seat of desire, lust and self-identity seated somewhere within us. As the French philosopher Michel Foucault argued in the first volume of his influential *History of Sexuality*, writing of the distinction between acts and identities in the history of same-sex desire, 'The sodomite had been a temporary aberration; the homosexual was now a species': an aphorism that helped to consolidate the view of sexual identity as an inherently modern dimension of the human subject.[1] Despite Foucault's considerable influence on the field, other strands of scholarship in this area have developed more flexible conceptions of sex and sexuality and their discursive analogues in the medieval world. As Karma Lochrie asks of medieval culture more broadly, 'What might sexualities have looked like before heterosexuality and the normal?'[2] Mark Miller suggests that we see sexuality 'less as a sphere of desire and behavior that provided Chaucer with the underlying causes of human behavior than as a highly charged and tropologically rich site on which he explored the drive to autonomy and the grief that attends it'.[3]

It is also the case that Chaucer says remarkably little about the procreative aspects of human sexuality. If anything, Chaucerian sexualities are consistently non- or even *anti*-procreative in their representation and in the ways they unfold within particular narratives. Monogamous, marital and reproductive wantings and couplings captivated the least of his attention. For Chaucer, the realm of sex seems to be governed less by what Foucault would call biopolitics and more by the heavy pressures and constant urges of lust. 'Venus me yaf my lust, my likerousnesse' (*CT*, III.611), says the (child-free) Wife of Bath.

Chaucer was an avid and inventive theorist and narrator of lust in its many emotional, affective and incarnate permutations. Indeed, it can be quite difficult to find a piece of Chaucer's writing that does not thematise the perils and pleasures of lust in some sustained way. It is no mistake that the words *lust* and *lechery*, as well as their cognates (*lust, lusty, lustyness, lustiheed*; *likerous, likerously, likerousnesse*; etc.) appear hundreds of times in the *Canterbury Tales* alone, and many dozens in *Troilus and Criseyde* and the shorter poems. Lust is a foundational idiom in the Chaucerian corpus as in medieval moral writing more broadly, a remarkably rich reservoir of terms and concepts for exploring such subjects as the nature of good and evil, the boundaries of community, the formation of character, and the mysteries of desire.

We get an intriguing glimpse at the complex workings of Chaucerian lust in a much discussed passage from Book II of *Troilus and Criseyde*. Here Criseyde, having been manipulated by Pandarus into agreeing to an initial encounter with Troilus, deliberates with herself over the proper course of action, deciding that the lesser evil will be to meet '[i]n honour' with Troilus and 'maken hym good chere' rather than risk her uncle's life:

> 'Of harmes two, the lesse is for to chese;
> Yet have I levere maken hym good chere
> In honour, than myn emes lyf to lese.
> Ye seyn, ye nothyng elles me require?'
> 'No, wis', quod he, 'myn owen nece dere'.
> 'Now wel', quod she, 'and I wol doon my peyne;
> I shal myn herte ayeins my lust constreyne'.
>
> (*Tr*, II.470–6)

At this moment, as Criseyde gives her first words of consent to a liaison with Troilus, she does so precisely on the terms of her 'lust', as the couplet's penultimate word has it. Yet here her lust directs her to avoid a romantic entanglement with her prospective lover, while her 'herte' compels this loving niece to save her uncle, who vows that he will die if she fails to comply with his wishes (and, by extension, those of Troilus). Far from a synonym for excessive sexual desire, lust here seems to connote the will precisely to *avoid* carnal entanglements – though Chaucer is clearly playing with the reader's expectations that love and lust should mobilise the subject in very different directions indeed. Lust, then, is both a simple human desire for some end (a successful joust, a good meal, a proper encounter with an admirer) as well as a direct pathway to sin, and as the poem progresses, of course, Criseyde's love and lust soon become directed to similar ends.

One of the most extended and influential discussions in medieval writings of the nature and operation of *luxuria* comes in Thomas Aquinas's *Summa theologiae*, which devotes five articles to lust in general (*De luxuria*, 2a2ae, q. 153, arts. 1–5), and another twelve to what Aquinas codifies as 'the types of lust' (2a2ae, q. 154, arts 1–12).[4] The questions *de luxuria* broaden the category of lust beyond the straightforward notion of sexual impulses and acts. Does lust consist simply in the venereal wants and pleasures that we as fallen humans pursue, Aquinas asks, or is there more to the vice than this? The philosopher's answers to these questions are a qualified *yes* to the first and a reluctant *no* to the second, and in this philosophical ambivalence we can see the amorphous power of *luxuria* to shape so much of medieval discourse on desire and sin.

In the third objection Aquinas cites Alexander of Hales, whose own *Summa theologiae* opts for a broad and all-encompassing notion of luxurious pleasure: 'Further, lust is defined "as the desire of wanton pleasure". But wanton pleasure regards not only venereal matters but also many others. Therefore lust is not only about venereal desires and pleasures' (2a2ae, q. 154, art. 1.3). In the subsequent reply to the third objection, the authority of Augustine serves to accord sexual *luxuria* a special place in the pantheon of human passions: 'Although wanton pleasure applies to other matters, the name of lust has a special application to venereal pleasures, to which also wantonness is specially applicable, as Augustine remarks' (2a2ae, q. 154, art.1, r. 3). From the beginning of Aquinas's extended enquiry, then, lust has a special inherence in venereal matters. The reverse holds true as well. While lust can be generalised to embrace the full spectrum of human wants, the sexual component of lust lurks always beneath, a burden that other forms of lust carry with them as they go about their nasty work of inducing us to sin.[5]

This simultaneously diffuse and specific sense of lust is also at play in Aquinas's subsequent typology of the many forms of *luxuria* in question 154, particularly his views of nocturnal emissions and rape – the first a victimless crime of the self, the second an embodiment of human-on-human violence. 'Whoever has the use of reason can sin', he writes. 'Now a man has the use of reason while asleep, since in our sleep we frequently discuss matters, choose this rather than that, consenting to one thing, or dissenting to another. Therefore one may sin while asleep, so that nocturnal pollution is not prevented by sleep from being a sin' (2a2ae, q. 154, art. 5). The question of sin here is one of culpability, and in the response to this objection the philosopher suggests that since our reason is impeded during sleep, we do not have the free judgement necessary to sin despite the physical manifestation suggestive of lust:

> The use of reason is more or less hindered in sleep, according as the inner sensitive powers are more or less overcome by sleep, on account of the violence or attenuation of the evaporations. Nevertheless it is always hindered somewhat, so as to be unable to elicit a judgment altogether free.

Aquinas thus settles on a semi-exoneration of nocturnal emissions as a type of minor lust: not precisely a sin in itself, but perhaps caused by prior sinful behaviour or enacted lust. As he puts it, 'it is manifest that nocturnal pollution is never a sin, but is sometimes the result of a previous sin' (2a2ae, q. 154, art. 6).

Rape, on the other hand, is most emphatically a sin of lust according to the *Summa*. Indeed, as Aquinas puts it in the reply to the second objection (art. 7): 'The employment of force would seem to arise from the greatness of concupiscence, the result being that a man does not fear to endanger himself by offering violence.' That a man would 'endanger himself' through an act of sexual violence against a woman is one of the cruel ironies of this view of lust as beastly capacity to sin, though it speaks directly to the disturbing representation of rape and its consequences in works such as the *Wife of Bath's Tale*. This story begins when a 'lusty bacheler' (*CT*, III.883) in King Arthur's household commits a brutal but somewhat dismissively represented act of rape against a maiden in the countryside – the glib adjective 'lusty' enlisted as efficient explanation and cause of the atrocity.

Here and elsewhere in the Chaucerian corpus lust becomes the master moral trope of the human subject: that innate postlapsarian capacity to 'turn' the human from the right course into the crooked path of deviance and sin. This is the sense of lust that inspires the influential treatise by Alan of Lille, *De planctu Naturae*, which contains an elaborate psychological war between lust and reason. For Alan, lust

> leads the human mind into the ruin of vices, so that it perishes; the former, reason, bids it, as it rises, to ascend to the serenity of virtue. The one dishonors man, and changes him to a beast; the other mightily transfigures him into a god. Reason illuminates the darkness of the brain by the light of contemplation; lust extinguishes the radiance of the mind by the night of desire. Reason makes man to talk with angels; lust forces him to wanton with brutes. Reason teaches man to find in exile a home; lust forces him in his home to be an exile. And, in this, man's nature cannot reproach me for my ordering and management. For, out of the council of wisdom, I have set such a war of opposition between these antagonists that if, in this strife, reason bend down lust to defeat, the victory will not be without its following reward. For prizes won by victories shine more fairly than other presents.[6]

Here the soul is a psychic theatre of reason and lust, in which the two inner antagonists war over the moral disposition of humanity. Are we brute beasts or are we gods? Do we reach for the skies or revel in the mud? It is no mistake that the language of exile figures so strongly in such pronouncements about the power of lust, which threatens to alienate us from our 'homes', the familiar and controllable qualities of our reason.

Chaucer's poetics of lust was hardly circumscribed by the conventions of medieval moral philosophy, of course, and if the philosophical tradition most often opposes lust to reason, it also has a powerful counterpart and frequent opponent in narrative elaborations of love. The relationship between love and lust was a frequent point of debate among philosophers, though it took a good story to limn the contours of this relationship with the full complexity and colour it demands. There is a moving passage in the *Knight's Tale* that wrestles implicitly with the tension between love and lust by placing an internal monologue on the subject in the mind of Palamon, who laments his fate as a prisoner condemned to endless gazing at his love, Emily:

> What governance is in this prescience,
> That giltelees tormenteth innocence?
> And yet encresseth this al my penaunce,
> That man is bounden to his observaunce,
> For Goddes sake, to letten of his wille,
> Ther as a beest may al his lust fulfille.
> And whan a beest is deed he hath no peyne;
> But man after his deeth moot wepe and pleyne,
> Though in this world he have care and wo.
> Withouten doute it may stonden so.

The answere of this lete I to dyvynys,
But wel I woot that in this world greet pyne ys.
(*CT*, I.1313–24)

Unlike Arcite, who, now that he is freed, may raise an army and assault the forces of Theseus, Palamon must suffer the lustful agonies of proximity to his beloved. The passage is also a powerful statement on the potential endurance of lust even beyond the death of the body. A lustful beast will die without worrying about the post-mortem goad of his want. For a human being, by contrast, death in the face of earthly lust is only the first stage in a desirous agony that could potentially last forever. Lust here as elsewhere in Chaucer's writings is not licence but constraint; our inability to satisfy or quench it defines us as well as the bounds of our suffering.

Palamon is afflicted in part with what medieval theologians termed *concupiscentia oculorum*, or 'the lust of the eyes': as A. C. Spearing puts it, the suggestion in clerical writings 'that looking might itself constitute a sexual goal'.[7] Spearing cites an illuminating passage from Robert Mannyng's manual for preachers, *Handlyng Synne*, in which the act of looking only increases the goad of *luxuria* as the subject gazes upon the desired object:

more synne hyt ys
Whan þou sekest þy wyl of flessh
To þe lust of lecherye,
Yn handlyng or dremyng of folye,
Þurgh þoghtes or syghtes þat þou ses
And yn alle ouþre pryuytes.
God hymself forbedeþ al þys:
Þey gete no part of heuene blys.[8]

'Scopophilia', a psychoanalytic term enlisted by film critics to denote the often perverse pleasures taken in visual provocation, seems an apt way of describing such ocular provocations to lust and its perilous fulfilment. Such afflictions by lustful looking abound in Chaucer's writings, working across generations, sexes and species to define *luxuria* as a visual as much as moral category.

Of all Chaucer's representations of lust, few rival the *Parson's Tale* in intricacy and anatomical precision. Modelled on a number of Latin penitential treatises and noted for its dry, non-narrative approach to its subjects, the *Parson's Tale* seems an unlikely source for the sorts of lustful provocations found in Chaucer's more blatantly sexual works. Yet the tale contains the poet's most extensive and detailed observations on the sin of *luxuria*, cataloguing the various manifestations of lust in the lives of the sinful while revelling in the spectacle of the flesh they create:

> Allas! somme of hem shewen the boce of hir shap, and the horrible swollen membres, that semeth lik the maladie of hirnia, in the wrappynge of hir hoses; and eek the buttokes of hem faren as it were the hyndre part of a she-ape in the fulle of the moone. And mooreover, the wrecched swollen membres that they shewe thurgh disgisynge, in departynge of hire hoses in whit and reed, semeth that half hir shameful privee membres weren flayne. (*CT*, x.422–4)

Ostensibly directed at immodest dress on the part of men, this bit of invective flaunts the very grotesquery it condemns. The attempt at 'disgisynge' the protuberance of the 'boce' (bulge) through the camouflage of parti-coloured hose emphasises those anatomical details it is intended to obscure; and all of this is conveyed through the over-interested enthusiasm the Parson himself displays in condemning these transgressions of dress. Such prurient hyperbole is a staple of penitential discourse on lust and sexual aberration, which so often delights in the transgressions of the flesh it purports to abjure, and in the *Parson's Tale* Chaucer subtly sends up the tradition in the voice of a modest and abstemious parish priest.

As a London poet attuned to the rhythms of city life in all their diversity, Chaucer was closely aware of the operations of lust within the various earthly institutions it afflicts and helps to define. Lust is at work in the court, the household and the church; on the street, in the parish and in the shop. In the final lines of the (uncompleted) *Cook's Tale* a Cheapside apprentice is expelled from his master's shop and takes lodging in a household dependent on the medieval sex-trade for its upkeep:

> Anon he sente his bed and his array
> Unto a compeer of his owene sort,
> That lovede dys, and revel, and disport,
> And hadde a wyf that heeld for contenance
> A shoppe, and swyved for hir sustenance.
> (I.4418–22)

We learn no more about this 'swyving' wife, nor about the particular modes of *luxuria* inspiring her unrepresented clientele. The sobering passage gives us the barest glimpse at an urban geography of lust that in part defines Chaucer's corpus and a good part of his world. It is but one among myriad lustful imaginings that shaped Chaucer's literary production and continue to inspire allure and repulsion among the lust-ridden readers of his works.

NOTES

1 Michel Foucault, *The History of Sexuality*, Vol. 1: *An Introduction*, trans. Robert Hurley (New York: Random House, 1978), p. 43.

2 Karma Lochrie, *Heterosyncrasies: Female Sexuality when Normal Wasn't* (Minneapolis: University of Minnesota Press, 2005), p. xxiv.

3 Mark Miller, *Philosophical Chaucer: Love, Sex, and Agency in the 'Canterbury Tales'* (Chicago: University of Chicago Press, 2004), p. 4.

4 St Thomas Aquinas, *Summa theologiae*, ed. and trans. Thomas Gilby (Oxford: Blackfriars, 1964–75). Citations hereafter will be internal by part, question and article.

5 On these discussions in the *Summa* see Simon Blackburn, *Lust: The Seven Deadly Sins* (Oxford: Oxford University Press, 2004), pp. 65–70.

6 Alan of Lille, *De planctu Naturae*, prosa 3, trans. Douglas M. Moffat (New York: Henry Holt, 1908), p. 26.

7 A. C. Spearing, *The Medieval Poet as Voyeur: Looking and Listening in Medieval Love-Narratives* (Cambridge: Cambridge University Press, 1993), p. 6.

8 *Ibid.*

CHAPTER 25

Animals in Chaucer

Gillian Rudd

Animals abound in Chaucer; like his contemporaries, he was surrounded by a range of ways of writing about animals, from the compendia of beast lore found in bestiaries and books on hunting, through fables and myths of metamorphosis, to allegory and heraldic symbols, as well as the simpler use of animals as part of a scene, as farm animals, working animals or pets. So, although he never wrote a text about animals per se (whatever else *Parliament of Fowls* is, it is not a straightforward study of birds), they do appear throughout his works. In fact, it becomes quite a challenge to find a text by Chaucer that contains no animal at all. Even the *Treatise on the Astrolabe* (a manual for a complicated astronomical gadget) includes a simile describing the lines etched into the discs as 'like to the clawes of a loppe': like the claws of a spider (*Astrolabe* 2.19.3).

As this casual use of the spider indicates, one of the main ways animals feature in Chaucer is as vehicles for thought. Normally, similes do not require detailed knowledge of the animal concerned, since the likeness they depend upon is drawn from our interpretation of stereotypical behaviour (timid as a mouse); common associations (brave as a lion); or familiar sayings, as when being like a fish out of water is used in the *General Prologue* to criticise the Monk for being out of his cloister (*CT*, I.179–81). That said, Chaucer rarely uses similes in an entirely straightforward way. Often, as with the *Astrolabe*'s spider, the point of comparison makes us pause before acknowledging the fitness of the simile. We may not commonly think of spiders as having claws, but claws fit perfectly with the grooves on the astrolabe's metal discs. The image is thus wonderfully complex, as the patterns etched in the metal summon up both a web and the shape of a spider's legs, making the spider both the creator of the pattern and the result of it. In other instances, the simile itself is direct enough, but used in a way that adds a level of subtlety. Arcite and Palamon are shown to be well-matched by comparing Palamon to a 'wood leon' (I.1656) and Arcite to a 'crueel tigre' (line 1657) before both become 'wilde bores' (line 1658). Then as now, the exotic lions and tigers signal ferocious strength and are usually encountered only through literature or heraldry; boars, however, were indigenous and found in certain forests where they were kept for hunting purposes. Chaucer's succession of similes thus brings these two knights out of the world of classical romance and into the realm of everyday experience for his medieval audience. They remain figures in fiction, but just as their battle in the bushes takes place in the kind of grove that was a feature of forests used for hunting deer in medieval England (which is how Theseus comes across them), so the animals they are finally compared to become beasts one might actually find in such a wood.

Bestiaries offer one good short-cut to the diversity of knowledge and association available to a medieval author when dealing with animals.[1] These books bring together all kinds of knowledge about the animals listed within, from observation of behaviour, to biblical references and allegorical meaning. All such information is equally important, which encourages a habit of holding several modes of meaning in play simultaneously. Thus, the hen is a domestic soul, guarding her chicks under her wing; a fussing bird farmed in a group; and easy prey for foxes. But she is also a symbol of divine wisdom, a figure of the Church taking care of her congregation (chicks). Add to this the fable of the Cock and the Fox as found in Aesop and Marie de France, and it is immediately apparent that the *Nun's Priest's Tale* connects with a rich vein of animal literature combining moral fable (with the cock representing the proud, gullible man) with Christian allegory (the bestiary tells us that the fox symbolises the devil), while also being a credible depiction of the livestock a widow and her daughters might well own.

Another compendium offers yet more information on how Chaucer and his contemporaries thought about animals. Isidore of Seville's *Etymologies* (*c.* 615–36) remained an influential source for a century, with bestiaries often drawing on it for their own definitions. As its title indicates, *Etymologies* is about the meanings and roots of words, so it includes close consideration of the terms used for classifications of animals, as well as remarks on specific species. Here we find a particularly interesting distinction that is reflected in Chaucer's poetry. Book VII, *De animalibus* (on animals), differentiates livestock from beasts. Significantly, it is under livestock and beasts of burden (*De pecoribus et iumentis*) that the term 'animal' is considered: 'In Latin they are called animals (*animal*) or "animate beings" (*animans*), because they are animated (*animare*) by life and moved by spirit.'[2] Being moved by spirit may indicate simply that they breathe, but it also allows animals to have some apprehension of a power beyond themselves. Isidore and others would baulk at attributing full spiritual self-awareness to animals, but the distinction between animal and beast implied here indicates how we humans concede that some animals are quite like us, recognising in them individuality, not just species traits. The kind of awareness Isidore reflects here helps illuminate Chaucer's use of an animal in his lyric *Truth*.

Truth recommends renouncing the pressures of courtly life in favour of the true qualities found in a simple life. The poem owes much to Boethius and expresses familiar sentiments, including the lines:

> Forth, pilgrim, forth! Forth, beste, out of thy stal!
> Know thy contree, look up, thank God of al;
> Hold the heye wey and lat thy gost thee lede.
> (lines 18–20)

Despite Chaucer's use of the word 'beste', this animal is clearly 'livestock' in Isidore's terms; it is kept in a stall, and the pun on 'Vache' in the next verse indicates Chaucer has a cow in mind. The *Riverside Chaucer* editors comment (p. 1085) that beasts look down, humans look up, making these lines an instruction to people to understand their difference from animals and act accordingly, but Isidore's definition of 'animal' offers us an alternative reading, focusing on the defining characteristic of being moved by spirit. The line that urges us to be pilgrims also reminds us that we are beasts. Admittedly, the implication is that we are beast-like because we are boxed in by our preoccupations with worldly affairs, just as an animal is boxed into its stall, but rather than seeing the ability to 'look up' as exclusive to humans, Isidore allows us to see this as an invitation to be more like animals, and reject the obsessions of human courtly affairs in favour of the real truths of heaven. Just as animals are moved by spirit, so we should be led more by our own 'gost'. For a fleeting moment, the common hierarchy of human over animal is inverted: animals have an innate sense of where they belong; in humans that instinct has been overwritten by the lures of social gain. This lyric urges us to correct that by returning to a simpler, better, more animal mode of being.

This analogy allows both Chaucer's contemporaries and his latter-day readers 'a chance to think about the lives of animals'.[3] Lisa Kiser points out the danger to animals of being absorbed into human mindsets (a beast of burden that is also an allegory for sinning human flesh can be beaten with impunity), but *Truth* offers an alternative to this danger. Here the important point is that the animal is an animal and not an allegory of something else, and that allows an attentive reader to think about the beast concerned in more complex and respectful ways.

Isidore is again illuminating when considering the description of Arcite and Palamon fighting mentioned above. According to Isidore's section on beasts (*De bestiis*):

> 1. The term 'beast' properly speaking, includes lions, panthers, tigers, wolves, foxes, dogs, apes, and other animals that attack either with their mouth or their claws, excepting serpents. They are called beasts (*bestia*) from the force (*vis*) with which they attack. 2. They are termed wild (*ferus*) because they enjoy a natural freedom and are driven (*ferre*) by their own desires – for their wills are free and they wander here and there, and wherever their spirit leads, there they go.[4]

Suddenly a new layer of association is revealed in apparently straightforward similes. The lion that is Arcite and the tiger that is Palamon do indeed attack each other with force, but even more appropriately they are driven by their desire, not governed by codes of combat, as Theseus would have them be. Even the detail of wandering free is significant, as both are at this point out of prison, each following his spirit as he tries, rather pointlessly at this juncture, to secure Emily. Such layers of association betray our still prevailing habit of considering animals as less aware, less complex and so less valuable than humans. When it suits us, we recognise in animals emotions, reactions, intentions and agency that dissolve any notion of a firm divide between human and animal; but when that proximity becomes uncomfortable we revert again to thinking of animals as little more than animated symbols.

The *Knight's Tale* and *Nun's Priest's Tale* mark two ends of a figurative scale, from the simple, one-point comparison of the Knight's 'wood leon' to the fully worked-through fable of Chauntecleer. Neither of these presents an animal as simply an animal, and in fact it is hard to find such a beast in Chaucer's work. Even the Prioress's pet dogs are included in order to comment on her character, and the imagined mouse in the trap, which comes closest to being simply an animal, is dead and mentioned only to mock her sensitivity (I.114–49). This process, whereby animals are associated with attributes that are then credited to humans connected with those animals, has been termed the 'symbolic loop' by Susan Crane and seems to be inherent in literary writing about animals[5] – so much so, that the question of how far animals can be 'simply themselves' in literature has been raised by critics such as Lisa Kiser and Jeffrey Jerome Cohen. Elsewhere, attention has been drawn to the way that readers from a paper – even paperless – age too easily overlook the economic importance of animals not just as a food source but as parchment.[6] This particular commercial use of animals does not figure at all in Chaucer; the most explicit reference to farmed animals comes in the list describing the widow's life in the *Nun's Priest's Tale*, and even there the livestock is mainly scene-setting before the narrative moves into the chicken coop and the sphere of fable. Once within that world the concept of livestock is forgotten and the anthropomorphism of the fable world becomes dominant.

Anthropomorphism means it is common for animals to speak in fables, although it is not an absolute requirement of the genre, and speech encourages us to regard these characters as human, often forgetting their animal bodies. This creates scope for comedy, such as when Chauntecleer tricks Russell into mocking his pursuers and then flies free; it takes a moment for us to link the fact that speech involves opening the mouth to the fact that a fox carries its prey in its jaws. This deft switch from anthropomorphism to observed animal behaviour results in a neat denouement to the tale, which forces us to focus on the animal as itself, as we re-establish the division between human and animal worlds. The very fact that we can be caught out like this hints that the human–animal boundary is less secure than we might think and may lead us to ponder what it is exactly that divides human from other animals – speech? capacity for forward planning? – yet these beasts have displayed both.

It is only when the fable ends and the fox needs to be dispatched that we are finally brought back from a world in which animals talk and have character (Chauntecleer, Pertelote, Russell) to one in which they may have names but do not have individual personalities (Colle, Talbot, Gerland). That return is not quite as simple as it may seem, as the grammar of the lines that name dogs and widow alike for the first time reveals: 'Ran Colle, oure dogge, and Talbot and Gerland, / And Malkyn, with a dystaf in hir hand' (VII.3383–4). Briefly, we bundle Malkyn in with the dogs, until the distaff corrects our mental image, adding to the comedy of the moment, but also demonstrating how porous that human–animal boundary is – are the dogs in the human, realist sphere, or is the widow in the animal, fabular one?

The function of names at the beginning of this tale is similarly ambiguous. While the widow and her daughters are not named, their one sheep, Malle, is. Chauntecleer's name, which invokes his fine crowing, indicates his value in the estimation of both human and bird, and befits the fable mode in which the fox also gets a name, albeit the type-name Russell. Pertelote's name is more complex. We learn the hen's name just as the narrative segues from the realist world of the widow who 'hadde a cok, hight Chauntecleer' (VII.2849) to the fable world in which Chauntecleer 'hadde in his govenaunce / Sevene hennes for to doon al his plesaunce' (2865–6). Pertelote is the fairest of these seven, but it is unclear whether that judgement is the cock's, the widow's or both, and likewise whether she was named by Chauntecleer, who addresses her by name several times (3122, 3158, 3200), or by the widow, who presumably named the other animals of the household. Names may serve to place humans and animals in the same sphere, but we oversimplify matters if we assume that they automatically endorse the human–animal hierarchy.

There remains one animal whose very ubiquity makes it easy to overlook: the horse. The sheer variety of horses in Chaucer's works indicates how central horses were to human life. References range from the 'good' that laconically describes the Knight's horse of the *General Prologue* (I.74) to the 'amblere' (I.469), whose broad back ensures a comfortable ride for the Wife of Bath, and the Shipman's 'rouncy' (carthorse), which marks him as a man unaccustomed to the saddle (I.390). If the kind and condition of the horses ridden by the Canterbury Pilgrims is used to signal their social and financial status, the 'courser' (*Tr*, V.85) that Troilus chooses as his mount to accompany Criseyde as she is handed over to the Greeks indicates his need to appear as a warrior to be reckoned with even at this moment of truce. Changes in terms used for the same animal signal changes in function; thus, the horse borrowed by the students in the *Reeve's Tale* begins as simple beast of burden ('hors' (I.4017)), only to become a superior riding mount ('palfrey' (line 4073)) when John fears its loss. He is right to be worried: the 'wehee' of the liberated horse on seeing the wild mares in the fen (lines 4064–5) hints at a beast responding to animal instinct, not one keen to retain its association with men. The image raises a laugh, but it also exemplifies Chaucer's habit of linking animals to human concerns. Although the sources at his command offer ways of writing about animals that accord them some autonomy, this is not a route Chaucer himself ever takes. Despite this, readers may find in his texts a rich demonstration of the many ways animals figure in our world and shape our thoughts.

NOTES

1 See *Bestiary: Being an English Version of the Bodleian Library, Oxford, MS Bodley 764*, trans. Richard Barber (Woodbridge: Boydell Press, 2010 [1992]); and the online Aberdeen Bestiary: www.abdn.ac.uk/bestiary (last accessed 9 December 2018).

2 Isidore of Seville, *The Etymologies of Isidore of Seville*, trans. Stephen, A. Barney, E. J. Lewis, J. A. Beach and O. Berghof (Cambridge: Cambridge University Press, 2006), XII.i.3 (p. 247).

3 Lisa Kiser, 'Margery Kempe and the Animalization of Christ', *Studies in Philology*, 106 (2009), 299–315 (p. 315).

4 Isidore, *Etymologies*, XII.ii.1–2 (p. 251).

5 Susan Crane, 'For the Birds', *Studies in the Age of Chaucer*, 29 (2007) 21–42 (pp. 27–30).

6 See Barbara A. Hanawalt and Lisa J. Kiser, eds., *Engaging with Nature: Essays on the Natural World in Medieval and Early Modern Europe* (Notre Dame: University of Notre Dame Press, 2008). For discussion of animals as walking parchment, see Sarah Kay, 'Legible Skins: Animals and the Ethics of Medieval Reading', *postmedieval*, 2 (2011), 13–32; and Bruce Holsinger, 'Of Pigs and Parchment: Medieval Studies and the Coming of the Animal', *PMLA*, 124 (2009), 616–23.

PART IV

Culture, Learning and Disciplines

CHAPTER 26

Childhood and Education

Nicholas Orme

Chaucer's life and work reflected the history of childhood and education in fourteenth-century England. Little can be inferred about his own upbringing apart from what is suggested by his rank in society, but that rank and his later career suggest that he learnt to read and then mastered Latin at a public or private grammar school in London; which school is unknown. His rank and education are likely to have introduced him to reading and speaking French, and during his teens, he received vocational training as a page in a noble household. As an adult writer, he noticed and alluded to the literacy and education of his own day, and his literary works were subsequently considered to have an educational value for young people. He also wrote a treatise, the *Astrolabe*, with a more strongly instructive purpose.

REARING AND SOCIAL EDUCATION

No written works gave much advice about how medieval children should be raised. The process was traditional and informal, but it may be roughly divided into rearing and education, and education into that which was social, religious, literary and vocational. After birth, babies were breast-fed for some two years – longer than nowadays – usually by their mothers, but by wet-nurses in the case of the nobility and gentry, and possibly in that of the merchant elites of towns to which Chaucer's family belonged. Babies were swaddled in bands for warmth and protection, and in a wealthy household might also have a dry-nurse to care for them. Equipment was available for children in such households: cradles, children's clothes, small chairs and toys. As they were weaned, they were introduced to normal foods: milk, bread, eggs and apples being mentioned. Infant mortality was high, although not necessarily higher than in early modern times. Statistical evidence from the sixteenth century suggests that as many as 25 per cent of children died in their first year, half as many (12.5 per cent) between one and four, and a quarter as many (6 per cent) between five and nine. By the age of ten, 43 per cent (two-fifths) might be dead, like the child in the *Summoner's Tale* (*CT*, III.1851–3).[1] There is no evidence, however, that this led parents to be indifferent to children's survival or importance, and Chaucer movingly describes the grief of a bereaved mother in the *Prioress's Tale* (VII.586–606).

Social education involved developing speech, skills, knowledge and relationships to adults and other children. The study of fatal accidents shows that children soon grew conscious of their gender. Boys tended to follow their fathers around, leading to injuries from tools, carts or farm animals, while girls suffered mishaps at the hearths and wells to which they went with their mothers. Infancy was considered to last from birth to the age of seven, after which gender differences hardened. Boys and girls were likely to be dressed differently from that age and to have a more overtly male or female upbringing. Boys could be tonsured as clergy when seven, which gave them clerical status, and in Chaucer's day this was regarded as appropriate for choristers and even boys at school. The seven-year-old schoolboy hero of the *Prioress's Tale* is described as a 'clergeon', 'a little clerk' (VII.503).

Childhood brings a continuous flow of advice and comment from adults. Most of this is impossible to recapture, but Chaucer mentions it on three occasions. One concerns a boy in the *Pardoner's Tale*, who recalls that his mother told him always to be ready for death when it comes (vi.680–4). Another occurs in the *Manciple's Tale* where a mother's advice to be discreet in speech is made the vehicle for a philosophical discussion (IX.309–62). The third is a remark of the Wife of Bath that one of her strategies for handling men was learnt from her mother (III.574–5). More formally, upbringing emphasised the acquisition of good manners, especially for boys of higher rank. Courtesy literature was produced, at first in Latin but later in English, most of which was aimed at such boys and included rules about praying on rising in the morning, table manners and general deportment. Courtesy literature for girls of status is rarer and chiefly survives from the fifteenth century, but this does not mean that they did not learn good behaviour, merely that they acquired it informally from mothers, sisters or other guardians. Manners could also be valued among the lower orders but this no doubt varied among families, from those who were polite to those who were churls and did churls' deeds, like the peasant in the *Summoner's Tale* (III.2207).

RELIGIOUS EDUCATION

English society in the fourteenth century was a religious society, and it followed that growing up was influenced by Christian teaching and practice. Birth was immediately followed by baptism, which made a child a Christian from the very first day of its life without any possibility of not being so. Every child at baptism acquired three godparents, two of its own gender and one of the other, and the senior godparent of the child's gender announced the forename of the child during the ceremony. Certain families, chiefly among the aristocracy, kept to distinctive forenames but the commonest practice seems to have been for the senior godparent to give his or her own name to the child. Chaucer was probably named in this way, since Geoffrey was not traditional within his family, and he probably followed the same custom with regard to his own son Lewis, whose principal godfather is likely to have been Geoffrey's friend, Sir Lewis Clifford.

A child's godparents were expected to help its parents to bring it up in Christian beliefs and practices. By the end of the Middle Ages the Salisbury or 'Sarum' service-books used in southern England included a charge for the priest to deliver after a baby's baptism. It told the godparents to ensure that the parents kept the child from harm until it was seven, while the godparents themselves should teach it (or see that it was taught) the three basic prayers of the Church and bring it to a bishop to be confirmed. These three prayers were the Paternoster (Lord's Prayer), Ave Maria (Hail Mary) and Credo (Apostles' Creed), and were normally learnt by heart in Latin until the Reformation. Confirmation was purely a ceremony without any element of a personal profession of faith. It could be administered at any time from baptism onwards, and in the case of the royal family and great nobility a bishop would confirm the child immediately after the baptism.

The nature of confirmation reflected the fact that little religious instruction was given to medieval children. Parish clergy were not usually expected to hold classes for this purpose, as they were after the Reformation. Children do not even seem to have been required to attend church, although they were sometimes taken or went there, because there are occasional complaints about their noise, especially that of babies brought by their mothers. A child's religion centred on learning religious behaviour rather than religious knowledge. The Paternoster, for example, was often said by adults when they were triggered to do so by passing a standing cross; it was good manners to do so. The schoolboy in the *Prioress's Tale* is taught by his mother to kneel down and recite the Ave Maria whenever he sees an image of the Virgin Mary (VII.505–12). At meals it was often the custom to get a child to say grace before eating began.

Since the twelfth century the Church had come to define and distinguish childhood and adulthood to a greater extent than before. A baptised child was believed to be regenerate from sin. If it died, it was buried in consecrated ground and its salvation was assured, hence the friar's claim in the *Summoner's Tale* that he saw a dead child 'borne to bliss' with God (III.1854–8). Children were thought incapable of committing mortal sins until they reached puberty and gained the mental and physical power to do so. They were therefore not required to attend confession and did not qualify to receive unction when dangerously ill. They were also exempt from fasting in Advent and Lent, along with Fridays and the vigils of saints' days. Theologians considered that they could not understand the miracle of transubstantiation, the conversion of bread and wine to the body and blood of Christ at the Eucharist, and so unlike adults they were not allowed to receive communion on Easter Sunday or at moments of danger.

All this changed at puberty, which was reckoned to take place at twelve for girls and fourteen for boys. The Church developed no rite of passage in connection with puberty, but it seems likely that parish clergy required their young parishioners as they approached or reached these ages to join the adults in coming to the confessions held during Lent and in receiving the bread of the Eucharist at Easter, as all adults did. In this way boys and girls made the passage from childhood to adulthood alongside their elders, not as a group on their own. From now on they were subject to adult rules and required to fast, pay Church dues when appropriate, attend confession and carry out the penances that might be imposed in that process. Many parish churches in the later Middle Ages came to have organised groups of young men and maidens, who represented the adolescents and young adults from puberty to marriage, which usually took place in the mid twenties. These groups raised money towards church expenses, held social activities and might venerate a particular image within the church building.

VOCATIONAL EDUCATION

Adolescence was also a time for learning to work, except (as we shall see) for those who went to school and university. Work might begin on a small scale when children were young: caring for siblings; helping with household chores; and doing light tasks out of doors such as bird-scaring, driving ducks or geese, and gleaning at harvest time. In an agricultural society, however, children could not be fully employed until they reached puberty and had sufficient strength. Then, unless their labour was needed at home, they were likely to be sent into service elsewhere. For most of the population this meant girls working as indoor servants and boys as personal attendants, farm servants or labourers. There was a wide demand for cheap juvenile labour. The great household of a prelate or magnate might employ a dozen or more 'pages' or 'boys' as assistants in its kitchen, bakery, stables and other departments. Even craftsmen, artisans or wealthy unmarried men might keep a young man as a servant, like the 'knave' Robin who works for the carpenter in the *Miller's Tale* (I.3431, 3466–9), or the 'knave' (also called a 'boy' and 'child') who serves the riotous young men in the *Pardoner's Tale* (VI.666, 670, 686).

Going away to work was also customary in the higher levels of society. Relatively prosperous families sent sons (and occasionally daughters) to become apprentices to crafts or trades in towns. This option was not easily available to the poor. Manorial law prohibited villeins (unfree tenants) from apprenticing their children without permission, lest the lord of the manor lose a useful worker, and the Statute of Cambridge (1386) required that any person, male or female, who had been used to working at the plough, cart or other agricultural labour up to the age of twelve should continue in the same work and not be put to learn a trade or craft. Later, in 1406, a statute forbade parents to apprentice their children in towns unless they possessed land or rent worth at least 20s. a year. Apprenticeships also cost money in the form of a down-payment made by parents to the employer. It follows that Perkyn Revelour, the apprentice in the *Cook's Tale*, was not poor but privileged, and his story (whatever it would have been) was not about a young man of low origins but one who made a descent into low life. Like apprentices were parish clerks, exemplified by Absolon in the *Miller's Tale* (I.3312–51). They too were usually adolescents or young adults, learning how to lead worship by assisting an adult priest and often aiming to be ordained as such when they reached the minimum age of twenty-four. Posts of this kind were also relatively elevated ones, gained through status and influence.

Youths and maidens of the nobility and gentry followed a parallel path in the great households of the aristocracy. Some were wards who, by the law of feudal tenure, came under the government and control of their lords if their father died before they reached adulthood, and were sometimes brought up in their lords' households. Others were placed with lords by their families at about the age of puberty: the boys as pages or 'henchmen' (a term developing in the mid fourteenth century) and the girls (without a specific title) as boarders in households where there was a wife or widow in charge. Chaucer himself spent part of his adolescence in the household of the Countess of Ulster, and he portrays similar young people in the *Canterbury Tales*. The Squire is one such example (I.79–100), as are Arcite (when in disguise) in the *Knight's Tale* (I.1415–41) and Jankyn in the

Summoners' Tale (III.2243–5), while the women described as attending on Ypolita and Canacee in the *Knight's Tale* and *Squire's Tale* (I.1750; V.382–3) doubtless included maidens of a corresponding age. Canacee herself has a 'mistress' or governess (V.374–7), and Chaucer includes advice to such mistresses in the *Physician's Tale* (VI.72–92), perhaps inspired by the fact that his wife's sister, Katherine Swynford, held this role in the family of John of Gaunt. Youths and maidens in noble households were partly upper servants waiting personally on their employers, and partly pupils undergoing training. Boys were taught to serve at table, ride and use weapons; and girls to spin, sew, and make textiles and clothes. Both sexes were likely to learn or practise reading in French or English, singing, dancing, and the playing of instruments: well summed up in the list of skills ascribed to the Squire.

LITERACY

The world in which young people grew up was, by Chaucer's lifetime, a literate world. This does not mean that everyone could read or write, but everyone's life was dependent upon written materials in one way or another. During previous centuries, the quantity and scope of these materials had steadily increased. Church services were conducted from written books. The royal government issued commands, grants of offices and privileges, parliamentary proceedings and statutes, legal documents, and financial accounts, all of them sent or preserved in writing. Similar records were produced in the Church (with the notable addition of wills), by town councils, on rural manors, in noble households and among the merchant class. A growing volume of devotional and recreational literature was also being created: prayer books such as primers and Books of Hours, spiritual treatises, saints' lives, handbooks, romances, and poetry. Texts of a temporary nature might be written on reusable tablets, but those that needed to be kept required a permanent format. It is a sign of the huge increase in written material during Chaucer's lifetime that parchment, which was the traditional medium of writing, became inadequate for the purpose, and the new and cheaper format of paper was developed, through which the proliferation of texts grew even further.

People were stimulated to learn to read for two reasons. There was a practical advantage to be gained and social status to be maintained or acquired. Kings, noblemen and gentlemen read in part because it was noble to do so, a tradition going back to the Romans. They also needed to access documents, to check the work of their subordinates and to correspond with other people. Their wives and daughters did not have so many needs, but both sexes wished to use prayer books, and to read religious works and works of entertainment. Much the same was true in the middling ranks of society: clergy, merchants, lawyers, craftsmen and wealthy farmers of the kind who would come to be known as yeomen. Women of these ranks might also want to read for piety or for pleasure, and men and women alike gained status from their skill. How far literacy extended to the majority of people – peasants, artisans and labourers – is still unclear. There were certainly some examples of low-born readers and even writers. The earliest version of *Piers Plowman* in the 1360s implies that a ploughman could read, and a villein on the Somerset manor of Shapwick was reported to be teaching children in 1372–3. William Smith of Leicester, an early Lollard in the 1380s who is said to have been named from his occupation, wrote religious works in English in his own hand. But even if the majority of the population could not read, all came into contact with written texts. All heard the clergy read in church. Any might buy or sell land by charter, have the grant of a tenancy recorded on a manorial court roll, make a will, be listed in a rental or taxation list or be named in legal documents if they became involved in crime or litigation.

Literacy in medieval England was complicated by issues of language. Written material might be in Latin, French or English. A full understanding of Latin was confined to boys and men of the prosperous classes. They required it to function as clergy or, as laity, to read formal administrative, financial and legal documents, especially those of the crown and the Church, which were normally kept in Latin. Women generally knew little Latin, although they might use Latin prayer books such as the Book of Hours. French was widely read among the aristocracy, clergy and merchant class up to about the time of Chaucer's death, both by men and women. It was employed for less formal documents such as private letters and financial records, as well as for reading devotional works and imaginative literature. English was read for the same purposes as French, but less extensively when Chaucer was born because its varying dialects made its works more difficult to circulate. During Chaucer's life, however, the relative popularity of French and English was completely reversed, so that when he died in 1400 it was becoming more natural to read and write in English for common purposes. The reading of French narrowed into texts and romances that had not yet been translated, and its speaking into the English law courts and interaction with people in France.

LITERARY EDUCATION

The kinds of people who learnt to read reflected the uses of literacy. As has been observed, they came largely from the upper and middle ranks of society, male and female, but not excluding some (chiefly men) from the lower orders. The simple skill of reading could be acquired in many places. Parents could teach it at home, or other literate adults in great households. Nunneries received small boys and girls from the wealthier classes, and boarded and taught them. Schools were held in some churches by parish clerks, and there were private schoolmasters and -mistresses in towns teaching elementary schools in their own houses. One began to learn to read in Latin. The alphabet was the Roman alphabet, and the first texts that learners encountered were the three basic Latin prayers, followed by other religious material such as Latin psalms and antiphons. Once these texts had been mastered, one could use the skill of reading to access texts in a familiar language such as English or French. Latin, however, required further study, because someone who had merely learnt to recognise Latin words and pronounce them would not understand their meaning. Chaucer makes this point in the *Prioress's Tale*. A boy is learning a Latin antiphon by heart but cannot yet translate it: 'I lerne song; I kan but small grammeere', meaning Latin (VII.536). Many men and most women could only read a Latin prayer book with devotion rather than full understanding.

The understanding of Latin was gained at a grammar school. This was virtually limited to boys of the wealthier classes. It cost more than learning to read and needed at least three or four years of study. Since most grammar schools were in towns, those living in the countryside faced the further expense of boarding away from home, which, then as now, was much greater than school fees alone. A grammar-school education involved learning the morphology of Latin, its vocabulary, its syntax (how to compose and speak it) and its prosody (the writing and pronunciation of verse). One also learnt linguistics, because the teaching of grammar emphasised the understanding of terminology and categories. Literature was read in the form of Latin poetry. In Chaucer's time this normally included only one work from classical Rome: the *Disticha Catonis*, a third-century collection of wise maxims, to which he refers several times in his works (e.g. *MerT*, IV.1377; *Mel*, VII.1280). The other poems read were all from the Middle Ages and centred on imparting wisdom, ethics and good manners, not on recounting stories. This emphasis is reflected in the romances of Chaucer and his contemporaries, which are concerned to raise moral or logical issues rather than being merely tales.

Grammar schools imparted two other skills besides Latin. One was writing, which was therefore chiefly a male accomplishment. Wealthy women usually had their writing done by male scribes, and although Chaucer describes women writing letters, this was typically done for private purposes such as conducting a love affair (*MerT*, IV.1996; *Anel*, 208–10; *Tr*, V.470–2). The other skill was French, which was often used by schoolmasters for teaching Latin in Chaucer's youth, up to about the middle of the fourteenth century. This practice came about because most of the wealthy pupils typical of grammar schools lived in households where French was spoken, and French, being a significantly unified language, was easier for a master to use than English, which had not yet acquired a standard form or many grammatical terms. After about 1350, however, this practice declined. Latin was taught in English, and French had to be learnt as a foreign language from specialised teachers outside grammar schools. Teachers of this kind were to be found in large towns and could also teach business studies: accounting and the writing of legal documents. Such studies were not taught in grammar schools, and most boys learnt them as part of their job when they became apprentices to merchants, or secretarial clerks in a great household.

Of the minority of boys who went to grammar schools, a further small minority went on to higher education. This too required wealth, because attending a university involved living away from home for lengthy periods. The basic degree course at Cambridge and Oxford, the 'arts course', took seven years with a requirement to spend two further years as a lecturer, but many students stayed for shorter periods and did not graduate. All were technically 'clerks' or clergy while at university, and most entered the Church, but not all. There must have been many like Jankyn, the fifth husband of the Wife of Bath, who left their studies for a life in the world and ended by marrying (*CT*, III.527–9). During Chaucer's lifetime, the common lawyers in London who practised English secular or 'common' law were beginning to gather in communities, known as the Inns of Court and Chancery. These communities became popular places in the fifteenth century for wealthy young men to board and receive some legal training as a prelude to life as gentlemen or to becoming lawyers themselves. But this development was hardly yet visible when Chaucer described the Inns in his portrait of the Manciple, and he did not allude to their educational function (*GP*, I.567–86).

CHAUCER AS EDUCATIONIST

It remains to examine how far the poet himself was aware of childhood and education, and how far he may be called a writer on these subjects.

The concern of his works with adult characters and issues necessarily meant that he made only casual references to children and their activities. Nevertheless, education plainly interested him. His description of an elementary school in the *Prioress's Tale*, though short, is perceptive, and rare in literature (VII.495–550). He praises the moderation and good sense of Seneca in tutoring Nero (*MkT*, VII.2495–518), offers advice to parents and mistresses of young noble girls (*PhyT*, VI.72–104), and includes a long piece of guidance from a mother to a son in the *Manciple's Tale* (IX.316–62). His portraits of the Squire in the *General Prologue* (I.79–100) and of Virginia in the *Physician's Tale* (vi.30–71) are typical examples of how medieval writers described well-educated young men and women. The Squire is praised for his accomplishments, and Virginia for her virtues, an apparent discrepancy that was not true in reality. As Chaucer shows elsewhere, women learnt plenty of skills: social, physical, literary and artistic.

Most notable is his interest in university students, of whom there are seven in his works: the Clerk of Oxford; Nicholas in the *Miller's Tale*; Alan and John in the *Reeve's Tale*; Jankyn, the husband of the Wife of Bath; and Aurelius's brother and the magician in the *Franklin's Tale*. Chaucer was evidently well acquainted with both Oxford and Cambridge as towns, and his placing of his ten-year-old son Lewis at Oxford in the 1390s, probably in one of the grammar schools for which the city was well known, may have been intended as a preparation or substitute for studying the arts course. He expresses indulgence or approval towards these men, in a way that is qualified or withheld in the case of monks and friars. Finally, Chaucer's *Astrolabe* (*c.* 1391) may be classified as an educational work, since it was undertaken at Lewis's request to teach him how to use the instrument. It also adopted the format of a father teaching his son, a format found in some other medieval treatises.

Four of the manuscripts of the *Astrolabe* are prefaced by the title 'bread and milk for children' which suggests that it was used in the fifteenth century as a text in which children could practise reading in English. Chaucer's East Midland dialect had the advantage for this purpose of resembling the standard English that was evolving during that century. Others of Chaucer's works were recommended to young people or read by them for pleasure. The courtesy poem 'Little Child', composed between 1450 and 1477, advises the boy for whom it was written to read any of Chaucer's works. In 1477 Thomas Spurleng of Norwich, a youth of about sixteen, assisted his father in making a copy of the *Canterbury Tales*, while the poet John Skelton, soon after 1500, credited Joan Scrope, a knight's daughter, with having read the *Tales*, singling out the *Knight's Tale*, *Wife of Bath's*

Tale and *Nun's Priest's Tale*. Chaucer was therefore both a writer on specific aspects of education and a writer whose works became regarded as generally educational. The historian of education may learn much from him.

NOTE

1 E. A. Wrigley and R. S. Schofield, *The Population of England 1541–1871* (London: Edward Arnold, 1981), pp. 248–9, 528.

CHAPTER 27

Philosophy

Stephen Penn

Early in the first book of his *Didascalicon de studio legendi*, an influential guide to the study of the arts that appeared during the twelfth century, the philosopher and exegete Hugh of St Victor famously quotes Boethius quoting Pythagoras, who, Boethius declares, was the first to define philosophy as the love and study of wisdom. This broad definition, based on the Greek etymology of the Latin term *philosophia*, was influential throughout the medieval period, and was enshrined in Isidore of Seville's *Etymologiae*, an encyclopedic glossary that most medieval scholars would have known. It would almost certainly have been known to Chaucer, who may have had no direct acquaintance with the rather forbidding *Didascalicon* itself. The very breadth of Hugh's definition gives an indication of the capacious nature of the discipline of medieval (and classical) philosophy. Though it encapsulated many of the concerns of its modern counterpart (the nature of being, knowledge and truth, for instance), it also embraced issues as diverse as the nature of musical harmony and the motions of the planets. As Hugh goes on to explain, however, the main purpose of philosophy in the period when Chaucer was writing was to prepare its student for a career in the supreme science of theology.

Chaucer had the scholarly resources of neither an ecclesiastic nor a student or fellow of one of the colleges of Oxford or Cambridge, and it seems that most of his formal education would have been received at a London grammar school, possibly the Almonry School of St Paul's Cathedral, where he would have learnt Latin. It appears likely that much of his knowledge of philosophy would have been gained from textual fragments reproduced in miscellanies, notes and encyclopedias, or from scholarly acquaintances, but his poetry reveals a strong familiarity with a small number of complete philosophical sources. His Middle English translation of the *De consolatione philosophiae* of Boethius identifies the most important philosophical treatise that he knew, and seemingly the one about which he thought at greatest length.

Chaucer's friendship with Ralph Strode, the 'philosophical Strode' to whom, with John Gower, he dedicated *Troilus and Criseyde*, must have brought him into contact with some of the elements of contemporary philosophical debate, though disappointingly little is known about their relationship. Strode was a fellow of Merton College between 1359 and 1360, and possibly also in 1361; he later became Common Sergeant of London. It is not impossible that the philosophical and the legal Strodes were in fact entirely different people, but Strode's departure from Oxford and the subsequent appearance of a London lawyer of the same name in 1373 seems unlikely to be coincidental. For two years from 1374, he lived above the gatehouse in Aldersgate, to the west of the city; Chaucer resided above the gatehouse in Aldgate, to the east, from May in that same year (a lease was made in his name until 1386), shortly before his appointment as customs controller of the port of London.[1] Strode had entered into an amicable debate with John Wyclif on the popular question of free will and divine foreknowledge in 1374, gently resisting the predestinarianism that Wyclif, drawing heavily on Thomas Bradwardine's *De causa Dei*, had famously defended in *De volitione Dei*, *De universalibus* and in many of his sermons.[2] That he should be identified in a poem that owes so great a debt to the philosophical musings of Boethius's *De consolatione philosophiae* is hardly a coincidence (Strode is known to have read a draft of the poem), and nor, it would seem, is the close verbal parallel between Troilus's claim that 'al that comth, comth by necessitee' (*Tr*, IV.958) and Wyclif's famous proclamation that 'omnia quae eveniunt de necessitate eveniunt', which appears in his *Responsiones ad argumenta Radulfi Strode*.[3] Placed in the mouth of a character so blind to Boethian reasoning, it may have served as an oblique endorsement of Strode's critique. An echo of Wyclif's words is also found in the *Nun's Priest's Tale*: 'what that Got forewoot mote nedes be' (*CT*, VII.3234). These words, describing the belief of 'certein clerkis' (VII.3235), are carefully challenged by the events of the tale itself. This belief in predeterminism, the Priest reveals, has given rise to 'greet altercacioun' and 'greet disputisoun' (VII.3237–8) in the schools (and no example can have been more familiar to Chaucer than the debate between Wyclif and his friend), but he modestly protests that he 'ne kan nat bulte it to the bren / As kan the hooly doctour Augustyn, / Or Boece, or the Bisshop Bradwardyn (VII.3241–2). Like Boethius, neither Augustine nor Bradwardine, nor indeed Wyclif, claimed that divine foreknowledge was incompatible with free will, but the teaching of the last two scholars was widely regarded as being inescapably deterministic. Strode certainly seemed to think so, as Wyclif's *Responsiones* confirm, and Chaucer's own knowledge of the position that Bradwardine had outlined in the *De causa Dei* must have owed something to this interpretation.

The resources on which Chaucer drew as a translator of *De consolatione*, including Jean de Meun's French vernacular translation, *Li livres de confort*, and the Latin commentary of the Dominican scholar Nicholas Trevet, together with his own vernacular glosses on the translated text, attest to the efforts that such a project must have entailed. The philosophy of Boethius shares its neo-Platonic foundations with many of Chaucer's other principal philosophical sources, such as the texts of Roman orator Cicero and his commentator Macrobius, together with the works of the Chartrian philosophical poets Bernardus Silvestris, Alanus de Insulis (Alan of Lille) and Andreas Capellanus, the last three all active during the philosophical 'renaissance' of the twelfth century. All of these writers, like Plato in the *Timaeus*, offer a vision of a universe rationally ordered and structured by the creator or craftsman (the *demiourgos*), and through whose nature and attributes, which the creator fashioned according to his eternal model, divine truths may be apprehended by the diligent student. Scipio is shown the cosmos by his adoptive grandfather, Scipio Africanus the Elder, in Cicero's *Somnium Scipionis*, and hears the mellifluous harmonies of the planetary spheres that ordinary mortals, restrained by the 'fetters of [the] body', are unable to discern; Prudence journeys through the ether to the heavens in pursuit of the perfect human soul in Alan of Lille's *Anticlaudianus*; Nature explains how the motions of the planetary and celestial bodies are guided by her in Alan's *De planctu Naturae*; and Nous, a personification of the Platonic intellect, reveals the universe to Natura in Bernardus Silvestris's philosophical allegory, the *Cosmographia*. It is not unlikely that Chaucer would have been familiar with the incomplete Latin translation of Plato's *Timaeus* produced in the fourth century CE by Chalcidius, who also wrote an extensive commentary on the text, though it seems likely that most of his Platonism would have derived from these later sources, amongst others.

Though Chaucer was hardly a philosopher, much less a dedicated Platonist, the neo-Platonic sources on which he drew leave a vivid philosophical residue in his writing. Much of the 'new science' that the scholarly and inexperienced narrator of Chaucer's *Parliament of Fowls* acquires from his ancient books, for example, is knowledge of a broadly philosophical kind. His reading of Macrobius's rendering of Cicero's *Somnium Scipionis*, the 'olde boke' that he chooses to examine prior to sleeping, is the most detailed that any of Chaucer's narrators provides. The *Somnium Scipionis* was originally part of the sixth and final book of a longer work by Cicero, the *De re publica*, but the portion preserved by Macrobius (not always entirely faithfully) was all that was known of this text in the later medieval period. The summary that Chaucer offers in lines 32–91 of his poem describes the Platonic universe revealed to Scipio by the 'African' (Scipio Africanus the Elder) in Chapters 3 and 4 of the original text, with the 'lytel erthe' at its centre, beneath nine concentric planetary and stellar spheres. A similar depiction of the universe is described by Nature in Jean de Meun's continuation of the *Roman de la Rose*, in which the figure of Nature and her priest Genius are fashioned after figures appearing in Alan of Lille's twelfth-century narrative, *De planctu Naturae*. In the narrator's summary of Cicero's text in the *Parliament of Fowls*, as in the Latin text, Scipio is urged to direct his thoughts away from the earth, 'so lyte / And dissevable and ful of harde grace' (*PF*, 64–5) towards the permanence of the heavens. In the *House of Fame*, the Dreamer is offered a similar perspective on his tiny world and the vastness of the surrounding universe by the eagle, after his professedly unphilosophical lecture about upward motion of speech-sounds. The earth is perceived to be so small by Geffrey that it 'No more semed than a prikke' (*HF*, 907). Alastair Minnis suggests that Boethius is the likely source here, highlighting the verbal parallel between 'prikke' and the term used in *De consolatione* to describe the earth ('punctus', which Chaucer translates as 'prikke' in the *Boece*).[4] Earlier in Book II, the eagle explains how everything in the universe has its 'kyndely stede' (line 731) – an idea that has obvious philosophical resonances and, he says, 'ys knowen kouth / Of every philosophres mouth' (lines 757–8), including both Plato and Aristotle. The 'eyryssh bestes' (line 932) that he gestures towards in the air above him are mentioned in Plato, he suggests, though it seems likely that Alan of Lille (whose 'Anteclaudian' is mentioned in line 986) is the immediate source here.[5] Chaucer was obviously keen to create often ironic parallels between the eagle's commentary on the universe and those found in his philosophical sources, but also to highlight the absurdity of his position as a figure of philosophical authority. In assuring Geffrey that neither Alexander the Great nor Scipio, in whose own dream he supposedly saw 'Helle and erthe and paradys', flew half so high as this (line 917), his hollow boasts have an ironic echo of Nature's words in the *Roman de la Rose*, in which dreamers who say that they have seen 'enfer et paradis', and who claim to have experienced dreams like those of Scipio, are mocked. Geffrey's experience in the claws of such a figure is all the more farcical, of course, when compared with that of Prudence in the *Anticlaudianus*.

A philosophical issue closely related to the questions about the structure of the universe and the nature of reality is that of divine foreknowledge and human agency, an issue that preoccupies Chaucer in a variety of texts. Boethius is once again, of course, the most relevant philosophical source here, and *Troilus and Criseyde* is the text that has attracted most critical attention.[6] Troilus's fatalistic responses to the perceived machinations of Fortune, as articulated in his dialogues with Pandarus and in his soliloquy on predestination, tend to identify him with the naïve persona of Boethius in his discussions with Philosophy (whose role is generally taken by Pandarus). Verbal borrowings from Boethius are often clearly visible, especially in Troilus's extended exchange with Pandarus in Book I, in which he complains of the malevolent influence of fortune and is offered Boethian philosophical advice from Pandarus, and in his lengthy soliloquy in Book IV. In the latter, Boethian borrowings are particularly conspicuous:

O welaway, so sleighe arn clerkes olde
That I not whos opynyoun I may holde.
'For som men seyn, if god seth al biforn –
Ne god may nat deceyued ben, parde –
Than moot it fallen, theigh men hadde it sworn,
That purveiance hath seyn byfore to be.
Wherfore I sey that from eterne if he
Hath wist byforn oure thought ek as oure dede,
We han no fre chois, as thise clerkes rede.'
(*Tr*, IV.972–98)

'It semeth', quod I, 'to repugnen and to contrarien gretly, that God knoweth byforn alle thinges and that ther is any freedom of liberte. For yif so be that God loketh all things byforn, ne God ne mai nat ben desceyved in no manere, thane moot it nedes ben that alle thinges betyden the which that the purveyance of God hath seyn before to comen. For whiche, yif that God knoweth byforn nat oonly the werkes of men, but also hor conseilles and hir willes, thane ne schal ther be no liberte of arbitrie.'
(*Bo*, V, pr. 3.5–16)

The verbal parallels between the two texts are so striking here that it would be tempting to look no further for philosophical sources. Even where verbal parallels are not so close, Boethian influence is tangible throughout the fourth book of the *Troilus*, and not merely in relation to Pandarus and Troilus. But another source that Chaucer knew very well incorporates a lengthy meditation on the relationship between fortune and free will: the *Roman de la Rose*. In spite of his minimal elaboration on the appearance and characteristics of Nature in the *Parliament of Fowls*, Chaucer must have been familiar with Jean de Meun's depiction of Nature's confession to her priest, Genius, in the tenth chapter of the text. Whilst Nature's discussion of the relationship between fate and free will is clearly Boethian, and she reaches a conclusion comparable to the one offered by Philosophy, the discussion is nevertheless distinctive. Though God sees everything that will happen, Nature suggests, individual volition remains free.[7] Jean uses the example of a man who sees another man doing something, arguing that the first man's knowledge can have no effect on the other man's actions; if this is true when knowledge is acquired as the action takes place, so it must be true if knowledge of the other man's actions is present in the man's mind in advance.[8]

The vision of the physical and the neo-Platonic universes that features in Macrobius also informs his thinking about the nature and philosophical value of dreams: those that have their sources in the world (*visa* and *insomnia*) are held to have little or no philosophical value, whereas those that embody truths, often under a veil of fiction (*oracula*, *visiones* and *somnia*) are held to be of great philosophical interest.[9] There is little compelling evidence that Chaucer paid any attention to the details of Macrobius's five-fold distinction, but he did recognise the fundamental division between truthful and untruthful dreams. His earliest dream vision, the *Book of the Duchess*, makes only a brief mention of Macrobius, which finds a close parallel in the first ten lines of Guillaume de Lorris's *Roman de la Rose*. In Chaucer's poem, however, the Dreamer anticipates that even Macrobius will be inadequate to explain this dream about the Black Knight, even though his authority is explicitly acknowledged (lines 284–9). The proem of Book II of the *House of Fame* offers a more detailed account of the typology of dreams, but with no direct reference to Macrobius. Allusions here to the *sweven*, *fantome* and *oracle* have close parallels in the *Roman de la Rose*, but the narrator makes no attempt to discover their causes. He enumerates a wide range of possibilities nevertheless, including physical disorders ('gret feblenesse' of the brain, distress, 'impressions' in the mind), and prophetic impulses ('spirites' of the soul, revealing what 'ys to come') or warning of future events through 'avisiouns or figures' (literal or figurative dreams, corresponding broadly to Macrobius's *oracula* and *visiones*) (lines 23–48). But he commits himself to none of these, and mentions 'noon opinion' of the 'gret clerkys' who have studied dreams, wishing only that 'the holy roode / Turne us every drem to goode!' (lines 57–8).

An equally detailed exploration of the nature of dreams, which also looks beyond Macrobius as an authority (though dutifully acknowledges him) appears in the *Nun's Priest's Tale*. Here, Chaucer drew on stories used by both Cicero and Valerius Maximus, either of whom could be 'Oon of the gretteste auctor that men reade' (VII.2984), the only indication that Chauntecleer gives as to the identity of the authority on which he draws for the two stories that he uses to try to persuade Pertelote of the prophetic nature of his dreams. In an influential article in *Speculum* in 1977, Robert Pratt argued persuasively that the stories and their prophetic interpretations were taken from *lectiones* 103 and 202 of Robert Holcot's

Wisdom commentary. On this basis, he assumed that their origin lay with Cicero, rather than Valerius Maximus, even though Valerius is named in the second narrative.[10] Though Chauntecleer has a genuine belief in the possible veracity of certain dreams, he has little more credibility as a philosopher than any of the narrators of Chaucer's dream poems.

The Platonic commitment to truth that underpins Macrobius's discussion of the nature and typology of dreams, and that lingers uncomfortably behind Chaucer's dream poems and *Nun's Priest's Tale*, also finds its way into other parts of the *Canterbury Tales* narrative and a number of his short poems. Towards the end of the *General Prologue*, in order to justify his plain speaking, Chaucer the pilgrim alludes to Plato: 'Eek Plato seith, whoso kan hym rede, / The words mote be cosyn to the dede' (I.741–2). Marc Pelen argues that the words 'cosyn to the dede' were especially attractive to Chaucer, as they appear at two other points in the *Canterbury Tales* narrative in a slightly different form.[11] The first stanza of *Lak of Stedfastnesse* likewise laments the lack of correspondence between 'word and deed'. Whether any of this identifies Chaucer with a particular philosophical position must remain open to question, but the playful treatment of Platonic realism in the shorter poems and *Troilus* inevitably complicates any attempt to classify him as a thoroughgoing Platonist.

The Platonic commitment to a universe of eternal ideas, forms or archetypes was challenged in the twelfth century by the controversial French monk Roscelin of Compiègne, and perhaps most famously in the fourteenth century by the English Franciscan William of Ockham, who died only years after Chaucer's birth. This is often seen to have led to a shift in philosophical thinking. Some critics have sought to argue that such a paradigmatic shift in ontological theory must have had repercussions in other cultural arenas, including the literary. Unfortunately, as many have conceded, this is virtually impossible to demonstrate in a vernacular author like Chaucer. Debates about the ontological status of universals were conducted in abstruse documents behind the walls of cathedrals, monasteries and universities. Moreover, unlike debates about real presence or papal dominion, they were of little concern to the layperson. Russell Peck, one of the most prominent commentators on Chaucer and nominalist thought, seemed unconcerned about this in his 1978 article 'Chaucer and the Nominalist Questions'. The debate about universals, he concedes there, is 'probably a matter that lies apart from Chaucer's particular interests', but this need not suggest, he goes on to argue, that Chaucer and Ockham have nothing in common.[12] Ockham's interest in 'empirical thought' (the world of particulars), he contends, is matched by the poet's interest in the authority of experience (as evidenced through the *Wife of Bath's Prologue* and the prologue to the *Legend of Good Women*).[13] Such an approach, whilst not uninteresting, can only ever be broadly speculative, but critical debate about 'nominalist questions' in Chaucer's writing (and in other Middle English literature) continues.[14]

Whatever his opinion of philosophy and its students, Chaucer offers an idealised portrait of the medieval scholar in his depiction of the Clerk in the *General Prologue* to the *Canterbury Tales* (and also, it could be argued, in his portrait of the Parson). As Jill Mann has remarked, the portrait is in many respects an inversion of the more common satirical stereotype, which generally associated student life with drinking, gambling, concubinage and intellectual apathy.[15] Nicholas and Absolon in the *Miller's Tale* satisfy important aspects of this stereotype, both seeking principally to satisfy lustful rather than intellectual curiosity. The Clerk, on the other hand, is identified explicitly as a 'philosophre' (I.297), and his emaciated appearance reveals not only the extent of his dedication to 'logyk' (I.286) and other aspects of philosophical learning, but also his eschewal of secular pleasures. Though he has not yet secured a living, he has no desire for secular employment, and what little money he is able to gain from his friends is spent on 'books and lernynge' (I.300). In return for these charitable gifts, he prays assiduously for the souls of his donors.

The philosophical elements in Chaucer's poetry reveal a close familiarity with the philosophical poetry of antiquity and the Middle Ages, and though there is little evidence that he had any detailed knowledge of the intricacies of scholastic debate, his writing reveals a close engagement with the important philosophical questions posed by Plato, Macrobius and Boethius, and the poets of the twelfth-century Renaissance in particular. His detailed familiarity with the *Roman de la Rose* brought him into contact with other literary authors who were philosophically engaged, and his friendship with Ralph Strode clearly provided him with some insight into contemporary academic debate. Chaucer's own philosophical position, if indeed he had one, is difficult to discern beneath the words of his narrators and the often complex ironies at work in his texts, but his fascination with popular philosophical issues is everywhere apparent in his work.

NOTES

1 *L-R*, pp. 144–5.
2 For a list of the many formulations of this expression in Wyclif's Latin writings, see W. R. Thomson, *The Latin Writings of John Wyclif* (Toronto: Pontifical

Institute of Medieval Studies, 1983), p. 100 n. 1. See also Richard Utz, *Literarischer Nominalismus im Spätmittelalter* (Frankfurt: Peter Lang, 1990), p. 178.

3 John Wyclif, *Johannis Wyclif opera minora*, ed. J. Loserth (London: Wyclif Society, 1910–11), p. 181 (line 20).

4 A. J. Minnis with V. J. Scattergood and J. J. Smith, *Oxford Guides to Chaucer: The Shorter Poems* (Oxford: Clarendon Press, 1995), p. 188.

5 The eagle's use of the term 'citizeyn[s]' to describe these creatures has a parallel in Alan's 'aereos cives', which was first identified by W. P. Ker. See 'Chaucer, "House of Fame" (ii. 417–426)', *Modern Quarterly*, 1 (1899), 38–9.

6 But see Mark Miller, *Philosophical Chaucer: Love, Sex and Agency in the 'Canterbury Tales'* (Cambridge: Cambridge University Press, 2004) for a detailed study of the philosophical issues surrounding agency in the *Canterbury Tales*.

7 *Roman de la Rose*, 17, 105–28.

8 *Ibid.*, 17, 401–24.

9 *Commentary on the 'Dream of Scipio' by Macrobius*, trans. W. H. Stahl (New York: Columbia University Press, 1990 [1952]), pp. 87–8.

10 Robert Pratt, 'Some Latin Sources of the Nonnes Preest on Dreams', *Speculum*, 52 (1977), 538–70.

11 Once when the Host addresses the Canon's Yeoman in the prologue to his tale (VIII.636–8), and once in an incidental comment made by the Manciple in the course of his narrative (IX.207–10). See Marc Pelen, 'Chaucer's "cosyn to the dede": Further Considerations', *Florilegium*, 19 (2002), 91–107 (p. 91). For an earlier philosophical interpretation of this phrase, see Paul B. Taylor, 'Chaucer's *Cosyn to the Dede*', *Speculum*, 57 (1982), 315–27.

12 Russell Peck, 'Chaucer and the Nominalist Questions', *Speculum*, 53 (1978), 745–60.

13 Peck refers to the expression 'Man shal not wenen every thing a lye / But yf himself yt seeth, or elles dooth' in the prologue to the *Legend of Good Women*, lines 12–13. See 'Chaucer and the Nominalist Questions', p. 749.

14 A selection of studies appears in Hugo Keiper, Christoph Bode and Richard Utz, eds., *Nominalism and Literary Discourse: New Perspectives* (Amsterdam: Rodopi, 1997). For a detailed refutation of claims made by critics about the influence of nominalism on vernacular literature, see Robert Myles, *Chaucerian Realism* (Cambridge: D. S. Brewer, 1994), pp. 1–32.

15 Jill Mann, *Chaucer and Medieval Estates Satire* (Cambridge: Cambridge University Press, 2008 [1997]), pp. 74–85.

CHAPTER 28

The Medieval Universe

Seb Falk

Chaucer's universe was an interconnected system, in which all things had their divinely ordered place. This conception of the cosmos was not simply a backdrop to his work; rather, his scientific interests fed directly into the overarching themes and specific details of his poetic, philosophical and didactic writing. A lifelong learner, his later works in particular reflect his growing knowledge of the natural sciences. Given the interweaving of celestial sciences throughout medieval culture, and Chaucer's particular predilection for astronomy, it is not surprising that, late in life, he wrote a guide to the quintessential medieval astronomical instrument: the astrolabe. If we are to grasp the multi-layered allusions that appear throughout his writings, we need an understanding of the complex and cohesive medieval sciences.

The widely accepted medieval picture of the universe was developed from a canon of authoritative works, as Chaucer explains: 'out of olde bokes ... / Cometh al this newe science that men lere' (*PF*, 24–5). Chaucer's 'science', it must be stressed, did not correspond closely to modern definitions of science: the Latin word *scientia* could describe any system of knowledge, and exploring the cosmos through systematic study and active practice took scholars into fields that we might not recognise as part of modern science. Moreover, disciplinary boundaries existed that might seem strange to modern scientists. The most important of these was between cosmology – an overarching science that speculated on the physical structure of the universe and the place of all things within it – and astronomy – a mathematical discipline that used geometrical models to track and predict motions in the heavens. Cosmology provided the essential structure to Chaucer's world-view, while his stories were shaped by his interest in astronomy and its applied cousin astrology (the two words were often used interchangeably).

Plato made cosmology an essential component of education, encouraging his readers to look beyond this earth to a greater reality that could be grasped by thought alone. His description of a cohesive cosmos that accounted for all existence was supplemented by three works written around 500 CE: Macrobius's neo-Platonic commentary on Cicero's *Dream of Scipio*, which vividly portrayed the ordered spheres of the heavens; *The Marriage of Philology and Mercury* by Martianus Capella, which catalogued the seven liberal arts (the *trivium* of verbal sciences (grammar, rhetoric and logic), and the *quadrivium* of mathematical arts (arithmetic, geometry, astronomy and music)); and the *Consolation of Philosophy* by Boethius, which despite containing little scientific detail left a clear mark on Chaucer's world-view with its vision of an ordered universe in which even 'muable nature' was part of a larger stability: 'the stablenesse of the devyne thought' (*Bo*, II, pr. 6.44–7). Most important was Aristotle, whose *On the Heavens* and *Metaphysics* laid out a model of the cosmos and motion within it that was not seriously challenged until the seventeenth century. Chaucer cites all the above authorities by name, but their ideas circulated widely in encyclopedic and literary presentations, and readers could easily encounter them in digested form, including in Dante's *Divine Comedy*. When it came to astronomy, the most popular manual was John of Sacrobosco's *On the Sphere*, which was a set text for students studying the *quadrivium* in the universities. Chaucer, however, drew on more specialist texts, above all the work of Ptolemy – 'the wise astrologien, Daun Ptholome' (*WBT*, III.324), which had been supplemented by many medieval scholars, some in the Islamic world.

Aristotle's authoritative cosmology was founded on a distinction between the earth and the heavens. The earthly region, sometimes known as *sublunary* because the moon's was the lowest heavenly sphere, was composed of the four elements: earth, water, air and fire. These had natural motions, in straight lines up or down (*HF*, 733–6), in contrast to the circular motions of the stars. The sublunary 'wrecched world' was a region of change and decay, in contrast to the 'pleyn felicitie / That is in hevene above', incorruptible and eternal (*Tr*, V.1817–19). Medieval people were in no doubt the earth was round, and Boethius had mused on its tiny size in relation to the vast heavens (*Bo*, II, pr. 7.23–31). Chaucer emphasises this fact in retelling Cicero's tale of Scipio's dream:

> Thanne shewede he hym the lytel erthe that here is,
> At regard of the hevenes quantite;
> And after shewede he hym the nyne speres;
> And after that the melodye herde he
> That cometh of thilke speres thryes thre,
> That welle is of musik and melodye
> In this world here, and cause of armonye.
>
> (*PF*, 57–63)

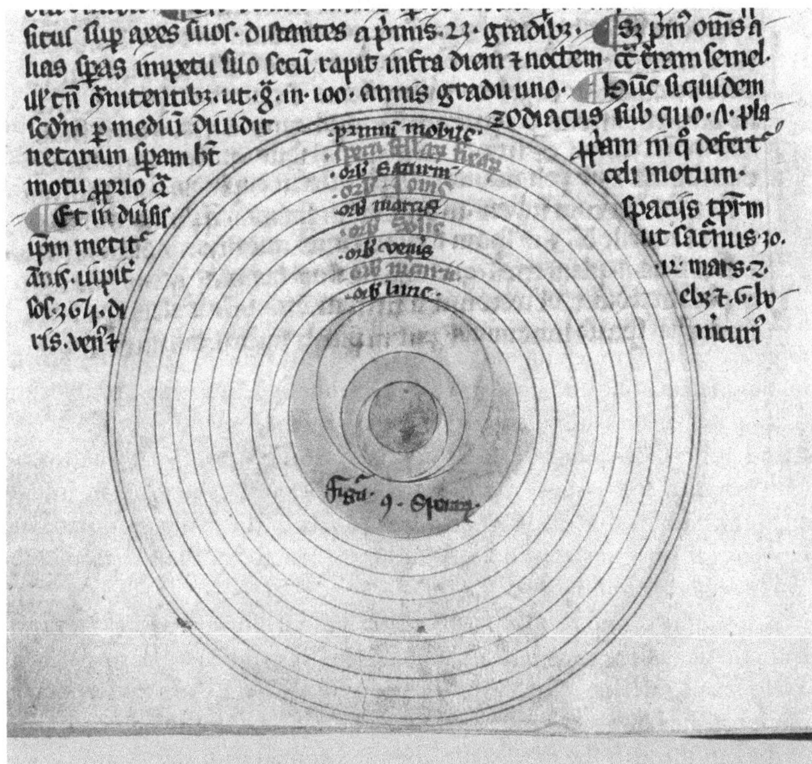

Figure 28.1 The nine spheres, in John of Sacrobosco, *De sphera* (*c.* 1230), Cambridge University Library, MS Ii.3.3, fol. 25v (*c.* 1276); this manuscript also contains a copy of Ptolemy's astrological *Quadripartitum* (*Tetrabiblos*).

The nine spheres were those of the seven planets (the moon, Mercury, Venus, the sun, Mars, Jupiter and Saturn), the 'fixed' stars and the *Primum Mobile* (Figure 28.1). The fixed stars were not wholly fixed, as astronomers of Chaucer's proficiency knew, but were called so to distinguish them from the wandering stars – the planets. The *Primum Mobile*, or 'Unmoved Mover', was necessitated by the Aristotelian principle that all motion in the universe must ultimately be caused by something that does not itself move. The 'music of the spheres' – the planets' emission of mathematically defined notes – was proposed in the myth of Er, in Plato's *Republic*, and developed by later writers: some were attracted by the way it could unify the four disciplines of the *quadrivium*, while others, like Chaucer in this passage, made a simpler connection between the harmonious balance of creation and music, within a poem that climaxes in the harmonious singing of the fowls.

As above, so below: Aristotle's cosmological separation of heaven and earth was counterbalanced by their astrological unity. Each of the four elements had two qualities: hot or cold, wet or dry (e.g. earth is cold and dry, and air hot and moist); the same pairs of qualities characterised the four seasons on earth, the planets (e.g. Mars is hot and dry, and Venus cold and wet) and, in groups of three (*triplicities*), the twelve signs of the zodiac. In mankind, they described the four humours of medical theory: blood, phlegm, black bile and yellow bile, and the four *complexions* or temperaments that correspond to them: sanguine, phlegmatic, melancholic and choleric (so the Franklin's 'sangwyn' complexion (*CT*, I.333) makes him red-faced, cheery and energetic). As Chaucer's friend John Gower emphasised, man was a microcosm of the universe (the macrocosm): illness or an uneven temper was caused by an imbalance of humours, but also reflected imbalances in the configuration of the heavens.[1] It was thus essential for Chaucer's Doctor of Physic (medicine) to know his astronomy (*CT*, I.414).

Astronomy centred on the mathematical modelling of celestial motions, laid out in tables, calendars and calculating instruments (leaving a relatively small role for observation of the stars). There were two principal motions: the daily rising and setting of the heavens, and the annual path of the sun through the fixed stars. The sun's annual path was known as the ecliptic circle, a line marking the middle of the wider band of the zodiac (Figures 28.2 and 28.3). This ecliptic circle is set at an angle to the celestial equator (a projection of the earth's equator onto the sky), so that as the sun moves around the ecliptic in the course of the year it crosses the equator twice, moving north and south of it. The two crossing points are the equinoxes, when day and night are equal length; the equator itself was often called the equinoctial circle (*Astr*, I.17.15–24). The vernal (spring) equinox, when the Sun crossed to the north of the equator, was the start of the astronomical year (*NPT*, VII.3187–8) and the starting point for measurement: angles around the ecliptic from this point were celestial longitude, and angles above or below the ecliptic were latitude. The sun was always on the ecliptic, but the other planets (including the moon) moved a few degrees north or south of it. An eclipse could only occur when the moon's latitude was zero; that is the origin of the word *ecliptic*, as Chaucer tells us (*Astr*, I.17.24–7).

The 360° of the ecliptic were divided into twelve *signs* – segments of exactly 30° – named by the ancient Greeks according to the twelve

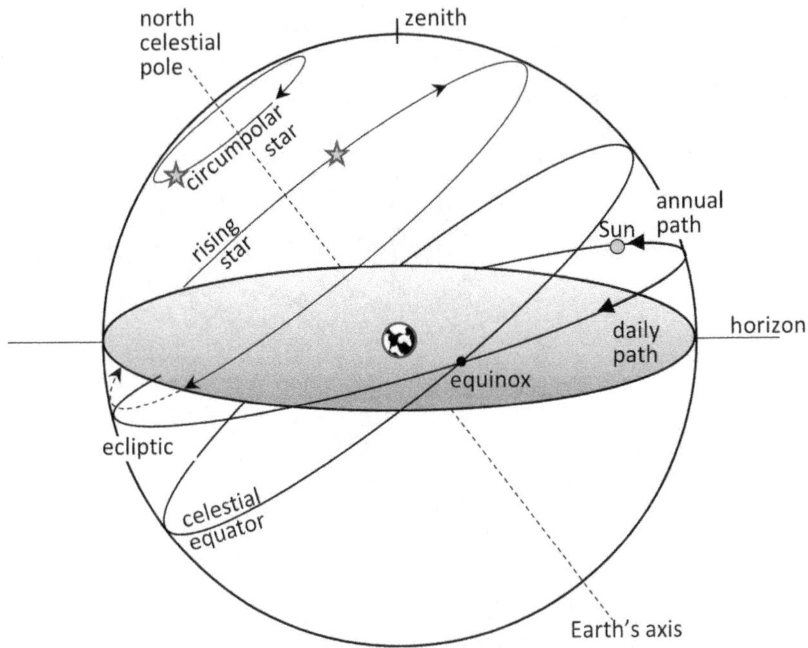

Figure 28.2 The daily and annual rotations of the heavens.

constellations closest to the ecliptic. The first sign the sun enters after the vernal equinox in March is Aries, so the vernal equinox was also known as the Head (start) of Aries; position in longitude was usually given in signs and degrees, so that if the 'sonne / … in the signe of Taurus had yronne / Twenty degrees and oon' (*NPT*, VII.3193–5) this meant that the sun had travelled 21° into Taurus, and as Taurus is the second sign, the sun's longitude would be 30 + 21 = 51° from the Head of Aries. However, that did not mean that the sun was among the stars of the constellation Taurus: the uniform 30° signs were different from the unevenly spaced constellations with which they shared their names. This was owing to the slow motion of the fixed stars (or the eighth sphere on which they sat). While remaining fixed in relation to each other, they had drifted around the ecliptic from their positions (relative to the equinox) at the time the ancient Greeks had named them, at a rate of around a degree per century. So while the first 30° of the ecliptic remained the sign of Aries, by Chaucer's day more than half the constellation Aries had moved off into the sign of Taurus. This is what the Franklin (who protests that 'I ne

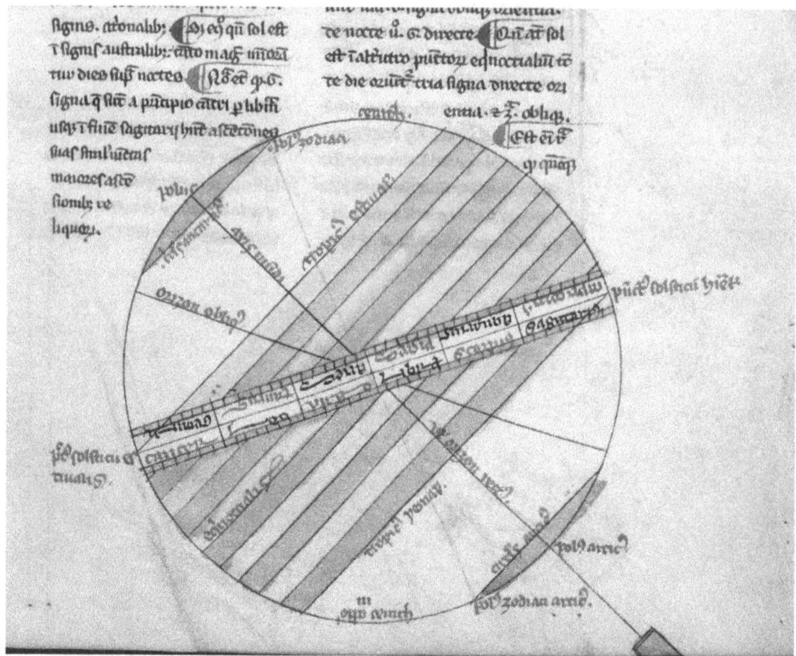

Figure 28.3 The heavens, in John of Sacrobosco, *De sphera* (*c.* 1230), London, British Library, MS Harley 3647, fol. 29r (*c.* 1300). Note that the celestial sphere is presented as an instrument with a handle; this portrayal was made even more explicit in the earliest printed versions of the *Sphere*. This manuscript also contains tables and a number of instrument treatises, including the astrolabe treatise attributed to 'Massahalla' (Māshā'allāh ibn Atharī (*c.* 740–815)), which was the principal source of Chaucer's *Astrolabe*.

kan no termes of astrologye' (*FranT*, v.1266)) means when he says of the expert astronomer of Orleans that:

> ... by his eighte speere in his wirkyng
> He knew ful wel how fer Alnath [a star[2]] was shove
> Fro the heed of thilke fixe Aries [the sign] above,
> That in the ninthe speere considered is.
> (lines 1280–3)

These principles underlay the calculations made by astrologers, of which the most fundamental was the *ascendant*: the degree of the ecliptic rising above the horizon at a particular moment (*Astr*, II.4). The ascendant was the basis of the division of the ecliptic into twelve astrological *houses*, each of which governed certain facets of human experience. The division could

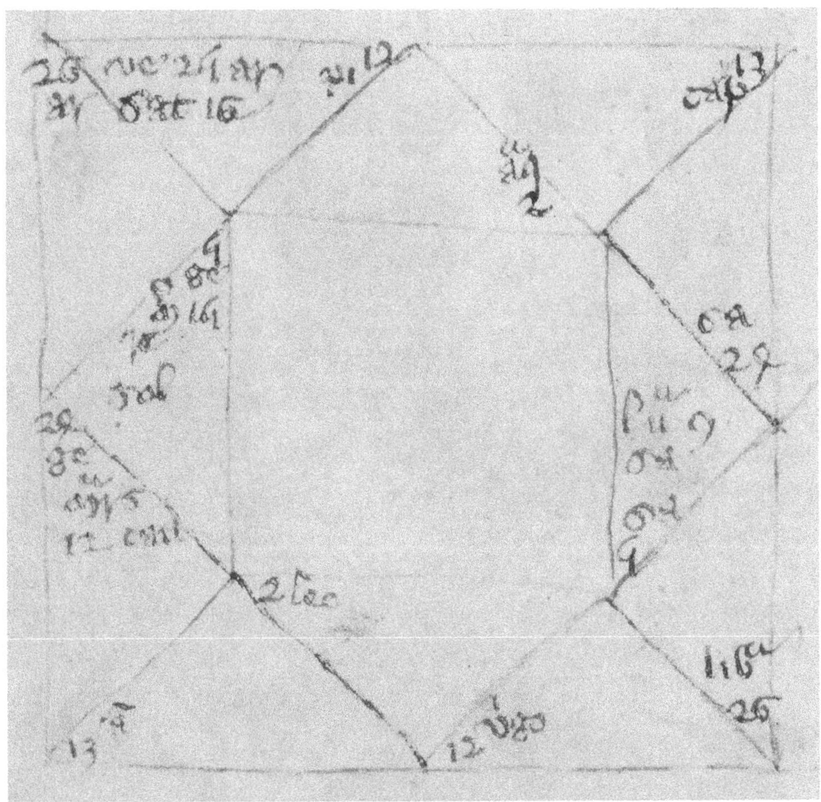

Figure 28.4 Horoscope diagram, adapted from one by Māshā'allāh ibn Atharī (*c.* 740–815), Cambridge, Peterhouse, MS 75.I, fol. 64v (1393).

be done in various ways but always started from the ascendant and midheaven (the position of the sun at noon on a given day). The locations of the planets within the houses were the basis of horoscopes; these were often recorded in schematic diagrams such as the one in Figure 28.4.[3]

As the ascendant degree changed constantly with the daily rotation of the heavens, such diagrams could never be too precise, and dividing the houses was difficult. Medieval astronomers devised ingenious tables to simplify the processes. The Toledan Tables used by the Franklin's Orleans astrologer (*FranT*, v.1273) were one (somewhat outdated) kind of table, but there were many others with different contents, presentations and levels of detail. Some, like those of the 'reverent clerkes' John Somer and Nicholas of Lynn (*Astr*, Pro.85), were presented as calendars valid for several decades;

Figure 28.5 '[A] suffisant Astrolabie as for oure orizonte, compowned after the latitude of Oxenforde' (*Astr*, Pro.8–10), London, British Museum, 1909, 0617.1 (1326). This astrolabe has plates for the latitudes of Jerusalem, Babylon, Rome, Montpellier, Paris and Oxford. The Y-style of the astrolabe rete is characteristic of 'Chaucerian' instruments.

other tables broke down celestial motions into simpler components and allowed users to find positions just by adding a few numbers.

Even more user-friendly than tables were instruments. Chaucer conveys the late medieval fascination with them: sundials (*ShipT*, VII.206); globes (*Astr*, II.26.1); clocks (*NPT*, VII.2854); and above all the portable, multifunctional and elegant astrolabe (Figure 28.5; *MilT*, I.3209). Instruments could be used for observation – to measure the altitude of a star – but this was the least of their functions. From a simple altitude an astrolabe could tell its user the time, the height of a building and the direction of north, and of course identify the ascendant and thereby divide the astrological houses. It could not provide data so precise as that found in tables, as Chaucer himself admits (*Astr*, Pro.74–6), but it was quick and easy to use. Indeed, precision was often less important than process: astrolabes and other instruments were used as much to model or demonstrate the workings of the universe as to calculate positions. An astrolabe could teach, for example, why the summer signs from Cancer to Sagittarius rise more vertically than the 'tortuous' winter signs from Capricorn to Gemini (*MLT*, II.302). Furthermore, they had a wider symbolism, reminding users of the order of the cosmos and their place within it. They could be devotional objects (astrolabe calendars were often personalised with particular local saints' days) or reflect artistic or architectural fashions in their design; they always lent scholarly prestige to their user. An astrolabe could not compute the positions of the planets, but Chaucer had access to tables that did – and instruments known as *equatoria* were invented to simplify the labour of computing planetary positions. One treatise on an equatorium was long attributed to Chaucer;[4] although it is unlikely that he wrote it, he certainly did write a treatise on the astrolabe, ostensibly to teach the use of that instrument to his ten-year-old son Lewis (*Astr*, Pro.1–24).

When astronomical knowledge of celestial positions was combined with cosmological principles of macrocosm and microcosm, astrological determination was possible. Every position was given significance, following meanings that were remarkably consistent across the wide-ranging astrological literature. Much astrological theory stemmed from the *Tetrabiblos* of Ptolemy, but fourteenth-century astrologers are most likely to have read the introductory texts written in the Islamic world, chief among them the *Introductorium* of al-Qabisi (d. 967), whom Chaucer knew as Alkabucius (*Astr*, 1.8.13); this was translated into Latin in the twelfth century and into Middle English in the fourteenth century. Each planet was ascribed benign or malign powers: Saturn and Mars were maleficent, Jupiter and Venus were beneficent, the sun and moon were broadly neutral, and Mercury would take its character from whichever planet or sign it was linked with at a particular time. The effects depended on which astrological house they were in: for example, according to al-Qabisi, the first, ascendant house indicated beginnings and speech, while the twelfth 'derkeste hous' (*MLT*, II.304) was the place of enemies, stratagems and riding animals. The planets' positions in the zodiac signs also had an effect: each planet had its *domus*, or home sign, where it was strongest, its *exaltation* where it was also strong, and its detriment where it was particularly weak. For example,

Venus was at home and thus particularly powerful in Taurus (*WBPro*, III.609–18). The real astrological complexity came when the influences of planets were interpreted according to their *aspect* – their relative position in the houses. For example, planets opposite each other in the sky were in conflict, but a separation of 60° was a benign aspect.

Such interpretations were particularly important in medical practice. Each sign of the zodiac governed a part of the body – Taurus, for example, was responsible for the neck (see Figure 28.6), and individual degrees within each sign also had subtle qualities. Astronomy also overlapped with other sciences. For example, practitioners of alchemy, a wide-ranging discipline that ran from mineralogy to occult philosophy, associated each planet with a metal from silver to lead; Chaucer explains this and a litany of alchemical techniques and tools (*CYT*, VIII.826–9). Likewise, natural magic exploited the hidden properties of plants and stones, often linking them to the stars.

Although medical astrology was universally accepted in Chaucer's day, other kinds of astrological interpretation were more controversial. The limits of astrology – both its validity and its acceptability – had been debated since its earliest development, and Christian thinkers such as St Augustine and Thomas Aquinas had discussed its relationship to theological questions. Aquinas worked out a careful compromise that acknowledged the evident influences of heavenly motions, while still respecting the crucial Christian doctrine of free will. Astrologers, he wrote, could quite lawfully observe the stars in order to predict the weather; it was widely accepted, for example, that a 'great conjunction' of Jupiter and Saturn heralded heavy rain (*Tr*, III.624–8). Further, since human will is affected by bodily appetites, celestial bodies could have an effect on human actions: dealings in business or politics; love, marriage and children; travel; death. However, human actions – let alone chance events – could not be predicted with certainty, and to attempt to do so was superstitious and unlawful.[5] Nevertheless, theological proscription did not prevent astrology being at least a popular diversion, and often a serious practice, in scholarly and courtly circles. John Somer's Calendar (noted above) was dedicated to Joan, mother of Richard II, and the King himself owned a book of divination and a quadrant instrument. Despite Chaucer's protestation in his *Treatise on the Astrolabe* that 'my spirit hath no feith' in such 'rytes of payens' (*Astr*, II.4.58–9), they were clearly doctrines that he took very seriously and, through the *Astrolabe*, wanted to teach his son. Chaucer – and his poetic narrators – ascribe varying powers to astrological determinism and free will (e.g. *WBPro*, III.615–16; *MLT*, II.194–6; *Tr*, IV.960–1078).

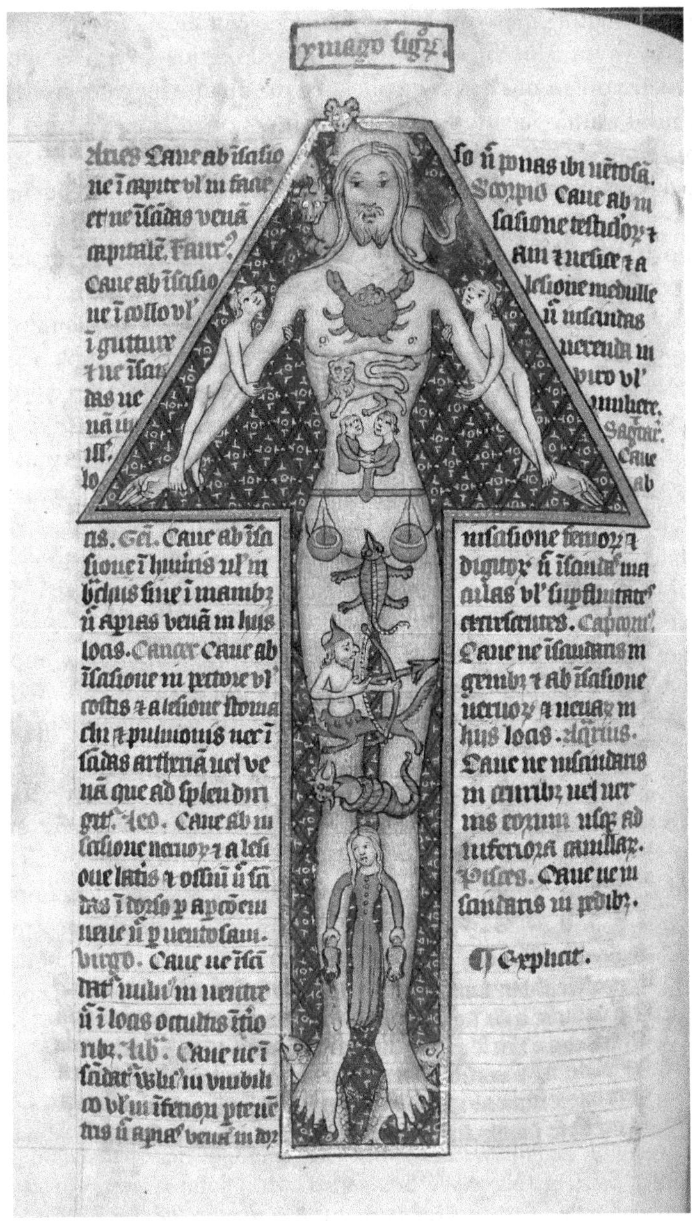

Figure 28.6 'Zodiac man' showing the parts of the body governed by each sign, in a copy of the Calendar of John Somer (1380), Cambridge, St John's College, MS K.26, fol. 41v (1397 x 1400).

Serious or not, most readers of Chaucer will encounter his astrology in the form of allusions in his poetry. Alongside overt references to instruments or famous books that he used to enhance his characters, he also introduced numerous subtle details that functioned as intellectual puzzles to amuse his readers and perhaps demonstrate his learning. For example, the cock Chauntecleer in the *Nun's Priest's Tale* 'knew ech ascencioun / Of the equynoxial' (*CT*, VII.2855–6), so that on 3 May (3190), when the sun had moved along the ecliptic 21° into the sign of Taurus, like an astrolabe he could find its altitude and deduce the time of day. Chauntecleer is coloured 'lyk the burned gold' (line 2864) and 'ful coleryk of compleccioun' (line 2955); the sun's metal was gold, and it was linked to choleric illness. It is unsurprising that a cock who sings with the sunrise (line 2878) should be associated with that planet, but the wealth of detail is striking. It is also likely that Chauntecleer's seven wives represent the seven stars of the Pleiades, which had a longitude of 21° in Taurus and were commonly known as hens in the Middle Ages. The colour of the malefic planet Saturn was black, so the black-eared fox (line 3215) who takes Chauntecleer by the throat (line 3335) may represent that planet; and we recall that Taurus, where the sun is, was medically responsible for that assaulted neck.

Other astrological connections could be highlighted, but it is important to stress that Chaucer's allusions do not dominate this – or any other – story, nor exclude different levels of interpretation, which might in this case focus on the Nun's Priest's moral regarding the fruit of knowledge (lines 3440–3) or his discussion of predestination (lines 3230–51). Nevertheless, it is clear that the sciences, and astronomy in particular, were of great interest to Chaucer, worthy of serious study both for their practical potential and their philosophical or ethical implications (see, for example, *Bo*, IV, m. 1.1–17; and *KnT*, I.2987–3089). His especial interest in instruments was typical of the age, and, in producing the first complete manual on a scientific instrument in Middle English, Chaucer made his own contribution to the exact sciences.

NOTES

1 I am grateful to Hilary Carey and Stephen Rigby for their comments on an earlier draft of this paper. See, for example, John Gower, *Vox clamantis*, VII.8.637–716, and *Confessio Amantis*, VII.380–462, in *The English Works of John Gower*, ed. G. C. Macaulay, 2 vols., EETS os 81–2 (London: Oxford University Press, 1900–1).

2 β Tauri, the bright star on the tip of the northern horn of Taurus. The name *al-nath* comes from the Arabic word for butting.

3 Chaucer uses the word 'horoscopum' simply to mean 'ascendant' (*Astr*, II.3, 4).
4 Known as the *Equatorie of the Planetis*. A facsimile, transcription, translation, virtual model, commentary and bibliography are available online at https://cudl.lib.cam.ac.uk/view/MS-PETERHOUSE-00075-00001 (last accessed 10 December 2018).
5 Thomas Aquinas, *Summa theologiae*, 2.2.95.5, 1.115.4, ed. Fundación Tomás de Aquino, www.corpusthomisticum.org (accessed 5 December 2017); Aquinas was drawing on St Augustine, *De civitate Dei*, v.6.

CHAPTER 29

Medicine and the Mortal Body

Samantha Katz Seal

From infancy to old age, the human body in medieval Europe was always first and foremost a dying one. At conception, each human life received its mortality as inheritance from Adam and Eve in consequence of their transgenerational sin. In the twelfth-century *On the Misery of the Human Condition* (translated by Geoffrey Chaucer as *Of the Wretched Engendrynge of Mankynde*), Pope Innocent III therefore characterised the human progression as one of ever-encroaching death. 'The future is forever being born, the present forever dying, and what is past is utterly dead. We are forever dying while we are alive; we only cease to die when we cease to live.'[1] While medical care might do much to alleviate the suffering of the human body or cure it 'temporarily' of its disease, such pessimism about the human body created a fundamental ambivalence about the value of medicine. Medical practitioners were required to engage directly with the theological implications of their work and, often, to acknowledge the inferiority of their abilities in comparison with those of the Church. The hierarchy may perhaps be best visualised in Arcite's death scene in Chaucer's *Knight's Tale*:

> Nature hath now no dominacioun.
> And certeinly, ther Nature wol nat wirche,
> Fare wel phisik! Go ber the man to chirche!
> (*CT*, 1.2758–60)

Medical remedies were certainly something to be attempted, but their power was limited and restrained in a way that that of God and his earthly servants could never be.

Christ was the ultimate physician, one whose capacity to heal far exceeded that of His earthly imitators. And yet, many medieval physicians were themselves members of the Church and thus entrusted not only with the care of their patients' fleshly bodies, but also of their souls. Danielle Jacquart has identified a 'clericalisation' of the medical profession within the fourteenth century.[2] Her estimate places the number of French medical practitioners in religious orders in the second half of the fourteenth century at over 11 per cent, with almost 24 per cent of students receiving ecclesiastical benefices.[3] In England, the percentage of medical students who also were members of the clergy was probably even higher. The Church's influence on medical practice in England was significantly augmented by the dominance that the academic study of theology maintained at the two English universities. Both the University of Oxford and the University of Cambridge still primarily functioned as doctoral institutions in theology and law; their medical faculty in comparison was quite limited in number and their coursework thereby limited in scope (the extent of this disparity was far less prominent at the more prestigious medical programmes of the University of Paris and the Italian universities). Nevertheless, the university remained the sole source of degree accreditation required for medieval physicians, and the title doctor of medicine carried specific educational (and, by extension, class) implications.

In terms of class and status, the physician stood at the top of a hierarchy of medical practitioners; there was plenty of patient demand for the skills of surgeons, barbers, apothecaries and midwives, but because their training happened through practical apprenticeships rather than academic study, members of these professions typically came from less elevated levels of society and received less compensation for their work. However, while the scholarly background of medieval physicians ensured their higher social status, it also served to stimulate criticism from their medical peers. The association of physicians with the *study* of medicine rather than its *practice* was often the focal point of anti-physician rhetoric. When a physician is mocked in Giovanni Boccaccio's *Decameron*, for example, his stupidity with regard to worldly matters is explicitly contrasted with his high-status education in Bologna.[4] Likewise, in a particularly vitriolic fourteenth-century attack on the knowledge of physicians, the author of an anonymous English poem writes:

> And yit ther is another craft that toucheth the clergie,
> That ben thise false fisiciens that helpen men to die;
> He wole wagge his urine in a vessel of glaz,
> And swereth that he [the patient] is sekere than evere yit he was …
> Though he wite no more than a gos wheither he wol live or die.[5]

Physicians, for all their education, could offer neither guarantee of recovery nor certainty of diagnosis to their patients. Even the best university education was powerless in the face of the human body's ultimate unknowability, as their critics were all too eager to note.

And yet, if they did not have divine knowledge of life and death, nevertheless by the fourteenth century English physicians did have access to a much wider assortment of medical scholarship than previous generations. Classical medical texts were among the many scientific treatises reintroduced to the Latin West from the Arab world from the twelfth century on. In addition, the fourteenth century saw an increase in the publication and dissemination of original medical texts and commentaries by European doctors and surgeons, many of which were quickly added to the common canon. When Chaucer tells us of his Physician he attests not only to the quality of his university education, but also to his impressive breadth of textual command:

> Wel knew he the olde Esculapius,
> And Deyscorides, and eek Rufus,
> Olde Ypocras, Haly, and Galyen,
> Serapion, Razis, and Avycen,
> Averrois, Damascien, and Constantyn,
> Bernard, and Gatesden, and Gilbertyn.
> (*CT*, I.429–34)

Chaucer's Physician has read not only the classical works of Galen and Hippocrates, but also the medical compendia and commentaries of Arab scholars (here referred to by the western corruptions of their names) of Averroes, Rhazes, Avicenna and Holy Abbas. Even more significantly, he has read the work of English or French physicians whose lives were relatively contemporaneous with his own (albeit fictional) one. By invoking Bernard de Gordon (d. after 1318), John of Gaddesden (d. 1361) and Gilbertus Anglicus (d. *c.* 1250), Chaucer references a genealogy of medical scholarship that had begun to evolve quite rapidly in England by the fourteenth century.

The increased proliferation of medical writings in the later Middle Ages allowed for the diffusion of medical beliefs about the composition and structure of the human body into popular texts. In particular, the Hippocratic theory of humoralism, which argued that the human body contained four different humours (blood, phlegm, yellow bile, black bile) needing to be in perfect balance in order for the body to be in a state of health, enjoyed pre-eminence as an accepted explanation for the differences between individuals and for their general ill health. Chaucer references this theory within the *General Prologue* in identifying the Reeve as a 'colerik man' (I.587); significantly, Chaucer also appears to expect that his audience will be familiar enough with humoral theory to understand what an excess of choler indicates about the Reeve's physical state and his personality.

According to this theory, most bodies were, if not explicitly sick, certainly not well. As Galen, whose commentary on Hippocrates's work was essential for popularising the theory in the medieval West, wrote: 'With respect to the more common mixtures of the body, it is shown that at some times in some single part the humors are mixed with each other neither equally nor similarly throughout the whole. And even when the function has clearly not yet deteriorated, still the health is compromised, even when there is not yet any illness.'[6] Here imperfection becomes the norm and all bodies appear to require a physician.

To heal these imbalances, physicians traditionally applied materials designed to offset the excess of one humour with its opposite. Chaucer attests to this practice within the *Tale of Melibee*, when he has the physicians remark that 'maladies been cured by hir contraries' (*CT*, VII.1017). In order to treat the excessive humour, the physician was first required to determine which humour was mixed out of balance. The classic image from medieval art of the physician examining a container of urine is a visualisation of one of the most common methods for determining an answer to that question. The colour, texture and smell of the patient's urine were all considered major indicators of which of his or her humours was out of balance. Gilbertus Anglicus, for example, advises in his medical writings that when trying to differentiate between a 'frenesy' and some other medical problem, the medical man should look to see if the 'urin is white and thinne. The cause therof is, for the hote colerik mater that shulde make the uryn reed and shulde com donward with the uryn, and it passeth upward into the heed and that maketh a man frentike.'[7] The urine was a key diagnostic tool, for it was directly impacted by the movement and quantity of the humours in the body, and might thus reveal which humour specifically needed to be moderated.

However, humours were not the only components of the body that could be out of balance. Hippocrates and Galen also attested to the importance of four elements in each individual's corporeal mixture. These elements (heat, cold, moisture and aridity) provided a medical explanation for the distinction between men and women. The male physiological composition was naturally hot and dry, the female cold and wet. The author of the *Trotula*, the most influential medieval gynaecological text, attributed these elemental distinctions to the divinely authorised necessity for reproduction: 'So that from them there might emerge fertile offspring, he endowed their complexions with a certain pleasing commixtion, constituting the nature of the male hot and dry. But lest the male overflow with either one of these qualities, He wished by the opposing frigidity and humidity of the woman to rein him in from too much excess.'[8] The healthy, fertile body is thus designed to require a form of 'medical' intervention. By creating the corporeal elements and dividing them according to biological sex, God acts almost as a physician, applying an opposite material to counterbalance excess. Just as in humoral theory, the theory of sex-specific elements serves to figure the human body as fundamentally imperfect and 'ill', incapable of moderating itself without mediation.

The *Trotula*'s depiction of God as a sort of physician, balancing out the human body's natural excess, speaks to a general medieval willingness to invoke a medical vocabulary when speaking of religious matters, and vice versa. The blurring of the line between the dominion of each profession spoke to the relatively synchronous roles that their practitioners assumed when dealing with the ill. As the lines quoted from the *Knight's Tale* at the beginning of this chapter attest, once the physician had failed to heal the body the priest was called to minister to the soul. Both were considered healers, negotiating the potential responses to the body's intrinsic mortality. Perhaps, because of this linkage around the deathbed, confessors in particular were highlighted as the spiritual equivalents of physicians. The author of the late-fourteenth-century *Piers Plowman*, for example, uses the allegory of a physician dispensing medical remedies when referring to a confessor and his strict penances.[9] Likewise, the author of the fourteenth-century French advice manual *Le Ménagier de Paris* couches an appeal about how one should select and treat a confessor with frequent comparisons to the process of interacting with a physician. He makes the analogy particularly explicit: 'Since every creature must wish for health of the body, that fleshly and transient material, all the more reason should he be anxious about the noble soul … thus, he ought to select a virtuous, wise, and most excellent physician to recoup immediately the health of the wounded or ill soul.'[10] When counselling men and women to follow religious strictures carefully for the sake of their souls, the language of corporeal medical treatment may have appeared to be a naturally efficacious tool. And, indeed, some readers may have reflected that if they had not done a particularly good job in selecting a skilled physician, surely that was all the more reason to have an exceptional confessor!

The blurring of this line between priest and doctor extended in both directions. Late medieval descriptions of famous physicians often seem almost indistinguishable from the description of a religious notable, despite the fact that many of these famous physicians had historically been either pagan or Muslim. By the late Middle Ages, the Christianisation of a figure like Hippocrates was so complete that in a popular representation such as the fifteenth-century *Dicts and Sayings of the Philosophers*, Hippocrates could appear to resemble a Christian preacher. All references to pagan gods have of course also been removed. This version of Hippocrates was not only (or even primarily) concerned with the health of the body; in the medieval imagination of the text's author, even famous doctors apparently deferred the healing of the body to the healing of the soul. For example, the text's Hippocrates preaches 'lyffe is shorte and the peyne is longe, experience is perylous and jugement is daungerous. And [he] seith that the helthe of body is in hem that wole nat be ydell, but putte hemself in excercyse of doynge gode dedis, and that he shulde nat fille his bodye with superfluyte of meetis and drynke.'[11] While the advice to avoid too much meat and drink may be understood as a reference to a humoral understanding of health (although it may also be tied to the sin of gluttony), the exhortation to do good deeds and reflect on the transience of life and longevity of hell would not appear out of place in a contemporaneous devotional manual.

And yet, no medical practitioner, no matter how educated, skilled or devout, had access to the types of remedies available to his spiritual counterpart, the confessor. Christ was the true healer of mankind; human medicine would only delay the inevitable death of the body, while adherence to Church dogma would ensure eternal life. Medieval writers were not shy to draw this comparison or to point out medical failures. Famous physicians like Hippocrates might be lauded and visualised in religious terms, but average medical practitioners might be mocked for their inability to heal. After all, medical authorities had done little to halt the destructive progress of the Black Death across Europe, not only in 1348, but in successive lethal waves as well. It is no wonder, for example, that Boccaccio's story-tellers, in retreat from the plague, would tell a tale that mocks the stupidity and powerlessness of a physician (although of course corrupt religious officials receive even more of their derision). By its very nature, medicine requires its patients to have faith in its efficacy, and such faith had probably been stretched very thin in fourteenth-century Europe. Disease, childbirth and battle were real threats to human life – threats that the practice of medicine could only partially ameliorate.

When Death confronts the Physician in the late medieval poem *The Dance of Death*, he laughs, 'Ayeyne my might yowre crafte mai not endure', and the Physician agrees: 'A-yens dethe is worth no medicine.'[12] By the late Middle Ages, medieval medicine possessed a strong canon of authoritative texts, a dominant vision of the composition of the human body, and powerful claims to wealth and status for its practitioners (particularly physicians). And yet, medieval authors consistently critiqued medicine for its ultimate impotence in the face of death. The bodies that medical craft was designed to treat were after all defined by their mortality, and thus deserving of only limited consideration in comparison with the eternal human soul. Men might be attached to their flesh, but even the most skilled doctor would be unable to preserve it for them indefinitely. Indeed, they could not even preserve their own. One could only pity those therefore, like Chaucer's Physician, whose focus was on earthly medicine and whose 'studie was but litel on the Bible' (1.438).

NOTES

1 Pope Innocent III, *On the Misery of the Human Condition: De miseria humane conditionis*, ed. Donald R. Howard, trans. M. M. Dietz (Indianapolis: Bobbs-Merill, 1969), p. 26.

2 Danielle Jacquart, *Le milieu médical en France du XIIe au XVe siècle* (Geneva: Librairie Droz, 1981), pp. 268–9.

3 *Ibid.*, pp. 269, 278–80.

4 Giovanni Boccaccio, *The Decameron*, ed. Jonathan Usher, trans. Guido Waldman (Oxford: Oxford University Press, 2008), pp. 528–40.

5 Peter Coss, ed., *Thomas Wright's 'Political Songs of England': From the Reign of John to that of Edward II* (Cambridge: Cambridge University Press, 1996), p. 333.

6 Galen, 'On Hippocrates' *On the Nature of Man*', ed. and trans. W. J. Lewis, chapter 61, *Medicina Antiqua* (Wellcome Trust Centre for the History of Medicine at UCL), www.ucl.ac.uk/~ucgajpd/medicina%20antiqua/tr_GNatHom.html (last accessed 29 October 2013).

7 Faye Marie Getz, ed., *Healing and Society in Medieval England: A Middle English Translation of the Pharmaceutical Writings of Gilbertus Anglicus* (Madison: University of Wisconsin Press, 1991), p. 11.

8 Monica H. Green, ed. and trans., *The 'Trotula': An English Translation of a Medieval Compendium of Women's Medicine* (Philadelphia: University of Pennsylvania Press, 2002), p. 71.

9 William Langland, *Piers Plowman: The C-Text*, ed. Derek Pearsall, 2nd edn (Exeter: University of Exeter Press, 1994), p. 374.

10 Gina L. Greco and Christine M. Rose, eds. and trans., *The Goodwife's Guide (Le ménagier de Paris): A Medieval Household Book* (Ithaca, NY: Cornell University Press, 2009), p. 64.

11 John William Sutton, ed., *The Dicts and Sayings of the Philosophers* (Kalamazoo: Medieval Institute Publications, 2006), p. 29.

12 Florence Warren Brown, ed., *The Dance of Death*, EETS os 181 (Oxford: Oxford University Press, 1931), lines 422, 432.

CHAPTER 30

The Law

Richard W. Ireland

Before telling his tale, the Man of Law takes the opportunity to rebuke Chaucer for the latter's deficiencies as a poet (*CT*, II.39–96). The joke is a good one, but why should it be given to the lawyer in particular? Perhaps it is because lawyers are traditionally simply an arrogant bunch, but those of us schooled in their art (for art it is) may think there is rather more to it than that. Though their public images are poles apart, poets and lawyers are essentially in the same line of work: their tools are words, they deploy them before an audience and hope to construct a compelling and effective narrative. The Man of Law prefers prose to verse, and may work for clients rather than patrons (although that distinction would not be so easily made in the Middle Ages), but he recognises a rival when he meets one. English law is adversarial: he puts Chaucer down.

The law has, at its very core, certain essential contradictions that it prefers not to talk about, though practitioners of imaginative fiction have long exploited them. Law looks forward, setting norms for future behaviour and practice, but often acts retrospectively, settling disputes that have already arisen over those norms. It embraces the idea, a socially important one, of the justice of certainty that inheres in the general rule, but often finds that generality to be at odds with the particular justice of the individual case. And it pursues that contradictory but essentially legal virtue, justice, whilst entrusting that pursuit to those whose immediate aims may be more grubbily personal and pragmatic. Lawyers, parasites on others' difficulties, are seldom popular: if they win your case they charge you a lot for getting what you always thought was rightly yours; if they lose it (or even win it when you know it wasn't rightly yours) then they are incompetent (or venal). Corrupt judges, ambiguous agreements, contradictory obligations: this was the world of the medieval lawyer as well as the teller of tales.

It would be banal to say that law was particularly significant in Chaucer's day: social norms, of which laws form an important subset, are always important, but the law is constantly changing (despite its pretence of stability, another of its contradictions) and some of the characteristics of law and its administration in the fourteenth century will undoubtedly help us understand the world in which Chaucer lived and may well illuminate some of the things he wrote. In a chapter as short as this it will be impossible to discuss in depth all the details of that law and legal system, although fuller doctrinal histories are available to those who wish to pursue specific points.[1] What follows here is an attempt to bring out certain general themes.

THE PLACE OF LAW

The first point to be understood about law and justice in the medieval world is that it is an imperfect simulacrum of the real thing, which is the preserve of God, not man. Chaucer's conclusion to the translation of that seminal medieval text, Boethius's *Consolation of Philosophy*, reminds the reader 'that ye worken and don (*that is to seyn, your dedes or your werkes*) byforn the eyen of the juge that seeth and demeth all thinges' (*Bo*, v, pr. 6.307–10). The most enduring philosophical exploration of the link between human law and God's law had been articulated by St Thomas Aquinas in the thirteenth century. It matters rather less for the purposes of this chapter exactly what that theory, and indeed competing philosophical ideas, entailed, or how much they may have influenced Chaucer's ideas. The important point to note here is that for Chaucer and his contemporaries, whether or not it lay at the front of their minds as they drew up their deeds, entered their contracts or disputed in the courts, human law was not the only or the ultimate measure of behaviour, nor the determination of its officials the only source of reward or punishment.

Let us pause to examine some concrete ramifications of this relationship to a higher law. The oath remained central to the legal system and occurs in a variety of social and legal settings, marking out formal from informal undertakings and, in 'pledging one's faith', invoking an eschatological guarantee of performance. Yet a central problem in all legal systems, and it is one that often occurs in literature too, is that of proof. How do we know what was agreed, who owns this field, who killed this man? Such questions lie at the very heart of legal disputes, but they are questions *for* law, rather than *of* law (or, as in the second example they may involve both sorts of question). A party's oath could be supported by the oaths of others who swore to his (and it is mostly his) reliability as a man whose oath was to be trusted. Such a way of proceeding made perfect sense in a face-to-face local context, or when undertaken within a specifically ecclesiastical one: neighbours would be unwilling to perjure themselves for another they knew to be dishonest. It worked less well in a court at Westminster, the home of the Common Law. Some weighty matters necessitated God's more immediate intervention. The divine judgement could be invoked in a unilateral ordeal (such as by hot iron or cold water) or in a bilateral one (trial by battle) in which it was made manifest. The former sort of ordeal had long disappeared by Chaucer's time, having been prohibited by Pope Innocent III's Fourth Lateran Council of 1215, though the latter remained possible, if less regularly used, in certain classes of land action and certain types of criminal prosecution throughout the fourteenth century and beyond. But the epistemological problem (how do we discover the truth?) that these archaic procedures dramatised remained to trouble the lawyers throughout the Middle Ages. The jury was the answer favoured by the Common lawyers, but the oft-stated 'Englishman's right to be tried by jury' is an absolute distortion of reality. The right remained, in these gravest of cases, to be tried by God (who, as Chaucer and Boethius testified, saw and could decide everything). A defendant in a serious criminal case, for example, could only be tried by a jury (persons whose judgement was necessarily fallible) if he chose to waive his right to be tried by God. The law could seek to 'persuade' him to do so, by a technique that involved pressing him under heavy weights, but no medieval government felt it possible to remove the defendant's right to trial by ordeal, even long after its use had become impossible. Such a finding is more than a historical curiosity: it sheds light on the relative competencies of God and man and of the difficulties of discovering the truth. Similar difficulties, of course, may exercise the poet as well as the lawyer.

A second point that arises from this desired, but necessarily imperfect, correspondence between divine and human law is the fact that the human judge is supposed to discard his baser humanity when acting officially. Yet the figure of the unjust judge is a common one in medieval representations, including in the *Physician's Tale*, and indeed in reality – Chief Justice Tresilian was hanged in 1388: the story that he was hanged naked after necromantical charms were found upon him highlights the spiritual danger connoted by such a crime.[2]

A further dimension of the place of law in medieval society is social rather than philosophical. Musson has considered the rise of 'legal consciousness' in the period, arguing that even lay members of society might have, depending on their position and experience, considerable familiarity with legal concepts and procedures. We know that Chaucer had significant exposure, in a variety of roles (Justice of the Peace, litigant, victim, defendant) and we may presume the same in at least some of his audience. There are undoubtedly elements of that knowledge within the works, and anyone approaching Chaucer without some appreciation of the place of law in medieval society will miss something.[3] The question as to whether the poet had any formal legal training is a debated one, but, in truth, is largely unimportant.[4] The works almost never pretend, as far as I can see, to contain anything in the nature of technical legal commentaries:[5] whether they are written by an experienced layman, or by a trained lawyer writing for experienced laymen, or indeed a trained lawyer writing as a person rather than the product of a professional training (lawyers too can talk of love, life and fun without writing a brief on them) seems to me, for the most part, immaterial.

One other observation on the social place of law is important. Although law was a significant element in the resolution of disputes, so too was 'love', often characterised as its antithesis. Private agreements, arbitrations and self-help were essential and important components of the medieval normative landscape.

THE LAW

The very title of this chapter is misleading, in that it implies a single body of law and, by extension, a single, unified, set of courts. Neither of these propositions holds true for the Middle Ages. A unified, national law in the form of the Common Law did exist in England, but it had limitations on its application. Maturing since the reign of Henry II, the Common Law, which had developed in particular to cover the two fundamental matters of land law and crime, employed professional judges and practitioners. The fourteenth century saw considerable extension, through the development of particular forms of trespass writ, of its jurisdictional reach into an expanding number of 'private' wrongs and agreements, and of its penetration into the lives of people in the local communities. Justices of the Peace took an important role in the administration of criminal justice, particularly after the regularisation and extension of their powers in the reign of Edward III, complementing the assize courts of royal judges, which took the Common Law out into the countryside. (Chaucer, himself, had, of course, served as a Justice of the Peace, as does his Franklin, whilst the Man of Law had sat on Assize.) Another important development was an increased use of legislation, of which we learn the Man of Law has an improbable mastery, though his description stresses the very real prestige and opportunity that the senior Common lawyers had by then attained.[6] The growth of the Common Law had seen a fundamental transition in the nature of the lawyer's task from the days of local oral custom as the basis for dispute settlement. Yet the old pre-Common Law local courts, of shire and hundred, still survived in the late fourteenth century, although their procedures increasingly resembled the royal courts. Land matters concerning unfree tenants ('villeins') were administered in manorial courts, which also exercised a 'disciplinary' jurisdiction. Much law concerning trade was carried out too in courts of boroughs (important chartered urban centres, including London), and of fairs and markets, the rules and procedures of which had adapted to the needs of the mercantile sector of the economy before the Common lawyers became interested. There was even a body of international trading custom, the *lex mercatoria*.[7] Perhaps the most important transnational jurisdiction, however – one with which all Chaucer's readers become familiar – is the Canon Law, a representative of which, the Summoner, appears in the *Canterbury Tales*. The Canon Law, crucially, had jurisdiction over a variety of causes and persons categorised as 'ecclesiastical', though the interpretation of the boundary with secular jurisprudence was sometimes disputed and sometimes loosely interpreted by both sides in the Middle Ages. The crucial point to note is that this wide jurisdiction touched ordinary members of society, not merely the clergy, in their everyday lives. An indication of the range of matters dealt with in Archdeacons' courts, the lowest in the Canon Law hierarchy, is provided in the *Friar's Tale* (*CT*, III.1301–74).

Paradoxically, given what has been said about the transnational dimensions to some laws and to Chaucer's career and literary interests, English Common Law was an increasingly insular phenomenon. Canon Law was influenced by Roman (civil) law, which itself had undergone a significant revival of interest, commentary and application in continental Europe. Such developments, though of academic interest in England, had little effect on the substantive Common Law, which had already begun the process of growth. Taught originally through experience of practice, later combined with study in the Inns of Court, English law was never a university subject: its practitioners were learned, but their skills were pragmatic ones of pleading and the writs (procedure, not abstract 'rights', was the lifeblood of the Common Law) rather than the elegance of classical juristics. Yet part of their learning was necessarily linguistic in the fourteenth century. Latin was the language of authority and record, and English of everyday speech, but lawyers (and, Musson argues, laymen with experience of the system)[8] would also be obliged to master their professional register, Anglo-Norman (later to be known as Law French). Despite a statute of 1362 mandating the use of English in oral pleading in court, a knowledge of Anglo-Norman remained a necessity for legal practitioners in Common Law courts.[9]

Does a knowledge of medieval law add anything to an appreciation of Chaucer's work? Law was undoubtedly an important element of social, intellectual and economic life in the fourteenth century, its centrality dramatically highlighted, for example, by the position it occupied in the agitation of the Peasants' Revolt.[10] It may indeed be interesting to know whether, when one of Chaucer's characters makes or breaks a promise, he or she is using a formula that creates a binding legal contract – including, perhaps, one of marriage.[11] Yet it is possible on occasion to worry too much about technicalities: a person who breaks their word is, in the absence of excusing or mitigating factors, generally speaking, doing a bad thing, and though we may legitimately claim that an appreciation of the legality or otherwise of that act 'adds another layer' to our understanding, it may do so only to a rather limited extent. Sometimes the additional perspective may have a greater explanatory power. I have argued, for example, in relation to the question of rape, that a clearer grasp of a contemporary understanding of legal principle may explain why modern readers experience anxiety in trying to resolve an ambiguity over the nature of the offence that medieval lawyers would simply not recognise as juridically important, and it may also explain why Chaucer should on occasion depart significantly from his source.[12] So an understanding of medieval law, its language, limits, conceptual structures, and the creativity and intelligence of its practitioners may indeed provide specific insights. More generally, however, such an understanding (to some extent) would form an integral part of Chaucer's own mentality. His modern readers should be encouraged to make it part of theirs.

NOTES

1 The soundest starting place is J. H. Baker, *An Introduction to English Legal History*, 4th edn (London: Butterworths, 2002). More temporally specific studies include Anthony Musson and W. M. Ormrod, *The Evolution of English Justice: Law, Politics and Society in the Fourteenth Century* (Basingstoke: Macmillan, 1999); Robert C. Palmer, *English Law in the Age of the Black Death, 1348–1381: A Transformation of Governance and Law* (Chapel Hill: University of North Carolina Press, 1993); and Edward Powell, *Kingship, Law and Society: Criminal Justice in the Reign of Henry V* (Oxford: Clarendon Press, 1989). Anthony Musson's *Medieval Law in Context: The Growth of Legal Consciousness from Magna Carta to the Peasants' Revolt* (Manchester: Manchester University Press,

2001) takes a less doctrinal stance, as does Richard Firth Green's *A Crisis of Truth: Literature and Law in Ricardian England* (Philadelphia: University of Pennsylvania Press, 2002), which latter outstanding work is particularly important for students of literature. I am obliged to David Seipp for a helpful conversation on this subject. A detailed legal analysis of legal material within Chaucer's work is to be found in Joseph Allen Hornsby, *Chaucer and the Law* (Norman, OK: Pilgrim Books, 1988).

2 See Richard W. Ireland, '"He hanged Rumbold": The Iconology of Judicial Partiality in the Middle Ages', *Law and Critique*, 7 (1996), 3–33.

3 Musson, *Medieval Law*, esp. chapter 3.

4 See Hornsby, *Chaucer and the Law*, pp. 16f., but cf. J. H. Baker, *The Legal Profession and the Common Law: Historical Essays* (London: Hambledon Press, 1986), p. 6.

5 An exception is the use of Peñafort's Canon Law *Summa* in the *Parson's Tale*.

6 I have no doubt (*pace* the suggestion at *Riverside Chaucer*, p. 811) that Chaucer's description is satirical: for example, scholars who have been pleased to spot the reference to all being 'fee simple' as a legal term of art should note that the more obvious pun survives that technicality. Hornsby suggests, unusually, that the character may be a London Common Sergeant, rather than a Royal Court one (*Chaucer and the Law*, p. 71). Note however that although legislation, introducing conscious change into the law, is important, so too is the idea, which seems to have been voiced in the Peasants' Revolt, that old law was good law, and vice versa. Such an idea underlies the invocation of a past 'Golden Age' (cf. Chaucer's *The Former Age*) in an early text of legal criticism, *The Mirror of Justices*.

7 Note in this context the international trade of the *Shipman's Tale*. For domestic local courts see Marjorie Keniston McIntosh, *Controlling Misbehavior in England, 1370–1600* (New York: Cambridge University Press, 1998). Another body of domestic law, which was to become known as Equity and intended to ameliorate the rigour of the Common Law, was developing in the later fourteenth century too: see Baker, *Introduction to English Legal History*, chapter 6.

8 Musson, *Medieval Law*, p. 121.

9 For the statute see W. M. Ormrod, 'The Use of English: Language, Law and Political Culture in Fourteenth Century England', *Speculum*, 78 (2003), 750–87; and W. Rothwell, 'English and French in England after 1362', *English Studies*, 82 (2001), 539–59.

10 For which see Musson, *Medieval Law*, chapter 6; and Green, *Crisis of Truth*, chapter 5.

11 See the analysis in Hornsby, *Chaucer and the Law*, chapters 2 and 3, for examples.

12 See R. W. Ireland, 'Lucrece, Philomela and Cecily: Chaucer and the Law of Rape', in T. S. Haskett, ed., *Crime and Punishment in the Middle Ages* (Victoria, BC: University of Victoria Press, 1998), pp. 37–61; or see the arguments and references in R. M. Houser, 'Alisoun Takes Exception: Medieval Legal Pleading and the Wife of Bath', *Chaucer Review*, 48 (2013), 66–90.

CHAPTER 31

Art

Julian Luxford

The picture of late Plantagenet art seen through the lens of recent scholarship is composed of conventional, largely hermetic categories such as architecture, woodwork, textiles, sculpture, stained glass, mural painting, panel painting, manuscript illumination, metalwork and so on. The roots of these categories are historical: while some individuals, particularly painters, worked in more than one medium, what we know of later medieval artistic praxis suggests a high degree of specialisation. However, if art is approached with reference to the viewing consciousness – something encouraged by the current 'cultural turn' in art history, with its reduced emphasis on connoisseurship and sharper focus on historical context – then the categories tend to lose definition and run together in a process of integration familiar from experience of our own material environments. From this perspective, the constitutive stake that art had in its spatial, social and historical settings emerges. This observation can be illustrated with a felicitous example.

The protracted trial of 1385–90 conducted in the Court of Chivalry between Sir Richard Scrope (the plaintiff) and Sir Robert Grosvenor (the defendant) is well known to students of Chaucer for the poet's appearance at it.[1] At stake in such trials was the entitlement to bear a given coat of arms (here *azure a bend or*), a matter that went to the heart of ancestral and personal honour and could also have serious financial consequences.[2] The most potent material evidence produced by deponents in the Scrope–Grosvenor case took the form of what would now be classified as works of art: sculpted tombs; glazed windows displaying imagery, heraldry and inscriptions ('verrures'); ecclesiastical vestments; altarpieces and other types of panel ('tablez'); painted banners; and seal-impressions. (Chaucer himself mentioned 'ban[er]s en v[er]rures en peyntures en vestementz', as well as a painted sign hanging outside a hostel in London.) In each case the object was cited because it had a historical or genealogical association with one of the litigants, and also because it displayed the contested arms. The Abbot of Easby Abbey, by Richmond in Yorkshire, testifying for Scrope, stated that his church contained a carved tomb bearing the stone effigy of a knight painted with the arms, and that this knight was Henry Scrope, one of the abbey's founders. Around this were several other tombs of Scropes, each embellished with their images and heraldry. The arms permeated the space around the tombs, existing on 'tables', in windows, on vestments and on a corporal case; and they also occupied windows in the canons' refectory and various chambers elsewhere in the abbey.[3] Other deponents offered similar testimony with reference to other religious houses and parish churches: in total, sixty-three locations containing objects emblazoned with the arms were cited. Where, as for Easby, the testimony is detailed, the impression of a collection of objects embedded in a broader material environment and related to one another through a synthesis of locational, historical and sentimental agency is palpable. Their circumstantial, forensic value for the court was a function of deeper, more complex associations. Even though some materials of manufacture are noted (stone, glass, paint), the deponents did not try to disaggregate the things they mentioned according to the taxonomy of modern art history, and neither do other voices on art during the period.

The point to stress here is that medieval art, no less than its modern kin, was conceptually fluid and functionally contingent on context and human psychology. This should not necessarily be taken to suggest that the medium-centred categories mentioned above are either impractical or methodologically obsolete. Linnaean structures of this type will be useful as long as scholars seek typological approaches to their material. The stylistic terms associated with these structures will also remain important as criteria for dating objects in the absence of documents (even though no such term adequately describes the properties of a specific work or works). A word about them will not be out of place here. In the broadest sense, art of the mid-to-later fourteenth century is classified as 'Gothic' in style. Because this term is applicable throughout the later Middle Ages, a series of adjectives based on the date or form of architecture is used to refine it according to period. Thus, in architecture, sculpture, embroidery and painting, 'Decorated' Gothic held sway in England from the second half of the thirteenth century until the Black Death, and for a decade longer north of the River Trent. The Decorated style is characterised by mannered, curving forms and a lushness and copiousness of detail that was expensive to produce.[4] It was supplanted in architecture by the starker Perpendicular style, but, unlike Decorated, this term is not transferrable to the other arts: we never speak of Perpendicular painting, for example, or even Perpendicular sculpture.

Rather, from the second half of the fourteenth century, art historians often use the term 'International Gothic' (or 'International style') in connection with the non-architectural arts, especially the different forms of sculpture, painting and metalwork. International Gothic combined stylistic features current in French and Italian art, particularly the types and styles of art associated with the patronage of courts of rulers. It was technically complex and abundantly decorative – gold is a leitmotif – and is associated in representations of the human figure with benign psychology; mannered gestures; and complicated, often fluttering draperies. The highly wrought objects persuasively connected by Joan Evans with passages in Chaucer's writings are likely to have been examples of International Gothic workmanship, and represent a category of art that frequently passed across the English Channel.[5] In England, the term is applicable to the better-quality alabaster sculptures such as those from Flawford in Nottinghamshire (*c.* 1380); the stained glass images of kings in the west window of Canterbury Cathedral (1396–1411); panel paintings such as the portrait of Richard II in Westminster Abbey (1394–5) and the Despenser retable at Norwich Cathedral (executed between 1370 and 1406); and manuscript illumination such as that of the Sherborne Missal (*c.* 1400–10), what remains of the Carmelite Missal (*c.* 1395–8) and the famous scene, reproduced on the cover of this book, of Chaucer (or at the very least the Chaucerian narrator) preaching at the beginning of the *Troilus and Criseyde* manuscript in Corpus Christi College, Cambridge (*c.* 1415–25). While the term 'International Gothic' is becoming unfashionable among art historians, some of its relevance is suggested by the Wilton Diptych (*c.* 1395–9), whose artist had absorbed the stylistic idioms of his courtly milieu so thoroughly that it is still unclear if he was English, French or Netherlandish.[6]

It is well known that English medieval art suffered dreadfully from deliberate destruction in every century from the mid-sixteenth to the nineteenth. But it should be remembered that the mass-refurbishment of churches and domestic buildings that occurred in the 200 years before the Reformation had already swept away a great deal of earlier art. The Middle Ages destroyed more medieval art than any subsequent period. Consequently, survivals from the second half of the fourteenth century are probably in the order of less than 1 per cent of the original total, although in a few areas, particularly tomb-sculpture, the proportion is higher. The artistic vigour of the period and enthusiasms of its patrons are thus lost from immediate view (except, of course, in the domain of architecture), and it is rather difficult now to imagine what the interior of a church or castle looked like in the years leading up to 1400. Inventories provide some purchase on the matter. That drawn up in 1397 at Pleshey Castle in Essex after the attainder of Thomas of Woodstock, Duke of Gloucester, indicates the place of art in an aristocratic residence.[7] It begins with a list of 'cloths of Arras work': sumptuous tapestries displayed in the castle chambers according to inclination and occasion. These represented chivalric narratives such as the history of Charlemagne (the longest, probably for the great hall), Godfrey de Bouillon's conquest of Jerusalem, the battle of Gawain and Lancelot, the siege of the Castle of Love and the history of St George, moral themes such as Judith and Holofernes and what was presumably Enyas and the Wild Man (it is called 'lestorie dun discomfiture dun Wodewose'), and religious scenes including episodes in the infancy of Christ and the Holy Sepulchre. Individually, the pieces measured up to 72 feet in length, and were valued as highly as £48 12s., although this probably represented only a fraction of their cost when new. A great tapestry with the arms of Edward III and his sons, plus those of the Earls of Hereford (valued at £20), is also listed, along with two groups of beds (one group made of silk and cloth of gold, the other of worsted), of which the most remarkable is 'a great bed of gold' ('un grant lit dor') valued at £182 3s. Copious vestments for use in the castle chapel are specified, some with religious imagery, others with motifs such as leopards, and still others with heraldry. There is also a diptych with the Crucifixion of Christ and Coronation of the Virgin, a triptych with 'various images', many liturgical and devotional books with illumination and precious clasps, and a commensurate quantity of liturgical silver. More books – eighty-three in total – are then listed under the heading 'Books of various romances and histories'. Many of these, including a 'large livre de Godefray de Boillou[n]', which resonated with the iconography of the Arras hangings, had illumination and highly-wrought fastenings.

A briefer inventory from the Abbot's chapel at Bury St Edmunds reveals the artistic affinities of a spiritual lord. It was made in 1429, but the things it lists were not new. Here, too, one encounters the customary later medieval affection for vestments, and also service books. As a rule, and with the addition of metalwork, these things are noted first in ecclesiastical inventories and the lists of benefactions included in chronicles. Where the Abbot of Bury's chapel differed from the Duke of Gloucester's was in the range of its imagery. It had a 'beautiful table' ('pulcra tabula') – probably the altarpiece – with an image of the Virgin Mary; another table with painted figures on parchment; alabaster statues of St John the Evangelist, St Christopher, and the Holy Trinity; 'a beautiful wooden image of the Virgin in an ingeniously wrought tabernacle'; and two further wooden sculptures representing Saint Edmund (the spiritual patron of the monastery) and

Edward the Confessor.[8] The contrasting emphases on chivalry and sanctity in the two inventories look like a text-book example of the way that social status conditioned taste. However, just as a layman such as Thomas of Woodstock was attracted to religious imagery, so a prelate might also demonstrate enthusiasm for secular romance through art. Walter of Monington, Abbot of Glastonbury from 1342 to 1375, had three carpets embroidered with the arms of King Arthur in his chapel, hangings in his hall depicting the Nine Worthies and wars of King Edward III, and a further hanging at one of his manor-houses with a description of the arms of King Arthur in French.[9]

While parish churches sat lower down the social scale, they contained, collectively, vastly more art than the sum total of monasteries and castles. A sizable village church of the later fourteenth century, as at Attleborough in Norfolk or Yeovil in Somerset, had wall-paintings, altarpieces, stained glass, an array of architectural and freestanding sculpture, screens and other furnishings in wood (the period saw the rise of pews in parish church naves), its own collection of vestments, silver plate, sepulchral monuments, painted banners, and books with at least a modicum of illumination.[10] These things were products of individual and collective patronage, and commonly bore donor-inscriptions, heraldry or other identifying marks. As this may suggest, their function was often commemorative as well as laudatory and utilitarian. Parish church art was more typical of the period in terms of quality than much of what is indicated in the inventories from Pleshey and Bury St Edmunds. Although scholars tend to light on the finer examples, most later medieval English art was neither technically nor aesthetically distinguished. The sculpted alabaster figures and panels that survive in relatively large numbers from the fifteenth century, and that had their genesis in the period addressed by this chapter, probably give an accurate impression of normal qualitative and technical standards.[11]

A remarkable set of inventories of parish churches in Norfolk survives from 1368. There are over 350 entries, each listing service books, vestments and metalwork, along with other items of value given to churches by specified donors.[12] They exclude much that is countable as art: with sporadic exceptions, stained glass, woodwork, wall-painting and sculpture do not appear. However, the modern reader gets a vivid impression, in quantitative and sometimes qualitative terms, of the embellishment associated with the parochial liturgy, and also the corporate nature of much local art-patronage. At Salle church, for example, there was a cope or chasuble of red silk with embroidered gold animals and green velvet orphreys with little moons and stars, the gift of one Sampson Bussell. St Mary's Church at Elsing, a new building, possessed a cope of gold material for use in the choir 'with the arms of Sir Hugh Hastings', jointly given by a relative of Hugh's and the rector. Among the thousands of books listed, Brandeston had a 'beautiful' breviary, All Saints Ber Street in Norwich 'a new missal of the best quality', and Upton a fine psalter given by one of the vicars on condition that his obit was celebrated for as long as the book should last. At Great Walsingham, there were banners depicting the Assumption and Coronation of the Virgin Mary; at Ranworth, banners with St Helen and the Holy Trinity; and at Holy Cross, Norwich, two banners painted with the Crucifixion. The latter church, along with those at Swanton Morley and Horstead, had alabaster altarpieces, that at Horstead new and purchased jointly by the rector and parishioners. There were figures of Virgins and the arms of the Earl of Suffolk on the high altar-frontal at Cawston; a mitre for a boy bishop 'of great value' at St Peter Mancroft in Norwich; and a red cope with peacocks and squirrels picked out in gold thread at St Etheldreda's at Thetford, a gift of one William Bernham. The sense of pride as well as hope invested in such objects emerges powerfully from these accounts. Through donation and use, artworks of metal, cloth, alabaster, parchment and wood, painted and unpainted, beautiful and otherwise, helped to bind people into the web of social and religious life, as well as mediating between the worshipper and the objects of his or her devotion.

Practically all of this material has been lost. There is, however, a major category of medieval art not mentioned in the inventories that has fared better. Sepulchral monuments, much discussed in current scholarship, played a large part in conditioning the appearance and spatial organisation of contemporary church interiors. In particular, the monumental brass, whose origins lay in the late thirteenth century, became widespread between 1350 and 1400. There was also a steep rise in three-dimensional tombs, with or without sculpted effigies.[13] The elevated monuments of Edward III and Richard II and Anne of Bohemia in the Confessor's Chapel at Westminster Abbey, with gilded bronze effigies of the highest quality upon them, represent the pinnacle of a division of art that played almost as important a part in the fabric of religious life as devotional images, but whose popularity transcended the Reformation. In their sculpture, engraving and chased detail, these objects convey many of the material and aesthetic qualities not now accessible in other categories of painting, sculpture and metalwork. Their geographical distribution, the various occupations of those they commemorate, and the gamut of their formal and aesthetic characteristics suggest a depth of social engagement with art that has not been surpassed in any subsequent period.

NOTES

1 *L-R*, pp. 370–4.
2 Maurice Keen, *Origins of the English Gentleman: Heraldry, Chivalry and Gentility in Medieval England, c. 1300–c. 1500* (Stroud: Tempus, 2002), pp. 25–70.
3 N. H. Nicolas, ed., *De controversia in curia militari inter Ricardum le Scrope et Robertum Grosvenor, milites*, 2 vols. (London: Samuel Bentley, 1832), Vol. 1, pp. 95–6 (Easby), 178–9 (Chaucer).
4 Paul Binski, *Gothic Wonder: Art, Artifice and the Decorated Style 1290–1350* (London and New Haven, CT: Yale University Press, 2014).
5 Joan Evans, 'Chaucer and Decorative Art', *Review of English Studies*, 6 (1930), 408–12.
6 Dillian Gordon, *Making and Meaning: The Wilton Diptych* (London: National Gallery Publications, 1993), pp. 72–3.
7 Viscount Dillon and W. H. St John Hope, 'Inventory of the Goods and Chattels Belonging to Thomas, Duke of Gloucester, and Seized in His Castle at Pleshey, Co. Essex, 21 Richard II. (1397)', *Archaeological Journal*, 54 (1897), 275–308.
8 London, British Library, Add. MS 14848, fols. 29v–31v (images listed on fol. 30r).
9 J. M. Luxford, '*Nichil ornatus in domo domini pretermittens*: The Professional Patronage of Walter of Monington, Abbot of Glastonbury', in Paul Binski and Elizabeth A. New, eds., *Patrons and Professionals in the Middle Ages* (Donington: Shaun Tyas, 2012), pp. 237–60 (pp. 251, 255).
10 Architectural sculpture is sculpture inseparably carved into or onto an architectural element.
11 See Francis Cheetham, *English Medieval Alabasters* (London: Victoria and Albert Museum, 1984); and, by the same author, *The Alabaster Images of Medieval England* (Woodbridge: Boydell and Brewer, 2003). For iconography see Richard Marks, *Image and Devotion in Medieval England* (Stroud: Alan Sutton, 2004).
12 Aelred Watkin, ed., *Inventory of Church Goods temp. Edward III*, 2 vols. (Norwich: Norfolk Record Society, 1947–8).
13 Nigel Saul, *English Church Monuments in the Middle Ages* (Oxford: Oxford University Press, 2009). For Chaucer's own tomb in Westminster Abbey see Derek Pearsall, 'Chaucer's Tomb: The Politics of Reburial', *Medium Ævum*, 64 (1995), 51–73.

CHAPTER 32

Architecture

Richard Fawcett

The fourteenth century opened with a period of artistic tension that was a prelude to developments that took English architecture along a path markedly different from the rest of Europe. A notable aspect of the period is the increase in the documentation that permits identification of named master masons as individual creative personalities,[1] especially in the case of the buildings designed by craftsmen of the Royal Office of Works.[2] But, at a time when design processes were increasingly systematically organised, unnamed identifications can also be attempted through forensic analysis of architectural detail.

The phase in which the germs of two rather different approaches to design were tentatively explored is well illustrated by the two-storeyed chapel of St Stephen in the Palace of Westminster, of which only the modified lower storey survives, but which is well documented and whose appearance was partly recorded before the fire of 1834.[3] The chapel was started for Edward I in 1292 by the mason Michael of Canterbury, and in a building intended to rival the French King's Sainte-Chapelle, every effort was made to show English architecture at its most innovative. The ogees (double-curves) to the window light-heads, previously employed only in decorative situations, along with the complexity of the lower chapel vault with its additional lierne (decorative) ribs, were particularly striking features.

The ogees at St Stephen's were the forerunners of the richly curvilinear tracery that typified the 'Decorated style'.[4] Such tracery was to be inventively developed at large scale in examples such as the east window of Carlisle Cathedral, of around 1318, and the west window of York Minster, of the 1330s. It was also deployed in many parish churches into the third quarter of the fourteenth century, especially in the eastern counties, as at Grantham and Boston in Lincolnshire, or at Patrington and Hull in the East Riding of Yorkshire.[5]

A particularly complex example is the west window of Snettisham in Norfolk, possibly built for the dowager Queen Isabella in the second quarter of the fourteenth century (Figure 32.1). Close similarities of detail

Figure 32.1 Snettisham Church, the west window.

Figure 32.2 Ely Cathedral, Lady Chapel, interior.

with the choir and crossing of Ely Cathedral, where reconstruction followed the collapse of the central tower in February 1322, suggest that masons working there also built Snettisham.[6] The choir at Ely has been convincingly attributed to William Ramsey,[7] a figure of outstanding importance for fourteenth-century architecture, who in 1326 was appointed chief mason and surveyor of the King's castles south of the Trent. In 1337, he took over responsibility for the building of St Stephen's Chapel.

Another royal craftsman at Ely was the carpenter William Hurley, who was appointed chief carpenter and surveyor south of the Trent in the same year that Ramsey became chief mason and surveyor. He was at Ely in 1334 and was presumably responsible for the brilliantly cantilevered timberwork over the new octagon. Like Ramsey he was also involved at St Stephen's, presumably designing the timber vault of 1347–8 over the upper chapel.

Another aspect of the Decorated style is demonstrated in the rectangular Lady Chapel to the north of Ely's choir, started in 1321 but only ready for dedication in 1352 (Figure 32.2). Here the soft clunch stone employed internally encouraged a highly enriched treatment. The framework for this is a network of niches capped by nodding (forward-projecting) ogee arches, with interplay between the planes of decoration best seen in the way that shafts supporting the vault or the rear plane of niches are extended down behind the outer plane of arches. Elements of this were foreshadowed in the upper chapel at St Stephen's, where arcading below the windows was capped by nodding ogees, with the window mullions extended down behind that arcading. The proliferation of ribs to the Lady Chapel vault, which emphasised the unity of the vault as a whole, may also reflect William Hurley's designs for St Stephen's upper-chapel timber vault.

If the richness and complexity of the Decorated style were anticipated at St Stephen's Chapel, however, so was an altogether more rigorously austere approach to design, which is generally characterised as the 'Perpendicular style'.[8] This is seen in the way that the mullions of the upper-chapel windows were externally extended down behind a string course, before reappearing in blind arcading to the walls above the lower-chapel windows; they were then extended down as free-standing stone bars in front of the lower windows. In the latter, there was probably an awareness of French work such as the 'harp strings' that decorate the west front of Strasbourg Cathedral, started in 1277. A related interest in strong vertical lines was demonstrated in the blind arcading of the internal spandrels of the upper-chapel windows, which is probably attributable to William Ramsey after he assumed responsibility for the chapel masonry in 1337.

Ramsey had already experimented with such ideas in the lost chapter house and cloister of St Paul's Cathedral in London, which he started to build in 1332. The chapter-house doorway had blind arcading comparable with the spandrels of the St Stephen's upper-chapel windows, while the window mullions were similarly extended down across the lower wall. But the most striking feature of the chapter house and cloister walks was that the preference for vertical lines was extended to the window tracery, where supermullions (short verticals in the tracery field) replaced the circlets or ogee curves that might have been expected.

The next stage in this chain of ideas is seen at Gloucester Cathedral. Following Edward II's murder at Berkeley Castle in 1327, his body was taken to Gloucester, where a superb tomb was constructed on the north side of the choir. It was subsequently decided to remodel the eastern parts of the cathedral, at least partly with funds provided by pilgrims to Edward's tomb; work started in the south transept around 1331, before moving on to the choir, which was completed in 1367 (Figure 32.3).[9]

Funding was perhaps not unlimited, and instead of demolishing the existing Romanesque choir the arcade and gallery stages were retained,

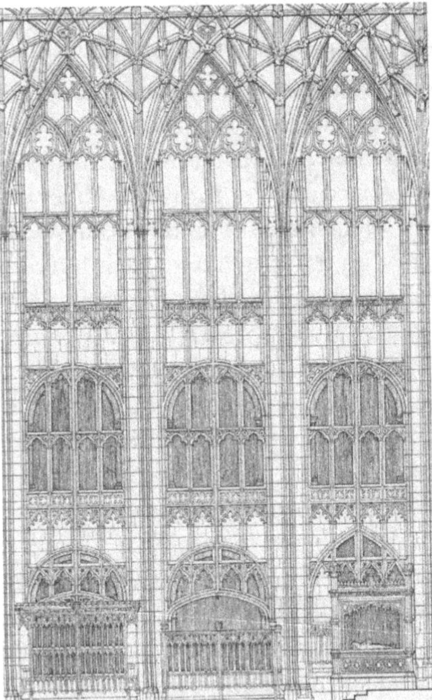

Figure 32.3 Gloucester Cathedral, choir elevation, from Francis Bond, *Gothic Architecture in England* (London: Batsford, 1905), p. 59.

and only the clerestory was replaced, to a height over twice that of the original. At the same time the inner walls of the apse were removed, and the arcade walls extended along to a vast new tripartite window occupying the whole east end. The internal choir elevations were then entirely faced with a skin of new masonry. It was not an altogether new idea to remodel an existing building by retaining the lower parts while replacing the upper parts: a related approach had been adopted at nearby Tewkesbury Abbey in the 1330s. But Gloucester was different in several important respects.

Gloucester's new skin of masonry was designed as a rectilinear grid of slender verticals and horizontals spread uniformly across both walls and voids, with only the vaulting shafts given greater emphasis. The grid was even extended across the retained round-headed gallery openings and the upper part of the arcade arches, so that the central vessel of the choir was visually isolated from the flanking spaces. It was nevertheless flooded with light from the vast east window and the new clerestory. The sense of spatial homogeneity that all this gave to the central vessel was further emphasised by the vault, which rose well above the apices of the clerestory windows, and whose surface was covered by a continuous net-like pattern of ribs.

Such systematic articulation of elevations through the definition of the component elements by clearly marked horizontals and verticals had its origins in the phase of French architecture usually described as Rayonnant. As seen in the reconstructed choir of the Royal Abbey of Saint-Denis, where work started in 1231, French architects increasingly chose to give a seemingly logical expression to the structure of their buildings in this way, with pronounced interlinkage of the levels by interpenetrating verticals. One of the fullest expressions of this approach was the choir of the Burgundian priory church of Saint-Thibault, rebuilt between 1290 and 1320, where the grid of verticals and horizontals is almost as all-embracing as at Gloucester.

French masons, however, never extended this rectilinearity into the window tracery; it was English masons who did that, and it is at St Paul's and Gloucester that we see how. The new approach to tracery design, in which vertical supermullions dictated the overall pattern, was in due course to fire the imagination of the nation's masons and patrons, and was eventually to become the norm in England for the rest of the Middle Ages. Indeed, such tracery was to become a defining leitmotif of the many increasingly light-filled and spacious parish churches rebuilt or enlarged in towns and villages across the country.

A further step taken at Gloucester in the process of extending tracery to masonry faces was to apply its patterns to vaulting surfaces in the rebuilt cloister, where work was started in the east walk around 1351. The vaults were designed as a succession of concave conoids meeting tangentially above the central axis of the walks and between the bays, and these were covered with radiating tracery like that seen in rose windows. This is a form now known as fan vaulting. Partial precedents for the conoids may be seen in a number of centralised chapter houses, and one wonders if that at St Paul's had something similar. A striking feature of the approach taken at Gloucester is the way that the vaults were constructed of coursed masonry in which the ribs were an integral part of each block, rather than with a structural framework of ribs supporting webbing.

A later building where retention of existing work conditioned the design was the nave of Winchester Cathedral (Figure 32.4). The decision to remodel the Romanesque nave was initiated in 1366 by Bishop William Edington, but most of the work was carried out for Bishop William Wykeham after 1394, and was executed by Wykeham's favoured master mason, William Wynford. The core of the Romanesque arcade piers was retained, together with the wall core above them at gallery and clerestory

Figure 32.4 Winchester Cathedral, nave interior, from Robert Willis, *Proceedings at the Annual Meeting of the Archaeological Institute* (London: Longman, Brown, Green and Longmans, 1846), p. 71.

levels, and the arches of the gallery stage.[10] Unlike at Gloucester, however, no earlier work was to remain visible. The result was an elevation of two approximately equal storeys: tall, steeply pointed arcade arches, with blind tracery in the spandrels, rise to an arcaded balustrade; the clerestory is recessed from the lower wall plane, and blind panelling extends the tracery of the window across the whole wall, masking the blank area at the level of the aisle roofs.

Considering the difficulties entailed in retaining but masking the Romanesque masonry, Wynford's nave is a successful exploration of what could be achieved with the new architectural forms, though the great masses of masonry that inevitably resulted, which limited inter-visibility between central vessel and aisles, cannot have been regarded as ideal. A different approach had earlier been adopted when it was decided to rebuild Canterbury Cathedral's nave in 1378 (Figure 32.5), almost certainly to the designs of the royal master mason Henry Yevele,[11] and it is attractive to imagine that Chaucer's pilgrims would have witnessed the process of reconstruction.

Figure 32.5 Canterbury Cathedral, nave interior.

Canterbury's nave shows many similarities with Winchester's; indeed, since the two master masons are known to have worked together elsewhere, it is likely Wynford was aware of Yevele's design. Tall arcades open into the aisles, and at clerestory level panelling extends across the walls below the windows. At Canterbury, however, there is far less sense of the weight of masonry. The piers are slender and allow clear views into the aisles; the arcade arches appear particularly thin, though much of their width is in fact concealed by the aisle vaults; and the clerestory level continues the plane of the arcades, so that overall the elevations appear lighter and more two-dimensional than at Winchester.

The buildings considered so far have all been religious: it is generally in the well-funded opportunities offered by the Church that we best see how the most inventive master masons took their ideas forward. Nevertheless, the fourteenth century witnessed remarkable innovations in secular architecture, both in the ways that buildings were planned and in their overall forms.[12] A striking feature of aristocratic residences is the novel forms given to some; thus, in about 1377 the Earl of Northumberland's great tower at Warkworth, in Northumberland (Figure 32.6), was given a cruciform plan,

Figure 32.6 Warkworth Castle, the great tower.

while around 1393 Lord Lovell's tower at Wardour in Wiltshire was designed as a hollow hexagon. Elsewhere, the multiplicity of lodgings and imposing public rooms required in the houses of the great were accommodated in regularly disposed quadrangles of ranges afforded prominence by towers at the four corners, as at Lord Scrope's Bolton in Yorkshire of around 1378, and the castle of 1389 that bore Lord Lumley's name in County Durham.

In much of this, virtuoso display was of prime importance, as supremely demonstrated in Richard II's remodelling of William Rufus's great hall at Westminster. Between 1394 and 1401 its upper walls were remodelled by Henry Yevele, and, once the original arcades had been removed, the great width of the hall was bridged by an arch-braced and hammer-beam roof. This unequalled triumph of engineering was the work of the carpenter Hugh Herland.

Herland had earlier designed a splendid arch-braced roof over the hall of the great new palace built for Edward III in the upper ward of Windsor Castle between 1357 and 1368, where the overall design was the responsibility of the master masons John Sponlee and William Wynford, and the operation was overseen by Bishop William Wykeham.[13] The palace has been so extensively modified that its original form is now barely recognisable, and the hall roof is long gone, though the impressive treatment of the long façades, with regularly disposed fenestration centring on a twin-towered entrance, is recorded in a view by Wenceslaus Hollar of 1672.

The lessons learnt at Windsor on the merits of unified designs were to be reflected in the 1380s and 1390s in two projects where Wykeham, Wynford and Hurley are again thought to have worked together. These were Wykeham's foundations of New College in Oxford, and Winchester College in his cathedral city, where he made simultaneous provision for the lower and higher education of future Church leaders. Winchester College was the work of Wynford, as was probably New College, though it was presumably jointly decided by patron and master mason that the chapel and hall should be united within a single impressive range. Most of Herland's timberwork for the colleges has been lost, apart from a timber fan vault over Winchester College's chapel that is almost certainly attributable to him.

Returning finally to aristocratic residences, it must be asked how far the militaristic repertory of towers, gatehouses and crenellation retained any serious function, one place where this question has often been raised being Bodiam Castle in Sussex, built around 1385 for Sir Edward Dallingridge (Figure 32.7). Set out to a compact square plan, it has round towers at all four corners and central towered gatehouses capped by machicolation on

Figure 32.7 Bodiam Castle.

two fronts. It is surrounded by a broad moat crossed by causeways, and within the walls elegant accommodation extends around a central courtyard.

The traditional understanding is that Bodiam was planned as a strongpoint in the defences of England's southern counties by a hardened war leader who understood the French threat. A more recent view is that it was a handsome country house with defensive trappings that were little more than an ostentatious expression of high status.[14] On balance, it may be suspected that Dallingridge had both those ends in view, albeit with a particular emphasis on his personal amenity. But it is an indicator of the fascinating complexity of fourteenth-century architecture that we only partly understand how the aspirations of patrons at a time of great innovation were expressed in the fine buildings raised for them.

NOTES

1 John Harvey, *English Medieval Architects: A Biographical Dictionary down to 1550*, 2nd edn (Gloucester: Alan Sutton, 1984).

2 R. A. Brown, H. M. Colvin and A. J. Taylor, *The History of the King's Works: The Middle Ages*, 2 vols. (London: Her Majesty's Stationery Office, 1963).

3 J. M. Hastings, *St Stephen's Chapel and Its Place in the Development of the Perpendicular Style in England* (Cambridge: Cambridge University Press, 1955).

4 The terms 'Decorated style' and 'Perpendicular style' (see below) were coined by Thomas Rickman in his *Attempt to Discriminate the Styles of English Architecture, from the Conquest to the Reformation*, in James Smith, ed., *Panorama of Science and Art* (Liverpool: Nuttall, Fisher, 1815). Those terms remain widely current. Recent discussions of the Decorated style include Jean Bony, *The English Decorated Style: Gothic Architecture Transformed 1250–1350* (Oxford: Phaidon, 1979); Nicola Coldstream, *The Decorated Style: Architecture and Ornament 1240–1360* (London: British Museum Press, 1994); and Paul Binski, *Gothic Wonder: Art, Artifice and the Decorated Style 1290–1350* (London and New Haven, CT: Yale University Press, 2014).

5 D. Etherton, 'The Morphology of Flowing Tracery', *Architectural Review*, 140, no. 823 (1965), 177–80.

6 Richard Fawcett, 'Snettisham Church', in John McNeill, ed., *King's Lynn and the Fens: Medieval Art, Architecture and Archaeology*, British Archaeological Association Conference Transactions, 31 (Leeds: Routledge for the British Archaeological Association, 2008), pp. 134–47.

7 John Maddison, 'The Gothic Cathedral: A New Building in a Historic Context', in Peter Meadows and Nigel Ramsey, eds., *A History of Ely Cathedral* (Woodbridge: Boydell Press, 2003), pp. 113–41 (pp. 124–37).

8 Discussions of the Perpendicular style include John Harvey, *The Perpendicular Style 1330–1485* (London: Batsford, 1978); and Christopher Wilson, 'The

Origins of the Perpendicular Style and Its Development to *circa* 1360', unpublished Ph.D. thesis (University of London, 1979).

9 David Welander, *The History, Art and Architecture of Gloucester Cathedral* (Stroud: Alan Sutton, 1991).

10 R. Willis, 'The Architectural History of Winchester Cathedral', *Proceedings of the Annual Meeting of the Archaeological Institute of Great Britain and Ireland at Winchester, September* MDCCCXLV (London: Longman, Brown, Green and Longmans, 1846).

11 Francis Woodman, *The Architectural History of Canterbury Cathedral* (London: Routledge and Kegan Paul, 1981), pp. 151–64.

12 John Goodall, *The English Castle 1066–1650* (New Haven, CT: Yale University Press, 2011), pp. 229–337.

13 Christopher Wilson, 'The Royal Lodgings of Edward III at Windsor Castle: Form, Function and Representation', in Laurence Keen and Eileen Scarff, eds., *Windsor: Medieval Archaeology, Art and Architecture of the Thames Valley*, British Archaeological Association Conference Transactions, 25 (Leeds: Routledge for the British Archaeological Association, 2002), pp. 15–94; Steven Brindle, 'Edward III's Windsor, c. 1365–1377', in Steven Brindle, ed., *Windsor Castle, a Thousand Years of a Royal Palace* (London: Royal Collection Trust, 2018), pp. 102–17.

14 Charles Coulson, 'Some Analysis of the Castle of Bodiam, East Sussex', in C. Harper-Bill and R. Harvey, eds., *The Ideals and Practice of Medieval Knighthood, 4: Papers from the Fifth Strawberry Hill Conference, 1990* (Woodbridge: Boydell, 1992), pp. 51–107.

CHAPTER 33

Heraldry, Heralds and Chaucer

Katie Stevenson

Heraldry is a system of identification that developed during the Middle Ages, principally as the result of the need to distinguish men in full armour. Indeed, Chaucer himself observed that 'by hir cote-armures … / The heraudes knewe hem best' (*KnT*, I.1016–17). Heraldry encapsulated status, genealogy and affinity, through the use of symbols and drawings; it was the language of an inherently international chivalric culture. The use of a coat of arms could signify subscription to the cult of chivalry, but more importantly it also indicated loyalty, lineage and personal ownership. As a mode of communication it was highly effective and quickly developed to have wider applications beyond the battlefield. Its omnipresence within elite material culture – on coins, seals, portraits, buildings, decorative objects and jewellery – demonstrates that heraldry was a quintessential part of the medieval world.

The fourteenth century was a particularly important period in the development of heraldry. By 1300 coats of arms were widely diffused amongst the knights of Western Europe, and the proliferation of rolls of arms from the 1270s established heraldry as a mainstay of chivalric culture. Indeed, so established were armorials and rolls of arms by Chaucer's time that the poet described an exaggerated armorial in the *House of Fame* (lines 1320–40). At the turn of the fourteenth century, heraldry was still understood principally within military contexts as a system of distinguishing individuals and retinues in battle, on campaign and in the chivalric tournament. For example, the carved front of the Courtrai Chest, now in the Ashmolean Museum, shows scenes from the Battle of the Golden Spurs in July 1302, an unexpected victory over the French by a Flemish urban militia, whose members are depicted here marching under the banners of several important Courtrai guilds. The *Great Roll of Arms* of *c.* 1308 is another remarkable survival, not only for the sheer number of English knights represented in the roll, but also because the arms are given in blazon, the codified written description of heraldry. Nevertheless, the problems of an unregulated system of heraldry were readily identifiable by contemporaries, especially from the fourteenth century. Episodes where men on opposing sides met in battle displaying the same heraldry were frequently reported. For example, the chronicler Jean Froissart relates an angry argument on the eve of the Battle of Poitiers in 1356 between the English knight Sir John Chandos and the Marshal of France, Sir Jean de Clermont.[1] Both knights had adopted an identical badge and each offered to fight in the field – to duel – to defend their right to display it. This became one of the standard methods of resolving chivalric and heraldic disputes.

During the fourteenth century heraldry had increased in popularity at an exponential rate and appeared in more commonplace contexts. The use of a visual code of ownership, identity, lineage and allegiance was increasingly useful in this wider variety of settings. Moreover, with its increased usage and lack of regulation the problems of maintaining heraldry's individuality had been quickly manifested. A complex system of regulation and law thus developed, concerned not only with the bearing of arms but also, more crucially, with their granting. This became one of the principal concerns of fourteenth-century elites: coats of arms signified heredity and lineage, and were property that could be inherited. Protection of the rights to arms was thus increasingly contested over the course of the century, and the officers of arms (the kings of arms, heralds and pursuivants) became correspondingly important figures in crown service.

Nevertheless, an important development with particular relevance to the Chaucerian world is that by the fourteenth century heraldry was not exclusive to knights on the battlefield, but was also widely used by urban elites and the gentry. This is witnessed, for example, in the use of armorial escutcheons on over half of the surviving fourteenth-century Londoners' personal seals, which favoured aristocratic-looking heraldry over the use of merchants' marks.[2] Chaucer, firmly of mercantile stock, was himself armigerous and used the arms *per pale argent* and *gules a bend* counterchanged. Evidence suggests that in the fourteenth century it was quite normal for the urban patriciate and the nobility to join together to celebrate chivalry. It was in this kind of urban context that Chaucer must have seen and understood heraldry in his everyday life.

Chaucer was the son of a wealthy but decidedly nouveau riche London vintner with enough capital to acquire some increase in social standing. By 1357 he was in the household of Elizabeth de Burgh, Countess of Ulster. He undertook his first military campaign to France in early 1360 in the retinue of Lionel, Earl of Ulster, during which the young Chaucer was captured and ransomed by Edward III. This experience of war no doubt had a profound effect on his understanding of the martial world of chivalry and heraldry.

Chaucer's exposure to heraldic culture and knowledge became even more intense in 1366 upon his marriage to Philippa de Roet. Philippa was of a higher social status than Chaucer, and her father – Sir Payn de Roet – is the key to understanding Chaucer's knowledge of chivalry and heraldry. Sir Payn was not only a knight, he was also a king of arms, the most senior heraldic officer. Sir Payn held the inaugural office of Guyenne King of Arms, the title indicating the jurisdictional authority of Aquitaine that had been restored to Edward III in the Treaty of Brétigny of 1360. A copy of the ratification of this treaty was kept in a superb wooden oak coffer, heavily decorated with brilliantly coloured coats of arms, and is typical of the way in which heraldry was ever present as a visual language in the Middle Ages.[3] Thus to signal the formal removal of French authority under this treaty, Edward III created Guyenne King of Arms. The creation of significantly titled heralds was a common practice emerging across Europe at this time, as new officers of arms were invented and named to signify territorial acquisitions or other claims to sovereign power and authority.

Little is known of Sir Payn, but he had another daughter, Katherine, who married Sir Hugh Swynford. Katherine then became the mistress of John of Gaunt, whom she eventually married in 1396 after the death of his second wife Constance of Castile. This marriage legitimised their four Beaufort children, with the caveat that they were barred from succession to the throne of England. Katherine had been in the household of Gaunt's first wife, Blanche, daughter of Henry Grosmont, Earl of Derby. Both Philippa and Geoffrey Chaucer also held positions in Blanche's household, and Chaucer wrote his first major poem, the *Book of the Duchess*, to commemorate Blanche's death in 1368. It is evident that Chaucer's close proximity to the Roets and the Lancasters gave him a privileged understanding of heraldic culture.

While Sir Payn de Roet's position as Guyenne King of Arms reveals to us a great deal about the potential sources of Chaucer's understanding of heraldry, this was not the only area that fell under the remit of officers of arms. Heralds spent the majority of their time occupied by work that included translation, legal, political, ceremonial, genealogical and diplomatic functions. The rapid expansion of heraldry in the fourteenth century was mirrored in the increasing professionalisation and swelling of the ranks of the officers of arms.

Chaucer's legal and intellectual understanding of heraldry was presumably enhanced by his personal relationships, and this may have exposed him to the legal literature that was circulating in contemporary elite society. Indeed, the second half of the fourteenth century was a crucial period in developing the law of arms and it seems probable that it was much discussed in intellectual circles. In the middle of the fourteenth century there were two quite distinct schools of thought on the right to bear arms. Bartolus Saxoferrato, a Paduan civil lawyer, wrote the earliest-known treatise on heraldry in the 1350s, *De insigniis et armis*, which was certainly known in England and was the tract upon which Nicholas Upton based his mid-fifteenth-century *De studio militari*.[4] But Saxoferrato's views were not universally endorsed and the rival view was explicit: no one could simply assume arms; instead they must be granted by a heraldic authority. The English commentator Johannes de Bado Aureo laid out a similar case in the *Tractatus de armis*, written around 1394 for Anne of Bohemia, the consort of Richard II.[5] This articulated the desire for increased regulation of armorial bearings in the latter part of the fourteenth century and explains the expansion of the ranks, duties and importance of the heralds at this time.

In 1386 Chaucer was considered expert enough in matters of heraldry to be called as a witness in one of the best-known cases of the nascent English High Court of Chivalry, *Scrope* v. *Grosvenor*. Jointly presided over by the Lord High Constable and the Earl Marshal, the High Court of Chivalry had emerged by 1348 and was a civil court that heard military cases. It had a broad jurisdiction that included unjust detention of prisoners of war, the exchange of prisoners, payments of ransom and the settlement of disputes over armorial bearings.

The problem at issue in the *Scrope* v. *Grosvenor* case was discovered in 1385, when amongst the banners of an English army preparing to invade Scotland were two identical banners, *azure a bend or*, belonging to Sir Richard Scrope, first Lord Scrope of Bolton, and to Sir Robert Grosvenor, a knight of the Palatinate. The hearing was to determine who had the legitimate claim to the arms and it ran for four years. The case was remarkably well documented and over 200 depositions have survived.[6]

Chaucer's deposition provides information unlike any of the others. The context in which most of the deponents had first seen these arms being borne was military; Chaucer, however, reveals an urban setting for the unfurling of the arms. The court initially asked Chaucer whether the arms belonged to Sir Richard Scrope. Chaucer 'said yes, for he saw him so armed in France before the town of Retters, and Sir Henry Scrope armed in the same arms with a white label, and with banner; and the said Sir Richard armed in the entire arms, and so during the whole expedition'.

However, this evidence was not enough for the court, and Chaucer was also asked how he knew the arms belonged to Sir Richard. Chaucer responded 'that he had heard old knights and esquires say that they had had continual possession of the said arms; and that he had seen them displayed on banners, glass, paintings, and vestments, and commonly called the arms of Scrope'. The crucial testimony was that Chaucer

> was once in Friday Street, London, and walking through the street, he observed a new sign hanging out with these arms thereon, and inquired "what inn that was that hung out these arms of Scrope?" And one answered him, saying, "They are not hung out, Sir, for the arms of Scrope, nor painted there for those arms, but they are painted and put there by a Knight of the county of Chester, called Sir Robert Grosvenor", and that was the first time that he ever heard speak of Sir Robert Grosvenor, or his ancestors, or of any one bearing the name of Grosvenor.[7]

Despite the obvious legal implications of the case and its inherent testing of the Saxoferratan view of the right to assume arms, Chaucer's testimony reveals to us the ways in which heraldry was encountered in everyday urban contexts. It also suggests that Chaucer and the passer-by, neither of whom was of the noble estate, were nevertheless familiar with heraldry. Indeed, it seems unthinkable that heraldry was not part of the visual language through which urban dwellers communicated, a conclusion supported by the striking example in 1377 of a mob of angry Londoners who hung the arms of John of Gaunt upside down on the doors of Westminster Hall and St Paul's Cathedral, alongside bills that declared Gaunt's illegitimacy.

The *Scrope* v. *Grosvenor* case was of significant legal importance, bringing into sharp relief the desperate need for the recording, monitoring and regulating of arms in the kingdom. In the event, the Constable found in favour of Scrope, but granted Grosvenor permission to bear the same arms with a *bordure argent*. Both parties were displeased with this resolution, and the matter dragged on until finally a settlement was made, over a year later, and the Grosvenor arms were assigned as *azure a garb or*. The issue of ownership of arms was thus not trivial to fourteenth-century elite society, but was considered of such significance that the men of highest standing in the kingdom were prepared to testify in such cases. Moreover, the costs involved in taking a dispute to court were crippling. It is no coincidence, then, that after the conclusion of this case there was an immediate increase in the number and the jurisdiction of the officers of arms, with growing powers to monitor and grant arms.

By the 1380s, during the running of the *Scrope* v. *Grosvenor* hearing, Chaucer was a seasoned royal officer and bureaucrat; in 1389 he was appointed Clerk of the King's Works. The significance of his appointment in heraldic terms may seem opaque, but part of the work that Chaucer undertook in this role involved an expansive knowledge of heraldry and how it was communicated in chivalric contexts, including the organisation and staging of tournaments and the meetings and ceremonies of the chivalric orders. As Clerk of the King's Works, Chaucer was responsible for overseeing the erection of the royal scaffolds for the tournament at Smithfield in 1390 during which Richard II distributed badges of the White Hart (his personal device) in a strategy to promote his royal authority. Likewise, Chaucer's knowledge of the Order of the Garter (founded in 1348) must have been considerable and necessary to oversee the repair of the meeting place of the order, the Chapel of St George at Windsor, drenched in the heraldic devices of the royal house and the companions of the premier English chivalric order.

Yet despite Chaucer's visual world being heavily heraldic, the translation of this into his literary works was minimal, but nevertheless revealing. He was inherently informed by heraldic language and imagery, but there is little explicit engagement with chivalry in his writing. The *Knight's Tale*, the most obvious place in which Chaucer might deploy his knowledge to colour the story of Arcite and Palamon, and to an extent the *Squire's Tale*, are the clear exceptions to this, and it is possible that both were compiled to be read at Garter feasts on St George's Day. Chaucer's intimate understanding of chivalry and his heraldic sensibility are nevertheless evident, however passingly, subtly or intermittently, in many of his works. Nevertheless, Chaucer's works tend to reflect the 'older' roles of heralds and the outmoded fashions of knighthood, whereas his own experiences exposed him to the new range of roles that heralds undertook as diplomats, legal administrators and the guardians of the golden age of chivalry.

NOTES

1 Jean Froissart, *Froissart's Chronicles*, ed. and trans. John Jolliffe (London: Penguin, 2001), p. 165.

2 Roger H. Ellis, *Catalogue of Seals in the Public Record Office: Personal Seals*, 2 vols. (London: Public Record Office, 1978, 1981).

3 The National Archives, Kew, E 27/8.

4 See London, British Library, MS Cotton Nero A VIII, fols. 122r–129r; Add. MS 14857; RP 8318; MSS Arundel 487, 473. Bartolo di Sassoferrato, *De insigniis et armis tractatus*, in Evan J. Jones, ed., *Medieval Heraldry: Some Fourteenth-Century Heraldic Works* (Cardiff: William Lewis, 1943), pp. 221–52. For Upton see London, British Library, MS Cotton Nero C III, fols. 4–75; Nicholas Upton,

Nicolai Vptoni de studio militari, ed. Edward Bysshe (London: Typis Rogeri Norton, 1654), pp. 257–8; Nicholas Upton, *The Essential Portions of Nicholas Upton's 'De studio militari', before 1446, Translated by John Blount, Fellow of All Souls (c. 1500)*, ed. F. P. Barnard (Oxford: Clarendon Press, 1931).

5 See London, British Library, Add. MSS 37526, 34648, 29901, 61902.

6 The National Archives, Kew, C 47/6/2–3. See also Nicholas Harris Nicolas, ed., *The Controversy between Sir Richard Scrope and Sir Robert Grosvenor in the Court of Chivalry, AD MCCCLXXXV–MCCCXC*, 2 vols. (London: Samuel Bentley, 1832).

7 Nicolas, *The Controversy*, Vol. II, pp. 411–12.

PART V

Political and Social Contexts

CHAPTER 34

Dissent and Orthodoxy

John H. Arnold

In one sense, 'heresy' is very straightforward: 'an opinion chosen by human perception contrary to holy Scripture, publicly avowed and obstinately defended', as Robert Grosseteste defined it in the thirteenth century.[1] There was heresy in late medieval England, most famously and influentially that of the Oxford theologian John Wyclif (1328–84). In 1377, Pope Gregory XI issued a condemnation of Wyclif's teachings, principally regarding the Church, lordship and the ecclesiastical ownership of property, declaring them erroneous and heretical; Wyclif responded but did not recant.

So Wyclif was a heretic. But what this meant in practice was rather less straightforward. Whether his theology was 'contrary to holy Scripture' was precisely at the heart of the debate: the core of Wyclif's theology was to read the Bible for 'the literal sense', rather than allegorically or anagogically, and to hold that there was no other scriptural authority than the Bible (contrary to the wider sense of authority that the Catholic tradition had accumulated, from the works of the Patristic writers to the pronouncements of the popes themselves). So, heresy also involved acts of interpretation – both theological and textual. One could only be a heretic if one was also, paradoxically, a Christian; heresy is a divergence from what is held as Christian truth, rather than a different set of ideas altogether.

It also involved power. 'Heretic' is a label ascribed, not self-applied; and to make the label stick it was necessary to speak from a position of authority. The Pope did, of course, have authority, but not, perhaps, overwhelmingly so. Earlier in 1377, Simon Sudbury, the Bishop of London, had attempted to conduct an inquisition into Wyclif's beliefs, but Wyclif had protection from major political players (including John of Gaunt) and the trial collapsed. The papal condemnation in May 1377 called for Wyclif to be examined by the Archbishop of Canterbury and the Bishop of London, but in the event, the University of Oxford objected to any imposition of external authority, and he was initially simply kept to halls. The struggle continued in a complex fashion, but the point is simply this: heresy was a political matter as well as a spiritual one.

Finally, the ideas and activities labelled 'heresy' are not necessarily static or unitary. Following the attempted trials of 1377, various events occurred: Edward III died, Pope Gregory XI died, and the papacy split into schism (with different popes elected by rival bodies of cardinals). Wyclif's theology and political thought became more radical, with a more pronounced hostility to the papacy and mendicant orders, and a more fundamental questioning of religious tenets that did not have clear scriptural authority: most importantly, whether the Eucharist was Christ's material body, or something made in spiritual commemoration of Him. Moreover, Wyclif began to ensure that his ideas were ever more 'publicly avowed': whereas previously he had written mostly in Latin, and spoken primarily to a university audience, he began to write in English, and to produce or at least inspire a vernacular translation of the Bible. Quite what was Wyclif's own work, what was that of his immediate circle of followers, and what was inspired by their example but perhaps at one remove (Wycliff*ite* or even Wycliff*ish*) becomes harder to discern as we move towards the later years of the fourteenth century. What also took place was the Peasants' Revolt of 1381 – almost certainly not inspired by Wyclif's theology (despite some contemporary chronicle reports alleging that the radical preacher and rebel leader John Ball had declared himself a follower) but nonetheless rendering the political situation much more fraught, such that the prospect of the ordinary laity listening to radical preaching sent a shiver down the spine of orthodox bishops and royal officials alike.

This kind of 'heresy' – popular preaching, in the vernacular, beyond the sight of the bishops or the crown (and hence possibly, innately, seditious?) – was what began to worry secular and ecclesiastical authority more. In 1382, Archbishop Courtenay, writing to the Bishop of London against unauthorised preachers, emphasised that just as sacred Canon Law institutes that in each city and diocese there should be an inquisitor into heretical depravity, 'so should you [bishops] similarly be present in your dioceses, and therefore should similarly inquire and proceed against heresy'.[2] In 1397 there was a petition to Parliament that 'as in other realms subject to the Christian religion, when anyone is condemned by the church for the crime of heresy they are then delivered to secular judgement to be done to death'.[3] And by 1401, with the statute *Ex heretico comburendo*, English law formalised the death sentence for heresy; the first victim was a priest, William Sawtre, connected to Wycliffite circles.

Others, in the fifteenth century, would be prosecuted in greater numbers, as 'Lollards' – understood to mean lay followers of Wyclif's ideas – and some of them would be executed also.

But whilst the legislative framework hardened, as the fourteenth century drew to a close the line between 'heresy' and 'orthodoxy' was in various ways still hard to discern, because it was always in the process of being drawn and redrawn. Whilst an important element (perhaps particularly after 1377) of Wycliffite thought was condemnatory and negative – against the fictional 'poverty' of the mendicants, against the claims of papal power, against the ways in which the Church was embedded in civil dominium – there was as much to it that was enthusiastic, reformist and evangelical, and, as such, emotionally (if not theologically) in concert with other strands of vernacular religiosity. The problematic issue of the Eucharist is instructive in this regard. Wyclif could not see that the Bible gave authority to believe that the Host became, in its material substance, the body and blood of Christ, and he did not think that this should be taught to the laity. His reasoning was partly scriptural, but also pastoral: that the laity did not really hold this belief, as it was too unreasonable, and that they should therefore be taught something theologically stronger and (he felt) spiritually sturdier – that Christ was spiritually present, and that the Eucharist commemorated this fact. This 'heresy' thus did not reject the Eucharist, but rather attempted to refigure it, and thus strengthen it.

Chaucer was writing during these years, and was connected to some within the Wycliffite circle. But the haziness that heresy has within his work may tell us as much about the lack of clarity within the spiritual/political landscape of his day as it does anything about his own beliefs and predilections. We catch glimpse, in the *Canterbury Tales*, of the smell of a 'Lollere in the wynd' (II.1173), but whether this indicates a stereotype of Lollardy as an organised sect, or whether it speaks to a much looser meaning of 'Loller' (from the Dutch *Lollaert*) as something like 'spiritually overenthusiastic person', is extremely unclear. The mendicants come in for some degree of satire; but then, so do many other groups, and in any case criticism of mendicancy and its apparent failure to live up to its original tenets of voluntary poverty was not by any means limited to Wycliffism. At moments, we see elements of theology treated, it would appear, with cavalier disdain: the alleged indivisibility of a fart, and the ability of all those present to share equally in its sound and stink (as explored in somewhat sniggering detail in the *Summoner's Tale*), plays upon a very common exposition of the Eucharist, the universal experience of which is frequently likened in pastoral theology to the sound of a bell or the sight of a candle.[4]

One can try to use these threads to tie Chaucer to 'dissent', and nudge him into the same broad vicinity as 'heresy'; but it is effortful, and as an interpretation not only depends on reading a lot into a few moments, but also rests implicitly upon a set of presumed oppositions (enquiring vernacular literature/credulous Latinate orthodoxy, the 'English' Church/the 'continental' papacy) that arose in the later polemics of the Reformation.

More useful, then, is to take the fluidity of attitude towards aspects of religion in Chaucer as, whatever else it is, a sign of his times. For 'dissent' can encompass more than that which is solidly decried as heresy, and 'orthodoxy' can turn out to be more than one mode of religious thought and expression. To take the latter point first: whilst there were essential tenets to medieval Christianity, as expressed in the Creed and emphasised by regular episcopal pronouncements (and, they hoped, reinforced by regular parochial preaching), these allowed a considerable area for further exploration and expression. What the general laity were expected to do and believe was not, as a minimum, all that restrictive or demanding: to be baptised, to attend confession once a year, to know by heart the basic prayers (Pater Noster and Ave Maria) and the Creed, to shun work and attend church on Sundays and feast days, and not that much more.[5] But this then provided considerable room for individual or (more often) collective embellishment and elaboration. Many people joined religious guilds or confraternities: in part for the annual feast, no doubt; in part to provide provision for their eventual burial; but also to allow acts of collective piety and communal religious patronage, such as bestowing a stained-glass window on a church or undertaking locally tailored acts of charity. Guilds were a common vehicle of lay piety, but varied in their social composition, specific purposes and spheres of operation. There were many highly local guilds within parishes, raising small amounts of money to keep lights burning in front of an image of a particular saint; and at the same time major guilds in cities, increasingly synonymous with the ruling oligarchy, acting as a major financial player within the town's economy. The difference that financial resources made affected other activities also. Pilgrimage could include journeys that required substantial investments of time and money, as to Canterbury and the other major shrines in Rome and the Holy Lands, and at St James of Compostela. In the early fifteenth century, Margery Kempe, daughter of the Mayor of Bishop's Lynn (now King's Lynn), travelled to Rome, Jerusalem and Compostela; and later in her life, she again went on pilgrimage to shrines at Wilsnack and Aachen. But many people made much more local 'pilgrimages' to shrines closer to home, fashioning their own sense of spiritual journey from more meagre resources.

Pilgrimage, acts of charity and guild membership – these are pious *practices* above all else, even if informed by theological ideals. But late medieval England also saw a rich literature of religious instruction and reflection, with much that was unconnected to Wyclif or Lollardy nonetheless written in the vernacular. Books of Hours, for example, were common particularly among the more elite in society, and invited private use and reflection as well as providing a foundation for religious instruction and devotion for the household as a whole. There are numerous instructional texts, many focused on 'handling sin' (as Robert Mannyng's fourteenth-century manual on confession put it), most derived from two thirteenth-century vernacular texts, the *Manuel des pechiez* and *Somme le Roi*. Herein, lay readers (or auditors of those reading aloud) would find not only instruction on the varieties of sin and the necessity of confession and penance, but also reflections on virtue, 'sobriety' (meaning a spiritual balance of appetites) and encouragement to interior reflection. Some texts particularly invite or direct inward reflection, giving us simultaneously a sense that late medieval lay piety could be interior as well as exterior, and that it could be *encouraged* and *shaped* to be so. There is a host of late medieval vernacular religious poetry, some emphasising tenets of belief, but some exploring aspects of faith more imaginatively and emotionally. There are rare but precious examples of laypeople who collected and collated the religious writings that spoke to them, such as the commonplace book kept in the later fifteenth century by Robert Reynes, a Norfolk reeve. We are thus reminded that people engaged with and made choices within their orthodoxy. Whilst those dealing directly with the written word were in the minority, some element of audience-agency must also be admitted to the very much larger number who regularly attended Sunday sermons and went to hear mendicant preaching and the like.

At the same time, there were those who made different choices. Whilst many of those prosecuted in the fifteenth century as 'Lollards' were inspired (in the emotional as well as relational sense of the word) by the legacy of Wycliffism, a few caught up in the trial processes seem to have had a more individual and less enthusiastic faith. The difficulty of believing that the Eucharist was other than a material piece of bread was, for some, a recurrent issue; similarly, the idea that the bones of dead saints could bring any benefit to health or happiness was intermittently rejected. There could be, in other words, 'dissent' of a more sceptical kind, not built into an alternative theology but rooted in the material conditions of everyday life, and a rejection of at least some of the supernatural. There could be, also, dissent built upon disaffection, alternative priorities and a notable lack of affect, as among those who failed to attend church on Sunday with their neighbours, preferring to labour, play games or simply stay at home in bed.[6]

To return to Margery Kempe: her autobiography, or perhaps we might say attempted auto-hagiography, immerses the reader at certain points in mystical reflection on Christ's Passion, in a style of interiorised piety developed to the maximum extent. Margery, an allegedly illiterate laywoman (though clearly enmeshed in a fairly elite religious culture drawing upon continental as well as English traditions), had the imaginative, spiritual and perhaps social resources to fashion herself into the story of Christ. Her piety was active and public, a kind of performance at times (she annoyed other pilgrims with her very public wailing and crying), but also reflective, interiorised, bodily and deeply *felt*. At the same time, Margery's faith was extreme, and provoked comment and intermittent censure as such. She was several times challenged by bishops over her faith, and accused by laypeople of being a 'Lollard' – an accusation that again illustrates the blurred outlines of heresy and of orthodoxy.

NOTES

1 Quoted in Matthew Paris, *Chronica majora*, ed. Henry Richards Luard, Rolls Series, 57, 7 vols. (London: Longman, 1872–83), Vol. v, p. 401; translation from Malcolm Lambert, *Medieval Heresy: Popular Movements from the Gregorian Reform to the Reformation* (Oxford: Blackwell, 1992), p. 5.

2 David Wilkins, *Concilia Magnae Britanniae et Hiberniae* (London, 1737), Vol. III, p. 159.

3 *Ibid.*; H. G. Richardson and G. O. Sayles, 'Parliamentary Documents from Formularies', *Bulletin of the Institute of Historical Research*, 11 (1933–4), 147–62 (p. 154): 'en autres roiaumes subgitz a la religion critiene quant aucuns sont condempnez par leglise de crime de heresie ils sont tantost liuerez a seculer iuggement pour estre mys a mort e leur biens temporales confiskez' (London, British Library, Add. MS 24062, fol. 189v).

4 Fiona Somerset, 'Here, There, and Everywhere? Wycliffite Conceptions of the Eucharist and Chaucer's "Other" Lollard Joke', in Fiona Somerset, Jill C. Havens and Derrick G. Pittard, eds., *Lollards and Their Influence in Late Medieval England* (Woodbridge: Boydell Press, 2003), pp. 127–38.

5 Norman Tanner and Sethina Watson, 'The Least of the Laity: The Minimum Requirements for a Medieval Christian', *Journal of Medieval History*, 32 (2006), 395–423.

6 John H. Arnold, 'The Materiality of Unbelief in Late Medieval England', in Sophie Page, ed., *The Unorthodox Imagination in Late Medieval Britain* (Manchester: Manchester University Press, 2010), pp. 65–95.

CHAPTER 35

The Church, Religion and Culture

Rob Lutton

By contemporary standards Chaucer was not a religious writer, but the Christian faith and the laws and teachings of the Church, if not always the subjects, are never far beneath the surface of his works, providing their cultural and ethical underpinning. Chaucer's explicitly religious poems demonstrate an appreciation of late medieval devotion in their attention to the cult of the Virgin Mary and the increasingly emotionally charged focus of the period on Christ's suffering. If there is an overriding Christian message to these religious works, however, it is a moral one: that it is one's actions that count and that belief in God's grace, providence and ultimate judgement allow for the making of meaning from the suffering and chaos of life. The individual's duty, expressed in the lives of Chaucer's female saints, is to remain constant in faith, submit to God's will and transcend the fleeting pleasures of this world. They provide a striking contrast with the corruption and malpractice of the religious professionals of the *Canterbury Tales* who, with one exception, are the objects of Chaucer's sharpest satirical criticisms.

The exception, the Parson, is idealised in the *General Prologue*, with no hint of irony, as the exemplary poor parish priest. Chaucer clearly held to the ideal of the priestly vocation that this portrait enshrines and he also appears to have shared the Parson's privileging, in the prologue to his tale, of pilgrimage as a metaphor for the spiritual life (*CT*, x.48–51). The *Parson's Tale* itself sets out the correct way to follow. It is not actually a tale at all, but a lengthy treatise on penance and confession that draws on well-known Latin penitential handbooks. In detailing the Seven Deadly Sins and their remedies it provides the doctrinal basis for the Christian life.

There is little doubt that the *Parson's Tale* was intended as an entirely sincere statement. Chaucer reinforced its seriousness in the *Retractions* that immediately follow it, which revoke all but his spiritual writings and ask forgiveness for 'my translacions and enditynges of worldly vanitees' (x.1083–4), which it goes on to name. It thereby puts into action the penitential message that precedes it. Nevertheless, it remains a literary device that forms the logical conclusion to the *Parson's Tale* and that only has effect when read against those secular 'tales of Caunterbury, thilke that sownen into synne' (x.1089–90) that Chaucer apparently never suppressed. This seeming double-mindedness of the *Canterbury Tales*, which is often so puzzling to the modern reader, exemplifies the dualism of a medieval culture that juxtaposed the sacred and the profane without undermining faith, but Chaucer also had deeper concerns with the nature of the Christian faith itself. So, with the exception of the *Parson's Tale*, he does not entirely commit himself to the claims of the overtly religious tales, but stands back and casts a sceptical eye on the sort of religion – much of it sensationalist, fantastical and emotionally manipulative – that they represent, and invites his readers to do the same. Whilst this was informed by Chaucer's extensive learning, socially elevated position and cultural milieu, it was also a sincere, if sceptical, attempt to explore the meaning of faith.

A good example of Chaucer's scepticism is found in the epilogue of the *Man of Law's Tale* when the Shipman exclaims 'We leven alle in grete God' (II.1181). The Shipman's declaration is provoked by an excess of religious and moral seriousness on the part of the Parson, who reprimands the Host for swearing on 'Goddes bones' and 'dignitee' (II.1166–71). In response, the Host mischievously berates the Parson for preaching at them and calls him 'this Lollere' (II.1177). Scholars have debated the intended meaning of this word. It could be one or all of 'idler', 'heretic' and, specifically, 'Lollard'. Possibly deriving from a Middle Dutch word meaning 'mumbler', which appears to have been used as a general term for religious dissenters across northern Europe, in its Latin form, 'lollardi', this word is recorded for the first time in 1382, as a term of abuse for the late-fourteenth-century followers of the Oxford academic John Wyclif. It was in this year that Wyclif's teachings were first condemned as heresy by the English Church. Among other things, Lollards were known for their strict opposition to swearing, as well as for their preaching and teaching of the Bible in English. Whatever Chaucer's precise attitude was to Lollardy, at the time when he was writing, two rival popes claimed supreme authority over the western Church and Richard II's court contained Wycliffite sympathisers known as the 'Lollard knights', some of whom Chaucer knew personally. In this context, the Shipman's assertion that all believe in God has a distinctly hollow ring to it. His appeal to a comfortable, universally shared and uniform Christian faith rebuts the discomfort of religious zeal and controversy but prompts more questions than it answers. By casting doubt on the Shipman's glib assertion of collective belief Chaucer called on his readers to scrutinise the myriad professions and acts of faith that they witnessed on a daily basis and to ask 'what is it to be Christian?'.

How Christian was late medieval England? On the surface, it had all the appearances of a society thoroughly steeped in Christian culture, but as twenty-first-century observers we must ask, like Chaucer, how deep that culture went, how sincere English people were in their religious beliefs and actions, and to what extent they really meant what they said and did. It is helpful to distinguish between what people were obliged to do and believe, and what they assented to and did of their own volition. To take obligatory religion first, the Fourth Lateran Council of 1215 produced one of the most important statements of the western Church's expectations of lay observance. Most famously, Canon 21 of Lateran IV made it obligatory for all Christians to confess annually to their parish priest. Confession, together with the subsequent absolution effected by the priest and satisfactory acts performed by the penitent, was one of the seven sacraments of the Church. In the wake of Lateran IV numerous manuals were written for priests to school them in the art of confession. Chaucer's *Parson's Tale* is just one English example of the final stage in a long process of translation of these penitential manuals from Latin into vernacular languages, first Anglo-Norman and then English, and their dissemination to an expanding lay audience. This literature and the efforts of the clergy to communicate its message to the laity seem to have ensured that by the fourteenth century the majority of parishioners confessed annually prior to receiving the Eucharist at Easter. Confession also became a mechanism of doctrinal instruction, but the Church generally operated a light touch when it came to prescription of minimal levels of required religious knowledge. The Creed and the Lord's Prayer made up the bare minimum, and particularly active and pastorally minded bishops instructed their clergy to extend this basic knowledge. John Mirk's *Instructions for Parish Priests*, written only a decade or so after Chaucer's *Parson's Tale*, is typical of the extent of this ideal of more extensive doctrinal instruction: the priest should teach his parishioners the articles of the faith and the seven sacraments, and use the Ten Commandments, the Seven Deadly and Seven Venial Sins as a framework for confession.[1]

Generally, though, provided they remained within the bounds of orthodoxy, the religious knowledge and understanding of the lay Christian were not considered to be as important as humble obedience to the authority of the Church and participation in its rites. Increasingly, clerical concerns focused on whether confession involved genuine contrition, a sorrow for one's sin rather than just a fear of eternal punishment, which was essential for its absolution and satisfaction. In counselling confessors as to what penance to prescribe, Mirk advises:

> But first take hede, by god a-vys,
> Of what contrycyone þat he ys,
> Ȝef he be sory for hys synne,
> And fulle contrite as þou myȝt kenne;
> Wepeþ faste, and ys sory,
> And asketh ȝerne [earnestly] of mercy,
> A-bregge hys penaunce þen by myche.
> For god hym-self for-ȝeueth syche.[2]

This demand for emotional or affective engagement with the faith was indicative of the general direction of lay piety in the fourteenth and fifteenth centuries. It was accompanied by an increasing tendency for introspection through practices of self-examination and imaginary meditation, but it is treacherously difficult to make firm judgements as to how many people were willing or able to feel, reflect and contemplate in these ways. It is likely, for example, that for the vast majority of people, annual confession was no more than a perfunctory affair. There is, however, abundant evidence for voluntarism or 'lay initiative', and very large numbers of individuals acted in ways that exceeded the minimum requirements of the Church. An important aspect of this was the investment of considerable amounts of money, time and other resources in the building, rites and communal activities of the parish church; in charitable giving to the poor and sick in gifts to the clergy and religious orders of monks, nuns and friars; in devotion to saints; and in the practice of pilgrimage to shrines and holy sites, whether nearby or, for the sufficiently wealthy, as far afield as Jerusalem.

Religious voluntarism raises questions about motives, not least because all types of investment in religious life implicitly formed part of a belief-system built on the late medieval doctrine of purgatory. This held that all but the most exceptional individuals must make satisfaction for sins committed in life by enduring suffering in purgatory, before proceeding to heaven. However, good deeds and intercessory prayers and rites, especially the Mass, could shorten the time spent there. These could be carried out by individuals themselves or by others after their death. Belief in purgatory should not, however, cause us to dismiss such giving as lacking in true religious conviction or sincerity. Even if largely selfishly motivated, such acts arose out of deeply held aspirations and fears about one's prospects in the afterlife, and were often accompanied by more generous and outward-looking sentiments that valued community and charity as ends in themselves.

A good example of the mixed motives for religious action is the membership of pious fraternities or guilds, which proliferated from the late thirteenth century. The reasons for joining a guild included the benefits of a good burial and proper intercessory commemoration; the opportunity to attend Mass regularly and to express devotion to the patron saint of the guild; financial support for members who fell on hard times or for pilgrimage; the pleasures of eating and drinking together at the fraternity feast; opportunities for networking in the contexts of business, governance and politics; and the social esteem that accrued to members of prominent guilds, particularly in urban centres. However, not all guilds served all of these functions at once, and some were more religious than others in their benefits and focus. For example, the late-fourteenth-century St Mary's guild in Nottingham appears to have been founded with overwhelmingly religious aims in mind: in particular, devotion to the Virgin. This guild can be contrasted with the Holy Trinity guild situated in the same parish church in the same city. This fraternity grew out of the town's merchant guild, which had been granted by the crown in 1189, as such serving administrative, economic and judicial functions, and its membership essentially comprised the urban oligarchy. Although both of these fraternities were ostensibly religious in their aims, the reasons for joining each of them were distinct. The Trinity guild still had a religious dimension but was probably more about wealth, status and power than the fraternity of St Mary.[3] Piety was, therefore, a complex thing often identified with respectability rather than any intensity of spirituality.

Such intensity of belief and feeling that did exist was by no means limited to the better-off, but wealth and the advantages that came with it certainly helped individuals to make the most of opportunities to engage more fully with the spiritual life. Perhaps the single greatest factor in shaping degrees of involvement in an increasingly rich devotional culture was literacy. On the whole, education remained one of the most important advantages of wealth. Literate abilities varied enormously across a wide spectrum, ranging from full competence in reading, writing and speaking Latin to the recognition of a few words or letters in English, but there was a fundamental distinction drawn between those schooled in Latin – the 'lered', or learned – and those who only knew English – the 'lewd', or unlearned. Because of the ways in which education was organised in the Middle Ages literacy was strongly associated with the clergy and illiteracy with the laity. There was an enormous amount of snobbery about the possession or lack of literate competency.

This cultural gulf between the 'lered' and the 'lewd' endured well beyond the fifteenth century and gives the impression that there were two cultures in the Middle Ages: an 'elite' culture and a 'popular' culture. However, medieval society was actually much more complicated than the snobbery of contemporary commentators would have us believe. It involved daily interaction between the clergy and laity and considerable overlap in the religious beliefs and practices of different social groups, from the peasantry right up to the aristocracy. One example of this overlap is the Book of Hours, which enabled the literate layperson to partake in the Church's daily cycle of prayer. From the early fifteenth century, this began to be mass-produced; its contents were standardised and it became affordable for anyone with reasonable means, in other words the middling ranks of society beneath the level of the gentry. The commonality of religious experience across the social scale that this process of acculturation points to is further evidenced by the similarity of the prayers in Latin and English added to Books of Hours by owners at either end of the social spectrum.

This said, before the late sixteenth century the majority of the population probably had insufficient literate abilities to read the English prayers in Books of Hours, let alone their standardised Latin contents, and for those who could read, or could find someone to read to them, devotional literacy increasingly stretched far wider than the Book of Hours. The ongoing work of translation into English of religious literature, mainly by the clergy and monastic orders, opened up rich opportunities for spiritual advancement. This ranged from basic doctrinal treatises such as *The Lay Folks' Catechism*, through penitential texts such as Chaucer's *Parson's Tale*, to more contemplative and mystical works by writers such as the earlier-fourteenth-century hermit and mystic Richard Rolle. Writers, and the ecclesiastical establishment, actively responded to popular demand for devotional and contemplative literature. One of the most important examples is the Carthusian monk Nicholas Love who, in the first decade of the fifteenth century, wrote his *Mirror of the Blessed Life of Jesus Christ*, which offered meditations on the life and sufferings of Jesus based on sources harmonising the Gospels, with the endorsement of Thomas Arundel, Archbishop of Canterbury. The *Mirror* survives in sixty-four late medieval manuscripts, which can be compared to the eighty-two containing complete copies or parts of the *Canterbury Tales*, but the most widely copied religious work of the period was the Wycliffite English Bible, surviving in over 200 manuscripts. This was sought after by not just Lollards but those more orthodox believers who wanted to read the Scriptures in English.

A final example serves to illustrate how there remained a cultural gulf between the 'lered' and the 'lewd' despite interaction between the clergy and laity. It also draws attention to types of religious practice that may well have involved sincere faith but were more about doing and belonging than intellectual understanding. In the late fourteenth century, John Buckingham, Bishop of Lincoln, wrote to William of Banbury, Rector of the parish church of Nettleham, condemning 'a very foul abuse, hateful to God' that was carried out each Easter before the reception of the Eucharist by his parishioners. Buckingham claimed they had cause 'to be blessed solemnly by the priest, in church, swine's flesh commonly called Bacun … and many shelled hardboiled eggs', and that these were provided at Banbury's expense and were 'carried to every house in the parish as a sort of holy offering, to the great scandal and dishonour of the Church of Christ and its sacraments, to the danger of the souls of these idolaters and, by example, to the souls of others'.[4] In response to this charge, would these parishioners – would Banbury even – have shared the Shipman's sentiment that 'we leven alle in grete God', and to what extent would they have been right?

NOTES

1 *John Mirk's Instructions for Parish Priests*, ed. Gillis Kristensson (Lund: CWK Gleerup, 1974), pp. 92–103, 108–63.
2 *Ibid.*, p. 153 (lines 1511–18).
3 Richard Goddard, 'Medieval Business Networks: St Mary's Guild and the Borough Court in Later Medieval Nottingham', *Urban History*, 40 (2013), 3–27.
4 Cited in Dorothy M. Owen, 'Bacon and Eggs: Bishop Buckingham and Superstition in Lincolnshire', in G. J. Cuming and Derek Baker, eds., *Popular Belief and Practice* (Cambridge: Cambridge University Press, 1972), pp. 139–42 (pp. 141–2).

CHAPTER 36

England at Home and Abroad

Anne Curry

For almost the whole of Chaucer's life England was at war. In 1340, a few years before his birth, Edward III had declared himself King of France. The conflict between England and France continued for much of the remainder of the century and was complicated by the involvement of allies of both sides. The fourteenth-century phase of the Hundred Years War (a term developed in France in the early nineteenth century) was truly a pan-European war. We see a good example of this in 1385, when a French invasion of the south coast was coordinated with a Franco-Scottish invasion of northern England. The English response was to launch a counter-invasion of Scotland. By exploiting the feudal powers of the crown, a huge army of 13,744 soldiers was raised, the largest army of the period. With so many members of the English military classes present, it is not surprising that some found they had been using the same coats of arms without realising. In the following year, the Court of Chivalry dealt with the dispute between Sir Richard Scrope and Sir Robert Grosvenor over the use of the arms *azure avec une bende d'or*. Chaucer appeared as a witness for Scrope, telling the court that when fighting in France near Réthel, a campaign on which he had been captured, he had seen Sir Henry Scrope with those very arms.[1] Chaucer therefore had first-hand experience of English ambitions in France. The campaign about which he reminisced had been launched by Edward III in 1359 with a view to capturing Rheims and effecting his coronation as King of France.

Chaucer's death in 1400 occurred a few months after Henry IV had invaded Scotland with an army almost as large as that of 1385, and within weeks of the eruption of Owain Glyndwr's rebellion in Wales. Henry had been able to seize the English throne easily in 1399 because Richard II was absent on campaign in Ireland and had been forced to return quickly without his army, but for the first half of Henry's reign England was racked by major internal unrest. After 1410, the new Lancastrian dynasty was secure enough to resume open hostilities with the French, encouraged by civil war in France. Even if Chaucer himself did not live long enough to see it, his son Thomas served as a man-at-arms in the Welsh wars in 1403 and engaged to serve on Henry V's great invasion of France in 1415.[2]

At every turn, both for the kingdom of England as a whole and for its gentry classes as epitomised by the Chaucers, warfare and international relations were a major shaper of life. The central relationship with France had a long pedigree. Although the lands of the Norman and Angevin rulers of England had been lost in the early thirteenth century, there remained the territories in south-west France and, from 1279, thanks to the inheritance of Edward I's queen, the county of Ponthieu around the mouth of the Somme. In the Treaty of Paris of 1259 Henry III had given up his claims to Normandy, Maine and Anjou and agreed to pay homage to the French crown as Duke of Aquitaine. This gave the French kings the advantage: they could manipulate their feudal authority to declare the English duke-king a contumacious vassal and to confiscate his lands. This happened in 1294, 1324 and 1337. On the first two occasions, a short war followed but the status quo was restored. On the third occasion Edward III was able to play a new card against French aggression – a claim to the French throne itself. It had been decided at the death of Louis X in 1316 that a woman could not inherit the French crown. When Charles IV died in 1328 the crown passed exclusively through males to a cousin, the Count of Valois, who became Philip VI. However, the right of a woman to *transmit* the inheritance was still a grey area. Therefore, Edward III, as the nephew of Charles IV by his sister, was able to put forward a claim. The French did not take this seriously, and Philip was able to put pressure on Edward to pay homage for his French lands. In 1337 Philip confiscated these lands on the grounds that Edward was harbouring an enemy of the French state, Robert of Artois. By now, thanks to military successes in Scotland, Edward was strong enough to take advantage of his French royal claim. Most importantly, they facilitated an alliance with the townsmen of Ghent, Bruges and Ypres, then in rebellion against the Count: Flanders was itself a fief of the French crown but England's premier trading partner. This explains why it was in Ghent, on 26 January 1340, that Edward formally assumed the title King of France and quartered his arms to produce the well-known shield of fleur-de-lis and leopards used by rulers of England for most of the years between 1340 and 1603, when James VI of Scotland's accession to the English crown added the Scottish arms.

The importance of Scotland in the age of Chaucer must not be overlooked. England regularly faced an enemy on two fronts. Scotland's survival as an independent kingdom in the face of English aggression had much to owe to its alliance with the French, which Philip VI also exploited in the opening phases of the Hundred Years War. This was in response to Edward III's own efforts to increase his control in Scotland in the early 1330s by supporting a Balliol claimant against the Bruce King, David II. Indeed, Edward's first taste of success in battle was at Halidon Hill near Berwick-upon-Tweed in 1333: a handful of those giving testimony in the Scrope–Grosvenor case in 1386 had military experience dating back that far. In 1346 David II invaded England as revenge for the French defeat at Crécy. Although David was defeated and captured at Neville's Cross, Edward was persuaded to release him in 1357 for the sake of concentrating on France.

The late 1350s, the time of Chaucer's military baptism, were arguably Edward III's greatest hour. Successes in the 1340s in Brittany, at Crécy and in the capture of Calais had prepared the way, but exceptional pressure was put on the French by the capture of King John II at the Battle of Poitiers (1356). In negotiations, and by means of a final military invasion, Edward pushed for expanded French lands to be held in full sovereignty in return for his putting aside his royal claim. Such a settlement was reached in the Treaty of Brétigny in May 1360, which also encompassed the allies of each party, including the Scots. The territorial extent of Edward's gains was substantial, almost restoring the whole of the old duchy of Aquitaine, as well as Ponthieu and Calais. Edward had achieved the aim of his ancestors to end the demeaning act of homage to the French. The star of England and the English was in the ascendant: in the Parliament of 1363 the Commons thanked Edward for delivering them from subjection to other lands and lifting the costs of war that they had suffered in the past.[3] In Europe Edward sought to expand his influence through a series of planned marriages, including that of Chaucer's erstwhile master, Prince Lionel, to Violante of Milan in 1368. Peace with France had also enabled a renewed interest in Ireland, to which Lionel was dispatched as viceroy in 1361, Chaucer possibly being in his company.

The French reneged on the Treaty of Brétigny in 1369: by taking Edward by surprise, within a few years they had recovered almost all of the territory that he had gained. The English were reduced to what they had held at the opening of the Hundred Years War, plus Calais. Until 1399, different methods were tried by the English to restore their position: major *chevauchées* across French territory, which failed to entice the French to give battle; efforts to capture additional bridgeheads on the French coast; Hong Kong-style purchases of temporary bases at Cherbourg and Brest; alliances with third parties, including the Bretons, the Ghentois and the

Portuguese, against the French and their allies; and exploitation of other dynastic claims, such as that of John of Gaunt, by marriage, to the throne of Castile. This was the most international phase of the Hundred Years War, and also the phase in which England's maritime position was the most threatened, thanks to the French alliance with the Castilians. As a result, the war was brought to England itself through raids on the south coast. An extra international element was introduced through the papal schism from 1378: since the English and French supported different popes it was even possible to launch an invasion of Flanders in 1383 as a crusade.

By 1389 a stalemate had been reached. No permanent peace could be found because neither side would compromise on the sovereignty of the lands in France. But it was possible to come to a truce in 1396 that promised a cessation of hostilities for the next thirty years and that was cemented by the marriage of Richard II to Isabella, daughter of Charles VI of France. To understand why this did not come to fruition requires us to turn to domestic affairs. Richard II, whose reign had seen a recurrence of conflict between the crown and nobility, used the long truce to his advantage, since without war he had no need to curry the support of Parliament or the military classes. His actions, verging on the tyrannical, contributed to his removal from the throne in 1399. Henry IV's weakness, as a usurper, forced him to continue the truce, but by 1410 there was renewed interest in an invasion of France, encouraged by the madness of the French King Charles VI and the factional struggle between Armagnac and Burgundy for control of him. Both sides sought the support of the English. In 1412 Henry IV was seduced by promises of the restoration of Aquitaine into sending an army to assist the Armagnacs. Generally, his son preferred a Burgundian alliance, but his own invasion of France in 1415, which culminated in victory at Agincourt, was undertaken without any French assistance and saw a revival in both the success of and enthusiasm for English interests in France.

This, then, was a highly militarised period that saw major changes in English armies. The emphasis was on professionalism. By 1335 all troops serving the crown were paid: feudal service had come to an end. After 1369 there was no further use of shire levies outside England, although they were regularly called out to defend the coasts and to deal with Scottish incursions. When Edward campaigned in person he expected troops to be provided for as long as he needed them. When others were in command, the system of indenture was used, whereby leaders entered into contracts with the crown to provide specified numbers and types of troops for agreed lengths of time. From 1369 onwards, indentures were used for virtually all expeditions and garrison commands. In order to check that leaders had fulfilled their terms of contract, musters were taken of the troops they provided. These form an exceptional source for the study of army personnel, revealing lengthy careers across many different war theatres.[4]

There was ample opportunity for paid military service. The garrison of Calais housed hundreds of men, especially when under threat from the French, as in the immediate aftermath of the reopening of the French war in 1369. It was further protected by a ring of other garrisons in the Calais march – Oye, Guînes, Sangatte, Hammes and the Tour de Rysbank. From the late 1370s to the late 1390s the English also garrisoned Brest and Cherbourg, thanks to leases from the Duke of Brittany and the King of Navarre. Further troops were also required in the garrisons of the Scottish frontier, and in Ireland. Glyndwr's rebellion also increased the need for troops in Wales. In 1403 Thomas Chaucer was one of 580 soldiers under his cousin, John Beaufort, Earl of Somerset, then royal lieutenant in south Wales, detailed to the defence of Carmarthen and its region. Expeditionary armies were sent to northern France on many occasions, but there were also opportunities for service in campaigns to Castile, Portugal and the Low Countries, and an occasional reinforcing of the English position in Gascony, although locals also played a key role in defence of that area. Soldiers were needed too for service at sea. The phase of the Hundred Years War from 1369 saw high levels of naval action as the English tried to counterbalance Castilian naval support for the French.

When opportunities for royal service dried up after the Treaty of Brétigny, some English soldiers sought alternative employment elsewhere in Europe as routiers. The most famous is Sir John Hawkwood, whose service to Florence is commemorated by a memorial in the Duomo. When in 1393 Richard II was showing his intention to come to truce, the gentry of Cheshire rebelled because he was depriving them of their livelihood as soldiers. Military training enabled a man to rise socially and to enjoy the generous wages the crown offered: 1s. a day for a man-at-arms, equivalent to the income from a small manor, and 6d. a day for an archer – at least as much, if not more, than that of a skilled craftsman. Knights were paid 2s. a day, barons and knights banneret 4s., earls 6s. 8d., and dukes 13s. 4d. In addition, the crown shared war profits with its soldiers. Ransoms could also be valuable, although for Englishmen unfortunate enough to be captured, they could also be damaging.

From the 1330s onwards we see the rise of the mixed retinue, where captains were expected to provide men-at-arms as well as archers. Here it is significant that Chaucer presented his Knight not as an individual but as part of a group (*CT*, I.43, 79, 101). The first three of Chaucer's pilgrims in the *General Prologue* – the Knight, the Squire and the Yeoman – represent the archetypal military retinue of the late fourteenth century. Men-at-arms were commonly called 'esquires' (*armigeri*) and archers 'yeomen' (*valetti*) in the muster rolls. All were mounted, although in battle situations it was common to fight on foot: hence the popularity of the foot joust as a way of training. The contribution of each kind of soldier varied according to what the King and his commanders decided was militarily advantageous. Most of the long *chevauchées* in France from 1369 to 1389 had equal numbers of men-at-arms and archers, producing armies of between 3,000 and 5,000 men. When large armies were needed, which was always the case when the King campaigned in person, the proportion of archers was increased. In Edward III's French campaign of 1346 (an army of perhaps 14,000) there were five archers for every man-at-arms; for Henry IV's invasion of Scotland in 1400 (an army of 13,085 men), there were seven. In the Welsh wars of the early fifteenth century a ratio of three archers for every man-at-arms was established and remained the norm for English armies until the 1440s. Thomas Chaucer contracted to bring twelve men-at-arms (including himself) and thirty-six archers in 1415.

The high level of military activity also affected royal authority. It made the crown dependent upon the nobility and gentry for the provision of troops, and on Parliament for granting taxes to pay wages, or, in reality, to secure loans in order to fund war. Increasingly it was the merchant elite of London that lent money to the crown. But these elements also enhanced royal power by making war a national as well as a business endeavour. Soldiers came from all parts of England: armies were the largest gatherings of Englishmen united in the service of the crown, all obliged to wear the cross of St George and to abide by a common set of disciplinary ordinances from at least 1385.[5] Victuallers, ship-owners, craftsmen – all benefited from the needs of armies and campaigns.

Success in war, as under Edward III and Henry V, boosted royal authority, but failure had the opposite effect. In the reversals of the 1370s there was much criticism of mismanagement of funds voted for war, which led to the first use of impeachment of ministers in the Parliament of 1376. That Parliament is also notable for the first election of a Speaker of the Commons, Sir Peter de la Mare, an experienced soldier who represented a group hostile to the prospect of negotiations with the French. It is also in the records of Parliament that we see the various lobbies. Merchants, for instance, were keen to maintain good relations with Flanders because of trade links, and were critical of a government that could not guarantee security at sea from French attack. The importation of Gascon wine into England was of great significance here. An aggressive stance was also seen as beneficial: the rising of 1381 was in part triggered by failures in France that had encouraged French raids on England. With war percolating so many areas of life it is not surprising that it contributed to the growth of national identity. All kings had the Church arrange prayers and processions for their successes overseas. By the same token, England's overseas interests encouraged an international outlook. English soldiers found themselves serving alongside Genoese, Gascons, Germans, Spaniards and Portuguese. War generated diplomacy and intercultural contacts. English envoys were sent to a wide range of European courts, and foreign envoys came to England. Chaucer's visit to Italy in 1372–3 was to negotiate a commercial treaty between Genoa and the English crown, and he later went on royal business to Flanders, France and Milan. Just as Chaucer's Knight is made to traverse Europe for the sake of crusade, so did several hundred Englishmen, known to have served in the Mediterranean as well as in Prussia. Sir Ralph Basset was even at Gallipoli in 1366–8, serving with the Count of Savoy.[6] Such experiences created real internationalism.

NOTES

1 Nicholas Harris Nicolas, ed., *The Controversy between Sir Richard Scrope and Sir Robert Grosvenor in the Court of Chivalry, AD MCCCLXXXV–MCCCXC*, 2 vols. (London: Samuel Bentley, 1832), Vol. 1, pp. 178–9.

2 The National Archives, Kew, E 101/43/21, membrane 4d (1403); E 101/45/5, membrane 3.

3 *PROME*, Vol. v: *Edward III 1351–1377*, ed. Mark Ormrod, p. 160.

4 See *The Soldier in Later Medieval England*, www.medievalsoldier.org (last accessed 11 December 2018).

5 Anne Curry, 'Ordinances for English and Franco-Scottish Armies in 1385: An International Code?', *Journal of Medieval History*, 37 (2011), 269–94.

6 Timothy Guard, *Chivalry, Kingship and Crusade: The English Experience in the Fourteenth Century* (Woodbridge: Boydell Press, 2013), p. 218.

CHAPTER 37

Chaucer's Borders

Anthony Bale

The words we now use to indicate foreignness, to separate someone else's identity from our own, are not the same as those used in Chaucer's England. In the early 1380s, when the English translators of the Wycliffite Bible came to render the Latin noun *alienigena* (in Ecclesiasticus 45:16), they had limited choices in Middle English. We might now say *foreigner, outsider, gentile, stranger*, one of a different community. However, *foreyn* (foreigner) had connotations of travellers or non-members of a group, and the adjective *forein* was more often used, legalistically, to describe those outside a guild or parish. The older English *outlond* and the adjectival *outlondish* did not necessarily connote strangeness and wonder but rather a hostile foreign power or military enemy. The noun *enemi* signified a more individual, and malicious, kind of foreignness: an evil spirit, an adversary in a feud, a member of a foreign army. The usual noun (and the one used in this case in the later Douay-Rheims translation) would perhaps have been *straungere* – used in Middle English to connote a foreigner, a traveller or simply someone *else*, 'if he coome fro a fer lond'[1] – which points to the inherently shifting unfamiliarity of identifying belonging and non-belonging. 'Straunge' lands were those visited by travellers: the 'straunge strondes' sought by pilgrim palmers (*CT*, 1.13), the 'many a straunge strem' passed by the itinerant Wife of Bath (1.464).

The solution the Wycliffite Bible translators settled on when translating *alienigena* was to use the Latinate word *alyen* – the precursor of the Modern English *alien*. It was not quite a neologism – Richard Rolle and Robert Mannyng had used the word in the 1340s, and *alien* was a common word in Anglo-Norman to refer to any kind of stranger or foreigner. It was frequently used in its Latinate and Romance forms to indicate an 'alien' priory, that is an English priory that owed its allegiance to a mother-house abroad (the adverb *abroad*, incidentally, just meant something like 'over a wide area', 'far apart', or away from one's home, rather than overseas!). Whilst maps were sometimes used to prove or assert limits or borders, the borders of national territories were rarely firmly established: affiliation, language and religion were more important indices of belonging. For those writing in fourteenth-century English, such as the Wycliffites and Chaucer, the very definition of belonging and foreignness was rather different from ours. In general, 'foreignness' in the Middle Ages was measured in local, rather than national, terms, and borders – those symbols of modern colonialism and the nation-state – were almost always porous.

Whilst Chaucer rarely used words such as *foreyn*, *alyen* or *enemi*, the crossing of borders and the interrogation of identity are absolutely crucial to his poetics. The borderlands of identity – and, in particular, crossings of borders, movements between identity – can be a helpful way of thinking about, and taking apart, received ideas of nation. We are now well used to thinking about and identifying transgression, the going beyond a limit or border, in order to understand how power works in literary texts.[2] John Ganim has explored how some of 'the most affecting moments in Chaucer's works are meditations on borders':[3] Ganim takes as his examples Troilus looking from Troy for Criseyde's return from the Greeks; Dorigen, in the *Franklin's Tale*, staring at the seas, waiting for her husband to return home; and Alcyone, in the *Book of the Duchess*, dreaming of crossing the border between living and dead. As Ganim's examples show, these are not modern, regulated borders, with guards and passports: rather, thresholds and limits of identity one crosses in encountering another person. Indeed, 'border' and 'boundary' did not have the same, rather definite, meanings they now have: a *bordure* was any edge; a *bounde* could mean any limitation on a piece of land, or simply the outer area of a space. Can we even think in terms of medieval borders when this was a world without formal borders? And does crossing a border always equate to transgression, a change of identity, or an encounter with the Other?

The most striking examples of Chaucerian border-crossing have been discussed copiously in recent criticism.[4] Most egregiously, the Asian cityscape of the *Prioress's Tale*, with its flux of Jewish and Christian bodies, stages a world of transgressed borders, not least in the Jewish street 'free and open at eyther ende' through which 'men myghte ride or wende' (VII.494, 493) and in the little Christian boy's 'throte … kut unto [the] nekke boon' (VII.649); the *Prioress's Tale* is replete too with attempts to institute boundaries, such as the provost's binding of the Jews (VII.620) and the 'tombe of marbul stones cleere' in which 'enclosen they' the dead child's 'litel body sweete' (VII.681–2).[5] Noteworthy too is the marvellous, magical and exotic Tartar court of Cambyuskan at Sarai, and the magical gifts received there from 'the kyng of Arabe and of Inde' in the *Squire's Tale*

(V.110).[6] Similarly, the Syrian, Roman and Northumbrian worlds of exoticism and cruelty in the *Man of Law's Tale* stage a world in which borders are evoked in order to be crossed; the Syrian court is a place of travelling merchants whilst the heroine, Constance, 'saileth in the salte see' (II.444–5), 'thurghout the See of Grece unto the Strayte / Of Marrok' (II.464–5), passing from one empire – the eastern one of the 'Barbre nacioun' (II.281) to 'oure occian' (II.505) and the coast of Northumberland.[7] There the nearest thing to a formal border is the sea, the medium for the movement of identity.[8] It is noteworthy that here the invocation of the East and of the Mediterranean prompts the Man of Law to self-define 'oure occian' – 'our' ocean is differentiated from 'their' sea, and 'here' becomes 'here' because it is not 'there'. Or, in the terms of contemporary border theory, 'cultural borders are effects produced in the mental operation that pulls two groups of people together … (con)fusing them in order to contrast them'.[9]

Such instances may be seen as Chaucerian 'heterotopias', to use Michel Foucault's term for 'other spaces', those provisional and liminal 'in-between' places of difference – such as the cemetery, barracks or prison – in which hierarchy and hegemony are both disturbed and confirmed. Such a heterotopia – a utopia of difference – is not separate, but rather contingent; as Foucault writes, heterotopias 'always presuppose a system of opening and closing that both isolates them and makes them penetrable'.[10] The Prioress's Asia, the Squire's Tartary and the Man of Law's Syria are not oppositional, 'other' spaces to western, Latin Europe, but rather worlds in which location, placement and identity are negotiable and mutable.

Identity, in Chaucer's poetry, is usually flexible and often circumscribed by its reaction to a border or a hierarchy. In the first story told on the Canterbury pilgrimage, the *Knight's Tale*, the 'race' of Amazons disappears. The Knight's story shows how identity – an identity based at once on the prerogatives of gender, nationalism, royal power and violence – can suddenly cease to exist. The tale opens with the 'lord and governour' Theseus, 'swich a conquerour / That gretter was ther noon under the sonne' (I.860–2). The opening lines of the *Knight's Tale* seem at first to celebrate masculine 'wysdom' and 'chivalrie' (I.865), but these lines also describe imperialist subjection: 'He conquered al the regne of Femenye, / That whilom was ycleped of Scithia' (I.866). The narration of Theseus's ascendant identity is tied directly to the conquest and erasure of the land of women, of the 'gret bataille' (I.879) between the Athenians and the Amazons of Femenye. This is marked through the enforced border-crossing and physical movement of the Scythian Queen, Ypolita, and her younger sister Emily: Theseus 'broghte hire hoom with hym in his contree / With muchel glorie and greet solempnytee' (I.869–70). Such a pattern might also be discerned in *Troilus and Criseyde*, in which Criseyde passes between the Greek and Trojan worlds. Thus, the project of the *Knight's Tale* – a story of courtly love, desire and competition between men – is based on subjection, conquest and the elimination of a nation. Borders here are not so much crossed as erased. In the *Knight's Tale*, Chaucer makes this vanished, subjugated identity a very eloquent, if muted, presence in the tale: Emily never speaks. Indeed, identity as narrated by Chaucer's Knight is a violent thing indeed, and this violence is directly linked to travel. The Knight himself is defined in the *General Prologue* by his roving violence – 'at many a noble armee hadde he be' (I.60) from Prussia to Turkey – and, in the tale, the 'progress' of Palamon and Arcite is defined by battles, incarceration and eventually slaughter.

Identities can disappear, but the human traces remain: Emily, a beautiful exhibit, becomes a silent but desirable vestige of the Amazonian nation, the memory of *translatio imperii* (the transfer of rule from empire to empire). Likewise, in the *Prioress's Tale*, the Jews are not converted by the miracle of the little boy who sings after his murder, but rather are put to death. Yet the hard stones of the boy's tomb endure, implicitly a sign of the permanence of the Jews' violence against him and the retributive violence that erases the Jews from the city.

On most medieval world maps, England appears, if it appears at all, at the edge: a marginal archipelago, a modest afterthought.[11] On the celebrated Hereford *mappa mundi* (*c.* 1290), England and Scotland appear at the bottom-left corner of the map, whilst Jerusalem is at the centre and paradise at the top. England, far from Jerusalem, Constantinople and Rome, and almost as distant from paradise as could be, *was* the margin. At several points in his poetry, Chaucer uses formulae for describing the extent of the world: in *Troilus*, 'Bitwixen Orkades and Inde' (*Tr*, V.971); the Wife of Bath's world of wives 'from Denmarke to Ynde' (*CT*, III.824); the Shipman's travels 'from Hulle to Cartage' (*CT*, I.404). Such formulations place the British Isles and Western Europe at the periphery. Their phrases mirror the dominant format of the kind of travel narrative known to Chaucer, in which a traveller set out from the western side of the world either to Jerusalem or to the wonders of the East. Chaucer's poetry, with its dazzling internationalism, marks England out as a place from which to depart in order to appraise one's home: to cross a border in order to think about oneself.

Chaucer's inspiration – or sources – for such a journey from home through time and space may have included Dante's *Divine Comedy* (*c.*

1308–20), Boccaccio's pilgrimage narrative in his *Decameron* (1350–3) and Petrarch's *Itinerarium* (1358). We can be certain that Chaucer knew Dante's text, itself a journey (in part modelled on the Jerusalem pilgrimage) through meaningful allegorical spaces.[12] Boccaccio's pilgrimage satire (VI.10) describes the smooth-talking Frate Cipolla, who describes various foreign places that are foolish fantasies (including visits to non-existent places called 'Truffia' and 'Buffia', suggesting swindling (*truffa*, fraud) and silliness (*buffa*, comic).[13] Meanwhile Petrarch's *Itinerarium*, which Chaucer may have known, is an imagined journey to Jerusalem, but one that tells us a lot more about Italy.[14] In these texts, the idea of foreign travel and the generic form of the travel narrative involve a reappraisal of the narrator's self – and the narrator's home. Even the knight-narrator of Mandeville's *Book of Marvels and Travels* (*c.* 1356), a text that probably informs the exoticism of the *Squire's Tale*, starts from and returns to Hertfordshire, and repeatedly uses marvels and wonders as a way of critiquing the habits and failings of European Christians.

The *Canterbury Tales* presents a view of religion in the British Isles focused on England and that most English of saints, Thomas Becket (martyred 1170). Becket's shrine at Canterbury was not only the pre-eminent national shrine but had, by Chaucer's day, become famous throughout Europe. Chaucer is also distinctively English inasmuch as he wrote in the English language and translated from French, Italian and Latin into English – but it is easy to misunderstand this as a kind of nationalism. As Derek Pearsall writes, 'Chaucer's idea in using English was ... not to assert an independent national identity but to enable England to take its place among those more advanced nations of Europe.'[15] In writing in English, Chaucer was part of a movement of English culture from the periphery of Europe towards its centre. And yet the stimulus towards a coherent national group is at the very heart of the Canterbury pilgrims' enterprise, and the fragility of the status of English as a literary language can be seen as a mirror to the difficulties and hierarchies involved in forming an 'all-inclusive *compagnye*', as described by David Wallace.[16]

Moreover, within the national polity we can discern highly distinctive and somewhat separate local and regional identities and affiliations. The British Isles then contained two separate, if tensely interconnected, kingdoms – England and Scotland – as well as the principality of Wales (largely Welsh-speaking, locally ruled by local lords and princes) and Ireland (ruled by the English in the Pale of Settlement, around Dublin, but otherwise ruled by Gaelic lords). There was certainly a literary and historical concept of Britishness, as fostered through Geoffrey of Monmouth's history of Arthur and the ancient kings of pre-Norman Britain.[17] But, historically, in late-fourteenth-century Britain, we must think in terms of a regionalism that contained a variety of different cultures and identities. This is used to mock the provincial 'sclendre colerik' Reeve (*CT*, I.587), who is 'Of Northfolk … / Biside a toun men clepen Baldeswelle' (I.619–20);[18] *his* provincialism is put into relief by that of his characters, the Northumbrian students of his tale and their dialect speech.

However, we should bear in mind too Chaucer's own regionalism: he was writing in southern English, for a London and south-eastern audience, probably a London elite (on the Canterbury pilgrimage, the Pardoner, Prioress, Manciple, Cook and Host are all from around the London area). Chaucer never really mentions the Irish, Scots or Welsh in his poetry; any Chaucerian Britishness can at most be said to be cryptic. Scotland appears in the penumbra of the *Man of Law's Tale* as a hostile kingdom adjacent to Northumbria;[19] Wales appears in the same tale as the place to which 'fledde the Cristyanytee / Of olde Britons dwellynge in this ile' (II.544–5). But these are asides. The name 'Scot' appears twice, but, enigmatically, as a horse's name (both the Reeve's horse and one of the horses in the *Friar's Tale*)! Such a silence may well be telling: as Simon Meecham-Jones has suggested in terms of the absence of Wales from late medieval English literature, '[i]t would seem that English medieval textual culture is inextricably implicated in the development of a colonial culture through its enactment of a (probably semi-conscious) erasure of the problems raised by the existence of Wales and the presence of English troops there'.[20] Chaucer's very English pilgrims, moving slowly from Southwark towards Canterbury, energetically narrate an international world outside themselves, a storied world, with a cosmopolitan eclecticism that looks far beyond Britain.

Chaucer's Shipman – by definition a navigator or sailor and thus a traveller – is a kind of counterpart to the Knight in that both are very well travelled around Europe. The Shipman is defined in his portrait not only by his wayfaring but also by his placelessness: he lives 'fer by weste' – way out west – 'for aught I woot, he was of Dertemouthe' (I.389). The Shipman's expertise is in maritime motion: 'tydes … stremes … herberwe … moone [and] lodemenage' (I.401–3). Whilst the Knight's journeys have taken him to borderlands of religious conflict – Prussia and the Baltic, Spain, the Holy Land – the Shipman's geography is one of trade and commerce – 'from Gootlond to the cape of Fynystere, / And every cryke in Britaigne and in Spayne' (408–9), from the Baltic harbours of the Hansards to the vintners' entrepôts and pilgrimage ports of France and Spain, whence he has drawn 'ful many a draughte of wyn … / Fro Burdeux-ward' (I.395–6).

The Shipman, who 'knew alle the havenes' (I.407), is a figure of movement and circulation, defined not by place but by his itinerant maritime life; this is mirrored in his transgressive lack of 'nyce conscience' (I.398) and his immorality.

These themes of physical and moral movement and circulation continue in the *Shipman's Tale*, which deals with a merchant of Saint-Denis, near Paris; his beautiful wife; and a young monk, John. The tale hinges not only on the movement of its characters between the merchant's house in Saint-Denis, the markets at Bruges and the Lombard money-lenders of Paris, but also on the mobile international coinage of Flemish shields and French franks; the financial circulation of the wife's borrowing of money from John; and the circulation of the wife's body, sexually, between the two men (represented in the recurring pun of 'taille', as both a debt and the sexual organs).[21] This kind of circulation is extended into the tale's generic form, which is that of a hybrid *fabliau*: the *Shipman's Tale* has all the ingredients of a *fabliau*, but rather than ending in humiliation or disclosure, it ends with all the characters, or consumers, being happy. The Shipman's mercantile world revolves around the circulation of money and bodies. Moreover, the Shipman invokes a world in which transgression – spatial and moral – not only goes unpunished, but appears to be rewarded.

The fact that the *Shipman's Tale* was probably originally designed to be told by the Wife of Bath does not change this reading,[22] for she is also a serial traveller, a tradeswoman with an international outlook, a mixer of genres: 'she koude muche of wandrynge by the weye' (I.467). Both the Shipman and the Wife of Bath can be read as cosmopolitan characters, defined by what we might now call their 'border thinking': challenging structures and spaces, crossing given boundaries. Such thinking may now look to us like decolonialism, but, in the premodern era, such 'border thinking' may be a hallmark of looking outwards into the world, of the movement of English people into the world and the embryonic stirrings of colonialism.[23]

Contrary to the ways in which Chaucer was appropriated as 'national laureate' in the fifteenth and sixteenth centuries, Chaucerian Englishness and Chaucer's definition of nationhood are hard to locate, often finding their most eloquent expression through internationalism: for instance, an English Knight who travels through Europe and tells a story, translated out of Boccaccio's Italian, of love and death in ancient Greece; an English prioress who tells a story, translated out of transnational Latin preachers' tales, of a Christian boy killed by Jews in an Asian city; an English shipman who tells a mutant *fabliau* of travel, commerce and circulation moving between

Saint-Denis and Bruges. As John Ganim writes, 'what is interesting about Chaucer's sense of a nation is his openness to expressions of multiple, competing, and overlapping identities, of which national identity is by no means preeminent'.[24] It is fair to say that Chaucer is interested in interrogating forms of nationhood, rather than simply celebrating English nationalism – and we must concur with Derek Pearsall that the 'idealisation of Chaucer as the poet of Englishness has little or no basis in his poetry'.[25] If this disappoints, confuses or surprises the modern reader, that perhaps says more about our own ideas of nation and belonging than those of Chaucer.

NOTES

1 The Wycliffite Bible translation of 2 Paralipomenon 6:32, translating the Latin *externum*. For an extended discussion of Chaucer's use of the term *straunge* see Derek Pearsall, 'Chaucer and Englishness', in Kathryn L. Lynch, ed., *Chaucer's Cultural Geography* (London: Routledge, 2002), pp. 281–301 (pp. 282–3).

2 The classic study is Allon White and Peter Stallybrass, *The Poetics and Politics of Transgression* (London: Taylor and Francis, 1986).

3 John Ganim, 'Cosmopolitan Chaucer; or, The Uses of Local Culture', *Studies in the Age of Chaucer*, 31 (2009), 3–21 (p. 14).

4 For a useful conspectus, see Kathy Lavezzo, 'Complex Identities: Selves and Others', in Elaine Treharne and Greg Walker, eds., *The Oxford Handbook of Medieval Literature in English* (Oxford: Oxford University Press, 2010), pp. 434–56.

5 On the Prioress see Louise O. Fradenburg, 'Criticism, Anti-Semitism, and the *Prioress's Tale*', *Exemplaria*, 1 (1989), 69–115; Anthony Bale, *The Jew in the Medieval Book: English Antisemitisms 1350–1500* (Cambridge: Cambridge University Press, 2006), pp. 81–8.

6 See Susan Crane, 'For the Birds', *Studies in the Age of Chaucer*, 29 (2007), 23–41; Scott Lightsey, *Manmade Marvels in Medieval Culture and Literature* (Basingstoke: Palgrave, 2007); Louise O. Aranye Fradenburg, 'Simply Marvellous', *Studies in the Age of Chaucer*, 26 (2004), 1–27.

7 Susan Schibanoff, 'Worlds Apart: Orientalism, Antifeminism, and Heresy in Chaucer's "Man of Law's Tale"', *Exemplaria*, 8 (1996), 59–96; Geraldine Heng, *Empire of Magic* (New York: Columbia University Press, 2003); Shayne Aaron Legassie, 'Among Other Possible Things: The Cosmopolitanisms of Chaucer's "Man of Law's Tale"', in John M. Ganim and Shayne Aaron Legassie, eds., *Cosmopolitanism and the Middle Ages* (Basingstoke: Palgrave, 2013), pp. 181–205.

8 See Sebastian Sobecki, ed., *The Sea and Englishness in the Middle Ages: Maritime Narratives, Identity and Culture* (Woodbridge: Boydell and Brewer, 2011).

9 David E. Johnson and Scott Michaelsen, 'Border Secrets: An Introduction', in *Border Theory: The Limits of Cultural Politics* (Minneapolis: University of Minnesota Press, 1997), pp. 1–39 (p. 10).

10 Michel Foucault, *Of Other Spaces: Heterotopias*, www.foucault.info/doc/documents/heterotopia/foucault.heterotopia.en/ (last accessed 11 December 2018).
11 See Kathy Lavezzo, *Angels on the Edge of the World: Geography, Literature, and English Community 1000–1534* (Ithaca, NY: Cornell University Press, 2006).
12 See John G. Demaray, 'Pilgrim Text Models for Dante's *Purgatorio*', *Studies in Philology*, 66 (1969), 1–24.
13 Giovanni Boccaccio, *The Decameron*, ed. Jonathan Usher, trans. Guido Waldman (Oxford: Oxford University Press, 1993), pp. 403–11.
14 *Petrarch's Guide to the Holy Land*, ed. and trans. Theodore J. Cachey (Notre Dame: University of Notre Dame Press, 2002), esp. pp. 1–2, on the 'interaction between mental and material travel'.
15 Pearsall, 'Chaucer and Englishness', pp. 290–1.
16 David Wallace, *Chaucerian Polity: Absolutist Lineages and Associational Forms in England and Italy* (Stanford: Stanford University Press, 1997), pp. 66, 79.
17 Alan MacColl, 'The Meaning of "Britain" in Medieval and Early Modern England', *Journal of British Studies*, 45 (2006), 248–69.
18 Thomas Jay Garbáty, 'Satire and Regionalism: The Reeve and His Tale', *Chaucer Review*, 8 (1973), 1–8.
19 R. James Goldstein, '"To Scotlond-ward his foomen for to seke": Chaucer, the Scots, and the "Man of Law's Tale"', *Chaucer Review*, 33 (1998), 31–42.
20 Simon Meecham-Jones, '"Englyssh Gaufride" and British Chaucer? Chaucerian Allusions to the Condition of Wales in the *House of Fame*', *Chaucer Review*, 44 (2009), 1–24.
21 Gerhard Joseph, 'Chaucer's Coinage: Foreign Exchange and the Puns of the "Shipman's Tale"', *Chaucer Review*, 17 (1983), 341–57.
22 See Helen Cooper, *The Canterbury Tales* (Oxford: Oxford University Press, 1991), p. 278.
23 On 'border thinking', see Walter Mignolo, 'The Many Faces of Cosmo-polis: Border Thinking and Critical Cosmopolitanism', *Public Culture*, 12 (2000), 721–48.
24 Ganim, 'Cosmopolitan Chaucer', p. 12.
25 Pearsall, 'Chaucer and Englishness', p. 288.

CHAPTER 38

Rank and Social Orders

Chris Given-Wilson

The England into which Chaucer was born around 1342 was a land of some 6 million people; the England in which he died in 1400 contained less than half this number, probably about 2.5 million. What made the difference was of course the Black Death, the great plague that swept across Europe between 1347 and 1353, wiping out around half of its population. At least five further plagues between 1361 and 1390 stalled demographic recovery, and it was not until around 1500 that the population began to rise, and not until the eighteenth century that it once again attained its early fourteenth-century level.

Depopulation on such a massive scale rebalanced the market forces of society: a surplus of labour, leading to low wages and under-employment, gave way to a shortage of labour, with wages rising and a growing compulsion-to-work ethic; greater availability of land meant that peasant holdings grew in size while rents declined; grain and other staple prices fell with demand, pushing up standards of living for the majority of the population. The later-fourteenth and fifteenth centuries, sometimes described as the golden age of the peasantry, thus saw a narrowing of the wealth-gap between rich and poor, the virtual disappearance of serfdom from England, social unrest driven by rising expectations, and the decline of feudal structures.

In short, late-fourteenth-century England was a land of opportunity and ambition. Enterprising peasants took advantage of land-abundance to accumulate holdings that in time would lead to the formation of the 'yeoman' class, a peasant aristocracy that aspired to gentility. One such family was the Pastons, the survival of whose voluminous correspondence has made them one of the best-known families in fifteenth-century England. Clement Paston (d. 1419), possibly a serf and certainly a peasant, bought up neighbouring properties to construct a substantial estate in Norfolk, and sent his son William to study law. William became a sergeant-at-law, married an heiress and eventually rose to be a royal justice; by the time his grandson John (d. 1479) was knighted, the Pastons were fully fledged members of the East Anglian gentry.

Net immigration to towns, high industrial wages resulting from a shortage of skilled labour, and the rapid rise of the cloth industry for both domestic and foreign markets created similar opportunities for urban dwellers. Although no more than 20 per cent of England's population lived in towns by 1400, the relative contribution of the urban economy outstripped this figure by far, and nowhere more markedly than in Chaucer's London, which during his lifetime definitively established its position as the economic and political hub of the realm. The King cast a covetous eye on the wealth of great merchants such as Richard (i.e. Dick) Whittington, Mayor of London three times between 1397 and 1420, and in return for loans and other favours would grant them socially advantageous privileges or even occasionally knighthood. It was in London too that the Inns of Court were located – the career of William Paston serving as a reminder of how important the legal profession had become as a route to economic and social self-betterment. Meanwhile, the Hundred Years War (1337–1453) spawned the rise of a professional mercenary class whose deeds, riches and accumulated honours sometimes eclipsed those of their social superiors – men such as the *condottiere* Sir John Hawkwood, the younger son of an Essex tanner, whose reputation at his death in 1394 was said to match that of the greatest men on earth.[1]

Traditional assumptions about hierarchy thus came under strain, and social stratification became a more scrupulous and delicate exercise, especially at the upper end of the scale, where fine distinctions mattered. Before 1337, the only heritable title in England apart from the King's was that of earl, the preserve of an exclusive group of between ten and twenty men at any one time; by 1450, England had dukes, marquises, earls and viscounts, in that order. This period also witnessed the development of a parliamentary peerage consisting of some fifty magnate families who claimed (by now as a hereditary right) privileges, offices, and possession of the sort of authority that drew a line between them and the knightly or gentry class. This was not an impermeable line: among the families to cross it were the Chaucers, rising in two generations from esquire (Geoffrey) to duchess (his granddaughter Alice, Duchess of Suffolk). Yet it was not a line that was crossed unobtrusively, and it usually necessitated an explicit royal act of promotion to do so.

This vogue for more precise stratification crept down the social scale, although its effects on the remainder of the landholding class were less clear-cut. The number of knights in England declined from around 5,000 or 6,000 in the twelfth century to little more than 1,000 by the early fifteenth, with a roughly equivalent number of the greater esquires making up what has been termed the 'county gentry'; these were the men who exercised the major political and administrative offices in the localities, such as Sheriff, Justice of the Peace and knight of the shire, and whose landed holdings, opulent households and personal service to the King or some other great lord differentiated them from their inferiors. Beneath them came the 'parish gentry', a group numbering perhaps 7,000 or 8,000, some of whom described themselves as esquires but most of whom, by the fifteenth century, had begun to call themselves gentlemen. The parish gentry tended to discharge the lesser shire offices (coroner, escheator, tax-collector) to be less wealthy and to have narrower horizons; what they aspired to was not nobility so much as its watered-down relation, gentility. There was plenty of movement between these groups, however, for the demarcation lines among knights, esquires and gentlemen were never inscribed in bold.

The term 'gentleman' only gained popularity as a social designation in the late fourteenth century, but by the second decade of the fifteenth century was in common use. One reason for this was that those who claimed gentility wished to differentiate themselves from those whom they regarded as undeserving (or at least less deserving) of it. Among the latter were the yeomen and franklins. Neither term was applied very precisely at this time, but essentially they referred to minor landholders, free but not noble-born (as a gentleman might be), whom some might think of as wealthy peasants but others (themselves doubtless included) as the lower rungs of the landholding class. They were the men like Clement Paston who had taken advantage of the opportunities presented by post-Black Death England, men whose hard-earned wealth belied their undistinguished origins and who, in the opinion of their betters, should not be allowed to forget that fact.

Uncertainty about the status of yeomen and franklins is reflected in the *General Prologue* to the *Canterbury Tales.* The portrait of the Yeoman – an archer, forester and servant to the Squire – reflects common usage of the term through the thirteenth and fourteenth centuries, as found for example in the Robin Hood ballads, but by the 1380s and 1390s 'yeoman' was acquiring another, wider, meaning, roughly equivalent to that of *kulak*, or peasant proprietor, in-early twentieth-century Russia. Chaucer's Yeoman thus seems a little outdated. His Franklin, on the other hand, is by contemporary standards simply misleading: that a franklin – a free-born, but definitely lesser landholder compared to a knight or esquire – might serve as sheriff or 'ful ofte tyme' represent his county in Parliament was unheard of. Chaucer's emphasis on his Franklin's well-stocked wine cellar and high office-bearing is thus symbolic of his aspirations rather than indicative of his actual standing or lifestyle. Whether Chaucer was attempting to present accurate and up-to-date social 'types' is of course another matter.[2]

If yeomen and franklins were trying to lever open the door to gentility, some merchants, lawyers and professional soldiers had already forced entry and, indeed, passed onwards and upwards. William de la Pole, the merchant of Hull who made a fortune syndicating loans to Edward III in the early stages of the Hundred Years War, was knighted for his services and lived just long enough to see his son Michael summoned to Parliament as a peer; twenty years later Michael was elevated to the earldom of Suffolk, but such nimble-footed promotion caused resentment (he was, remarked one snobbish contemporary, 'more suited to the world of commerce than to knighthood'), and in 1388 he was appealed of treason and fled abroad, although his family was later restored. Indeed, it was his grandson William, Duke of Suffolk, who married Alice Chaucer and thus made a duchess of her.[3] More fortunate than Earl Michael were the lawyers Geoffrey Lescrope (d. 1340) and his brother Henry (d.1336), each of whom served as Chief Justice under Edward III and founded a dynasty of parliamentary peers; in 1397, Henry's grandson William became Earl of Wiltshire, if only briefly. Among English soldiers, the most remarkable career apart from Hawkwood's (which was spent mainly in Italy) was that of Sir Robert Knolles, the son of a burgess or yeoman from Cheshire, whose formidable reputation as a war-captain led to his appointment in 1370 as the first man below the rank of earl to command a major royal expedition abroad. Weathering the inevitable jealousy, he went on in his later years to devote much of his vast wealth to charitable and religious foundations – the very paradigm of *noblesse oblige*.

Exceptional as such cases were, they are symptomatic of the social fluidity of late-fourteenth-century England and the fears to which it gave rise. The forces of reaction duly reacted. Just as Parliament (an unashamedly upper-class body) passed statute after statute trying to regulate the wages, geographical mobility and contractual obligations of labourers to the benefit of landlords, so too did it pass legislation aimed at curbing social mobility. The most famous such act was the sumptuary ordinance of 1363. Responding to a petition from the commons complaining that 'various people of various conditions wear various apparel not appropriate to their estate', Parliament drew up a schedule specifying the sort of clothes and personal adornments that different social and economic groups were allowed to wear. At the bottom of the list came agricultural workers, grooms and servants (who were also enjoined to eat only basic foodstuffs); then craftsmen and 'people called yeomen' (the form of words is revealing); then lesser merchants, burgesses and poorer esquires; then wealthy merchants and esquires; then knights and rich clerks. Above the level of knights, no restrictions were imposed. Although unsuccessful as legislation (the ordinance was abolished in the next Parliament), it is a notable attempt to produce a hierarchy that integrated landholders and townsmen, with the economic bar naturally set much higher for the latter to compensate for their social deficit.

Sixteen years later Parliament drew up a schedule for contributions to the graduated poll-tax that it had just granted. Lawyers were now included too, and royal justices, strikingly, were ranked above earls and below only dukes in their ability to pay, while 'sergeants and great apprentices of the law' were ranked with peers and wealthy knights, and 'other apprentices [of law]' with the wealthier esquires. The Mayor of London was reckoned to be able to pay as much as an earl, and an alderman as much as a peer. Middling (*suffisantz*) merchants were expected to pay twice as much as 'esquires of lesser estate'. There is an inevitable artificiality about these attempts to tabulate social relationships, but the presumption of professional and mercantile wealth is unmistakable. So too are the social assumptions that surface repeatedly in the legislation of the period. In 1390, for example, artisans, labourers and other persons holding less than 40s.' worth of land a year were prohibited by statute from keeping hunting dogs or any device that might be used in 'the sport of gentlemen'. Chaucer's well-to-do Monk, who 'loved venerye [hunting]' (*CT*, 1.166), would doubtless have approved.[4]

Chaucer's declared aim in the *General Prologue* to the *Canterbury Tales* was to describe the 'condicioun' and 'degree' of each of his thirty pilgrims, 'and eek in what array that they were inne' (1.38–41). That he tends to dwell on their 'array' is indicative of the transparency and topicality of personal attire as a marker of status (particularly, for example, in the case of the five artisans, the Haberdasher, Weaver, Dyer, Carpenter and Tapicer, who were arrayed well above their station). There are of course many other ways – table manners, quality of horses, physiognomy – in which he subtly or not so subtly delineates the 'sondry folk' (1.25) whom he chose to depict as accompanying him to Canterbury. His portrait gallery of pilgrims is in effect a topped-and-tailed cross-section of a society in transition: topped-and-tailed because it includes no great magnate or prelate (too exalted to ride in such company) nor any serf or explicitly landless labourer (too poor or soil-bound to go on such a journey), but a cross-section nevertheless because it includes representatives from the three orders (nobles, clerics and labourers); from town and country; from rich and poor; from education, the law and medicine; from both regular and secular clergy; and from both sexes – although women, it must be said, feature sparingly, and only well-to-do women feature at all. Yet as a celebration of the rapidly evolving diversity of late-fourteenth-century English society, it resonates admirably with its age: the stately, fork-bearded Merchant who 'sat high on his horse' (1.270–1); the 'wise and wary' Sergeant-at-Law who knew all his statutes by heart (1.309, 327); the Doctor of Physic who carefully hoarded the gold gleaned from plague victims (1.442–4); the *parvenu* Franklin hoping to impress his neighbours by keeping open house (1.353–4) – all these must have been stereotypes instantly recognisable to Chaucer's audience.

Although Chaucer's satire is gentle and subtle, most of his pilgrims are, to a greater or lesser degree, portrayed as suffering from the faults typical of their rank or profession. Three, however – one from the top of the social scale, two from the bottom – are idealised: the Knight (the personification of chivalric virtue), the Ploughman (a God-fearing and honest labourer) and the Parson (the very model of a parish priest). Clearly Chaucer was trying to relate his picture of late-fourteenth-century England's social diversity to the traditional 'Three Estates' (or 'Three Orders') division of society: those who fought (the nobility), those who prayed (the clergy) and those who worked (the rest). That is one reason why, for example, he places the three estates in their traditional order. At the heart of this enduring but ossified model lay the notion that each estate had complementary functions to perform, and what Chaucer shows us in his three idealised portraits is how those functions ought to be performed, measures of perfection compared to which most (including their companions) inevitably fell short.

Yet what Chaucer also understood was that the traditional model was increasingly unsatisfactory as a way of classifying contemporary society. The use of literary evidence to corroborate or question historical reality (inasmuch as the latter can be determined) is naturally fraught with problems, but what the *General Prologue* does show is that the new diversity of English society led to the questioning of old certainties, and a good deal of jostling for elbow-room. More titles, more professions, more grades, lists and demarcation lines might give the appearance of a more rigid hierarchy, but in reality this society, in which it increasingly mattered where people stood in relation to each other, was a society with more, not less, social mobility.

The more opportunities there were for people to rise, the more necessary it became to find ways of trying to keep them in their place.

NOTES

1 I am grateful to Michael Alexander for his comments on an earlier draft of this paper. Thomas Walsingham, *The St Albans Chronicle: The 'Chronica maiora' of Thomas of Walsingham*, ed. John Taylor, Wendy R. Childs and Leslie Watkiss, 2 vols. (Oxford: Clarendon Press, 2003, 2011), Vol. I: *1376–1394*, pp. 4–5.

2 Nigel Saul, 'The Social Status of Chaucer's Franklin: A Reconsideration', *Medium Ævum*, 52 (1983), 10–26.

3 Walsingham, *St Albans Chronicle*, Vol. I, p. 782.

4 *PROME*, Vol. V: *Edward III 1351–1377*, ed. Mark Ormrod, pp. 166–8; Vol. VI: *Richard II 1377–1384*, ed. Geoffrey Martin and Chris Given-Wilson, pp. 115–16; Vol. VII: *Richard II 1385–97*, ed. Chris Given-Wilson, p. 166.

CHAPTER 39

Chivalry

Craig Taylor

For Chaucer, the word *chivalry* held a very different meaning than it does for modern readers of the *Canterbury Tales*. In Middle English, *chivalrie* was a collective noun referring to mounted and fully armed knights and squires, equipped for battle.[1] Less commonly, English writers used the word to refer to the bravery and prowess of such warriors. In the *General Prologue*, for example, Chaucer described the Knight as:

> ... a worthy man,
> That fro the tyme that he first bigan
> To riden out, he loved chivalrie,
> Trouthe and honour, fredom and curteisie.
> (*CT*, 1.43–6)

This limited medieval usage of the term *chivalry* focused upon the military and social identity of the aristocracy, an elite with whom Chaucer was very familiar despite his humble origins as the son of a vintner. The poet was even summoned to testify before the Court of Chivalry in 1386 in a dispute between Sir Robert Grosvenor and Sir Richard Scrope over the right to bear a particular set of heraldic arms. Chaucer carefully set out his credentials as a witness, highlighting his own status as an esquire of the King's chamber and citing his military service in Artois and Picardy in 1359.[2]

Since the Middle Ages, the term *chivalry* has come to refer more broadly to the military and courtly culture of the aristocracy of Western Europe during the high and late Middle Ages. Most famous and defining of this period, at least for modern audiences, were the romances that first emerged towards the end of the twelfth century, and that married traditional heroic themes with ideas of love and courtesy inspired by classical learning and theology. Yet there were other important changes and developments in courtly activities, such as tournaments and knightly orders, and the rise of heraldry. Chaucer was intimately familiar with both the remarkable tradition of chivalric romances and court culture in general. As Clerk of the King's Works for Richard II, for example, he was responsible for the oversight of various parks and hunting lodges, as well as the mews for the royal falcons at Charing Cross, and he played a key role in the preparations for the great feasts and international jousts held at Smithfield in October 1390. The most prominent English participants in this grand event were the knights of the famous chivalric Order of the Garter, led through the City of London to Smithfield by ladies of the Garter, pulling each knight by a golden chain. It is possible that the experience of this remarkable event helped to shape Chaucer's description of the great joust that marked the spectacular climax of the *Knight's Tale*.[3]

For most modern readers of the *Canterbury Tales*, the term *chivalry* is associated above all with the moral and social codes underpinning this aristocratic society and culture. Influenced by the romantic notions of writers such as Sir Walter Scott, modern audiences often imagine that medieval knights lived by a chivalric code characterised by selfless bravery, honour and courtesy. This is a nostalgic and warm fantasy of a world of noble warriors who treated war as a courteous game and constantly sought to impress and to romance ladies with their elevated and courtly manners. As an ideal of elegant and civilised masculinity, such a notion of chivalry continues to exercise a great power over the modern imagination. Yet, there were very few medieval knights or squires who actually lived up to such lofty ideals. During the lifetime of Chaucer, for example, English armies ravaged the French countryside, deliberately targeting non-combatants. During the 1346 Crécy campaign, Edward III led his army across Normandy in a trail of destruction that stretched up to 15 or even 20 miles across. Such raids, or *chevauchées*, were extremely popular amongst soldiers and largely self-financing, drawing supplies and plunder from the local populations. They also served a military purpose in weakening the enemy's resources, destroying crops, livestock and even the peasants who worked the land. In addition they intimidated the enemy, undermining the authority of the King and aristocracy, who were failing in their duty to protect their people. Indeed, their ultimate goal was to draw out the enemy's military forces, in order to bring them into a decisive encounter on the battlefield, as happened at Crécy (1346) and Poitiers (1356).[4] Such ruthless behaviour betrays the lie of the notion that medieval knights were more ethical and civilised than warriors in other periods of history.

The most obvious response to the brutal reality of such aristocratic behaviour would be to denounce both chivalric culture in its broad sense, and the chivalric code in particular, as hypocrisy by the ruling elites: either an escape from reality or, worse, an effort to justify their power and status both to themselves and to the rest of medieval society. Yet it is essential to recognise that our modern vision of chivalry was very much a product of postmedieval commentators who preferred to highlight the new themes of love and courtesy in the chivalric romances that emerged from the twelfth century, while ignoring the central importance of prowess, courage and competition for honour both in literature and in the wider aristocratic culture. As Richard W. Kaeuper in particular has carefully demonstrated, medieval romances and other chivalric texts were imbued with a level of violence and brutality that makes uneasy reading alongside the more romantic and civilised themes.[5]

In truth, throughout the age of chivalry, writers offered complex and shifting visions of the code of chivalry. Most agreed that knights should display a range of virtues and qualities such as prowess, loyalty, honour, generosity (*largesse*), courtesy, magnanimity, mercy and prudence. Yet while each of these values may seem to be unproblematic at first glance, their precise meaning was subject to constant debate and analysis by medieval authors. For example, while accepting that prowess was essential to knighthood, chivalric writers offered very different views about the circumstances in which knights could resort to violence: was it better to perform deeds of arms in tournaments, in the defence of the realm or on crusade? Was it either shameful or unlawful to take up arms in more mundane matters, such as defending one's honour? Moreover, the precise list of qualities required of the ideal knight varied from one writer to another, with shifting emphasis placed upon martial qualities such as prowess, loyalty and courage, and the moderating influence of other virtues and values such as mercy, *mesure* (moderation), magnanimity, prudence and discipline.

Indeed, there were profound tensions inherent in these models. How could the masculine model of warrior aggression sit alongside the more restrained, civilised and even effeminate notion of the courtier? How could a knight demonstrate the humility and piety expected of a true Christian given the vainglorious importance of honour and reputation in chivalric culture? Was the ideal knight an energetic, enthusiastic but sometimes rash young man, or the wise and experienced older man who could lead others but no longer win personal honour through the performance of great deeds of arms? In short, normative models of masculinity like the knightly ethos may appear to offer solid and stable images of manhood, but it would be extraordinary to imagine a static and simple model of masculine behaviour that remained unchallenged for hundreds of years, immune to changing social contexts. From the twelfth to the fifteenth century, the practical function of knights in military, political and social terms was subject to important changes and pressures, and the precise identity of the aristocratic class itself was in constant flux, as old families died out and new men rose to replace them. Given such circumstances, it was inevitable that the ideal of knighthood would change and also be subject to debate, even if core values such as honour, prowess, loyalty and courage remained constant.

It is important to stress that romances were only one of the many genres in which the values and norms of chivalry were debated, alongside other kinds of texts such as chronicles, biographies, sermons, polemical letters, manuals and treatises on both war and knighthood.[6] At the same time as Chaucer was writing romances such as *Troilus and Criseyde*, *Sir Thopas* and the tales recounted by other Canterbury pilgrims, including the Knight, the Squire and the Wife of Bath, Jean Froissart was composing his *Chroniques*, which offered a history of the wars between the kings of France and England during the first half of the Hundred Years War. Meanwhile, the Chandos Herald was preparing a biography of the Black Prince, Edward of Woodstock, son of Edward III.[7] Both works offer important visions of knighthood, though, like other kinds of chivalric writing, each must be understood not merely as a mirror to the values of the aristocracy, but also as an attempt to shape and influence them. In the prologue to his great work, Froissart explicitly declared his intention to inspire young men through his presentation of stories of chivalric prowess and deeds of arms, while the biography of the Black Prince was very much a political work, designed to encourage his son Richard II to live up to a romanticised ideal of his father. Neither offers a simple window into the values and norms of the chivalric elite.

Treatises and manuals of chivalry were rarer in fourteenth-century England than in France. The most famous chivalric manuals were the late-thirteenth-century *Libre del orde de cavayleria* by a Majorcan knight named Ramon Llull, and the so-called *Livre de chevalerie* composed by the French knight Geoffroi de Charny around 1350.[8] These two books are often treated by scholars as definitive statements of the code of chivalry and anchors against which to view the writings of individuals like Chaucer, but in fact both were polemical and reformist texts, quite explicitly designed to persuade their aristocratic audience to change their behaviour. Llull had experienced a dramatic religious conversion in 1263, after which he had abandoned his career as a knight and dedicated his life to scholarly pursuits, teaching and writing. Charny composed the *Livre de chevalerie* in around 1350 as part of a reform programme initiated by King John

II in an effort to turn French military fortunes against the English and to rally noble support behind the crown at a time of mounting division and tension. More importantly, neither of their works was well known in England during the time of Chaucer. Llull's was translated into Latin and French in the fourteenth century, but was only made available to English readers at the end of the fifteenth century when it was printed by William Caxton. Charny's was markedly less successful in the Middle Ages, surviving in just two manuscripts. There is no evidence at all that this work was known in England during the lifetime of Chaucer.

There is no oral history from which to reconstruct the lived form of the social codes of the aristocracy during the age of chivalry. The surviving evidence for the values and beliefs of the chivalric classes derives almost exclusively from texts written by clerics and intellectuals rather than by knights or ladies. Yet chivalric texts were not simple mirrors to the values of their aristocratic audiences, because such works consistently sought to educate and to shape attitudes, advancing ideals for what the aristocracy ought to become. Indeed, the principal danger inherent in the study of chivalry is the assumption that such texts simply replicate the attitudes, values and beliefs of their lay audiences. There is no doubt that the two were intimately related, just as the surviving texts of medieval sermons and lives of saints provide a window into the religious beliefs of the laity. Yet they are not the same thing, despite the modern, romantic assumption that chivalric narratives in particular were direct reflections of the values of the medieval aristocracy. The difficulties of recovering aristocratic reactions to such writings cannot be underestimated. In a sense, Chaucer dramatised this problem in the *Canterbury Tales*, with the juxtaposition of the representations of 'real' members of the aristocratic audience such as the Knight and the Squire with powerful examples of chivalric literature in their tales, raising difficult questions about the relationship between the life stories of these men and the visions of knighthood that they articulated in front of the other pilgrims.

NOTES

1 For the knightly class and the aristocracy in England, see three books by Peter Coss: *The Knight in Medieval England, 1000–1400* (Stroud: Sutton, 1993); *The Lady in Medieval England, 1000–1500* (Stroud: Sutton, 1998); *The Origins of the English Gentry* (Cambridge: Cambridge University Press, 2003).

2 Nicholas Harris Nicolas, ed, *De controversia in curia militari inter Ricardum Le Scrope et Robertum Grosvenor milites: Rege Ricardo Secundo,* MCCCLXXXV–MCCCXC (London: S. & R. Bentley, 1832), Vol. 1, pp. 178–9.

3 Sheila Lindenbaum, 'The Smithfield Tournament of 1390', *Journal of Medieval and Renaissance Studies*, 20 (1990), 1–20; and Hugh E. L. Collins, *The Order of the Garter 1348–1461: Chivalry and Politics in Late Medieval England* (Oxford: Oxford University Press, 2000).

4 Clifford J. Rogers, *War Cruel and Sharp: English Strategy under Edward III, 1327–1360* (Woodbridge: Boydell Press, 2000).

5 Richard W. Kaeuper, *Chivalry and Violence in Medieval Europe* (Oxford: Oxford University Press, 1999).

6 Craig Taylor, 'English Writings on Chivalry and Warfare during the Hundred Years War', in Peter R. Coss and Christopher Tyerman, eds., *Soldiers, Nobles and Gentlemen: Essays in Honour of Maurice Keen* (Woodbridge: Boydell Press, 2009), pp. 64–84.

7 Jean Froissart, *Chroniques de Jean Froissart*, ed. S. Luce, G. Raynaud, L. Mirot and A. Mirot, 15 vols. (Paris: Société de l'Histoire de France, 1869–1975); and Chandos Herald, *La vie du Prince Noir* [*The Life of the Black Prince*], by *Chandos Herald: Edited from the Manuscript in the University of London Library*, ed. D. B. Tyson (Tübingen: Max Niemeyer, 1975).

8 Ramon Llull, *The Book of the Order of Chivalry*, trans. Noel Fallows (Woodbridge: Boydell Press, 2013); and Geoffroi de Charny, *The Book of Chivalry of Geoffroi de Charny: Text, Context and Translation*, ed. Richard W. Kaeuper and Elspeth Kennedy (Philadelphia: University of Pennsylvania Press, 1996).

CHAPTER 40

Chaucer and the Polity

Gwilym Dodd

Chaucer belonged to a generation that witnessed the very best and very worst of late medieval English kingship. He, and others of similar age who were born in the middle decades of the fourteenth century and lived long enough to see the opening decade of the fifteenth century, experienced the high-water mark of royal magnificence and achievement in the 1360s, political instability and royal humiliation in the 1370s and 1380s, and final catastrophe with the deposition of 1399. If, at the end of his life, Chaucer had mused on the characteristics of the late-fourteenth-century English polity (i.e. its form or system of government), he would undoubtedly have reflected on its extraordinary changeability. These years demonstrated that the English polity was not fixed or absolute, but was in a constant state of flux. Fundamentally, this was because its nature and shape were almost wholly dependent on the (changeable) abilities and personality of one individual: the King. But it was more complicated than this, for royal authority – or the way the King ruled – was being constantly negotiated between the King and his subjects. The political system of the England of Geoffrey Chaucer was not some form of antecedent twentieth-century despotic dictatorship, but was a 'limited monarchy', in which royal power depended upon the ability of the King to manage his people successfully and gain their consensus for his rule and policies. In other words, a late medieval King did not rule *over* his subjects; he ruled with their help, cooperation and approval. He ruled, but much was expected of his rule. The King was head of the polity, but the polity incorporated a broad political community whose members had a profound interest in how effectively England was governed. Without the confidence of his subjects, the King could expect his rule to be questioned, sometimes challenged and occasionally even overthrown. These are the factors that made politics and government in the period of Chaucer's lifetime so changeable.

In the 1360s England enjoyed a period of almost unprecedented peace and prosperity. In political terms, these were the golden years of the fourteenth century. Edward III, King of England since 1327, was at the pinnacle of his success. In 1360 the French had been forced to the negotiating table, and if the English had not attained all the war aims they had harboured since the outbreak of war in 1337, the terms of the Treaty of Brétigny did at least signal the commanding position England now held over France. In these years the King ceased imposing a heavy burden of tax on his subjects to fund his overseas campaigns. Instead, his attention was focused elsewhere. Windsor Castle was rebuilt to become a magnificent venue for meetings of the Order of the Garter, and the royal court (which cost a staggering £35,000 per annum to maintain) gained international renown as a centre of culture and literary sophistication. (In part, this was because it now included over half-a-dozen senior members of the French nobility acting as surety for the ransom of their King, John II, who had been captured by the English at Poitiers in 1356.) Above all, Edward enjoyed the loyalty and affection of his people. The nobility were united behind his rule, sharing with him the glory and spoils of a successful war, and the people rejoiced in the benefits of a prolonged period of peace: in 1363 the Commons in Parliament declared their satisfaction at the prospect of a 'Great Peace' and thanked their King for delivering them 'from being subject to other lands', and for freeing them 'from the many charges [of taxation] which they had sustained in times past'.[1]

Edward III was a great King, but even great kings grow old. In the 1370s, the single most important challenge faced by the political community was having to cope with the lack of effective royal leadership in a political system depending almost wholly on the personal dynamism of its King to function properly. By the mid 1370s Edward was no longer an effective political entity. He was losing his mental grip and was increasingly distracted by the attentions of his notorious mistress, Alice Perrers. She and other unpopular courtiers were impeached in the Good Parliament of 1376, which saw a groundswell of discontent aimed at the now unpopular and discredited government. But the difficulties faced by the political community were about to become even more challenging. Until 1376, Edward's eldest son, the Black Prince – a strong and capable man who looked likely to build on his father's successes – had been in line to succeed his father, but he tragically died of illness in this year. This meant that on the death of Edward III almost exactly a year later, in June 1377, England faced the prospect of the rule of the Black Prince's son, Richard of Bordeaux, who was then only 10 years old. The political vacuum that had been created by Edward III's dotage thus transferred seamlessly into the 'non-age' of Richard II.

Officially, Richard II ruled in his own right from his succession, but in reality the governance of the realm was in the hands of his advisers, of whom his uncle John of Gaunt, Duke of Lancaster, was the most powerful. There was also increasing emphasis on more collective forms of governance, as the political community sought to ensure that power was exercised prudently and appropriately in the absence of an adult King. Councils were set up to advise Richard, and Parliament, which contained the spiritual and temporal Lords, as well as representative members of the gentry and urban elites, held royal ministers to account and monitored government more generally. This worked well to begin with, but as Richard grew older and sought to exercise his own will, significant problems emerged. In essence, they centred on the question of whether Richard was capable of ruling in his own right. In the course of the 1380s, the political community fractured into two bitterly opposed sides: one upheld the King's prerogative to choose his own councillors and break loose from the impositions placed on him in the early years of the reign; the other maintained that the King was still not capable of ruling responsibly and ought therefore to continue to have his authority subjected to external control for the sake of the common interest and welfare of the kingdom (or so it was argued). Eventually, the King's opponents, known as the Lords Appellant, staged a coup in the so-called Merciless Parliament of 1388, in which they purged the royal household of the King's favourites (eight were executed) and all power and authority were removed from him. At this time, England teetered on the brink of full-scale civil war and deposition: Richard himself was utterly humiliated. However, in the end, the momentum of the Appellants dissipated and from 1389 the King resumed his rule, albeit in an atmosphere of uneasy political truce.

These were the tumultuous times through which Geoffrey Chaucer lived and wrote much of his poetry. How he was affected by these events has long interested scholars. His political career, as opposed to his literary career, suggests a surprising degree of involvement. Whatever he thought about what was happening (and we will consider this shortly), Chaucer will undoubtedly have been fully aware of, and to some extent immersed in, the political events of the late fourteenth century, by virtue of his employment by the crown and his connections with a number of the key political actors of the time. We think of Chaucer primarily as a poet; but for much of his adult life, until he gained fame for his writing, he would have been known in a public context as a gifted and able servant of the King, an esquire of the royal household and an associate of some key members of the royal court. To many, he may simply have been identified as the man married to Philippa de Roet, who was lady-in-waiting to John of Gaunt's second duchess, Constance of Castile, and whose sister, Katherine Swynford, later became Gaunt's mistress. From 1367, Chaucer was paid an annuity out of the exchequer and became an esquire of the royal household, a position he retained for the rest of his life. This does not in itself indicate that he was intimately acquainted with whoever sat on throne (i.e. Edward III, Richard II or Henry IV), but it does signify in broad terms an association with the court, and it provided Chaucer with access to those who attended it.

Thus, it is widely believed that some of Chaucer's earliest works were strongly influenced by the burgeoning of French literary tastes at the English court in the 1360s, as a result of his contact with the French writers and their noble patrons who were there as hostages for the French King's ransom. Later, in the 1380s, when the household became the focus of the bitter power struggle between Richard II and his opponents, Chaucer's associations took on a sharper political hue. While there is nothing to indicate that Chaucer had any association with the five Lords Appellant, there is clear evidence to show that he did have connections with eight out of the eleven men whom the Appellants condemned in 1388, including the notorious courtiers Nicholas Brembre, Robert Tresilian and Simon Burley, who were all executed. It was Sir Simon Burley, the King's former tutor, who was responsible for introducing Chaucer into the affairs of the county of Kent in the 1380s, where he was appointed as Justice of the Peace in 1385 and then elected as Member of Parliament to the 'Wonderful Parliament' of 1386. This Parliament was a key moment in Richard's reign. When Richard II looked back in 1397 at the humiliations he had suffered since his succession, he pinpointed the Wonderful Parliament of 1386, rather than the Merciless Parliament of 1388, as the nadir of his fortunes, for it was in this assembly that royal power was effectively suspended, as the King's enemies took over the running of government and forced Richard into political exile. Chaucer was there, in person, to witness this severest of attacks on the royal prerogative.

His career suggests that he would have strongly sympathised with the plight of the King in these years – that he was one of the 'King's men'. He was, after all, a member of the royal affinity and he counted amongst his friends and acquaintances men who paid with their lives for their involvement in Richard's regime. Even if it is now accepted that the misfortunes to befall Chaucer's career in the late 1380s – that is, his removal from the customs office in December 1386 and his resignation of his annuity on 1 May 1388 – were self-imposed rather than forced upon him as 'punishment' by the Appellants, the fact that Chaucer on his own initiative decided to disengage from politics and administration suggests that he was acutely aware of the vulnerability of his position, as an individual who might have been perceived as a partisan of the court. His most lucrative office to date, that of Clerk of the King's Works, was secured only a matter of months after the King had regained his authority in May 1389, which further strengthens the impression that Chaucer's personal circumstances and the political fortunes of the King and court closely coincided.

And yet, it is a striking characteristic of Chaucer's poetry that one will search in vain to find overt topical references to these political events: this is one reason why the dating of many of his poems has proved to be so problematic. It is symptomatic of the absence of overt political commentary in his work that perhaps the most clearly 'topical' of his poems, the *Parliament of Fowls* (*c.* 1380), did not concern the political turmoil of the day but the theme of courtly love, to mark the occasion of Richard II's suit for the hand of Anne of Bohemia in 1381. The clearest indication of Chaucer's reluctance to engage directly with what we might describe as 'current affairs' is the almost complete absence in his poetry of direct allusion to the Peasants' Revolt of 1381. This was arguably the most cataclysmic political event of the English Middle Ages. It threatened to overturn completely the established political system, as well as the social and religious hierarchy. Chaucer himself was almost certainly in London when the rebels stormed the capital. And yet he confined direct references to the rebellion to just a few lines of the *Nun's Priest's Tale* (*c.* 1390s), where allusion was made to the wholesale slaughter of the Flemings in the capital (*CT*, VII.3394–6).

Self-evidently, Chaucer was not a political poet. He wrote principally about human nature rather than historical events. Some scholars have assumed that this is because he was either little affected by these events, or else little interested in them. While the first view is patently untrue, the second hardly seems plausible, given his membership of the royal household and his reliance on the crown for a living. Rather, whatever political views Chaucer had, it seems he chose not to grandstand them in his work. Perhaps this reflected the literary tastes of his audience, who preferred not to 'mix politics with pleasure'. Perhaps, also, it indicated Chaucer's desire to make his work appeal to a broad audience whose members espoused a variety of different and conflicting political standpoints. Another possibility is that it was simply dangerous for Chaucer to make his writing too political. Scholars have commented on his uncanny ability to withdraw himself from public life at times of acute political stress. Perhaps this sense of self-preservation also extended to his poetry. Paul Strohm has highlighted the stark contrast in the fortunes of Chaucer and those of a contemporary of his, Thomas Usk, with whom he was acquainted.[2] Both men were confronted with the potential risks and rewards of factional affiliation in the 1380s, but whereas Chaucer exercised discretion and distanced himself from overt alignment to the royal cause, Usk heavily implicated himself in factional politics (by serving the unpopular London Mayor Nicholas Brembre) and was executed for his troubles by the Appellants in 1388. It should be stressed that Usk was not executed for his writing; but, by using his work to ingratiate himself with the court party, he effectively nailed his political colours to the mast and gave himself little chance of denying his factional affiliation once the tables were turned and the Appellants had the upper hand. Chaucer's poetical political allusions were, by contrast, far too subtle to implicate him in a similar way.

His reluctance to engage in politics suggests that there was only a low level of expectation that royal servants should conspicuously demonstrate their loyalty to the King. Chaucer's desire to avoid writing anything that might have offended the King's opponents evidently outweighed any pressure he felt as an esquire of the royal household to use his writing to show unfailing allegiance to Richard II. We may surmise that Chaucer did not feel he needed to use his poetry to maintain (or enhance) his position. We might also conclude that, from the point of view of the crown, Chaucer's value lay in his administrative abilities, not his literary talents: there is no evidence to indicate that Richard II showed any interest in Chaucer's work, or that there was any personal or special connection between the two. Other factors, however, may be pertinent. Rather than seeing Chaucer's lack of direct political engagement as part of a self-preservation strategy, it is possible that it reflected a more complex set of attitudes towards the political unrest of these years, and a support of Richard that was nevertheless conditioned by misgivings about the King's actions and his evident failings. Chaucer was no enthusiast of the Appellant programme of 1388, nor the concerted opposition to Richard's rule before this. Insofar as any political meaning can be discerned from his poetry, it is possible to identify an underlying suspicion of populist forms of government which the King's opponents stood for. For example, collective decision-making, of the sort to be found in Parliament at this time, is implicitly criticised in the *Parliament of Fowls* and *Troilus and Criseyde* (*c.* 1385–6). In the latter, the kingdom of Troy is led to ruin as a result of the people's intransigence in a parliamentary-type assembly. But equally, Chaucer was no advocate of unbridled royal excess. In the *Legend of Good Women* (*c.* 1386) the duties of a king are set out, and they are strikingly conventional in form and intention. A king is exhorted to be honourable; he must cherish his people and hate extortion; he should protect his estate; he must fear God, provide justice and love truth; and he should lead his subjects to steadfastness. Much of the significance of these lines hinges on whether one sees them as flattery for qualities the King was already felt to possess, or an exhortation to him to *acquire* these qualities. Perhaps Chaucer meant their meaning to be ambiguous. Either way, the clear message appears to be that a king was expected to rule within certain permissible boundaries, and that just as his subjects had obligations towards him, so too the King had obligations to his subjects.

What I am suggesting, therefore, is that, politically speaking, Chaucer inhabited a middle ground – that he was, in essence, a fence-sitter. He rejected the 'tyranny' of Appellant rule, because their ruthless purge of Richard's courtiers threatened the stability of the realm, but he was also uncomfortable with the prospect of a king whose policies did not serve the common interest and whose favouritism was destabilising the political community. Such a standpoint has tended to be ignored by historians, who have focused attention on the polarised views of either the 'court party' or the King's opponents. Yet, the more neutral standpoint of Chaucer – if this is how we can label it – was probably the more typical. Only the most committed and most ambitious members of the political community gambled with their careers and lives by actively seeking the destruction of the side they opposed. The remainder, like Chaucer, watched the struggle for power with anxiety, but maintained a discreet distance. They remained loyal to the King, insofar as he was God's chosen representative on earth, but they did not feel any great personal attachment, such that they were willing to put their heads on the block for him. For Chaucer, and a large section of society, what mattered most was the preservation of the integrity of the crown, because it was this that ensured political stability and social harmony. Although both Richard and the Appellants could be said to have damaged this integrity, Richard, as the ordained King, still represented the best hope of restoring political consensus, and so people's natural loyalties, including those of Chaucer, lay with the King.

It is interesting to reflect that this was probably the standpoint of John of Gaunt, with whom, as we have seen, Chaucer had connections. Gaunt remained staunchly loyal to Richard throughout the latter's reign, even though one suspects he had grave reservations about the ability of his nephew to rule effectively. When the usurpation came in 1399, it was the non-alignment of large sections of the population that enabled

Gaunt's son, Henry Bolingbroke, to depose Richard without fighting a battle. Chaucer for his part, and for the reasons discussed above, probably felt no great sense of sorrow at the demise of King Richard. A recent suggestion that Henry IV had Chaucer murdered because of his Ricardian credentials is completely without foundation.[3] On the contrary, it is possible that Chaucer's Lancastrian connections were far more influential on the poet during Richard's reign than has been acknowledged. Alongside his royal annuity, from 1374 Chaucer was also in receipt of an annuity from the duchy of Lancaster. His wife Philippa remained in the Duke's household from 1369 until her death in 1387. Their son, Thomas, grew up alongside Gaunt's Beaufort sons (by Katherine Swynford) and very quickly became staunchly loyal to the Duke, serving him in Spain from 1386 to 1389 and in return receiving an extremely generous annuity. The lucrative offices given to Thomas by Gaunt were confiscated by Richard II early in 1399, when the Duke died and the duchy of Lancaster was taken into the King's hands, so Geoffrey Chaucer would have directly observed – through his son – the arbitrary nature of Richard's rule. There is no evidence to suggest that Gaunt was ever formally Geoffrey Chaucer's patron, but in its careful avoidance of factional politics and its qualified support for the principles underpinning royal authority there is much to be said for the view that Chaucer's poetry mirrored an essentially Lancastrian political perspective: politically, it was non-aligned, cautious and subtle. If Chaucer avoided direct political commentary, this probably reflected the uncertain and delicate position that Gaunt himself held in Richard II's polity, for Gaunt supported the King but was a political outsider, having no affiliation to either the court or the court's opponents, who viewed him equally with suspicion bordering on contempt.

The title of this chapter is 'Chaucer and the Polity', but in some ways it ought to read 'Chaucer *in* the Polity'. His poetry is not overtly political, but this does not mean that Chaucer himself was not heavily politicised. I have suggested that his views and his poetry did not correspond with the extreme political perspectives of either the 'court party' or those who sought to destroy it, but this does not preclude the possibility that he felt passionately about the disintegration of the political consensus from the 1370s and the dangers this posed for the wellbeing of the kingdom, as well as his own career. In this, I suspect he held views shared by large segments of the political community, of which Chaucer can be considered to be a member. Unlike other topics covered in this volume, there is a whole body of 'historical' evidence that helps contextualise the views and values Chaucer expressed about politics and governance. But discerning the significance of his professional and political connections is not a straightforward matter, just as discerning the meaning and purpose of the political allusions in his poetry requires care. Chaucer was a royal esquire, but this did not make him a committed 'courtier'. The apparent mismatch between his privileged position in the King's entourage and his reluctance to express anything other than indirect and often very subtle support for the King has traditionally been the source of perplexity, but it makes sense if we understand political loyalty in the late fourteenth century to have been highly complex, gradated and variable. This was undoubtedly an age of *personal* kingship and *personal* ties of loyalty, but the life and career of Chaucer indicate that this operated on a sliding scale of intensity and that it was perfectly possible to have a successful career in the service of the crown without embroiling oneself in the life-and-death struggles of a relatively small minority intent on achieving political hegemony. In this, Chaucer was not unusual, but was representative of a large swathe of the political community whose members simply wanted to get on with their lives and prosper.

NOTES

1 *PROME*, CD-ROM version, Parliament of 1363, item 8.
2 Paul Strohm, 'Politics and Poetics: Usk and Chaucer in the 1380s', in *Literary Practice and Social Change in Britain, 1380–1530*, ed. Lee Patterson (Berkeley and Los Angeles: University of California Press, 1990), pp. 83–112.
3 Terry Jones, Robert Yeager, Terry Dolan, Alan Fletcher and Juliette Dor, *Who Murdered Chaucer? A Medieval Mystery* (London: Methuen, 2003).

CHAPTER 41

The Economy

Christopher Dyer

Geoffrey Chaucer can be portrayed as a sophisticated and cosmopolitan writer living in an agrarian society with an underdeveloped economy. The simplicity of that picture should not be overstated, as closer examination reveals many complexities in the rural economy as well as in the urban world of commerce and high finance.

Chaucer's wealthy and educated audience had small interest in the peasants, and their word for them, *cherl*, could be applied to anyone regarded as uncultured and ill-mannered. Following the convention of dividing mankind into estates (nobles, clergy and workers) with distinct functions and duties, the poet chose a 'ploughman' as the ideal representative of those who worked. William Langland makes a ploughman the central figure in his poem *Piers Plowman*, and describes him as a peasant of some substance who owns his own plough with animals to pull it. The peasant pilgrim of the *General Prologue* to the *Canterbury Tales*, as well as possessing a plough, rides on his own mare. He would be tenant of at least 15 acres of land, which would mean engaging in such back-breaking tasks as ditching and manure spreading, but he has spare time to help the less fortunate, and does his duty by paying a tenth of his crops to the Church (I.530–41).

The humble peasant father of Griselda in the *Clerk's Tale* is described as 'poor', though his circumstances appear to resemble the Ploughman's, as his buildings include an ox stall (which implies a plough), and he owns a small flock of sheep (IV.204–7, 291). Of the 400,000 rural households of low status in England revealed by the poll-tax of 1377, about 250,000 belonged to the type represented by these two fictional figures. With 15 acres or more they could feed themselves and their families, and their collective surplus of crops and animal products (such as cheese and wool) satisfied most of the needs of the rest of society, especially the townspeople and country-dwellers without adequate amounts of land. This last category is well represented in the *Canterbury Tales* by the 'poor widow' of the *Nun's Priest's Tale*, who keeps herself and her two daughters with seven animals and some poultry, but has, apparently, no arable land, only a garden. As a dairy maid, or *deye*, working presumably for the lord of the manor, she would receive a modest cash wage and enough grain to feed her small family. Chaucer highlights her frugality as an ironic comment on the luxury of the aristocratic lifestyle (VII.2821–48). Such smallholding peasants who also earned wages (often described in general as cottagers) accounted for about 150,000 rural households in 1377.[1]

The peasants who appear in our mundane administrative documents seem rather less virtuous than Chaucer's ideal types. Tenants cultivating more than fifteen acres would have been producing for the market, lending and borrowing money, buying and selling land, and being drawn into the commercial world.[2] A poor widow would often have taken up brewing and would sell the ale above the legally fixed price.[3] After the Black Death epidemic of 1348–9 the number of tenants was reduced and holding sizes tended to increase. In addition, peasants kept more animals as the area of grazing land expanded. These tendencies reinforced the commercial and profit-seeking outlook of peasants. The Ploughman in the *General Prologue* meets his obligations without grumbling, but peasants are known to have avoided paying rents and dues.[4] The Ploughman's willingness to work for neighbours without wages would surprise an audience accustomed to widespread demands for higher pay. Chaucer is making an ironic point about the gap between the ideal and the perceptions of society prevailing among his audience. Less subtlety was needed in the case of reeves and millers, who provide extreme examples of acquisitive and dishonest countrymen.

Chaucer briefly indicates the mechanisms by which peasants hand over cash or goods to make up the revenues of their social superiors: the poor widow pays rent; the Ploughman contributes tithes; the Miller takes tolls from those bringing him corn to grind. The fullest account of the flow of wealth from peasants to lords comes from the Parson's conventional sermon, which itemises sins, including the pride of lords whose households feast on elaborate dishes while being entertained by minstrels. These extravagances are funded by avaricious demands for high cash payments from tenants, such as tallages (annual lump sums paid collectively) and amercements (paid by offenders in the manor court). The Parson hints at more responsible standards of lordship, by reminding the rich that they should protect their subordinates, and not devour tenants' possessions without restraint (X.435–47, 751–60, 773–5).

The treatment of manorial tenants by lords and their officials caused persistent controversy throughout Chaucer's lifetime. Lords held manors and estates in which a proportion of the land – often a fifth or a quarter – was controlled by the lord (the demesne), and up to the 1370s much of it was managed directly to produce food for the lord's household, or for sale. Most of the manorial land was divided among free and unfree tenants who paid rents in cash, labour and kind. The combined value of their various payments contributed more than half of lords' income. Their contribution to labour on the lord's land was dwindling in importance during the period 1340–1400, and most work on the demesne was done by hired labour. Peasants paid most rents in money, which they acquired by selling produce from their own holdings, or by earning wages.[5] A particular point of friction between lords and peasants, as the *Parson's Tale* indicates, lay in the payments made through the manor court, such as the amercements, and the dues associated with servile status, such as tallage and marriage fines. Serfs made up a substantial minority in the 1340s, but everyone might be required to pay amercements or contribute to collective fines. When the population was halved after the plague epidemic of 1348–9, rents ought to have been reduced, but many were fixed by custom. Lords could even increase their revenues by maximising the number and value of amercements and other dues that depended on the 'lord's will'.[6] The absence of controls over lords' demands gave opportunities for corrupt officials, like the devil-bailiff in the *Friar's Tale*, to extort money (III.1429–33). A miller could also take for himself a toll of corn and flour in addition to the fraction (typically a twentieth) allowed to the lord by custom.[7]

The exploitation of demesnes provided another source of contention. Before 1349 reeves and bailiffs made decisions about crops and livestock, hired labour, and were responsible for making the land profitable for the lord.[8] This system of direct management between 1200 and 1348 gave the lords the benefit of the high market-price produce, which could be grown with cheap wage-labour. The Black Death reduced the number of mouths to be fed, which ought to have led to low corn prices. Wages should have increased as workers were in short supply. For various reasons, such as a run of poor harvests, the full impacts of these changes were delayed, which enabled manorial demesnes in the 1350s and 1360s under the rule of reeves to generate quite high profits.[9] Chaucer's Norfolk Reeve was skilled at outwitting the auditors, stealing without being discovered and persuading his lord to be well satisfied with his efficiency (I.587–612). Chaucer here was reflecting anxieties about the running of manors at a time when the disadvantages of direct management were becoming fully apparent. Eventually, lords gave up the role of agricultural entrepreneurs, and passed the mantle on to the farmers or lessees who agreed to pay a fixed rent for each demesne.

An example of these changes at work comes from a part of the country with which Chaucer must have been familiar: Essex and East Anglia, where fourteen scattered properties formed the bailiwick of Clare, one of four divisions of an estate belonging to Elizabeth de Burgh, who died in 1360.[10] These lands were held afterwards by successive members of the Mortimer family, Earls of March. In the late 1330s the total of land under crops in the demesnes of these manors exceeded 2,300 acres, and between them they generated annual income of at least £650. Through the 1340s, 1350s and 1360s rents from one of those manors, Claret in north Essex, brought in £10 annually; between £1 and £3 came from the profits of the courts, and there were rents from various other assets such as pastures. The demesne produced wool worth £2–£3, and corn with a value of at least £32. The labour costs were, however, increasing in the twenty years after the Black Death, until in 1369 the lord gave up producing for the market and the demesne was leased for £10 per annum. Lords' income fell by about 10 per cent in the thirty years after the Black Death, which in the potentially disastrous circumstances of falling population and the threats to the profitability of agriculture shows a remarkable skill in adapting to circumstances.

The numerous peasant holdings added together and the thousands of acres in the lords' demesnes made the English countryside very productive. At the time of the poll-taxes around 1380 about 7 million acres were devoted to the cultivation of field crops, which were most abundant in the east, the Midlands and central southern England.[11] Corn fields needed to be linked with grassland, as animals were essential to pull ploughs and carts, and to provide the manure that kept the arable fertile. Pastures were carefully managed to prevent overgrazing and to protect the vital hay crop used for winter feed. Woods were coppiced on a cycle for fuel, and fenced to stop animals causing damage. Moorlands, fens and marshes, which appear to have been wild, were exploited and managed for grazing and as sources of raw materials and fuel. The corn fields provided food, but the animals and especially wool were sold for cash.[12]

When contemporaries, like Chaucer, imagined landscapes they did not pay so much attention to the corn fields and the pastures stocked with sheep and cattle. The *Parliament of Fowls* is located in a man-made space – a park surrounded by a stone wall, but within the enclosure are trees and streams abounding with fish; here rabbits play and deer wander (lines 120–210). A similar countryside with meadow, daisies, flower beds and singing birds is described in the *Legend of Good Women* (G 35–60). These were not just literary fantasies, as many lords at the time were maintaining or creating ideal places with parks, gardens, warrens and ponds as prestigious backdrops to a residence. Such spaces were capable of yielding some material advantage, from renting out the grazing of the park; from felling trees for timber; and from consuming the deer, rabbits and fish. Nonetheless, lords who chose to use land in this way were opting for pleasure and status – above all hunting – rather than giving priority to agricultural production.[13]

The economy that Chaucer knew best was the urban and commercial world of London. He spent time at Westminster both early and late in his life, and when he was appointed controller of the customs he lived above Aldgate in the City. From his travels on the Continent he would have appreciated that London's size, role as a capital and function as a major port made it comparable with the greatest European cities.[14] When Chaucer was a customs official, the amount of wool being taken through London to the Continent fell from about 12,000 sacks in the accounting year 1374–5 to 7,000 sacks in 1385–6. The number of woollen cloths exported through London increased from an annual total of between 2,000 and 3,000 in the early 1370s to 4,000–6,000 in 1391–5.[15] We know that these trends belong in the early phases of England's transformation from a producer of raw wool to a manufacturer of cloth. By the year of Chaucer's death in 1400, total English cloth exports were near to 1 million yards, and four times this figure would have been sold within the country. Chaucer was evidently aware of the industry, as he refers to a number of cloth-making artisans in the *General Prologue*, including the Wife of Bath.

The pilgrims travelling to Canterbury included a range of people making their living in towns: Merchant, Shipman, guildsmen (who were prosperous artisans), Manciple, Clerk of Oxford, Pardoner, Man of Law and Doctor. A number of the tales are about merchants and townspeople, and the author assumes that the audience will regard as commonplace the passage of ships with cargoes or passengers to the Low Countries, Bordeaux, Compostella, Rome and Jerusalem. It seems natural that the Wife of Bath's cloth should be compared with that made in Ypres and Ghent. Money is pervasive, beginning with the early lines of the *Canterbury Tales* when the Host sets out his plan for story-telling only when all the bills are paid, and he proposes that the reward for the pilgrim telling the best tale would be a free meal funded by the rest of the party (I.760–821). Sums of money are quoted exactly, such as £40 owed for stone to build a friary in the *Summoner's Tale* (III.2106), or the pan worth 12d. that the summoner in the *Friar's Tale* takes from a poor widow (III.1603–15). The precision of each sum has a purpose, demonstrating the friar's materialism and the summoner's uncharitable ruthlessness, just as Chaucer uses possessions (especially horses and garments) to define the mentality and social aspirations of the pilgrims.

Although Chaucer focused on London, England as a whole was relatively highly urbanised (by fourteenth-century European standards), as towns in all contained about 100,000 households, a little below one in five of the whole country. Besides London, which stood out with its 40,000–50,000 people, there were 50 large towns (among them Canterbury and Oxford appear in Chaucer's writing) and about 600 small towns with populations ranging from a few hundred to 2,000, including the small port of Dartmouth and the market town of Bath.[16] The towns interacted with the surrounding countryside, allowing the rural population to sell produce and buy manufactured goods. Towns had suffered a reduced population after the mid-century plagues, but they seem to have maintained their prosperity, and a few were expanding. Towns benefited from supplying consumer goods, which more people could afford as peasant holdings expanded and wages increased. The Parson was indignant about 'superfluity of clothing', which could be indecent as well as extravagant (X.411–34), and dressing above one's station was (unsuccessfully) made illegal in 1363.

A high proportion of the urban population consisted of employees of various kinds, including labourers and more skilled workers hired by the day, as well as large numbers of servants. The servants included domestic staff, and young people learning a trade, who were not always formally registered as apprentices.[17] Chaucer takes the existence of wage-earners and servants for granted. His contemporaries, however, were much exercised by the scarcity of labour after the Black Death. They attempted unsuccessfully through legislation and special courts to enforce the rates of pay prevailing before the pestilence, and to compel workers to accept contracts when they were offered. Chaucer makes no comment about this controversy, but at least indirectly he seems to reflect the growing prominence of women in the work force. The Wife of Bath asserts her lack of subservience to successive husbands, and makes her own living from weaving, and there is no shortage of independently minded women elsewhere in Chaucer's writing. In the towns of late-fourteenth-century England, encouraged by the high demand for labour after the epidemics, we find wives pursuing their own trades, for example as brewsters, and those who took over their former husbands' businesses in their widowhood. Women usually earned lower wages than did men doing similar work, but the pay gap was narrowing.[18]

Chaucer relies on contracts and credit as key elements in some of his narratives, which was in accord with his audience's experience. In the *Franklin's Tale*, a wife makes a marriage contract with a social inferior; she then promises herself to a young admirer if he can remove the dangerous rocks around the coast of Brittany (where she lives); he makes an agreement for the removal of the stones for £1,000 with a magician, who succeeds in the endeavour and demands his money. The young man faces ruin in borrowing this enormous sum, but eventually the contracts are cancelled and social disaster avoided. The *Shipman's Tale* revolves around a payment of 100 francs by a monk to a merchant's wife in return for sexual favours; the monk obtains the money as a loan from the merchant (VII.181, 201). Both stories hinge on love and sex being bought with money, but this 'commodification' of human relationships is shown to be immoral. At the end of the *Franklin's Tale* chivalric values are reasserted over commercial values.[19]

Chaucer assumed that if money was needed, a loan could be negotiated. The economy depended on credit arrangements, as few people had enough cash available to buy goods, and merchants in particular had to advance large sums to obtain expensive commodities. Small town traders were often found to owe a few shillings (for a sack of grain, or a length of cloth) when they were sued for payment in the borough court, while London merchants, such as grocers dealing in spices for aristocratic kitchens, or imported dyestuffs for cloth-making, would keep a formal record of debts that varied through the decades of Chaucer's life between £80 and £280.[20] Owing money was not a source of shame, or the prelude to ruin – it was an integral part of economic activity.[21]

Finally, Chaucer reflects the conventional morality by which economic activity was judged. Restraint in expenditure and a rejection of worldliness were admired, and indulgence in luxuries by the Friar, Monk and Prioress were regarded as inconsistent with their calling. At the same time, people were expected to live up to the standards of dress and lifestyle appropriate to the gradations of wealth and status. Trade for profit, collecting rents fairly, and cultivating the land efficiently were all legitimate, but not cheating, extortion and deception for private profit.[22] Lords were expected to show moderation in their treatment of their subjects, and the rich were under an obligation to help the poor.

NOTES

1 R. H. Hilton, *The English Peasantry in the Later Middle Ages* (Oxford: Oxford University Press, 1975), pp. 37–41.

2 Richard H. Britnell, *The Commercialisation of English Society 1000–1500* (Cambridge: Cambridge University Press, 1993), pp. 201–3; Chris Briggs, *Credit and Village Society in Fourteenth-Century England* (Oxford: Oxford University Press, 2009), pp. 29–64; John Mullan and Richard Britnell, *Land and Family: Trends and Local Variations in the Peasant Land Market on the Winchester Bishopric Estates, 1263–1415* (Hatfield: University of Hertfordshire Press, 2010), pp. 118–31.

3 Judith M. Bennett, *Ale, Beer and Brewsters in England: Women's Work in a Changing World, 1300–1600* (New York: Oxford University Press, 1996), pp. 37–59.

4 Phillipp R. Schofield, *Peasant and Community in Medieval England* (Basingstoke: Palgrave, 2003), pp. 42–4.

5 Richard Britnell, *Britain and Ireland 1050–1530: Economy and Society* (Oxford: Oxford University Press, 2004), pp. 429–50.

6 Christopher Dyer, 'The Social and Economic Background to the Rural Revolt of 1381', in Christopher Dyer, *Everyday Life in Medieval England* (London: Continuum, 2000), pp. 191–220 (pp. 199–214); Peter L. Larson, *Conflict and Compromise in the Late Medieval Countryside: Lord and Peasant in Durham 1349–1400* (New York: Routledge, 2006), pp. 77–110.

7 Richard Holt, *The Mills of Medieval England* (Oxford: Blackwell, 1988), pp. 90–8, 105–6.

8 David Stone, *Decision-Making in Medieval Agriculture* (Oxford: Oxford University Press, 2005), pp. 13–14, 89–120.

9 Richard Britnell, 'English Agricultural Output and Prices, 1350–1450: National Trends and Regional Divergences', in Ben Dodds and Richard Britnell, eds., *Agriculture and Rural Society after the Black Death: Common Themes and Regional Variations* (Hatfield: University of Hertfordshire Press, 2008), pp. 20–39 (pp. 20–31).

10 G. A. Holmes, *The Estates of the Higher Nobility in Fourteenth-Century England* (Cambridge: Cambridge University Press, 1957), pp. 86–93, 114, 147, 148, 149–50.

11 Bruce M. S. Campbell, *English Seigniorial Agriculture, 1250–1450* (Cambridge: Cambridge University Press, 2000), pp. 386–90.

12 Joan Thirsk, ed., *The English Rural Landscape* (Oxford: Oxford University Press, 2000), pp. 112–14, 197–8.

13 Oliver H. Creighton, *Designs upon the Land: Elite Landscapes of the Middle Ages* (Woodbridge: Boydell Press, 2009), pp. 122–53, 167–94; S. A. Mileson, *Parks in Medieval England* (Oxford: Oxford University Press, 2009), pp. 15–44.

14 Caroline M. Barron, *London in the Later Middle Ages: Government and People 1200–1500* (Oxford: Oxford University Press, 2004), pp. 97–101.

15 E. M. Carus-Wilson and Olive Coleman, *England's Export Trade 1275–1547* (London: Oxford University Press, 1963), pp. 51, 52, 84–5.

16 D. M. Palliser, ed., *The Cambridge Urban History of Britain*, Vol. 1: *600–1540* (Cambridge: Cambridge University Press, 2000), pp. 396–7, 506–8, 758–9.

17 P. J. P. Goldberg, 'Urban Identity and the Poll Taxes of 1377, 1379 and 1381', *Economic History Review*, 2nd series, 43 (1990), 197–208 (p. 199).

18 Marjorie Keniston McKintosh, *Working Women in English Society, 1300–1620* (Cambridge: Cambridge University Press, 2005), pp. 29–42.

19 L. Farber, *An Anatomy of Trade in Medieval Writing* (Ithaca, NY and London: Cornell University Press, 2006), pp. 68–82.

20 Pamela Nightingale, 'Monetary Contraction and Mercantile Credit in Later Medieval England', *Economic History Review*, 43 (1990), 560–75; Jim L. Bolton, *Money in the Medieval English Economy 973–1489* (Manchester: Manchester University Press, 2012), pp. 274–7.

21 Briggs, *Credit and Village Society*, pp. 214–21.

22 James Davis, *Medieval Market Morality: Life, Law and Ethics in the English Market Place, 1200–1500* (Cambridge: Cambridge University Press, 2012).

CHAPTER 42

Towns, Villages and the Land

Mark Bailey

Geoffrey Chaucer's life spanned one of the most dramatic and volatile periods in the economic, social and environmental history of England. At the time of his birth in *c.* 1342, the English countryside was more populous, and more of its land under the plough, than ever before. By the time he reached the age of majority in *c.* 1363, half of his compatriots had died in successive outbreaks of the Black Death. The arrival of plague in 1348–9 opened a golden age of pathogenic activity, with subsequent epidemics in 1361–2, 1369, 1375–6 and 1390–1. The only relief was that the epidemics became progressively less virulent, lethal and widespread with time, and so their impact and disruptiveness gradually diminished. We cannot know how many of those who lived through this bacterial assault (including Chaucer himself) survived because they simply failed to catch the disease or because they were infected but subsequently recovered.

The Black Death is the worst recorded catastrophe in English history. Many contemporaries regarded it as the agent of divine retribution and the portent of worse yet to come. Their fears must have been exacerbated by a sudden and severe deterioration in the weather in the 1350s, which became persistently cold, wet and short of sunlight. The Black Death created its own climate of anxiety, uncertainty and dread. Daily life in every town and village was dominated by the need to cope with those fears, to make sense of the huge and arbitrary loss of life, and to adjust to its immense repercussions.

Historians agree that the process of adjustment was not completed until around the time of Chaucer's death in 1400, but disagree about the immediate impact of the first two outbreaks of plague. The orthodox interpretation downplays their importance, arguing that little appears to have changed in the generation after 1348–9. The period *c.* 1350–*c.* 1375 has been dubbed an 'Indian summer', in which grain prices and rural rental incomes remained buoyant; landholdings were largely reoccupied; and domestic and overseas trade, and the war against France, quickly resumed. In the villages, landlords stridently enforced serfdom, a social system in which half the population rendered demeaning personal incidents and services in return for land, and were restricted in their freedom of time and action. The government introduced new legislation to restrict wage rises everywhere. In this interpretation, significant and enduring socio-economic change was not apparent until the last quarter of the century, when the inevitable consequences of the reduced population finally emerged. In the 1380s and 1390s the economy contracted sharply, characterised by falling output and profits, a shrinking trade in basic commodities, and a spike in abandoned landholdings and houses. The scarcity of labourers and tenants increased their bargaining power to a point where landlords could no longer resist, which hastened the decline of serfdom and resulted in some redistribution of income down the social scale, thus stimulating demand for basic consumer goods – such as clothing and household furnishings – and the creation of larger farms.

This orthodoxy is increasingly at odds with a mounting body of evidence pointing to substantial changes within English towns and villages immediately after the first epidemic. For example, the so-called 'Indian summer' is now known to have been stormy and troubled, not calm or balmy. The period when Chaucer was a young man – the 1350s to the mid 1370s – is increasingly regarded as an age of instability and volatility, when both society and the economy were struggling to assimilate the immense impact of plague. In contrast, Chaucer's older years – the late 1370s to his death – were characterised by greater stability and predictability, when the new social and economic paradigms of the post-plague era had finally settled.

This revised categorisation of the immediate post-plague era is exemplified by recent discoveries about the ways in which the British climate underwent change. Between the mid 1340s and the mid 1370s temperatures tended to be below the long-term average for the Middle Ages, summers were wetter and cooler and references to flooding were common. Levels of temperature and rainfall were volatile, varying markedly from one year to the next, so that a succession of cold and damp years was punctuated by occasional warm and dry ones. For example, the grain harvests of 1349–52 and 1367–9 were dire, the former the consequence of one of the coldest snaps of the entire millennium, whereas between 1362 and 1364 yields were good and summers were warm. The persistently poor weather meant that grain prices were high. Yet the harvests of 1376, 1377 and 1378 were all bountiful and mark a turning-point in the climate. During the 1380s and 1390s the variability of the weather from one year to the next diminished, average temperatures rose and references to flooding disappear. The rate at which trees grew reached one of the peaks of the last millennium, and grain harvests were consistently generous. Grain prices were lower and less volatile. The stability and benevolence of the climate when Chaucer was writing the *Canterbury Tales* are so striking, especially when compared with the unsettled and harsher environment of the previous thirty years, that Bruce Campbell has dubbed it 'The Chaucerian Anomaly'.[1]

The deaths of tenants in successive plagues, and the reduction in the size of the labour force, increased opportunities for the survivors to construct sizable landholdings and to obtain as much paid work as they desired. Opportunities were further enhanced by the commercialised nature of agriculture and the availability of work in the expanding industrial and service sectors. Rural dwellers routinely travelled to local markets and fairs to buy or sell basic goods, and they routinely travelled up to a dozen miles or so for employment, usually paid on day rates. The turnover of land tenants increased after 1348–9, as many people left their home village to claim the inheritance of a distant, deceased relative, or to acquire a larger holding or a more attractive rent package as strangers in a new place. Tenants were also choosy about the terms on which they held customary land, prompting landlords to remove some of its demeaning servile incidents and language in order to make it more appealing. Furthermore, whenever customary land remained unoccupied for any length of time it was converted to fixed-term tenures such as leasehold, in which the unpopular dues of serfdom were replaced with a commercial money rent. Leases were now used on an unprecedented scale, and were particularly attractive to outsiders and first-time buyers, because they offered a flexible and low-risk mode of entry into the land market.

Between *c.* 1350 and *c.* 1375 the combination of poor harvests, disturbed marketing networks, labour shortages and the high turnover of tenants contributed to an air of change and instability in rural communities. Newcomers were not steeped in the rules and traditions of their communities, and their pushy individualism could undermine customary notions of collective responsibility and spirit. Manor courts issued sensible by-laws to reinforce basic communal agricultural and trading practices, which locals increasingly flouted: they grazed their livestock illegally (unsupervised sheep and geese were particular scourges), encroached on the land of others, enclosed slivers of land, traded illegally and, in some places, behaved violently and disrespectfully towards each other. As Peter Larson observes laconically, some villagers in County Durham 'were doing quite unneighbourly things'.[2]

The disruption to and shortages in the labour market caused by successive epidemics between 1348 and 1375–6 increased the opportunities for young women to obtain paid employment, providing them with greater social and economic freedom than before. The wages and earnings of labourers everywhere rose, which worked to the disadvantage of employers. The initial response of the authorities was to introduce ambitious and wide-ranging legislation, whose purpose was to restore the conditions of the pre-plague labour market and to impose upon the lower orders the discipline of manual labour deemed essential to the common good and ordained within medieval estates theory. The Statute of Labourers of 1351 (and its regular subsequent revisions) attempted to fix a national maximum wage based on pre-plague rates, to impose annual rather than daily contracts of employment, to compel able-bodied men and women to work if ordered to do so, to regulate the behaviour of the lower orders, and to address the difficulty of retaining serfs on their home manor. During the 1350s and 1360s the ruling elite hoped this legislation would turn back the clock to the golden days of the pre-plague labour market, but from the 1370s the dawning realisation that it was not working, and that peasant power – epitomised by the Peasants' Revolt of 1381 – was rising, triggered intense debate about the remedies for society's ills. These issues attracted the attention of contemporary moralisers and poets.

After the mid 1370s the benign climate, greater market certainty and monetary deflation caused grain prices to rest at a persistently lower level. Arable production settled into a low-level equilibrium, more prone to fall further than to rise. This encouraged the emergence of a more settled structure of landholding in most rural communities, which became polarised between two groups. The first comprised a small number of wealthier peasants, who held well in excess of 20 acres of land, generated surpluses of agricultural produce for the market, and hired labourers and servants to help work their land. The second group comprised smallholders and the landless, who earned a living in craftwork or wage labour. The attitude of the authorities to labourers was now more realistic and less idealistic, and the obsession with turning back the clock to the 1340s had been replaced with a pragmatic determination to address specific concerns relating to poverty, vagrancy and public order. This changing attitude to labour is exemplified in the contrast between Gower's disdain for the lower orders and his yearning for a golden age of compliant peasants, and the absence of such commentary in the *Canterbury Tales*: Gower's views are those of an arch-reactionary writing mainly in the mid-to-late 1370s, whereas Chaucer was writing in the period when society's post-plague contours had become more solid and secure, and when the debate on labour had moved on.

In *c.* 1380 around one-fifth of the population of England lived in towns, none of which was especially large, but their inhabitants possessed greater freedom to determine their own affairs than did many rural dwellers. Towns faced formidable problems in the third quarter of the fourteenth century. As Richard Britnell notes, 'many of the practical problems posed by the epidemics were exceptionally grim in towns ... [which consequently] bore the scar of plague for many years'.[3] Deceased councillors, borough officers and guild officials had to be replaced, and their experience and expertise – accumulated over many years – were sorely missed. Urban officials were now elected from a smaller pool of talent, which was short of experience and knowledge of civic government, but they faced far greater problems and challenges than their experienced predecessors ever had to address.

The main challenge facing the urban authorities was to integrate the wave of migrants who flooded into towns looking for a fresh start: perhaps one-half of all town populations had originated from the countryside. They were attracted by the availability of both work and vacant properties, but newcomers had to be inducted into the daily habits, customs and rules essential to ensuring that the environmental and behavioural nuisances of urban life were minimised. Officials struggled to impose order, because towns contained more alehouses where disturbances might occur than villages did; they also provided a greater degree of anonymity for subversive behaviour and sexual misconduct, and offered richer pickings for drifters, beggars and criminals. Urban officials faced the additional challenge of enforcing the raft of new and ambitious government legislation, which extended well beyond the Statute of Labourers to include the Sumptuary Laws (1363) – designed to regulate the consumption patterns of ordinary people – and a series of intrusive parliamentary statutes that effectively tried to enforce national standards for the price and quality of processed food and drink.[4] It was not until the 1380s and 1390s that this government interference diminished, thus allowing consumer choice and the traders themselves to regulate the market. The result was a reduction in the number of part-time and occasional producers in the food and drink trades, and the rise of specialist professionals.

Thus adjustments to the new, and still uncertain, trading environment were slow and varied during the third quarter of the fourteenth century, hindered by the intervention of government and urban officials. Most towns struggled to overcome the dramatic contraction in aggregate levels of their staple trades, and the shift in the market for basic foodstuffs towards higher-quality bread and ale, and towards greater consumption of meat and dairy produce. Most towns were physically smaller. In 1365 Lincoln was suffering from a sharp decline in trade and its public streets were in a poor state through neglect.[5] Empty houses were gradually dismantled, leaving vacant plots in the less desirable locations, although some desirable plots were amalgamated and larger buildings constructed across them. A few towns, such as Hadleigh (Suffolk), seized the opportunities presented by the surge in demand for lower-grade woollen textiles, caused by the rising disposable incomes of ordinary people and lower prices for wool, to increase production and their size drastically. Others, such as Thaxted (Essex) slowly shifted production towards leather goods, clothing and household goods. Both developments encouraged immigration from villages and struggling towns into nascent manufacturing centres.

The high turnover of populations in urban and rural communities throughout Chaucer's lifetime created opportunities for social mobility, as Chris Given-Wilson shows in Chapter 38, and it also contributed to a general sense of *Wanderlust*: the population of England may have been halved, but a higher proportion of it was on the move, geographically and socially. Many used family connections to establish themselves in new places, although the plagues had reduced the density and range of such links, while others just tried their luck wherever opportunity knocked. Migrants and strangers everywhere sought to construct a network of personal and professional contacts, and to establish roots and a presence in their new locality. To aid the processes of socialisation and integration, communities adapted and developed existing institutions, of which the most important were the religious guild and the parish.

The foundation of religious guilds, each based on a parish church, increased during the second half of the fourteenth century, and the rise was especially pronounced in towns. By *c.* 1500 many rural parishes in Cambridgeshire contained one or two such confraternities, while the borough of Cambridge had over thirty, at least eight of which first appeared in the generation after the Black Death. The majority of these guilds possessed limited means – a little property, some livestock and petty cash – and their membership comprised ordinary men and women. Their primary objectives were to offer rudimentary insurance policies for death and disability, and to provide good fellowship, as the example of the Guild of the Nativity of St John the Baptist of Stow-cum-Quy (Cambridgeshire) reveals. This humble guild was founded in the 1350s, based on a side altar within the parish church, and its objectives were to provide a decent burial for every member, attended by the rest of the guild, to hasten the soul of the departed through purgatory and on to heaven; to provide poor relief to any member suffering 'indigence and poverty arising from any misfortune, and [who] cannot live honestly by his means'; and to raise money for the maintenance and improvement of the fabric of the parish church.[6]

Many rural guilds were open to all residents within the parish, while urban guilds tended to be more focused upon particular needs. Some encouraged the membership of young women or of entire households, while others catered for young journeymen. Beyond their religious dimension, urban guilds facilitated social integration to civic life by providing the chance to form friendships, to seek marriage partners, to find work and to acquire a degree of respectability. Guilds also promoted harmonious relations among members, and served as an effective means of resolving disputes between them. The importance of fellowship is evident from the inventories and activities of fifteenth-century guilds, which include donations and paraphernalia to support communal feasts and celebrations. The parish community supplemented such events with convivial fundraisers, in which bread and ale were sold to parishioners after church services with all profits to the parish chest. Thus the guild and the parish provided opportunities for networking, confraternity and conviviality within the context of religious observance and charitable works: a winning combination because it was socially and spiritually, individually and collectively, efficacious.

The settling of a new social order within rural and urban communities in the 1380s and 1390s did not necessarily mean that social relations within them were benign. In towns, access to urban office was becoming increasingly restricted to a smaller number of people, and the widening influence of narrowing oligarchies was often resented. In the countryside, newcomers with limited social capital held important local offices whose interests, and those of the emerging peasant elite, could be at odds with those of the labouring smallholders, mainly because they clashed over contracts of employment. So it would be wrong to equate the emergence of a new social order with social unity. However, social relations were more solid than they had been in the immediate post-plague era, and they incorporated new concepts of community, including the promotion of good relations between neighbours and the need to resolve disputes informally and amicably. Social commentators increasingly emphasised the noble qualities of labour rather than denouncing its vices. Chaucer's Ploughman in the *Canterbury Tales* may be seen as a simple but powerful model for labourers *and* the new peasant elite, both of whom were being encouraged to cooperate, to collaborate and to shoulder their wider social responsibilities.

NOTES

1 Bruce M. S. Campbell, 'Grain Yields on English Demesnes after the Black Death', in Mark Bailey and S. H. Rigby, eds., *Town and Countryside in the Age of the Black Death: Essays in Honour of John Hatcher* (Turnhout: Brepols, 2012), pp. 121–71 (pp. 150–1).
2 Peter L. Larson, *Conflict and Compromise in the Late Medieval Countryside* (London: Routledge, 2007), p. 181.
3 R. H. Britnell, 'The Black Death in English Towns', *Urban History*, 21 (1994), 195–210 (p. 201).
4 *Ibid.*, pp. 195–210.
5 J. W. F. Hill, *Medieval Lincoln* (Cambridge: Cambridge University Press, 1948), pp. 251–3.
6 J. P. C. Roach, ed., *Victoria County History of Cambridgeshire and the Isle of Ely*, Vol. III (London: Oxford University Press for the Institute of Historical Research, 1959), pp. 133–5; Virginia R. Bainbridge, *Gilds in the Medieval Countryside: Social and Religious Change in Cambridgeshire, c. 1350–1558* (Woodbridge: Boydell, 1996).

CHAPTER 43

London's Chaucer
A Psychogeography

John J. Thompson

Now have I toold you soothly, in a clause,
Th'estaat, th'array, the nombre, and eek the cause
Why that assembled was this compaignye
In Southwerk at this gentil hostelyre
That highte the Tabard, faste by the Belle.
(CT, I.715–19)

> I am haunted by a mythology of gates: as metaphors and as facts. Gates cut into the Wall's continuity, truces of going and coming: exchanges with the idea of outside, with the field and the garden. Instants of risk and betrayal, capture and farewell. Anticipations of journeys and pilgrimages.[1]

When examining the importance of the idea of London to a writer such as Chaucer, it is attractive to consider the general idea of the city being a palimpsest. The term is normally used in book history to describe a repurposed page from a wax tablet, manuscript or scroll that has had its original text scraped off and replaced with something fresh, but I am using it here in the sense in which Iain Sinclair deploys it. For Sinclair, twenty-first-century London offers an absorbing urban space, supporting many half-erased layers and repeated patterns relating to centuries of metropolitan human activity and achievement upon which fresh significances and new meanings can be added. And I think it is fair to follow the analogy of the city as palimpsest through to Chaucer since, in both the *Canterbury Tales* and *Troilus and Criseyde*, we get a sense of specific metropolitan environments set in a time and space contrived by the poet through a blend of different kinds of historical, biographical and literary juxtaposition, narrative patterning, erasures (or absences) and creative overlay. The poetic effect is pleasing and subtle, precisely because London, or Troy – or, sometimes perhaps, a distant view of London as *Troia Nova* – is never much more than an inviting but unfulfilled idea or prospect in the landscape of Chaucer's verse. Moreover, London's Chaucer offers the promise of a complex social and urban setting from which to explore not just the larger narrative development of the *Canterbury Tales* but also the repeated patterns of metropolitan activities that impose themselves on our understanding of the place of Chaucer and his achievement in late medieval and early modern book history.

London and its suburban environs enjoy their strongest geographical presence in the *Canterbury Tales*. Southwark, south of the river over London Bridge, is on the poet's itinerary in the *General Prologue*, for example, providing the metropolitan backdrop for Chaucer's account of 'th'estaat, th'array, the nombre, and eek the cause' that brought together his extraordinary band of tale-tellers as a 'compaignye' of Canterbury pilgrims (*CT*, I.716, 717). The Middle English term *compaignye* is a direct borrowing from the French *compaignie*, and had a range of meanings, including connotations of companionship or friendship based on sharing a common purpose. It is with this primary sense in mind that I frequently use the term in what follows below. *General Prologue*, line 716 also identifies a set of promisingly charged socio-political terms, suggestive of a potentially robust metropolitan attitude relating to issues of religion; dress; rank; and the rights, or otherwise, of different interest groups in the city and its suburbs, especially their licence to meet together in free and public assembly for whatever purpose they desire. These hint at the types of legal matters that have been examined in much recent modern historical research, particularly in relation to the contemporary understanding in Chaucer's day of the nature and threat presented by London's growing population and the city's flourishing underworld.[2] To the evident frustration of scholarly endeavours to implicate Chaucer's verse in this discussion, however, such topics provided Chaucer with a rich source of comedy for the pilgrim descriptions in the *General Prologue*: the joke is on us if we take his apparently nuanced but also fictive probing into character and motive too seriously. The suggestive juxtaposition of London and Southwark as the setting for the meeting together of the Canterbury pilgrims for the first time is similarly underplayed in the *General Prologue*. We are left with a sense that we are reading a poem set in and around London but with no clear idea of the poet's attitudes to some of the most pressing metropolitan concerns of his day regarding the wealth, status and privilege of citizens, visitors and newcomers in late medieval England's fastest-growing major urban sprawl.

On the other hand, we know from the surviving records that Chaucer had a metropolitan identity, linked with the city since birth and childhood, and, for much of his adult life, with his work at court through his service in the royal household. He was married to John of Gaunt's future sister-in-law, Philippa, sister of Katherine Swynford (Gaunt's third wife), and was also the beneficiary of a series of life annuities from the Lancastrian household.[3] As long-time controller of the wool custom in the port of London (1374–86), he was expected to spend considerable periods of time at the Wool Wharf, managing its business or transcribing legal documents. For this period, he was also granted the right to live rent-free in rooms over Aldgate. But his offices at court and in metropolitan public service undoubtedly overlapped also with his identity as a much-travelled English vernacular poet-translator. It was Chaucer who, as a result of his royal service in Italy, became known as the first English poet to imbibe the verse of Dante, Petrarch and Boccaccio, and make their cultural background and achievement fully part of his own.

His good fortune in this respect was not lost on contemporary London writers such as Thomas Usk, a clerk of the Goldsmiths' Livery company in Cheapside until the early 1380s. In his *Testament of Love* (*c.* 1387) Usk names Chaucer as the pre-eminent English poet of his day who 'passeth al other makers'; it is also Usk who has the God of Love describe Chaucer as 'the noble philosophical poete in Englissh'.[4] The lines are written in the knowledge that Chaucer had earlier bestowed the epithet 'philosophical' on his fellow poet Ralph Strode, to whom, jointly with John Gower, Chaucer dedicates *Troilus and Criseyde* (v.1856–7). Strode was also Common Sergeant at the London Guildhall (1373–82) and enjoyed the right to live rent-free in rooms over Aldersgate to the west during the same period that Chaucer enjoyed his Aldgate privileges in the east of the City. 'Moral' Gower, in turn, had lodgings south of the Thames within the priory of St Mary Overie in Southwark, not far from the geographical location of the Tabard Inn. In an early recension of *Confessio Amantis* he speaks of living in a land filled with Chaucer's verse, 'whereof to him in special / aboue alle other I am most holde'.[5] The mutuality and reciprocal exchange of such complimentary gestures offer evidence of 'th'estaat, th'array, the nombre, and eek the cause' of a select *compaignye* of London poets, thinkers and public servants, all of whom knew each other and were the begetters of the living European heritage of texts and genres that Chaucer is credited, in large part, with having transformed into an English poetical tradition.

The late-fourteenth-century metropolitan culture that granted Chaucer laureate status found a natural later home in the life of public service associated with the next generation of Chaucer admirers in fifteenth-century London and its environs. The London Chaucer legacy took on many different forms. We can see a striking example in the case of the poet Thomas Hoccleve. He was a clerk in the office of the Privy Seal associated with Westminster Hall from 1387 until about 1426. Hoccleve wrote about his London life and personal circumstances with much more autobiographical verisimilitude than any of his contemporaries. He tells us that he resided 'at Chestre Ynne, right fast be the Stronde' in the western suburbs of the city, presumably granted him as one of the perks for being part of another London *compaignye* of unmarried clerks in public service.[6] His residency there and his travel to or from Westminster Hall to his 'pore cote', or around the city on foot and on the river by boat, are documented in poems such as *La male regle*.[7] It may have coincided with the short period in 1399 when Chaucer spent his last year not far distant from roads habitually travelled by Hoccleve, in a house in the garden precinct of Westminster Abbey.

Hoccleve claims to have met the older poet and known him well but, whether this was true or not, the autobiographical register of much of his poetry allows him to play out the drama of a metropolitan life spent finding and enhancing one's own poetical voice along the lines already suggested by London's Chaucer. This is especially evident in Hoccleve's fond remembrance of the deceased laureate poet in the *Regiment of Princes*. Chaucer is characterised as the absent father-friend who engaged deeply with the professional and literary preoccupations that also marked the younger poet's career. Along with making provision for a visual representation (see Figure 1.1) of the dead poet to be inserted in the *Regiment*, Hoccleve takes on the role of quasi-legal petitioner on behalf of Chaucer in the court of heaven. He does so in a manner reminiscent of the witty adaptations of the metropolitan public voice found elsewhere in both his own petitionary verse and also that of Chaucer: in Chaucer's 'Envoys' to Bukton and Scogan, or his *Complaint to His Purse*, *Truth*, *Gentilesse* or *Lak of Stedfastnesse*. Because of the potentially overlapping *compaignye* of friends and professional metropolitan associates that both poets enjoyed, they were probably readily enough identified with such petitionary discourses precisely because they held responsible public office.

One would also like to think that they were widely known in their day-to-day life in London for their self-effacing wit, their acute observations of the human condition, their broad interests in near-contemporary European literature, the promise of their own vernacular and their good ear for English poetry.

In the years following his death in 1400 Chaucer's works also remained part of a living metropolitan literary culture, largely because of the efforts of his fifteenth-century copyists. Recent codicological research has emphasised the extent to which the transmission of London's Chaucer and its marketing alongside other vernacular literature in the capital and beyond its gates was largely dependent on the activities of scribes in the city of London, 'busy about the supply of reading matter for a coterie audience of civil servants and literary-minded gentry'.[8] These were often legal clerks working for the mayor, aldermen or sheriffs, servicing their courts while they were in session and also perhaps performing legal duties for the great London Livery companies. They were presumably also encouraged to undertake other more literary scribal commissions, such as London chronicle texts or the Middle English prose *Brut* versions, as time permitted and when opportunities arose. In other words, the making of an English past that glorified the city in which they lived and worked was often left in their hands. Such later reader-copyists have occasionally been imagined as particularly sensitive to the dynamics of reader response already present in Chaucer's verse, and it is assumed they sometimes paid particular attention to the clues he had left regarding the unfinished nature of his work. But the London Chaucer copyists were perhaps more pragmatic readers than this modern critical assessment suggests. Working in *compaignye*, they are known to have consulted the different Chaucer manuscript versions available to them as part of an editorial process that attempted to make good the apparently flawed textual fabric of their London textual inheritance. Such a process had probably already begun in Chaucer's lifetime, possibly with the task proceeding apace under the general guidance of different members of the dying poet's coterie.

The palaeographical identification of Adam Pinkhurst as Chaucer's own scribe and as a member of one such possibly closely-knit metropolitan *compaignye* has caused a flurry of excitement among Chaucer scholars.[9] Palaeography is not simply a forensic science but also a discipline whose findings remain susceptible to subjective critical judgement. It is fair to say at the time of writing that the scribal identification leading to Pinkhurst's identification is still not beyond question, so caution is required in building upon this detail. What is beyond dispute is that the hand attributed to Pinkhurst not only appears in the Hengwrt and Ellesmere manuscripts, the two earliest surviving *Canterbury Tales* copies, but is also identified as scribe B in the Cambridge, Trinity College, MS R.3.2 copy of John Gower's *Confessio Amantis*. This is a manuscript for which Thomas Hoccleve also completed a short stint, his contribution originally characterised by modern palaeographical scholarship as that of scribe E until its identification was confirmed as Hoccleve's by close palaeographical scrutiny of other autograph copies of his verse. Both copyists shared the task of transcribing Gower's verse with three other scribes, including scribe D, who undertook the bulk of the transcription. He has been tentatively identified as John

Marchaunt, clerk of the chamber or 'controller' of the City of London from 1380. Marchaunt was common clerk in the Guildhall until his retirement in 1417 when he was succeeded by John Carpenter. And Carpenter was the person to whom Hoccleve eventually dedicated a petitionary *ballade*, adding 'Master John Carpenter' to his title over an erasure – a palimpsest – in the holograph copy for this short poem now extant only in San Marino, Huntington Library, MS HM 111. The London Guildhall precinct is as likely a place as any in which to assume that much of the scribal activity associated with establishing the fifteenth-century Chaucer tradition took place; however, the trajectory of literary interest in English poetics among those who revered both the city of London and its laureate poet extended far beyond these confines. It must have taken in the many routes leading from Westminster into and around the City, including the gateways, workplaces, hostels and taverns sometimes mentioned in Hoccleve's verse, presumably also often used as familiar journey markers for metropolitan itineraries planned by the poet and other likeminded associates.

The advent of metropolitan printing with movable type brought a new technological dynamic to the task of securing the body of Chaucer's work for the City of London. Chaucer's first printer was also the father of English printing, William Caxton. He was a mercer by trade who had served his apprenticeship in London before moving to Bruges in the service of the English 'nation' of Merchant Adventurers. In 1471 Caxton then travelled to Cologne, where he learnt the art of printing. In September 1476 he set up his first printing shop in the precincts of Westminster Abbey, not far from the place where the long-dead Father of English Poetry had ended his days. Between 1477 and 1483 Caxton then produced seven Chaucer prints (work that was not completed without difficulty), including two editions of the *Canterbury Tales* (1478 and 1483), the *Parliament of Fowls* (1477 or 1478?), *Boece* (1478), the *House of Fame* (1483) and *Troilus and Criseyde* (1483).

Caxton's second edition of the *Canterbury Tales* includes a preface explaining his anxiety to get things right; he reports that a gentleman reader had complained of his first edition that 'this book was not accordyng in many places vnto the book that Gefferey chaucer had made / To whom I answerd that I had made it accordyng to my copy'.[10] His comments in 1483 show some prescience, since Caxton was describing an issue that was to preoccupy many later London printers of Chaucer's works, who variously tried to make good the fragmentary and incomplete nature of the *Canterbury Tales* and other apparent gaps in the rapidly expanding Chaucer canon. Some of their efforts in this respect drew the derision of other later Chaucer editors but also created the space for them to make their own selections of material from the manuscripts available to them or to insert their own often spurious additions. Much was gleaned by Caxton's sixteenth-century successors, such as William Thynne, John Stow and Thomas Speght, from their reports to each other of the investigations that proceeded as important early manuscript collections containing works attributed to Chaucer or associated with his verse came to their attention.[11]

The example of Speght's editorial interactions with Stow for both his 1598 and 1602 Chaucer editions is particularly instructive, since it shows how both London printers worked closely together (in *compaignye*) to secure and promote the idea that Chaucer's verse lived on in recognisably classical form for a new generation of early modern readers. Speght's 1598 edition offers readers 'The Workes of our Antient and Learned / English Poet, Geffrey Chavcer', with the new additions promised on the title page including 'His [Chaucer's] Portraiture and Progenie shewed … His Life Collected'. In effect, Speght is here printing the first biography of the London vintner's son who became the Father of English Poetry. From Speght's own comments in 1598 and 1602, it is clear that it was Stow, the London Merchant Tailor, who had better knowledge of the details of Chaucer's life and better manuscript access to some of the best or only extant texts of works ascribed to Chaucer, especially those few he authenticated that had hitherto failed to enter the printed canon, such as 'Chauciers wordes a Geffrey vnto Adame his owen scryveyne' (added in Stow's 1561 edition), or the 'ABC to the Virgin' (added in Speght's 1602 edition).[12]

The idea of London's Chaucer having a psychogeography comes to fruition in John Stow's works. Like his fifteenth-century scribal predecessors, he keenly felt a responsibility for the making of the English past in the immense shadow of the city in which he lived and through which he had walked for over sixty years, even as the world he had grown up in was apparently slipping away. Stow responded in various ways to the imperative to preserve a public record of metropolitan literary, architectural and historical achievement. On the one hand, he did so by reconstructing a version of Chaucer's life and canon, while, on the other, he became the most prolific (and probably most derided) writer of chronicles and annals and other histories of his age. But, of course, Stow is best remembered for his topographical *Survey of London*, written in the year 1598 and based on a series of nostalgic itineraries that took him to every ward in the city; to the metropolitan centres of power and influence, the great Livery companies, the churches, hospitals and lazar houses; to the gates of the city and beyond; to Westminster Abbey and its precincts; and to Westminster Hall, along the Strand and past hostels and taverns. We find him in the borough of Southwark on his journey home towards London Bridge, on an itinerary marked by a multitude of tavern signs – 'the Spurre, Christopher, Bull, Queenes head, Tabarde, George, Hart, Kinges Head, &c'.[13] It is, of course, the Tabard that captures his attention as the oldest of these inns. Having explained the origin of 'tabarde' as an item of clothing once worn by the nobility during wartime but now only worn by heralds, he proceeds to quote his version of lines 19–29 of the *General Prologue*. These lines belong to the ventriloquised 'I' voice of Chaucer the pilgrim in the fiction of the *Canterbury Tales*, but at this moment in the *Survey of London* they surely also belong simultaneously to Stow, acting in his capacity as the sixteenth-century chronicler of London's Chaucer.

NOTES

1 Iain Sinclair, *Lights Out for the Territory* (London: Penguin, 2003), p. 102.

2 Frank Rexroth, *Deviance and Power in Late Medieval London* (Cambridge: Cambridge University Press, 2007).

3 *L-R.*

4 Thomas Usk, *Testament of Love*; for its place in the panoply of contemporary metropolitan praise for the poet see Derek Brewer, ed., *Chaucer: The Critical Heritage*, 2 vols. (London: Routledge and Kegan Paul, 1978), Vol. 1, p. 43.

5 *Ibid.*, p. 43.

6 Thomas Hoccleve, *Regiment of Princes*, line 5; conveniently extracted in Derek Pearsall, ed., *Chaucer to Spenser: An Anthology* (Oxford: Blackwell, 1999), pp. 322–34.

7 *Ibid.*, pp. 319–22.

8 Jane Roberts, 'On Giving Scribe B a Name and a Clutch of London Manuscripts from *c.* 1400', *Medium Ævum*, 80 (2011), 247–70 (p. 252).

9 Linne R. Mooney, 'Chaucer's Scribe', *Speculum*, 81 (2006), 97–138, with much further development of the Pinkhurst identification and that of his London Guildhall Chaucer *compaignye* in Linne R. Mooney and Estelle Stubbs, *Scribes and the City: London Guildhall Clerks and the Dissemination of Middle English Literature, 1375–1425* (Woodbridge: York Medieval Press, 2013).

10 William Caxton, *The Prologues and Epilogues of William Caxton*, ed. Walter John Blythe Crotch, EETS os 176 (London: Milford, 1928), pp. 90–1.

11 Paul G. Ruggiers, ed., *Editing Chaucer: The Great Tradition* (Norman, OK: Pilgrim Books, 1984).

12 Geoffrey Chaucer, *The Workes of Geffrey Chaucer … with Divers Addicions*, ed. John Stow (London, 1561); Geoffrey Chaucer, *The Workes of Our Antient and Lerned English Poet, G. Chaucer*, ed. Thomas Speght (London, 1602).

13 John Stow, *A Survey of London*, introd. C. L. Kingsford, 2 vols. (Oxford: Clarendon Press, 1908), Vol. II, p. 62.

CHAPTER 44

Everyday Life

Wendy Childs

Material surroundings and the structure of daily life in Chaucer's England varied widely according to rank, wealth, occupation, location and gender. For brevity, this chapter focuses on the everyday life of urban groups from which Chaucer drew some of his Canterbury pilgrims, especially the Merchant, the craftsmen and the Shipman, which offer examples of rich, modest and poorer folk.

I

No merchant housing in the late fourteenth century could approach the scale of the urban palaces of nobles and bishops. Nonetheless, the better urban houses, especially in London, were by this time symbols of affluence and centres of increasing comfort. Wealthy merchants (with estates perhaps worth £1,000 and business turnovers of several hundreds of pounds, on a par with knights and some barons) had large houses, often set round courtyards with space for stables and store-rooms, and possibly their own brew-houses and ovens. Many were of stone or part stone, as towns, including London, required chimneys and roofs to be of stone or tile to decrease fire risks. Such houses might still have a great hall with a central hearth, but would also have multiple rooms for living and sleeping, some of which by now had fireplaces against the walls. Richer merchants probably had separate counting houses for themselves and their clerks, and the largest houses would also have gardens and orchards. Lesser merchants and craftsmen, with incomes ranging down to £20 or £10 a year, would be more likely to hold long, narrow burgage plots, with a shop and workshop in front and multiple rooms upstairs or further back for living space, more work space and stores. Servants and journeymen earning perhaps £2 a year lived in their masters' houses. Poorer townsmen could rent a room or two in buildings of multiple occupancy.

Furnishings also reflected wealth. The best piece of furniture was normally a great bed. For the wealthiest it would be four-posted and canopied with a full set of matching curtains and coverlet, linen sheets, feather mattresses and pillows. The less well-off had simple frame-beds with a rope lattice to keep bedding off the ground, or possibly built-in cupboard beds. The poor might have simply a straw mattress on the floor, and lesser servants and stable boys would sleep wherever they could find space. Dressers to display plates were only for the rich; others used simple open shelves for utensils. Chests (elaborately decorated for the wealthy) were used for storage by all ranks. Warmth and colour could be given to rooms with wall hangings (tapestries, woven textiles or 'painted cloth'). Benches and stools were more usual than chairs in modest houses, and permanent tables were relatively few, since rooms were used for multiple purposes. Trestles set up for meals were easily removed afterwards.

People at all levels of society normally ate two meals a day: dinner around noon and a lighter supper some time before bed. Breakfast was not a formal meal and food taken then would have been eaten informally, 'on the hoof', before the day's work. A formal dinner in the richer households normally had one or two 'courses' each of several dishes, but supper was simpler and might be simply leftovers. Serving dishes in the houses of rich townsmen might be of silver and pewter, but many used pottery or wood. Food was often eaten off trenchers of bread, but platters of wood and earthenware increased at the end of the Middle Ages. For those who did not have large kitchens with roasting hearths, much food was cooked in pots as soups and stews, or in oven-baked pies. Pies of varying qualities could be bought from professional cooks, such as Chaucer's pilgrim. Eating was done with knife, spoon and fingers. Knives were generally personal items and not provided by the host. Hygiene etiquette demanded that knives used to spear meat from communal bowls should not be put in the mouth, and hand-washing was encouraged wherever fingers were to be put into communal dishes.

Food was reasonably plentiful in late-fourteenth-century England, and City authorities were keen to ensure sufficient supplies of reasonable quality and price. Weights and measures were checked; forestalling the market and hoarding were strictly forbidden, as was the adulteration of food (such as the addition of chalk to bread flour, or the addition of colouring and resins to old wine). Thus the urban housewife or her servants would find plenty of meat, poultry, fish (fresh, dried and smoked), dairy products and commercially produced bread available in markets, shops, and from street hawkers. Richer families would certainly be able to afford additional imported luxuries, such as dried figs and raisins, sugar, saffron, and spices. Ale was by far the most widely used beverage. Water was suspect in the crowded and unhygienic urban conditions, and milk was considered suitable only for children and the sick. Ale stayed in good condition for not much more than a week, so was regularly brewed by professional brewers or at home and, retailing at around 1d. or less per gallon, was in everyone's range. Wine was also plentiful. Most was imported from Gascony, England's French dominion, but smaller amounts came from Spain, Portugal, La Rochelle and the Rhineland. It was more expensive, retailing in taverns at about 6s. 8d. a gallon, but was still within range for occasional drinking by the moderately well-off merchant and craftsman. Sweet wines (malmsey, romney, bastard and others) from the Mediterranean and Iberia were more expensive still and remained a drink for the rich.

Clothing also varied according to rank and wealth. Few townsmen or their wives would wear luxurious Italian fabrics. These were mainly for the very rich, but could be used in great civic processions. Most people wore woollen cloth, which was available in many qualities and prices, from the finest coloured broadcloth to the poorest undyed homespun. Fashions in clothing began to change more quickly in the fourteenth century, and moralists decried the extremes of ever-lower necklines for women, long-piked shoes and figure-hugging, bum-freezer doublets for men. These were popular at court, but townsfolk dressed more plainly, even if still colourfully. Women wore long gowns and kerchiefs of varying elaboration on their heads. Men wore knee- or calf-length gowns that allowed easy movement for riding and walking, and most men of standing wore hats; those of lower ranks wore hoods. Underclothing, essential because heavy wool was difficult to wash regularly, was made from fine linen or coarse hemp fabrics according to wealth. Furs and sheepskin provided extra warmth, and leather provided the best protection against rain. Shoes and boots were of leather, laced or buckled, and wooden patens would raise the wearer above the mud in streets and courtyards. Merchants who were comfortably off and their wives could show taste and wealth not only through clothing, but also through accessories: belts, buckles, buttons, hairpins and jewellery. People carried purses, pouches for personal seals, and small scabbards with table knives hanging from their belts. When travelling, men normally carried weapons, as did Chaucer's Shipman in the *Canterbury Tales*. Travel outside the town might be for business or to visit distant families or to make a pilgrimage. Although inns might not be comfortable, and winter travelling could be difficult, roads were not too bad in good weather (they were certainly good enough to sustain large numbers of carts and pack-horses for long-distance bulk trade in wool, cloth, wine and victuals), and once 'sweet April' arrived journeys might become a pleasure. People normally travelled in groups for protection and mainly on foot or horse (ladies increasingly riding side-saddle, but some still riding astride, like the Wife of Bath in the Ellesmere miniature). Carts were primarily for goods and only the very rich had carriages. Distances covered in a day depended on weather, terrain and the mix of the group. Walkers and riders together probably covered no more than 15 miles, but a group of riders might easily cover 20, and those in haste, regularly changing horses, could cover over 40 miles a day.

Health was a constant problem in towns. Infectious diseases spread easily and plague became endemic after 1348. Hygiene was encouraged by the washing of hands before meals, the preference for ale and wine, and urban ordinances controlling the disposal of garbage. Water was available from wells and occasionally through conduits, and could be delivered to houses by water-carriers. Many houses had internal latrines that emptied into cesspits, which were regularly emptied by 'gongfermers', but human waste in densely populated towns was always a problem. Inadequately lined pits leaked into neighbouring cellars, and waste could contaminate wells. Bathing was probably more frequent than once thought. The rich could bathe in privacy with servants bringing plenty of hot water; others could go to public baths, some of which were respectable, although often they became centres of prostitution and thus out of bounds for respectable women. Fine soap was imported from Castile, teeth were cleaned with twigs and cloths, and for much of the Middle Ages it was fashionable for men to be clean-shaven. Despite efforts at cleanliness, the smell of privies, body odour, cooking, smoke, rotting floor rushes, garbage and animals must have nearly always exceeded the sweeter smells of flowers, herbs and spices in bouquets and pomanders.

Surviving children in well-off households had a comfortable childhood with toys and freedom to play, but childhood was short by modern standards. By the age of seven those who were to be educated would start their schooling, and by the age of twelve childhood was over for most; they became increasingly engaged in the family business and household duties or became servants or apprentices outside the family. Those in commercial occupations benefited if they were to some degree literate. Children learnt their numbers and letters at home or in schools or during their apprenticeships. Some learnt to write as well as to read. Many merchants learnt the languages of the countries they dealt with when they were factors and junior partners. Merchants and some craftsmen acquired enough Latin to deal with formal accounts, legal matters (the contracts and lawsuits that inevitably accompanied business) and administrative duties that required Latin records. They could employ clerks and scribes to read and write for them but it was without doubt better to be able to read contracts and letters and to keep accounts oneself. Readers might also get pleasure from books, but for most urban families reading matter outside business was the prayer book; books were expensive, and frivolous works (such as romances) rarely appear in urban wills.

Early marriage was relatively rare in urban families. Young men had to establish enough wealth to support a family, and young women either learnt the skills of household management at home or, working outside the family, earned money to contribute to a new household. Once married, urban women often played a full part in their husbands' businesses. They might be expected to run these while husbands were away, and to continue them as widows. Married women could carry on working independently as *femmes soles*, and this independent employment was probably essential in poorer families.

II

The structure of the day varied considerably according to rank and occupation but everyone depended much more on the seasons and the length of daylight than people do today. Telling the time was done by the passage of the sun combined with the tolling of monastic church bells for timed services. By the end of the fourteenth century some people would also hear the chimes of mechanical clocks, set up on secular buildings as well as in the great churches. Most people rose at dawn and retired soon after dusk. Moving around outside after dark was difficult without servants to carry torches, and in towns movement was also discouraged by urban curfews. A further major limitation to nightlife was the expense of lighting. Richer people who could afford plenty of candles and torches could extend their day as long as they liked, but the poorest families managed by firelight and perhaps a single candle or oil lamp and retired early. The best wax candles, held on a 'pricket', or spike, until the fifteenth century when socket candlesticks began to appear, lasted for hours, but they were three or four times more expensive than tallow candles, which smoked, smelt, burnt dimly and needed constant trimming. Rush lights (rushes dipped in tallow and held by a clip) were cheaper still, but probably lasted no longer than half an hour. Even with good candles, light at night was never as good as daylight, and craftsmen were forbidden from night working by their guilds because the quality of work done then was less good.

The day began in the houses of the better-off merchants and craftsmen with the servants stirring up the fire, preparing washing facilities, helping with dressing and providing simple food for breakfast. A prosperous merchant who had often travelled when young and who might still make an occasional journey abroad to keep in touch with markets, customers and agents, could now run his business from home. Such a man might spend all or part of the day in his counting house (perhaps with his clerk) on 'paperwork': drawing up accounts, checking contracts, writing letters and dictating instructions to his factors abroad. He might also spend time in his store-rooms checking goods and showing them to prospective buyers. His wife would run the household and servants, supervising the marketing, preserving, brewing, baking, and laundering and repair of the house textiles. She would also care for the health and early education of the children. The merchant had plenty of business outside the house too. He might walk through the London streets (some paved, others no more than muddy lanes) to the city's wharves to check shipping arrangements, customs payments and the loading of his goods if he dealt overseas, or perhaps to a tavern to meet customers or to grumble with friends about the high war taxes of Richard's reign that brought so little success in France or Spain. He might need to attend the Mayor's court or the central courts at Westminster (for merchants were bound at some time to be caught up in lawsuits). He would also take part in public activities. The wealthiest merchants became mayors, aldermen and sheriffs, and became heavily involved with City administration and politics. They might also become office-holders within their companies or in charitable fraternities, and they would be expected to play a full part in parish affairs. Although the Church demanded that parishioners take communion only once a year, it encouraged frequent attendance and, moreover, the parish was the social and charitable centre for the local community. Parishioners gave time and money for such things as the maintenance of the church fabric, parish charities and bequests for the poor. Finally, at the end of the day, at curfew, as the city gates were shut and dusk fell, the merchant would return home to his family, a light supper, perhaps some talk and leisure by candlelight, and bed.

The lives of craftsmen had a more circumscribed routine than those of merchants. They needed to spend more time within their workshops producing goods for their livelihoods. On most days the families would similarly rise early, take an informal breakfast, work at their craft with apprentices until midday and dinner, work again until the light was gone, take a simple supper, and soon go to bed. But craftsmen too had outside interests. They needed to source their raw materials, and they also took part in the administration of their craft guilds, in parish life and in religious fraternities. Office-holding within these institutions brought responsibilities but also prestige, as Chaucer shows with the five aspiring craftsmen in the *Canterbury Tales*.

The Shipman, of course, led a much less predictable life. Whether he worked in coastal trade, fishing or overseas trade, much of his time was spent away from home. He could be away days, weeks or months. A short trip across the North Sea to the Low Countries could take days, but might take weeks as he waited in port for favourable winds and then for his ship to unload and reload (charter-parties normally allowed about thirty days for turnaround times). Voyages to the Baltic, Bordeaux or Iberia meant absences of perhaps three or four months. Seamen (already reputed to have a girl in every port) probably remained unmarried when young and lived when they came home with parents or siblings or in temporary lodgings or rooms in inns. Those who prospered by a little trading might afford to marry and rent a room or two, especially if wives continued to work independently. A master, especially if he was part-owner of his vessel, became financially secure, but the sea was always a risky occupation and maritime families could be flung on to fraternity or parish charity at any time.

Greater per capita money supply and the scarcity of labour after the Black Death, together with visibly increasing commercialisation and consumerism in the period, brought the possibility of greater material comfort to many, but nonetheless everyday life in both material possessions and daily structure still varied widely according to wealth and occupation, even within the urban population.

CHAPTER 45

Household and Home

Peter Fleming

The word 'household' appeared in Middle English, as *hous(e)hold*, in the later fourteenth century, when it could mean both the group of people who habitually shared the same physical space – who were co-resident – and that physical space itself, together with the material possessions it contained. While a thing may exist long before the word that signifies it comes into existence, in this case the appearance of 'household' probably reflects a deepening sense that this 'private' domestic space is different from the 'public' space beyond its walls. This new sense of the distinctiveness of the domestic was, it has been suggested, particularly clearly articulated and realised among the lay urban elite, the *burgeiserie*, a word closely related to the modern 'bourgeoisie': in other words the burgess class of merchants and wealthier craftsmen who exercised economic and political mastery over their less-favoured fellow town-dwellers – sometimes the majority.

Chaucer's own family came from such a background, and it was probably from within this milieu that most members of his early audience were drawn.[1] Chaucer was the poet of this nascent bourgeois culture, and the household was one of the crucial arenas in which it was embodied, displayed and performed. This same culture, with its ideals and modes of behaviour, has established itself as the norm within western capitalist society. This chapter concentrates on the urban bourgeois household, the one with which Chaucer would have been most familiar, but does not ignore the domestic arrangements of those above and below this level in the socio-economic hierarchy of later-fourteenth-century England, both urban and rural.

Closely tied to notions of the 'household' were those of 'home' and 'family'. In Chaucer's England 'home' and 'homely' denoted 'familiarity, friendship, nurturing and intimacy', and were closely associated with notions of Christ's meekness and simplicity; indeed, religion played a crucial role in the genesis and evolution of all three terms.[2] Of these, 'family' is perhaps the word whose modern meaning is most distant from its origins. In contemporary western society 'family' can usually be defined as a cohabiting group of close kin, or unmarried cohabiting partners and their children. By contrast, for Chaucer and his contemporaries such a mode of living was expected only among the poor (but who, it must be remembered, formed the majority of the population). For wealthier members of the laity, the household invariably included servants and, often, apprentices. These lived with the cohabiting kin-group, a clumsy phrase made necessary by English's lack of an equivalent to 'family' before the fifteenth century, the closest parallel being the Latin *familia*, which, perhaps significantly, means 'household', in the sense both of cohabiting kin-group and of servants and apprentices.[3]

As in any age before our own, when machines have effectively taken their place, servants were essential to comfortable living. Chaucer's peers were yet to develop that notorious Victorian and Edwardian unease among their servants. Rather, it was a life unattended that presented the truly disquieting prospect. To contemporaries, the knowledge that Nicholas, the student in the *Miller's Tale*, lived in his single room 'Allone, withouten any compaignye' (*CT*, I.3203–4), or that the 'povre wydwe' in the *Nun's Priest's Tale* lived in a 'narwe cotage' accompanied only by 'hir doghtren two' (VII.2822–9), would immediately have identified them as occupying a disadvantaged socio-economic position.

Most servants were in their teens or early twenties, and served a succession of masters for a year at a time. The difference between servants and apprentices was essentially that the latter were contracted to serve in return for training in their master's particular craft. Service or apprenticeship was part of the life-cycle of many, perhaps most, of the male laity. Most rural servants were male, as were apprentices, but in towns it is probably the case that more young women were employed as domestic servants. Service and apprenticeships were among the most important means by which towns attracted new blood. While most people did not travel long distances in one journey, cities and large towns such as London, Norwich, York and Bristol attracted servants and apprentices from a wide region, reflecting family and business links and the ease or otherwise of travel. For young country people making their first acquaintance with a big city in this way, their first few months must often have been both exciting and bewildering. Their masters acted *in loco parentis* towards them, and their moral health would often have been of great concern.[4]

The presence of servants and apprentices aside, households in Chaucer's England were generally of a similar size and composition to their modern counterparts: an 'average' family (a description that, of course, hides considerable variations), might consist of husband and wife (separated in age by only a few years), and perhaps two to four children surviving beyond infancy, while first marriages tended to be contracted when the couple were in their early-to-mid twenties, and lasted, on average, less than twenty-five years. However, the reasons for the prevalence of this modern-looking 'nuclear' family are very different from those determining modern families. In very general terms, the same results today achieved through contraception, abortion and divorce were produced in Chaucer's day through death. Infant mortality was terrifyingly high: even among the nobility, around one-third of all babies did not survive their first five years. Life expectancy from birth was accordingly very low, but those who survived childhood could expect to live into their late forties or early fifties. To high infant mortality was joined relatively low fertility for most mothers, although better diets and the employment of wet nurses (thereby reducing the impact of lactation) meant that the elite probably enjoyed higher average fertility rates. For most people, marriage had to wait until they were able to establish a new, separate household. For eldest sons, this was often achieved through inheriting the deceased father's estate. Marriage was generally forbidden to servants or apprentices, which also delayed the age at which a family could be started.[5]

Ideally, the married couple constituted a companionate partnership, but this was not to be a partnership of equals. Men, as fathers, husbands and masters, were expected to exert discipline over their children, wives and servants, and not to spare the rod if necessary. Indeed, if inflicted within such 'legitimate' household contexts, physical abuse had to be practically life-threatening before the perpetrator could be prosecuted. While Prudence exerts a benign influence over her husband in *Melibee*, she is still careful to refer to him as her lord, while in the *Franklin's Tale*, arguably, it is the surrender of his mastery over Dorigen, his wife, by Arveragus that plunges the couple into near catastrophe, when in his absence she enters into an unwise bargain with Aurelius.[6]

The wife's role in the 'family business' varied, naturally, depending on circumstances. Lower-rank women living in the countryside – 'peasants' – were expected to attend to the cottage garden, chickens and pigs, as well as the domestic chores, while their husbands laboured in the fields. Spinning was also a near-universal household activity for women. Wives of gentry and noble husbands supervised the servants, but could also involve themselves in such 'masculine' concerns as the political, marital and economic management of the family affairs, particularly if their husband was away or otherwise incapacitated. Among those below the elites, food preparation was a traditional part of the wife's domestic labour, and in some cases, particularly in relation to ale-brewing, produce that exceeded the requirements of the household was sold, thereby involving her in marketing and retail activities. Both in towns and villages, within the households of craftsmen, artisans and merchants, wives would play an important role in helping to run the business. Production of manufactured goods typically took place in the workshop, part of the family home, and hence there was no room for the development of the 'separate spheres' associated with the 'industrial revolution', whereby the male breadwinner went out to work, leaving the woman within the home. Usually, the full extent of female participation is obscured by the legal assumption that she was subsumed into the identity of her husband, so that only his name appears on most legal documents, including business contracts. There are exceptions, however. In some towns and cities, London among them, wives could register as *femme sole*, thereby allowing them to trade in their own right, but all the time with their husbands' permission. The number of wills made by wives whose husbands are still alive is tiny (for one thing, since married women could not own movable property, the scope of such wills ought to have been severely limited), but they do exist, although they always include the assurance that they were made with the husbands' permission. Among the most telling of these exceptions is the appearance of the wife's name on apprentice contracts, whereby both she and her husband record agreed terms with the family or guardian of an apprentice they have taken on. The expectation that wives would participate in the apprentice's training was not restricted to socialisation, instruction in etiquette and general education, as is shown by frequent instances of widows carrying on the craft training of apprentices after their husband's death. Bourgeois husbands usually appointed their wives as the executors of their wills, demonstrating their confidence in them as dependable people who knew the family business well, and could be relied upon to conclude their affairs effectively. Some widows went further, and carried on their husbands' trade long after his death. All of this evidence demonstrates that marriages within such milieux were usually real business partnerships, with the wife fully engaged in her husbands' affairs, admittedly as the junior partner. As such, we may see these craft, artisanal and mercantile households as being considerably less gendered, in terms of the distribution of work and responsibility, than those of the rural masses and the landed elite. Typically, these households occupied timber-framed structures of several storeys, with a workshop/shop on the ground floor and accommodation above, and stables, outhouses and warehouses in the yard behind. The more substantial contained a hall, whose function was probably at least as much symbolic – denoting authority and prestige, on the pattern of gentry and noble great halls – as practical.[7]

Above the 'middle-classes', among the gentry and nobility, households were highly gendered and highly structured. The households of great magnates contained between 60 and 700 people, but the average for lesser landowners was in double figures: for knights, a figure of around 20, or fewer, would be common. These households were divided: not just 'above' and 'below stairs', into those servants who attended the lord personally and those menial servants who provided domestic labour, but also between the 'great household' – the permanent establishment in the lord's main residence – and the 'riding household', which accompanied him on his travels. Among the latter's functions was to impress and overawe, and, at times, to act as a bodyguard; and so men, if possible of an impressive physique, were chosen to ride with the lord: in the fifteenth century, they would often be referred to as the 'tall men'. To enhance the visual impact of the noble household, servants were increasingly provided with livery, in the form of either a badge or a matching set of clothes. The semi-military nature of noble households is one reason why women were few and far between: the personal entourage of the lady of the house apart, these were overwhelmingly masculine environments. Typically, noble households were divided into four departments: the pantry, responsible for bread and table linen; the buttery, responsible for wine and ale; the kitchen, overseeing food preparation; and the marshalsea, dealing primarily with the horses, but with a wider responsibility over a range of other household matters. The senior officers presiding over this structure were the steward, in overall control; the wardrober, looking after the family's clothes and personal effects; a marshal, looking after the stables and dogs; and a treasurer, or financial controller. There would also have been at least one family chaplain. Below them were a varied host of lesser servants, from pantlers and butlers (working in the pantry and buttery respectively) down to laundresses and their assistants, who were usually the only female menial servants.

An average day in the noble household was as carefully structured as the household itself. The chief officers and catering staff would rise between four and seven in the morning (depending on the season) to open the gates, prepare fires and food, and cast the daily accounts. Matins would also be heard first thing. Breakfast was then taken, but only by the family and senior servants: it was a mark of seniority, and so everyone else had to wait until lunch/dinner (*prandium*), usually taken by midday, for any kind of substantial meal. Around 3 p.m. evensong was heard, followed by supper/dinner (*cena*). Bedtime was between 8 and 10 p.m., depending on the season. Food would have been plentiful, with large amounts of animal protein and spices, both regarded as status symbols. Meals could be very formal occasions, with strict etiquette and ceremonial. In the fourteenth century there was an increasing tendency for the family to distance itself from the rest of the household. This growing appreciation of privacy is reflected in the architecture of great houses and castles. The traditional arrangement of domestic space centred on the great hall: a long room, open to the roof, with a screened passage crossing it at one end and connecting to a door on either side, off which led the pantry, buttery and, beyond a short corridor, the kitchen. The hall was once the focus of nearly all household activity, being not only the place where food was eaten, but also where the household slept. By Chaucer's time these functions were being taken into separate rooms: the family slept in their own bedchambers and lived in private suites made up of parlours and withdrawing rooms, while servants might also be provided with their own sleeping accommodation. The hall remained important, but was increasingly reserved for large-scale ceremonial banquets or, conversely, became the servants' mess-hall. The extent to which bourgeois households borrowed, in a scaled-down form, from these aristocratic exempla is debated, but in a period of considerable social fluidity, it is likely that there was at least some aping of their social superiors by the mercantile and artisanal elites.[8]

At the other extreme in the socio-economic hierarchy, discounting those homeless whose numbers and living conditions are almost unknowable, many, both individuals and families, both in town and countryside, lived in one room. For them there could have been little opportunity to structure time or space, since sleeping, working and childcare were confined to one place. Many of the humblest rooms lacked hearths, and so cooking was impossible, with the result that their inhabitants were dependent on 'fast food' shops, which were very common in urban areas. Often these single rooms would be rented as part of a larger house occupied by a more substantial household, as was the case with Chaucer's Nicholas, who rented his chamber in the 'hostelrye' of a wealthy carpenter (1.3187–203).[9]

NOTES

1 These two paragraphs draw on P. J. P. Goldberg and Maryanne Kowaleski, 'Introduction. Medieval Domesticity: Home, Housing and Household', in P. J. P. Goldberg and Maryanne Kowaleski, eds., *Medieval Domesticity: Home,*

Housing and Household in Medieval England (Cambridge: Cambridge University Press, 2008), pp. 1–13; Felicity Riddy, '"Burgeis" Domesticity in Late-Medieval England', in *ibid.*, pp. 14–36; and P. J. P. Goldberg, 'The Fashioning of Bourgeois Domesticity in Later Medieval England: A Material Culture Perspective', in *ibid.*, pp. 124–44.

2 Goldberg and Kowaleski, 'Introduction', p. 1.

3 David Herlihy, 'Family', *American Historical Review*, 96 (1991), 1–16.

4 P. J. P. Goldberg, 'Marriage, Migration and Servanthood: The York Cause Paper Evidence', in P. J. P. Goldberg, ed., *Woman Is a Worthy Wight* (Stroud: Sutton, 1992), pp. 1–18; P. J. P. Goldberg, *Women, Work and Life-Cycle in a Medieval Economy: Women in York and Yorkshire, c. 1300–1520* (Oxford: Clarendon Press, 1992), pp. 158–202.

5 Generally forbidden, but not entirely so: Philippa C. Maddern, '"In myn own house": The Troubled Connections between Servant Marriages, Late-Medieval English Household Communities and Early Modern Historiography', in Stephanie Tarbin and Susan Broomhall, eds., *Women, Identities and Communities in Early Modern Europe* (Aldershot: Ashgate, 2008), pp. 45–60. This and the following paragraph are based on Peter Fleming, *Family and Household in Medieval England* (Houndmills: Palgrave, 2001), p. 20. A comprehensive discussion of marriage in medieval England is provided by Conor McCarthy, *Marriage in Medieval England: Law, Literature, and Practice* (Woodbridge: Boydell Press, 2004).

6 Barbara Hanawalt, *The Ties that Bound: Peasant Families in Medieval England* (Oxford: Oxford University Press, 1986), pp. 182–3, 206, 214; Christopher N. L. Brooke, *The Medieval Idea of Marriage* (Oxford: Clarendon Press, 1989), pp. 29–30. This aspect of the *Franklin's Tale* is discussed in McCarthy, *Marriage in Medieval England*, pp. 102–6.

7 Christopher Dyer, *Standards of Living in the Later Middle Ages* (Cambridge: Cambridge University Press, 1989), pp. 114–18, 132–3; Jennifer Ward, 'Townswomen and Their Households', in Richard Britnell, ed., *Daily Life in the Late Middle Ages* (Stroud: Sutton, 1998), pp. 27–42; P. J. P. Goldberg, *Medieval England: A Social History, 1250–1550* (London: Hodder Arnold, 2004), pp. 100–13.

8 For this and the previous paragraph, see Kate Mertes, *The English Noble Household, 1250–1600: Good Governance and Politic Rule* (Oxford: Basil Blackwell, 1988); C. M. Woolgar, *The Great Household in Late Medieval England* (New Haven, CT: Yale University Press, 1999); Mark Gardiner, 'Buttery and Pantry and their Antecedents: Idea and Architecture in the English Medieval House', in Goldberg and Kowaleski, *Medieval Domesticity*, pp. 37–65.

9 Jane Grenville, 'Urban and Rural Houses and Households in the Late Middle Ages: A Case Study from Yorkshire', in Goldberg and Kowaleski, *Medieval Domesticity*, pp. 92–123.

CHAPTER 46

Marriage

Sally Dixon-Smith

Over a century since George Kittredge proposed the idea of a 'marriage group' within the *Canterbury Tales*, scholars continue to be fascinated by the depiction of marriage in Chaucer's works, as well as debates and discoveries about the role of Christian marriage in medieval society. Although it is estimated that around 15 per cent of the population of northern Europe did not marry in this period, largely because of religious vows, marriage was the norm for the majority and shaped their lives, households, finances, social status and connections. So, what was marriage in Chaucer's time – how was it formed, what did it involve, how could it be ended, who did it and why? *Mariage* and *wedded*, like so many *faux amis* in Middle English, may look like straightforward cognates, but describe often significantly different social, religious and legal practices then and now.

In the fourteenth century, what was a valid and legally binding marriage was defined and enforced by the Church rather than secular law courts. Although this is often taken as read, active ecclesiastical jurisdiction over marriage was a medieval development and it was hardly a foregone conclusion that twelfth-century theologians would decide that marriage – a secular, social, sexual and financial partnership – was a holy sacrament. Two centuries later, there was still a wide range of views on the subject among churchmen teaching at the flourishing universities: for instance, Peter of Anchorano (*c.* 1330–1416, Bologna) questioned whether marriage truly was a sacrament, while John Wyclif (*c.* 1330–84, Oxford) argued that since marriage was indeed holy and created by God, it was rather strange that the clergy were expected to remain celibate. Despite continuing debates about how holy matrimony really was, the English had been early adopters of Church authority over marital matters, and both the Church courts and the Canon Law they implemented were very well established by Chaucer's time. Through sermons, Christians were also regularly exposed to a vast amount of Church teaching and law, including on marriage, at a time when preaching was so ubiquitous that it can be considered a means of mass communication. It seems that Chaucer and, presumably, many in his audience were well aware of the way the clergy and Church courts were supposed to regulate sex and marriage, otherwise presenting this in parody (*FrT*, III.1354–74; *GP*, I.649–662) would have no effect. Chaucer was well acquainted with the nitty-gritty of Canon Law itself, using Peñafort's *Summa* (1234, part of the standard collection of law and legal precedent used by canon lawyers) very extensively in the *Parson's Tale*, while many of the key teachings and debates on marriage underpin the *Wife of Bath's Prologue*.

Marriage law was based on fairly clear principles, some more surprising to modern eyes than others: the consent of the couple alone made a marriage; people could marry from puberty onwards (twelve for women, fourteen for men);[1] marriage was indissoluble and lasted until the death of one partner; Christians could only marry Christians, and could only be married to one person at a time; marriage was a vitally important way of creating new social and spiritual bonds, and to make the most of its potential for peace-making, Christians should practice exogamy (marrying outside their existing kinship group); kinship, or the group of people an individual should not marry as they were already bound together, was defined by degrees of consanguinity (blood relationship) and affinity – a term covering ties created by sex, marriage ('in-laws') and certain vows, for instance godparenthood; marriage was the only acceptable place for sex: both parties should be physically capable of having penetrative sex, and each spouse 'owed' sex to the other – the 'marriage debt'; and, overall, the union of a man and woman in marriage and sex not only could, but ideally should, represent the mystical union of Christ and the Church. How these principles should apply in practice, and which to enforce at the expense of another, created a web of rules and regulations that could leave people genuinely confused about who was actually married. In Chaucer's time, untangling marriage disputes provided Church courts in southern England with between a quarter and a third of their business. Canon Law, and the theology it was based upon, could have a profound impact on the most personal aspects of people's everyday lives.

For fourteenth-century Christians, it was almost dangerously easy to get married. To create a legally binding, valid, indissoluble, till-death-us-do-part marriage, all that was required was the consent of the couple involved. They did not need a ring, witnesses, a priest, or to be in or near a church (although all these might be strongly recommended). This was a society in which certain words and deeds were absolute and legally binding, and contracting a marriage was no exception. Consent to marry could be expressed verbally in the present tense (*per verba de praesenti*), usually as simple as 'I, [name], take you as mine.' No set formula was required, but priests were expected to teach their parishioners something appropriate in English or French, a measure that demonstrates that a priest was not necessarily present when couples married. Court records show marriages being contracted in informal, secular settings: round at a friend's, on the road or in bed. While sex was not necessary to validate or complete a 'present consent' marriage, for couples who had already promised to marry each other (*per verba de futuro*), sex was taken as a physical expression of present consent and so transformed their status from engaged to married. Unmarried couples brought up before the courts as serial fornicators were made to get engaged so that if they had sex again they would be married whether they liked it or not. Consent could also be expressed through gesture, specifically giving a subarrhation – a gift that indicated the exchange of consent to marry – an object known in Middle English as a 'wed'. A wed could be anything but was often a ring offered by the man and accepted by the woman, and this 'wedding' created the marriage. Fooling around with such a potent gesture – 'pleyinge entrechaungeden hire rynges' like *Troilus and Criseyde* (*Tr*, III.1368) – could be ill-advised. According to the Statutes of Salisbury (1217–19), a highly influential set of English Church legislation, no man should 'place a ring of reeds or another material, vile or precious, on a young woman's hands in jest, so that he might more easily fornicate with them, lest, while he thinks himself to be joking, he pledge himself to the burdens of matrimony'. Couples who exchanged present consent in any of these ways – verbally, sexually or through gift-exchange – were married before God, the ultimate witness, and were legally bound.

However, for clarity's sake, Christians were expected to marry not only before God, but *in facie ecclesiae* – in the presence of the Church. This could be interpreted in several ways: having other Christians as witnesses (the Church as the Christian community); being married by a priest (the Church as the clergy); or, particularly in England, quite literally in front of a church building – as the Wife of Bath declares in her prologue, she was married five times at the 'chirche dore' (*CT*, III.6). The longstanding practice of using physical proximity to the sacred to confer spiritual legitimacy on vows or oaths was reflected in the marriage liturgy used most widely in England, the Sarum Use. Most of the marriage service, including the vows, took place at the church door, and many English churches were equipped with strikingly large and fancy porches that could accommodate nuptials. Being married at church was the norm in Chaucer's time, although it seems likely that some, perhaps most, couples who were married with full solemnities by a priest were, in fact, married already as they had previously exchanged present consent elsewhere. This duplication was seen by many couples and their friends as a natural progression, part of a process of widening publicity for the union, moving from a personal commitment to full social recognition.[2]

Publicity was essential to establish the union on a secure foundation. While it was very simple to contract a marriage using words or gesture, there was an awful lot of red tape regarding who was in a position to give the consent that formed a marriage and who was able, and available, to marry. Some of these rules were absolute and immutable, creating 'diriment impediments' that would automatically invalidate a marriage. For instance, marrying while already married to someone else, or bound by a religious vow that 'married' someone to the Church, was bigamy and completely nullified the second contract. Such an annulment (*divortium a vincula* – separation from the bond) ended the marriage – but only because, legally, it had never existed in the first place. *Divortium a mensa et thoro* (separation from bed and board) meant a legal separation where the parties were permitted to live separately, but remained married. It was granted very rarely, usually as a result of extreme domestic violence. Divorce, in the modern sense of ending a perfectly valid marriage, simply did not exist. Other rules were more akin to strict guidelines creating 'prohibitive impediments' that could be waived to a greater or lesser extent, in specific circumstances, but at a spiritual cost. For example, ideally, couples like the Wife of Bath and her fifth husband, Jankyn, whose relationship started as adultery, should not have married, as this legitimised a sinful affair. However, such a marriage could be permitted on certain conditions: Chaucer's patron John of Gaunt married his long-term mistress, Chaucer's sister-in-law Katherine Swynford, but only after receiving dispensation from the impediment of adultery and performing penance to atone for the sinful beginnings of their relationship.

It is worth noting that the 'speak now or forever hold your peace' part of the marriage service, which creates such drama in *Jane Eyre*, was introduced later. In Chaucer's time, although the congregation and the couple were exhorted to reveal any concerns during the marriage service, any impediments undeclared or unknown at that time could still be raised years afterwards and, potentially, undermine the marriage completely. Reading the banns (announcing forthcoming marriages on three successive holy days with at least one normal day in between) was a practical way to reduce this risk by notifying the parish community so that the marriage could be called off if necessary. Covert, secretive, unpublicised marriages were strictly prohibited because unaired impediments could threaten the union later on. Such clandestine marriages were punishable by penance and any children born would be illegitimate (although they would be legitimised in the eyes of the Church, but not the secular courts, if their parents went on to marry openly). Contrary to what is sometimes said, what made a marriage clandestine in this period was not where it took place (whether it was a secular or sacred space), or whether a priest officiated. The key question was whether it was done openly with the full knowledge of the wider community: in other words, had the banns been read? Banns followed by a church marriage represented the most clear-cut way to achieve an irrefutable level of openness.

Although clandestine marriages were prohibited, they would, nevertheless, be upheld in court. The idea that such a marriage could be illegal but also valid at the same time seems contradictory but was motivated by the principle that any marriage, even one contracted covertly, was a commitment for life. This logic could cause major upheaval when applied to real cases. For instance, when she was twelve, Joan of Kent, the future mother of Richard II, contracted a clandestine marriage with a knight who then left on campaign. About a year later, she publicly married an aristocrat. When her 'secret husband' returned to the country he was ignored. Several years later he had the money to pursue his case at the papal court, where he won. Joan's public, church, marriage was annulled in favour of her first, clandestine, marriage contract. She was returned to her 'secret husband', even though her 'public husband' had considered himself legitimately married to her for the previous eight years or so. Around 90 per cent of marriage cases in southern England were disputes over clandestine marriages, many of them concerning this type of 'pre-contract'. Being married to two people at the same time was legally, and spiritually, an impossible state that could only be resolved, as in Joan's case, by upholding the indissolubility of the first contract. Assuming an adulterous couple were willing to commit perjury, this system was open to abuse – as a false claim of pre-contract could be used to end an unwanted marriage and (re-)establish a preferred union. It was not until the early modern period that clandestine marriages were made invalid and could no longer overturn properly publicised marriages.

Some couples intentionally contracted a clandestine marriage when they knew full well there was a prohibitive impediment, for instance kinship. Their hope was that, presented with a *fait accompli*, the community at large would accept the marriage and the Church might grant a dispensation after the fact, upholding the bond rather than breaking it over a waivable offence. The Council of London (1342) ruled that couples who temporarily moved 'to cities and well-populated towns in which they do not have an advance reputation', so that the banns could be read without the impediment coming to light, should be excommunicated. This council described runaway, incognito marriages as a 'very common vice', especially for couples who were too closely related. This is perhaps surprising, as in 1215 the Church had made its incest rules far more manageable by slashing the forbidden degrees of consanguinity (blood relationship that prevented marriage) from seven degrees (having a great-great-great-great-great-grandparent in common) to four (great-great-grandparent in common). Joan of Kent provides a good example: as a young widow, in 1361, she entered an impossibly high-profile clandestine marriage with the heir to the throne, Edward, the Black Prince. As both were descended from Edward I – Joan's grandfather – they were too closely related. The couple were granted a papal dispensation and allowed to marry openly and correctly on the understanding that they would undertake penance, endow two chapels in recompense for their illicit marriage and never support, or ever again enter into, another clandestine marriage. Joan was particularly censured for her Pope-bothering marital antics as this was her second clandestine marriage: the first had also ended up in the papal courts, and she should have known better. Among contemporary chroniclers, and some historians since, Joan's somewhat dodgy marriage history has lent her a rather salacious sexual reputation.[3]

The idea that there was something vaguely improper, or even louche, about second and subsequent marriages is one of the (many) things the Wife of Bath takes issue with (*WBPro*, III.10–58). Around half of all marriages were remarriages, and Chaucer was rather unusual in not remarrying after he was widowed – certainly his mother remarried within a year of his father's death. Although remarriage was very common, 'bigamye' could be used to describe this type of serial monogamy (*WBPro*, III.33). This was due to a 'defect' in the symbolism of remarriage: only a first marriage was the union of 'one with one' and could fully signify the union of Christ and the Church. Remarriages always had the ghost of the previous union(s) in the background spoiling the symbolism and so did not receive the sacramental blessing. Although this was only one of many blessings in the ceremony, when it was left out, the most visually arresting element of the service disappeared too. At first-time marriages, a special cloth referred to as a pall or veil was held over the couple, who prostrated themselves on the floor to receive the blessing. Such dramatic staging signposted the most critical, sacred and transformative moment in a ceremony: for instance, the anointing at a coronation, which marked the recipient as God's chosen leader, the Lord's anointed, was, and still is, done under a pall. In a world where gesture carried so much weight, it is likely that omitting the pall and its drama, rather than skipping over one of a series of blessings, made remarriage appear significantly less holy. Also, as it was customary in England that any illegitimate children the couple had were legitimised by joining their parents under the pall, this substantial benefit was not available at remarriages either. Interestingly, like Joan of Kent, many people who remarried chose to be buried next to their first spouse – perhaps reflecting the view that first marriage was more sacred and ritually potent, rather than indicating more love and affection for the first spouse than subsequent marriage partners.

While the Church as legislator and enforcer was concerned with spiritual appropriateness, for most people there were many other considerations in their choice of marriage partner. Although under Church law it was only the consent of the couple themselves that mattered, it was generally expected that they would seek formal permission from others too: peasant women, or their families, paid a 'merchet' fine to their lord for permission to marry, while at the other end of the social scale, tenants-in-chief were expected to ask the King's permission and the King was expected to consult over his own, and his children's, marriages. Consenting to a marriage was not the same as having complete freedom of choice, and most marriages were formed with a good deal of input from parents, families, affinities and lordship networks as part of a 'marriage strategy' to preserve and further group interests. Consent was not the only exchange at marriage: it was standard at all levels of society to have a 'pre-nup' involving gifts, agreements or settlements to provide for the marriage itself, any children and future widow-/widowerhood. While the Church wanted Christians to avoid marrying relations, most people were far more worried about 'social miscegenation'. Unions between people of different classes were regarded with visceral disapproval and there was a high level of social endogamy, particularly among aristocrats. Joan of Kent provides a striking example: her first 'secret' husband and 'public' husband both fought on the Crécy campaign alongside her future husband, the Black Prince, and all three men became knights of the new, ultra-elite, Order of the Garter (twenty-six members, including the King). Socially motivated endogamy and spiritually motivated exogamy were bound to clash. One nobleman thought it so improbable that he would find an acceptable marriage partner to whom he was not already related that he sought a blank-cheque dispensation before even looking for a wife.[4] Despite the theological principle that men and women had equal rights when it came to consent to marriage, and equal claims over each other's bodies sexually, marriage in this period was nonetheless a fundamentally unequal relationship. It is interesting that, a century on from Kittredge, scholars have proposed that Chaucer's discursive and varied portrayal of marriage may be not about marriage at all, but a way of tactfully examining the problems inherent in another, far more politically sensitive, unequal relationship – that between lord and retainer.[5]

NOTES

1 My thanks to Historic Royal Palaces for allowing time away from my desk to write; to David d'Avray, who introduced me to the fascinating study of medieval marriage; and to the St Andrews students who put so much into 'Sex, Marriage and the Law'. On marrying high-status children under the age of consent, see D. L. d'Avray, *Papacy, Monarchy and Marriage, 860–1600* (Cambridge: Cambridge University Press, 2015).

2 Shannon McSheffrey, 'Place, Space, and Situation: Public and Private in the Making of Marriage in Late-Medieval London', *Speculum*, 79 (2004), 960–90 (pp. 965–7, 971).

3 W. M. Ormrod, 'In Bed with Joan of Kent: The King's Mother and the Peasants' Revolt', in Jocelyn Wogan-Browne *et al.*, eds., *Medieval Women: Texts and Contexts in Late Medieval Britain: Essays for Felicity Riddy* (Turnhout: Brepols, 2000), pp. 277–92 (pp. 282–3).

4 Joel T. Rosenthal, 'Aristocratic Marriage and the English Peerage, 1350–1500: Social Institution and Personal Bond', *Journal of Medieval History*, 10 (1984), 181–94 (pp. 183–4).

5 Kathleen E. Kennedy, *Maintenance, Meed, and Marriage in Medieval English Literature* (New York: Palgrave Macmillan, 2009), pp. 11–12, 31–59.

CHAPTER 47

Dress

Laura F. Hodges

English sumptuary laws (1363), in effect for less than a year before being rescinded, illustrate the socio-economic, and sometimes moral, debate concerning appropriate apparel for each social class while they also inform our comprehension of Geoffrey Chaucer's works.[1] Despite being ineffective, this 1363 legal text is now informative about the medieval attitudes that produced these laws, as well as those that opposed them. Across the western world in the Middle Ages such sartorial laws were promulgated, defeated in actual practice, reissued and again rendered useless by a variety of stratagems. Updated versions were issued yet again. In England, for example, another similar set of sumptuary laws was proposed in 1378–9, but was not passed.

These 1363 sumptuary laws were the only ones to have been in effect, however briefly, during Geoffrey Chaucer's lifetime. Nevertheless, he surely was aware of the ongoing social, political and economic controversy concerned with the mode of dress appropriate to each stratum of society. The proponents of sumptuary laws held that members of the ideal society dressed in garments that would inform onlookers of their socio-economic rank. Frances Elizabeth Baldwin posits that the advocates of these laws presumed that honest and straightforward dealings would proceed from this knowledge; that the laws would check immoral luxury and extravagance; that they would inhibit purchase of foreign wares (and thus subsidise foreign economies); and that they would encourage thrift at home, producing savings that could be taxed for the King's wars.[2] However, many recognised that wearing the proper set of garments could be effective in achieving upward social mobility. Chaucer's *Canterbury Tales* portrays such social climbers, for example in the *Reeve's Tale* the miller Symkyn and his family, dressed in their Sunday best: 'As any pecok he was proud and gay', in his red hose, displaying three bladed weapons and a hood draped in *chaperone* fashion (a gentleman's style of headcovering). Symkyn's wife, too, is 'proud, and peert as is a pye', dressed in her red 'gyte' (outer garments)

(I.3926–33, 3950–5). Similarly, in the *General Prologue* Chaucer's Physician dresses in imported red and blue silks, advertising his flourishing practice (I.439–40), and the Merchant wears neatly fastened boots, and fashionable yet ambiguous *mottelee* (multi-coloured cloth of difficult-to-determine quality), topped by a beaver hat from Flanders (I.271–3). Each of these characters illustrates the knowledge that one could 'dress for success', with the hope that one who looked prosperous might be treated with more deference. The sumptuary laws addressed socially nimble persons of this sort and attempted to control dressing above one's station.[3]

In many of his works Chaucer employs clothing and fabric images to create a complex socio-economic and moral context for his audience. In doing so, he goes beyond the ordinary medieval author's rhetorical decoration of his text. His knowledge of rhetoric and current sartorial practices and attitudes is the underpinning of his works. He knows what his contemporary audience does not need to be told.

The stipulations for clothing and adornment in the 1363 laws exist in Items VIII–XIV of that document, dealing respectively with seven groupings of English society: (1) servants (grooms), 'Servants of Lords, as they of Mysteries, and Artificers'; (2) handicraftsmen and yeomen; (3) esquires and 'all Manner of Gentlemen' (below the rank of knights); (4) merchants, citizens, burgesses and handicraftsmen; (5) knights; (6) clergy (clerks of various sorts); and finally (7) ploughmen, carters, drivers of the plough, oxherds, cowherds, shepherds, keepers of beasts, threshers of corn, 'all Manner of People of the Estate' and others of similar incomes. Overall, the law stipulates that wives and children are subject to the same rules as their husbands or fathers. In each case, the person's income determines the kind of clothing he, his womenfolk and offspring should wear.

The first of these, item VIII pertaining to servants, specifies the reason behind all of these laws: they were written to correct 'the Outragious and Excessive Apparel of divers People, against their Estate and Degree, to the great Destruction and Impoverishment of all the Land'.[4] Then this item provides that servants' clothes ('Vesture' and 'Hosing'), which would be provided by their employers, should be limited to 2 marks in price; they were to wear clothes made of no higher price even if they paid for them with their own money. Beyond that, they were forbidden anything made of gold or silver, embroidery, or anything enamelled or made of silk. The set price limit was problematic, given that servants sometimes received as reward or payment the cast-off clothing of their masters, such as the coat and hood, and the long *surcote* (outer garment worn over a tunic) of *pers* (expensive dark blue cloth), worn as a second-hand garment by Chaucer's

Reeve (I.612, 617). In any case, item VIII reveals, through those things specifically forbidden to servants, the adornments in which some servants must have aped their employers – the gold and silver, perhaps used in the embroidered patterns on garments, so popular among the nobles in that period; the enamelled items (rings? brooches?); and the silk, an imported, costly fabric. Moreover, the family females are instructed not to wear veils worth more than 12d. each. Such an instruction indicates the probability that some servants' wives or daughters must have previously done just this – worn a veil of finer fabric and/or fussier construction than what was deemed appropriate.

The 'People of Handicraft, and Yeomen' received similar limitations (item IX). This law proclaims that their clothing and hosing must not cost more than 40s. for the whole *cloth* (a term of legal measure) when it was purchased. They must not wear 'Stone' (gemstones); 'Cloth of Silk nor of Silver' (silk woven of or embroidered with silver thread); 'Girdle [belt], Ring, Garter, Owche [necklace, jewel, collar], Ribband, Chains, nor no such other Things of Gold nor of Silver, nor no Manner of Apparel embroidered'; anything enamelled; or silk of any kind. Females, besides following the above rules, are again forbidden to wear silk veils. They were repetitively instructed (because silk was not produced in England at this time) to wear only veils woven from yarns produced in England. Also, they must not wear any kind of fur, including 'Budge' (lambskin with fur turned to the outside); they were allowed to wear lamb (a garment with a lamb lining would have the wool side turned to the body for warmth), cony (rabbit), cat and fox furs.[5] Clearly Alison, the wife of the elderly carpenter in the *Miller's Tale*, wears a costume that would be transgressive if judged only by this law, precisely because of her girdle, her smock's double-sided embroidery with black silk threads and her provocative brooch (I.3235–67). That Chaucer dresses her in this manner, whether or not a sumptuary law was in force to forbid it, suggests his expectation that Alison would be judged by the moralists in the court of contemporary opinion, and found to be excessive in her dress, prideful and lacking in the decorum suitable to her social status.

Esquires, gentlemen of lesser ranks than knights, having incomes of less than £100 per annum (item X), were restricted to buying cloths valued at 'Four Marks and a Half' for their clothing. They were not allowed cloths of gold or silver; silk; or any decoration of garments or self, including embroidery, ribband, jewellery such as a ring or 'owche of Gold'; girdles enhanced with precious metallic threads or gemstones; or any manner of fur. However, esquires with a yearly income of 200 marks might wear cloths priced at 5 marks per cloth, including silk, and adorn them with silver, ribbons and complementary girdles. Their womenfolk and children might wear fur of miniver (white belly fur of squirrels), turned up, for their headdresses, but were forbidden the furs of 'Ermins' (white fur from a stoat with a black-tipped tail) or 'Letuse' (white pelts of the snow weasel), as well as any gemstone decoration. We cannot know if Chaucer's Squire (I.89–93), in his embroidered gown, would pass muster in the court of public opinion according to item x, because we do not know his income. Assuming that his income derives from his father, the Knight, the recipient of numerous prizes, it follows that the Squire was probably not dressing above his status. At the same time, we note the Franklin's gentlemanly accessories of 'anlaas' (type of dagger), girdle and 'gipser' (purse) of white silk, fully consistent with his office of 'knyght of the shire' (I.357). Further, Chaucer omits describing the Knight's general habits of dress, but he would have been subject to social standards of seemliness regarding his station in society, and Chaucer often characterises noble dress in terms of silk fabrics, enhanced with gold decoration and jewelled embroidery, all of which possess surfaces that reflect light, as in the *Legend of Good Women*, where Dido is dressed 'al in gold and perre wrye', while Eneas's appearance is compared to Phebus, the god of the sun (*LGW*, 1201–2, 1206–7). In the *House of Fame*, Chaucer describes nobles in jewelled crowns, ribbons and fringes, and heralds who represent these nobles in their *cote-armure*, embroidered 'wonderliche ryche', probably with gold and/or silver thread (*HF*, 1316–40). Beyond these we find Criseyde's widow's habit of 'samyt broun' in *Troilus and Criseyde* (I.109), a gleaming garment that is an important part of her sheen, as mentioned throughout this poem.[6]

Item XI prescribes the sartorial limits for merchants, citizens, burgesses and handicraftsmen, again with the deciding factor in each category being economic means. The first grouping deals with those having 'Goods and Chattels' valued at £500. They are restricted to the same sartorial limitations as esquires and gentlemen whose rental incomes yield '*C. li*' per year. A second grouping of merchants, citizens and burgesses, with 'Goods and Chattels' worth '*M. li*', may dress in the manner of esquires and gentlemen having incomes of '*ii. C. li*' each year. As usual, the women and children of these men were mandated to follow suit. As a result of income being the determining factor in both items x and XI, the appearance of members of these groups dressed in their designated clothing would proclaim both their social status and their relative economic status. Two of Chaucer's pilgrims who might be evaluated by the above two items are the Wife of Bath and the Merchant, but again we lack knowledge of their incomes, that determining factor. If the Wife travels to Canterbury wearing both hose *and* a gown of her favoured fabric of red *scarlet* (most expensive woollen cloth available, dyed 'in graine'), as the prologue to her tale suggests she might (III.559), then she is indeed expensively dressed, but it is likely that this is not beyond her economic status as a well-to-do cloth-maker. The Merchant's 'mottelee' costume (I.271) treads carefully (such cloth might be woven partly of threads of lesser cost and questionable quality). It portrays current style, seeming prosperity and qualitative discretion. We do not know his true economic status, and his outward appearance gives nothing away.

Next, item XII addresses the highest category within the 'Estate of Temporal Rulers': knights. Knights are divided into two economic categories: those with land or rental income of '*ii.C*', and those of 'land and rent over *iv. C.* Mark by Year, to the Sum of *M. li*'. The first group may only spend 6 marks per cloth for their clothing. They are forbidden to purchase cloth of gold for garments and/or mantles, or to have gowns furred with miniver or ermine, and any garment embroidered with gemstones or 'otherwise'. Their wives, however, may wear headdresses displaying gemstone embroidery. In contrast, the second, more affluent group of knights may dress 'at their Pleasure', with the exceptions of wearing ermines and *letuses*, and they may wear pearls and gemstones on their headgear. Chaucer scholars might rejoice at having these sartorial standards for a 'rule of thumb' to use in evaluating his knights, except that Chaucer, most often, does not elaborately and rhetorically dress his knights. The exceptions are Lygurge and Emetreus in the *Knight's Tale* (I.2140–52, 2160–78), and Thopas (VII.730–5, 752–3, 857–83); the first two are foreign knights garbed for Theseus's tournament, set well into the past, in ancient Greece, and the last is Flemish and the target of Chaucer's elaborate parody of romance *descriptio*. As such, they are not suitable subjects for a judgement by contemporary English clothing standards.[7]

Addressing a different medieval estate, that of spiritual rulers, item XIII concerns the clergy. Clerks having a 'Degree in any Church, Cathedral, Collegial, or Schools … [and clerks] of the King, that [hath] such Estate that requireth Furr' may wear this fur in accordance with that institution's constitution. Another group of clerks, who receive '*ii. C.Marks*' of income per annum, may dress the same as knights of the same income. The same correspondence in income and dress holds true for Clerks and knights of '*C.li*' in yearly rents. All those who may wear fur within these specifications may also wear 'Lawn' ('Linure', fine linen) during the summer. In any case, the only one of Chaucer's clergy who wears fur is the Monk in the *General Prologue* (I.193–4). The Monk, in the purfiling (trimming, edging) of the sleeves of his habit, illustrates the apparently widespread clerical practice of displaying the forbidden expensive squirrel fur known as *gris* (the backs of winter pelts of grey squirrel fur). This fur elicited complaints in monastic records and even a rule forbidding its use, suggesting that it was used often enough to be deemed a serious problem within the religious community. The Monk's sparing use of *gris* only as trim and not in a full lining perhaps alludes to this trend, which no quantity of Church rulings managed to snuff out.[8] Item XIII does not address issues of style or fashion. Thus we cannot know exactly how the Friar's short and bell-shaped cape might fare under secular rulings.[9] Religious dress, in general, was prescribed in each order's religious rules, their constitutions, and this item concurs.

The last estate mentioned (item XIV) is that of the providers: 'Carters, Ploughmen, Drivers of the Plough, Oxherds, Cowherds, Shepherds (Deyars, [swineherds, dairymen]) and all other Keepers of Beasts, Threshers of Corn, and all Manner of People of the Estate (of a Groom, attending to Husbandry) and all other People', with possessions worth less than 40s. These persons were ordered to buy only *blanket* and *russet* (classified as rough cloths) costing 12d. (per cloth or per piece?). They were to wear only the linen girdles consistent with their estate. The penalty for dressing in excess of these rules was confiscation of the offending garment or accessory. Chaucer's Ploughman (I.541), in his tabard, that all-purpose over-garment of the Middle Ages, illustrates, so far as we can tell, compliance with these rulings. Chaucer's poorest characters, including the Clerk (I.290) and, most notably, Griselda in the *Clerk's Tale* (IV.913–17), correctly wear clothing made of old and/or worn, rough fabric.

For a moralist's point of view, we may consider the diatribe of Chaucer's Parson, for whom Chaucer provides no costume, except a pilgrim-type walking stick, an accessory illustrating his manner of serving his parish (I.495–7). In his tale the Parson presents a catalogue of the most frequently committed 'clothing sins' of his day (X.409–35). His complaints, many of which are concerned with the decoration of garments, including dagging,[10] are deemed an original Chaucerian addition,[11] and may have been compiled by Chaucer from contemporary sermons against sartorial sins and 'pious' literature of all types. Collectively, this diatribe condemns sins of excess as well as sins of scantiness in the sartorial practices of the society of Chaucer's time.

NOTES

1 *The Statutes of the Realm*, Vol. 1 (London, 1810), pp. 380–2, available at https://catalog.hathitrust.org/Record/012297566 (last accessed 13 December 2018); Frances Elizabeth Baldwin, *Sumptuary Legislation and Personal Regulation in England* (Baltimore: Johns Hopkins University Press, 1926), pp. 10–65.
2 Baldwin, *Sumptuary Legislation*, p. 10.
3 I have discussed the implications of the costumes of Chaucer's pilgrims in *Chaucer and Costume: The Secular Pilgrims in the 'General Prologue'* (Cambridge: Boydell and Brewer, 2000); *Chaucer and Clothing: Clerical and Academic Costume in the 'General Prologue' to the 'Canterbury Tales'* (Cambridge: Boydell and Brewer, 2005); and *Chaucer and Array: Patterns of Fabric and Costume Rhetoric in the Canterbury Tales, Troilus and Criseyde and Other Works* (Cambridge: Boydell and Brewer, 2014).
4 *Statutes of the Realm*, p. 380.
5 For fur definitions see Elspeth M. Veale, *The English Fur Trade in the Later Middle Ages* (Oxford: Clarendon Press, 1960), Glossary, pp. 216–29.
6 See Sarah-Grace Heller, 'Light as Glamour: The Luminescent Ideal of Beauty in the *Roman de la Rose*', *Speculum*, 76 (2001), 934–59.
7 I address these topics in *Chaucer and Array*, pp. 14–32, 140–66.
8 Hodges, *Chaucer and Clothing*, pp. 112–32.
9 *Ibid.*, pp. 133–59.
10 Regarding dagging, see Andrea Denny-Brown, 'Rips and Slits: The Torn Garment and the Medieval Self', in Catherine Richardson, ed., *Clothing Culture, 1350–1650* (Burlington, VT: Ashgate, 2004), pp. 223–37. See also her *Fashioning Change: The Trope of Clothing in High- and Late-Medieval England* (Columbus: Ohio State University Press, 2012).
11 Nicole D. Smith, 'The Parson's Predilection for Pleasure', *Studies in the Age of Chaucer*, 28 (2006), 117–40 (p. 120); see too her *Sartorial Strategies: Outfitting Aristocrats and Fashioning Conduct in Late Medieval Literature* (Notre Dame: University of Notre Dame Press, 2012), pp. 137–75.

PART VI

Chaucer Traditions

CHAPTER 48

The First Chaucerians
Reception in the 1400s

Robert J. Meyer-Lee

In several ways, Chaucer was an invention of the early fifteenth century. Of course, through October 1400 there lived a Geoffrey Chaucer who, when not otherwise occupied by his work for the royal government, wrote some poetry and prose. But however much he may have impressed his circle of readers with these amateur literary efforts, this circle was a small one, and hence if it were not for the energetic activities of his emulators, copyists and readers in the first two decades or so after his death, his literary achievements might have been lost to history. Instead, in the early fifteenth century these agents of Chaucer's legacy fashioned him into the Father of English Poetry, and ever since, rightly or not, he has occupied a permanent originary spot in the English literary historical imagination. Chaucer the person died at the end of the fourteenth century, but at the beginning of the next his successors gave birth to his literary authority by figuring him as the fountainhead of a high-culture English literary tradition – one that they were in fact in the very process of creating.

Until relatively recently, literary historians considered this establishment of Chaucer's place in the literary tradition as a merely passive accomplishment of his fifteenth-century successors: incapable of matching his poetic genius, these successors – according to this view – at least had the good sense to recognise his excellence and transmit it to later generations. But we now understand that to recognise literary excellence is to define it, and to define it is to produce the idea of it in engagement with a specific historical context for specific purposes, not all of which are literary. Hence, Chaucer's constitution as the Father of English Poetry in the early fifteenth century was a complexly creative historical act, one whose motives, character and shaping influences have had foundational effects that persist in some fashion to the present.

In the most practical sense, the fifteenth-century invention of Chaucer was a matter of manuscripts. Although one or two of the very earliest Chaucer manuscripts may date to the final years of the poet's life, virtually the entire corpus of witnesses to his writings is a product of the fifteenth century. Significantly, this turning-point of 1400 in respect to Chaucer manuscripts coincides with a sudden increase in the production of manuscripts of English poetry more generally: before 1400, there are a few dozen such manuscripts; by the end of the fifteenth century, there are many hundreds.[1] While this spike in production results from a number of large-scale historical trends, such as a general increase in lay literacy, some of the details of this production point to more specific reasons, for which the reception of Chaucer's poetry is integral. In particular, it is no coincidence that the most widely disseminated English poets of the early fifteenth century – Thomas Hoccleve (*c.* 1367–1426) and John Lydgate (1371–1449) – self-identify in their works as disciples of Chaucer. These poets made quite substantial contributions to the expansion of English poetic production in their own authorship, as well as in other ways. Hoccleve, as clerk of the Privy Seal, was a professional scribe who we know lent his skills to the copying of English poetry, including, perhaps, Chaucer's.[2] Lydgate, a monk of Bury St Edmunds, had close working relations with some of his copyists, especially the proto-publisher John Shirley, one of the key figures in the early circulation of Chaucer's writings; and the remarkable volume of Lydgate's poetic output served in part as a conduit for Chaucer's works, with the latter often appearing alongside Lydgate's in manuscript anthologies. Thus, traditionally labelled Chaucerian poets, Hoccleve and Lydgate earn this epithet in a double sense: they not only self-identify as Chaucer's poetic disciples, but through this emulation and their disseminating activities they also are agents of interpreting and transmitting Chaucer's poetry, becoming the first Chaucerians in the modern, academic sense.

Crucially, however, the circumstances of Hoccleve's and Lydgate's composition of poetry were rather different from Chaucer's. In contrast with their predecessor, they wrote literature in much more direct engagement with the sphere of political power, and their poetry, especially Lydgate's, circulated broadly in their own lifetimes. Writing under stated or informal royal sponsorship, they were quasi-official, public vernacular poets, in which position both turned to Chaucer as an authoritative precedent, despite the fact that Chaucer's poetic career did not resemble theirs. Hoccleve and Lydgate, at roughly the same time, inked poetic paeans to their master Chaucer, and they did so in capacious, politically freighted, culturally aspirant works addressed to princes of the Lancastrian dynasty, and especially to Prince Henry of Monmouth, later Henry V. In this way, the Chaucerian tradition emerges at the beginning of the century not merely as recognition of Chaucer's aesthetic achievement but also as a consequence of an unprecedented collision, with respect to literature in English, between the realms of royal politics and literary culture.

Following the *coup d'état* in 1399, the new Lancastrian dynasty showed much more interest in English poetry than did Richard II, who, although an implicit looming presence in much Ricardian verse, left at best ambiguous traces of direct royal concern with what have turned out to be the English literary masterpieces of his day. Scholars have ascribed this Lancastrian innovation to the new dynasty's need for public legitimation from whatever sources available, and, however programmatic or merely opportunistic their activities were in this regard, this motive was doubtlessly part of the impetus – although certainly also contributing were, among other factors, renewed conflict with France; growing royal concern with heresy (in which writing in English was a key issue); intra-dynastic jostling for power and recognition; and the simple fact that Richard's usurper, Henry IV, was the first king since the Norman Conquest whose mother-tongue was English. For Hoccleve and Lydgate, this Lancastrian cultural innovation meant that they were asked to produce works that spoke both *for* a prince and *to* a prince: works that carried a literary authority notionally equivalent to the authority of the sovereign whom those works addressed, and that conceived of this authority as residing in the poet as a conduit of a literary tradition. To achieve this, both Hoccleve and Lydgate shrewdly transformed the literary ambition and achievement of Chaucer into what we would now call cultural capital, thereby fashioning themselves a basis upon which to claim authority as poets writing in an English literary tradition, which in turn provided the ground upon which they could claim the right to address, advise and even admonish a sovereign. In the process, by necessity and almost as a side-effect, they invented a high-culture English literary tradition with Chaucer as its father.

Such self-authorising triangulation of poet, prince and poetic predecessor occurs in several key places in the works of Hoccleve and Lydgate; here I touch on just one particularly notable instance for each. Late in the *Regiment of Princes* (1410–11), a sprawling poem whose stated purpose is to advise Prince Henry of Monmouth on political and other matters, Hoccleve includes a section on what is in this context the delicate topic of how good kings should receive counsel 'in omnibus factis'. The obviously self-promoting nature of this advice puts especially heavy pressure on the advising poet's implicit claim to authority. Cannily, Hoccleve deflects this pressure backwards, digressing to identify the recently deceased Chaucer as the ideal embodiment of literary authority. After insisting that the Prince not hold counsels on 'holy dayes' lest he offend God – and going as far as to suggest that a king who does so thereby forfeits political authority – Hoccleve ascribes this and other such pointed counsel to Chaucer:

> The firste fyndere of our fair langage,
> Hath seid, in cas semblable, and othir mo,
> So hyly wel that it is my dotage
> For to expresse or touche any of tho.
> Allas, my fadir fro the world is go,
> My worthy maister Chaucer – him I meene.[3]

To emphasise his personal acquaintance with Chaucer, Hoccleve then recalls the physical appearance of his 'worthy maister', next to which stanza he has the famous portrait of Chaucer (see Figure 1.1) positioned. It hardly matters that Chaucer, as Hoccleve well knew, was not a poet prone to giving direct political advice to his sovereign; his purpose is to refashion Chaucer into such a poet, one who, as the 'first fyndere' and 'fadir', stands as the point of origin of a specifically English ('our fair langage') tradition of literary excellence – as it is this tradition that Hoccleve is implicitly claiming to extend to his own work, even while he is in fact inventing it.

Of the many corresponding moments in Lydgate's writing, especially influential ones occur in his massive *Troy Book* (1412–20), which also was written for Prince Henry. As a comprehensive telling of the rise and fall of Troy – the ancient narrative underlying medieval Western European claims to royal power, including that of England – the *Troy Book* would under any circumstances have held immense cultural and political prestige. Its ambition and significance are thus so much the greater given the royal commissioning that Lydgate details in the prologue, and specifically Henry's desire that

> The noble story openly wer knowe
> In oure tonge, aboute in euery age,
> And y-writen as wel in oure langage
> As in latyn and in frensche it is;
> That of the story þe trouthe we nat mys
> No more than doth eche other nacioun.[4]

Lydgate imagines poetic composition here as national public service of the highest order, and this entails a tacit claim to authority that, for a poet writing in 'oure tonge' rather than in 'latyn' or 'frensche', requires a legitimating precedent. In the prologue, Lydgate refashions for this purpose the comments of his source about the authority and tradition of writers in general. Just like Hoccleve, however, he identifies Chaucer in key moments later in the work as his more specific and germane precedent.

One such moment occurs in Book III, when, reaching the point in the story when Criseyde must leave Troy, Lydgate digresses to recall Chaucer's *Troilus and Criseyde*. This evolves into an elaborate eulogy of his predecessor that in effect tells of the birth of a high-culture English literary tradition:

> For he owre englishe gilte with his sawes,
> Rude and boistous firste be olde dawes,
> ...
> Til þat he cam & þoruȝ his poetrie
> Gan oure tonge firste to magnifie
> And adourne it with his eloquence.
> (III.4237–43)

Chaucer, these lines declare, inaugurated the 'gilte' English poetic tradition, thereby lifting the language from its 'boistous' status in the 'olde dawes' into the same league of 'eloquence' as that of the French and Latin that Lydgate mentions in the prologue, thereby creating the medium necessary for the national public service that Lydgate proposes for his own *Troy Book*. Accordingly, as Lydgate goes on to imagine, Chaucer lifted *himself* into a position of national cultural authority that Lydgate conceives Petrarch to have held (following Chaucer's own comments in this regard from the prologue to the *Clerk's Tale*): 'So þat þe laurer of oure englishe tonge / Be to hym ȝoue for his excellence', Lydgate proclaims, 'Riȝt as whilom ... / ... / To Petrak Fraunceis was ȝouen in Ytaille' (III.4244–51). Significantly, that Chaucer was not in fact crowned with a 'laurer' is evident in Lydgate's phrasing; Chaucer's precedent may only be recognised (which is to say, invented) belatedly. An actual poet laureate receives his crown, like 'Petrak Fraunceis', in his lifetime as a marker of his achievement and his ongoing, authoritative public service. The implication is clear: if Chaucer established the literary language that makes an English poet laureate possible, then Lydgate – in the very act of using this language to create an epic account of Troy for an English prince – deserves the office of the laureate itself.

Thus, Lydgate and Hoccleve, asked or otherwise encouraged by reigning princes to write public poetry for the good of the realm, imagined Chaucer's literary achievement in these terms, thereby supplying themselves their needed authoritative precedent and coincidentally establishing the conceptual and terminological basis for a high-culture English literary tradition, with Chaucer as its fountainhead. Throughout the rest of the fifteenth century and into the sixteenth, subsequent English poets consistently adopt (or otherwise respond to) these concepts and terms. In the middle of the fifteenth century, for example, George Ashby, writing a poetic advice-text for exiled Lancastrian Prince Edward (son of Henry VI), plainly recognises the principle of inheritance that Lydgate implies in his praise of Chaucer, at once emulating Lydgate and including him among the founding fathers:

> Maisters Gower, Chauucer & Lydgate,
> Primier poetes of this nacion,
> Embelysshing oure englisshe tendure algate,
> Firste finders to oure consolacion
> Off fresshe, douce englisshe.[5]

Such a eulogistic address to the founding triumvirate of English poetry was by no means a stale convention at this point; Ashby was only the second to versify this formulation and the first to do so in the years after Lydgate's death, preceded only by Osbern Bokenham's somewhat more ambivalent celebration of the triumvirate in the last years of Lydgate's life. (Notably, in the epithet 'Firste finders' Ashby draws on Hoccleve's phrasing from the advice-text written for the grandfather of Ashby's own addressee, but denies Hoccleve membership among the English poetic fathers, inaugurating a literary historical erasure of Hoccleve that is one of the curiosities of the later fifteenth century.) From this point well into the next century, this formulation became shorthand for marking one's participation in the high-culture tradition of English poetry as it was first conceived in Hoccleve's and Lydgate's reception of their Ricardian predecessor. For example, in a spectacularly self-congratulating amplification of this convention, John Skelton's *Garlande or Chapelet of Laurell* (1523) depicts the English poetic triumvirate ushering Skelton into the court of the Queen of Fame.

In stark contrast, Sir Thomas Wyatt, Skelton's younger contemporary in Henry VIII's court, wholly effaces Chaucer's fifteenth-century mediators (perhaps to forestall comparison with contemporary poets like Skelton), writing the lyric verse that would come to mark in English literary history the break between medieval and Renaissance. Nonetheless, Hoccleve's and Lydgate's laureate poetic ideals did not simply vanish with the early-sixteenth-century elevation of private and courtly over public and clerkly; they merely temporarily dropped from prominence. They are again fully evident in the work of Edmund Spenser and, indeed, reappear in sometimes unexpected places down to the present. For example, they are readily apparent in the poem that Robert Frost intended but failed to read for the inauguration of John F. Kennedy, which anticipates in its concluding lines, 'A golden age of poetry and power / Of which this noonday's the beginning hour'.[6] Although readers today, influenced by the postmedieval reception of Chaucer, are not likely to imagine him as a laureate striding the realms 'of poetry and power', the legacy of the very first Chaucerians still haunts the English poetic tradition and its sense of what poetry might be.

NOTES

1 See John H. Fisher, *The Emergence of Standard English* (Lexington: University Press of Kentucky, 1996), pp. 16–35.

2 See A. I. Doyle and M. B. Parkes, 'Paleographical Introduction', in Paul G. Ruggiers, ed., *The 'Canterbury Tales': A Facsimile and Transcription of the Hengwrt Manuscript, with Variants from the Ellesmere Manuscript* (Norman: University of Oklahoma Press, 1979), pp. xix–xlix.

3 Thomas Hoccleve, *The Regiment of Princes*, ed. Charles R. Blyth (Kalamazoo: Medieval Institute Publications, 1999), lines 4978–83.

4 John Lydgate, *Lydgate's 'Troy Book'*, ed. Henry Bergen, 4 vols., EETS es 97, 103, 106, 126 (London: Kegan Paul, Trench, Trübner, 1906–35), Pro.112–17. Further citations in text.

5 George Ashby, 'Active Policy of a Prince', in *George Ashby's Poems*, ed. Mary Bateson (London: Kegan Paul, Trench, Trübner, 1899), EETS es 76, lines 1–5.

6 Robert Frost, 'For John F. Kennedy His Inauguration', in *The Poetry of Robert Frost*, ed. Edward Connery Lathem (New York: Henry Holt, 1979), lines 76–7.

CHAPTER 49

The Reception of Chaucer in the Renaissance

Alex Davis

In the engraving entitled *The true portraiture of GEFFREY CHAUCER the famous English poet*, produced by John Speed and included in Thomas Speght's 1598 edition of his *Workes*, Chaucer is depicted full-length, framed by the coats of arms of his descendants (Figure 49.1). His right hand touches his penner, or pen-case, which is strung around his neck; the gesture directs the hand towards his breast, as if he were pointing towards himself in order to endorse the identification of image and name. Below, a tomb decorated with further armorial shields stands on a chequered marble floor. A motto indicates that this is the resting place of Thomas Chaucer, the poet's son.

The image is structured around a contrast. Chaucer's progeny are reduced to heraldic emblems and monumental effigies, while he appears as when alive. This vivificatory impulse is a recurrent feature of sixteenth- and seventeenth-century invocations of the poet. Alexander Neville praised his verse, writing that 'by this doth famous *Chaucer* lyue'.[1] Samuel Daniel's *Musophilus* eulogised '*Chaucer* … who yet liues and yet shall' (Spurgeon, p. 160). And in Speght's second edition of the *Workes* in 1602, Speed's engraving is accompanied by a poem 'Vpon the picture of Chaucer', which ends:

> Then *Chaucer* liue, for still thy verse shall liue,
> T'unborne Poets, which life and light will giue.
> (Spurgeon, p. 170)

The motif also existed in darker variants. Shakespeare and Fletcher's *The Two Noble Kinsmen*, adapted from the *Knight's Tale*, opens with a prologue that nervously imagines Chaucer's reaction should the play fail to reproduce the dignity of its original:

> How will it shake the bones of that good man,
> And make him cry from under ground, 'Oh fan
> From me the witless chaff of such a writer
> That blasts my bayes, and my famed works makes lighter
> Then Robin Hood!'[2]

Figure 49.1 *The true portraiture of GEFFREY CHAUCER the famous English poet*, from *The Workes of Our Antient and Learned English Poet, Geffrey Chaucer*, ed. Thomas Speght (London: Adam Islip, 1602), facing sig. b1r.

That unquiet grave was a reality. In 1556, Nicholas Brigham had arranged for Chaucer's remains to be exhumed and moved a short distance to an elaborate new tomb in Westminster Abbey – one that again featured a portrait of the poet.

So this is the Renaissance Chaucer: dead, and buried; and yet somehow not so. The origins of this restlessness lie as much in the cultural dynamics of the age as with Chaucer himself. We name this period 'the Renaissance', with the implication that it sought cultural revival through a humanistic rebirth of classical culture and a rejection of medieval forms. Negative assessments of earlier writing are certainly not hard to find in this period. One of the Earl of Surrey's poems elegises Thomas Wyatt as the man who 'reft Chaucer the glory of his wit' (Spurgeon, p. 84), whilst in 1555 Robert Braham unfavourably compared the 'grosenesse and barbarousenesse of [Chaucer's] age' with 'our time, where in all kindes of learnyng … haue as much flouryshed as they euer did in anye former dayes' (Spurgeon, p. 93). This periodising manoeuvre has been challenged in modern criticism by scholars who emphasise the continuities linking 'medieval' and 'Renaissance' England. But even within the humanistic model, the relation between past and present is more conflicted than it appears at first glance. Precisely to the extent that one of humanism's key ambitions was to fashion English into a medium of cultivated expression comparable with Latin and Greek, or the continental vernaculars – precisely to the extent, that is, that this was an anxious and an aspirational Renaissance – its relationship with the Chaucerian inheritance was necessarily more complex than one of mere disavowal. Chaucer was important because he represented the most notable example of literary achievement in the vernacular before the sixteenth century. His age might be denigrated as rude or barbarous, but the image of precocious Ricardian literary excellence embodied in Chaucer's writing offered the point of origin for an imagined lineage of national achievement in English, and a mirror for humanistic aspirations in the present. The repeated rehearsal of hesitations over Chaucer's status – dead or alive? – responds to this historical double bind: medieval Chaucer represented everything that the newest tendencies of the age aspired towards.

What was at stake in the reaction to Chaucer, therefore, was cultural legitimacy. This issue is foregrounded through a second system of motifs, in which Chaucer is depicted as a father. Speed's engraving is again representative: it positions Chaucer above his son's funeral monument, festooned about with armorial bearings and lines of genealogical connection. We might compare the epilogue to William Caxton's edition (*c.* 1479) of

Chaucer's *Boece*, a translation of Boethius's *Consolation of Philosophy.* This describes how

> the worshipful fader & first founder & embelissher of ornate eloquence in our english. I mene Maister Geffry Chaucer hath translated this sayd weke out of latyn in to our vsual and moder tonge.
>
> (Spurgeon, p. 58)

Like the idea of a living Chaucer, this trope harboured complexities. The metaphor of fatherhood, which presents Chaucer as a source of hereditary authority, at the same time opens to view the extent to which this authority was being propagated through means that diverge from the channels of inheritance imagined by conventions of genealogical succession. The last decades of the fifteenth century, when Caxton was writing, represented the moment at which Chaucer's texts began to migrate from a world of scribal copying into the medium of print. Exploiting the new technology of mechanical reproduction, Caxton evokes a conventionally biologistic family romance, in which Chaucer figures as the 'father' of vernacular eloquence, productively allied to our 'moder tonge', the English language. The imagery was itself inherited: writing after Chaucer's death, the fifteenth-century poet Thomas Hoccleve had imagined him as a literary father figure (Spurgeon, p. 21), and praise of his activity as a translator was equally commonplace. Moving into the sixteenth century and beyond, however, print multiplied the image of 'father Chaucer' more extensively and more intensively than ever before. Thus, in 1570, John Foxe noted that 'Chaucers woorkes bee all printed in one volume, and therefore knowen to all men' (Spurgeon, p. 105). Christopher Cannon has argued that Chaucer represents a primary source for the 'holographic' seductions of authorial genealogy and canon-building. His term puns on 'holograph' as authorial manuscript: the illusion of literary authority, produced by the technology of manuscript writing.[3] Chaucer's entry into the networks of print reproduction only intensified these dilemmas of cultural inheritance.

The Renaissance Chaucer was a multi-faceted figure, therefore. Outright attacks were rare, except from religious voices seeking to promote godly reading. It was in this context that the schoolmaster John Wharton denounced the 'stale tales of Chaucer' (Spurgeon, p. 111). Other readers complained about the obscurity and difficulty of Chaucer's language. Writing in 1546, Peter Ashton declared that 'Chaucers words … by reason of antiquitie be almost out of vse' (Spurgeon, p. 87). Others still presented him as only as learned as the 'barbarous rudeness' of his age would permit (Spurgeon, p. 105). Yet at the same time Chaucer was celebrated. He was praised as a translator and stylist, the culture hero who 'first began to reduce the confused garden of our language into some proportion' (Spurgeon, p. 177), and who produced the first 'pure' style in English (Spurgeon, p. 145). He might even be presented as a vernacular classic, fully comparable to anything the ancient world had to offer: Roger Ascham's *Toxophilius* refers to 'our *English Homer*' (Spurgeon, p. 85). Francis Kynaston's 1635 *Amorum Troili et Cressidae* may look like an outright oddity: a translation of Chaucer's *Troilus and Criseyde* into rhymed Latin verse, printed facing the English text. In many ways, though, it encapsulates the divergent impulses governing the reception of Chaucer in this period. We see here the desire to align Chaucer with antique precedents; assertions in the prefatory matter of Chaucer's 'seeming rudenesse' (Spurgeon, p. 215); and then the reciprocal fear that it is in fact modern sensibility that 'growes barbarous' (p. 211) in its inability to appreciate the vernacular classic. Nor were reactions confined to strictly literary issues. Chaucer was celebrated by the likes of Foxe as a proto-Protestant 'who (no doubt) saw in Religion as much almost, as euen we do now, and vtterth in hys works no lesse, and semeth to be a right Wicleuian' (Spurgeon, p. 106). Meanwhile, Gabriel Harvey catalogued the 'Notable *Astronomical descriptions* in Chawcer' (p. 127).

Some of the strongest claims for Chaucer's importance are made by editions of his works. Chaucer is one of the first English authors in print. Caxton produced editions of the *Canterbury Tales* in 1478 and 1483, and of *Troilus and Criseyde* in 1483. The *Parliament of Fowls* and *Anelida and Arcite* were printed in 1477 or 1478. The *House of Fame* came out in 1483, and the translation of *Boece* was published in 1478. Chaucer's writing was also printed by Caxton's successors, Richard Pynson and Wynkyn de Worde. Later still, there were the ground-breaking volumes of collected 'workes' that Foxe refers to: ground-breaking because Chaucer was the first author in English to be honoured in this way. These were published in 1532 (by William Thynne – reprinted in 1542 and 1550), 1561 (John Stow), 1598 (Thomas Speght), and 1602 (Speght again). A key impulse here was the expansion of the canon of Chaucer's writing. Thus, the anti-clerical *Plowman's Tale* – one of two such pseudo-Chaucerian texts in existence – first appeared in the second edition of Thynne's *Works* in 1542; Speght was the first to print the fifteenth-century poem *The Floure and the Leaf* as Chaucer's. (Other texts are missing: Chaucer's *Retractions* were not printed in a volume of *Works* until 1721.) Editions of Chaucer could even incorporate avowedly non-Chaucerian material as a way of heightening the prestige of his work: Lydgate's *Siege of Thebes* is a regular inclusion after 1561.

The technology of print thus opened up new opportunities for circulating the image of Chaucer's authority. These Renaissance editions are large prestigious volumes, printed in folio, generously supplemented with paratextual material and decorative features such as woodcuts and engraved plates. It is during this period that many of the conventions governing the presentation of Chaucer's work were put in place: to read a sixteenth-century edition of Chaucer is to encounter a volume that in some ways looks disconcertingly like a modern one, such as *The Riverside Chaucer*. We can count off the similarities: a table of contents, a biographical sketch of the author, a note on language and short introductions ('arguments') for each poem. It is Speght's 1598 *Workes*, for instance, that begins the practice of inserting a list of 'The old and obscure words of Chaucer, explained', followed by similar glosses to French phrases, a list of authors cited and explanatory endnotes. The rationale for these additions is telling, however. In a letter to Speght, printed in the prefatory material to the edition, Francis Beaumont notes that 'all Greeke and Latine Poets haue had their interpretours, and most of them translated into our tongue'. So too with the continental poets: du Bartas, Petrarch, Ariosto. 'Shall onely *Chaucer*', he asks, 'our ancient poet, nothing inferior to the best, amongst all the Poets of the world, remaine always neglected, and neuer be so well vnderstood of his owne countriemen, as Strangers are?'.[4] Beaumont's letter lays bare the emulousness that underpins Chaucer's reputation in this period. Is the annotation a genuine attempt to illuminate the obscurities of 'ancient' Chaucer, or does it function to claim him as a revered father figure, a homegrown English classic?

Chaucer also played a key role as a stimulus to new literary production in this period. For the first generation of Tudor poets – Skelton, Wyatt and Surrey – Chaucer was a central figure, frequently referenced and invoked. He appears as an interlocutor, for instance, in Skelton's long poem *A Garland of Laurel*. And he remained pivotal into the later sixteenth century and beyond. Allusion to and adaptations of his works were frequent. Edmund Spenser produced a continuation of the *Squire's Tale* in Book IV of *The Faerie Queene*. Shakespeare dramatised both *Troilus and Criseyde* and the *Knight's Tale*, whilst the songs of winter and spring that conclude *Love's Labour's Lost* adapt the ending of the *Parliament of Fowls*. Ben Jonson made Chaucer a character in his masque *The Golden Age Restor'd*.

It is notable, however, how frequently these adaptations of Chaucer frame themselves in ways that highlight the ambivalence at play in the movement between medieval and Renaissance texts. Thus, Richard Tottel's seminal collection of lyric verse, the *Songes and Sonettes* (1557), prints Chaucer's ballad *Truth*, but anonymously, prefacing it with another poem, 'A comparison of his love wyth the faithful and painful love of Troylus to Creside', which sardonically distorts the tale it purports to tell by recasting it as one of happy and faithful love.[5] Book IV of Spenser's *Faerie Queene* completes the unfinished tale of Cambalo and Canace, told by Chaucer's Squire. The narrative is introduced with wholehearted praise of 'Dan *Chaucer*', the 'well of English vndefyled', at the end of which we read that Spenser dares to produce his continuation only because of the 'infusion sweete / Of thine owne spirit'.[6] This may sound modest and self-effacing. Yet the tale that follows presents a hyperbolically violent reworking of the motif of spiritual infusion. Spenser invents three brothers with one shared soul: Priamond, Diamond and Triamond. As each brother is killed by Chaucer's Cambello, his vital spirits are distributed amongst the survivors. Triamond ends up filled with 'double life, and griefe'.[7] 'Infusion', here, emerges as inextricably bound up with fraternal loss, as Spenser produces a disquieting revision of both the vitalism and of the genealogical plots that channel praise of the Renaissance Chaucer.

We have already seen the uncanny quality ascribed to the Chaucerian voice in the prologue to *The Two Noble Kinsmen*. We might also consider a more obliquely related text such as *A Midsummer Night's Dream*. *A Midsummer Night's Dream* is not a direct Chaucerian adaptation. It positions itself within the interstices of Chaucer's *Knight's Tale*, offering an account of events preceding the marriage of Theseus and Hipploya, whose conquest by Theseus opens Chaucer's text. As David Wallace has noted, however, the adventures of the Athenian mechanical Bottom also rework the *Tale of Sir Thopas*.[8] They might be read as an expansion of Sir Thopas's exclamation:

> Me dremed al this nyght, pardee
> An elf-queene shall my lemman be
> And slepe under my gore [*cloak*].
> (*CT*, VII.787–9)

A forest setting, dreams of an elf-queen, a clash between high and low idioms, the superimposition of nobility onto extreme naiveté: all these elements are drawn into Shakespeare's play. *Sir Thopas* is one of the two *Canterbury Tales* self-deprecatingly narrated as if by 'Chaucer' himself. Bottom's dream, and Shakespeare's *Dream*, are therefore genetically related to the 'dreme' of Sir Thopas, and through it to its creators, Chaucer the pilgrim and Chaucer the author. Do the parallels suggest an admiring Shakespearean tribute to his source's sly wit and indirection, or do they enact a drama of supersession, in which the dreams of the Father of English Poetry are identified with the helpless Athenian 'mechanical' Bottom – half man and half ass – whose liaison with the queen of the fairies is mockingly bereft of reproductive potential?

In books of 'Works' and for his readers, on both fronts the Renaissance Chaucer possessed an ambivalent quality that kept him poised between presence and absence. The moment could not last. Chaucer's eventual safe consignment to the past was the product less of increased historical distance than of the growing self-assurance of vernacular writing. In his *Defence of Poesy*, the Elizabethan Philip Sidney had declared himself uncertain 'whether to merueile more, either that he in that mistie time, could see so clearly, or that wee in this cleare age walke so stumblingly after him' (Spurgeon, p. 122). By the later seventeenth century, a very different cultural climate prevailed: for John Dryden, writing in 1700, Chaucer is the author who 'follow'd Nature every where; but was never so bold to go beyond her' (Spurgeon, p. 276). The loss of edge from the motif of *vestigia*, 'following in the footsteps', is palpable. 'Nature', for Dryden, provides the formula under which Chaucer can be decorously universalised, even whilst he emerges as the suitable candidate for modernisation in the adaptations contained within *Fables Ancient and Modern*. 'He is the Father of *English* poetry', Dryden writes, 'so I hold him in the same Degree of Veneration as the *Grecians* held *Homer*, or the *Romans* Virgil' (Spurgeon, p. 276) – both translated by Dryden into a heroic-couplet idiom distantly descended from one of Chaucer's own favourite verse-forms. 'Father Chaucer' had thus secured the canonical status that his sixteenth-century admirers had hopefully claimed for him, and was laid to rest.

NOTES

1 Caroline F. E. Spurgeon, *Five Hundred Years of Chaucer Criticism and Allusion (1357–1900)*, 3 vols. (London: Chaucer Society, 1914–25), Vol. 1 (hereafter Spurgeon), p. 98. Spurgeon collects a host of allusions to Chaucer. Further references to this volume appear parenthetically in the main body of the text.

2 William Shakespeare and John Fletcher, *The Two Noble Kinsmen*, ed. Lois Potter (London: Thomas Nelson, 1997), Prologue, lines 17–21.

3 Christopher Cannon, *The Grounds of English Literature* (Oxford: Oxford University Press, 2004), pp. 198–209.

4 Geoffrey Chaucer, *The Workes of Our Antient and Learned English Poet, Geffrey Chaucer*, ed. Thomas Speght (London: Adam Islip, 1598), 'F. B. to his very louing friend, T. S.'.

5 Richard Tottel, ed., *Tottel's Miscellany: Songs and Sonnets of Henry Howard, Earl of Surrey, Sir Thomas Wyatt and Others*, ed. Amanda Holton and Tom MacFaul (London: Penguin, 2011), poems 206 and 207.

6 Edmund Spenser, *The Faerie Queene*, ed. A. C. Hamilton (London: Longman, 1977), IV.ii.32–4.

7 *Ibid.*, IV.iii.22.

8 See the discussion in David Wallace, *Chaucerian Polity: Absolutist Lineages and Associational Forms in England and Italy* (Stanford: Stanford University Press, 1997), pp. 121–4; and also E. Talbot Donaldson's *The Swan at the Well: Shakespeare Reading Chaucer* (New Haven, CT and London: Yale University Press, 1985), pp. 7–29.

CHAPTER 50

The Reception of Chaucer from Dryden to Wordsworth

Bruce E. Graver

Eighteenth-century interest in the poetry of Chaucer begins with John Dryden's *Fables Ancient and Modern* (1700). There, scattered among translations and paraphrases of Ovid and other classical authors, are five versions of Chaucerian poems: *Palamon and Arcite* (based on the *Knight's Tale*), *The Cock and the Fox* (based on the *Nun's Priest's Tale*), *The Wife of Bath, Her Tale*, the pseudo-Chaucerian *The Flower and the Leaf* and a paraphrase of the Parson's portrait from the *General Prologue*. In his Preface, Dryden writes at length about Chaucer's literary achievement. Chaucer

> is the Father of English Poetry, so I hold him in the same Degree of Veneration as the Grecians held Homer, or the Romans Virgil. He is a perpetual Fountain of good Sense; learn'd in all Sciences; and therefore speaks properly on all Subjects: As he knew what to say, so he knows when to leave off; a Continence which is practis'd by few Writers, and scarcely any of the Ancients, except Virgil and Horace.[1]

But Chaucer's reputation was in decline, primarily because of the difficulty of his language and the failure of his editors to include adequate commentary. 'How few are there who can read Chaucer', lamented Dryden,

> So as to understand him perfectly? And if imperfectly, then with less Profit, and no Pleasure ... I think I have just Occasion to complain of them, who because they understand Chaucer, would deprive the greater part of their Countrymen of the same Advantage, and hoard him up, as Misers do their Grandam Gold, only to look on it themselves, and hinder others from making use of it ... I have translated some part of his Works, only that I might perpetuate his Memory, or at least refresh it, among my Countrymen.[2]

So Dryden hoped to make Chaucer accessible to a reading public incapable of understanding Middle English, so that his literary achievement could at last be widely appreciated. The translations themselves show that Dryden believed extraordinary measures were necessary: they are among the freest he ever attempted, as much as twice as long as the Chaucerian original, and often with much material of Dryden's own invention. He defends this procedure in the Preface:

> I have not ty'd myself to a Literal Translation; but have often omitted what I judg'd unnecessary, or not of Dignity enough to appear in the Company of better Thoughts. I have presumed farther in some Places, and added somewhat of my own where I thought my Author deficient, and had not given his Thoughts their true Lustre, for want of Words in the beginning of our Language.[3]

Dryden, then, is producing a modern-dress Chaucer, preserving the broad outlines of his plots, while freely omitting or adding details and figures. Rather than an authentically medieval Chaucer, Dryden tries to present the poet as he would have written, had he been an English poet of the Augustan age.

Dryden's efforts had their desired effect: British poets began to read Chaucer again. As a result, it became clear to the publisher, Bernard Lintot, that a new edition of Chaucer's works would be both desirable and profitable: one that would supersede the 1687 black-letter Speght edition, the only one then available. The Speght edition was essentially a reprint of the Elizabethan edition of 1594, with an expanded, 2,000-word glossary, made up mostly of one-word definitions, and with some attempts to regularise spelling. This, Lintot believed, was inadequate for the modern reader, so he commissioned John Urry of Christchurch, Oxford to edit the volume. When Urry died in 1716, the work was finished by Timothy Thomas, who was responsible for the glossary, and his brother William; it was published in a fine folio volume in 1721. The Urry edition advanced Chaucer's reputation in a number of important ways. First, it was the first complete edition of Chaucer's works to eschew black-letter typeface: Lintot had it set in a clear roman font, to remove one of the chief barriers to reading Chaucer: one Dryden specifically complained about. Second, the volume was prefaced with John Dart's new 'Life of Geoffrey Chaucer', an important work that distilled much seventeenth-century research into Chaucerian biography, and thus helped to contextualise Chaucer's writings for the general reader. Third, Thomas's glossary was far more extensive and accurate than Speght's, and in it there are several attempts to consider variant manuscript readings, something the editors of the 1687 Chaucer did not do at all. And finally, and most controversially, Urry (who had largely finished the text at the time of his death) regularised Chaucer's spelling and attempted to regularise his metre, the latter by adding or subtracting syllables here and there. The aim was to make Chaucer's metre conform more closely to the expectations of ears attuned to the smooth regularity of the neoclassical couplet. The Urry edition, then, like Dryden's modernisations, was an attempt to deliver Chaucer to a wider reading audience; like Dryden, it presents a modern-dress Chaucer, and is designed to make his verse more than the exclusive domain of antiquarians and scholars.[4]

In this respect, the Urry edition was successful: many more could read Chaucer's poems, thanks in large part to the improved glossary, and many contemporary poets followed Dryden's lead in either modernising or imitating Chaucer's works. The best of the modernisations were collected by George Ogle in 1741, in a three-volume collection entitled *The Canterbury Tales of Chaucer, Moderniz'd*.[5] Ogle reprinted Dart's 'Life' from Urry, and included, in the last volume, his own critical assessment of Chaucer's achievement. There he echoes Dryden's remarks about the supposed crudeness of his versification. But rather than looking to Chaucer as an English Virgil or Homer, Ogle sees him as part of a comic-satiric tradition stretching back to different classical models: to Aristophanes, Terence and Horace. 'You can name no author even of Antiquity, whether in the Comic or in the Satiric Way, equal … to [Chaucer]', Ogle asserted. Chaucer's particular genius, he continued, is for characterisation: his characters are carefully defined, and his way of 'introducing them properly on the Stage … and … supporting them agreeably to the Part they were formed to personate' is unmatched.[6] Ogle's collection is not a complete *Canterbury Tales*; only about a third of the work is included. And given Ogle's remarks about the poet, it is not surprising that his collection is concentrated on the bawdy Chaucer – on the Wife of Bath and the tales of the Miller and Reeve – rather than on more solemn works. This is the Chaucer he presents to the general reader.

But if the Urry edition did much to revive Chaucer's reputation by inspiring collections such as Ogle's, from a scholarly point of view it was a disaster. Urry based his text primarily on printed editions, particularly the 1687 Speght, and worked very little with Chaucerian manuscripts. He did not, for instance, check lines from the printed texts against manuscripts, to determine better or worse readings. As a result, his attempts to regularise spelling, and especially his attempts to fix Chaucer's supposed metrical irregularities, produced a hopelessly corrupt text. He regularised words in the genitive case to end in *-is*, to distinguish them from plurals ending *-es*, in spite of the fact that Chaucer rarely used that spelling. Many of his corrections to Chaucer's metre were made in utter ignorance of Middle English grammar and resulted in lines that either altered the plain sense of Chaucer's verse or made no sense at all, however nicely iambic they may have seemed to the eighteenth-century ear. So, although his efforts increased the readership of Chaucer's poems, the Chaucer Urry presented was mangled and deformed. Scholars were quick to point out the flaws, and turned back to their black-letter editions in disgust. But in pointing out the flaws, they brought into public debate textual and grammatical matters that few had known before. And that debate laid the foundation for one of the great scholarly achievements of the eighteenth century: Thomas Tyrwhitt's edition of the *Canterbury Tales*.[7]

Tyrwhitt, a trained classical philologist, brought to the editing of a medieval English text the same kind of scholarly procedures practised by classical scholars since the late Renaissance: he understood the necessity of studying original manuscripts, of mastering Middle English grammar and of comparing Chaucer's use of language with that of his contemporaries in order to determine his meaning. That is, he understood that, to edit Chaucer adequately, he must possess the same depth of knowledge that a Bentley or a Scaliger would bring to the editing of a Greek or Latin author. He outlined his procedures in his preface:

> The first object of this publication was to give the text of *The Canterbury Tales* as correct as the MSS. within the reach of the Editor would enable him to make it. The account of former Editions … will shew, that this object had hitherto been either entirely neglected, or at least very imperfectly pursued. The Editor therefore has proceeded as if his Author had never been published before. He has formed the text throughout from the MSS. and has paid little regard to the readings of any edition, except the two by Caxton, each of which may now be considered as a Manuscript. A list of the MSS. collated, or consulted, upon this occasion is subjoined.[8]

Thus Tyrwhitt's edition is based on the comprehensive analysis of the Chaucerian manuscript tradition, and like an edition of a classical author, begins with a manuscript census, the first time any such analysis had been performed on Chaucer's works. The result was a transformed text, swept clean of two centuries of errors and misprisions passed from printed edition to printed edition and made worse by Urry's uninformed emendations. Tyrwhitt also standardised the order of the tales, based on manuscript evidence, and included an expanded glossary providing linguistic information as well as definitions.

In addition to his textual work, Tyrwhitt provided his readers with a lengthy 'Essay on the Language and Versification of Chaucer'.[9] It is fair to say that he was the first modern editor to have a thorough understanding of Chaucer's language, and certainly was the first to understand the sophistication of Chaucer's metre. He begins by tracing the historical relationship between Norman French and Anglo-Saxon, in part to counter uninformed charges that Chaucer corrupted his English by introducing French words and phrases. Then Tyrwhitt lays out, simply and systematically, the grammatical peculiarities of what he calls Chaucer's 'Norman-Saxon dialect', providing the reader with a useful summary of Middle English grammar.[10] No editor of Chaucer had done anything like this before. His aim was to demonstrate that Chaucer's French borrowings were all thoroughly absorbed into the Saxon grammatical system. But the effect was different: he at last provided his readers with the means to read and understand Middle English. His treatment of Chaucer's metre is handled similarly: he begins with a historical survey of English metre and the use of rhyme, then turns to Chaucer's own metrical compositions and explains, simply and clearly, how the metre works. 'We should always have in mind', he writes,

> that the correctness and harmony of an English verse depends entirely upon its being composed of a certain number of syllables, and its having the accents of those syllables properly placed. In order therefore to form any judgement of the Versification of Chaucer, it is necessary that we should know the syllabical value ... of his words, and the accentual value of his syllables, as they were commonly pronounced in his time.[11]

Self-consciously employing the reasoning and methods of a classical philologist (and citing the hypothetical example of Ennius as he does so), Tyrwhitt asserts that

> The great number of his verses, sounding complete even to our ears, which is to be found in all the least corrected copies of his works, authorizes us to conclude, that he was not ignorant of the laws of metre. Upon this conclusion it is impossible not to ground a strong presumption that he intended to observe the same laws in the many other verses which seem to us irregular.[12]

He then argues that most of these irregularities can be resolved by consulting the best manuscripts, in order to sort out copyists' errors, something his edition has already done. The rest can, for the most part, be resolved by attending to differences of pronunciation. And here he articulates a few simple rules: that there is no silent *-e* in Middle English, except in cases of elision (he calls these the 'feminine e'), that the *-ed* in past-tense verbs is always pronounced, and that there is a tendency in Middle English to place the accent on later syllables, as the French would do – thus *licóur* rather than *líquour*.[13] In one blow, Tyrwhitt disposed of a century of uninformed criticism of Chaucer's metre and language and at last made it possible for serious readers to appreciate the full range of Chaucer's genius.

Tyrwhitt's *Canterbury Tales* went into several printings, and was the standard edition of the poem well into the nineteenth century. But this was not the only way it was distributed: his text and glossary were reprinted in the massive anthologies of British poets that began to appear in the 1770s. John Bell (1778), Robert Anderson (1793) and Alexander Chalmers (1810) all based their texts of the *Canterbury Tales* on Tyrwhitt and included many of his notes and essays, and their relatively cheap volumes dramatically increased the readership of Chaucer's poetry. William Blake, who engraved the frontispiece to Volume XIII of Bell's Chaucer (1782), may have first read and studied Chaucer from this edition.[14] But Blake objected to Tyrwhitt's exclusion of the Lollardite *Plowman's Tale*, and thus came to prefer earlier editions. His magnificent painting and engraving of *The Canterbury Pilgrims* depicts himself as the Ploughman, and his brilliant commentary on the poem in his *Descriptive Catalogue* specifically cites the 1687 Speght.[15] William Wordsworth, like Blake, began his lifelong engagement with Chaucer in an anthology text, found in Robert Anderson's *British Poets*. But Wordsworth took a more scholarly approach than Blake, and his engagement with Chaucer's poetry is more representative of Chaucerian reception during the Romantic period.

According to *The Prelude*, a young William Wordsworth first read Chaucer while a student at Cambridge:

> Beside the pleasant Mills of Trompington
> I laugh'ed with Chaucer; in the hawthorn shade
> Heard him (while birds were warbling) tell his tales
> Of amorous passion.[16]

The allusion, of course, is to the *Reeve's Tale*, as well as to the opening lines of the *General Prologue* ('smale foweles maken melodye' (I.9)), and it is clear that as a youth, Wordsworth, like most eighteenth-century readers, preferred the bawdier tales. His direct engagement with Chaucer began about a decade later, in 1801, when he acquired Anderson's anthology and began reading Chaucer aloud with his sister and with his future wife, Mary Hutchinson. These evening sessions led quickly to his composing modernisations: first the sexually frank *Manciple's Tale*, followed days later with the *Prioress's Tale* and the pseudo-Chaucerian *Cuckoo and the Nightingale*, and about the same time he also composed a modernisation of 168 lines from *Troilus and Criseyde*. All of these relied on the texts and glossary in Anderson, as marginal notes in two family copies of the anthology reveal.[17]

Wordsworth's modernisations demonstrate how deeply Tyrwhitt's philological and editorial achievement had affected the subsequent reception of Chaucer's works. Unlike Dryden, Wordsworth attempted to translate Chaucer line for line, preserving even his rhymes as often as possible, and much of his diction and syntax. According to Wordsworth, 'the affecting parts of Chaucer are almost always expressed in language pure and universally intelligible even to this day'.[18] Thus he strove to reproduce that language in his translation. The opening lines of the *Manciple's Tale* exemplify his procedures:

When Phoebus took delight on earth to dwell
Among mankind as ancient stories tell
He was the blithest Bachelor I trow
Of all this world, and the best Archer too:
He slew the serpent Python as he lay
Sleeping against the sun upon a day
And many another worthy noble deed
Wrought with his bow as men the same may read.
Whan Phebus dwelled here in erth adoun,
As olde books maken mentioun,
He was the moste lusty bachelor
Of all this world, and eke the best archer:
He slow Phiton the serpent as he lay
Sleping agains the sonne upon a day
And many another noble worthy dede
He with his bow wrought, as men mowen rede.[19]

Of particular interest here is line 6, which Wordsworth renders word for word, even preserving the archaic idiom 'sleeping against the sun'. Elsewhere in his modernisations he uses such words as 'certes', 'lemman' and 'eke', and phrases like 'I wis' and 'I trow': these can be found almost nowhere else in his verse. Rather than produce a modern-dress Chaucer, like Dryden or Ogle, Wordsworth employs a self-consciously archaic idiom, bending his language out of its natural shape, to give contemporary readers as much of the experience of Chaucer's English as he thought possible.

Wordsworth's version of *The Cuckoo and the Nightingale*, a poem now attributed to John Clanvowe, further shows his indebtedness to eighteenth-century advances in Chaucerian scholarship. Anderson based his text on Urry's edition of the minor poems, which reprinted the text of the poem from Speght (1687), with alterations that further corrupted an already problematic text. Wordsworth sensed these difficulties in 1802, and left his modernisation incomplete, stopping at line 260. But in revising the poem for publication in 1840, he inserted Bodleian Library manuscript readings supplied in a letter to the *Gentlemen's Magazine* (January 1839), noting that these additions were 'necessary to complete the sense'. The letter was signed 'H. H.', and was written by Robert Southey's son-in-law, Herbert

Hill, who before his marriage had held a position at the Bodleian Library, and knew Wordsworth personally. As I have written elsewhere, this makes Wordsworth's modernisation an important event in the publishing history of this poem. When it appeared in 1841, it was the first published text of the poem to depart from the corrupt texts of printed editions of Chaucer, and to restore more accurate manuscript readings.[20]

Although Wordsworth largely composed his modernisations in 1801–2, he left them unpublished for many years. The first to appear was the *Prioress's Tale,* which he included in his 1820 *River Duddon* volume. His decision to publish was probably motivated by the public discussion of Chaucer's poetry conducted by William Hazlitt and Leigh Hunt.[21] Hazlitt devoted one of his *Lectures on the English Poets* (1818) to 'Chaucer and Spenser', and he praised Chaucer for his 'equal eye for truth of nature and discrimination of character', and wrote at length about his 'power of observation' and the '*gusto*' of his 'descriptions of natural scenery'.[22] Of the *Prioress's Tale,* he wrote: 'It is simple and heroic to the last degree.'[23] Writing about the same time, Leigh Hunt specifically criticised Dryden and other modernisers of Chaucer for 'divert[ing] attention from the illustrious original', and argued instead that one should alter 'only just as much as is necessary for comfortable intelligibility, and preserving all the rest, that which appears quaint as well as that which is more modern'.[24] The principles Hunt lays out here are almost exactly those Wordsworth practised, and in his 1820 headnote, Wordsworth echoes Hunt directly:

> In the following Piece I have allowed myself no farther deviations from the original than were necessary for the fluent reading, and instant understanding, of the Author: so much however is the language altered since Chaucer's time, especially in pronunciation, that much was to be removed, and its place supplied with as little incongruity as possible. The ancient accent has been retained in a few conjunctions ... from a conviction that such sprinklings of antiquity would be admitted, by persons of taste, to have a graceful accordance with the subject.[25]

So Wordsworth's decision to prepare his modernisations for publication seems to have been a direct response to the critical revival of Chaucer taking place among London literati. But his view of the *Prioress's Tale* was not exactly Hazlitt's: in a note to the poem added in 1827, he remarked on 'the fierce bigotry of the Prioress', which contrasts oddly with her 'tender-hearted sympathies with the Mother and Child'.[26]

The Romantic-era reception of Chaucer culminated with the publication of *The Poems of Geoffrey Chaucer, Modernized*, under the editorship of R. H.

Horne, the 'Farthing Poet'. This volume appeared in 1841, exactly a century after George Ogle's collection. Among the contributors were Wordsworth (*The Cuckoo and the Nightingale* and the excerpt from *Troilus*), Leigh Hunt (the tales of the Manciple, Friar and Squire), and Elizabeth Barrett (*Anelida and Arcite*); the collection also included a new life of Chaucer, written by the German scholar Leonhard Schmitz. There is a much greater range of Chaucer's verse than in Ogle, who published just *Canterbury Tales* excerpts; several of the minor poems are translated, and although there is a clear preference for the bawdy tales, several of the serious tales are included as well. In his preface, Horne promises a greater standard of accuracy than in earlier modernisations, and takes Ogle's collection to task for its cavalier treatment of the plain sense of Chaucer's poems. He also hoped to bring out a second volume, one that would include his version of the *Knight's Tale*, if his initial effort proved successful.

But it did not. For besides the prominent poets he had engaged, Horne worked closely with the literary hack and forger Thomas Powell, and was not much better than a hack himself. Powell had been instrumental in promoting the project, and had personally coaxed Wordsworth to contribute his modernisations; Powell's own contributions were the pseudo-Chaucerian *Flower and the Leaf* and three selections from the *Legend of Good Women*. The reviewers of *Chaucer Modernized* praised the efforts of Wordsworth and Hunt, but for Horne and Powell had little but contempt. In the *Athenæum* Henry Chorley called Horne's *General Prologue* 'a counterfeit presentment'. J. A. Grimes, in the *Monthly Review*, complained that Horne knew little 'of the difficulty of translation' and was ill 'fitted for such an undertaking', and Barron Field, in an unpublished review sent directly to Wordsworth, took both Horne and Powell to task for their lack of learning, and chided Wordsworth for letting his excellent work be thrown on such a 'dung-hill'.[27] So there was no second volume, and Horne's *Knight's Tale* remained unpublished. But the volume he did publish shows, in its unevenness of quality, the state of Chaucer reception between the ground-breaking work of Tyrwhitt and its later refinement by Furnivall and Skeat. For serious students of Chaucer, like Wordsworth and Hunt, it was possible to gain a depth of understanding of Chaucer's language and art that had not been available before; for lesser talents, like Horne and Powell, there were wordlists and glossaries that could allow them easy access to Chaucer, even if their understanding was poor. Chaucer had been taken off the scholar's shelf and out of the library, which was a good thing, but at the same time his verse had been exposed to the soil of Grub Street.

NOTES

1 John Dryden, *Fables, Ancient and Modern* (London, 1700), p. vii.
2 *Ibid.*, pp. xii–xiii.
3 *Ibid.*, pp. xi–xii.
4 This account of the Urry edition is based on William L. Alderson's 'Urry's Edition (1721)', in William L. Alderson and Arnold C. Henderson, *Chaucer and Augustan Scholarship* (Berkeley: University of California Press, 1970), pp. 69–140. Alderson notes that, besides Urry and the Thomas brothers, at least five other men contributed to the volume in one way or another.
5 Geoffrey Chaucer, *The Canterbury Tales of Chaucer, Moderniz'd by Several Hands*, ed. George Ogle, 3 vols. (London, 1741).
6 *Ibid.*, Vol. III, p. vii.
7 Alderson, 'Urry's Edition (1721)', pp. 121–9.
8 Geoffrey Chaucer, *The Canterbury Tales of Chaucer. To which are added; an Essay on His Language and Versification; an Introductory Discourse; and Notes*, ed. Thomas Tyrwhitt, 4 vols. (London: T. Payne, 1775), Vol. I, p. i.
9 *Ibid.*, Vol. IV, pp. I–III.
10 *Ibid.*, Vol. IV, p. 28.
11 *Ibid.*, Vol. IV, p. 88.
12 *Ibid.*, Vol. IV, p. 91.
13 *Ibid.*, Vol. IV, pp. 91–106.
14 Gerald Bentley, *Blake Books* (Oxford: Oxford University Press, 1977), pp. 539–40.
15 Alexander S. Gourlay, 'What Was Blake's Chaucer?' *Studies in Bibliography*, 42 (1989), 272–83.
16 William Wordsworth, *The Thirteen-Book Prelude*, ed. Mark L. Reed, 2 vols. (Ithaca, NY: Cornell University Press, 1991), III.276–9.
17 William Wordsworth, *Translations of Chaucer and Virgil*, ed. Bruce E. Graver (Ithaca, NY: Cornell University Press, 1998), pp. 11–12.
18 Cited in *ibid.*, p. 10. The statement appears in a footnote to the 1800 Preface to *Lyrical Ballads*.
19 Wordsworth, *Translations*, p. 10.
20 *Ibid.*, pp. 23–5.
21 *Ibid.*, pp. 17–18.
22 William Hazlitt, *Lectures on the English Poets, Delivered at the Surrey Institution* (London: Taylor and Hessey, 1818), pp. 46, 53.
23 *Ibid.*, p. 63.
24 Leigh Hunt, *The Round Table*, Vol. I (Edinburgh, 1817), p. 135. Cited in Wordsworth, *Translations*, p. 17.
25 Wordsworth, *Translations*, p. 36.
26 Cited in *ibid.*, pp. 18–19.
27 *Ibid.*, pp. 27–8.

CHAPTER 51

The Reception of Chaucer from the Victorians to the Twenty-First Century

David Matthews

The accession of Queen Victoria in June 1837 did not mark the end or beginning of any new phase in the understanding of the works of Geoffrey Chaucer. In fact, those few early Victorian scholars who were interested in Chaucer lamented that the study of the poet had stagnated since the landmark new edition of the *Canterbury Tales* edition by Thomas Tyrwhitt sixty years earlier, which had helped to give Chaucer some currency among the Romantic poets. In the 1840s things were much as they had been for decades: it was easy enough for an interested individual to lay hands on Chaucer's poems, but the existing editions were unscholarly and full of recycled, often erroneous assumptions about Chaucer and his works.

The new reign, however, *did* mark a new sympathy for the medieval period. The 1840s were a time of intense interest in the Middle Ages: neo-Gothic buildings were springing up everywhere (most notably the new Houses of Parliament); poets, novelists and painters worked on medievalist themes.[1] In this context, fresh scholarship on Chaucer began to flourish. While popular medievalism led increasingly away from scholarship and towards works of the imagination (such as Tennyson's Arthurian *Idylls of the King*), others who had grown up with the new climate of acceptance for medievalism, such as Frederick Furnivall, Henry Bradshaw and Walter Skeat, devoted themselves to scholarship. Thirty years after Victoria's accession, they reorientated Chaucer studies and laid the foundations of the modern discipline.

In 1851, Ford Madox Brown completed a large painting, *Chaucer at the Court of Edward III*. In it, Chaucer is represented as reading at the heart of the royal court. The original design envisaged a triptych, in which other great English poets would appear. But Chaucer was always to have been central, representing the Pre-Raphaelite sense of the poet's importance. But was this generally true? Was Chaucer thought of as parallel with, say, Shakespeare? This chapter looks at Chaucer's fortunes, beginning with the Victorian transformation in the study of Chaucer, before pausing with the Edwardian period to see what Chaucer studies had become at the beginning of the twentieth century, just as English studies was becoming a professionalised university discipline. It then concludes with a summary of Chaucer reception between the First World War and the present day. In the 1840s, there was hardly any Chaucer scholarship, as currently understood, and very little popular reception of the poet. In this chapter I examine what has changed in this respect between then and now.

In the 1840s and 1850s there were no professional scholars or students in late medieval studies in Britain. Chaucer was certainly not studied in universities, and most people's needs were met by the standard, if faulty, editions of the day. In these, Chaucer was routinely said to have been born in 1328 (when in fact he was most probably born after 1340). His importance was mythologised with the exaggerated opinion that he had almost single-handedly turned English into a proper language for poetry. Several works that were certainly not written by him were usually included as his, even by editors who did not believe he had written them. The *Tale of Gamelyn*, for example, was frequently included as the Cook's tale, though Tyrwhitt had left it out as spurious in 1775. Even the most scholarly of early Victorian editions of the *Canterbury Tales*, that of Thomas Wright published by the Percy Society in 1847–51, included *Gamelyn* (though set apart in a smaller typeface than the genuine tales). Evidently, some ideas about Chaucer were too deeply seated for anyone to worry too much about rejecting them.

This changed entirely in the second half of the century, when a great deal of effort was devoted to trying to find out exactly who Chaucer was, what he wrote and when. The Chaucer Society, founded by Furnivall in 1868, unearthed many new details of Chaucer's life, as well as what were then two disregarded manuscripts of the *Canterbury Tales*, now central to all scholarship on them. These are the Ellesmere manuscript (San Marino, Huntington Library, MS EL 26 C 9) and the Hengwrt manuscript (Aberystwyth, National Library of Wales, MS Peniarth 392 D). The society was also instrumental in the production of the first modern complete Chaucer edition, Skeat's Clarendon Chaucer of 1894.

Chaucer scholarship was not, however, an exclusively British affair. In fact, British Chaucer studies was some distance behind that of German scholars – as the British scholars themselves frequently acknowledged. Bernhard ten Brink published far more on Chaucer than any British scholar, and the establishment of university chairs in English philology in Germany was more extensive than in Britain.[2]

Scholarship was not, however, the only expression of late Victorian interest in Chaucer. There was a long tradition of translating and modernising Chaucer that had intensified in the eighteenth century (after the translations by John Dryden, which had appeared in 1700) so that by 1795 a more or less complete translation of the *Canterbury Tales* was available. These translations were often loose and idiosyncratic, and the Victorian period saw a shift towards more literal renditions. R. H. Horne's 1841 anthology, *The Poems of Geoffrey Chaucer, Modernized*, collected several works of Chaucer's, as translated by William Wordsworth, Leigh Hunt, Elizabeth Barrett and other, less well-known poets. A different tradition was initiated by Charles Cowden Clarke, who produced his *Tales from Chaucer, in Prose* in 1833. Specifically addressed to 'young readers', this work was unmistakably concerned with moral improvement; Clarke hoped that his readers would 'become wise and good, by the example of the sweet and kind creatures' in the tales, and that they 'might derive improvement by the beautiful writing'.[3]

Unspoken here was a particular concern of Victorian Chaucer popularisations: the idea that Chaucer, viewed in the original, presented too much morally dubious material, not just for children, but for adults as well. Clarke's *Tales from Chaucer* appeared in a second edition in 1870, which proved to be a more propitious time for such modernised and bowdlerised retellings of the poet's work. During the following fifty years, a series of versions of Chaucer's work appeared, explicitly aimed at children.

Hence, the notional Edwardian reader of Chaucer was in a very different position from readers at the beginning of Victoria's reign. Edwardian scholars could, at a price, acquire Skeat's scholarly edition, which more closely represented Chaucer's texts as they were in the manuscripts than any previous edition. Many basic facts of Chaucerian biography had been clarified and some of the myths cleared away. This Edwardian reader had perhaps gained some acquaintance with Chaucer as a child in the nursery; perhaps the same reader's own children were reading Chaucer in one of the dozens of cheap, illustrated children's versions of the *Canterbury Tales* that succeeded Clarke's. These children would later be able to study Chaucer as a university discipline: the new field of English studies began to take off in the years after the First World War, and it is at this time that we can see the direct origins of what is understood today as Chaucer studies.

By the end of the Edwardian period, most of the work on Chaucer in the British tradition was empirical: devoted to establishing a chronology of Chaucer's work, for example, and the hierarchy of manuscripts. This form of study was obviously dominated by the idea of the single great author, a figure who was worth listening to for the powerful truths in his work. This is partly why it was so important to the late Victorians to weed out what had been spuriously attributed to Chaucer. It is also why it was felt Chaucer needed to be expurgated, so that young readers could appreciate the great author before they were confronted with his unaccountable lapses in good taste. Before the First World War there was very little that we would recognise today as *literary* study of Chaucer. What did exist was written in German, and so was reserved for specialists.

The postwar period, however, saw the emergence of a new force in Chaucer studies. There had been considerable interest in medieval English literature in some of the universities of the north-eastern United States of America for several decades. In its early years, the Chaucer Society (which relied on subscriptions to survive) had struggled for funds, and it was in America rather than Britain that the society most rapidly prospered, at one point being bailed out by a cash donation from the eminent Harvard University medievalist Francis James Child. Later, Child's protégé and successor, George Lyman Kittredge, established himself as the leading Chaucerian of his time, confirming the centrality of Harvard to the new discipline. Before the First World War, American scholars were very open to German methods and scholarship. This was a period when a scholar could relatively easily read all of the existing criticism on Chaucer, and Kittredge clearly did this – including that in German, in which he was fluent.

The important thing about Kittredge's lectures on Chaucer – published in 1915 as the influential monograph *Chaucer and His Poetry* – was his essentially *literary* approach to the poet. He offered 'a full-blown *interpretation* of Chaucer', rather than source study, historical contextualising or 'philological explication'.[4] He expected his hearers to approach Chaucer the same way they approached the modern novel: by thinking about character, theme, irony, psychology. Kittredge did not stress the *difference* of the medieval past, but rather Chaucer's modernity. While it was nothing new to claim that Chaucer was the first modern poet, Kittredge gave the statement real force, arguing that the fourteenth century was in fact more familiar to us than the eighteenth, and claiming that he was struck more by the familiarity of Chaucer's time than by the strangeness.[5]

Practically, this meant that when he analysed *Troilus and Criseyde*, Kittredge was concerned not so much with its links back to the classical period as with the way it anticipated modern literature: he called the poem 'an elaborate psychological novel', and it was, he said, 'the first novel, in the modern sense, that ever was written in the world, and one of the best'.[6] *Troilus and Criseyde*, with its troubling sexual morality, had puzzled nineteenth-century readers, who tended instead to favour the *Canterbury Tales*, thinking that work more realistic. For Kittredge, by contrast, Troilus,

Criseyde and Pandarus are simply characters with whom we are supposed to sympathise, recognising their emotional dilemmas much as we might recognise those of the characters in a novel by George Eliot or Henry James.

Kittredge's book has had long influence and is still cited. After it, a rapidly expanding Chaucer industry arose in American universities. German scholarship declined after the war and US–German relations deteriorated, American English studies detaching itself from German influence. It prospered, so that not only did American critics dominate literary critical trends, but the major initiatives in editing also shifted away from Britain to the USA. The successor to Skeat's complete Chaucer edition was that of the Harvardian F. N. Robinson, produced in 1933, with a second edition in 1957, used by generations of students and leading directly to the current standard, *The Riverside Chaucer*, another Harvard enterprise under the general editorship of Larry D. Benson. The edition of the *Canterbury Tales* by J. M. Manly and Edith Rickert, with its exhaustive descriptions of all the manuscripts known at the time, was produced by the University of Chicago Press in 1940. Of course, there were and are major Chaucerians based in British universities, from C. S. Lewis in the 1950s and 1960s to Helen Cooper more recently. But from Kittredge onwards, the major publishing initiatives tended to emerge from American university presses, while some of the most important critical trends were represented in the work of critics based in American universities.

Kittredge, as we have seen, emphasised the *modernity* of Chaucer's writing. This opened the way for the work of Chaucer to join the canon of English literature and, when the methodology of New Criticism became dominant in many American English departments from the mid twentieth century onwards, to be studied just as one would study Wordsworth or, even more aptly, Shakespeare. But the New Critical method of such a leading Chaucerian as E. T. Donaldson – with its emphasis on the self-sufficiency of the individual poem as a verbal icon – was not uncontested in Chaucer studies in the 1960s. There were others, such as D. W. Robertson, who maintained that what Chaucer wrote should be seen as originating in medieval religious doctrine. By locating Chaucer thoroughly in his context (albeit a context relatively narrowly understood) exegetical criticism, as it was called, was obviously a form of historicism.[7] Ultimately, exegetical criticism was judged by most critics to be too exclusively concerned with a narrowly conceived sense of Chaucer's originary context.

A more decisive swing to historicism in Chaucer criticism took place in the 1980s and thereafter, in the work of critics reacting against New Criticism – by then dominant – and concerned to place Chaucer in his social and political context in a way more expansive than Robertson: David Aers, Sheila Delany, Stephen Knight, Lee Patterson, Paul Strohm, among others. At the same time, a range of explicitly theoretical initiatives was seen in Chaucer studies: queer and gender studies in the work of Carolyn Dinshaw, for example, and psychoanalysis in that of L. O. Aranye Fradenburg, while the work of David Wallace opened Chaucer (so often thought of as a quintessentially English writer) to broader European currents of thought.

University study was, then, a dominant factor in reception of Chaucer up until the present day. But there remained, and remains, a wider sense of Chaucer in the popular domain. The idea that Chaucer ought to be made more accessible had some currency among the generation of mid-twentieth-century critics who had grown up surrounded by Edwardian translations. An Oxford don, Nevill Coghill, presented a series of verse translations of the *Canterbury Tales* on BBC radio between 1946 and 1949, before publishing them with Penguin Classics in 1951 as perhaps the most influential translations of Chaucer ever to appear. They led to a musical stage version of the *Tales* that ran for several years in London and toured the world. By the time Pier Paolo Pasolini's film *I racconti di Canterbury* appeared in 1972, Chaucer's most famous work was more widely available and in more varied media than ever before. In more recent times, animated versions of the tales of the Nun's Priest, Knight, Wife of Bath and others have been created for television by Jonathan Myerson (1998, 2000), while very free modern adaptations of six tales appeared on British television in 2003. In 2005 the Royal Shakespeare Company presented a dramatic version of the *Tales* directed by Gregory Doran, Rebecca Gatward and Jonathan Munby, which went on to a successful world tour.

These productions suggest a rising fame for Chaucer in the popular sphere to match his undoubted prominence in scholarship. The relative difficulty of reading Chaucer in the original, however, qualifies the suggestion that there is a Chaucer industry comparable with that surrounding Shakespeare. On the south bank of the Thames in London, it is Shakespeare's Globe that dominates literary tourism, not the Tabard Inn. Arguably, Chaucer is relatively obscure 'in our culture at large', which Steve Ellis attributes to various factors, including Chaucer's language, a patronising attitude on the part of later writers and Chaucer's appropriation by academics.[8] This obscured Chaucer is seen in the 2001 film *A Knight's Tale*, when the poet (Paul Bettany) is encountered walking naked down the road, having lost his shirt (and everything else) while gambling.

The hero of the film, William Thatcher, and his companions fall into conversation with the poet, who tells them he is a writer:

WAT: A what?
CHAUCER: A wha— a what? A writer. You know, I write, with ink, and parchment. Geoffrey Chaucer's the name, writing's the game. You've probably read my book? the Book of the Duchess? [blank looks] No? Well, it *was* allegorical.
ROLAND: Well, we won't hold that against you, that's for every man to decide for himself.[9]

Later in the film, apart from one brief scene with a summoner and a pardoner, there is little sense of Chaucer's role as future poet and instead he becomes a warm-up man for William's jousting bouts. The gags are knowing ones that suggest the film-maker's knowledge about the poet, but this is a Chaucer who, just as Ellis concludes, is 'everywhere and nowhere'.[10] A film featuring Shakespeare will (like *Shakespeare in Love* (1998)) lead to quoting of the bard's lines and perhaps the staging of a play. But when Chaucer appears it does not become an occasion for the declaiming of his verse. At the beginning of the twenty-first century, then, there remains a significant split between popular and scholarly receptions of Chaucer. Popularly, he is known *about* but not much read. Just as in the 1840s, it is in the domain of scholars and students that Chaucer's afterlife continues most vigorously.

NOTES

1 See further David Matthews, *Medievalism: A Critical History* (Cambridge: D. S. Brewer, 2015), pp. 49–59.
2 See Richard Utz, *Chaucer and the Discourse of German Philology: A History of Reception and an Annotated Bibliography of Studies, 1793–1948* (Turnhout: Brepols, 2002), pp. 82–102.
3 Charles Cowden Clarke, *Tales from Chaucer, in Prose: Designed Chiefly for the Use of Young Persons* (London: Effingham Wilson, 1833), p. iii.
4 Kathy Cawsey, *Twentieth-Century Chaucer Criticism: Reading Audiences* (Farnham: Ashgate, 2011), p. 22 (emphasis in original).
5 G. L. Kittredge, *Chaucer and His Poetry* (Cambridge, MA: Harvard University Press, 1915), pp. 8–9.
6 *Ibid.*, pp. 109, 112.
7 See Lee Patterson, *Negotiating the Past: The Historical Understanding of Medieval Literature* (Madison: University of Wisconsin Press, 1987), chapter 1.
8 Steve Ellis, *Chaucer at Large: The Poet in the Modern Imagination* (Minneapolis: University of Minnesota Press, 2000), p. 153.
9 Brian Helgeland, dir., *A Knight's Tale*, produced by Todd Black, Brian Helgeland and Tim van Rellim (Columbia Pictures, 2001).
10 Ellis, *Chaucer at Large*, p. 154.

CHAPTER 52

Cyber-Chaucer

Stephen Kelly

Cyber-, comb. form.

Chiefly prefixed to nouns. Originally: forming words relating to (the culture of) computers, information technology, and virtual reality, or denoting futuristic concepts. Later also: spec. forming terms relating to the Internet. (*OED*)

I

But as I slepte, me mette I was
Withyn a temple ymad of glas,
In which ther were moo ymages
Of gold, stondynge in sondry stages,
And moo ryche tabernacles,
And with perre moo pynacles,
And moo curiouse portreytures,
And queynte maner of figures
Of olde werk, then I saugh ever.
(*HF*, 119–27)

It is perhaps the predicament of all 'great' literature that it heralds the nature of its future appropriations. For what else is Chaucer's narrator dreaming of in that 'temple ymad of glass', full of 'curiouse portreytures', than computer screens, where 'olde werk', including his own, circulates and persists in the endless reproducibility and connectivity of the network? The web is here prefigured as a house of fame, in which textual knowledge provokes its own dissemination and interconnection, as myths of fame succeed and echo one another. Too regularly labelled a Borgesian Library of Babel, isn't the web in fact Chaucer's 'temple', realised in computers, smartphones and tablets, re-mediated across always-on networks?

Earlier in this volume, we read how sixteenth- and seventeenth-century publishers and admirers of Chaucer, from John Speed and Thomas Speght to Alexander Neville and Samuel Daniel, articulated the relevance of the poet to their contemporary audiences in terms of what Alex Davis called a 'vivificatory impulse' (p. 410). Such an impulse may be one of the inaugurating gestures of any literary history. How will Chaucer be newly 'alive' to us in the increasingly technologically augmented circumstances of twenty-first-century literary studies? The 'digital humanities' (hereafter DH) promises to revivify Chaucer, but in what ways? And what is at stake?

Of course, DH has not emerged *sui generis*; it replaced what was once called 'humanities computing' – a field in which medievalists played a pioneering role. From Roberto Busa's concordances of the works of Thomas Aquinas in the 1950s, to the myriad medieval studies 'portals' of the late 1980s and early 1990s – Labyrinth, NetSerf, Orb, Luminarium, Medieval Sourcebook – to more sophisticated projects such as the Hyperbibliography, Digital Scriptorium and the *Canterbury Tales* Project, medievalists have had few qualms about recognising the potential and reach of computer technologies for the enhancement of their research. Broadly speaking, humanities computing provided the traditional activities of literary studies with technological facilitation. Its work was undertaken by information-technology specialists or humanities graduates who had side-stepped into computer science. The sovereign intelligence here remained that of the critic; computing was merely a tool: its outputs typically consisted of concordances, corpora and digitised texts. However, with digitisation, represented pre-eminently by the Text Encoding Initiative (TEI), which emerged in the late 1980s, information technology was beginning to be perceived less as the sacred fire of technicians before which literary scholars genuflected than as an instrument in itself – a method – to be deployed by critics and historians for articulating new research questions.

What marks the transition from humanities computing to DH? The terms of any response will probably be contested by the exceedingly broad church of scholars and computing specialists who make up the field. Might it be suggested that 'humanities computing' names a phase when information technology was leveraged as a means of expanding the purview of traditional humanities research questions, while DH promises to explore the implications of doing research digitally in the first place? Humanities computing recognised the potential of information technology to automate large-scale, and typically tedious, data-related tasks, such as the collation of corpora and concordances – hence, the centrality of the database to such research. The first transcendental virtue that guided humanities computing was the enhancement of accessibility. Digital platforms promised to liberate materials traditionally under the archivist's lock and key for use and reuse by myriad academic and student audiences (the fabled promise of 'open access' or the liberal licensing rights of Creative Commons). The benefits were self-evident; in the case of Chaucer, scholars and students could enjoy unprecedented access to the manuscripts of Chaucer's works, or reprocess and repurpose Chaucerian texts digitised in TEI-compliant XML. However, such a libertarian spirit was arguably framed by the brash utopianism of the market place: of computing and software companies whose market capitalisation fed symbiotically on their claims to democratisation. Hence, we might be wise to resist the rhetoric of novelty, nascency or latency, accompanying first humanities computing and now DH. Too often, champions of DH take the extraordinary success of the personal computer over the past forty years and its current ubiquity and mobility as means to pretend to futurity. As David Berry comments, 'The digital assemblages that are now being built not only promise great change at the level of the individual human actor, they provide destabilising amounts of knowledge and information.'[1] Such utopian rhetoric accompanied the first self-conscious stirrings of the digital humanities: 'hypertext … presages a potential revolution in literary studies', Paul Delany and George Landow excitedly declared in *Hypermedia and Literary Studies*, published in 1991.[2] According to Berry, 'computer code enables new communicative processes, and, with the increasing social dimension of networked media, the possibility of new and exciting forms of collaborative thinking arises'.[3] While the intellectual novelties of DH may indeed be exciting, their complicity with a neo-liberal fantasy of a market place of boundless availability and opportunity must be submitted to that foundational reflex of humanities thinking, scepticism. That information technology and the World Wide Web have been enormously transformative is a truism, but the misty-eyed liberalism of DH's exponents crashes against the new elitisms – not to mention modes of surveillance and commercial exploitation – that network technologies have brought into being.

II

Men loven of propre kynde newefangelnesse,
As briddes doon, that men in cages fede,
For though thou nyght and day take of hem hede,
And strawe hir cage faire and softe as silk,
And yeve hem sugre, hony, breed, and milk,
Yet right anon as that his dore is uppe,
He with his feet wol spurne adoun his cuppe,
And to the wode he wole and wormes ete;
So newefangel been they of hir mete,
And loven novelrie of propre kynde.

(*SqT*, v.610–19)

So says Chaucer's Squire. Novelty here repudiates the consolations of the familiar; the delights of the 'wode' and its 'wormes' overwhelm the cosseted attachments of habit or tradition. Has DH let us out of our disciplinary cages? In a 2012 lecture at the University of Oxford, medievalist Andrew Prescott, then head of the Department of Digital Humanities at King's College London, the leading centre for DH in the UK, commented, 'to judge from the projects it produces, the digital humanities as formally constituted has been party to a concerted attempt to reinstate an outmoded and conservative view of the humanities'.[4] The technology may be new, but the ideas underpinning it wouldn't have bothered F. R. Leavis. While Prescott's views have provoked vigorous debate online, in the case of medieval studies, many of the highest-profile DH projects have proceeded precisely from revered notions of canonicity and authority. Take, for example, the *Canterbury Tales* Project, initiated by the late Norman Blake and brought to fruition by one of the leading DH advocates then working in Britain, Peter Robinson. The *Canterbury Tales* Project's laudable aim was to digitise the extant manuscripts of the *Canterbury Tales*, and at least initially the project hoped to elaborate a new model for editing the tales based on the application of cladistics – a method of animal classification derived from evolutionary biology – to the manuscript corpus of Chaucer's tales. In such a gesture is captured one of the utopian goals of the emergent DH and its second transcendental virtue: transdisciplinarity. Here, the humanities work in concert with the sciences and need no longer cling to Wilhelm Dilthey's conception of *Geisteswissenschaften*, now increasingly spurious in the context of a society and academy in which the humanities are continually traduced. Instead, humanities scholars can hide in plain sight, basking in the empirically demonstrable successes of the 'hard sciences'. Robinson's methodology was subjected to devastating critique by Ralph Hanna, in a paper presented at the launch of the project in Leicester in 1999. Published subsequently as 'The Application of Thought to Textual Criticism in All Modes – with Apologies to A. E. Housman', the sarcastic title of Hanna's essay captures what is its central argument: that critical thought is eclipsed in the application of scientific models,

> I am initially bemused by Robinson's choice of tool, a striking form of cyclical 'historicism' whereby the post-modern 'machine' replicates its archaic origins. For Robinson implicitly appeals to analogy – the development of manuscript tradition should be like the development of species – and in so doing, thoughtlessly replays the same Late Romantic fascination with origins and organic growth which produced this kind of thinking in the first place.[5]

Regardless of the success or failure of Robinson's model, Hanna asserts that a humanist notion of critique – with its supposedly careful, sceptical and unbiased motivations – is the defining first principle of humanities research.[6] What he insistently refers to as the 'machine' cannot make the subjective judgements that instantiate the difference between the humanities and sciences. But need he have worried? In a response to Hanna's trenchant essay, Robinson betrays that his own values as a digital editor aren't as far from Hanna's as they seem: 'better to learn how to use these new methods to make better editions, editions which give the reader something of the same excitement we have felt in seeing patterns emerge within the vast quantities of data, and in encountering readings where Chaucer's own hand seems at work'.[7] The traditional goal of literary scholarship – to recuperate the Author – counteracts the supposed radicalism of the method of recuperation.[8] Is, then, the Chaucer of the digital humanities the Chaucer we always knew? Even in the pedagogical application of digital tools, the values of old-fashioned literary criticism reign supreme: witness METRO, developed by leading medievalists at Harvard University.[9] This resource uses online quizzes and hypertextual essays to train undergraduates in the traditional skills of medieval studies; its Chaucer pages provide 'platforms' for the study of Chaucer's language and manuscripts, and for the traditional techniques of manuscript study, palaeography and codicology. At no point in METRO does one have the sense that the Chaucer imagined here has been affected by the digital. Cyber-Chaucer awaits other midwives.

III

This wrecched worldes transmutacioun,
As wele or wo, now povre and now honour,
Withouten ordre or wys discrecioun
Governed is by Fortunes errour.
(*Fortune*, lines 1–4)

Digital Humanities is now a firmly established 'discipline' in its own right. Our students are so-called 'digital natives', reading texts on e-readers or iPads when they are not tweeting, Instagramming, Facebooking or gaming. Academics prepare their research using JSTOR, Project Muse and Google Books, and deliver their teaching, via VLEs and MOOCs, in electronic form; the lecture, as an educational medium, is under increasing attack as antiquated (even 'medieval') and unfit for purpose. The tendency to cling to traditional critical values even when mediated digitally is perhaps understandable; the humanities seem to have entered an archaeological and curatorial phase. Creativity is disaggregated (not democratised; this is a toxic myth of the new digital order) across myriad platforms. Poetry is produced by exploiting the algorithmic vagaries of Google Search. For DH advocates, it is a moment of dizzying possibility that places us on the cusp of a Copernican revolution in which 'computation' will do the majority of the heavy lifting previously undertaken by archivists, editors, textual critics and historians, as David Berry claims:

> If software and code become the condition of possibility for unifying the multiple knowledges now produced in the university, *then the ability to think for oneself*, taught by rote learning of methods, calculations, equations, readings, canons, processes and so forth, *might become less important*.[10]

One can hear their teeth grinding, those humanists from Geoffrey Chaucer to Ralph Hanna who prize learning and thoughtful, critical reflection. We might contrast Berry's breathless excitement with the rather more measured views of Willard McCarty, one of DH's most eminent and intelligent theorists:

> Reduction of text to data is a trade-off: manipulability, including quantification and other transformations, is gained; meaning, and with it 'context' as a meaningful term, is lost. Effectively all would indeed be lost as far as the humanities are concerned if the change were one-way, the machine substituted for human intelligence. Nothing like that is the case for scholarship. Like other tools, computing augments it, gives it greater reach … Computing machines and scholarly intelligence change each other, recursively.[11]

McCarty might remind both advocates and critics of DH that culture has always been transmitted; digital cultural productions are no less mediated than the texts of the Hengwrt manuscript of the *Canterbury Tales*. 'Shaped', says Bonnie Mak, 'by social forces of the twenty-first century, and marked by the cultural, bibliographic, and computational codes of the past and present … digitised pages are witness to their own course through time and space'.[12] Digital artefacts are hence no less material than their physical counterparts, as any effort to utilise the CD-ROMs of the *Canterbury Tales* Project on a modern computer will demonstrate. What was once (close to) state-of-the-art technology now appears bloated, clumsy and dated: images are not photographed at sufficient resolution to drive contemporary high-definition displays, and browsers that support web standards dislike the proliferating frames of a user-interface (UI) where user experience (UX) seems to have been given little thought. While the late Steve Jobs characterised the work of Apple as the 'intersection of technology and the liberal arts', the liberal arts, as represented by DH, struggle to reach an ever-receding horizon of technological development in which academics have little or no investment and to which they make little contribution.[13] (No wonder the impact of scholarship on computing is, in McCarty's term, recursive!) As the authors of the 2012 Digital_Humanities manifesto put it,

> All future scholarly projects that do not aspire to the highest design standards are unlikely to achieve public impact or enduring results. This is the reason why meticulous attention to design also provides new opportunities: namely, that good design breeds rich and robust digital tools and resources, and can make specialized forms of knowledge and inquiry comprehensible to expanded audiences and user groups.[14]

Brilliant new tools such as Manuscripts Online enable the retrieval of data produced by a variety of collaborative research projects in ways that allow new knowledge of medieval textual cultures to emerge.[15] DigiPal has the potential to enhance enormously our understanding of medieval scripts and hence transform our understanding of literary history.[16] In turn, scholars are working with experts in artificial intelligence to develop tools to identify scribal hands automatically. In other words, important digital research is under way, and lessons have been learnt about the design and implementation of such platforms. But the question of how the digital might fundamentally transform our understanding of culture, and cultural history, remains.

How, then, might Chaucer be read, studied, researched digitally? This chapter has suggested that to date, DH projects – whether digital editions, concordances, transcriptions or e-learning tools – have in general reaffirmed the traditional attachments of the 'analogue' humanities to canonicity and authority. The paradigm of fixity and textual stability promulgated (disingenuously, of course) by print never affected a manuscript culture 'governed ... by Fortunes errour', and yet it continues to underpin scholarship of Chaucer. While Chaucer may have feigned horror of *mouvance* at the end of *Troilus and Criseyde* or in his witty scolding of Adam Scriveyn/Pinkhurst, he was more than aware that, in Patrick Connor's terms, 'the essence of a collective human textuality is – and always has been – its potential to be a hypertext'.[17] Digital textuality, incorporating sound, vision and written word, is still working out how to 'revivify' Chaucer for the Age after the Book. Erik Weiscott's *Mapping Chaucer*, a Google 'mash-up' produced for an undergraduate course at Boston College and influenced, presumably, by David Wallace's landmark project *Europe: A Literary History, 1348–1418*, translates the *Canterbury Tales* from text to a series of itineraries, and is richly suggestive of the intertexts and cultural and intellectual crossroads of the *Tales*.[18] It is at the interface of the visual and performing arts that new iterations of Chaucerian narrative, new mash-ups, are emerging. Baba Brinkman's *The Canterbury Tales Remixed*[19] or the Confraternity of Neoflagellants' multimedia *thN Lng folk 2go* (performed at the University of St Andrews in July 2013 and subsequently published by Punctum Books) model the influence and reception of Chaucer in ways that DH scholarship has yet to begin to imagine.

But the question of whether we have yet begun to understand who 'cyber-Chaucer' might be remains. If there is anything genuinely revolutionary in DH, it is in demoting the significance of hermeneutic commentary as a primary activity of humanities research. Scholarship, as it emerged in classical culture and developed in the so-called Middle Ages and Renaissance, has proceeded upon the myth of a hierarchy of 'primary' and 'secondary' texts. As Stuart McWilliams puts it,

> 'Primary' texts are maintained as being capable of nothing more than referential inwardness. The designation of 'primary', which seems to confer so much esteem, in fact silences the text – it becomes esoteric. If scholars are to be reflexive in their construction of history, so texts must be permitted their exotericism; their outwardness.[20]

The supposed 'primary' text does not 'speak' for itself but rather must be articulated by scholarly commentary. The scholar-archon assumes a powerful role of arbitration. If it is not legislated out of existence under the influence of 'Big Publishing' or the war on 'net neutrality',[21] digital culture promises – for it is always a promise – to collapse this distinction definitively: the boundaries between author, commentator, publisher, scribe, coder, designer and between text and page and screen will dissolve into multiple continua of text. It is in such a context that a 'cyber-Chaucer' will eventually emerge.

NOTES

1 David M. Berry, 'Introduction', in *Understanding Digital Humanities* (London: Routledge, 2012), p. 8.

2 Paul Delany and George P. Landow, eds., *Hypermedia and Literary Studies* (Boston, MA: MIT University Press, 1991), p. 6.

3 Berry, 'Introduction', p. 5.

4 Published on Prescott's blog as 'Making the Digital Human: Anxieties, Possibilities, Challenges', http://digitalriffs.blogspot.co.uk/2012/07/making-digital-human-anxieties.html (last accessed 10 July 2013).

5 Ralph Hanna, 'The Application of Thought to Textual Criticism in All Modes – with Apologies to A. E. Housman', *Studies in Bibliography*, 53 (2000), 163–72 (pp. 171–2).
6 Perhaps such a model of scholarship is itself in a terminal phase; see Rita Felski, *The Limits of Critique* (Chicago: University of Chicago Press, 2015).
7 Peter Robinson, 'Making Electronic Editions and the Fascination of What Is Difficult', *Linguistica computazionale*, 20–1 (2004), 415–38 (p. 438).
8 It is striking that much work in DH side-steps or simply ignores the radical critique of the humanities undertaken by literary and cultural theory.
9 METRO: Middle English Teaching Resources Online, http://metro.fas.harvard.edu/icb/icb.do (last accessed 31 March 2013).
10 Berry, 'Introduction', p. 10 (my emphasis).
11 Willard McCarty, *Text and Genre in Reconstruction: Effects of Digitalization on Ideas, Behaviours, Products and Institutions* (Cambridge: OpenBook Publishers, 2010), 'Introduction', p. 2.
12 Bonnie Mak, *How the Page Matters* (Toronto: University of Toronto Press, 2011), p. 70.
13 'It is in Apple's DNA that technology alone is not enough. That it's technology married to the liberal arts, married to the humanities, that yields us the result that makes our hearts sing.' Apple, Inc., 'iPad introduction', March 2006, www.youtube.com/watch?v=KlI1MR-qNt8 (last accessed 31 July 2013).
14 Anne Burdick, Johanna Drucker, Peter Lunenfeld, Todd Presner and Jeffrey Schnapp, *Digital_Humanities* (Cambridge, MA: MIT Press, 2012), p. 119.
15 www.manuscriptsonline.org/ (last accessed 14 December 2018).
16 www.digipal.eu/ (last accessed 14 December 2018).
17 Patrick Connor, 'Hypertext in the Last Days of the Book', *Bulletin of the John Rylands University Library of Manchester*, 74 (1992), 7–24 (p. 8).
18 https://mediakron.bc.edu/mappingchaucer/ (last accessed 14 December 2018).
19 https://music.bababrinkman.com/album/the-canterbury-tales-remixed (last accessed 14 December 2018).
20 Stuart McWilliams, *Magical Thinking: History, Possibility and the Idea of the Occult* (London: Bloomsbury, 2012), p. 2.
21 On 'Big Publishing' see David Matthews, 'Will Other Countries Follow Germany into Battle with Elsevier?', *Times Higher Education Supplement*, 1 February 2018. On the ongoing controversies, especially in the USA, regarding net neutrality, see www.theverge.com/net-neutrality (last accessed 14 December 2018).

Further Reading

1 WHAT WAS CHAUCER LIKE?

Crow, Martin M. and Clair C. Olson, eds., *Chaucer Life-Records* (Oxford: Clarendon Press, 1966). [=*L-R*]

Pearsall, Derek, *The Life of Geoffrey Chaucer: A Critical Biography* (Oxford: Blackwell, 1992).

2 CHAUCER'S LIFE AND LITERARY 'PROFESSION'

Crow, Martin M. and Clair C. Olson, eds., *Chaucer Life-Records* (Oxford: Clarendon Press, 1966). [=*L-R*]

Green, Richard Firth, *Poets and Princepleasers: Literature and the English Court in the Late Middle Ages* (Toronto: University of Toronto Press, 1980).

The Oxford Dictionary of National Biography (Oxford: Oxford University Press, 2004–), www.oxforddnb.com/ (entries on many relevant figures).

Pearsall, Derek, *The Life of Geoffrey Chaucer: A Critical Biography* (Oxford: Blackwell, 1992).

Strohm, Paul, *Chaucer's Tale: 1386 and the Road to Canterbury* (New York: Viking, 2014).

Wallace, David, *Chaucerian Polity: Absolutist Lineages and Associational Forms in England and Italy* (Stanford: Stanford University Press, 1999).

3 CHAUCER'S LINGUISTIC INVENTION

Brewer, D. S., 'Chaucer's Poetic Style', in Piero Boitani and Jill Mann, eds., *The Cambridge Chaucer Companion*, 1st edn (Cambridge: Cambridge University Press, 1986), pp. 227–42.

Burnley, J. D., *A Guide to Chaucer's Language* (Basingstoke: Macmillan, 1983).

Cannon, Christopher, 'Chaucer's Style', in Piero Boitani and J. Mann, eds., *The Cambridge Chaucer Companion*, 2nd edn (Cambridge: Cambridge University Press, 2004), pp. 233–50.

Copeland, Rita, 'Chaucer and Rhetoric', in Seth Lerer, ed., *The Yale Companion to Chaucer* (New Haven, CT: Yale University Press, 2006), pp. 122–46.

Donaldson, E. Talbot, 'Idiom of Popular Poetry in *The Miller's Tale*', in *Speaking of Chaucer* (London: Athlone, 1970), pp. 13–29.

Duffell, Martin J., '"The craft so long to lerne": Chaucer's Invention of the Iambic Pentameter', *Chaucer Review*, 34 (2000), 269–88.

Horobin, Simon, *Chaucer's Language* (Basingstoke: Palgrave Macmillan, 2007).

4 CHAUCER AND LONDON ENGLISH

Burnley, J. D., *A Guide to Chaucer's Language* (Basingstoke: Macmillan, 1983).

Butterfield, Ardis, *The Familiar Enemy: Chaucer, Language and Nation in the Hundred Years War* (Oxford: Oxford University Press, 2009).

Horobin, Simon, *Chaucer's Language* (Basingstoke: Palgrave Macmillan, 2007).

Horobin, Simon, and J. J. Smith, *An Introduction to Middle English* (Edinburgh: Edinburgh University Press, 2002).

Sandved, Arthur O., *Introduction to Chaucerian English* (Woodbridge: Boydell and Brewer, 1985).

Wogan-Browne, Jocelyn *et al.*, *Language and Culture in Medieval Britain: The French of England, c. 1100–c. 1500* (Woodbridge: Boydell and Brewer, 2009).

5 MANUSCRIPTS AND MANUSCRIPT CULTURE

(See also the recommendations for Chapter 6.)

De Hamel, Christopher, 'The Hengwrt Chaucer', in *Meetings with Remarkable Manuscripts* (London: Penguin, 2018), pp. 426–65.

Doyle, A. I., and M. B. Parkes, 'The Production of Copies of the *Canterbury Tales* and the *Confessio Amantis* in the Early Fifteenth Century', in M. B. Parkes and Andrew G. Watson eds., *Medieval Scribes, Manuscripts and Libraries: Essays Presented to N. R. Ker* (London: Scolar Press, 1978), pp. 163–210. Reprinted in M. B. Parkes, *Scribes, Scripts and Readers* (London: Hambledon Press, 1991), pp. 201–48.

Edwards A. S. G., review of Linne R. Mooney and Estelle Stubbs, *Scribes and the City*, *The Library* 15, no. 1 (2014), 79–81.

Griffiths, Jeremy and Derek Pearsall, eds., *Book Production and Publishing in Britain 1375–1475* (Cambridge: Cambridge University Press, 1989).

Hanna, Ralph, *Pursuing History: Middle English Manuscripts and Their Texts* (Stanford: Stanford University Press, 1996).

Mooney, Linne R. and Estelle Stubbs, *Scribes and the City: London Guildhall Clerks and the Dissemination of Middle English Literature, 1375–1425* (Woodbridge: York Medieval Press, 2013).

Mosser, Daniel W., *A Digital Catalogue of the Pre-1500 Manuscripts and Incunables of the 'Canterbury Tales'*, 2nd edn, www.mossercatalogue.net/ (last accessed 12 August 2018).

Warner, Lawrence, *Chaucer's Scribes: London Textual Production*, 1384–1432 (Cambridge: Cambridge University Press, 2018).

6 CHAUCER'S BOOKS

Coleman, Joyce, *Public Reading and the Reading Public in Late Medieval England and France* (Cambridge: Cambridge University Press, 1996).

De Hamel, Christopher, *Scribes and Illuminators* (London: British Museum Press, 1992).
Gillespie, Alexandra and Daniel Wakelin, eds., *The Production of Books in England 1350–1500* (Cambridge: Cambridge University Press, 2011).
Morgan, Nigel J. and Rodney M. Thomson, eds., *The Cambridge History of the Book in Britain*, Vol. II: *1100–1400* (Cambridge: Cambridge University Press, 2008).

7 AUTHORITY

Galloway, Andrew, 'Authority', in Peter Brown, ed., *A Companion to Chaucer* (Oxford: Blackwell, 2000), pp. 23–39.
Hanna III, Ralph, '*Compilatio* and the Wife of Bath: Latin Backgrounds, Ricardian Texts', in *Pursuing History: Middle English Manuscripts and Their Texts* (Stanford: Stanford University Press, 1996), pp. 247–57.
Kinch, Ashby, ' "Mind like wickerwork": The Neuroplastic Aesthetics of Chaucer's House of Tidings', *postmedieval*, 3 (2012), 302–14.
Minnis, A. J., *Medieval Theory of Authorship: Scholastic Literary Attitudes in the Later Middle Ages* (London: Scolar Press, 1984; 2nd edn with a new preface by the author, Philadelphia: University of Pennsylvania Press, 2010).
'The Author's Two Bodies? Authority and Fallibility in Late-Medieval Textual Theory', in P. R. Robinson and R. Zim, eds., *Of the Making of Books: Medieval Manuscripts, Their Scribes and Readers. Essays Presented to M. B. Parkes* (Aldershot: Scolar Press, 1997), pp. 259–79.
Translations of Authority in Medieval English Literature: Valuing the Vernacular (Cambridge: Cambridge University Press, 2009).
Minnis, A. J. and A. B. Scott, with the assistance of David Wallace, *Medieval Literary Theory and Criticism c. 1100–c. 1375: The Commentary Tradition* (Oxford: Clarendon Press, 1988).
Sidney, Sir Philip, *An Apology for Poetry; or, The Defence of Poesy*, ed. G. Shepherd, 2nd edn (Manchester: Manchester University Press, 1973).
Steiner, Emily, 'Authority', in P. Strohm, ed., *Middle English* (Oxford: Oxford University Press, 2007), pp. 142–59.
Terrell, Katherine H., 'Reallocation of Hermeneutic Authority in Chaucer's *House of Fame*', *Chaucer Review*, 31 (1997), 279–90.
Utz, Richard J., ' "As writ myn auctor called Lollius": Divine and Authorial Omnipotence in Chaucer's *Troilus and Criseyde*', in H. Keper, C. Bode and R. J. Utz, eds., *Nominalism and Literary Discourse: New Perspectives* (Amsterdam and Atlanta: Rodopi, 1997), pp. 123–44.
Wheeler, Bonnie, ' "As the French book seyeth": Malory's *Morte Darthur* and Acts of Reading', *Cahiers de recherches médiévales et humanistes*, 14 (2007), 115–25.
Wogan-Browne, Jocelyn, Nicholas Watson, Andrew Taylor and Ruth Evans, eds., *The Idea of the Vernacular: An Anthology of Middle English Literary Theory 1280–1520* (Exeter: University of Exeter Press, 1999).
Ziolkowski, Jan, 'Cultures of Authority in the Long Twelfth Century', *Journal of English and Germanic Philology*, 108 (2009), 421–48.

8 LITERARY THEORY AND LITERARY ROLES

Copeland, Rita and Ineke Sluiter, eds., *Medieval Grammar and Rhetoric: Language Arts and Literary Theory, AD 300–1475* (Oxford: Oxford University Press, 2009).

Minnis, A. J., *Medieval Theory of Authorship: Scholastic Literary Attitudes in the Later Middle Ages* (London: Scolar Press, 1984; 2nd edn with a new preface by the author, Philadelphia: University of Pennsylvania Press, 2010).

Minnis, Alastair and Ian Johnson, eds., *The Cambridge History of Literary Criticism*, Vol. II: *The Middle Ages* (Cambridge: Cambridge University Press, 2005).

Parkes, M. B., 'The Influence of the Concepts of *Ordinatio* and *Compilatio* on the Development of the Book', in J. J. G. Alexander and M. T. Gibson, eds., *Medieval Learning and Literature: Essays Presented to R. W. Hunt* (Oxford: Clarendon Press, 1976), pp. 115–41.

9 METRE AND VERSIFICATION

Barney, Stephen A., *Studies in 'Troilus': Chaucer's Text, Meter, and Diction* (East Lansing, MI: Colleagues Press, 1993).

Duffell, Martin J., *A New History of English Metre* (London: MHRA and Manley, 2008).

Gaylord, Alan T., ed., *Essays on the Art of Chaucer's Verse* (New York: Routledge, 2001).

Minkova, Donka, 'Chaucer's Language, Pronunciation, Morphology, Metre', in Steve Ellis, ed., *Chaucer: An Oxford Guide* (Oxford: Oxford University Press, 2005), pp. 130–58.

Putter, Ad, 'In Appreciation of Metrical Abnormality: Headless Lines and Initial Inversion in Chaucer', *Critical Survey*, 29 (2017), 65–85.

Shannon, Edgar F., 'Chaucer's Use of the Octosyllabic Verse in *The Book of the Duchess* and *The House of Fame*', *Journal of English and Germanic Philology*, 12 (1913), 277–94.

Ten Brink, Bernhard, *The Language and Metre of Chaucer*, trans. M. Bentinck Smith (London: Macmillan, 1901).

10 DIALOGUE

Lawton, David, *Voice in Later Medieval Literature: Public Interiorities* (Oxford: Oxford University Press, 2017).

Nielsen, Melinda E., 'Translating Lady Philosophy: Chaucer and the Boethian Corpus of Cambridge, University Library MS Ii.3.21', *Chaucer Review*, 51 (2016), 209–26.

Pugh, Tison, 'Gender, Vulgarity, and the Phantom Debates of Chaucer's Merchant's Tale', *Studies in Philology*, 114 (2017), 473–96.

Wetherbee, Winthrop, 'The *Consolation* and Medieval Literature', in John Marenbon, ed., *The Cambridge Companion to Boethius* (Cambridge: Cambridge University Press, 2009), pp. 279–302.

11 ROMANCE

Barron, W. R. J., *English Medieval Romance* (London: Longman, 1987).

Beer, Gillian, *The Romance: The Critical Idiom* (London: Methuen, 1970).

Cooper, Helen, *The English Romance in Time: Transforming Motifs from Geoffrey of Monmouth to the Death of Shakespeare* (Oxford: Oxford University Press, 2004).

Rubenstein, Richard E., *Aristotle's Children: How Christians, Muslims, and Jews Rediscovered Ancient Wisdom and Illuminated the Middle Ages* (New York: Harvest Books, 2003).

Saunders, Corinne, ed., *A Companion to Romance: From Classical to Contemporary* (Oxford: Blackwell, 2004).

Shepherd, S. H. A., 'Middle English Romance', in *The Oxford Encyclopedia of British Literature* (Oxford: Oxford University Press, 2006), 5 vols., Vol. III, pp. 483–90.

12 LOVE

Donaldson, E. Talbot, 'The Myth of Courtly Love', in E. T. Donaldson, *Speaking of Chaucer* (London: Athlone Press, 1970), pp. 154–63.

Hume, Cathy, *Chaucer and the Cultures of Love and Marriage* (Cambridge: D. S. Brewer, 2012).

Jaeger, C. Stephen, *Ennobling Love: In Search of a Lost Sensibility* (Philadelphia: University of Pennsylvania Press, 1999).

Klassen, Norm, *Chaucer on Love, Knowledge and Sight* (Cambridge: D. S. Brewer, 1995).

Lewis, C. S., *The Allegory of Love: A Study in Medieval Tradition* (Oxford: Oxford University Press, 1936).

Mitchell, Jerome, and William Provost, eds., *Chaucer the Love Poet* (Athens: University of Georgia Press, 1973).

Paxson, James J. and Cynthia A. Gravlee, eds., *Desiring Discourse: The Literature of Love, Ovid through Chaucer* (Selinsgrove: Susquehanna University Press; London: Associated University Presses, 1998).

Saunders, Corinne, 'Love and the Making of the Self: *Troilus and Criseyde*', in Corinne Saunders, ed., *A Concise Companion to Chaucer* (Oxford: Blackwell, 2006), pp. 135–56.

'Mind, Breath and Voice in Chaucer's Romance Writing', in Stephanie M. Hilger, ed., *New Directions in Literature and Medicine Studies* (London: Palgrave Macmillan, 2017), pp. 119–41.

Wack, Mary Frances, *Lovesickness in the Middle Ages: The 'Viaticum' and Its Commentaries* (Philadelphia: University of Pennsylvania Press, 1990).

Weisl, Angela Jane, *Conquering the Reign of Femeny: Gender and Genre in Chaucer's Romance* (Cambridge: D. S. Brewer, 1995).

13 CHAUCER AND THE CLASSICS

Anderson, David, *Before the Knight's Tale: Imitation of Classical Epic in Boccaccio's 'Teseida'* (Philadelphia: University of Pennsylvania Press, 1988).

Baswell, Christopher, *Virgil in Medieval England: Figuring the 'Aeneid' from the Twelfth Century to Chaucer* (Cambridge: Cambridge University Press, 1995).

Cannon, Christopher, *From Literacy to Literature: England 1300–1425* (Oxford: Oxford University Press, 2016).

Clark, James G., Frank Thomas Coulson and Kathryn L. McKinley, eds., *Ovid in the Middle Ages* (Cambridge: Cambridge University Press, 2011).

Copeland, Rita, ed., *The Oxford History of Classical Reception in English Literature*, Vol. 1: *800–1558* (Oxford: Oxford University Press, 2016).

Davis, Isabel and Catherine Nall, eds., *Chaucer and Fame: Reputation and Reception* (Cambridge: D. S. Brewer, 2015).

Fumo, Jamie Claire, *The Legacy of Apollo: Antiquity, Authority and Chaucerian Poetics* (Toronto: University of Toronto Press, 2010).

Grafton, Anthony, Glenn W. Most and Salvatore Settis, eds., *The Classical Tradition* (Cambridge, MA: Belknap Press of Harvard University Press, 2010).

Lawton, David, *Voice in Later Medieval English Literature: Public Interiorities* (Oxford: Oxford University Press, 2017).

Minnis, Alastair and Ian Johnson, eds., *The Cambridge History of Literary Criticism*, Vol. II: *The Middle Ages* (Cambridge: Cambridge University Press, 2005).

14 THE FRENCH CONTEXT

Butterfield, Ardis, *The Familiar Enemy: Chaucer, Language and Nation in the Hundred Years War* (Oxford: Oxford University Press, 2009).

Calin, William, *The French Tradition and the Literature of Medieval England* (Toronto: University of Toronto Press, 1994).

Muscatine, Charles, *Chaucer and the French Tradition: A Study in Style and Meaning* (Berkeley: University of California Press, 1957).

Wimsatt, James I., *Chaucer and His French Contemporaries: Natural Music in the Fourteenth Century* (Toronto: University of Toronto Press, 1992).

15 THE ITALIAN TRADITION

Boccaccio, Giovanni, *Tutte le opere di Giovanni Boccaccio*, ed. Vittore Branca, 10 vols. (Milan: A. Mondadori, 1964–98).

The Decameron, trans. G. H. McWilliam, 2nd edn (London: Penguin, 1995).

The Filostrato, trans. Robert P. apRoberts and Anna Bruni Benson, in Geoffrey Chaucer, *Troilus and Criseyde*, ed. Stephen A. Barney (New York: W. W. Norton, 2006).

Boitani, Piero, ed., *Chaucer and the Italian Trecento* (Cambridge: Cambridge University Press, 1983).

Clarke, K. P., *Chaucer and Italian Textuality* (Oxford: Oxford University Press, 2011).

'Chaucer and Italy: Contexts and/of Sources', *Literature Compass*, 8 (2011), 526–33.

'Florence', in David Wallace, ed., *Europe: A Literary History*, 2 vols. (Oxford: Oxford University Press, 2016), Vol. 1, pp. 687–707.

Correale, Robert M. and Mary Hamel, eds., *Sources and Analogues of the 'Canterbury Tales'*, 2 vols. (Cambridge: D. S. Brewer, 2002–5).

Dante, *La commedia secondo l'antica vulgata*, ed. Giorgio Petrocchi, 2nd edn, repr. with corrections, 4 vols. (Florence: Le Lettere, 1994).

The Divine Comedy of Dante Alighieri, ed. and trans. Robert M. Durling, introduction and notes by Ronald L. Martinez and Robert M. Durling, 3 vols. (Oxford: Oxford University Press, 1996–2011).

De Robertis, Teresa, Carla Maria Monti, Marco Petoletti, Giuliano Tanturli and Stefano Zamponi, eds., *Boccaccio autore e copista* (Florence: Mandragora, 2013).

Edwards, Robert R., *Chaucer and Boccaccio: Antiquity and Modernity* (Basingstoke: Palgrave, 2002).

Ginsberg, Warren, *Chaucer's Italian Tradition* (Ann Arbor: University of Michigan Press, 2002).

Havely, Nick, *Dante* (Oxford: Blackwell, 2007).

Kirkham, Victoria and Armando Maggi, eds., *Petrarch: A Critical Guide to the Complete Works* (Chicago: University of Chicago Press, 2009).

Kirkham, Victoria, Michael Sherberg and Janet Levarie Smarr, eds., *Boccaccio: A Critical Guide to the Complete Works* (Chicago: University of Chicago Press, 2014).

Kirkpatrick, Robin, *English and Italian Literature from Dante to Shakespeare: A Study of Source, Analogue and Divergence* (London: Longman, 1995).

McKinley, Kathryn L., *Chaucer's 'House of Fame' and Its Boccaccian Intertexts: Image, Vision, and the Vernacular* (Toronto: Pontifical Institute of Mediaeval Studies, 2016).

Milner, Stephen, Guyda Armstrong and Rhiannon Daniels, eds., *The Cambridge Companion to Boccaccio* (Cambridge: Cambridge University Press, 2014).

Minnis, Alastair, '"Dante in Inglissh": What *Il convivio* Really Did for Chaucer', *Essays in Criticism*, 55 (2005), 97–116.

Petrarch, *Francis, Petrarch's Lyric Poems: The Rime Sparse and Other Lyrics*, trans. Robert M. Durling (Cambridge, MA: Harvard University Press, 1976).

Rerum vulgarium fragmenta, in Francesco Petrarca, *Canzoniere: Rerum vulgarium fragmenta*, ed. Rosanna Bettarini, 2 vols. (Turin: Einaudi, 2005).

Rossiter, William T., *Chaucer and Petrarch* (Cambridge: D. S. Brewer, 2010).

Scott, John A., *Understanding Dante* (Notre Dame: University of Notre Dame Press, 2004).

Schless, Howard H., *Chaucer and Dante: A Revaluation* (Norman, OK: Pilgrim Books, 1984).

Taylor, Karla, *Chaucer Reads "The Divine Comedy"* (Stanford: Stanford University Press, 1989).

The Essential Petrarch, ed. and trans. Peter Hainsworth (Indianapolis: Hackett, 2010).

Wallace, David, *Chaucer and the Early Writings of Boccaccio* (Cambridge: D. S. Brewer, 1985).

Giovanni Boccaccio: 'Decameron' (Cambridge: Cambridge University Press, 1991).

Chaucerian Polity: Absolutist Lineages and Associational Forms in England and Italy (Stanford: Stanford University Press, 1997).

Witt, Ronald G., *Hercules at the Crossroads: The Life, Works, and Thought of Coluccio Salutati* (Durham, NC: Duke University Press, 1983).

16 THE ENGLISH CONTEXT

Duncan, Thomas G., ed., *A Companion to the Middle English Lyric* (Cambridge: D. S. Brewer, 2005).

Fisher, John H., *The Emergence of Standard English* (Lexington: University Press of Kentucky, 1996).

Mann, Jill, *Chaucer and Medieval Estates Satire* (Cambridge: Cambridge University Press, 1973).

Smith, D. Vance, 'Chaucer as an English Writer', in Seth Lerer, ed., *The Yale Companion to Chaucer* (New Haven, CT: Yale University Press, 2006), pp. 87–121.

Wallace, David, *Premodern Places: Calais to Surinam, Chaucer to Aphra Behn* (Oxford: Blackwell, 2004).

17 CHAUCER'S COMPETITORS

Lawton, David, ed., *Middle English Alliterative Poetry and Its Literary Background* (Cambridge: D. S. Brewer, 1982).

Turville-Petre, Thorlac, *The Alliterative Revival* (Cambridge: D. S. Brewer, 1977).

Edwards, A. S. G., ed., *Middle English Prose: A Critical Guide to Major Authors and Genres* (New Brunswick, NJ: Rutgers University Press, 1984).

18 BOETHIUS

Chadwick, Henry, *Boethius: The Consolations of Music, Logic, Theology, and Philosophy* (Oxford: Clarendon Press, 1981).

Cornelius, Ian. 'Boethius' *De consolatione philosophiae*', in Rita Copeland, ed., *The Oxford History of Classical Reception in English Literature*: Vol. 1, *800–1558* (Oxford: Oxford University Press, 2016), pp. 269–98.

Courcelle, Pierre, *La consolation de la Philosophie dans la tradition littéraire: Antécédants et postérité de Boèce* (Paris: Etudes augustiniennes, 1967).

Gibson, Margaret, ed., *Boethius: His Life, Thought, and Influence* (Oxford: Blackwell, 1981).

Glei, Reinhold F., Nicola Kaminski and Franz Lebsanft, eds., *Boethius Christianus? Transformationen der 'Consolatio Philosophiae' in Mittelalter und Früher Neuzeit* (Berlin: De Gruyter, 2010).

Hoenen, J. F. M. and Lodi Nauta, eds., *Latin and Vernacular Traditions of the 'Consolatio Philosophiae'* (Leiden: Brill, 1997).

Jefferson, B. L., *Chaucer and the 'Consolation of Philosophy'* (Princeton: Princeton University Press, 1917).

Kaylor, Noel Harold, Jr. and Philip Edward Phillips, eds., *A Companion to Boethius in the Middle Ages* (Leiden: Brill, 2012).

Machan, Tim William, *Techniques of Translation: Chaucer's 'Boece'* (Norman, OK: Pilgrim Books, 1985).

with the assistance of A. J. Minnis, *Sources of the 'Boece'* (Athens: University of Georgia Press, 2005).

Marenbon, John, *Boethius* (Oxford: Oxford University Press, 2003).

Minnis, A. J., ed., *The Medieval Boethius: Studies in Vernacular Translations of 'De consolatione Philosophiae'* (Cambridge: D. S. Brewer, 1987).

ed., *Chaucer's 'Boece' and the Medieval Tradition of Boethius* (Cambridge: D. S. Brewer, 1993).

Walton, John, *Boethius: 'De consolatione Philosophiae'*, ed. Mark Science, EETS os 170 (London: Oxford: Oxford University Press, 1927).

19 CHAUCER'S GOD

Mann, Jill, 'Chance and Destiny in *Troilus and Criseyde* and the *Knight's Tale*', in *Life in Words: Essays on Chaucer, the Gawain-Poet, and Malory* (Toronto: University of Toronto Press, 2014), pp. 42–61.

Shepherd, Geoffrey, 'Religion and Philosophy in Chaucer', in Derek Brewer, ed., *Geoffrey Chaucer* (London: Bell, 1974), pp. 262–89.

Utz, Richard, 'Philosophy', in Steve Ellis, ed., *Chaucer: An Oxford Guide* (Oxford: Oxford University Press, 2005), pp. 158–73.

Watts, W. H., 'Chaucer's Clerks and the Value of Philosophy', in Hugo Keiper, Christoph Bode and Richard J. Utz, eds., *Nominalism and Literary Discourse: New Perspectives* (Amsterdam: Rodopi, 1997), pp. 145–55.

20 HOLINESS

Bestul, Thomas H., 'Chaucer's Parson's Tale and the Late-Medieval Tradition of Religious Meditation', *Speculum*, 64 (1989), 600–19.

Bynum, Caroline Walker, *Christian Materiality: An Essay on Religion in Late Medieval Europe* (New York: Zone Books, 2011).

Duffy, Eamon, *The Stripping of the Altars: Traditional Religion in England, c. 1400–c. 1580* (New Haven, CT: Yale University Press, 1992).

Finucane, Ronald C., *Miracles and Pilgrims: Popular Beliefs in Medieval England* (New York: St Martin's Press, 1977).

Phillips, Helen, ed., *Chaucer and Religion* (Woodbridge: D. S. Brewer, 2010).

Jonathan Sumption, *Pilgrimage: An Image of Mediaeval Religion* (London: Faber and Faber, 1975).

Nicholas Watson, 'Chaucer's Public Christianity', *Religion and Literature*, 37, no. 2 (2005), 99–114.

21 SECULARITY

Carey, Hilary, *Courting Disaster: Astrology at the English Court and University in the Later Middle Ages* (Basingstoke: Macmillan, 1992).

Minnis, Alastair, '*I speke of folk in seculer estaat*: Vernacularity and Secularity in the Age of Chaucer', *Studies in the Age of Chaucer*, 27 (2005), 25–58.

Moran, Bruce T., *Distilling Knowledge: Alchemy, Chemistry, and the Scientific Revolution* (Cambridge, MA: Harvard University Press, 2005).

North, John, *God's Clockmaker: Richard of Wallingford and the Invention of Time* (London and New York: Hambledon and Palgrave Macmillan, 2005).

Patterson, Lee, 'Perpetual Motion: Alchemy and the Technology of the Self', in *Temporal Circumstances: Form and History in the 'Canterbury Tales'* (New York: Palgrave Macmillan, 2006), pp. 159–76.

Rigby, Stephen H., *Wisdom and Chivalry: Chaucer's 'Knight's Tale' and Medieval Political Theory* (Leiden: Brill, 2009).

Rosenfeld, Jessica, *Ethics and Enjoyment in Late Medieval Poetry: Love after Aristotle* (Cambridge: Cambridge University Press, 2010).

Turner, Ralph V., 'The *Miles literatus* in Twelfth- and Thirteenth-Century England: How Rare a Phenomenon?', *American Historical Review*, 83 (1978), 928–45.

22 THE SELF

Blamires, Alcuin, 'Individuality', in Elaine Treharne, Greg Walker and William Green, eds., *The Oxford Handbook of Medieval Literature in English* (Oxford: Oxford University Press, 2010), pp. 478–95.

Bullón-Fernández, María, 'Poverty, Property, and the Self in the Late Middle Ages: The Case of Chaucer's Griselda', *Mediaevalia*, 35 (2014), 193–226.

Dinshaw, Carolyn, 'Chaucer's Queer Touches/A Queer Touches Chaucer', *Exemplaria*, 7 (1995), 75–92.

Ganim, John M., 'Chaucer, Boccaccio, Confession, and Subjectivity', in L. M. Koff and B. Deen Schildgen, eds., *The 'Decameron' and the 'Canterbury Tales': New Essays on an Old Question* (Madison, NJ: Fairleigh Dickinson University Press, 2000), pp. 128–47.

Leicester, H. Marshall, Jr., *The Disenchanted Self: Representing the Subject in the 'Canterbury Tales'* (Berkeley: University of California Press, 1990).

Lochrie, Karma, *Covert Operations: The Medieval Uses of Secrecy* (Philadelphia: University of Pennsylvania Press, 1999).

Miller, Mark, 'Subjectivity and Ideology in the *Canterbury Tales*', in Peter Brown, ed., *A Companion to Medieval English Literature and Culture, c. 1350–c. 1500* (Malden, MA: Blackwell, 2007), pp. 554–69.

Patterson, Lee, 'Perpetual Motion: Alchemy and the Technology of the Self', *Studies in the Age of Chaucer*, 15 (1993), 25–57.

'"What is me?" Self and Society in the Poetry of Thomas Hoccleve', *Studies in the Age of Chaucer*, 23 (2001), 437–70.

Spearing, A. C., *Textual Subjectivity: The Encoding of Subjectivity in Medieval Narratives and Lyrics* (Oxford: Oxford University Press, 2005).

Raskolnikov, Masha, 'Confessional Literature, Vernacular Psychology and the History of the Self in Middle English', *Literature Compass*, 2 (2005), 1–20.

Strohm, Paul, *Conscience: A Very Short Introduction* (Oxford: Oxford University Press, 2011).

Van Dyke, Carolynn, *Chaucer's Agents: Cause and Representation in Chaucerian Narrative* (Madison, NJ: Fairleigh Dickinson University Press, 2005).

Williams, Tara, *Inventing Womanhood: Gender and Language in Later Middle English Writing* (Columbus: Ohio State University Press, 2011).

23 WOMEN

Barron, Caroline M. and Anne F. Sutton, eds., *Medieval London Widows 1300–1500* (London: Hambledon Press, 1994).

Goldberg, P. J. P., 'Pigs and Prostitutes: Streetwalking in Comparative Perspective', in Katherine J. Lewis, Noel James Menuge and Kim M. Phillips, eds., *Young Medieval Women* (New York: St Martin's Press, 1999), pp. 172–93.

Goodman, Anthony, *Margery Kempe and Her World* (London: Longman, 2002).

Hanawalt, Barbara A., *The Wealth of Wives: Women, Law and Economy in Late Medieval London* (Oxford: Oxford University Press, 2007).

Karras, Ruth Mazo, *Common Women: Prostitution and Sexuality in Medieval England* (Oxford: Oxford University Press, 1996).

Lewis, Katherine J., ed., *Women in Medieval English Society* (Stroud: Sutton, 1997).

24 SEX AND LUST

Blackburn, Simon, *Lust: The Seven Deadly Sins* (Oxford: Oxford University Press, 2004).

Dinshaw, Carolyn, *Getting Medieval: Sexualities and Communities, Pre- and Postmodern* (Durham, NC: Duke University Press, 1999).

Karras, Ruth Mazo, *Sexuality in Medieval Europe: Doing unto Others* (New York: Routledge, 2004).

Newhauser, Richard, ed., *The Seven Deadly Sins: From Communities to Individuals* (Leiden: Brill, 2007).

Spearing, A. C., *The Medieval Poet as Voyeur* (Cambridge: Cambridge University Press, 2005).

25 ANIMALS IN CHAUCER

Barber, Richard, trans., *Bestiary: Being an English Version of the Bodleian Library, Oxford, MS Bodley 764* (Woodbridge: Boydell Press, 2010 [1992]).

Crane, Susan, 'For the Birds', *Studies in the Age of Chaucer*, 29 (2007), 21–42.

Flores, Nona, ed., *Animals in the Middle Ages* (New York and London: Routledge, 2000).

Hanawalt, Barbara A. and Lisa J. Kiser, eds., *Engaging with Nature: Essays on the Natural World in Medieval and Early Modern Europe* (Notre Dame: University of Notre Dame Press, 2008).

Holsinger, Bruce, 'Of Pigs and Parchment: Medieval Studies and the Coming of the Animal', *PMLA*, 124 (2009), 616–23.

Isidore of Seville, *The Etymologies of Isidore of Seville*, trans. Stephen A. Barney, E. J. Lewis, J. A. Beach and O. Berghof (Cambridge: Cambridge University Press, 2006).

Kay, Sarah, 'Legible Skins: Animals and the Ethics of Medieval Reading', *postmedieval*, 2 (2011) 13–32.

Kiser, Lisa, 'Margery Kempe and the Animalization of Christ', *Studies in Philology*, 106 (2009), 299–315.

Mann, Jill, *From Aesop to Reynard: Beast Literature in Medieval Britain* (Oxford: Oxford University Press, 2009).

Rowland, Beryl, *Blind Beasts: Chaucer's Animal World* (Kent, OH: Kent State University Press, 1971).

Salisbury, Joyce, *The Beast Within: Animals in the Middle Ages* (London: Routledge, 1994).

26 CHILDHOOD AND EDUCATION

Clanchy, Michael, *From Memory to Written Record: England 1066–1307*, 2nd edn (Oxford: Blackwell, 1993).

Nicholls, J. W., *The Matter of Courtesy* (Woodbridge: D. S. Brewer, 1985).

Orme, Nicholas, *From Childhood to Chivalry: The Education of the English Kings and Aristocracy 1066–1530* (London: Methuen, 1984).

'Chaucer and Education', *Chaucer Review*, 16 (1981), 38–59, repr. in Nicholas Orme, *Education and Society in Medieval and Renaissance England* (London and Ronceverte: Hambledon Press, 1989), pp. 221–42.

Medieval Children (New Haven, CT and London: Yale University Press, 2001).

Medieval Schools (New Haven, CT and London: Yale University Press, 2006).

articles on baptism, children, confirmation, education, literacy, parish clerks, schools, universities, in *The English Parish Church through the Centuries*, 1st edn (York: Christianity and Culture, 2010), CD-ROM.

'Childhood and Education in the Great Medieval Household', in C. M. Woolgar, ed., *The Great Household in Medieval England* (Donington: Shaun Tyas, 2018).

Salisbury, Eve, *Chaucer and the Child* (New York: Palgrave Macmillan, 2017).

27 PHILOSOPHY

Jefferson, Bernard L., *Chaucer and the 'Consolation of Philosophy' of Boethius* (Princeton: Princeton University Press, 1917).

Lynch, Kathryn L., *Chaucer's Philosophical Visions* (Cambridge: D. S. Brewer, 2000).

Miller, Mark, *Philosophical Chaucer: Love, Sex and Agency in the 'Canterbury Tales'* (Cambridge: Cambridge University Press, 2004).

Minnis A. J., ed., *Chaucer's 'Boece' and the Medieval Tradition of Boethius* (Cambridge: D. S. Brewer, 1993).

28 THE MEDIEVAL UNIVERSE

Boudet, Jean-Patrice, *Entre science et nigromance: Astrologie, divination et magie dans l'Occident médiéval* (Paris: Publications de la Sorbonne, 2006).

Carey, Hilary M., 'Astrology in the Middle Ages', *History Compass*, 8 (2010), 888–902.

Grant, Edward, 'Cosmology', in David C. Lindberg and Michael H. Shank, eds., *The Cambridge History of Science*: Vol. II, *Medieval Science* (Cambridge: Cambridge University Press, 2013), pp. 436–55.

Lewis, C. S., *The Discarded Image: An Introduction to Medieval and Renaissance Literature* (Cambridge: Cambridge University Press, 1964).

Lindberg, David C., *The Beginnings of Western Science: The European Scientific Tradition in Philosophical, Religious, and Institutional Context, Prehistory to AD 1450*, 2nd edn (Chicago: University of Chicago Press, 2007).

North, J. D., *Horoscopes and History* (London: Warburg Institute, 1986).

Chaucer's Universe (Oxford: Clarendon Press, 1988).

Thorndike, Lynn, ed., *The Sphere of Sacrobosco and Its Commentators* (Chicago: University of Chicago Press, 1949).

29 MEDICINE AND THE MORTAL BODY

Appleford, Amy, *Learning to Die in London, 1380–1540* (Philadelphia: University of Pennsylvania Press, 2014).

Biller, Peter and Joseph Ziegler, eds., *Religion and Medicine in the Middle Ages* (Woodbridge: Boydell and Brewer, 2001).

Cadden, Joan, *The Meanings of Sex Difference in the Middle Ages: Medicine, Science, and Culture* (Cambridge: Cambridge University Press, 1995).

Getz, Faye, *Medicine in the English Middle Ages* (Princeton: Princeton University Press, 1998).

Rawcliffe, Carole, *Medicine and Society in Later Medieval England* (Stroud: Sutton, 1995).

Talbot, C. H., *Medicine in Medieval England* (London: Oldbourne, 1967).

Ussery, Huling, *Chaucer's Physician: Medicine and Literature in Fourteenth-Century England* (New Orleans: Department of English, Tulane University, 1971).

30 THE LAW

Green, Richard Firth, *A Crisis of Truth: Literature and Law in Ricardian England* (Philadelphia: University of Pennsylvania Press, 2002).

Hornsby, Joseph Allen, *Chaucer and the Law* (Norman, OK: Pilgrim Books, 1988).

Musson, Anthony, *Medieval Law in Context: The Growth of Legal Consciousness from Magna Carta to the Peasants' Revolt* (Manchester: Manchester University Press, 2001).

31 ART

Alexander, Jonathan and Paul Binski, eds., *Age of Chivalry: Art in Plantagenet England 1200–1400* (London: Weidenfeld and Nicolson, 1987).

Marks, Richard, *Stained Glass in England during the Middle Ages* (London: Routledge, 1993).

Sandler, Lucy Freeman, *Gothic Manuscripts 1285–1385*, 2 vols. (London: Harvey Miller, 1986).

Scott, Kathleen L., *Gothic Manuscripts 1385–1485*, 2 vols. (London: Harvey Miller, 1996).

32 ARCHITECTURE

Alexander, Jonathan and Paul Binski, eds., *Age of Chivalry: Art in Plantagenet England 1200–1400* (London: Weidenfeld and Nicolson, 1987).
Binski, Paul, *Gothic Wonder, Art, Artifice and the Decorated Style 1290–1350* (New Haven, CT and London: Yale University Press, 2014).
Emery, Anthony, *Greater Medieval Houses of England and Wales*, 3 vols. (Cambridge: Cambridge University Press, 1996–2006).
Evans, Joan, *English Art 1307–1461* (Oxford: Oxford University Press, 1949).
Goodall, John, *The English Castle* (New Haven, CT and London: Yale University Press, 2011).
Harvey, John, *The Perpendicular Style 1330–1485* (London: Batsford, 1978).

33 HERALDRY, HERALDS AND CHAUCER

Coss, Peter, and Maurice Keen, eds., *Heraldry, Pageantry and Social Display in Medieval England* (Woodbridge: Boydell Press, 2002).
Crane, Susan, *The Performance of Self: Ritual, Clothing, and Identity during the Hundred Years War* (Philadelphia: University of Pennsylvania Press, 2002).
Jones, Robert W., *Bloodied Banners: Martial Display on the Medieval Battlefield* (Woodbridge: Boydell Press, 2010).
Keen, Maurice, *Chivalry* (New Haven, CT: Yale University Press, 1984).
The Origins of the English Gentleman: Heraldry, Chivalry and Gentility in Medieval England, c. 1300–c. 1500 (Stroud: Tempus, 2002).
Squibb, G. D., *The High Court of Chivalry: A Study in the Civil Law in England* (Oxford: Clarendon Press, 1959).
Stevenson, Katie, ed., *The Herald in Late Medieval Europe* (Woodbridge: Boydell Press, 2009).
Wagner, Anthony, *Heralds and Heraldry in the Middle Ages: An Inquiry into the Growth of the Armorial Function of Heralds*, 2nd edn (Oxford: Clarendon Press, 1956).
The Heralds of England: A History of the Office and College of Arms (London: Her Majesty's Stationery Office, 1967).

34 DISSENT AND ORTHODOXY

Bose, Mishtooni, 'Vernacular Philosophy and the Making of Orthodoxy in the Fifteenth Century', *New Medieval Literatures*, 7 (2005), 73–99.
Bryan, Jennifer, *Looking Inward: Devotional Reading and the Private Self in Late Medieval England* (Philadelphia: University of Pennsylvania Press, 2008).
Cole, Andrew, *Literature and Heresy in the Age of Chaucer* (Cambridge: Cambridge University Press, 2008).
Forrest, Ian, *The Detection of Heresy in Late Medieval England* (Oxford: Oxford University Press, 2005).
Ghosh, Kantik, *The Wycliffite Heresy: Authority and the Interpretation of Texts* (Cambridge: Cambridge University Press, 2002).

Goodman, Anthony, *Margery Kempe and Her World* (London: Longman, 2004).

Hornbeck, J. Patrick, *What Is a Lollard? Dissent and Belief in Late Medieval England* (Oxford: Oxford University Press, 2010).

Hudson, Anne, *The Premature Reformation: Wycliffite Texts and Lollard History* (Oxford: Oxford University Press, 1988).

Kerby-Fulton, Kathryn, *Books under Suspicion: Censorship and Tolerance of Revelatory Writing in Late Medieval England* (Notre Dame: University of Notre Dame Press, 2006).

McNiven, Peter, *Heresy and Politics in the Reign of Henry IV: The Burning of John Badby* (Woodbridge: Boydell, 1987).

Somerset, Fiona, *Feeling like Saints: Lollard Writings after Wyclif* (Ithaca, NY: Cornell University Press, 2014).

35 THE CHURCH, RELIGION AND CULTURE

Arnold, John H., *Belief and Unbelief in Medieval Europe* (London: Hodder Arnold, 2005).

Bossy, John, *Christianity in the West, 1400–1700* (Oxford: Oxford University Press, 1985).

Duffy, Eamon, *The Stripping of the Altars: Traditional Religion in England, 1400–1580*, 2nd edn (New Haven, CT: Yale University Press, 2005).

Hamilton, Bernard, *Religion in the Medieval West* (London: Arnold, 1986).

MacFarlane, K. B., *Lancastrian Kings and Lollard Knights* (Oxford: Oxford University Press, 1972).

McCormack, Frances M., 'Chaucer and Lollardy', in Helen Phillips, ed., *Chaucer and Religion* (Cambridge: D. S. Brewer, 2010), pp. 35–40.

Pantin, William Abel, *The English Church in the Fourteenth Century* (Cambridge: Cambridge University Press, 1955).

Swanson, Robert N., *Religion and Devotion in Europe, c. 1215–c. 1515* (Cambridge: Cambridge University Press, 1995).

Tanner, Norman and Sethina Watson, 'Least of the Laity: The Minimum Requirements for a Medieval Christian', *Journal of Medieval History*, 32 (2006), 395–423.

Webb, Diana, *Pilgrimage in Medieval England* (London: Hambledon, 2000).

36 ENGLAND AT HOME AND ABROAD

Ayton, Andrew and Philip Preston, *The Battle of Crécy* (Woodbridge: Boydell Press) 2005).

Bell, Adrian R., Anne Curry, Andy King and David Simpkin, *The Soldier in the Later Middle Ages* (Oxford: Oxford University Press, 2013).

Curry, Anne, *The Hundred Years War*, 2nd edn (Basingstoke: Palgrave, 2003).

Curry, Anne and Michael Hughes, eds., *Arms, Armies and Fortifications of the Hundred Years War* (Woodbridge: Boydell Press, 1994).

Sumption, Jonathan, *The Hundred Years War III: Divided Houses* (London: Faber and Faber, 2009).

37 CHAUCER'S BORDERS

Ganim, John M. and Legassie, Shayne Aaron, eds., *Cosmopolitanism and the Middle Ages* (Basingstoke: Palgrave, 2013).

Lavezzo, Kathy, *Angels on the Edge of the World: Geography, Literature, and English Community 1000–1534* (Ithaca, NY: Cornell University Press, 2006).

Lynch, Kathryn, ed., *Chaucer's Cultural Geography* (New York: Routledge, 2002).

MacColl, Alan, 'The Meaning of "Britain" in Medieval and Early Modern England', *Journal of British Studies*, 45 (2006), 248–69.

Sobecki, Sebastian ed., *The Sea and Englishness in the Middle Ages: Maritime Narratives, Identity, and Culture* (Woodbridge: Boydell and Brewer, 2011).

38 RANK AND SOCIAL ORDERS

Given-Wilson, C. *et al.*, *The Parliament Rolls of Medieval England 1275–1504*, 16 vols. (Woodbridge, Boydell Press, 2005). [= *PROME*]

Hanawalt, Barbara, ed., *Chaucer's England: Literature in Historical Context* (Minneapolis: University of Minnesota Press, 1992).

Keen, Maurice, *English Society in the Later Middle Ages 1348–1500* (London: Penguin, 1990).

Mann, Jill, *Chaucer and Medieval Estates Satire* (Cambridge: Cambridge University Press, 1993 [1973]).

Saul, Nigel, 'The Social Status of Chaucer's Franklin: A Reconsideration', *Medium Ævum*, 52 (1983), 10–26.

Rigby, Stephen. H., ed., with the assistance of Alastair J. Minnis, *Historians on Chaucer: The 'General Prologue' to the 'Canterbury Tales'* (Oxford: Oxford University Press, 2014).

Taylor, John, Wendy R. Childs and Leslie Watkiss, eds., *The St Albans Chronicle I: 1376–1394, and II: 1394–1422* (Oxford: Clarendon Press, 2003, 2011).

39 CHIVALRY

Jaeger, C. Stephen, *The Origins of Courtliness: Civilizing Trends and the Formation of the Courtly Ideals, 939–1210* (Philadelphia: University of Pennsylvania Press, 1985).

Ennobling Love: In Search of a Lost Sensibility (Philadelphia: University of Pennsylvania Press, 1999).

Kaeuper, Richard W., *Chivalry and Violence in Medieval Europe* (Oxford: Oxford University Press, 1999).

Holy Warriors: The Religious Ideology of Chivalry (Philadelphia: University of Pennsylvania Press, 2009).

Medieval Chivalry (Cambridge: Cambridge University Press, 2016).

Keen, Maurice, *Chivalry* (New Haven, CT: Yale University Press, 1984).

Saul, Nigel, *For Honour and Fame: Chivalry in England, 1066–1500* (London: Bodley Head, 2011).

Taylor, Craig, *Chivalry and the Ideals of Knighthood in France during the Hundred Years War* (Cambridge: Cambridge University Press, 2013).
Vale, Malcolm, *War and Chivalry: Warfare and Aristocratic Culture in England, France and Burgundy* (London: Duckworth, 1981).
Wollock, Jennifer G., *Rethinking Chivalry and Courtly Love* (Santa Barbara, CA: Praeger, 2011).

40 CHAUCER AND THE POLITY

Dodd, Gwilym, 'Changing Perspectives: Parliament, Poetry and the "Civil Service" under Richard II and Henry IV', *Parliamentary History*, 25 (2006), 299–322.
Pearsall, Derek, *The Life of Geoffrey Chaucer: A Critical Biography* (Oxford: Blackwell, 1992).
Roskell, J. S., Linda Clark and Carole Rawcliffe, *The House of Commons, 1386–1421* (Stroud: Sutton, 1992), 4 vols., Vol. II (biographies of Geoffrey Chaucer and Thomas Chaucer).
Sanderlin, S., 'Chaucer and Ricardian Politics', *Chaucer Review*, 22 (1987–8), 171–84.
Schlauch, Margaret, 'Chaucer's Doctrine of Kings and Tyrants', *Speculum*, 20 (1945), 133–56.
Strohm, Paul, *Social Chaucer* (Cambridge, MA: Harvard University Press, 1989).

41 THE ECONOMY

Barron, Caroline M., *London in the Later Middle Ages: Government and People 1200–1500* (Oxford: Oxford University Press, 2004).
Britnell, Richard, *Britain and Ireland 1050–1530: Economy and Society* (Oxford: Oxford University Press, 2004).
Dyer, Christopher, *Making a Living in the Middle Ages: The People of Britain, 850–1520* (New Haven, CT and London: Yale University Press, 2002).
Goldberg, P. J. P., *Women, Work and Life Cycle in a Medieval Economy: Women in York and Yorkshire c. 1300–1520* (Oxford: Oxford University Press, 1992).

42 TOWNS, VILLAGES AND THE LAND

Bailey, Mark and S. H. Rigby, eds., *England in the Age of the Black Death: Essays in Honour of John Hatcher* (Turnhout: Brepols, 2012).
Campbell, Bruce M. S., *The Great Transition: Climate, Disease and Society in the Late Medieval World* (Cambridge: Cambridge University Press, 2016).
Hatcher, John, 'England in the Aftermath of the Black Death', *Past and Present*, 144 (1994), 3–35.
Horrox, Rosemary, trans. and ed., *The Black Death* (Manchester: Manchester University Press, 1994).
Palliser, D. M., ed., *The Cambridge Urban History of Britain*, Vol. I: *600–1540* (Cambridge: Cambridge University Press, 2000).

Rigby, Stephen. H., ed., with the assistance of Alastair J. Minnis, *Historians on Chaucer: The 'General Prologue' to the 'Canterbury Tales'* (Oxford: Oxford University Press, 2014).

43 LONDON'S CHAUCER: A PSYCHOGEOGRAPHY

Bahr, Arthur, *Fragments and Assemblages: Forming Compilations of Medieval London* (Chicago: University of Chicago Press, 2013).

Barron, Caroline M., *London in the Later Middle Ages* (Oxford: Oxford University Press, 2004).

Burrow, John A., *English Writers of the Late Middle Ages: Thomas Hoccleve* (Aldershot: Variorum, 1994).

Lerer, Seth, *Chaucer and His Readers* (Princeton: Princeton University Press, 1993).

Pearsall, Derek, *The Life of Geoffrey Chaucer: A Critical Biography* (Oxford: Blackwell, 1992).

Sinclair, Iain, *Lights Out for the Territory* (London: Penguin, 2003).

Stow, John, *A Survey of London*, introduced by C. L. Kingsford, 2 vols. (Oxford: Clarendon Press, 1908).

Strohm, Paul, *Social Chaucer* (Cambridge, MA: Harvard University Press, 1989).

44 EVERYDAY LIFE

Brewer, Derek, *Chaucer and His World* (London: Eyre Methuen, 1978).

Britnell, Richard, ed., *Daily Life in the Late Middle Ages* (Stroud: Sutton, 1998).

Chew, Helena M. and William Kellaway, eds., *London Assize of Nuisance: A Calendar* (Chatham: W. and J. Mackay, 1973).

Dyer, Christopher, *Standards of Living in the Later Middle Ages: Social Change in England c. 1200–1520* (Cambridge: Cambridge University Press, 1989).

Making a Living in the Middle Ages: The People of Britain 850–1520 (London: Penguin, 2003).

Horrox, Rosemary and W. Mark Ormrod, *A Social History of England 1200–1500* (Cambridge: Cambridge University Press, 2006).

Pearsall, Derek, *The Life of Geoffrey Chaucer: A Critical Biography* (Oxford: Blackwell, 1992).

Piponnier, Françoise and Perrine Mane, *Dress in the Middle Ages* (New Haven, CT: Yale University Press, 1997).

45 HOUSEHOLD AND HOME

Britnell, Richard, ed., *Daily Life in the Late Middle Ages* (Stroud: Sutton, 1998).

Dyer, Christopher, *Standards of Living in the Later Middle Ages* (Cambridge: Cambridge University Press, 1989).

Goldberg, P. J. P., *Medieval England: A Social History, 1250–1550* (London: Hodder Arnold, 2004).
Goldberg, P. J. P. and Maryanne Kowaleski, eds., *Medieval Domesticity: Home, Housing and Household in Medieval England* (Cambridge: Cambridge University Press, 2008).
Mertes, Kate, *The English Noble Household, 1250–1600: Good Governance and Politic Rule* (Oxford: Basil Blackwell, 1988).
Woolgar, C. M., *The Great Household in Late Medieval England* (New Haven, CT: Yale University Press, 1999).

46 MARRIAGE

Brand, Paul, 'Family and Inheritance, Women and Children', in Chris Given-Wilson, ed., *An Illustrated History of Late Medieval England* (Manchester: Manchester University Press, 1996), pp. 58–81.
Brundage, J. A., *Law, Sex, and Christian Society in Medieval Europe* (Chicago: University of Chicago Press, 1987).
d'Avray, D. L., *Medieval Marriage: Symbolism and Society* (Oxford: Oxford University Press, 2005).
Fleming, Peter, *Family and Household in Medieval England* (Basingstoke: Palgrave, 2001).
Helmholz, R. H., *Marriage Litigation in Medieval England* (Cambridge: Cambridge University Press, 2007 [1974]).
Karras, Ruth Mazo, *Unmarriages: Women, Men, and Sexual Unions in the Middle Ages* (Philadelphia: University of Pennsylvania Press, 2012).
Kelly, Henry Ansgar, *Love and Marriage in the Age of Chaucer* (Ithaca, NY: Cornell University Press, 1975).
Murray, Jacqueline, *Love, Marriage and the Family in the Middle Ages: A Reader* (Peterborough, ON: Broadview Press, 2001).
Phillips, Kim M., *Medieval Maidens: Young Women and Gender in England, 1270–1540* (Manchester: Manchester University Press, 2003).
Reynolds, Philip L., *How Marriage Became One of the Sacraments: The Sacramental Theology of Marriage from Its Medieval Origins to the Council of Trent* (Cambridge: Cambridge University Press, 2016).
Sheehan, Michael M., *Marriage, Family and Law in Medieval Europe: Collected Studies* (Toronto: University of Toronto Press, 1996).

47 DRESS

Jenkins, David, ed., *The Cambridge History of Western Textiles* (Cambridge: Cambridge University Press, 2003).
Owen-Crocker, G., Elizabeth Coatsworth and Maria Hayward, eds., *Encyclopedia of Medieval Dress and Textiles in the British Isles c. 450–1450* (Leiden and Boston, MA: Brill, 2012).

48 THE FIRST CHAUCERIANS: RECEPTION IN THE 1400S

Ashby, George, *George Ashby's Poems*, ed. Mary Bateson, EETS es 76 (London: Kegan Paul, Trench, Trübner, 1899).

Boffey, Julia, and A. S. G. Edwards, eds., *A Companion to Fifteenth-Century English Poetry* (Cambridge: D. S. Brewer, 2013).

Bokenham, Osbern, *Legendys of Hooly Wummen*, ed. Mary S. Serjeantson. EETS os 206 (London: Oxford University Press, 1938).

Burrow, J. A., *Thomas Hoccleve* (Aldershot: Variorum, 1994).

Cannon, Christopher, *The Making of Chaucer's English: A Study of Words* (Cambridge: Cambridge University Press, 1998).

Doyle, A. I., and M. B. Parkes., 'A Paleographical Introduction', in Paul G. Ruggiers, ed., *The 'Canterbury Tales': A Facsimile and Transcription of the Hengwrt Manuscript, with Variants from the Ellesmere Manuscript* (Norman: University of Oklahoma Press, 1979).

Ebin, Lois A., *Illuminator, Makar, Vates: Visions of Poetry in the Fifteenth Century* (Lincoln: University of Nebraska Press, 1988).

Fisher, John H., *The Emergence of Standard English* (Lexington: University Press of Kentucky, 1996).

Frost, Robert, *The Poetry of Robert Frost*, ed. Edward Connery Lathem (New York: Henry Holt, 1979).

Hoccleve, Thomas, *Thomas Hoccleve: 'The Regiment of Princes'*, ed. Charles R. Blyth (Kalamazoo: Medieval Institute Publications, 1999).

Knapp, Ethan, 'Eulogies and Usurpations: Hoccleve and Chaucer Revisited', *Studies in the Age of Chaucer*, 21 (1999), 247–73.

Lerer, Seth, *Chaucer and His Readers: Imagining the Author in Late-Medieval England* (Princeton: Princeton University Press, 1993).

Lydgate, John, *Lydgate's 'Troy Book'*, ed. Henry Bergen, 4 vols., EETS es 97, 103, 106, 126 (London: Kegan Paul, Trench, Trübner, 1906–35).

Meyer-Lee, Robert J., *Poets and Power from Chaucer to Wyatt* (Cambridge: Cambridge University Press, 2007).

Nolan, Maura, *John Lydgate and the Making of Public Culture* (Cambridge: Cambridge University Press, 2005).

Pearsall, Derek, *John Lydgate (1371–1449): A Bio-Bibliography* (Victoria: University of Victoria, 1997).

Scanlon, Larry, 'Lydgate's Poetics: Laureation and Domesticity in *The Temple of Glass*', in James Simpson and Larry Scanlon, eds., *John Lydgate: Poetry, Culture, and Lancastrian England* (Notre Dame: University of Notre Dame Press, 2006).

Simpson, James, *Reform and Cultural Revolution* (Oxford: Oxford University Press, 2002).

Skelton, John, *John Skelton: The Complete English Poems*, ed. John Scattergood (Harmondsworth: Penguin, 1983).

Strohm, Paul, 'Hoccleve, Lydgate and the Lancastrian Court', in David Wallace, ed., *The Cambridge History of Medieval English Literature* (Cambridge: Cambridge University Press, 1999).

49 THE RECEPTION OF CHAUCER IN THE RENAISSANCE

Bishop, Louise, 'Father Chaucer and the Vivification of Print', *Journal of English and Germanic Philology*, 106 (2007), 336–63.

Cooper, Helen, 'Choosing Poetic Fathers: The English Problem', in Guillemette Bolens and Lukas Erne, eds., *Medieval and Early Modern Authorship* (Tübingen: Narr, 2011), pp. 29–50.

Krier, Theresa M., *Refiguring Chaucer in the Renaissance* (Gainesville: University Press of Florida, 1998).

Miskimin, Alice S., *The Renaissance Chaucer* (New Haven, CT: Yale University Press, 1975).

Spearing, A. C., 'Renaissance Chaucer and Father Chaucer', *English*, 34 (1985), 1–38.

Teramura, Misha, 'The Anxiety of *Auctoritas*: Chaucer and *The Two Noble Kinsmen*', *Shakespeare Quarterly*, 63 (2012), 544–76.

50 THE RECEPTION OF CHAUCER FROM DRYDEN TO WORDSWORTH

Alderson, William L. and Arnold C. Henderson, *Chaucer and Augustan Scholarship* (Berkeley: University of California Press, 1970).

Bentley, Gerald, *Blake Books* (Oxford: Oxford University Press 1977).

Brewer, Derek, ed., *Chaucer: The Critical Heritage*, 2 vols. (London: Routledge and Kegan Paul, 1978, 1995).

Espie, Jeff, 'Wordsworth's Chaucer: Mediation and Transformation in English Literary History', *Philological Quarterly*, 94 (2015), 377–403.

Gourlay, Alexander S., 'What Was Blake's Chaucer?', *Studies in Bibliography*, 42 (1989), 272–83.

Spurgeon, Caroline F. E., *Five Hundred Years of Chaucer Criticism and Allusion (1357–1900)*, 3 vols. (London: Chaucer Society, 1914–25).

Wordsworth, William, *Translations of Chaucer and Virgil*, ed. Bruce E. Graver (Ithaca, NY: Cornell University Press), 1998.

51 THE RECEPTION OF CHAUCER FROM THE VICTORIANS TO THE TWENTY-FIRST CENTURY

Barrington, Candace, *American Chaucers* (New York: Palgrave Macmillan, 2007).

Cawsey, Kathy, *Twentieth-Century Chaucer Criticism: Reading Audiences* (Farnham: Ashgate, 2011).

Clarke, Charles Cowden, *Tales from Chaucer, in Prose: Designed Chiefly for the Use of Young Persons* (London: Effingham Wilson, 1833).

Ellis, Steve, *Chaucer at Large: The Poet in the Modern Imagination* (Minneapolis: University of Minnesota Press, 2000).

Kittredge, G. L., *Chaucer and His Poetry* (Cambridge, MA: Harvard University Press, 1915).

Matthews, David, 'Infantilizing the Father: Chaucer Translations and Moral Regulation', *Studies in the Age of Chaucer*, 22 (2000), 93–114.

Medievalism: A Critical History (Cambridge: D. S. Brewer, 2015).
Patterson, Lee, *Negotiating the Past: The Historical Understanding of Medieval Literature* (Madison: University of Wisconsin Press, 1987).
Trigg, Stephanie, *Congenial Souls: Reading Chaucer from Medieval to Postmodern* (Minneapolis: University of Minnesota Press, 2002).
Utz, Richard, *Chaucer and the Discourse of German Philology: A History of Reception and an Annotated Bibliography of Studies, 1793–1948* (Turnhout: Brepols, 2002).

52 CYBER-CHAUCER

Berry, David M., *Understanding Digital Humanities* (London: Routledge, 2012).
Bryant, Brantley, *Geoffrey Chaucer Hath a Blog: Medieval Studies and New Media* (London: Palgrave Macmillan, 2010).
Burdick, Anne, Johanna Drucker, Peter Lunenfeld, Todd Presner and Jeffrey Schnapp, *Digital_Humanities* (Cambridge, MA: MIT Press, 2012).
Confraternity of Neoflagellants, eds. *thN Lng folk 2go: Investigating Future Premoderns™* (New York: Punctum, 2013).
Higl, Andrew, *Playing the 'Canterbury Tales': The Continuations and Additions* (Farnham: Ashgate, 2012).
Mak, Bonnie, *How the Page Matters* (Toronto: University of Toronto Press, 2011).
McCarty, Willard, ed., *Text and Genre in Reconstruction: Effects of Digitalization on Ideas, Behaviours, Products and Institutions* (Cambridge: OpenBook Publishers, 2010).
Schreibman, Susan, Ray Siemens and John Unsworth, eds., *A Companion to Digital Humanities* (Oxford: Wiley-Blackwell, 2008).
Siemens, Ray and Susan Schreibman, eds., *A Companion to Digital Literary Studies* (Oxford: Wiley-Blackwell, 2007).
Wallace, David, ed., *Europe: A Literary History, 1348–1418* (Oxford: Oxford University Press, 2016).

Index

accessus, 59, 68
Aers, David, 434
Aesop, 210
agriculture, *see* economy: rural economy
Alan of Lille (Alain de Lille, Alanus de/ab Insulis), 51, 61, 118, 232
  Anticlaudianus, 51, 232, 233
  De planctu Naturae, 15, 51, 191, 205, 232, 233
  waxen nose of authority, 61, 66
alchemy, 178–82, 248
'Alfredian' Old English translation of Boethius, *De consolatione philosophiae*, 150
aliens, 315–16, *see also* borders/identities
Alliterative Morte Arthure, 143
alliterative verse, 136–7, *see also* metre: alliterative long line
al-Qabisi, *Introductorium*, 247–8, *see also* universe
Anderson, Robert, 424–5
Andreas Capellanus, *De arte honesti amandi*, 98, 232, *see also* love
animals, 190, 209–14
  bestiaries, 210
  in Chaucer's works, 203–14
  fables and anthropomorphism, 213
  horses, 214, 328, 351, 373, 374, 382
  Isidore of Seville on animals, 210–11, 212
  livestock, 210–11, 213, 332, 346–9, 357
  names, 213–14
  as vehicles for human thought, 209–14
Anne of Bohemia, Queen of England, 17, 18, 138, 271, 289, 341
apprentices, 207, 223, 227, 253, 328, 374, 376, 379–81, *see also* households/home: servants and apprentices
Aquinas, Thomas, 260, 437
  Summa theologica/theologiae, 84, 149, 203–4, 248
Arabia/Arabs, 182, 316
  Arabic knowledge, 254, *see also* Islam: Islamic knowledge
architecture, 273–84
  religious architecture, 273–80
    Canterbury Cathedral, 279–80, 280f32.5
    Chapel of St Stephen, Palace of Westminster, 273–6
    Ely Cathedral, 275, 275f32.2
    Gloucester Cathedral, 276–9, 277f32.3
    Snettisham Church, 273–5, 274f32.1
    Winchester Cathedral, 278–80, 279f32.4
  religious styles
    Decorated Style, 273–6
    Perpendicular Style, 276–8
  secular architecture, 280–4
    Bodiam Castle, 283f32.7, 287–9
    Warkworth Castle, 280, 281f32.6
    Westminster Palace, great hall, 282, 290
aristocracy, *see* rank
Aristotle, 51, 60, 147, 179, 185, 240, 242
  Ethics, 184
  De interpretatione, 147, 148
  Metaphysics, 148, 240
  On the Heavens, 240
  Poetics, 148
  Physics, 51
  Politics, 184
  Praedicamenta (*Categories*), 148
  De sophisticis elenchis, 148
  De topiciis differentiis, 148
armies, *see* Hundred Years War: army recruitment and organisation
art, 266–72
  Gothic style, 267–8
    Canterbury Cathedral, 268
    Corpus Christi College Cambridge *Troilus* frontispiece, 268
    contemporaneous inventories of art, 268–71

art (*cont.*)
parish church art inventories, 270–1
Wilton Diptych, 268
sepulchral art, 271–2
socially engaged nature of art, 266–7
Arthur, legendary King of Britain, 91, 98, 102, 135, 143, 204, 270, 320, 429
Ascham, Roger, *Toxophilius*, 414
Ashby, George, *Active Policy of a Prince*, 407–8
Ashenden, John, *Summa astrologiae judicialis de accidentibus mundi*, 184
Ashton, Peter, 413
astrolabes, 16, 179, 183, 209, 239, 246–7, 246f28.5, 250
astrology, *see* universe: astrology
Auchinleck manuscript (Edinburgh, National Library of Scotland Advocates MS 19.2.1), 21, 30, 134–5, 136
Augustine, Saint, 51, 60, 150, 161, 203, 231, 248
City of God, 150, 152
author (*auctor*), *see* literary theory/literary roles: author
authority, 58–63, *see* Alan of Lille: waxen nose of authority
auctores, 59, *see also* literary theory/literary roles
Chaucer's redeployment of authority, 58–9
definitions, 59
transfer of literary authority, 61–3
autobiography, 196, 300, 366
Averroes, 51, 254
Avicenna, 51, 254
Awntyrs off Arthure, 150

ballade, *see* metre
Barrett, Elizabeth, 427, 431
Bartholomaeus Anglicus, *De proprietatibus rerum* (*On the Nature of Things*), 113
Beaumont, Francis, 415
Becket, Saint Thomas, 167, 168–72, 169f20.1, 170f20.2, 173, 174, 319
Bell, John, 424
Benoît de Sainte-Maure, *Roman de Troie*, 102, 129
Benson, Larry D., 433
Beowulf, 32
(de) Berkeley, Sir Edward, 126
Bernard Silvester (Bernardus Silvestris), 232
Cosmographia, 232
bestiaries, *see* animals
Bevis of Hampton, 135
Bible, 50, 59, 65, 66, 67, 134, 150, 152, 168, 180, 210, 258, 295, 297, 302, *see also* Wycliffites; Wycliffite Bible
Black Death, 324
depopulation, 324
impact, 355–9
see also economy: Black Death and socio-economic changes; economy: rural economy, impact of Black Death
Black Prince, *see* Edward of Woodstock
Blake, William, 424
Blanche, Duchess of Lancaster, 15, 99, 132, 188, 197, 199–200, 288
Boccaccio, Giovanni, 16, 55, 58, 60, 108, 126–30, 131, 135, 365
Caccia di Diana, 129
De casibus virorum illustrium, 127, 129
De claris mulieribus, 127, 129
De montibus, 129
Decameron, 127, 129, 130, 131, 253, 257, 319
Filocolo, 92
Filostrato, 33, 78, 102, 112, 120, 126, 129, 135
Genealogia deorum gentilium, 129
Teseida, 50, 66–7, 78, 91, 104, 110–14, 126, 129, 130, 321
Boethius, 2, 147–53
commentary on Aristotle's *De interpretatione*, 147
De arithmetica, 148
De consolatione philosophiae, 15, 46, 50, 58, 84–5, 87, 91–2, 104, 110, 121, 147, 148–53, 185, 211, 230, 231, 232, 237, 240
Christianity of the work, 150
reception and influence, 150
as source for Chaucer, 151–3
synopsis of the work, 148–9
De musica, 148
life, 147–8
Opuscula sacra, 148, 150
Bokenham, Osbern, 180, 408
Bologna, 130, 253, 385
Bonaventure, Saint, 65–6, 68, 70
borders/identities, 315–22
border-crossing in *Prioress's*, *Squire's*, and *Man of Law's Tales*, 316–17
English regionalism and Chaucer's literary works, 320
identities within British Isles, 319–20
identity, 317–18
Prioress's Tale, 318
Scotland/Scots, Ireland/Irish, and Wales/Welsh in Chaucer's works, 320
Shipman and *Shipman's Tale*, 320–1
Wife of Bath, 321
see also aliens
Bradshaw, Henry, 429

Bradwardine, Thomas, 161, 231
De causa Dei, 231–2
Braham, Robert, 412
Brembre, Nicholas, 340, 342
Brinkman, Baba, *The Canterbury Tales Remixed*, 443
Bromholm, Holy Rood of, 174, 175f20.3
Brut, The (anonymous prose), 144, 367
Buckingham, John, Bishop of Lincoln, 307
Burley, Sir Simon, 340

Canterbury, 169, 172, 199, 298, 319, 320, 351
Canterbury Cathedral, *see* architecture; art
Canterbury Tales Project, 437, 439–41, *see also* digital humanities and Chaucer
Carpenter, John, 368
Cato, 15, 55, 113
Disticha Catonis, 50, 53, 226
Caxton, William, 412, 414
translation of *Aeneid*, 29, 368–9
translation of Raymond Llull, *Libre del ordre de cavayleria*, 334–5
Cecilia, Saint, 102, 159, 172
Chalmers, Alexander, 424
Chandos Herald, *La Vie du Prince Noir* (*The Life of the Black Prince*), 334
Charles IV, King of France, 309
Charles V, King of France, 179
Charles VI, King of France, 17, 311
Charny, Geoffroi de, *Livre de la chevalerie*, 334–5
Chaucer, Alice, Duchess of Suffolk, 20, 325, 327
Chaucer, Geoffrey
biographical context
biographical details, 14–20
Chaucer's religious temper, 301–3
Chaucer's scribes, 366–8
education and reading, 15–16, 50–5
family and marital life/affiliations, 14, 15, 18
literary life and affiliations, 7–9, 15, 365–6, *see also* Chaucer's language/linguistic context: London English
commitment to writing in English, 20–2
London, 16, 136, 320, 325, 341, 363–70
narrative self-presentation, 9, 51–2
personal political contexts, 339–45
politics and his writings, 341–3
personality, 7–12
portraits of Chaucer and personal appearance
Hoccleve portrait, 8, 9f1.1, 406
portrait in Speght's 1598 edition, 369, 410, 411f49.1
Troilus frontispiece Corpus Christi College Cambridge, *see* front cover of *Geoffrey Chaucer in Context*, 43, 268
professional and military life, 11, 14, 16–17, 18–19, 136, 287, 291, 308, 332, 365
raptus allegation, 18
social affiliations, 14, 136
travel abroad, 16–17, 55, 126, 365
Westminster, 18, 35, 174, 261, 350, 368, 376
Palace of Westminster great hall, 366, 369
Westminster Abbey, 19–20, 173, 199, 366, 368, 369, 412
Lady Chapel, 19
Poets' Corner, 19
witness in Scrope-Grosvenor dispute, 15, 147
Chaucer's language/linguistic context
dialects, 36–7
French, 39
inventio/invention, 27–33
London English, 36–40
pronouns of power, 28–9
social class, 38–40
style, 29–33
use of English, 319
Chaucer manuscripts
Aberystwyth, National Library of Wales, MS Peniarth 392 D (Hengwrt Manuscript), 27, 36–7, 45, 47–8, 367, 430, 441
Cambridge, Cambridge University Library, MS Gg.4.27, 46
Cambridge, Corpus Christi College, MS 61, 43, 268
London, British Library, MS Harley 7333, 45–6
Manchester, John Rylands Library, MS Eng. 113, 43–4
Oxford, Bodleian Library, MS Arch Selden B.24, 46
Oxford, Bodleian Library, MS Digby 181 part 1, 43–4
Oxford, Bodleian Library, MS Rawlinson Poet.163, 46
San Marino, Huntington Library, MS EL 26 C 9 (Ellesmere manuscript), 36, 45, 47–8, 367, 374, 430
San Marino, Huntington Library, MS HM 114, 46, *see also* manuscripts and manuscript culture
editions and editors, 368–9, *see* reception/afterlife; *see also* Benson, Larry D.; Caxton, William; Manly, J. M. and Edith Rickert; *Riverside Chaucer*; Robinson, F. N.; Robinson, Peter; Skeat, Walter; Speed, John; Speght, Thomas; Thynne, William; Tyrrwhitt, Thomas; Stow, John; Tyrwhitt, Thomas; Urry, John

Chauncer, Geoffrey (*cont.*)
reception/afterlife, 19–20, 140, 366–7
Chaucer as Father of English poetry, 403, 412–13, 415–17, 419
reception from Dryden to Wordsworth, 419–28, *see also* Blake, William; Ogle, George; Tyrwhitt, Thomas; Urry, John
Dryden, John, 419–20
editions in eighteenth century, 420–4
Wordsworth, William: reception of Chaucer, 424–6, *see also* Blake
reception in fifteenth century, 403–9
context of Lancastrian dynasty, 404–5
fifteenth-century Chaucer manuscripts, 403–4, *see also* Ashby, George, Bokenham, Osbern; Hoccleve, Thomas; Lydgate, John; Shirley, John; Skelton, John
reception in Renaissance, 410–17, *see also* Speed, John; Speght, Thomas; Neville, Alexander; Daniel, Samuel; Wyatt, Sir Thomas; Caxton, William; Kynaston, Francis; Skelton, John; Spenser, Edmund; Shakespeare, William; Sidney, Sir Philip; Thynne, William; Ogle, George; Tyrwhitt, Thomas; Urry, John
reception from Victorians to twenty-first century, 429–35, *see also* Furnivall, Frederick James; Kittredge, George Lyman; Manly, J. M. and Edith Rickert; *Riverside Chaucer*; Robinson, F. N.; Skeat, Walter
Chaucer studies in the Edwardian era, 431–2
Chaucer studies in the Victorian era, 429–31
Chaucer studies from World War I to twenty-first century, 432–4
popular adaptations of Chaucer's works, 434–5
works
ABC to the Virgin, 121, 122, 137
Anelida and Arcite, 22, 44, 112, 126, 227, 414, 427
Boece, 16, 17, 48, 50, 51, 66, 84, 86, 120, 121, 144, 150, 152, 161–2, 192, 230, 232, 234, 240, 250, 260, 368, 413, 414
Book of the Duchess, 15, 29–30, 44, 51, 52, 76–8, 85, 95, 99–100, 102, 110–12, 119, 132, 151, 152, 188, 200, 235, 288, 316, 435
Canon's Yeoman's Prologue and Tale, 180–1, 248
Canterbury Tales, 7, 11, 18, 19, 27, 36, 44, 45, 47, 48, 68–9, 78, 86, 90, 92, 94, 100–1, 118, 122, 142, 152, 158, 167, 168, 196, 199, 202, 223, 228, 236–7, 263, 297, 301–2, 306, 319, 326, 328, 331–2, 335, 346, 350, 357, 358, 361, 363, 364, 367, 368, 370, 373, 377, 385, 393–4, 414, 416, 421, 429, 430, 431, 432, 433, 434, 437, 441, 442
Canterbury Tales pilgrims
Clerk, 228, 237, 350, 398
Cook, 320, 430
Franklin, 242, 262, 326–7, 329, 396
Friar, 352, 398
Harry Bailey, the Host, 11, 29, 95, 135, 142, 157–8, 302, 350
Knight, 10, 17, 38, 158, 214, 313, 314, 318, 320, 321, 329, 331, 334, 335, 396
Man of Law, 10, 11, 189, 259, 262–3, 329, 350
Manciple, 227, 320, 350
Merchant, 9, 329, 350, 371, 394, 397
Miller, 38, 158–9, 347, 421
Monk, 10, 136, 328, 352, 397, 398
Pardoner, 10, 46, 50, 118, 142, 167, 320, 350
Parson, 10, 137, 142, 173, 207, 237, 301, 302, 329, 347, 351, 419
Physician, 183, 254, 258, 329, 394
Ploughman, 329, 346, 347, 361–2, 398, 424
Prioress, 10, 21, 196, 198, 212, 317, 320, 321, 352, 426
Reeve, 75, 254, 320, 348, 395
Shipman, 214, 302–3, 307, 318, 320–2, 350, 371, 373, 377
Squire, 20, 223, 224, 228, 313, 317, 326, 334, 335, 396, 416
Summoner, 142, 263
Wife of Bath, 50, 62, 118, 196, 214, 227, 228, 321, 334, 350, 351, 374, 388, 397
Yeoman, 313, 326
Chaucers Wordes unto Adam, His Owne Scriveyn, 47, 48, 53, 66, 369, 442
Clerk's Prologue and *Tale*, 50, 61, 89, 127, 131, 165–6, 190, 346, 398, 407
Complaint of Chaucer to his Purse, 117
Complaint of Venus, 73–4, 121, 141
Complaint unto Pity, 77, 78
Cook's Tale, 199, 207, 223
Former Age, 151–2
Fortune, 141, 151, 440
Franklin's Tale, 62, 86, 89, 92–3, 101, 164–5, 182–3, 228, 316, 352, 380
Friar's Tale, 79, 180, 263, 320, 348, 350–1, 386, 427
General Prologue, 9–10, 17, 19, 21, 72, 77, 79, 135, 136, 142, 167, 170, 171, 196, 209, 214, 227, 228, 236, 237, 242, 254, 258, 301, 312–13, 315, 318, 320–1, 326, 328–9, 331, 346, 347, 350, 363,

364, 370, 386, 394, 395, 396, 397, 419, 424, 427
Gentilesse, 151, 366
House of Fame, 10, 11–12, 13n7, 16, 17, 22, 32, 44, 47, 50, 51, 58, 62, 63, 72, 76, 77, 106–8, 109–10, 115, 122, 126, 151, 152, 191, 192, 233, 235, 240, 286, 368, 396, 414, 436
Knight's Tale, 19, 50, 66–7, 75, 77, 78, 79, 80, 85, 89, 90, 91–2, 93, 94, 100–1, 103, 114, 126, 136, 151, 152, 162–3, 164, 184–5, 188, 205–6, 209, 212, 223–4, 228, 250, 252, 256, 286, 291, 317–18, 332, 397, 410, 415, 416, 419, 427, 434
Lak of Stedfastness, 151, 236, 366
Legend of Good Women, 10, 16, 17, 18, 22, 47, 51, 52, 56, 73, 75, 89, 95, 100, 101, 108–9, 114, 119–21, 137–8, 141, 151, 168, 180, 237, 342–3, 349–50, 396, 427
Lenvoy de Chaucer a Bukton, 152, 366
Lenvoy de Chaucer a Scogan, 366
Man of Law's Tale, Prologue, and *Epilogue*, 10–11, 18, 47, 89, 94, 114, 158, 189, 247, 248, 259, 302, 317, 320
Manciple's Tale, 220, 228, 424, 425, 427
Merchant's Tale, 61, 95, 101, 120, 188, 190, 226, 227
Merciles Beaute, 74–5
Miller's Prologue and *Tale*, 30–2, 66–7, 68–9, 75, 95, 101, 158, 159–60, 168, 171–2, 173, 194–5, 223, 228, 237, 246, 379, 383, 395, 421
Monk's Tale, 15, 17, 228
Nun's Priest's Tale, 16, 55, 62, 81, 142, 153, 160–1, 163, 164, 210, 212, 213–14, 229, 231, 235–6, 242, 243, 246, 250, 335, 341, 379, 419, 434
Pardoner's Prologue and *Tale*, 79–81, 158, 167–8, 173, 220, 223
Parliament of Fowls, 16, 17, 21, 28–9, 38–9, 44, 45, 46, 50, 51, 52, 74, 77, 78, 85, 86, 95, 100, 102, 122, 126, 140, 151, 209, 232–3, 234, 239, 240, 341, 343, 349, 368, 414, 415
Parson's Prologue and *Tale*, 40, 51, 75, 137, 144, 167, 206–7, 301–2, 303, 306, 347, 348, 386, 398
Physician's Tale, 102, 121, 224, 228, 261
Prioress's Tale, 171, 220, 221, 226, 228, 316, 318, 321, 424, 426
Reeve's Tale, 37, 46, 101, 174, 214, 228, 393–4, 424
Retractions, 47, 56, 69, 152, 168, 185–6, 301–2, 414
Romaunt of the Rose, 50, 117
Second Nun's Tale, 51, 79, 102, 159, 172–3
Shipman's Tale, 46, 77, 246, 321, 352
Sir Thopas, 11, 20, 73, 93–5, 97, 134, 135, 142, 334, 397, 416–17
Squire's Tale, 89, 94, 174, 182, 189, 224, 291, 316–17, 319, 415–16, 427, 438–9
Summoner's Tale, 73, 92, 220, 221–2, 297, 350
Tale of Melibee and *Prologue*, 51, 62, 86, 121, 135, 142, 226, 255, 380
Treatise on the Astrolabe, 51, 68, 144, 179, 184, 209, 219, 228, 239, 242, 244, 244f28.3, 245, 246–7, 248, 250
Troilus and Criseyde, 7, 17, 18, 32, 37–8, 43, 44, 45, 46, 53, 54, 58, 60, 63, 66, 72, 77, 78, 79, 85, 95, 98, 102–4, 109, 112, 114, 120, 126–7, 140, 144, 151, 152, 162–3, 164, 183, 184, 185–6, 188, 190, 202–3, 214, 227, 231, 234, 236, 240, 248, 268, 316, 318, 334, 343, 363, 365, 368, 387, 396, 407, 414, 424, 427, 432, 442
'Lollius', 58, 59, 112
Truth, 141, 151, 211–12, 366, 415–16
Wife of Bath's Prologue and *Tale*, 51, 53, 86, 89, 93–4, 95, 102, 151, 158, 180, 195, 201, 202, 204, 214, 220, 228, 237, 315, 318, 321, 334, 350–1, 374, 386–8, 390, 397, 419, 421, 434
Chaucer, John, 14
Chaucer, Lewis, 221, 228, 247
Chaucer, Philippa (née de Roet), 15, 18, 195, 197, 198, 199, 288, 340, 344, 365
Chaucer, Thomas, 8, 20, 312, 313, 344, 410
Chaumpaigne, Cecily, *see* Chaucer, Geoffrey: biographical context, *raptus* allegation
children/childhood, 219–28, 380, *see also* education of the young
chivalry, 331–5
brutality of warfare, 332–3
definitions, 331
role of romance in defining chivalry, 291, 316–17, 331
literature of chivalry, 334–5, *see also* heraldry
romanticised civilised chivalry, 332
tensions in models of chivalry, 333–5
tournaments and knightly orders, 331–2
Chrétien de Troyes, 89, 98
Le chevalier de la charrete, 98
Le chevalier au lion, 89
Erec et Enide, 98
Cligès, 98
Le conte du graal, 98

Christianity in late medieval England, 301–7
- confession, 21, 222, 298, 299, 303–4
- lay piety and religious observance, 303–7
- lay motives for religious behaviours, 304–5
- religious fraternities and guilds, 305, *see also* guilds
- educated and uneducated lay piety, 305–7, *see also* dissent; God; heresy; Lollards/Lollardy; orthodoxy; Wycliffites/Wycliffism

Christine de Pizan, 117, 122–3
- *Epistre au dieu d'Amours*, 122
- *Le livre de la cité des dames*, 61
- *Querelle de la rose*, 122

Church, *see* Christianity in late medieval England; dissent; God; heresy; orthodoxy

Cicero, 62, 232, 235–6
- *De inventione*, 27
- *Somnium Scipionis* (*Dream of Scipio*), 51, 53, 232–3, 240
- *Topics*, 148

cities, *see* economy: urban economy; everyday urban life; household/home; rank: immigration to towns; towns

Clifford, Sir Lewis, 54, 221

confession, *see* Christianity in late medieval England

Cooper, Helen, 433

Copton, Agnes de, 14

Court of Love, The, 20

Courtenay, William, Archbishop of Canterbury, 296

Clanvowe, Sir John, *The Cuckoo and the Nightingale*, 424, 425, 427

Clarke, Charles Cowden, *Tales from Chaucer, in Prose*, 431

class, *see* rank; dress

classical context and influence, 106–15
- classical gods, 94, 100–8, 109, 121, 122, 123, 129, 162, 202, 257, *see also* paganism/pagans: pagan gods
- mediation of classical through vernacular and non-classical elements, 100, 109, 111–13, 115
- mediation of Ovid, 106–15
- mediation of Virgil, 106–15

Claudian, 15, 106, 109
- *De raptu Proserpinae*, 15, 113

climate, 356–7
- 'Chaucerian Anomaly', 357

coats of arms, *see* heraldry and heralds

Coghill, Nevill, verse translations of the *Canterbury Tales*, 434

colonisation/colonialism, 132, 320–1

commerce, *see* economy

confession, *see* Christianity in late medieval England: confession

Confraternity of Neoflagellants, *thN Lng folk 2go*, 443

Constance of Castile, 15, 197, 288, 340

cosmology, *see* universe

courtesy, 220, 228, 331–3

credit, *see* economy: credit/debt

Cuckoo and the Nightingale, The, *see* Clanvowe, Sir John

Dance of Death, The, 257

Daniel, Samuel, *Musophilus*, 410, 436

Dante Alighieri, 16, 109, 110, 126–8, 130, 135, 151, 365
- *Convivio*, 62, 106, 128
- *De vulgari eloquentia*, 128, 129
- *Divine Comedy* (*Comedìa*, *Divina Commedia*), 50, 97, 100, 115, 126, 127, 128, 130, 150, 240, 318, 319
- *Monarchia*, 128
- *Vita nova*, 128, 130

Dart, John, *Life of Geoffrey Chaucer*, 420

David, King of Israel, 61

David II, King of Scotland, 310

de la Mare, Sir Peter, Speaker of the House of Commons, 313

de la Pole, Edmund, 20

de la Pole, John, Earl of Lincoln, 20

de la Pole, Michael, 327

de la Pole, William, 327

de la Pole, William, Duke of Suffolk, 20, 327

de Worde, Wynkyn, 414

debate, *see* dialogue

Delany, Sheila, 434

Deschamps, Eustache, 16, 117, 123
- *Ballade* to Geoffrey Chaucer, 33, 54, 55, 115, 117, 120
- *L'art de dictier*, 120
- *Miroir de marriage*, 120

dialogue, 83–7
- Boethian dialogue, 84–5
- Chaucer's involvement of readers in dialogue, 86–7
- Socratic *elenchus*, 83–4

Dicts and Sayings of the Philosophers, 257

digital humanities and Chaucer, 436–43
- debate about digital humanities and traditional/innovative scholarship, 439–40
- history and aspirations of humanities computing/digital humanities, 437–8

problems and opportunities in applying digital humanities to Chaucer, 436–43
problematics of digital editing of Chaucer, 439–40, *see also* *Canterbury Tales* Project
Dinshaw, Carolyn, 434
dissent, 295, 299, *see also* Christianity in late medieval England; God; heresy; Lollards/Lollardy; orthodoxy; Wycliffites/Wycliffism
Dives et Pauper, 178
Donaldson, E. T., 433
Douglas, Gavin, 89, 92, 95
dreams, *see* philosophy: dreams
dress, 393–8, *see also* rank
1363 sumptuary laws and dress of pilgrims, 393–8
social categorisation in 1363 law, 394
women and offspring categorised through menfolk, 394
affluent bourgeoisie, 396–7
Chaucer's deployment of costume rhetoric, 393–4
clergy, 397–8
clothing sins in *Parson's Tale*, 398
craftsmen and yeomen, 395
esquires and lesser gentlemen, 395–6
knights, 397
labourers, 398
servants, 394–5
Dryden, John, 19, 138, 140, 417, 420, 421, 425, 426, 431
Fables Ancient and Modern, 417, 419–20
see also Chaucer, Geoffrey: reception/afterlife, reception from Dryden to Wordsworth
Dutch language, 36, 121, 150, 297, 302, *see also* Flanders, Flemings

economy, 346–52
Black Death and socio-economic changes, 355–9
contracts, 352
credit/debt, 352
labour legislation, 358
morality in economic activity, 352
rural economy, 346–50
agricultural infrastructure and landscape, 349–50
estates management, 347–9
impact of Black Death, 347, 349
reeves and bailiffs, 348–9
peasants in economy, 346–7
urban economy, 350–1
London, 350–1, 371
urban workers, 351
wool trade, 350
editions of Chaucer's works, *see* Chaucer, Geoffrey: editions and editors; Chaucer, Geoffrey: reception/afterlife
education of the young, 219–29, 374
Chaucer as educationist, 227–9
child-rearing and social education, 195, 219–20
literacy and language learning, 224–5, 305–6, 374–5
literary education, 226–7
religious education, 220–2
vocational education, 222–4
Edward I, King of England, 273, 309, 390
Edward II, King of England, 276
Edward III, King of England, 14–15, 17, 19, 126, 132, 133, 136, 195, 262, 269, 270, 271, 282, 287, 288, 296, 308, 309–11, 313, 327, 332, 334, 338, 340, 429
Edward of Woodstock, the Black Prince, 14, 195, 334, 338, 390, 391
Edward the Confessor, King of England, 270
Elizabeth I, Queen of England, English translation of Boethius, *De consolatione philosophiae*, 150
Elizabeth de Burgh, Countess of Ulster, 14, 72, 223, 349
encyclopaedias, 68, 113, 144, 230, 240
England, *see* borders/identities: English regionalism and Chaucer's literary works/identities within British Isles
English context and influence, 132–8
Chaucer's debt to English tradition, 135–8
English writings' adaptation of French tradition, 137
French writing in English territories, 133–4
linguistic hybridity, 132–3
writing in English, 134, 141–4
Equatorie of the Planetis, 144
estates satire, 135
everyday urban life, 371–83
clothing and accessories, 373, *see also* dress
daily routines, 375–7
food and drink, 372–3
furnishings, 372
housing, 371, *see also* household/home
hygiene, 374, *see also* education of the young; women
travel, 373–4
Ex heretico comburendo, 296
experience, 63, 100, 108, 192, 236–7, 244, 257, *see* secularity: experience (observation)

family, *see* education of the young; everyday urban life; household/home
fate, 107, 149, 151, 152, 160–3, 164, 205, 233–5, *see also* Boethius: *De consolatione philosophiae*; fortune; philosophy: free will and divine foreknowledge; God: divine foreknowledge
Flemings, *see* Flanders
Fletcher, John: *see* Shakespeare, William
film adaptations, *see* Chaucer, Geoffrey: reception from Victorians to twenty-first century, popular adaptations of Chaucer's works
Flanders, 309, 311, 313, 314, 321, 394
  Flemings, 286, 397
    Flemings in London, 36, 341
Florence, 16, 126, 127–9, 130, 131, 312
  Florentines in London, 36
Flower and the Leaf, 427
foreigners, *see* aliens; *see also* borders/identities
foreknowledge, *see* fate; fortune; philosophy: free will and divine foreknowledge; God: divine foreknowledge
fortune, 91–2, 103, 104, 150, 151, 152, 162–4, 192, 234, 440, 442, *see also* Boethius: *De consolatione philosophiae*; free will; philosophy: free will and divine foreknowledge; God: divine foreknowledge
Foxe, John, 413, 414
Fradenburg, L. O. Aranye, 434
France, *see* French context and influence; Hundred Years War 308–14, *see also* Edward III
free will, 46, 69, 102, 104, 120, 149, 151, 152, 160–3, 183, 231–5, 248, *see also* Boethius: *De consolatione philosophiae*; fate; fortune; philosophy: free will and divine foreknowledge; God: divine foreknowledge
French context and influence, 15–16, 20–2, 54, 60, 73–5, 76, 78, 104, 110, 111–12, 117–23, 140, 141, 142, 152
  Chaucer's French-sourced/influenced works, 119–22
  see also Christine de Pizan; Deschamps, Eustache; Guillaume de Deguileville; Guillaume de Lorris; Guillaume de Machaut; Jean de Meun; Jean de la Mote; Froissart, Jean; Gower, John; Oton de Grandson
French language in England, *see also* Chaucer's language/linguistic context: French; French context and influence
  French language and education of young in England, 219, 224, 227
  French literacy in England, 225, 226
  French as language of law, 45
Frideswide, Saint, 171–2
Froissart, Jean, 16, 20, 21, 119, 120, 133
  Chronicles (*Chroniques*), 119, 287, 334
  Meliador, 119
  Paradys d'amours, 99, 100, 117, 119
Furnivall, Frederick James, 427, 429, 430

Galen, 254, 255, *see also* medicine
Gawain-poet, 90, 92, 137
  Sir Gawain and the Green Knight, 90–1, 93, 94, 137, 143
  Pearl, 137, 141–2
Geoffrey of Vinsauf, *Poetria nova*, 70
Gervase of Melkley, *Ars poetica*, 70
Giles of Rome, *De regimine principum*, 184, 185
Glyndwr, Owain, *see* Wales, Owain Glyndwr's rebellion
God, 157–66
  divine compassion in a cruel world, 163–6
  divine foreknowledge, 160–3, *see also* fate; fortune; philosophy: free will and divine foreknowledge; Boethius: *De consolatione philosophiae*
  human knowledge of God, 158–60
  invocations of God, 157–8, *see also* Christianity in late medieval England; dissent; heresy; holiness; Lollards/Lollardy; orthodoxy; Wycliffites/Wycliffism
gods, *see* classical context and influence: classical gods; paganism/pagans: pagan gods
Gothic, *see* art; architecture
Gower, John, 17, 18, 21, 75, 77, 78, 117, 123, 133, 135, 231, 358, 365
  Confessio Amantis, 47, 78, 123, 150, 181, 365, 367
  French *ballades*, 78
  In Praise of Peace, 78
  Mirour de l'homme, 133
  Vox clamantis, 242
Grosvenor, Sir Robert, *see* Scrope-Grosvenor Court of Chivalry dispute
Guido delle Colonne, *Historia destructionis Troiae*, 102, 129
guilds, 198, 286, 298, 299, 305, 315, 350, 359, 360–1, 375, 377
Guillaume de Deguileville, 117
  Pèlerinage de l'âme, 122
  Pèlerinage de la vie humaine, 121–2, 137
  Pèlerinage de Jésus-Christ, 122
Guillaume de Lorris
  Roman de la Rose, 99, 117, 118, 121, 187, 235

see also Jean de Meun, *Roman de la Rose* continuation; *Roman de la Rose*
Guillaume de Machaut, 16, 21, 100, 117, 119, 120, 135
Dit de la fonteinne amoureuse, 99, 110, 119
Jugement dou roy de Behaingne, 99, 119
Jugement dou roy de Navarre, 99
Remede de fortune, 119
Gutenberg, Johannes, 52
Guy of Warwick, 135
Guyenne King of Arms, *see* heraldry; *see also* Paon/Payn de Roet, Guyenne King of Arms

Hailes Abbey, 173
holy blood of Hailes, 173
Hanna, Ralph, 439–40, 441
Harvey, Gabriel, 414
Havelok, 89, 93
Hawkwood, Sir John, 17, 126, 312, 325, 327
Hazlitt, William, 426
heathens, 159, *see also* paganism/pagans
Henry II, King of England, 169, 262
Henry III, King of England, 173, 309
Henry IV, King of England, 19, 308–9, 311, 313, 340, 344
Henry V, King of England (earlier Henry of Monmouth, Prince of Wales), 19, 133, 198, 309, 311, 313, 404, 405, 406
Henry VI, King of England, 408
Henry VIII, King of England, 408
Henry of Monmouth, Prince of Wales, *see* Henry V, King of England
Henryson, Robert *Testament of Cresseid*, 150
heraldry and heralds, 286–91
Chaucer and Scrope-Grosvenor heraldic legal dispute, 289–90
Chaucer's coat of arms, 286–7
Chaucer's exposure to heraldic culture, 287–9
Chaucer's heraldic sensibility in literary works, 291
coats of arms, 286–7
definition of heraldry, 286
see also chivalry
heresy
definition, 295
Wycliffite heresy, 295–7
see also dissent; Christianity in late medieval England; God; Lollards/Lollardy; orthodoxy; Wycliffites/Wycliffism
Higden, Ralph, *Speculum curatorum*, 181, 183
Hippocrates, 254, 255, 256–7, *see also* medicine
Hoccleve, Thomas, 9, 12, 19, 27, 133, 365, 367, 368, 404–6, 407–9
Regiment of Princes, 7–8, 19, 27, 140, 150, 405–6, 413
La male regle, 366
Holcot, Robert, commentary on Wisdom, 236
holiness, 167–74
devotion to saints, 168–73, 224, 247, 269–70, 301, 304, 319, *see also* relics
holy blood of Christ, 173
meanings of holiness, 167–8
relics of Christ and Mary, 173–4, *see also* Bromholm, Holy Rood of; Hailes Abbey: holy blood of Hailes
saints' sacred sites, 171–2, *see also* Christianity in late medieval England
Holy Land, 298, 320, *see also* pilgrimage; Jerusalem
home, *see* everyday life; households/home
Homer, 19, 58, 97, 115, 414, 417, 419, 421
Iliad, 102
Horne, R. H., *The Poems of Geoffrey Chaucer, Modernized*, 426–7, 431
horses, *see* animals
households/home, 378–83
definition of urban bourgeois household and family, 378–9
gentry and noble households, 382–3
living arrangements of the poor, 383
privacy and domestic space, 383, *see also* everyday urban life; women
marriage and children, 379–80
servants and apprentices, 379
wives' economic activities, 380–1
How the Good Wife Taught Her Daughter, 194
Hugh of St Victor, *Didascalicon*, 67, 230
humanism/humanists, 63, 108, 127, 130, 147, 148, 412, 440, 441, *see also* scholasticism
humours, *see* medicine: humoral theory; universe, humoral theory and the heavens
Hundred Years War
Anglo-French wars, 136, 308–14, 355, 405
army recruitment and organisation, 311–13
Edward III's wars with France, 310–11
English possessions in France, 309–10
Henry IV and war with France, 311
Henry V and war with France, 311
political repercussions of French wars, 313–14
Richard II and war with France, 311
war and national identity, 310
war and international outlook, 314
see also chivalry; Edward III
Hunt, Leigh, 426–7, 431

identity, *see* borders/identities
industry, *see* economy
Innocent III, Pope, *On the Misery of the Human Condition*, 252

International Gothic, *see* architecture
inventio, *see* Chaucer's language/linguistic context: *inventio*/invention; Cicero, *De inventione*
Ireland/Irish, 319
  English interest and occupation, 310, 312
  Irish in London, 15
  Richard II's campaign in Ireland, 309
Isabella, Princess, 311
Isidore of Seville *Etymologiae* (*Etymologies*), 210–11, 230
  definition of 'beast', 212
Islamic knowledge, 178, 240, 247, 256, *see also* Arabia/Arabs
Italian context and influence, 78, 104, 126–31, *see also* Dante Alighieri; Boccaccio, Giovanni; Petrarch, Francis;
  Chaucer's Italian-sourced works, 126–7
Italy, *see* Italian context and influence

Jean de la Mote, 133
Jean de Meun, 16, *see also* Guillaume de Lorris; *Roman de la Rose*
  Old French translation of Boethius, *De consolatione philosophiae*, 121, 150–2, 232
  Roman de la Rose continuation, 99, 117–18, 121, 122, 233, 234
Jerome, Saint, 61
Jerusalem, 196, 199, 246f28.5, 296, 298, 304, 318, 319, 350
  celestial Jerusalem, 67, 142, 167
Jews, 316, 318, 321
  antisemitism, 321, 322n5
  Hebrew, 150
Joan of Kent, 389–91, *see also* marriage: Joan of Kent's marriage history
Joannes Januensis (John of Genoa), *Catholicon*, 66
Johannes de Bado Aureo, *Tractatus de armis*, 289
John II, King of France, 310, 334, 338
John of Garland, *Parisiana poetria*, 70
John of Gaunt, Duke of Lancaster, 15, 19, 20, 38, 99, 132–3, 195, 197, 199–200, 224, 288–90, 295, 311, 339, 340, 344, 364–5, 388
John of Sacrobosco, *De sphera* (*On the Sphere*), 240, 241f28.1, 244f28.3
John of Wales, *Communiloquium*, 113
Jonson, Ben, *The Golden Age Restor'd*, 415
jousting, 18, 203, 313, 332
Julian of Norwich, 61
Juvenal, 113

Kempe, Margery, 195–7, 198, 199, 298, 300
  Book of Margery Kempe, 62, 173, 196–7
Kittredge, George Lyman, 432–3
Knight, Stephen, 434
knighthood, *see* chivalry
Knight's Tale, A, dir. Brian Helgeland, 434–5
Kynaston, Francis, *Amorum Troili et Cressidae*, 414

labour, *see* economy; everyday urban life
laity/layfolk, *see* Christianity in late medieval England; God
land, *see* economy: rural economy
Langland, William, 135
  Piers Plowman, 21, 60, 136, 143, 150, 225, 256, 346
Latin context/sources, 50–5, 58–63, 65–70, 106–15, 118–21, 126–31, 147–53
  Latin language, 21, 36, 134, 137, 221, 225–7, 294, 296, 303, 305, 319, 374–5, 407, 412, 414
  Latin literature, 15, 54, 97, 133, 220, 321, 335
  Latin school-texts, 15, 50, 55
  see also authority; Boethius; classical context and influence; education of the young; French context and influence; Italian context and influence; literary theory and literary roles
law, 259–64
  canon law, 263
  Chaucer's legal knowledge, 261–2
  common law, 262–3
  human law in context of divine law, 260
  judges, 261
  languages of law, 263–4
  oaths, 260
  trials, 261
Lay Folks' Catechism, 306
Lescrope, Geoffrey, 327
Lescrope, Henry, 327
Lescrope, William, Earl of Wiltshire, 327
Lewis. C. S., 98, 433
Lintot, Bernard, 420
Lionel, Prince, Earl of Ulster, 14, 136, 287, 310
literacy, *see* education of the young: literacy and language learning; literary education
literary theory/literary roles, 65–70
  levels of meaning, 67
  literary roles
    author, 65–6, *see* authority: *auctores*
    commentator, 65–8
    compiler, 65, 68–9
    scribe, 65–6
    translator, 66–7
  rhetoric/prescriptive poetics, 69–70
littera, 67
Lollards/Lollardy, 2, 18, 21, 55, 168, 225, 297, 299, 300, 302, 306, 424
  Lollard knights, 302

see also Wycliffites/Wycliffism
London, *see* Chaucer, Geoffrey: biographical context, London; Chaucer, Geoffrey: Chaucer's language/ linguistic context: London English; economy: urban economy, London
Le Ménagier de Paris, 256
Lords Appellant, *see* polity
Louis X, King of France, 309
love, 97–104
love in Chaucer
Boethian elements, 104
classical models, 97
Christian elements, 100–1
fin' amor, 98–104
Love, Nicholas, *The Mirror of the Blessed Life of Jesus Christ*, 159, 172, 306
Low Countries, 312, 350, 377, *see also* Flanders
Lucan, 58, 115
lust (*luxuria*), 201–7
Alan of Lille on lust, 204–5
Aquinas on lust, 203–4
lust as Chaucerian theme, 202–3, 205–7
Lydgate, John, 12, 133, 404–6, 407–8
Complaint of the Black Knight, 47
Fall of Princes, 150
Siege of Thebes, 414
Troy Book, 8–9, 12, 406–7

Macrobius, commentary on Cicero's *Somnium Scipionis*, 232–3, 235, 236, 237, 240, *see also* philosophy: dreams
Malory, Sir Thomas, 150
Le Morte Darthur, 62, 63
Mandeville's Travels, 134, 319
Mannyng, Robert, 315
Handlyng Synne, 136, 206, 299
Manuel des pechiez, 299
Manly, J. M. and Edith Rickert, edition of *Canterbury* Tales, 433
manuscripts and manuscript culture, 43–8
circulation, 44–5
production, 43–4, 52–3, 55
scribes, 47–8
textual variation, 45–7, 53
see also Chaucer, Geoffrey: biographical context, education and reading
Map, Walter, 59–60
Marchaunt, John, 367–8
Marie de France, 98, 210
marriage, 195–6, 375, 385–92
Chaucer's understanding of marriage, 386
church authority on marriage, 385–6
church weddings, 387–8
clandestine marriage, 388–90
consanguinity, 390
divorce, 388
exogamy and endogamy, 391
impediments and annulments, 388
Joan of Kent's marriage history, 389–90
marriage law, sex and consent, 386–7, 391
permission/approval to marry, 391
second and subsequent marriages, 390–1
Martianus Capella, *The Marriage of Philology and Mercury*, 240
marvels, 92–3, *see* romance: marvels and the impossible
Māshā'allāh ibn Atharī ('Massahalla'), 244f28.3, 245f28.4, *see* universe
Matheolus, *Lamentations*, 61
Matthew of Vendôme, *Ars versificatoria*, 70
Maximian, *Elegies*, 113
Medici, Lorenzo de', 127
medicine, 252–8
clericalism of medical profession, 252–3
corporeal elements (heat, cold, moisture, aridity), 255
humoral theory, 254–5
medical writings, 254
mortality of human body, 252
physicians, 253–4
religious aspect of medicine, 256–8, *see also* Galen; Hippocrates
merchants, 16–17, 43, 54, 55, 126, 135, 136, 194, 196, 198, 219, 224, 225, 227, 305, 313–14, 321, 325, 327, 328, 350, 352, 368, 371, 373, 374, 376, 378, 381, *see also* dress; economy: urban economy; everyday urban life; rank
metre in Chaucer, 31–3, 72–81, 140–3
alliterative long line, 142–3
ballade, 73–4, 141–2
tail-rhyme, 142
Mirk, John *Instructions for Parish Priests*, 303–4
mirrors, 187–92
mothers, *see* education of the young: child-rearing and social education; women
music, 90, 148, 195, 230, 240
music of the spheres, 241–2
Myerson, Jonathan, TV animations of *Canterbury Tales*, 434

Narcissus, 187–92
nationalism, *see* borders/identities: English regionalism and Chaucer's literary works/identities within British Isles
Navicula de Venitiis, 144
neo-Platonism, *see* philosophy; philosophy: neo-Platonism in Chaucer's work
Neville, Alexander, 436
Nicholas of Lyra, *Postilla literalis*, 67
nobility, *see* chivalry; rank

Notker Labeo, Old High German translation of Boethius, *De consolatione philosophiae*, 150

Ogle, George, *The Canterbury Tales of Chaucer, Moderniz'd*, 421, 425, 427
Oresme, Nicole
  De causis mirabilium, 181–2
  De visione stellarum, 179
  Le livre de yconomque d'Aristote, 185
orthodoxy, 298–300, *see also* Christianity in late medieval England; dissent; God; heresy; Lollards/Lollardy; Wycliffites/Wycliffism
Oton de Grandson, 16, 20, 21, 117, 141
  Ballades, 73, 78, 121
Ovid, 15, 16, 58, 62, 97, 98, 106–15, 118, 120, 121, 419
  Amores, 97, 118
  Ars amatoria, 97
  Heroïdes, 97, 100, 106–10
  Metamorphoses, 50, 97, 99, 100, 107, 119, 187, 188–9
  Remedia amoris, 118
Ovide moralisé, 60, 100, 110
Owl and the Nightingale, 84

Padua, 16, 131, 289
paganism/pagans, 46, 91, 114
  pagan authors/texts, 60
  pagan gods, 182–3, *see also* classical context: classical gods; heathens
Paon/Payn de Roet, Sir, Guyenne King of Arms, 195, 288
Paris, 14, 246f28.5, 309, 321
Parliament, 18, 224, 296, 310, 311, 313–14, 325, 327–8, 338, 339, 340, 343, 429
Pasolini, Pier Paolo (director), *I Racconti di Canterbury*, 434
Paston, Clement, 324, 326
Paston, John II, 44, 324–5
Paston, William, 324, 325
Patterson, Lee, 434
Pearl, *see Gawain*-poet
peasants, *see* rank: peasantry; economy: rural economy, peasants in economy
Peasants' Revolt, 18, 264, 296, 314, 341, 358
Pecock, Reginald, *The Donet*, 61
Perrers, Alice, 338
Peter of Anchorano, 385
Petrarch, Francis (Francesco Petrarca), 16, 50, 55, 61, 108, 110, 127, 128, 130–1, 365, 407, 415
  Africa, 130
  De obediencia ac fide uxoria mythologia (*A Fable of Wifely Obedience and Faithfulness*), 127, 165
  Itinerarium, 319
  Rerum familiarum libri, 130, 131
  Rerum senilium libri, 407
  Rerum vulgarium fragmenta (Canzoniere), 102, 103, 127, 130–1
Philip IV, King of France, 121
Philip VI, King of France, 309–10
Philippa, Queen of England, 15, 133, 195, 199
Philippe de la Vitry, 133
philosophy, 230–7
  Chaucer's association with Ralph Strode, 231–2
  definition of philosophy, 230
  dreams, 235–6
  free will and divine foreknowledge, 231–2, 233–5, *see also* Boethius, *De consolatione philosophiae*; fate; fortune; philosophy; God: divine foreknowledge
  neo-Platonism in Chaucer's works, 232–3
  nominalism, 236–7
physicians, *see* medicine
Piers Plowman, *see* Langland, William
piety, *see* Christianity in late medieval England; God; holiness
pilgrimage, 167, 173, 196, 199, 211, 298–9, 304, 305, 373
  pilgrim souvenirs, 169f20.1, 175f20.3, 174
  pilgrimage in Dante and Boccaccio, 318–19
  pilgrimage as metaphor for life, 301
  pilgrimage narrative in Deguileville, 121–2
  pilgrims, 211, 276, 279, 315
Pinkhurst, Adam, 27, 47–8, 367, 442
plague, *see* Black Death
Plato, 148, 181, 233, 236, 237, 239–40
  Dialogues, 10, 83, 148
  Republic, 241
  Timaeus, 232
    Latin commentary on *Timaeus* by Chalcidius, 232
    Latin translation of *Timaeus* by Chalcidius, 232
political attitudes of Chaucer, *see* Chaucer, Geoffrey: biographical context, personal political contexts, politics and his writings
politics, *see* polity
polity
  increasing political instability of Richard II's reign, 339
  limited monarchy, 337
  Lords Appellant, 339–43
  Merciless Parliament, 339, 340
  political stability and instability during Edward III's reign, 337–8
  see also Hundred Years War: Anglo-French wars, political repercussions of French wars

Porphyry, *Isagoge*, 148
Powell, Thomas, 427
Prescott, Andrew, 439
Prick of Conscience, 21
print/print culture, *see* Chaucer, Geoffrey: biographical context, reception/afterlife, reception in Renaissance; Caxton, William; Speed, John; Speght, Thomas; Pynson, Richard; Thynne, William; de Worde, Wynkyn
purgatory, 128, 304, 361
Pynson, Richard, 173, 414

rank, 324–30, *see also* dress
  Chaucer's attitudes to rank in pilgrim portraits, 328–30
  gentry and gentlemen, 326
  graduated poll tax, 328
  immigration to towns, 325
  peasantry, 324
  social demarcation borders and mobility, 325–6, 327
  sumptuary laws, 327–8
  yeomen and franklins, 326–7
rape (*raptus*), 201
  Aquinas on rape, 204
  sexual violence in works, 201, 204, *see also* Chaucer, Geoffrey: biographical context, *raptus* allegation
readers/reading, *see* Chaucer, Geoffrey: biographical context, education and reading; education of the young: literacy and language learning, literary education; literary theory/literary roles: levels of meaning
rebellion, *see* Peasants' Revolt
relics
  Becket, Saint Thomas, 168–71
  fake relics, 46, 167
  St Thomas's Water (or Canterbury Water), 168–70
  see also Bromholm, Holy Rood of; Hailes Abbey: holy blood of Hailes; holiness: devotion to saints/holy blood of Christ/relics of Christ and Mary
religion, *see* Christianity in late medieval England; dissent; God; heresy; holiness; Lollards/Lollardy; orthodoxy; Wycliffites/Wycliffism
Remigius of Auxerre, glosses on Boethius, *De consolatione philosophiae*, 150, 152
Renaissance, *see* Chaucer, Geoffrey: biographical context, reception in Renaissance; humanism
Reynes, Robert, 299
rhetoric, *see* literary theory/literary roles: rhetoric/prescriptive poetics; Chaucer's language/linguistic context: *inventio*/invention/style
Richard II, King of England, 17, 18, 19, 40, 55, 197, 248, 268, 271, 282, 289, 291, 302, 308, 311, 312, 332, 334, 338–9, 340–1, 342, 343–5, 376, 389, 405
  instability and deposition, *see* polity
Richard III, King of England, 20
Rickert, Edith: *see* Manly, J. M. and Edith Rickert
Riverside Chaucer, 45, 47, 76, 211, 415, 433
Robertson, D. W., 433
Robinson, F. N., 433
Robinson, Peter, 439–40
Rolle, Richard, 306, 315
Roman de la Rose (*Romance of the Rose*), 50–99, 109, 111–12, 137, 150, 233, 235, 237, *see also* Guillaume de Lorris; Jean de Meun, *Roman de la Rose* continuation
romance, 89–96
  definition, 89
  marvels and the impossible, 92–3
Rome, 128, 129, 131, 147, 196, 199, 226, 246f28.5, 298, 318, 350
Royal Shakespeare Company dramatic adaptation of the *Canterbury Tales*, 434

St Erkenwald 136
saints, 97, 100, 102, 150, 335, *see also* holiness: devotion to saints; relics
Salutati, Coluccio, 108, 127, 130
Santiago de Compostela, 196, 199, 298, 350
Sawtre, William, 296
Saxoferrato, Bartolus, *De insigniis et armis*, 289
scepticism, 61, 63, 299, 302, 438, 440
Schmitz, Leonhard, life of Chaucer, 427
scholasticism/scholastics, 60, 62, 92, 93, 96, 147, 153, 178, 237
schools, *see* education of the young
science, *see* medicine; secularity: secular science; universe
Scotland/Scots, 318, 319, 320
  Anglo-Scottish wars, 308–10, 311, 312, 313
  Scots continuation of *Parliament of Fowls*, 45, 46
  Scots in London, 36
Scott, Sir Walter, 140, 332
scribes, *see* Chaucer, Geoffrey: biographical context, Chaucer's scribes; works, *Chaucers Wordes unto Adam, His Owne Scriveyn*; literary theory/literary roles: scribe; manuscripts and manuscript culture: scribes; Pinkhurst, Adam

Scripture, *see* Bible
Scrope, Sir Richard, *see* Scrope-Grosvenor Court of Chivalry dispute
Scrope-Grosvenor Court of Chivalry dispute, 14, 15, 123, 266–7, 289–90, 308, 310, 331, *see also* Chaucer, Geoffrey: biographical context, witness in Scrope-Grosvenor dispute; heraldry and heralds
sculpture, *see* art
secularity, 178–86
  definitions, 178
  experience (observation), 179–80
  natural marvels and the miraculous, 180–3
  predictions and horoscopes, 183–4
  secular philosophy of sexual pleasure, 185
  secular science, 178–85
self and self-awareness, 187–92
Seneca, 113, 115, 228
sensus, 67
sentence (*sententia*), 67
serfdom, *see* rank
servants, *see* households/home: servants and apprentices
sex, 201–7, *see also* lust; marriage
Shakespeare, William, 20, 140, 415, 429, 431, 433, 434
  A Midsummer Night's Dream, 416–17
  William Shakespeare and John Fletcher, *The Two Noble Kinsmen*, 410
Shirley, John, 44, 47, 404
shrines, *see* holiness: devotion to saints/saints' sacred sites; pilgrimage
Sidney, Sir Philip, *Defence of Poesy*, 63, 417
Simeon manuscript (London, British Library MS Add. 22283), 142
Simonie, The, 135–6
sin, 69, 181, 203–4, 206–7, 221, 252, 257, 299, 303–4, *see also* Christianity in late medieval England: confession
Sir Orfeo, 32, 90, 92, 93, 135
Skeat, W. W., 20, 427–33
Skelton, John, 228–9
  Garlande or Chapelet of Laurell, 408, 415
social mobility/socialisation, 360, *see also* rank
social orders, 324–30, *see also* rank
Socrates, 10, 115
  Socratic *aporia*, 83, 84, 85, 87
  Socratic *elenchus*, 83
soldiers, *see* Hundred Years War: army recruitment and organisation
Solomon, 61
Somme le Roi, 299
Southwark, 35, 44, 320, 364, 365, 370
  ale of Southwark, 68–9
Speculum devotorum (*A Mirror to Devout People*), 62–3
Speed, John, 410–12, 436
Speght, Thomas, 19–20, 369, 410–12, 414–15, 420–1, 424–5, 436
Spenser, Edmund, 408, 426
  The Faerie Queene, 415, 416
squires, *see* rank
stained glass, *see* art
Stanzaic Morte Arthure, 150
Statius, 58, 115
  Thebaid, 15, 110, 112
Stonde wel moder under rode, 137
Stow, John, 369–70, 414
Strode, Ralph, 54, 231–2, 237, 365
Strohm, Paul, 434
Stury, Sir Richard, 15, 17, 18
Sudbury, Simon, Bishop of London, 295
sumptuary laws, *see* dress; rank: sumptuary laws
Surrey, Henry Howard, Earl of, 412, 415
Swynford, Hugh, 195, 197
Swynford, Katherine (née de Roet), 15, 18, 195, 196, 197–8, 199, 224, 340, 344, 365, 388
Swynford, Margaret, 197, 198

television adaptations, *see* Chaucer, Geoffrey: reception/afterlife, reception from Victorians to twenty-first century, popular adaptations of Chaucer's works
Tale of Gamelyn, 430
Ten Brink, Bernhard, 430
theology, *see also* dissent; God; heresy; orthodoxy
Thomas, Timothy, 420
Thomas, William, 420
Thomas of Woodstock, Duke of Gloucester, 54, 269, 270
Thynne, William, 20, 369, 414
Tottel, Richard, *Songes and Sonettes*, 415–16
tournaments, 90, 286, 290–1, 331, 333, 397, *see also* chivalry; jousting; heraldry
towns, 359–60
  changing trading environment, 359–60
  socio-economic regulation, 359
  see also economy: urban economy; everyday urban life; households/home
translation/translators, *see* classical context and influence; English context and influence; French context and influence; Italian context and influence; literary theory/literary roles: literary roles, translator
Tresilian, Chief Justice Robert, 261, 340
Trevet, Nicholas, commentary on Boethius, *De consolatione philosophiae*, 16, 150, 152, 232

Trevisa, John
translation of *De proprietatibus rerum*, 144
translation of *De regimine principum*, 184
translation of *Polychronicon*, 144
Trotula, 255
Tyrrwhitt, Thomas, 422–5, 427, 429

universe 239–50
astrology 245f28.4, 247–50, 249f28.6
astronomical instruments, 246–7
astrolabes, 246–7, 246f28.5
astronomy, 242–7, 243f28.2, 244f28.3
cosmology, 239–42, 241f28.1
humoral theory and the heavens, 242
Treatise on the Astrolabe, 247
University of Cambridge, 227, 228, 253
University of Oxford, 16, 54, 93, 184, 227, 228, 231, 253, 282, 295, 302, 350, 385
University of Paris, 253
Upton, Nicholas, *De studio militari*, 289
Urry, John, 420–2, 425
Usk, Thomas, *Testament of Love*, 20, 342, 365

Valerius Maximus, 235–6
Valla, Lorenzo, 147, 148, 153
Vernon manuscript (Oxford, Bodleian Library, MS Eng. poet. a. 1), 134, 142
versification, *see* metre in Chaucer
Vincent of Beauvais, 113
Speculum historiale, 100
Virgil, 15, 19, 58, 97, 106, 115, 417, 419, 421
Aeneid, 29, 58, 62, 89, 100, 106–10, 115
Visconti, Archbishop Giovanni, 131
Visconti, Bernabò, 17, 126
Visconti dynasty, 127

Wales/Welsh, 319, 320
Anglo-Welsh wars
Owain Glyndwr's rebellion, 308, 309, 312, 313
Welsh absence from English literature, 320
Welsh in London, 36
Welsh language, 319
Wallace, David, 434
Walsingham, 174, 271
Walton, John, Middle English translation of Boethius, *De consolatione philosophiae*, 150
war, *see* chivalry; Edward III; Hundred Years War; Scotland/Scots: Anglo-Scottish wars; Wales/Welsh: Anglo-Welsh wars
weather, *see* climate
Weiscott, Erik, *Mapping Chaucer*, 442–3
Westminster
Palace of Westminster great hall, 282, 290
St Stephen's Chapel, 273
Westminster Abbey, 268, 271
see also Chaucer, Geoffrey: biographical context, Westminster
Wharton, John, 413
Whittington, Richard, Mayor of London, 35, 325
widows, *see* women
William of Aragon, commentary on Boethius, *De consolatione philosophiae*, 150
William of Conches, commentary on Boethius, *De consolatione philosophiae*, 150
William of Ockham, 236–7
windows, *see* art; architecture
wives, *see* women
women, 194–200, *see* Kempe, Margery; Swynford, Katherine, Wife of Bath, Prioress
domestic acculturation, 194–5
female piety, 197–9
nuns and lay sisters, 198–9
vowesses, 198
women pilgrims, 199
marriage, 195–6
middle-class woman, 196–7
upper-class mistress/wife, 197
women of the streets, 199
see also Kempe, Margery; Prioress; Swynford, Katherine; Wife of Bath
Wordsworth, William, 424–7, 431, 433
The Prelude, 424
translation of *The Cuckoo and the Nightingale*, 425–6
translation of the *Manciple's Tale*, 425
translation of the *Prioress's Tale*, 426
work, *see* economy; everyday urban life; household/home
Wyatt, Sir Thomas, 408, 412, 415
Wyclif, John, 161, 178, 231, 295–7, 299, 302, 385
Responsiones ad argumenta Radulfi Strode, 231
De universalibus, 231
De volitione Dei, 231
Wycliffite Bible, 21, 54, 134, 144, 296, 306, 315
Wycliffites/Wycliffism, 21, 59, 61, 296–7, 302, 316, 414, *see also* Christianity in late medieval England; dissent; God; Lollards/Lollardy; orthodoxy
Wykeham, William, Bishop of Winchester, 278, 282
Wynnere and Wastoure, 136

youth, *see* education of the young
Ywain and Gawain, 89

CPSIA information can be obtained
at www.ICGtesting.com
Printed in the USA
LVHW051639190321
681925LV00018B/326